Dimensions
of
Second Edition HUMAN
BEHAVIOR

To my mother, who is my model for
courage and tenacity in the face of both constancy and change

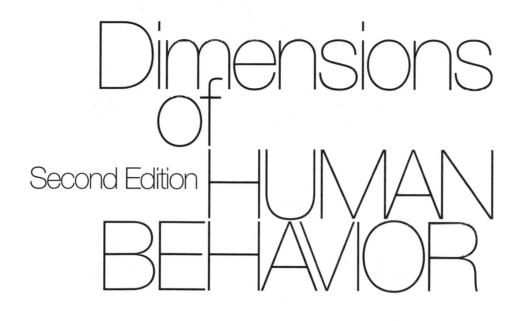

Dimensions of
of
Second Edition
HUMAN
BEHAVIOR

Person and Environment

Elizabeth D. Hutchison
Virginia Commonwealth University

SAGE Publications
International Educational and Professional Publisher
Thousand Oaks ■ London ■ New Delhi

For information:

Sage
2455 Teller Road
Thousand Oaks, California 91320
E-mail: order@sagepub.com

Sage Publications Ltd.
6 Bonhill Street
London EC2A 4PU
United Kingdom

Sage Publications India Pvt. Ltd.
B-42, Panchsheel Enclave
Post Box 4109
New Delhi 110 017 India

Printed in the United States of America

Library of Congress Cataloging-in-Publication Data
Dimensions of human behavior. Volume one, Person and environment / edited by Elizabeth D. Hutchison.— 2nd ed.
    p. cm.
Includes bibliographical references and index.
ISBN 0-7619-8765-7 (paper)
   1. Social psychology. 2. Human behavior. 3. Social structure.
4. Social service. I. Title: Person and environment. II. Hutchison, Elizabeth.
HM1033 .D56 2003
302—dc21

                                                     2003001684

05   10   9   8   7   6   5   4

Acquiring Editor:	Alison Mudditt
Editorial Assistant:	Mishelle Gold
Developmental Editor:	Rebecca Smith
Production Editor:	Claudia A. Hoffman
Typesetter:	C&M Digitals (P) Ltd.
Copy Editor:	Barbara Coster
Indexer:	Molly Hall
Cover Designer:	Michelle Lee

ABOUT THE AUTHOR

Elizabeth D. Hutchison, M.S.W., Ph.D., is Associate Professor in the School of Social Work at Virginia Commonwealth University. She has practiced in health, mental health, and child and family welfare. Her major areas of interest are child and family welfare, social work practice with nonvoluntary clients, and the human behavior curriculum. She has taught human behavior courses at the B.S.W., M.S.W., and doctoral levels, and currently teaches human behavior, social justice, and child and family policy courses.

BRIEF CONTENTS

CONTENTS

CHAPTER 4   ## The Psychological Person: Cognition, Emotion, and Self / 151

Joseph Walsh, Virginia Commonwealth University

CHAPTER 5

The Psychosocial Person: Relationships, Stress, and Coping / 185

Joseph Walsh, Virginia Commonwealth University

CHAPTER 6   **The Spiritual Person / 220**

Michael J. Sheridan, Virginia Commonwealth University

Key Ideas / 220

CASE STUDY: Sean's Search for Meaning and Connection / 221

CHAPTER 8   # Culture / 318

Linwood Cousins, University of North Carolina—Charlotte

CHAPTER 9   **Social Institutions and Social Structure / 356**

Elizabeth D. Hutchison, Virginia Commonwealth University
Amy Waldbillig, Virginia Commonwealth University

CHAPTER 13   Communities / 508

Elizabeth D. Hutchison, Virginia Commonwealth University

CHAPTER 14   Social Movements / 542

Elizabeth D. Hutchison, Virginia Commonwealth University

KNOWLEDGE INTO PRACTICE: Margaret Ryan at Sacred Heart Center / 573

Elizabeth D. Hutchison, Virginia Commonwealth University

PREFACE

In the Preface to the first edition of this book, I noted that I have always been intrigued with human behavior. I didn't know any social workers when I was growing up—or even know there was a social work profession—but I felt an immediate connection to social work and social workers during my junior year in college when I enrolled in an elective entitled Introduction to Social Work and Social Welfare. What attracted me most was the approach social workers take to understanding human behavior. I was a sociology major, minoring in psychology, and it seemed that each of these disciplines—as well as disciplines such as economics, political science, and ethics—added pieces to the puzzle of human behavior; that is, they each provided new ways to think about the complexities of human behavior. Unfortunately, it wasn't until several years later when I was a hospital social worker that I began to wish I had been a bit more attentive to my course work in biology, because that discipline holds other pieces of the puzzle of human behavior. But when I sat in that Introduction to Social Work and Social Welfare course, it seemed that the pieces of the puzzle were coming together. I was inspired by the optimism about creating a more humane world, and I was impressed with an approach to human behavior that clearly cut across disciplinary lines.

Just out of college, amid the tumultuous societal changes of the late 1960s, I became an M.S.W. student. I began to recognize the challenge of developing the holistic understanding of human behavior that has been the enduring signature of social work. I also was introduced to the tensions in social work education, contrasting breadth of knowledge versus depth of knowledge. I found that I was unprepared for the intensity of the struggle to apply what I was learning about general patterns of human behavior to the complex, unique situations that I encountered in the field. I was surprised to find that being a social worker meant learning to understand my own behavior, as well as the behavior of others.

Since completing my M.S.W., I have provided services in a variety of social work settings, including hospitals, nursing homes, state mental health and mental retardation institutions, community mental health centers, a school-based program, public child welfare, and a city jail. Sometimes the target of change was an individual, and other times the focus was on bringing about changes in dyadic or family relationships, communities, organizations, or social institutions. I have also performed a variety of social work roles, including case manager, therapist, teacher, advocate, group facilitator, consultant, collaborator, program planner, administrator, and researcher. I love the diversity of social work settings and the multiple roles of practice. My varied experiences have strengthened my commitment to the pursuit of social justice, enhanced my fascination with human behavior, and reinforced my belief in the need to understand human behavior holistically.

For over 20 years, I have been teaching courses in Human Behavior in the Social Environment to undergraduate students, M.S.W. students, and doctoral students. The students and I struggle with the same challenges that I encountered as a social work student in the late 1960s: the daunting task of developing a holistic understanding of human behavior, the issue of breadth versus depth of knowledge, and discovering how to use general knowledge about human behavior in unique practice situations. My experiences as student and teacher of human behavior led me to write this book.

Holistic Understanding of Human Behavior

Social work has historically used the idea of person-in-environment to develop a holistic understanding of human behavior. This idea has become popular with most social and behavioral science disciplines. Recently, we have recognized the need to add the aspect of time to the person-environment construct, to capture the dynamic, changing nature of person-in-environment.

The purpose of this book is to help you to breathe life into the abstract idea of person-in-environment. As I did in the first edition, I identify relevant dimensions of person and relevant dimensions of environment, and my colleagues and I present up-to-date reports on theory and research about each of these dimensions. All the while, we encourage you to link the micro world of personal experience with the macro world of social trends—to recognize the unity of person and environment. We help you make this connection by showing how several of the same theories have been used to understand dimensions of both person and environment. A companion volume to this book, *The Changing Life Course,* builds on the multiple dimensions of person and environment analyzed in this book and demonstrates how they work together with dimensions of time to produce patterns in unique life course journeys.

Breadth Versus Depth

The most difficult challenge I face as a student and teacher of human behavior is to develop a broad, multidimensional approach to human behavior without unacceptable sacrifice of depth. It is indeed a formidable task to build a knowledge base both wide and deep. After years of struggle, I have reluctantly concluded that although both breadth and depth are necessary, it is better for social work to err on the side of breadth. Let me tell you why.

Social workers are doers; we use what we know to tell us what to do. If we have a narrow band of knowledge, no matter how impressive it is in its depth, we will "understand" the practice situations we encounter from this perspective. This will lead us to use the same solutions for all situations, rather than to tailor solutions to the unique situations we encounter. The emerging risk and resilience literature suggests that human behavior is influenced by the multiple risk factors and protective factors inherent in contemporary social arrangements. What we need is a multidimensional knowledge base that allows us to scan widely for and think critically about risk factors and protective factors and to craft multipronged intervention programs to reduce risks and strengthen protective factors.

To reflect recent developments in the social and behavioral sciences, this book introduces dimensions of human behavior that are not covered in similar texts. Chapters on the biological and spiritual dimensions of person, the physical environment, social institutions, and social movements provide important insights into human behavior not usually covered in social work texts. In addition, we provide up-to-date information on the typically identified dimensions of human behavior.

General Knowledge and Unique Situations

The purpose of the social and behavioral sciences is to help us understand *general patterns* in person-environment transactions. The purpose of social work assessment is to understand *unique configurations* of person and environment dimensions. Those who practice social work must weave what they know about unique situations with general knowledge. To assist you in this process, as we did in the first edition, we begin each chapter with one or more case studies, which we then weave with contemporary theory and research. Most of the stories are composite cases and do not correspond to actual people known to the authors. In this second edition, we call more attention to the successes and failures of theory and research to accommodate human diversity related to gender, race and ethnicity, culture, sexual orientation, and disability.

About This Book

The task of developing a solid knowledge base for doing social work can seem overwhelming. For me it is an exciting journey, because I am learning about my own behavior as well as the behavior of others. What I learn enriches my personal life as well as my professional life. My colleagues and I wanted to write a book that gives you a state-of-the-art knowledge base, but we also wanted you to find pleasure in your learning. We have tried to write as we teach, with enthusiasm for the content and a desire to connect with your process of learning. We have developed some special features that we hope will aid your learning process.

The bulk of this second edition will be familiar to instructors who used the first edition of *Dimensions of Human Behavior: Person and Environment*. Many of the changes that do occur came at the suggestions of instructors who have been using the first edition. All chapters have been updated to reflect recent census data, developing trends, and cutting edge research. As in the first edition, key terms are presented in bold type in the chapters and defined in the Glossary.

Also New in This Edition

The more substantial revisions for this edition include the following:

- More content has been added on human diversity.

- New exhibits have been added and others updated.

- Some new case studies have been added to reflect contemporary issues.

- Web resources have been updated.

- Orienting questions have been added to the beginning of each chapter to help the student to begin to think about why the content of the chapter is important for social workers.

- Key ideas have been summarized at the beginning of each chapter to give students an overview of what is to come.

- Active learning exercises have been added at the end of each chapter.

- The order of presentation of dimensions of environment has changed. The new order is Chapter 7, "The Physical Environment," Chapter 8, "Culture," Chapter 9, "Social Institutions and Social Structure," Chapter 10, "Families," Chapter 11, "Small Groups," Chapter 12, "Formal Organizations," Chapter 13, "Communities," and Chapter 14, "Social Movements." This new order allows us to end with a hopeful discussion of the role of social movements in the pursuit of social justice.

One Last Word

I imagine that you, like me, are intrigued with human behavior. That is probably a part of what attracted you to social work. I hope that reading this book reinforces your fascination with human behavior. I also hope that when you finish this book, and in the years to come, you will have new ideas about the possibilities for social work action.

Learning about human behavior is a lifelong process. You can help me in my learning process by letting me know what you liked or didn't like about the book.

—*Elizabeth D. Hutchison*
School of Social Work
Northern Virginia Program
Virginia Commonwealth University
6295 Edsall Road
Alexandria, VA 22314
ehutch@atlas.vcu.edu

Acknowledgments

A project like this book is never completed without the support and assistance of many people. A second edition stands on the back of the first edition, and by now I have accumulated a large number of people to whom I am grateful.

Steve Rutter, former publisher and president of Pine Forge Press, shepherded every step of the first edition, and provided ideas for many of the best features of the book. Along with Paul O'Connell, Becky Smith, and Maria Zuniga, he helped to refine the outline for the second edition.

The contributing authors and I are grateful for the assistance of Dr. Maria E. Zuniga, of San Diego State University School of Social Work, who served as cultural competency consultant for the second edition. She contributed the Meza family case study in Chapter 9 and provided many valuable suggestions of how to improve the coverage of cultural diversity in each chapter. Her suggestions have improved the book immensely.

I am grateful once again to work with a fine group of contributing authors. They were gracious about tight time lines and requests for new features. Most important, they were committed to providing a state-of-the-art knowledge base for understanding the multiple dimensions of human behavior across the life course.

I was so fortunate to have the developmental editorial services of Becky Smith for both the first and second editions. She is such a joy to work with! She took our drafts and returned them to us in a much more coherent and polished form. The contributing authors and I appreciated her mastery of both language and ideas. We also appreciated her ability to give feedback in a kind and gentle manner. In addition, Becky served as editor for the visual essays.

In the later stages of this project, a whole host of people connected to Sage Publications became a part of my life and helped me with the many processes and procedures that are involved in getting a project like this into print. Alison Mudditt, Mishelle Gold, and Claudia Hoffman worked behind the scenes to bring the pieces of this complex project together. I am sure there are many more who played a role but who remain nameless to me. Barbara Coster competently provided further editorial refinement.

I am also grateful to Dr. Shirley Bryant, Program Director, and my colleagues at the VCU School of Social Work Program in Northern Virginia. They have provided me with much care and support through a difficult year and tolerated my preoccupation without complaint. My conversations about the human behavior curriculum with colleagues Holly Matto and Connie Laurent-Roy have produced new ideas that ended up in this book. I am lucky to have such colleagues.

My students over the past 20-plus years also deserve a special note of gratitude. They teach me all the time, and many things that I have learned in interaction with them show up in the pages of this book. They also provide a great deal of joy to my life journey. Those moments when I encounter former students doing informed, creative, and humane social work are special moments, indeed.

My deepest gratitude goes to my husband, Hutch. Since the first edition of this book was published, we have weathered several challenging years. Without his support, and his patience about forgoing vacations, this book could not have been completed in this year of loss.

—Elizabeth D. Hutchison
November 2002

CONTRIBUTING AUTHORS

Leanne Wood Charlesworth, M.S.W., Ph.D., is a senior associate with Caliber Associates, a research and consulting firm. She has held various child welfare and research positions. Her areas of interest include social welfare policy and child and family issues. She has taught human behavior and research courses.

Linwood Cousins, M.S.W., M.A., Ph.D., is Associate Professor of Social Work at the University of North Carolina at Charlotte. He is a social worker and an anthropologist who has practiced in child welfare and family services. His research, teaching, and practice interests include the sociocultural manifestations of race, ethnicity, and social class, as well as other aspects of human diversity in the community life and schooling of African Americans and other ethnic and economic minorities.

Elizabeth P. Cramer, M.S.W., Ph.D., L.C.S.W., A.C.S.W., is Associate Professor in the School of Social Work at Virginia Commonwealth University. Her primary research and service areas are domestic violence, lesbian and gay male issues, and group work. She teaches in the areas of foundation and clinical practice, social justice, oppressed groups, and lesbian and bisexual women. She lives with her partner, their adoptive daughter, and their pets.

Stephen French Gilson, M.S.W., Ph.D. in Medical Sciences, is Associate Professor in the School of Social Work at the University of Maine. Following receipt of his doctoral degree, he was awarded an Intramural Research Training Award Fellowship at the Addiction Research Center, Neuroscience Branch, Neuroimaging and Drug Action Section, National Institute on Drug Abuse. He is involved in three interrelated areas of scholarly inquiry: (1) legitimacy categorization and response applied to disability, domestic violence, and aging, (2) critical examination of local, state, national, and international health policy as it relates to diversity, categorical distribution of resources, and resulting disparities, and (3) human biology. He teaches courses in human behavior, health practice, health policy, and human biology and the social environment. He identifies as a disabled person, and is actively involved in disability advocacy.

Martin Schwartz, M.S.W., Ed.D., L.C.S.W., B.C.D., is Professor Emeritus in the School of Social Work at Virginia Commonwealth University. He previously taught at Columbia University School of Social Work and Yale University Department of Psychiatry. His major areas of interest are HIV/AIDS and the gay male identity process. He has taught human behavior, clinical practice, and social work with AIDS. He maintains a varied clinical practice, and was elected as a member of the Social Work Practice Academy.

Michael J. Sheridan, M.S.W., Ph.D., is Associate Professor in the School of Social Work at Virginia Commonwealth University. Her practice experience includes work in mental health, health, corrections, and youth and family services. Her major areas of interest are spirituality and social work, social justice, and the experiences and needs of persons who are incarcerated and their families. She teaches social justice, spirituality and social work, and research at the B.S.W., M.S.W., and doctoral levels.

Nancy R. Vosler, M.S.W., Ph.D., is Associate Professor in the George Warren Brown School of Social Work, Washington University, in St. Louis. Her research interests include the impact of unemployment and poverty on families, welfare reform, and non-marital coparenting. She is author of a book titled *New Approaches to Family Practice: Confronting Economic Stress* (Sage, 1996). She teaches social policy and family practice courses, and is Coordinator of the School's Family Therapy Specialization. She serves on the board of Fathers' Support Center, St. Louis, an agency addressing the service needs of unmarried fathers and their children.

Amy A. Waldbillig, M.S.W., L.C.S.W., is a doctoral student in the School of Social Work at Virginia Commonwealth University. She received her M.S.W. from the University at Albany. Her practice experience includes in-home services for foster care prevention, clinical case management with treatment foster care, and foster parent training. Her major areas of interest include foster care disruption, improvement of stability for youth in foster care, and intervention research.

Joseph Walsh, M.S.W., Ph.D., L.C.S.W., is Associate Professor in the School of Social Work at Virginia Commonwealth University. He was educated at Ohio State University and has worked for 25 years in community mental health settings. His major areas of interest are clinical social work, serious mental illness, and psychopharmacology. He teaches courses in social work practice, human behavior and the social environment, and research while maintaining a small clinical practice.

Maria E. Zuniga, M.S.W., Ph.D., is Professor in the School of Social Work at San Diego State University. She previously taught at Sacramento State University. Her areas of focus are direct practice, gerontological practice, and practice with multicultural populations, in particular practice with Latinos. She has taught human behavior courses. She was a member of the board of directors of the Council on Social Work Education (CSWE) and helped to develop a CSWE-sponsored conference on Cultural Competence held at the University of Michigan in 1999. She is a consultant on cultural competence for local, state, and national agencies and publishing houses.

PART I

A Multidimensional Approach for Multifaceted Social Work

- Caroline O'Malley is knocking at the door of a family reported to her agency for child abuse.

- Sylvia Gomez and other members of her team at the rehabilitation hospital are meeting with the family of an 18-year-old man who is recovering from head injuries sustained in a motorcycle accident.

- Mark Bernstein is on the way to the county jail to assess the suicide risk of an inmate.

- Helen Moore is preparing a report for a legislative committee.

- Juanita Alvarez is talking with a homeless man about taking his psychotropic medications.

- Stan Weslowski is meeting with a couple who would like to adopt a child.

- Andrea Thomas is analyzing the results of a needs assessment recently conducted at the service center for older adults where she works.

- Anthony Pacino is wrapping up a meeting of a cancer support group.

- Sam Belick is writing a social history for tomorrow's team meeting at the high school where he works.

- Sarah Sahair has just begun a meeting of a recreational group of 9- and 10-year-old girls.

- Jane Kerr is facilitating the monthly meeting of an interagency coalition of service providers for substance-abusing women and their children.

- Ann Noles is planning a fund-raising project for the local Boys Club and Girls Club.

- Meg Hart is wrapping up her fourth counseling session with a lesbian couple.

- Chien Liu is meeting with a community group concerned about youth gang behavior in their neighborhood.

- Mary Wells is talking with one of her clients at the rape crisis center.

What do these people have in common? You have probably guessed that they all are social workers. They work in a variety of settings, and they are involved in a variety of activities, but they all are doing social work. Social work is, indeed, a multifaceted profession. And because it is multifaceted, social workers need a multidimensional understanding of human behavior. This book provides such an understanding. The purpose of the two chapters in Part I is to introduce you to a multidimensional way of thinking about human behavior and to set the stage for subsequent discussion. In Chapter 1, you are introduced to the multiple dimensions of person, environment, and time that serve as the framework for the book. You are given some tools to think critically about the multiple theories and varieties of research that make up our general knowledge about these dimensions of human behavior. And you learn about the organization of the book. In Chapter 2, you encounter eight theoretical perspectives that contribute to multi-dimensional understanding. You learn about their central ideas and their scientific merits. Most important, you consider the usefulness of these eight theoretical perspectives for social work. The Knowledge Into Practice story for Part I illustrates the multifaceted nature of a day in the life of one social worker.

Looking at a Complex World

Consider a line.

It is a single-dimensional representation of reality but still is useful.

It can give direction, like an arrow.

It can make connections between two items to show a relationship.

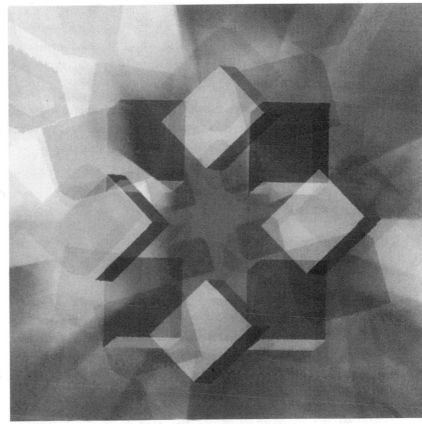

But a single-dimensional line still is limited in what it can tell us about the real world. The real world is multidimensional. It has spatial and temporal dimensions. And within these dimensions, people live out very complex and dynamic lives.

Now consider a cube.

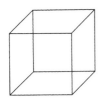

It too is useful for describing and analyzing aspects of the world. It shows not only direction and relationship, as a line does, but also depth.

But a cube is also limited in what it can tell us about the real world. Consider how your image of the cube might change if you looked at it interacting with many other elements, as in a kaleidoscope. So it is with the world in which social workers function.

This book urges you to look at the world as you might look at the ever-changing pattern in a kaleidoscope, appreciating its many elements and its complexity. The multiple aspects of human behavior—person, environment, and time—are explored throughout these pages. As you read, you will need to hold various dimensions of person, environment, and time in mind in order to develop a more complete picture of the world and of the way social workers interact with that world.

Furthermore, you will need to develop the ability to look at situations from as many different perspectives as possible. As a social worker, you will need to be able to look at each individual and situation from a variety of angles and positions.

Imagine that you have been called on to help a youngster having trouble adjusting to school. Naturally, you should look at the educational environment to understand the forces influencing the child.

As a social worker, though, you can't stop with the child's immediate environment. You also need to look at the child. Does the child have a health problem or a problem with vision or hearing or learning abilities that is influencing behavior in the classroom?

Another aspect of the situation to consider is the wider environment. Is turmoil in the child's home life seeping into the school environment? And what is the child encountering in the neighborhood?

As a social worker, you must always be on the lookout for the complex factors that shape human lives.

© Corbis.

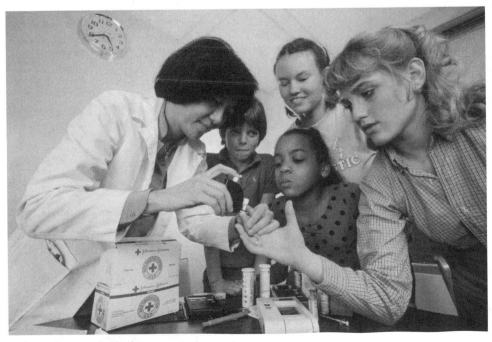

© Roger Ressmeyer/Corbis.

Social work services are also multidimensional. In looking for ways to assist the troubled child, you are also looking for ways to assist the family.

You might call on social service agencies that have helped other children and families through difficult periods.

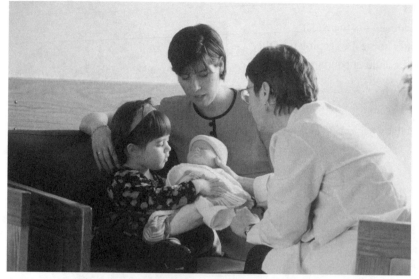

© Tom Stewart/Corbis.

You might also need to help link the child and the family with other organizations outside the school setting, so the child has positive interactions with other children and adults while trying to overcome school difficulties.

Social workers generally encounter a great many other situations and settings. However, every case can be approached, as this one has been, from multiple perspectives.

© Corbis.

As a social worker, you should also have a good grasp of general knowledge about human behavior and be able to apply that knowledge flexibly. General knowledge, which comes from both theory and research, helps social workers put their clients' lives into larger perspective.

© Alan Schein Photography, Inc./Corbis

Theory and research about social conditions and trends can give us a general perspective on the lives of these people.

However, only by discovering the unique details of their lives can we understand what brings individuals like these to us for help. Yes, they are part of a large group of poor people who share many traits. But each one has also experienced life in a unique way.

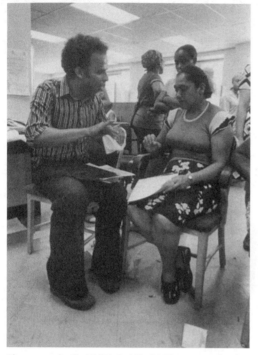

Photograph © AP/Wide World Photos.
Used by permission.

Photograph © Emily Niebrand.
Used by permission.

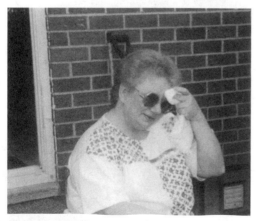

Photograph © Stacey Kowalski.
Used by permission.

General knowledge about human behavior and a good understanding of individuals' lives are the basic tools we need to do social work.

CHAPTER 1

Aspects of Human Behavior: Person, Environment, Time

Elizabeth D. Hutchison

Aspects of Human Behavior: Person, Environment, Time

Elizabeth D. Hutchison
Virginia Commonwealth University

What is it about people, environments, and time that social workers need to understand?

Why is it important for social workers to understand the role that diversity and inequality play in human behavior?

Key Ideas

As you read this chapter, take note of these central ideas:

1. This book provides a multidimensional way of thinking about human behavior in terms of changing configurations of persons and environments.

2. Although person, environment, and time are inseparable, we can focus on them separately by thinking about the relevant dimensions of each.

3. Relevant personal dimensions include the biological, the psychological, and the spiritual.

4. Nine dimensions of environment that have relevance for social work are the physical environment, culture, social institutions and social structure, dyads, families, small groups, formal organizations, communities, and social movements. These dimensions have been studied separately, but they are neither mutually exclusive nor hierarchically ordered.

5. Special attention should be paid to diversity, power relations, and patterns in opportunities and constraints.

6. General knowledge, as well as knowledge about the unique situation, is necessary for effective social work practice.

7. We use a number of ways to try to understand human behavior, but we draw heavily on two interrelated rigorous and systematic ways of building general knowledge: theory and empirical research.

CASE STUDY

SINA'S DETERMINATION TO SURVIVE

Sina grew up in a suburb of Phnom Penh, Cambodia. Because there were so many children in the family into which she was born, Sina and her two younger sisters were sent to be raised by relatives who lived nearby and who could not have children of their own. Sina had a happy childhood with these relatives and thinks of them as her parents (therefore, I will refer to them as her parents). Sina's parents were merchants, and she worked in the store with them. Her marriage at the age of 16 was arranged. Both Sina and her husband completed the equivalent of our high school education and were considered, in Cambodia, to be quite well educated. Sina's husband worked as a mechanic until they left the Phnom Penh area.

When the Khmer Rouge soldiers came to the outskirts of Phnom Penh in April 1975, Sina had no idea that her pleasant life was about to be so radically changed. The soldiers spread the word that the Americans were planning to bomb Phnom Penh and that everyone had to leave the area for a little while. The whole city was quickly evacuated. Sina, who was pregnant, headed for the countryside with her husband, 4-year-old daughter, and very large extended families from both sides. In the countryside, people were instructed to build houses, which most of them did not know how to do. Very soon, it became apparent that all was not well. The soldiers became very dictatorial and were particularly harsh with people who appeared educated and otherwise demonstrated "Western ways." Sina and her family started trying to hide their Western ways. They got rid of eyeglasses and books, changed their linguistic style to appear less educated, and tried to fake farming skills.

Things got worse. People, particularly men, began disappearing in the night, and gunshots were heard. Stories spread about terrible things happening. Rice began to disappear, and there was not enough to eat. The evacuees were forced to go to political meetings that lasted for hours. Fear was continual, but nighttime was the worst. That was when people disappeared and the gunshots were heard. The realization that they were

CASE STUDY

prisoners came slowly. But the atrocities intensified, and soon it was not uncommon to witness people, even family members, being shot in front of you. People had to work in the rice fields all day, but they were not allowed to eat the rice. Many people were starving to death. Malaria and dysentery were common. Members of Sina's extended family held up as well as could be expected, but her husband's brothers disappeared and were believed to be dead, and his sisters became ill and died. Sina's baby was underweight and sick at delivery, and Sina was relieved to have enough milk to feed her. Starvation and fear were constant companions.

Sina and her family stayed in the camp for about 3 years. She became pregnant again. Her husband's parents died of starvation. One night, Sina said to her husband, "We have to escape." Her husband said, "No, I am afraid." Sina insisted that they were going, that she could take no more, and she knew that there had to be a better life for her children. Sina rounded up her parents and her sisters and told them that they were going. They too were afraid and tried to dissuade her. But Sina was resolved to go, and they left in the middle of the night—pregnant Sina, her husband and two daughters, her parents, and her two sisters. Some of them were without shoes. They were very anxious about the possibility of being apprehended by the soldiers as they fled, and there were land mines everywhere.

Leaving camp, they entered the jungle. They ate whatever they could find—Sina is very vague when she talks about what they ate—and were constantly afraid of being apprehended by soldiers or stepping on a land mine. Night was still the most frightening time. Sina's husband was always near tears. After a few days, they could only travel a few miles per day, because they were too weak to walk and some were sick with malaria and dysentery. Sina is not sure how long it took them to get to Thailand, but she estimates 4 or 5 months. They just kept moving, with no clear idea where they were headed. In Thailand, they stayed in a United Nations camp for about 2 years. It was months before they could take solid food, and it took them a long time to recover from the aftermath of starvation and trauma. Sina gave birth to her third child soon after reaching the camp, and a fourth child before they left the camp to come to the United States.

Sina and her family were sponsored as immigrants by a refugee resettlement organization. With the help of a sponsor and an agency social worker, they were settled into an apartment when they first arrived, and Sina and her husband soon found jobs. The social worker also helped the family to understand and navigate the school system and the health care system and to make sense of their new world. Over the years, Sina has made

CASE STUDY

episodic contact with agency social workers to seek information about community organizations or to discuss challenges the family was facing. Recently, she came to the agency to talk with you about her husband's constant sadness.

Sina's husband is still employed by the same construction company that hired him as a newly arrived refugee. At first, Sina worked as a hotel maid, but she now has a job as a case aide with a social service organization. When money is tight, she still works part time as a maid. A fifth child was born after arriving in the United States, and all of the children have made good adjustments to their new environment. Sina and her husband put a high value on education, and the children have done well in school. Two of the children have graduated from college, and the youngest will soon graduate. The family's sponsor helped them to buy a house in the suburbs a number of years ago.

Sina and members of her extended family report that they still have trouble being in the dark, and they get very anxious if the food supply runs low. Sina's husband seems very sad all the time, and he sometimes suggests that he should have stayed and died. Sina, however, thinks they had no choice but to leave, for the sake of the children, and she is matter-of-fact about their struggles. Sina is always motivated to learn something new. She has become a U.S. citizen and is putting great efforts into learning English. She has converted from Buddhism to Catholicism, but her husband has not. Sina and her husband sometimes have a great deal of tension between them because he thinks she is more assertive than women should be. Sina is not sure if this problem would have arisen between them if they had been able to continue with their lives in Cambodia. Sina is more comfortable in her current environment than her husband is, but she sometimes wonders why Americans are so brash, so loud, so direct, so demanding, and so lacking in humility.

The Complexity of Human Behavior

As eventful as it has been, Sina's story is still unfolding. As a social worker, you will become a part of many unfolding life stories, and you will want to have a way of thinking about them. The purpose of this book is to provide a way for you to think about the nature and complexities of the people and situations that are at the center of social work practice. Three major aspects of this approach to human behavior are the person, the environment, and time.

If we focus on the *person,* we observe that Sina must have been blessed with a healthy biological constitution initially and must have been nurtured well in her childhood. She was able to carry babies to term through starvation, illness, and a journey through a jungle. She was able to recover in the hospital camp when many others died of damaged bodies and/or broken spirits. She has emotional resilience and a belief in her own capabilities. Sina and her husband have both survived physically, but she has survived spiritually as well, with a zest for life and hope for the future that he lacks.

If we focus on the *environment,* we see many influences on Sina's story. Consider first the physical environment: Sina moved from a comfortable suburban environment into a very primitive rural prison camp. From there, she wandered in the jungle, with tigers and snakes as her fellow travelers, and torrential rains, imagined soldiers, and land mines as foes. Her next stop was a hospital camp and, finally, a city in the United States.

Culture is a powerful influence in Sina's story. She faced no stigma for being given to relatives at birth, because that was not an unusual custom in Cambodia, where there was no birth control and extended families were close. Culture recommended that she be married at what may appear to us to be an early age and that her partner would be chosen for her. Culture also held that women lack power and influence, and yet Sina assumed a powerful role in her family's escape from the prison camp. Culture accorded a high value to humility, indirect communication, and saving face. The suburban, modernized lifestyle in which Sina was reared contributed a value on education that was not shared with Cambodians who lived in rural areas. And now, Sina lives biculturally. She assists the social workers at her agency to understand the communication patterns of Cambodian clients, and yet she is often baffled by the communication patterns of her native-born U.S. neighbors and coworkers. She is influenced by changing gender roles but is unhappy with the tension that such changes have produced in her marital relationship.

Sina's story has also been powerfully influenced by the geopolitical unrest of her early adulthood. Her relationships with social institutions have changed over time, and she has had to learn new rules based on her changing place in the social structure. Prior to evacuation, as an educated urban woman, she enjoyed high status and the respect that comes with it. In the prison camp, she had to learn to conceal that status and encountered greater powerlessness than she could have previously imagined. In the United States, she has often experienced the loss of status that comes from the language barrier, regardless of one's educational background.

Another dimension of the environment, family, is paramount to Sina. She was lucky that she did not have to leave many family members behind or see them die in the prison camp. Her husband was not so lucky. Sina's children are central to her life, and she suggests that they have motivated her to survive and reach beyond survival with hope. Sina and her husband are devoted to each other, but she is sorry about the tension in their relationship and her husband's enormous sadness. She is grateful, however, that her husband has not self-medicated his grief with alcohol as she has seen other Cambodian American men do in her work.

Small groups, organizations, and communities have been important forces in Sina's life, but she has had little direct contact with social movements. Sina's English as a second language (ESL) class is a small group that has become particularly important to her lately; she enjoys the companionship and the collegial sense of "we are all in the same boat" that she gets from the weekly classes. She has found several organizations particularly helpful in mediating her struggles with resettlement: the refugee resettlement program that sponsored her family, the social service organization for which she works, the Catholic church of which she is a member, and the schools her children attend. Sina has drawn strength and courage from her associations with these organizations, and she differs from her husband in this regard. Sina moved from a suburban community, where she was surrounded by extended family and long-term friends, to a prison camp, where fear was the driving force of relationships and loss of loved ones a common occurrence. Next she moved to a hospital camp, where recovery and taking note of losses took all the available energy. Finally, she moved to a city in the United States, where many people were willing to help but everything seemed strange and the language barrier was a serious impediment. Sina has heard about the antiwar movement that opposed U.S. involvement in Viet Nam, but she is not sure what to make of it.

If we now focus on the influence of *time*, we see that war and atrocity, escape, and resettlement have been powerful life events for Sina and her family. These events have left many trace effects in their current life. Experiences with past environments have left them with fear of the dark, panic regarding food shortages, and a preference for suburban environments. Both Sina and her husband have minor chronic medical problems from their years of hardship. Sina's husband has no surviving member of his family of origin, and his grief, and perhaps survivor's guilt, over the massive losses is severe. The language barrier is the most persistent reminder that this is not home. Luckily, Sina managed to smuggle some personal documents and photographs out of Cambodia, and she uses these to invite fond memories of past joyful events, including her traditional Cambodian wedding. These memories give her pleasure, but Sina lives mostly in the present while anticipating the future with confidence. To her husband, however, the past holds more positive meaning than either the present or future does.

Person, environment, and time interact dynamically. Relationships are reconfigured as the multiple influences on human behavior ebb and flow. The actions of one person can only be understood in relation to the actions of other people and in relation to ever-changing situations. A focus on changing relationships among inseparable aspects of a unity is often referred to as a transactional approach (Altman & Rogoff, 1987; Dewey & Bentley, 1949). A basic tenet is that person and environment depend on each other for their definition; the same person in a different environment, or the same environment with a different person, most likely will yield different behaviors. In reality, of course, any configuration or situation involves multiple persons and multiple environments.

Sina's story is a good illustration of the inseparability of person, environment, and time. What made her decide to attempt to escape from the prison camp? Was it something within her, something about her physical and social environment, or something about that time of her life? Or a combination of all three? Why has she chosen to acculturate more quickly than her husband? What leads her, now, to reach out for help for her husband? It is impossible to focus on person, environment, and time independently; they are inseparable.

A Multidimensional Approach

Thinking about human behavior as changing configurations of person and environment over time is a **multidimensional approach**. Such an approach is not new. Social work has historically recognized human behavior as an interaction of person with environment. The earliest social work practice book, *Social Diagnosis,* written by Mary Richmond in 1917, identified the social situation and the personality of the client as the dual focus of social work assessment. The Settlement House Movement put heavy emphasis on the environmental aspects of person-environment configurations, but environment was deemphasized, and intrapsychic factors emphasized, when social work began to rely on psychodynamic theory in the 1920s. In 1958, Herman Stein and Richard Cloward published an edited reader, *Social Perspectives on Behavior: A Reader in Social Science for Social Work and Related Professions.* In the Preface, they commented that social work had failed, in the midst of its fascination with dynamic psychology, to keep abreast of developments in sociology, cultural anthropology, and social psychology. In addition, in the late 1960s, general systems theory and other related formulations were incorporated into the way social work scholars think about human behavior (Anderson & Carter, 1974; Bloom, 1984; Germain, 1973; Hartman, 1970; Hearn, 1958, 1969; Meyer, 1976; Pincus & Minahan, 1973; Siporin, 1975). These approaches have renewed social workers' interest in the social sciences and helped social workers to understand the "pattern and flow" (Altman & Rogoff, 1987) of the processes and activities involved in the relationships between person and environment. The multidimensional approach of this book is rooted in the systems perspective.

We need, of course, to move beyond general statements about the inseparability of person and environment and about changing configurations to bring these ideas alive in our day-to-day experiences as social workers and to understand how to talk with clients like Sina about their concerns. A vast multidisciplinary literature, of both theory and research, is available to help us. The good news is that the multifaceted nature of this literature provides a broad knowledge base for the varied settings and roles involved in social work practice. The bad news is that this literature is highly fragmented, "scattered across more than thirty fields" (Kirk & Reid, 2002, p. 207). What we need is a structure for organizing our thinking about this multifaceted, multidisciplinary, fragmented literature.

The multidimensional approach provided in this book should help. This approach is built on the three major aspects of human behavior: person, environment, and time. Although in this book and in the companion volume, *Dimensions of Human Behavior: The Changing Life Course,* we focus on each of these aspects separately, keep in mind that no single aspect can be entirely understood without attention to the other aspects.

We can get a clearer picture of these three aspects if we think about the important dimensions of each—about what it is that we should study about person, about environment, and about time. Exhibit 1.1 is a graphic overview of the dimensions of person, environment, and time discussed in this book. Exhibit 1.2 defines and give examples for each dimension.

Keep in mind that **dimension** refers to a feature that can be focused on separately but that cannot be understood without also considering other features. The dimensions identified in this book are usually studied as detached or semidetached realities, with one dimension characterized as causing or leading to another. However, I do not see dimensions as detached realities, and I am not presenting a causal model. I want instead to show how these dimensions work together, how they are embedded with each other, and how many possibilities are opened for social work practice when we think about human behavior this way. I am suggesting that human behavior is **multidetermined**, or developed as a result of many causes. I do think, however, that

EXHIBIT 1.1

Person, Environment, and Time Dimensions

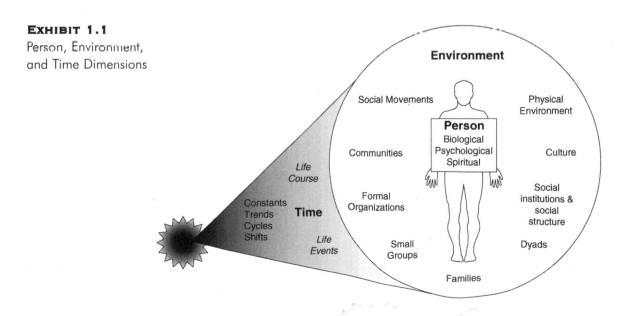

EXHIBIT 1.2

Definitions and Examples of Dimensions of Person, Environment, and Time

Dimension	Definition	Examples
Personal Dimensions		
The Biological Person	The body's biochemical, cell, organ, and physiological systems	Nervous system, endocrine system, immune system, cardiovascular system, musculoskeletal system, reproductive system
The Psychological Person	The mind and the mental processes	Cognitions (conscious thinking processes), Emotion (feelings), Self (Identity)
The Spiritual Person	The aspect of the person that searches for meaning and purpose in life	Themes of morality; ethics; justice; interconnectedness; creativity; mystical states; prayer, meditation, and contemplation; relationships with a higher power
Environmental Dimensions		
The Physical Environment	The natural and human-built material aspects of the environment	Water, sun, trees, buildings, landscapes
Culture	A set of common understandings, evident in both behavior and material artifacts	Beliefs, customs, traditions, values
Social Institutions and Social Structure	Social Institutions: Patterned ways of organizing social relations in a particular sector of social life Social Structure: A set of interrelated social institutions developed by humans to impose constraints on human interaction for the purpose of the survival and well-being of the collectivity	Social Institutions: family, religion, government, economy, education, social welfare, health care, mass media Social Structure: social class
Dyads	Two persons bound together in some way	Parent and child, romantic couple, social worker and client
Families	Groupings of two or more people who define themselves as family and assume obligations to one another	Nuclear family, extended family, fictive kin
Small Groups	Collections of people who interact with each other, perceive themselves	Friendship group, self-help group, therapy group, committee, task group

(continued)

EXHIBIT 1.2

Definitions and Examples of Dimensions of Person, Environment, and Time *(continued)*

Dimension	Definition	Examples
	as belonging to a group, are interdependent, join together to accomplish a goal, fulfill a need through joint association, or are influenced by a set of rules and norms	
Formal Organizations	Collectivities of people, with a high degree of formality of structure, working together to meet a goal or goals	Civic and social service organizations, business organizations, professional associations
Communities	People bound either by geography or by network links (webs of communication), sharing common ties, and interacting with one another	Territorial communities such as neighborhoods; relational communities such as the social work community, the disability community, a faith community, a soccer league
Social Movements	Large-scale collective actions to make change, or resist change, in specific social institutions	Civil rights movement, poor people's movements, disability movement, gay rights movement
Time Dimensions		
Trends	Long-term patterns of change that move in a general direction	Trend toward greater ethnic diversity in the U.S. Trend toward delayed child-bearing in advanced industrial countries Trend toward decline in manufacturing sector and increase in service sector in advanced industrial societies
Cycles	Short-term patterns of change that reverse direction repetitively	A weekly cycle of work interspersed with rest and relaxation Economic downturns and upturns
Shifts	Sudden abrupt changes of direction	Changes in patterns of living following a major loss Changes in the physical and social environment following a natural disaster (e.g., hurricane, flood, earthquake), or a human-made disaster such as September 11, 2001
Linear Time	Time in terms of a straight line	Past, present, future

focusing on specific dimensions one at a time can clarify general, abstract statements about changing configurations of person and environment.

Personal Dimensions

Any story could be told from the perspective of any person in the story. The story at the beginning of this chapter is told from Sina's perspective, but it could have been told from the perspectives of a variety of other persons: a Khmer Rouge soldier, Sina's husband, her mother, one of her children, a member of the sponsoring family, the social worker. You will want to recognize the multiple perspectives held by different persons involved in the stories of which you become a part in your social work activities.

You also will want tools for thinking about the various dimensions of the persons involved in these stories. For many years, social work scholars described the approach of social work as *psychosocial,* giving primacy to psychological dimensions of the person. Personality, ego states, emotion, and cognition are the important features of the person in this approach. Currently, however, social workers, like contemporary scholars in other disciplines (e.g., Clark, Anderson, Clark, & Williams, 1999; Kaplan & Sadock, 1998; Larivana et al., 2000; Longres, 2000; McInnis-Dittrich, 2002; Saleebey, 2001), take a **biopsychosocial approach**. In this approach, human behavior is considered to be the result of interactions of integrated biological, psychological, and social systems. Psychology is seen as inseparable from biology; emotions and cognitions affect the health of the body, and are affected by it.

In recent years, social work scholars as well as scholars in the social behavioral sciences and medicine have argued for greater attention to the spiritual dimension of persons as well. Recent developments in neuroscience have generated new explorations of the unity of the biological, psychological, and spiritual dimensions of the person. For example, recent research has focused on the ways that emotions and thoughts, as well as spiritual states, influence the immune system (Rice, 2001; "Spiritual Matters, Earthly Benefits," 2001). Thus, this book gives substantial coverage to all three of these dimensions.

Environmental Dimensions

Social workers have always thought about the environment as multidimensional. As early as 1901, Mary Richmond presented a model of case coordination that took into account not only personal dimensions but also family, neighborhood, civic organizations, private charitable organizations, and public relief organizations (see Exhibit 1.3). Like contemporary social workers, Richmond saw the environment as multidimensional.

Several models for classifying dimensions of the environment have been proposed more recently. Among social work scholars, Ralph Anderson and Irl Carter (1974) made a historic contribution to systemic thinking about human behavior with the first edition of their *Human Behavior in the Social Environment: A Social*

EXHIBIT 1.3

Mary Richmond's
1901 Model of
Case Coordination

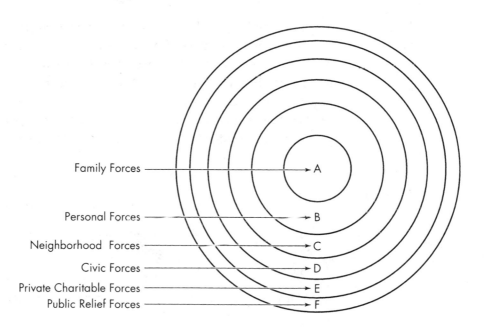

A. *Family Forces.*
   Capacity of each member for
   Affection.
   Training.
   Endeavor.
   Social development.

B. *Personal Forces.*
   Kindred
   Friends.

C. *Neighborhood Forces.*
   Neighbors, landlords, tradesmen.
   Former and present employers.
   Clergymen, Sunday-school teachers,
      fellow church members.
   Doctors.
   Trade-unions, fraternal and benefit
      societies, social clubs,
      fellow-workmen.
   Libraries, educational clubs, classes,
      settlements, etc.
   Thrift agencies, savings-banks,
      stamp-savings, building and loan
      associations.

D. *Civic Forces.*
   School-teachers, truant officers.
   Police, police magistrates, probation
      officers, reformatories.

Health department, sanitary
   inspectors, factory inspectors.
Postmen.
Parks, baths, etc.

E. *Private Charitable Forces.*
   Charity organization society.
   Church of denomination to which
      family belongs.
   Benevolent individuals.
   National, special, and general relief
      societies.
   Charitable employment agencies and
      work-rooms.
   Fresh-air society, children's aid
      society, society for protection of
      children, children's homes, etc.
   District nurses, sick-diet kitchens,
      dispensaries, hospitals, etc.
   Society for suppression of vice,
      prisoner's aid society, etc.

F. *Public Relief Forces.*
   Almshouses.
   Outdoor poor department.
   Public hospitals and dispensaries.

Systems Approach, one of the earliest textbooks on human behavior authored by social workers. Their classification of environmental dimensions has had a significant impact on the way social workers think about the environment. Anderson and Carter divide the environment into five dimensions: culture and society, communities, organizations, groups, and families. Social workers (see, e.g., Ashford, LeCroy, & Lortie, 2001) have also been influenced by Uri Bronfenbrenner's (1989, 1999) ecological perspective, which identifies four interdependent, nested categories or levels of systems:

1. Microsystems are systems that involve direct face-to-face contact between members.

2. Mesosystems are networks of microsystems of a given person.

3. Exosystems are the linkages between microsystems and larger institutions that affect the system, such as the family system and the parent's workplace or the family system and the child's school.

4. Macrosystems are the broader influences of culture, subculture, and social structure.

Some recent models have added the physical environment (natural and designed environments) as a separate dimension. Failure to include the physical environment has most notably hampered social work's ability to respond to persons with disabilities.

To have an up-to-date understanding of the multidimensional environment, social workers need knowledge about the eight dimensions of environment described in Exhibit 1.2 and presented as chapters in this book: the physical environment, culture, social institutions and social structure, families, small groups, formal organizations, communities, and social movements. We also need knowledge about dyadic relationships—relationships between two people, the most basic social relationships. Dyadic relationships receive attention throughout the book, are emphasized in Chapter 5, and are the focus of the Knowledge Into Practice reflection at the end of Part II. Simultaneous consideration of multiple environmental dimensions provides new possibilities for action, perhaps even new or revised approaches to social work practice.

These dimensions are neither mutually exclusive nor hierarchically ordered. For example, a family is sometimes referred to as a social institution, families can also be considered small groups or dyads, and family theorists write about family culture. Remember, dimensions are useful ways of thinking about person/environment configurations, but you should not think of them as detached realities.

Time Dimensions

When I was a doctoral student in a social work practice course, Professor Max Siporin began his discussion about social work assessment with the comment, "The date is the most important information on a written social work assessment." This was Siporin's way of acknowledging the importance of time in human behavior, of recognizing that person/environment transactions are ever-changing, dynamic, and flowing.

We are aware of the time dimension in the ongoing process of acculturation in Sina's story. As will be discussed in Chapter 8, **acculturation** is a process of changing one's culture by incorporating elements of another culture. Acculturation happens over time, in a nonlinear process, with new situations and opportunities to learn, negotiate, and accommodate. Sina has aggressively pursued learning about her new culture's roles while still keeping her culture of origin, becoming bicultural over time. Her husband, however, barely speaks the new language and is involved in a much slower acculturation process. There is some evidence that women who are immigrants often have a faster pace of acculturation than their spouses; there is considerable evidence that children usually have a faster pace of acculturation than their parents (Hernandez & McGoldrick, 1999).

Nancy Yattaw (1999) suggests four ways of thinking about time in changing configurations of persons and environment: constants, trends, cycles, and shifts. Constants and trends are long-term changes, and cycles and shifts are short-term changes. This is how they differ:

- **Constants** move invariably in one direction. It is hard to think of examples of constants in our contemporary global societies, but the aging process approximates the idea of a constant.

- **Trends** move in a general direction but are not as invariable as constants. Sina and her family are part of a trend toward greater cultural diversity in the United States. Chapter 9 examines trends in major social institutions and in patterns of social inequality.

- **Cycles** reverse direction repetitively. Cycles of behavior can recur in different patterns: daily, weekly, monthly, seasonally, annually, or in some other regular or partially regular pattern. Miriam Glucksmann (1998) suggests that cyclical time serves as the glue for social life: "[E]verybody does the same thing on the same day so they share a common daily or weekly cycle" (p. 256). Socially constructed cyclical time has a large impact on our lives. As I work on this book in mid-July, I am cognizant that summer "vacation" is more than half over, and soon my time will be spent preparing lectures, grading papers, and making visits to field agencies, all activities that I do not engage in during the summer. I am also remembering the rhythm of the school semester: the intense activity to get the semester up and rolling; the settling-in time when I think to myself, *I can handle this*; the accelerated pace beginning around mid-semester when I am determinedly focused on time management; and the hectic last weeks when, in spite of my best intentions, my health maintenance program is seriously compromised and I find myself wondering, *How did I let this happen again?* This cycle has been repeating for over 20 years, but it is never exactly the same. Stability, as well as change, comes with cyclical time. Another example of cycles comes from social movements. During "cycles of contention," protest movements build on each other. Such cycles are broken by periods of relative quiet, when little is happening in the way of social protest. In the United States, the last cycle of contention is the rights movements of the 1960s. In Eastern Europe, the late 1980s was the beginning of a cycle of contention.

■ **Shifts** are sudden abrupt changes in direction. Several shifts are evident in the story of Sina and her family: evacuation, escape, and resettlement. After September 11, 2001, we heard much talk about whether the terrorist attacks on the World Trade Center and the Pentagon will produce shifts in our patterns of social interactions. Early reports suggested that family life became more precious to us ("ACOG Assess Impact of September 11," 2002) and faith in each other increased ("Historical Perspective," 2002). It remains to be seen whether these immediate reactions result in longer-term shifts in social life.

Time orientation is another concept that has been used to describe time dimensions. It is the extent to which individuals and collectivities are invested in three temporal zones—past, present, and future time—known as **linear time**. Research indicates that cultures differ in their time orientation. More traditional cultures are more invested in the past, and advanced industrial cultures are more invested in the future (Hofstede, 1998). Some cultures, for example the Hopi of the U.S. Southwest, and some Arab cultures, do not distinguish past, present, and future (Newman, 1995). Research also indicates that there are age-related differences in time orientation, with older adults more past oriented than younger age groups (Shmotkin, 1991). There are also individual variations in time orientation. We noted earlier, for example, that Sina is invested in the future but her husband is oriented to the past. This difference is consistent with one recent research report that found that trauma survivors who had experienced the most severe loss were more likely than other trauma survivors to be highly oriented to the past (Holman & Silver, 1998).

Sometimes the pace of change is more rapid than at other times—for example, the pace of change accelerated in April 1975 for Sina and her family. There is also a temporal scope, or duration, to changing configurations. In linear time, the scope of some events is brief, such as a birthday party, an accident, termination from a job, winning the lottery, or a natural disaster. Werner, Altman, and Oxley (1985) refer to these brief events as *incidents;* in this book and the companion volume, they are called **life events.** Although life events are brief in scope, they may produce shifts and have serious and long-lasting effects. It is important to note the role of perception when discussing both the pace of change and the duration of an event (Rappaport, Enrich, & Wilson, 1985). It is easy to imagine that the 3 years spent in the prison camp seemed much longer to Sina and her family than the preceding 3 years in their suburban home.

Other events are long and complex transactions of people and environments. Werner et al. (1985) refer to these longer events as *stages;* it is this dimension of time that has been incorporated into life stage theories of human behavior. As explained in Chapter 2, however, life stage theories have been criticized for their overstatement of the consistency of the sequence of stages and of the timing of human behavior. In contrast, a **life course perspective** assumes that each person's life has a unique long-term pattern of stability and change but that shared social and historical contexts produce some commonalities (George, 1993). The life course perspective is the topic of Chapter 1 in the companion volume.

Diversity and Inequality

Kenneth Prewitt (2000), Director of the 2000 census, has suggested that the driving issue in the 2000 census was demographic diversity. The United States was 87% white in 1925, 80% white in 1950, 72% white in 2000, and by 2050, it is projected that we will be about 50% white. According to Prewitt: "The U.S. was a microcosm of all of Europe by 1920. With the 2000 census, we are the first country in the world's history to be a microcosm of the *world* in race, ethnicity, and religion." It is exciting to live in such times, but we face the great challenge of finding unity in such diversity.

Some of the diversity in our national social life is new. Clearly, there is increasing racial, ethnic, and religious diversity in the United States, and as Prewitt notes, the mix in the population stream has become much more complex in recent years (Alvarez, 2001). However, some of the diversity in our social life is not new but simply newly recognized. In the contemporary era, we have been developing a heightened consciousness of human differences— gender differences, racial and ethnic differences, cultural differences, religious differences, differences in sexual orientation, differences in abilities and disabilities, differences in family forms, and so on. We are experiencing a new tension to navigate the line between cultural sensitivity and stereotypical thinking about individuals. It is the intent of this book to capture the diversity of human experience in a manner that is respectful of all groups, conveys the positive value of human diversity, and recognizes differences *within* groups as well as differences *between* groups.

As you seek to honor differences, keep in mind the distinction between heterogeneity and diversity (Calasanti, 1996). **Heterogeneity** refers to individual-level variations, differences among individuals. For example, as the social worker whom Sina consults, you will want to recognize the ways in which Sina is different from you and from other clients you serve. An understanding of heterogeneity allows us to recognize the uniqueness of person-environment configurations. **Diversity**, on the other hand, refers to patterns of group differences. Diversity recognizes social groups, groups of people who share a range of physical, cultural, or social characteristics within a category of social identity. As a social worker, besides recognizing individual differences, you will also want to be aware of the diversity in your community, such as the distribution of various ethnic groups, including those of Cambodian heritage. Knowledge of diversity allows us to provide culturally competent practice.

Attending to diversity involves recognition of the power relations between social groups and the patterns in opportunities and constraints for social groups (Calasanti, 1996). If we are interested in the Cambodian community in our city, for example, we will want to note, among other things, the neighborhoods where they live, the quality of the housing stock in those neighborhoods, the comparative educational attainment in the community, the occupational profile of the community, and the comparative income levels. When we attend to diversity, we not only note the differences between groups, but we also note how socially constructed hierarchies are superimposed on these differences.

Recent scholarship in the social sciences has emphasized the ways in which three types of categorizations—gender, race, and class—are used to develop hierarchical social structures "within which people form identities and through which they realize their life chances" (Stoller & Gibson, 2000, p. 4). This literature suggests that these social categorizations create **privilege**, or unearned advantage, for some groups and disadvantage for other groups. In a much-cited article, Peggy McIntosh (1988/2001) has pointed out the mundane daily advantages of white privilege that are not available to members of groups of color, such as, "I can be sure that my children will be given curricular materials that testify to the existence of their race" and "Whether I use checks, credit cards, or cash, I can count on my skin color not to work against the appearance of financial reliability." We could also generate lists of advantages of male privilege, adult privilege, upper middle-class privilege, heterosexual privilege, ability privilege, Christian privilege, and so on. McIntosh argues that we benefit from our privilege but have not been taught to think of ourselves as privileged. Members of privileged groups take for granted that their advantages are "normal and universal" (Bell, 1997, p. 12).

It is important to note, however, that privilege and disadvantage are multidimensional, not one-dimensional. One can be privileged in one dimension and disadvantaged in another; for example, I have white privilege but not gender privilege. As social workers, we need to be attuned to our own configuration of privilege and disadvantage and how this might serve as an aid or a barrier when we work with particular client groups.

This is not easy for us, because in the United States, as a rule, we avoid the topic of class and don't like to admit that it shapes our lives (Sernau, 2001, p. 65). It is important for social workers to acknowledge social inequalities, however, because our interactions are constantly affected by inequalities. And there is clear evidence that social inequalities are on the rise in the United States. In the last couple of decades, the United States gained the distinction as the most unequal society in the advanced industrial world, and the gap continues to widen. Scott Sernau reports that the most unequal advanced industrial societies are "former frontier societies" (p. 49)—the United States, Canada, and Australia. He suggests that, interestingly, these societies have the strongest ethic of equal opportunity and suspicion of snobbery, but they also continue with a frontier bias toward limited federal government and unrestrained markets (Sernau, 2001). Thus, social workers face a great challenge in advocating for groups who are disadvantaged.

The General and the Unique

The tension between commonalities and individual differences is central to the multidimensional approach. Let's assume that your field instructor has asked you to meet with Sina regarding her concerns about her husband. How will you know how to talk with her and what to talk with her about? What questions will you have before you get started? What do you want to know more about? Most likely, you want to know something about Sina's unique life story, and you must decide how much of that to learn from agency records and your field instructor and how much to wait and hear from Sina herself. But you will probably want to know some other, more general types of information that will not be in the agency record and that you know your field instructor expects you to take some personal responsibility for learning. This general information might include aspects of Cambodian culture, the acculturation process, family functioning, Buddhism and Catholicism, grief reactions, post-traumatic stress reactions, clinical depression, and cross-cultural communication.

Carol Meyer (1993) suggests that effective social work practice involves balancing an individualized (unique) assessment of the specific person in a specific situation with general knowledge about human behavior. Professional social workers weave idiosyncratic details of a client's story with general knowledge about patterns of relationships between persons and situations. Although Meyer writes about work with one particular client, her suggestions about general knowledge and unique situations could apply equally well to work with families, small groups, neighborhoods, and so on. You might want, for example, to form a mutual aid group of Cambodian men or to develop an outreach program in a Cambodian neighborhood, drawing on both general knowledge about small group dynamics and community building and more specialized knowledge of Cambodian culture and the interpersonal dynamics in the group or neighborhood.

I want to emphasize two ideas about the relationship between general and unique knowledge: first, it is a person's unique story that suggests which general knowledge is needed. Second, the general knowledge suggests **hypotheses**, or tentative statements, to be explored and tested, not facts to be applied, in transactions with the person (Schutt, 1999, p. 36). For example, your examination of general knowledge may lead you to hypothesize that Sina's husband understands the tenets of Buddhism to direct him to hold himself personally responsible for his own suffering. You may hypothesize that, like many Southeast Asians, he would find it disgraceful to engage in direct conversation about his emotions. You may have learned that although seeking help for physical problems was acceptable in Cambodia, there were no special professions for addressing emotional problems. This understanding may lead you to hypothesize that Sina's husband would be more comfortable talking about his situation in terms of its biological aspects instead of its emotional aspects. Ultimately, of course, you want to understand how Cambodian culture, family functioning, Buddhism and Catholicism, grief reactions, post-traumatic stress reactions, clinical depression, cross-cultural communication, and all the rest come together to form a whole in Sina's unfolding life story. That is a lot to think about, but such complexity is what makes social work such a demanding and exciting profession.

Professional social workers must struggle continuously with the tension between the general and the unique. The multidimensional approach presented in this book is well suited to this struggle. A multidimensional approach allows examination of an idiosyncratic event from several perspectives and opens the possibilities for considering the variety of factors that contribute to a particular transaction. A multidimensional approach also facilitates social work's emphasis on human diversity.

To assist you in moving between general knowledge and unique stories, each chapter in this book begins, as this one does, with one or more case studies. Each of these unique stories suggests which general knowledge is needed. Then, throughout the chapter, the stories are woven together with the relevant general knowledge. Keep in mind as you read that general knowledge is necessary, but you will not be an effective practitioner unless you take the time to learn about the unique life course of each person or collectivity you serve.

General Knowledge: Theory and Research

Some suggest that there can be no "general" knowledge because all situations are unique. I think you can see, however, that the details of Sina's unique story are inadequate for guiding you in thinking about how to talk with her and what to talk about. You also need some general knowledge about human behavior as you try to understand the world and situations such as those facing Sina and her family.

We go about trying to understand human behavior in a number of ways. Christine Marlow (2001) has identified the following types of understanding: values, intuition, experience, authority, and science. Monette, Sullivan, and DeJong (1998) have suggested a slightly different classification: tradition, experience, common sense, and science. All these ways of understanding, or put another way, all these types of knowledge, have pitfalls as well as strengths. Exhibit 1.4 summarizes the ways of understanding presented by Marlow and by Monette, Sullivan, and DeJong and analyzes their strengths as well as their pitfalls.

EXHIBIT 1.4
Ways of Understanding

Way of Understanding	Definition	Strengths	Pitfalls
Authority (Marlow)	An outside source of knowledge that is recognized as indisputable for the matter at hand.	Authorities of various types can provide readily accessible knowledge on a variety of topics.	The knowledge gained is only as strong as the authoritative source.
Common Sense (Monette et al.)	Practical judgments based on the shared experiences and prejudices of a collectivity.	Common sense is readily available and can be valuable and accurate.	What is common sense in one culture may make no sense in another culture. What is considered common sense does not usually involve rigorous and systematic investigation.
Experience (Marlow; Monette et al.)	Firsthand, personal participation in similar events or activities.	Firsthand experience may help us understand aspects of a situation not grasped by other ways of understanding. Experience also helps us remember, because it involves all the senses.	Experience is vulnerable to perceptual biases, faulty inferences, vested interests, and faulty generalizations.
Intuition (Marlow)	An insight that is not based on special training or reasoning. May be based on past experiences.	Intuition can give us leads to follow for further investigation. It may involve perceptions that are not yet captured at the conscious level. It is highly valued in some cultures.	Intuition does not usually involve rigorous and systematic investigation, and is subject to a variety of biases.
Science (Marlow; Monette et al.)	A rigorous and systematic way of producing knowledge about the world.	Science attempts to put a check on biases. It reminds us to remain tentative and open to questions and possibilities. It allows us to accumulate accurate information over time.	Science is never fully free of bias. It is created by persons and institutions with power. Bias can occur at every stage of the scientific process.
Tradition (Monette et al.)	Customs, habit, and repetition.	Tradition can provide valuable information for moral	Tradition is extremely resistant to change. It

(continued)

Exhibit 1.4

Ways of Understanding (continued)

Way of Understanding	Definition	Strengths	Pitfalls
Values (Marlow)	Beliefs about what is right and wrong.	judgments and value decisions. Social work is based on values about what constitutes socially just relationships and social structures.	easily confuses "what is" with "what should be." Values are very culture-bound. They are accepted on face value and are not expected to be put to the test of skeptical inquiry.

Source: Based on Marlow, 2001; Monette et al., 1998.

Although all ways of understanding have both strengths and pitfalls, a profession such as social work should draw on general knowledge that is built in the most rigorous and systematic way (Kirk & Reid, 2002). As you can see from Exhibit 1.4, that way of understanding is what we call science. Two interrelated approaches to knowledge building, theory and empirical research, fit the scientific criteria of being rigorous and systematic. Together, they create the base of knowledge that social workers need to understand commonalities among their clients and practice situations.

Theory

Social workers use theory to help organize and make sense of the situations they encounter. A **theory** is a logically interrelated set of concepts and propositions, organized into a deductive system, that explains relationships between aspects of our world. *Theory* is a somewhat imposing word, seemingly abstract and associated with serious scholars, but it has everyday utility to social workers:

> Scratch any social worker and you will find a theoretician. Her own theoretical perspectives about people and practice may be informed by theories in print (or formal theories) but are put together in her own way with many modifications and additions growing out of her own professional and personal experience. (Reid & Smith, 1989, p. 45)

Thus, theory gives us a framework for interpreting person/environment transactions and planning interventions. Theories focus our attention on particular aspects of the person-environment-time configuration.

Other terms that you will often encounter in discussions of theories are *model, paradigm,* or *perspective. Model* usually is used to refer to a visual representation of the relationships between variables. *Paradigm* is usually used to mean a way of seeing the world, and *perspective* is an emphasis or a view. Paradigms and perspectives are broader and more general than theory.

If you are to make good use of theory, you should know something about how it is constructed. **Concepts** are the building blocks of theory. They are symbols that allow us to communicate about the phenomena of interest. Some relevant concepts in Sina's story are culture, family functioning, Buddhism, grief reaction, post-traumatic stress disorder, clinical depression, and cross-cultural communication.

Theoretical concepts are put together to form **propositions** or assertions. For example, attachment theory asserts that loss of an attachment figure leads to a grief reaction. This proposition, which asserts a particular relationship between the concepts of loss, attachment figure, and grief, may help us understand the behavior of Sina's husband.

Theories are a form of **deductive reasoning**, meaning that they lay out general, abstract propositions that we can use to generate specific hypotheses to test in unique situations. In this example, attachment theory can lead us to hypothesize that Sina's husband is still grieving the many losses he has suffered: loss of loved ones, loss of a homeland, loss of status, and so on.

Social and behavioral science theories are based on **assumptions** about the nature of human social life. These theoretical assumptions have raised a number of controversies, three of which are worth introducing at this point (Burrell & Morgan, 1979; Martin & O'Connor, 1989; Monte, 1999):

1. Do the dimensions of human behavior have an **objective reality** that exists outside a person's consciousness, or is all reality based on personal perception (**subjective reality**)?

2. Is human behavior determined by forces beyond the control of the person (**determinism**), or are persons free and proactive agents in the creation of their behavior (**voluntarism**)?

3. Are the patterned interactions among people characterized by harmony, unity, and social cohesion or by conflict, domination, coercion, and exploitation?

The nature of these controversies will become more apparent to you in Chapter 2. The contributing authors and I take a middle ground on all of them: we assume that reality has both objective and subjective aspects, that human behavior is partially constrained and partially free, and that social life is marked by both cohesion and conflict.

Empirical Research

Traditionally, science is equated with empirical research, which is widely held as the most rigorous and systematic way to understand human behavior. Research is typically viewed, in simple terms, as a problem-solving process, or a method of seeking answers to questions. Something that is empirical is something that we experience through our senses, as opposed to something that we experience purely in our minds. The process of **empirical research** includes a careful, purposeful, and systematic observation of events with the intent to note and record them in terms of their attributes, to look for patterns in those events, and to make our methods and observations public. Like theory, empirical research is a key tool for social workers: "The practitioner who just conforms to ongoing practices without keeping abreast of the latest research in his or her field is not doing all possible to see that his or her clients get the best possible service" (Rubin & Babbie, 1993, p. xxv).

Just as there are controversies about theoretical assumptions, there are also controversies about what constitutes appropriate research methods for understanding human behavior. Modern science is based on several assumptions, generally recognized as a **positivist perspective**: the world has an order that can be discovered; findings of one study should be applicable to other groups; complex phenomena can be studied by reducing them to some component part; findings are tentative and subject to question; scientific methods are value-free.

Quantitative methods of research are the preferred methods from the perspective of modern science. These methods use quantifiable measures of concepts, standardize the collection of data, attend only to preselected variables, and use statistical methods to look for patterns and associations.

Over the years, the positivist perspective and its claim that positivism = science have been challenged. Critics of these methods argue that quantitative methods cannot possibly capture the subjective experience of individuals or the complex nature of social life. Although most of these critics do not reject positivism as *a way* of doing science, they recommend other ways of understanding the world and suggest that these alternative methods should also be considered part of science. Various names have been given to these alternative methods. We will be referring to them as the **interpretist perspective**, because they share the assumption that reality is based on people's definitions of it.

Interpretists see a need to replace existing methods with **qualitative methods of research,** which are more flexible and experiential than quantitative methods (Reid & Smith, 1989, p. 87). Participant observation, intensive interviewing, and focus groups are examples of qualitative methods of research. Interpretists assume that people's behavior cannot be observed objectively, that reality is created as researcher and research participants interact. They are interested in capturing how research participants experience

EXHIBIT 1.5
Questions Asked by
the Active Reader

1. What is the evidence for this statement?
2. Is this true for all people (for me, for my client, for other people I know)?
3. How can I use this information in my practice?
4. Is there anything left out of this argument?
5. What is the main point of this section?
6. Can I summarize the argument?
7. How does this relate to other evidence about this topic?

Source: Based on Gambrill, 1990, p. 75.

social life rather than recording human behavior according to preselected categories. Researchers using qualitative methods are more likely to present their findings in words than in numbers and to attempt to capture the settings of behavior. They are likely to report the transactions of researcher and participant, as well as the values of the researcher, because they assume that value-free research is impossible.

In this controversy, it is my position that no single research method can adequately capture the whole, the complexity, of human behavior. In fact, "we must often settle for likely, approximate, or partial truths" (Kirk & Reid, 2002, p. 16). Both quantitative and qualitative research methods have a place in a multidimensional approach, and used together may help us to see more dimensions of situations. Alvin Saperstein (1996) has stated my view well: "Science is a fabric: its ability to cover the world depends upon the existence of many different fibers acting together to give it structure and strength" (p. 163).

Critical Use of Theory and Research

Theories of and research about human behavior are nearly boundless and constantly growing. This book presents an up-to-date account of the current state of knowledge about human behavior, but it is highly likely that some of this knowledge will eventually be found mistaken. Thus, you are encouraged to be an active reader—reading with a sense of inquiry and curiosity, but also with a healthy skepticism. Exhibit 1.5 lists some questions that the active reader should think about; I hope that you will incorporate these questions into your reading of this book.

As you read this book and other sources of general knowledge, you will also want to begin to think critically about the theory and research that they present. In other words, you will want to carefully deliberate about "whether to accept, reject, or suspend judgment" (Moore & Parker, cited in Gibbs, 1997, p. 82) about the credibility of the claims made. Let's look first at theory. It is important to remember that although theorists may try to put checks on their biases, they write from their own cultural frame of

EXHIBIT 1.6
Criteria for Evaluating Theory and Research

Criteria for Evaluating Theory

Coherence and conceptual clarity. Are the concepts clearly defined and consistently used? Is the theory free of logical inconsistencies? Is it stated in the simplest possible way, without oversimplifying?

Testability and evidence of empirical support. Can the concepts and propositions be expressed in language that makes them observable and accessible to corroboration or refutation by persons other than the theoretician? Is there evidence of empirical support for the theory?

Comprehensiveness. Does the theory include multiple dimensions of persons, environments, and time? What is included and what is excluded? What dimension(s) is emphasized? Does it account for things that other theories have overlooked or been unable to account for?

Consistency with social work's emphasis on diversity and power arrangements. Can the theory help us understand uniqueness and diversity? How inclusive is it? Does it avoid pathologizing members of minority groups? Does it assist in understanding power arrangements and systems of oppression? Can it be used to promote social justice?

Usefulness for social work practice. Does the theory assist in the understanding of person and environment transactions over time? Can principles of action be derived from the theory? At what levels of practice can the theory be used?

Criteria for Evaluating Research

Corroboration. Are the research findings corroborated by other researchers? Are a variety of research methods used in corroborating research? Do the findings fit logically with accepted theory and other research findings?

Multidimensionality. Does the research include multiple dimensions of persons, environments, and time? If not, do the researchers acknowledge the omissions, connect the research to larger programs of research that include omitted dimensions, and/or recommend further research to include omitted dimensions?

Definition of terms. Are major variables defined and measured in such a way as to avoid bias against members of minority groups?

Limitation of sample. Does the researcher make sufficient effort to include diversity in the sample? Are minority groups represented in sufficient number to show the variability within them? When demographic groups are compared, are they equivalent on important variables? Does the researcher specify the limitations of the sample for generalizing to specific groups?

Influence of setting. Does the researcher specify attributes of the setting of the research, acknowledge the possible contribution of the setting to research outcomes, and present the findings of similar research across a range of settings?

Influence of the researcher. Does the researcher specify the attributes of the researcher and the role of the researcher in the observed person/environment configurations? Does the researcher specify the possible contributions of the researcher to research outcomes?

Social distance. Does the researcher attempt to minimize errors that could occur because of literacy, language, and cultural differences between the researcher and respondents?

Specification of inferences. Does the researcher specify how inferences are made, based on the data?

Suitability of measures. Does the researcher use measures that seem suited to, and sensitive to, the situation being researched?

reference and from a particular location in the social structure of their society. So, when taking a critical look at a theory, it is important to remember that theories are generally created by people of privileged backgrounds who operate in seats of power. The bulk of theories still used today were authored by white, middle- to upper-class Western European men and men in the United States with academic appointments. Therefore, as we work in a highly diversified world, we need to be attentive to the possibilities of biases related to race, gender, culture, religion, sexual orientation, abilities/disabilities, and social class—as well as professional or occupational orientation. One particular concern is that such biases can lead us to think of disadvantaged members of society or of members of minority groups as pathological or deficient.

Social and behavioral science scholars disagree about the criteria for evaluating theory and research. However, I recommend the criteria presented in Exhibit 1.6 because they are consistent with the multidimensional approach of this book and with the value base of the social work profession. (The five criteria for evaluating a theory presented in Exhibit 1.6 are also used in Chapter 2 to evaluate eight theoretical perspectives relevant to social work.) There is agreement in the social and behavioral sciences that theory should be evaluated for coherence and conceptual clarity as well as for testability and evidence of empirical support. The criterion of comprehensiveness is specifically related to the multidimensional approach of this book. We do not expect all theories to be multidimensional in nature, but critical analysis of a theory should help us identify determinism and unidimensional thinking where they exist. The criterion of consistency with emphasis on diversity and power arrangements examines the utility of the theory for a profession that places high value on social justice. And the criterion of usefulness for practice is essential for a profession.

Just as theory may be biased toward the experiences of members of dominant groups, so too can research. The result may be "misleading and, in some cases, outright false conclusions regarding a minority" (Monette et al., 1998, p. 8). Bias can occur at all stages of the research process.

- Funding sources and other vested interests have a strong influence on which problems are selected for research attention. For example, several critics have suggested that governmental agencies were slow to fund research on acquired immune deficiency syndrome (AIDS) because it was associated in the early years with gay males (Shilts, 1987).

- Bias can occur in the definition of variables for study. For example, using "offenses cleared by arrests" as the definition of crime, rather than using a definition such as "self-reported crime involvement," leads to an overestimation of crime among minority groups of color, because those are the people who are most often arrested for their crimes (Hagan, 1994).

■ Bias can occur in choosing the sample to be studied. Because of their smaller numbers, members of minority groups may not be included in sufficient numbers to demonstrate the variability within a particular minority group. Or a biased sample of minorities may be used (e.g., it is not uncommon to make black/white comparisons on a sample that includes middle-class whites and low-income blacks).

■ Bias can occur in data collection. The validity and reliability of most standardized measuring instruments have been evaluated by using them with white, non-Hispanic respondents, and their cultural relevance with ethnic minorities is questionable. Language and literacy difficulties may arise with both written survey instruments and interviews. Several potential sources of errors when majority researchers gather data from members of minority groups are mistrust and fear, the motivation to answer what is perceived to be wanted, shame and embarrassment, joking or making sport of the researcher, answering based on ideal rather than real, and inadequacy of questions (e.g., asking about a monthly income with families that will have to do a complex computation of "part-time incomes of different family members, income from selling fruit and Popsicles on weekends, income from helping another family make cheese once every two to three weeks, extra money brought in by giving haircuts and permanents to neighborhood women, or occasional childcare and sewing") (Goodson-Lawes, 1994, p. 24).

As with theory evaluation, there is no universally agreed-upon set of criteria for evaluating research. We recommend the nine criteria presented in Exhibit 1.5 for considering the credibility of a research report. These criteria can be applied to either quantitative or qualitative research. Many research reports would be strengthened if their authors were to attend to these criteria.

Theory and Research in a Multidimensional Approach

As you travel the journey on which this book takes you, you should have a clear understanding of the assumptions the contributing authors and I make about the role of theory and research in understanding human behavior. That understanding will assist you to be a critical reader of the book. I have written about some of these assumptions earlier in the chapter, but I summarize them for you here for emphasis.

Our assumptions about theory are as follows:

■ Changing configurations of persons and environments may involve unique, unrepeatable events, but they also may involve consistencies and patterns of similar events. Therefore, general statements and theories are possible, but should not be expected to fit all situations or all aspects of a given situation.

■ Each situation allows examination from several perspectives, and using a variety of theoretical perspectives brings more dimensions of the situation into view. Different situations call for different combinations of theoretical concepts and propositions.

■ Theories, like situations, are unfolding and should be viewed as tentative statements. Theoretical propositions serve as hypotheses to be tested, not as factual statements about the situation under examination.

■ Given the complexity of human behavior, a given transaction is probably not predictable, but we do not rule out the possibility of prediction.

■ Our goal as social workers should be to develop maximum understanding of situations in terms of whatever theoretical concepts and propositions apply. Multiple theoretical perspectives are necessary when taking a multidimensional approach to human behavior. This point is the focus of Chapter 2.

■ Social life is fraught with contradictions as well as consistencies, so it is acceptable to use multiple theoretical approaches that introduce contradictions. You will discover some contradictions in the theories discussed in Chapter 2.

Our assumptions about research include the following:

■ Any setting is an acceptable research setting, but studying a variety of settings enhances the knowledge-building process.

■ The researcher should always consider the contribution of the setting to the research findings.

■ The characteristics, biases, and role of the researcher constitute aspects of the phenomenon under study and should be considered in interpretation of data. The meanings of the research activities to the participants are also important dimensions of the research situation and should also be considered in interpreting the data.

■ Standardized measures should be used only when they are suited to the situation under study.

■ Understanding of human behavior may be advanced by both traditional and nontraditional methods of research.

■ Research projects that exclude person, environment, or time dimensions may advance an understanding of human behavior, but the researcher should recognize the omissions in interpretation of the data.

Organization of the Book

This book covers two of the three aspects of human behavior: person and environment. The third aspect, time, is covered in a companion volume titled *Dimensions of Human*

Behavior: The Changing Life Course.

In this book, Part I includes two stage-setting chapters that introduce the framework for the book and provide a foundation for thinking critically about the discussions of theory and research presented in Parts II and III. A Knowledge Into Practice reflection at the end of Part I demonstrates the multifaceted nature of social work. Part II comprises four chapters that analyze the multiple dimensions of persons—one chapter each on the biological person, the psychological person (or the self), the psychosocial person (or the self in relationship), and the spiritual person. A Knowledge Into Practice reflection at the end of Part II emphasizes the importance of attending to all four dimensions of the person in social work practice. The eight chapters of Part III discuss the environmental dimensions: the physical environment, culture, social institutions and social structure, families, small groups, formal organizations, communities, and social movements. At the end of Part III, a Knowledge Into Practice reflection demonstrates how one social worker focuses on several dimensions of environment.

Presenting personal and environmental dimensions separately is a risky approach. I do not wish to reinforce any tendency to think about human behavior in a way that camouflages the inseparability of person and environment. We have taken this approach, however, for two reasons. First, the personal and environmental dimensions, for the most part, have been studied separately, often by different disciplines, and usually as detached or semidetached entities. Second, I want to introduce some dimensions of persons and environments not typically covered in social work textbooks and provide updated knowledge about all the dimensions. However, it is important to remember that no single dimension of human behavior can be understood without attention to other dimensions. Thus, frequent references to other dimensions throughout Parts II and III should help develop an understanding of the unity of persons, environments, and time.

IMPLICATIONS FOR SOCIAL WORK PRACTICE

The multidimensional approach outlined in this chapter suggests several principles for social work assessment and intervention, for both prevention and remediation services:

- In the assessment process, collect information about all the critical dimensions of the changing configuration of person and environment.

- In the assessment process, attempt to see the situation from a variety of perspectives. Use multiple data sources, including the person(s), significant others, and direct observations.

- Allow people to tell their own stories, and pay attention to how they describe the pattern and flow of their person/environment configurations.

- Use the multidimensional database to develop a dynamic picture of the person-environment configuration.

- Link intervention strategies to the dimensions of the assessment.

- In general, expect more effective outcomes from interventions that are multidimensional, because the situation itself is multidimensional.

- Pay particular attention to the impact of diversity and inequality on the unique stories and situations that you encounter.

- Allow the unique stories of people and situations to direct the choice of theory and research to be used.

- Use general knowledge to suggest tentative hypotheses to be explored in the unique situation.

- Think of social work practice as a continuous, dialectical movement between unique knowledge and general knowledge.

KEY TERMS

acculturation
assumptions
biopsychosocial approach
concepts
constants
cycles
deductive reasoning
determinism
dimension
diversity
empirical research
heterogeneity
hypotheses
interpretist perspective
life course perspective
life events

linear time
multidetermined
multidimensional approach
objective reality
positivist perspective
privilege
propositions
qualitative methods of research
quantitative methods of research
shifts
subjective reality
theory
time orientation
trends
voluntarism

ACTIVE LEARNING

1. We have used multiple dimensions of person, environment, and time to think about Sina's story. If you were to be the social worker who met with her to discuss her concerns about her husband, you would bring your own unfolding person-environment-time story to that encounter. With the graphic in Exhibit 1.1 as your guide, write your own multidimensional story. What personal dimensions are important? What environmental dimensions? What time dimensions? What might happen when these two stories encounter each other?

2. Select a social issue that interests you, such as child abuse or youth gangs. List five things that you "know" about this issue. Think about how you know what you know. Where does your knowledge fit in Exhibit 1.4? How would you go about confirming or disproving your current state of knowledge on this topic?

WEB RESOURCES

Each chapter of this textbook contains a list of Internet resources and Web sites that may be useful to readers in their search for further information. Each site listing includes the address and a brief description of the contents of the site. Readers should be aware that the information contained in Web sites may not be truthful or reliable and should be confirmed before being used as a reference. Readers should also be aware that Internet addresses, or URLs, are constantly changing; therefore, the addresses listed may no longer be active or accurate. Many of the Internet sites listed in each chapter contain links to other Internet sites containing more information on the topic. Readers may use these links for further investigation.

Information not included in the Web Resources sections of each chapter can be found by using one of the many Internet search engines provided free of charge on the Internet. These search engines enable you to search using keywords or phrases, or you can use the search engines' topical listings. You should use several search engines when researching a topic, as each will retrieve different Internet sites.

GOOGLE
www.google.com
ASK JEEVES
www.askjeeves.com
YAHOO
www.yahoo.com

EXCITE
www.excite.com
LYCOS
www.lycos.com

There are several Internet sites that are maintained by and for social workers, some at university schools of social work and some by professional associations:

World Wide Web Resources for Social Workers

www.nyu.edu/socialwork/wwwrsw

Site developed and maintained by Professor Gary Holden of New York University's School of Social Work contains links to many federal and state Internet sites as well as journals, assessment and measurement tools, and sites maintained by professional associations.

Social Work Access Network (SWAN)

www.sc.edu/swan
Site presented by the University of South Carolina College of Social Work contains social work topics, list of schools of social work, upcoming conferences, and online chats.

Social Work and Social Services Web Sites

gwbweb/wustl.edu/websites.html
Site presented by the George Warren Brown School of Social Work, Washington University, St. Louis, Missouri, contains links to resources for a wide variety of social issues and social service organizations.

Council on Social Work Education (CSWE)

www.cswe.org/onav.htm
Site presented by the Council on Social Work Education, the accrediting body for academic social work programs, contains information about accreditation, projects, publications, and links to a number of social work-related Web sites.

National Association of Social Workers (NASW)

www.naswdc.org
Site presented by the National Association of Social Workers contains professional development material, press room, advocacy information, and resources.

CHAPTER 2

Theoretical Perspectives on Human Behavior

Elizabeth D. Hutchison and Leanne Wood Charlesworth

Theoretical Perspectives on Human Behavior

Elizabeth D. Hutchison
Virginia Commonwealth University

Leanne Wood Charlesworth
Caliber Associates

What theories are needed to understand the multiple dimensions of person, environment, and time involved in human behavior?

What criteria should social workers use to evaluate theories of human behavior?

Key Ideas

As you read this chapter, take note of these central ideas:

1. The systems perspective sees human behavior as the outcome of reciprocal interactions of persons operating within organized and integrated social systems.

2. The conflict perspective draws attention to conflict, inequality, dominance, and oppression in social life.

3. The rational choice perspective sees human behavior as based on self-interest and rational choices about effective ways to accomplish goals.

4. The social constructionist perspective focuses on how people learn, through their interactions with each other, to classify the world and their place in the world.

5. The psychodynamic perspective is concerned with how internal processes such as needs, drives, and emotions motivate human behavior.

6. The developmental perspective focuses on how human behavior changes and stays the same across the life cycle.

7. The social behavioral perspective suggests that human behavior is learned as individuals interact with their environments.

8. The humanistic perspective emphasizes the individual's freedom of action and search for meaning.

CASE STUDY

INTERGENERATIONAL STRESSES IN THE CLARK FAMILY

You have been asked to investigate the possibility that Martha Clark's family caregivers are emotionally and physically abusing her, as well as neglecting her. Martha Clark is an 81-year-old Euro-American widow who has lived with her 58-year-old son, Al, and his wife, Betty, since moving from her one-story apartment in a senior housing project when her husband died 2 years ago. Mrs. Clark never held a job outside the home, and her current income consists of the $400 per month she receives from Social Security. She has no savings. Mrs. Clark has arthritis that limits her mobility, making it difficult for her to walk the stairs from the main floor of Al and Betty's home to her bedroom and to the only bathroom, both on the second floor. Mrs. Clark also has heart disease and diabetes. She has been challenged by periodic episodes of depression throughout adulthood, and she has been despondent since her husband died.

Nine months ago, Al Clark was laid off from the plant where he had worked for the past 15 years. He had a massive heart attack 6 months ago, and he remains very fearful of having a second heart attack. Betty Clark works an 8:30-to-4:30 shift at the factory where she has worked on and off for 30 years. Currently, there is a rumor that the company is planning to relocate the factory outside the United States. Al and Betty Clark have two young adult children, both of whom live out of town. Their son, father of two children, was recently divorced; their daughter is pregnant with her third child. Both children are struggling financially, and their son often turns to Al and Betty with his grief about the divorce.

Before she leaves for work every morning, Betty prepares breakfast for Al and Martha. Most mornings, Martha does not come down until it's almost time for Betty to leave for work, and then Martha only picks at her food. Al has become concerned that Martha usually eats no lunch, and he admits that on several occasions he has lost his temper, screamed at his mother, and even hit her a few times. He feels angry, frustrated, and ashamed for losing his temper, but he doesn't know how to get his mother to eat. He also discovered recently that she has not been taking her medication for depression. When he discovered that, he berated Martha, screaming that she is "just a useless old woman."

Since Al's heart attack, money has been tight. The family car needed an expensive repair, and the hot water heater had to be replaced. Martha's medications are not covered by Medicare, and for the past 2 weeks, Al and Betty have not renewed some of her prescriptions, hoping each week that the money situation will be better next week. Al and Betty often have harsh words about the money problems.

Martha Clark reports that Al and Betty are doing a good job caring for her. She says that she has lived too long anyway, and that Al is right: she is a useless old woman. The doctor tells her that walking would be good for both her arthritis and her heart disease, but she spends most of her time sitting in a chair in her bedroom. She says she does not eat because she has no appetite.

Multiple Perspectives for a Multidimensional Approach

The unfolding story of Martha Clark, her son, and her daughter-in-law may be familiar to you in some ways, but it is also unique in the way these particular persons and environments are interacting over time. As a social worker, you need to understand these details about the situation of the Clark family. However, if you are to be helpful in improving the situation, you also need some general knowledge that will assist you in thinking about its unique elements. As suggested in Chapter 1, the range of general knowledge offered by a multitheoretical approach is necessary when taking a multidimensional approach to human behavior. The purpose of this chapter is to introduce you to eight theoretical perspectives that are particularly useful for thinking about changing configurations of persons and environments: systems perspective, conflict perspective, rational choice perspective, social constructionist perspective, psychodynamic perspective, developmental perspective, social behavioral perspective, and humanistic perspective. In Chapter 1, we defined *theory* as a logically interrelated set of concepts and propositions, organized into a deductive system, that explain relationships among aspects of our world. We suggested that a perspective is broader and more general, an emphasis or view. Each of the perspectives discussed in this chapter comprises a number of diverse theories.

We have selected these eight theoretical perspectives because they have stood the test of time and have a wide range of applications. In this volume, margin notes are used to help you recognize ideas from specific perspectives. Our purpose in this chapter is to introduce the "big ideas" of the eight perspectives, and not to present the various theories within the perspectives. We want to lay a groundwork for your understanding of the variations of the perspectives discussed in subsequent chapters. If you are interested in a more in-depth look at these theoretical perspectives, you might want to consult an excellent book titled *Contemporary Human Behavior Theory: A Critical Perspective for Social Work* (Robbins, Chatterjee, & Canda, 1998a).

Besides presenting an overview of the big ideas, we analyze the scientific merit of the perspectives and their usefulness for social work practice. The five criteria for critical understanding of theory identified in Chapter 1 provide the framework for our discussion of perspectives: coherence and conceptual clarity, testability and empirical support, comprehensiveness, consistency with social work's emphasis on diversity and power arrangements, and usefulness for social work practice. Exhibit 2.1 summarizes this analysis, rating each perspective as low, moderate, or high on each of the criteria. Two ratings are given if there was considerable change as the perspective developed over time. In those cases, the first rating applies to the earlier versions of the perspective, and the second rating applies to more recent versions.

Four of the perspectives introduced in this chapter are based in sociology, four are based in psychology, and several have interdisciplinary roots. This diversity reflects the history of the social work profession: social work scholars began with a preference for sociological knowledge, moved over time to a preference for psychological knowledge, and have recently come to seek knowledge of both environmental and personal factors (Germain, 1994). This recent trend is consistent with the multidimensional approach of this book.

As noted in Chapter 1, diversity and inequality are major themes of this book. In earlier versions of the eight perspectives, few, if any, acknowledged the importance of looking at diverse persons in diverse environments. Each of the perspectives has continued to evolve, however, and the perspectives are being reconstructed to better accommodate diversity and inequality. Some theory critics suggest that this shift to greater emphasis on diversity and inequality represents a paradigm, or worldview shift (e.g., Schriver, 2001). Other theory critics, on the other hand, argue that the eight perspectives discussed here have undergone continual change, but not such revolutionary change as to be labeled a paradigm shift (e.g., Ritzer, 2000). These critics suggest that the perspectives have stood the test of time because they have, over time, become much more self-conscious about diversity and inequality. Whether or not the attention to diversity and inequality constitutes a paradigm shift, we agree that it has been a major

EXHIBIT 2.1

Eight Theoretical Perspectives Analyzed by Five Criteria

Theoretical Perspective	Coherence and Conceptual Clarity	Testability and Empirical Support	Comprehensiveness	Diversity and Power	Usefulness for Practice
Systems Perspective	Low	Moderate-High	High	Low-Moderate	Moderate
Conflict Perspective	Moderate	Moderate	Low-Moderate	High	Moderate-High
Rational Choice Perspective	Moderate	Moderate	Moderate	Moderate	Low-Moderate
Social Constructionist Perspective	Low	Moderate	Moderate	High	Moderate-High
Psychodynamic Perspective	Moderate-High	Low-Moderate	Low-Moderate	Low-Moderate	High
Developmental Perspective	High	Moderate-High	Moderate	Low-High	Moderate
Social Behavioral Perspective	High	High	Moderate	Low-Moderate	High
Humanistic Perspective	Low	Moderate	Low-Moderate	Moderate	Moderate

and positive trend in behavioral science theorizing. Another major trend in behavioral science theory is that although much of recent theorizing fits within existing categories of theoretical perspectives, theoretical synthesizing is blurring the boundaries between perspectives (Ritzer, 2000). As you read about each of the perspectives, think about not only how it can be applied in social work practice but also how well it represents all the complexities of human behavior in its current form.

Systems Perspective

When you read the case study at the beginning of this chapter, you may have thought of it as a story about a family system—a story about Martha Clark, her son Al, and her daughter-in-law Betty—rather than "Martha Clark's story." You may have noted how Martha's, Al's, and Betty's lives are interrelated, how they influence one another's

Exhibit 2.2
Big Ideas of the
Systems Perspective

- Systems are made up of interrelated members (parts) that constitute an ordered whole.
- Each part of the system impacts all other parts and the system as a whole.
- All systems are subsystems of other larger systems.
- Systems maintain boundaries that give them their identities.
- The dynamic interactions within, between, and among systems produce both stability and change, sometimes even rapid, dramatic change.

behavior, and what impact each of them has on the overall well-being of the family. You may be thinking that Al's treatment of Martha contributes to her despondence, and that her despondent behaviors are feeding his sense of failure and frustration. You also may note that this family, like other families, has a **boundary** indicating who is in and who is out, and you may be wondering if the boundary around this family is as closed as it appears, with minimal input from friends, extended family, neighborhood, church, and so on. You may also have noted the influence of larger systems on this family: the insecurity of the labor market, the limitations of the health care delivery system, and historical gender roles that influenced Martha to confine her work to the home.

You can see, in Exhibit 2.2, how these observations about Martha, Al, and Betty fit with the big ideas of the systems perspective. The **systems perspective** sees human behavior as the outcome of reciprocal interactions of persons operating within organized and integrated social systems. Its roots are very interdisciplinary. During the 1940s and 1950s, a variety of disciplines—including mathematics, physics, engineering, biology, psychology, cultural anthropology, economics, and sociology—began looking at phenomena as the outcome of interactions within and among systems. Mathematicians and engineers used the new ideas about system **feedback mechanisms**—the processes by which information about past behaviors in a system are fed back into the system in a circular manner—to develop military technology for World War II; scientists at the Bell Laboratories used the same ideas to develop transistors and other communication technology (Becvar & Becvar, 1996). Later, George Engel (1977) used the same ideas to develop a biopsychosocial model of disease.

Social workers were attracted to the systems perspective in the 1960s, as they shifted from a psychiatric model to a model more inclusive of environment. Social work has drawn most heavily on the work of sociologists Talcott Parsons and Robert Merton, psychologists Kurt Lewin and Uri Bronfenbrenner, and biologist Ludwig von Bertalanffy. The social workers who first adopted the systems perspective were heavily influenced by *functionalist sociology,* which was the dominant sociological theory during the 1940s and 1950s. In functionalism, social systems are thought to be orderly and remain in a relatively stable state, also known as *homeostasis* or *equilibrium.* Each part of the system serves an essential function in maintaining the system, and the functions of the various parts are coordinated to produce a well-functioning whole. System processes and structures such as rules and roles serve to maintain system stability. Although this systems approach did not deny the possibility of system change, it was more impressed with the mechanisms of system maintenance.

In the systems perspective, the structure of roles has been an important mechanism for maintaining system balance. **Role** refers to the usual behaviors of persons occupying a particular social position. Consider the roles played by each person in the Clark family and the stresses the family has faced as a result of role transitions over the past 2 years. Martha Clark went from being wife and comanager of her own home to a less well-defined role in the home of Al and Betty. Al has seen his relationship with his mother change toward a caregiver role, has lost his role as worker, and has taken on a "sick" role. We might anticipate that Betty is experiencing role overload in the roles of sole wage earner, primary housekeeper, and caregiver for both her mother-in-law and her husband.

There was substantial growth in interest in the use of the systems perspective in social work during the 1970s, but by the end of the decade, social workers became dissatisfied with the perspective on two counts. First, the perspective was seen as too abstract and, second, the emphasis on stability seemed too conservative for a profession devoted to social change. Throughout the 1980s, some social work scholars tried to correct for these shortcomings with the continual development of ecological and dynamic systems approaches (e.g., Germain & Gitterman, 1980). Social workers (e.g., Bolland & Atherton, 1999; Hudson, 2000; Warren, Franklin, & Streeter, 1998) took renewed interest in the systems perspective in the 1990s as they began to make use of chaos theory and the related complexity theory. Chaos theory emerged in mathematics in the 1960s, took hold in a number of natural science disciplines in the 1970s, and has also revitalized the systems perspective in the social sciences in the past 2 decades.

Whereas traditional systems theories emphasize systems processes that produce stability, **chaos theory**, and the closely related complexity theory, emphasize systems processes that produce change, even sudden, rapid, radical change. This difference in understanding about change and stability in social systems is explained by propositions central to chaos theory. Traditional systems theories proposed that system stability results from *negative feedback loops* that work like a thermostat to feed back information that the system is deviating from a steady state and needs to take corrective action. Chaos theory recognizes negative feedback loops as important processes in systems and their role in promoting system stability. In addition, it proposes that complex systems produce *positive feedback loops* that feed back information about deviation, or should we say innovation, into the steady state in such a way that the deviation reverberates throughout the system and produces change, sometimes even rapid change. The change-producing feedback may come from within the system or from other systems in the environment.

EXHIBIT 2.3
Closed and Open
Systems

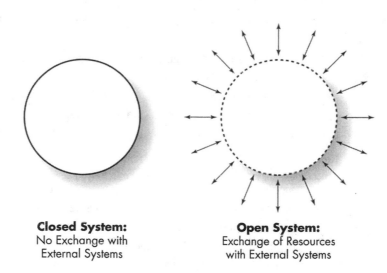

Closed System:
No Exchange with
External Systems

Open System:
Exchange of Resources
with External Systems

Like earlier systems theories, chaos theory emphasizes that all systems are made up of subsystems, and all systems serve, as well, as subsystems in other systems. Subsystems are always adjusting to each other and their environments, and the resultant changes are continuously being fed back. This results in a constant state of flux, and sometimes small changes in systems can reverberate in such a way as to produce very sudden and dramatic changes.

One issue about which the various versions of the systems perspective disagree is the permeability, or openness, of systems' boundaries to the environment. Functionalist sociology seemed to assume that interactions take place within a *closed system* that is isolated from exchanges with other systems. The idea of systems as closed was challenged by dynamic systems theories, most recently chaos theory, which assume a more *open system* as the healthy system. As Exhibit 2.3 illustrates, an open system is more likely to receive resources from external systems.

Recently, deep ecology has emerged with an emphasis on the notion of the total interconnectedness of all elements of the natural and physical world. Certainly, we were reminded of our interconnectedness with people in distant countries on September 11, 2001. On the other hand, recent theorizing in sociology has argued the case of the closed system. Niklas Luhman's (1987) general system theory, which has been popular in sociology in recent years, suggests that in highly complex societies, systems tend to become fragmented and closed to each other. They develop different languages and cultures and, consequently, cannot receive (hear and understand) feedback from each other. Luhman calls such systems *autopoietic systems.* Again, September 11, 2001, reminded us that even in a context of rapid international communication and a global economy, cultures may remain very isolated from the feedback of other cultures. The seemingly impermeable boundaries between the United States and Middle Eastern nations speak to this.

This is how the criteria for evaluating theory apply to the systems perspective:

■ *Coherence and conceptual clarity.* Although it has been popular over time, the systems perspective is often criticized as vague and somewhat ambiguous. Functional sociology has been particularly vulnerable to criticisms that its concepts are poorly, or inconsistently, defined. Although chaos theory and complexity theory have greater consistency in use of terms than earlier approaches did, concepts in these theories remain highly abstract and often confusing in their generality. In reality, chaos theory and complexity theory emerged in applied mathematics, and concepts from them are still being developed in the social sciences. There are recent attempts by social workers to extrapolate concepts from these theories (e.g., Bolland & Atherton, 1999; Hudson, 2000; Warren et al., 1998), but scholars have not yet stated or explained the concepts of these theories in the simplest and clearest way possible.

■ *Testability and evidence of empirical support.* Poorly defined and highly abstract concepts are difficult to translate into measurable variables for research. Nevertheless, a long tradition of research supporting a systems perspective can be found in anthropology and sociology. The systems perspective has been greatly strengthened in recent years with developments in brain research, epidemiology, and risk and resilience. Research methods have been developed in the natural and social sciences for studying concepts of chaos and complexity, methods such as lengthy time series analyses, but these methods are still rarely used in social work (Warren et al., 1998).

■ *Comprehensiveness.* Clearly, the systems perspective is devoted to the ideal of comprehensiveness, or wholism. It can, and has, incorporated the various dimensions of human systems as well as various dimensions of environmental systems. Systems theorists recognize—even if they do not always make clear—the social, cultural, economic, and political environments of human behavior. They acknowledge the role of external influences and demands in creating and maintaining patterns of interaction within the system. Early theorizing in the systems perspective did not deal with the time dimension—the focus was always on the present. But recent formulations have attempted to add a time dimension to accommodate both past and future influences on human behavior (see Bronfenbrenner, 1989; Ford & Lerner, 1992; Hannerz, 1992; Wachs, 1992). Certainly, chaos theory and complexity theory give implicit, if not always explicit, attention to time with their emphasis on dynamic change.

■ *Diversity and power.* Although diversity is not explicated in most systems theorizing, recent versions of the systems perspective, with their attention to complexity and continuous dynamic change, open many possibilities for unique and diverse person-environment configurations. And while most systems theorists do not explicate the role of power in systems transactions, some can accommodate the idea of power differentials better than others. Traditional systems theories that were influenced by functionalist sociology assumed that social systems are held together by social consensus and shared values. The emphasis on system equilibrium and on the necessity of traditional roles to hold systems together can rightly be criticized as socially conservative and oppressive to those who lack power within the system. Contemporary systems theory has begun to recognize power and oppression (see Longres, 2000; Martin & O'Connor, 1989), and conflict is seen as necessary for change in chaos theory.

■ *Usefulness for social work practice.* The systems perspective is more useful for understanding human behavior than for directing social work interventions, but several social work practice textbooks were based on the systems perspective in the 1970s and 1980s (see Germain & Gitterman, 1980; Meyer, 1983; Pincus & Minahan, 1973; Siporin, 1975). The primary value of the systems perspective is that it can be used at any level of practice. It also has merit because it surpasses other perspectives in suggesting that we should widen the scope of assessment and intervention (Allen-Meares & Lane, 1987) and expect better outcomes from multidimensional interventions (Ford & Lerner, 1992). Chaos theory can even be used by social workers to input information into a client system to facilitate rapid change, therefore enhancing possibilities for brief treatment, and group process can be used as reverberating feedback to produce change (Warren et al., 1998). In fact, social workers who work from a family systems perspective (e.g., Carter & McGoldrick, 1999a) have, for some time, used methods such as family genograms, and other forms of feedback about the family, as information that can produce change as it reverberates through the family system.

Conflict Perspective

In your case assessment with the Clark family, you have probably observed that Martha Clark is highly dependent on Al and Betty. Thus, another way of looking at her situation is to suggest that her lack of power in the family contributes to her problems. In a larger sense, Martha is a member of a class of people—old, poor, frail, single women—who hold little power in society. You may also note that Al and Betty, while holding more power in the family than Martha, hold little power in the labor market; they are vulnerable to the economic interests of other, more dominant, groups. You could be thinking about recent political debates about health care funding, noting the financial strain this family faces and its inability to pay for Martha Clark's medications. You may also note the authority associated with your role as protective investigator, and wonder how

EXHIBIT 2.4
Big Ideas of the
Conflict Perspective

1. Groups and individuals try to advance their own interests over the interests of others.
2. Power is unequally divided, and some social groups dominate others.
3. Social order is based on the manipulation and control of nondominant groups by dominant groups.
4. Lack of open conflict is a sign of exploitation.
5. Members of nondominant groups become alienated from society.
6. Social change is driven by conflict, with periods of change interrupting long periods of stability.

Martha, Al, and Betty will react to your power. Compare these observations with the central ideas of the conflict perspective, presented in Exhibit 2.4.

The **conflict perspective** has become popular over and over again in history, drawing attention to conflict, dominance, and oppression in social life (Collins, 1994). The conflict perspective typically looks for sources of conflict, and causes of human behavior, in the economic and political arenas. In sociology, the conflict perspective has two traditions: a utopian tradition that foresees a society in which there is no longer a basis for social conflict, and a second tradition that sees conflict as inevitable in social life (Wallace & Wolf, 1995).

The roots of contemporary conflict theory are usually traced to the works of Karl Marx and his collaborator Friedrich Engels and to the works of Max Weber. Marx (1887/1967) and Engels (1884/1970) focused on economic structures, but Weber (1904-1905/1958) criticized this singular emphasis in favor of a multidimensional perspective on social class. Contemporary conflict theory tends to favor Weber's multidimensional perspective, calling attention to a confluence of social, economic, and political structures in the creation of inequality (Collins, 1994; Ritzer, 2000; Wallace & Wolf, 1995). As you have probably noted, Weber's perspective is also more consistent than Marx and Engels's with the multidimensional approach of this book.

Power relationships are the focus of the conflict perspective. Some theorists in the conflict tradition limit their focus to the large-scale structure of power relationships, but many theorists also look at the reactions and adaptations of individual members of nondominant groups. These theorists note that oppression of nondominant groups leads to their *alienation,* or a sense of indifference or hostility. Jurgen Habermas (1984, 1987) and other **critical theorists** are interested in the connections between culture, social structure, and personality, paying particular attention to the role of individual perception. Lewis Coser (1956) proposes a **pluralistic theory of social conflict,** which recognizes that more than one social conflict is going on at all times, and that individuals hold cross-cutting and overlapping memberships in status groups. Social conflict exists between economic groups, racial groups, ethnic groups, religious groups, age groups, and gender groups. Thus, it seeks to understand life experience by looking at simultaneous memberships—for example, a white, Italian American, Protestant, heterosexual, male semiskilled worker, or a black, African American, Catholic, lesbian, female professional worker.

Although early social workers in the settlement house tradition recognized social conflict and structured inequality, and focused on eliminating oppression of immigrants, women, and children, most critics agree that social workers have not drawn consistently on the conflict perspective over time (Robbins et al., 1998a). Concepts of power and social conflict were revived in the social work literature in the 1960s (Germain, 1994). In the past decade or so, with renewed commitment to social justice in its professional code of ethics and in its curriculum guidelines, social work has drawn more heavily on the conflict perspective to understand dynamics of *privilege,* or unearned advantage, as well as discrimination and oppression. Social workers have used the conflict perspective as a base to develop practice-oriented **empowerment theories**, which focus on processes by which individuals and collectivities can recognize patterns of inequality and injustice and take action to increase their own power (e.g., Gutierrez, 1990, 1994; Lee, 2001; Rose, 1992, 1994; Solomon, 1976, 1987). Both in their renewed interest in domination and oppression and in their development of practice-oriented empowerment theories, social workers have been influenced by earlier **feminist theories**, which focus on male domination of the major social institutions and present a vision of a just world based on gender equity. Feminist theories, of course, are rooted in the conflict perspective.

Here is how the conflict perspective rates on the five criteria for evaluating social work theory:

1. *Coherence and conceptual clarity.* Most concepts of the conflict perspective are straightforward—conflict, power, domination, inequality—at least at the abstract level. Like all theoretical concepts, however, they become less straightforward when we begin to define them for the purpose of measurement. Across the various versions of the conflict perspective, concepts are not consistently used. One major source of variation is whether power and privilege are to be thought of as objective material circumstances, subjectively experienced situations, or both. In general, theories in the conflict tradition are expressed in language that is relatively accessible and clear. This is especially true of many of the practice-oriented empowerment theories developed by social workers. On the other hand, most recent conflict theorizing in the postmodern tradition is stated at a high level of abstraction.

2. *Testability and evidence of empirical support.* Conflict theory has developed, in the main, through attempts to codify persistent themes in history (Collins, 1990). The

preferred research method is empirical historical research that looks at large-scale patterns of history (see Mann, 1986; McCarthy & Zald, 1977; Skocpol, 1979; Wallerstein, 1974-1989). As with other methods of research, critics have attacked some interpretations of historical data from the conflict perspective, but the historical analyses of Michael Mann, Theda Skocpol, and Immanuel Wallerstein are some of the most influential works in contemporary sociology. In addition to historical analysis, conflict theorists have used experimental methods to study reactions to coercive power (see Willer, 1987) and naturalistic inquiry to study social ranking through interaction rituals (Collins, 1981). Contemporary conflict theorists are also drawing on network analysis, which plots the relationships among a group of people, and are finding support for their propositions about power and domination (see Burt, 1983).

3. *Comprehensiveness.* Traditionally, the conflict perspective focused on large-scale social institutions and social structures, such as economic and political institutions. In the contemporary era, Randall Collins (1990) is a conflict theorist who has made great efforts to integrate conflict processes at the societal level with conflict processes at the community, small group, and family levels. Collins suggests that we should recognize conflict as a central process in social life at all levels. Although early psychodynamic theory focused on intrapsychic conflicts, the sociological conflict perspective has not attended to personal dimensions. This omission is corrected by recent empowerment theories that give considerable attention to individual perceptions of power. Most conflict theories do consider dimensions of time. They are particularly noteworthy for recommending that the behavior of members of minority groups should be put in historical context, and indeed, as discussed above, empirical historical research is the research method that many conflict theorists prefer.

4. *Diversity and power.* The conflict perspective is about inequality, power arrangements, and systems of oppression. It helps us look at group-based patterns of inequality. In that way, it also assists us in understanding diversity. However, with the exception of the pluralist theory of social conflict, which recognizes that individuals have overlapping memberships in a variety of status groups, the conflict perspective is not helpful for understanding individual uniqueness. A major strength of the conflict perspective is that it helps us avoid pathologizing members of minority groups in the assessment process by helping us to put them in historical, cultural, economic, and political context. Empowerment theories guide us to engage in practice interventions that build on the strengths of members of minority groups.

5. *Usefulness for social work.* Concepts from the conflict perspective have great value for understanding power dimensions in community, group, and family relationships, as well as the power differential between social worker and client. Clearly, the conflict perspective is crucial to social work because (a) it shines a spotlight on how

domination and oppression might be affecting human behavior, (b) it illuminates processes by which people become estranged and discouraged, and (c) it encourages social workers to consider the meaning of their power relationships with clients, particularly nonvoluntary clients (Cingolani, 1984). In recent years, social workers have been in the forefront of developing practice-oriented empowerment theories, and the conflict perspective has become as useful for recommending particular practice strategies as for assisting in the assessment process. Empowerment theories provide guidelines for working at all system levels (e.g., individual, family, small group, community, and organization), but they put particular emphasis on group work because of the opportunities presented in small groups for solidarity and mutual support. With the addition of empowerment theories, the conflict perspective can not only help us to understand how the Clark family came to be discouraged but also help us think about how we can assist individual family members, as well as the family as a whole, to feel empowered to improve their situation. Social movement theories (see Chapter 14), which are based in the conflict perspective, have implications for the mobilization of oppressed groups, but the conflict perspective, in general, provides little in the way of policy direction.

Rational Choice Perspective

Another way to think about the Clark family is to focus on the costs and benefits that each of them derives from interacting with the others. You might suggest that Martha Clark receives the benefit of having most of her basic needs met but endures the cost of feeling that she has nothing to offer in exchange, as well as the blows to body and spirit delivered by her son. She seems to think that the care she is receiving is as good as she deserves, and probably sees no better alternative. Al Clark benefits from the household management that Betty provides but has recently endured the cost of feeling that his contributions, economic and otherwise, are not equal to hers, as well as the cost of feeling inadequate in his ability to meet his mother's needs. Now he must endure the embarrassment of an adult protective investigation. By virtue of the greater resources she brings to exchanges, Betty Clark holds a power position in the family, but she endures the cost of inadequate support from her husband and mother-in-law. Exhibit 2.5 reveals a fit between these observations about the Clark family and the central ideas of the rational choice perspective.

The **rational choice perspective** sees human behavior as based on self-interest and rational choices about effective ways to accomplish goals. The perspective is interdisciplinary, with strong roots in utilitarian philosophy, economics, and social behaviorism. Social workers are most familiar with the rational choice perspective as it is manifested in social exchange theory in sociology, rational choice models of organizations, public choice theory in political science, and the emerging social network theory.

EXHIBIT 2.5
Big Ideas of the
Rational Choice
Perspective

- People are rational and goal directed.
- Social exchange is based on self-interest, with actors trying to maximize rewards and minimize costs.
- Values, standards, expectations, as well as alternatives, influence the assessment of rewards and costs.
- Reciprocity of exchange is essential to social life.
- Power comes from unequal resources in an exchange.

The rational choice perspective is a very old tradition in social thought (Collins, 1994), but the roots of contemporary sociological theories of rational choice are generally traced to Claude Lévi-Strauss, George Homans, and Peter Blau. Other major theorists include John Thibaut and Harold Kelley, James March and Herbert Simon, Michael Hechter, James Coleman, James Buchanan, Richard Emerson, and Karen Cook.

Social exchange theory starts with the premise that social behavior is based on the desire to maximize benefits and minimize costs. Persons with greater resources in a social exchange hold power over other actors in the exchange. In the early development of social exchange theory, Homans (1958) insisted that behavior can be understood at the psychological level, denying the relevance of the cultural and social environments. Homans was particularly forceful in attacking the view that individuals are influenced in their behavior by role expectations that emanate from sociocultural systems. History, to Homans, is important only because the history of rewards for past behavior informs an actor about what is in his or her best interest. More recent formulations of social exchange theory have moved from this position toward a greater emphasis on the social, economic, political, and historical contexts of social exchanges (see Levi, Cook, O'Brien, & Faye, 1990). These formulations would emphasize how the Clark family conflicts are influenced by the structure of the labor market and political decisions about health care. Beginning with the work of Peter Blau (1964), social exchange theorists and researchers have taken a strong interest in how power is negotiated at all levels, from interactions between two people to Realpolitik among nations. Particularly noteworthy in this regard is Emerson's (1972a, 1972b) power-dependency theory and Cook's (1987) exchange network theory.

Rational choice theory is currently popular in sociology largely due to the work of one theorist, James Coleman (Ritzer, 2000). Coleman (1990) was dedicated to the idea that social theory should not be simply an academic exercise in trying to explain the social world, but it should also contain interventions for improving social life. A major feature of his work is his exploration of possible incentives to encourage actors to behave in ways more beneficial to others. For example, he has recommended financial incentives for providing nurturant care to children and adolescents who are at risk of becoming an economic drain on society—incentives that should increase with the potential hazard to society. He has also proposed lifting the legal immunity of members of corporate boards to encourage them to act in a more prosocial manner. This suggestion takes on new meaning whenever revelations of corporate fraud hit the media.

Some feminists have criticized exchange theory on the grounds that its emphasis on rational calculation of personal advantage is a male attitude and does not represent the female perspective (Collins, 1994). This criticism might be shared by ethnic groups who have traditionally been more collectivist, and less individualist, than white Anglo-Saxon Protestant Americans. In fact, Homans developed his American version of exchange theory partially in reaction to Lévi-Strauss's French collectivist version, which argued that social exchange is driven by collective, cultural, symbolic forces and not based simply on self-interest (Ekeh, 1974). Recently, Karen Cook and her colleagues (Cook, O'Brien, & Kollock, 1990) have undertaken a synthesis of social exchange and symbolic interaction theories (see the discussion of the social constructionist perspective), recognizing the possibility that different people hold different definitions of positive outcomes in social exchange.

Thibaut and Kelley's concepts of comparison level and comparison level alternatives are also useful in understanding different definitions of rewards and costs (Kelley & Thibaut, 1978; Thibaut & Kelley, 1959). *Comparison level,* a standard for evaluating the rewards and costs of a given relationship, is based on what the evaluator feels he or she deserves. Martha Clark's suggestion that she is receiving good care may well be based on such a standard; she may well believe that a woman in her situation deserves no better care. *Comparison level alternative* is the lowest level of outcomes a person will accept in light of alternative opportunities. Martha Clark might find her current situation less acceptable if she had another son or daughter who was in a position to provide a better quality of life.

Theorists in the rational choice tradition are also advancing **social network theory,** which actually has intellectual roots in the systems perspective. Still in the early stages of development, social network theory already provides useful tools for person/environment assessments and holds great promise for the future (Specht, 1986). Social networks are typically presented visually as sociograms, which illustrate the relations among network members (see Hartman, 1995; Meyer, 1993). Members of the network—individuals, groups, or organizations—are represented as points, and lines are drawn between pairs of points to demonstrate a relationship between them. Arrows are often used to show the flow of exchanges in a relationship. These graphic displays illuminate such issues as network size, density of relationships, strength of relationships, reciprocity of relationships, and access to power and influence. Sociograms are usually called **ecomaps** in the social work literature. An ecomap of the Clark family is presented in Exhibit 2.6.

EXHIBIT 2.6

Ecomap of the Clark Family

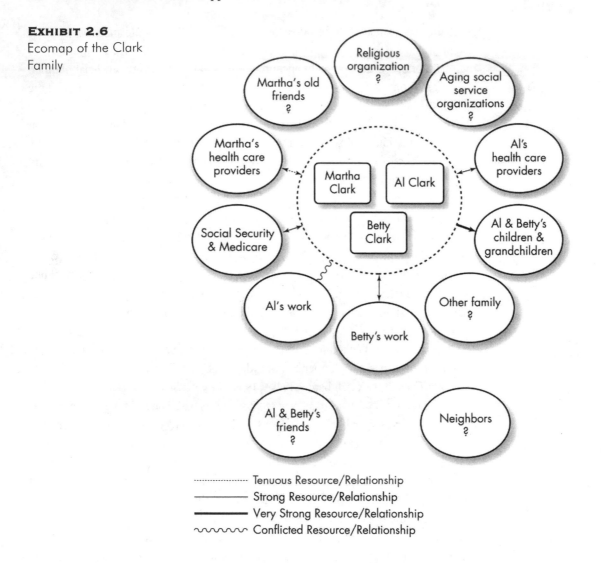

-------------------- Tenuous Resource/Relationship

——————— Strong Resource/Relationship

▬▬▬▬▬▬ Very Strong Resource/Relationship

∿∿∿∿∿ Conflicted Resource/Relationship

Here is an analysis of how well the rational choice perspective meets the criteria for judging social work theory:

■ *Coherence and conceptual clarity.* As the rational choice perspective has developed, two conceptual puzzles have emerged, one at the individual level and one at the collective level. At the individual level, there is a question about the individual's capacity to process information and make rational decisions. At the collective level, the question is how collective action is possible if each actor maximizes rewards and minimizes costs. To their credit, recent theorists have embraced these puzzles. New developments in the rational choice perspective emphasize the limits to rational choice in social life (see Cook et al., 1990; Levi et al., 1990; March & Simon, 1958). James Coleman (1990) is particularly noted for his attempts to employ rational choice theory to activate collective action for the purpose of social justice. There is still much internal inconsistency in most rational choice theories, however, about the nature and extent of rationality.

■ *Testability and empirical support.* The rational choice perspective has stimulated empirical research at several levels of analysis, with mixed results. Cognitive psychologists Daniel Kahneman and Amos Tversky (1982, 1984) dealt a blow to the rational choice perspective in the 1980s. They reported research findings that individual choices and decisions are often inconsistent with assumed rationality and that, indeed, situations are often too complicated for individuals to ascertain what is the most rational choice. On the other hand, more than modest support for the perspective has been found in research on dyads, families, and labor markets (see Adams & Jacobsen, 1964; Becker, 1981; Blood & Wolfe, 1960; Burgess & Nielsen, 1974; Carter & Glick, 1976). Randall Collins (1988) suggests that a serious problem for the rational choice perspective is the lack of a common metric for calculating the costs and benefits derived from social exchange. Contemporary theorists acknowledge the inherent imprecision of this metric and suggest that the rational choice perspective must find a way to incorporate both what people value and what factors are present in the situation in which they seek an exchange (see Cook et al., 1990).

■ *Comprehensiveness.* Although all strains of the rational choice perspective are interested in person-environment configurations, the different strains focus on different dimensions of those configurations. Homans as well as Thibaut and Kelley were primarily interested in dyads. Ivan Nye (1982) has used the rational choice perspective to understand family life. Peter Blau (1964) came to be interested in larger structures. Coleman (1990) is interested in how individual actions get aggregated into collective action at the organizational and societal level. Network theory focuses on social interactions at the community, organizational, and institutional levels. In general, the rational choice perspective is weak in exploration of personal dimensions, except for assumptions made about the psychological dimension and human motivation. The rational choice perspective has also ignored the time dimension, except to respect the history of rewards and costs in past exchanges.

■ *Diversity and power.* Although they were looking for patterns, not uniqueness or diversity, early rational choice theories provided some tools for understanding uniqueness and diversity in behaviors that come out of particular social exchanges. All theories in this perspective recognize power as deriving from unequal resources in the exchange process. Some versions of rational choice theory emphasize the ways in which patterns of exchange lead to social inequalities and social injustices. Although the rational choice perspective does not explicitly pathologize members of minority groups, those versions that fail to put social exchanges in historical, political, and economic contexts may unintentionally contribute to the pathologizing of these groups.

■ *Usefulness for social work practice.* Some versions of rational choice theory serve as little more than a defense of the rationality of the marketplace of social exchange, suggesting a noninterventionist approach. In other words, if all social exchanges are based on rational choices, then who are we to interfere with this process? This stance, of course, is inconsistent with the purposes of social work. However, some theorists in this tradition, most notably James Coleman, have begun to propose solutions for creating social solidarity while recognizing the self-interestedness that is characteristic of Western, industrialized societies. These attempts have led Collins (1994) to suggest that, out of all current social theories, contemporary rational choice theories have the greatest chance of informing social policy. On the other hand, Deborah Stone (2002) has skillfully demonstrated that the rational choice model is not a sufficient fit, and maybe not even a good fit, with the more messy, nonlinear policy-making process. Social workers make use of social network theory at the micro level, to assess and enhance the social support networks of individual clients and families (see Collins & Pancoast, 1976; Tracy & Whittaker, 1990). Social work administrators and planners use social network theory to understand and enhance the exchange of resources in networks of social service providers (see Streeter & Gillespie, 1992).

Social Constructionist Perspective

Both Martha Clark and her son sometimes think of her as a "useless old woman." You may be thinking that this idea could be contributing to Martha's growing despondency and passive approach to life and to her son's impatient treatment of her. Their current interactions help to reinforce this idea. It is likely, however, that both Martha and her son entered the current situation with a shared understanding about useless old women. This is an understanding that may have been developed and sustained across generations in their family, but it also clearly reflects traditional images of old women in the popular culture. You may also be wondering what kinds of ideas Martha, Al, and Betty have about gender roles and about heart disease, and how their current interactions are affected by these ideas. By considering these issues, you have begun to explore the central ideas of the social constructionist perspective (see Exhibit 2.7).

To understand human behavior, the **social constructionist perspective** focuses on how people learn, through their interactions with each other, to classify the world and their place in the world (Stryker, 1980). People are seen as social beings who interact with each other and the physical world based on *shared meanings,* or shared understandings

EXHIBIT 2.7
Big Ideas of
the Social
Constructionist
Perspective

- Human consciousness, and the sense of self, is shaped by continual social interaction.
- Social reality is created when people, in social interaction, develop a common understanding of their world.
- People perform for their social audiences, but they are also free, active, and creative.
- Social interaction is grounded in language customs, as well as cultural and historical contexts.
- People can modify meanings in the process of interaction.
- Society consists of social processes, not social structures.

about the world. In this view, people develop their understandings of the world and themselves from social interaction, and these understandings shape their subsequent social interactions.

The intellectual roots of the social constructionist perspective are usually traced to the German philosopher Edmund Husserl, as well as to the philosophical pragmatism of John Dewey and early theorists in the symbolic interaction tradition, including Charles Horton Cooley, W. I. Thomas, and George Herbert Mead. More recent theorists include Herbert Blumer, Erving Goffman, Alfred Schutz, Harold Garfinkel, Peter Berger, and Thomas Luckmann. Collins (1994) suggests that social constructionist theorizing is the type of sociology that American sociologists do best.

To the social constructionist, there is no singular objective reality, no true reality that exists "out there" in the world. There is, instead, the shared subjective realities that are created as people interact. Constructionists emphasize the existence of multiple social and cultural realities, developed in changing configurations of persons and environments. Both persons and environments are dynamic processes, not static structures. The sociopolitical environment and history of any situation play an important role in understanding human behavior, particularly if these are significant to the individual.

The importance of subjective rather than objective reality has often been summed up by the words of W. I. Thomas (Thomas & Thomas, 1928, p. 128): "If men define situations as real, they are real in their consequences." Actually, social constructionists disagree about whether there is, in fact, some objective reality out there. Radical social constructionists believe not. They believe that there is no reality beyond our personal experiences. More moderate social constructionists believe that there are "real objects" in the world, but those objects are never known objectively, but rather only through the subjective interpretations of individuals and collectivities (Mahoney, 1991).

Social constructionists also disagree about how constraining the environment is. Some see individual actors in social interactions as essentially free, active, and creative

(Gergen, 1985). Others suggest that individual actors are always performing for their social audiences, based on their understanding of community standards for human behavior (Berger & Luckmann, 1966; Goffman, 1959). The dominant position is probably the one represented by Schutz's (1932/1967) *phenomenological sociology*. While arguing that people shape social reality, Schutz also suggests that individuals and groups are constrained by the preexisting social and cultural structures created by their predecessors. Schutz does not provide theoretical tools for understanding social institutions and their links to individual constructions of reality, however.

The social constructionist perspective sees human understanding, or human consciousness, as both the product and the driving force of social interaction. Some social constructionists focus on individual consciousness, particularly on the human capacity to interpret social interactions and to have an inner conversation with oneself about social interactions (Cooley, 1902/1964; Ellis, 1989; Mead, 1934). They see the self as developing from interpretation of social interaction. Cooley (1902/1964) introduces the concept of "looking-glass self," which can be explained as "I am what I think you think I am." The looking-glass self has three components: (1) I imagine how I appear to others, (2) I imagine their judgment of me, and (3) I develop some feeling about myself that is a result of imagining their judgments of me. Mead (1959) suggests that one has a self only when one is in community, that the self develops based on our interpretation of the *generalized other*, which is the attitude of the entire community. Cynthia Franklin (1995) suggests that these cognitively oriented versions of social constructionism are best known as constructivism.

Other social constructionists put greater emphasis on the nature of social interactions, calling attention to gestures and language that are used as symbols in social interaction (Charon, 1998). These symbols take on particular meaning in particular situations. These social constructionists also see social problems as social constructions, created through claims making, labeling, and other social processes (Best, 1989).

Martha Clark's eating habits are serving as powerful symbols in the Clark family, but they probably are interpreted differently by different family members. This is something we might want to explore as we work with the family. We should also explore the meaning of the words "useless old woman" for both Al and Martha Clark. Most social constructionists believe that people can modify meanings in social interactions. Perhaps if Al Clark participated in a support group with other survivors of heart attacks, he would begin to modify some of the meaning he is making of the hold that heart disease has on his life.

This is how the social constructionist perspective measures against the criteria for judging theories:

■   *Coherence and conceptual clarity.* Social constructionism, particularly the original phenomenological and symbolic interactional concepts, is often criticized as vague and unclear. Over the past few decades, a great diversity of theorizing has been done within this broad theoretical perspective, and there is much fragmentation of ideas. Sociologists in the conflict and rational choice traditions have begun to incorporate social constructionist ideas, particularly those related to meaning making, which has further blurred the boundaries of this perspective. One challenge to the consistency of the social constructionist perspective is that it denies the one-absolute-truth, objective approach to reality while arguing that it is *absolutely true* that reality is subjective.

■ *Testability and evidence of empirical support.* Because of the vagueness of concepts, the social constructionist perspective has been criticized for being difficult to operationalize for empirical research. Social constructionists have responded in two different ways to this criticism. Some social constructionists argue that it is naïve to think that any theory can be evaluated based on empirical evidence (Cole, 1992). However, many social constructionist proponents have challenged the criticism and offered alternative criteria for evaluating theory (see Witkin & Gottschalk, 1988). They also propose an alternative research methodology, *constructivist research* (Lincoln & Guba, 1985), which is sensitive to the context of the research, seeks the views of key parties, and takes into account the interactions involved in the research process (Sherman & Reid, 1994). Social constructionism has stimulated a trend in the behavioral sciences to use a mix of quantitative and qualitative research methodologies to accommodate both objective and subjective reality (see Collins, 1990; Cook et al., 1990).

■ *Comprehensiveness.* Social constructionism pays little attention to the role of biology in human behavior, with the exception of a few constructivist biologists (Maturana, 1988; Varela, 1989). In some versions, cognitive processes are central (Mahoney, 1991), and the social construction of emotions is considered in others (Ellis, 1989). With the emphasis on meaning making, social constructionism is open to the role of religion and spirituality in human behavior. With its emphasis on social interaction, the social constructionist perspective is strong in attention to the social environment. It has been criticized, however, for failing to pay attention to the macro world of social institutions and social structure. Time, and the role of history, is respected in the social constructionist perspective, with many authors drawing attention to the historical era in which behavior is constructed.

■ *Diversity and power.* With its emphasis on multiple social realities, the social constructionist perspective is strong in its ability to accommodate diversity. It has been criticized, however, for failure to provide the theoretical tools necessary for the analysis of power relationships (Coser, 1975; Ritzer, 2000). Some critics have suggested that many contemporary postmodern versions of social constructionism, by ignoring power while focusing on multiple voices and multiple meanings in the construction of reality, reduce oppression to mere difference (Middleton, 1989). These critics suggest that this reduction of oppression to difference masks the fact that some actors have greater power than others to privilege their own constructions of reality and to disadvantage the constructions of other actors. This criticism cannot be leveled at all versions of social constructionism, however. Social work scholars have been particularly attracted to those versions of the social constructionist perspective that have incorporated pieces of the conflict tradition (Laird, 1994; Saleebey, 1994; Witkin & Gottschalk, 1988), particularly to the early work of Michel Foucault (1969) on the relationship between power and knowledge. They propose that in contemporary society, minority or "local" knowledges are denied credibility in majority-dominated social arenas and suggest that social work practitioners can bring credibility to minority viewpoints by allowing oppressed individuals and groups to tell their own stories.

■ *Usefulness for social work practice.* Social constructionism gives new meaning to the old social work adage "Begin where the client is." In the social constructionist perspective, the social work relationship begins with developing an understanding of how the client views the situation and what the client would like to have happen. The current strong interest in solution-focused and narrative and storytelling therapies is based on the social constructionist perspective. Solution-focused approaches attempt to help clients construct solutions rather than solve problems. They are based on the assumption that clients want to change and are capable of envisioning the change they would like to see (Gingrich & Eisengart, 2000). Narrative therapy starts with the assumption that we all tell ourselves stories about our lives, developing dominant story lines and forgetting material that does not fit into the dominant story line. A goal of therapy is to help clients see more realities in their story lines, with other possible interpretations of events (Kelly, 1996). The social worker should engage the client in thinking about the social, cultural, and historical environments in which their version of reality was constructed, which, for members of oppressed groups, may lead to empowerment through restorying, or revision of the story line (Laird, 1994; Saleebey, 1994). In your work with the Clark family, you might want to test this hypothesis by inviting Martha Clark to tell her story about how she came to see herself as just a useless old woman. In the process, she might realize that another interpretation of her status is possible. At the level of groups and organizations, the social constructionist perspective recommends getting discordant groups to engage in sincere discussion of their disparate constructions of reality and to negotiate lines of action acceptable to all (Fox & Miller, 1995) (see Chapter 12 for further discussion).

Psychodynamic Perspective

Martha Clark's despondence and her loss of confidence and hope are apparent—and easy to understand. Think about the losses she has recently experienced: loss of

EXHIBIT 2.8

Big Ideas of the
Psychodynamic
Perspective

- Emotions have a central place in human behavior.
- Unconscious, as well as conscious, mental activity serves as the motivating force in human behavior.
- Early childhood experiences are central in the patterning of an individual's emotions and, therefore, central to problems of living throughout life.
- Individuals may become overwhelmed by internal and/or external demands.
- Individuals frequently use ego defense mechanisms to avoid becoming overwhelmed by internal and/or external demands.

husband, loss of home, loss of privacy, loss of income, and loss of health. You may begin to wonder, given her long-term struggle with depression, about the possibility of early experiences with loss, deprivation, or trauma. You may also note her son's anger and frustration. Think about the losses he too has recently experienced: loss of father, loss of job, loss of income, loss of privacy, and loss of health. You also may wonder if he has a residue of anger toward his mother, perhaps related to childhood deprivation that he experienced during her episodes of depression. Is it possible that his label of "useless old woman" is a projection of his own sense of uselessness? As you explore the Clark family's situation from the psychodynamic perspective (see Exhibit 2.8), these and other possibilities emerge.

The **psychodynamic perspective** is concerned with how internal processes such as needs, drives, and emotions motivate human behavior. The perspective has evolved over the years, moving from the classical psychodynamic emphasis on innate drives and unconscious processes toward greater emphasis on the adaptive capacities of individuals and their interactions with the environment. The origins of all psychodynamic theories are in the work of Sigmund Freud; other prominent theorists in the evolving psychodynamic perspective include Carl Jung, Anna Freud, Melanie Klein, Margaret Mahler, Karen Horney, Heinz Hartmann, Robert W. White, Donald Winnicott, Otto Kernberg, Heinz Kohut, and Erik Erikson. More recent formulations of the perspective include ego psychology, object relations, and self psychology theories. *Ego psychology* gives primary attention to the rational part of the mind and the human capacity for adaptation. It recognizes conscious as well as unconscious attempts to cope. *Object relations theory* studies how people develop attitudes toward others and how those attitudes affect the view of the self as well as social relationships. *Self psychology* focuses on the individual need to organize the personality into a cohesive sense of self and to build relationships that support this cohesive sense of self. You will read more about the psychodynamic perspective in Chapter 4.

Freud looked at the human personality from a number of interrelated points of view; the most notable are his drive or instinct theory, topographical theory, structural theory, and psychosexual stage theory, summarized below. Freud revised each of these approaches to human personality over time, and different followers of Freud have attended to different aspects of his theoretical works, further revising each of them over time.

- *Drive or instinct theory.* Proposes that human behavior is motivated by two basic instincts, *thanatos,* or the drive for aggression or destruction, and *eros,* or the drive for life (through sexual gratification). Recent revisions of drive theory have suggested that human behavior is also motivated by drives for mastery and for connectedness (Goldstein, 1996).

- *Topographical theory of the mind.* Proposes three states of mind: *conscious* mental activities of which we are fully aware; *preconscious* thoughts and feelings that can be easily brought to mind; *unconscious* thoughts, feelings, and desires of which we are not aware but which have a powerful influence on our behavior. Although all psychodynamic theorists believe in the unconscious, the different versions of the theory put different emphases on the importance of the unconscious in human behavior.

- *Structural model of the mind.* Proposes that personality is structured around three parts: the *id,* which is unconscious and strives for satisfaction of basic instincts; the *superego,* which is made up of conscience and ideals and is the censor of the id; and the *ego,* which is the rational part of personality that mediates between the id and the superego. Freud and his early followers were most interested in the id and the pathologies that emanate from it, but later followers have focused primarily on ego strengths and the drive for adaptation. Both ego psychology and self psychology are in this later tradition.

- *Psychosexual stage theory.* Proposes a five-stage model of child development, based on sexual instincts: *oral phase* (birth to about 18 months), when the search for pleasure is centered in the mouth; *anal phase* (from about 18 months to 3 years), when the search for pleasure is centered in the anus; *phallic phase* (ages 3-6), when the search for pleasure is centered in the genitals; *latency phase* (ages 6-8), when erotic urges are repressed; and *genital phase* (adolescence onward), when the search for pleasure is centered in the genitals and sexual intimacy. Freud proposed that there was no further personality development in adulthood. Recent revisions of psychodynamic theory, starting with the work of Erik Erikson (1963), have challenged that idea. Although they still give primacy to the childhood years, they suggest that personality continues to develop over the life course. Recent theories put less emphasis on sexual instincts in stage development.

Psychodynamic theory is essentially a conflict theory of human behavior. All versions focus on the anxiety that arises from conflicts between individual needs and desires and environmental demands. Individuals are seen to defend against that anxiety by using *defense mechanisms,* or unconscious processes that keep intolerable threats from conscious awareness.

Here are the criteria for evaluating theories applied to psychodynamic theory:

■ *Coherence and conceptual clarity.* Criticisms that the psychodynamic perspective lacks logical consistency are directed primarily at Freud's original concepts and propositions, which were not entirely consistent because they evolved over time. Ego psychology and object relations theorists strengthened the logical consistency of the psychodynamic perspective by expanding and clarifying definitions of major concepts.

■ *Testability and evidence of empirical support.* Later psychodynamic theorists translated Freud's ideas into more measurable terms. Consequently, much empirical work has been based on the psychodynamic perspective. Contradictions in the research findings may be due in large part to the use of different definitions and measures. Some concepts, such as mastery or competence, have strong empirical support, but this support has been generated primarily by other schools of thought, such as developmental psychology and Albert Bandura's social behaviorism. Recent long-term longitudinal studies suggest that childhood experiences are important, but personality does continue to develop throughout life.

■ *Comprehensiveness.* Psychodynamic theories are primarily concerned with internal psychological processes. Strong attention is paid to emotions, and in recent formulations, cognitions are also accounted for. Although Freud assumed that biology determines behavior, psychodynamic theories have failed to incorporate new developments in neurological sciences about early brain development. With the exception of Carl Jung, psychodynamic theorists are not interested in the spiritual aspects of human behavior, typically viewing them as irrational defenses against anxiety. As for environments, the psychodynamic perspective conceptualizes them as sources of conflicts with which the individual must struggle. Recent formulations put greater emphasis on human behavior as a response to challenges in the environment than was found in classical theory, but theoretical propositions about internal processes continue to predominate. When environmental forces are considered, they include only passing mention of social forces beyond the family. Social, economic, political, and historical environments of human behavior are probably implied in ego psychology, but they are not explicated. This failure to expand the view of the social environment beyond the family has led to accusations that psychodynamic theories are "mother blaming" and "family blaming" (Luepnitz, 1988). As for time, the focus is how people change across childhood. There is no attempt to account for change after childhood or to recognize the contributions of historical time to human behavior.

■ *Diversity and power.* Traditional psychodynamic theories search for universal laws of behavior and their applicability to unique individuals. Thus, diversity of experience at the group level has been quite neglected in this tradition until recently. Moreover, in the main, "universal" laws have been developed through analysis of heterosexual men of white, Anglo-Saxon, middle-class culture. Feminists, as well as members of racial and ethnic minority groups, have criticized the psychodynamic bias toward thinking of people as autonomous individuals (Berzoff, 1989; Bricker-Jenkins, Hooyman, & Gottlieb, 1991; Gilligan, 1982; Ho, 1992; Sue & Sue, 1990). These critics suggest that viewing this standard as "normal" makes the connectedness found among many women and members of racial and ethnic minority groups seem pathological. Overemphasis on autonomy may also lead us to think of Martha Clark's growing dependence in pathological terms. Recently, proponents of the psychodynamic perspective have tried to correct for these biases and develop a better understanding of human diversity (Goldstein, 1996). Psychodynamic theories are strong in their recognition of power dynamics in parent/child relationships and in exploration of the life worlds of children. They are weak in looking at power issues in other relationships, however, including gender relationships. Early on, Freud recognized gender differences, even gender inequality, but attributed them to moral deficits within women. Erik Erikson's theory of psychosocial development has a somewhat greater emphasis on social forces. However, Erikson's work has been criticized for its lack of attention to the worlds of women, racial minorities, and sexual minorities (Berzoff, 1989; Chestang, 1972; Kravetz, 1982; Kropf & Greene, 1994; Schwartz, 1973; Wesley, 1975). It does not take into account the persistently hostile environments in which minority group members interact or the extraordinary coping strategies needed to negotiate those environments (Chestang, 1972).

■ *Usefulness for social work practice.* Most versions of the psychodynamic perspective have included clinical theory as well as human behavior theory. Differences of opinion about principles of practice reflect the theoretical evolution that has occurred. Practice principles common to all versions of the psychodynamic perspective include the centrality of the professional/client relationship, the curative value of expressing emotional conflicts and understanding past events, and the goals of self-awareness and self-control. Thus, you would be interested in having both Martha and Al discuss their past, as well as present, emotional conflicts. In contrast to the classical psychodynamic approach, recent formulations include directive as well as nondirective intervention, short-term as well as long-term intervention, and environmental manipulations—such as locating a day care program for Martha—as well as intrapsychic manipulations such as emotional catharsis. Ego psychology has also been used to develop principles for prevention activities in addition to principles of remediation (Goldstein, 1996). In general, however, the psychodynamic perspective does not suggest practice principles at the level of communities, organizations, and social institutions. Thus, it would not help you to think about how to influence public policy to secure coverage for Martha Clark's medications.

Developmental Perspective

Another way to think about the Clark family is to view their situation in terms of the developmental tasks they face. You might note that Martha Clark is entering late old age and struggling with the chronic illnesses and losses that people in this life stage frequently experience. She must make peace with the life that she has lived and find purpose to continue to live. You might also note that Al and Betty are part of the "sandwich generation," which must take on caregiving responsibilities for the older generation while also continuing to provide support to the generation behind them. They may be plagued with fears about their own vulnerability to the aging process. These observations are consistent with the central ideas of the developmental perspective, summarized in Exhibit 2.9.

The focus of the **developmental perspective** is on how human behavior changes and stays the same across the life cycle. Human development is seen as a complex interaction of biological, psychological, and social processes, which occurs in clearly defined stages. Each new stage brings changes in social roles and statuses. Currently, there are two streams of theorizing in the developmental perspective, one based in psychology and one based in sociology.

Life span or *life cycle theory,* based in psychology, focuses on the inner life during age-related stages. The study of life span development is rooted in Freud's (1905/1953) theory of psychosexual stages of childhood development, but Erikson (1963) has been the most influential developmental theorist to date because his model of development includes adult, as well as child, stages of development. Other early life cycle theorists include Margaret Mahler, Harry Stack Sullivan, and Jean Piaget. More recent developmental

EXHIBIT 2.9
Big Ideas of the
Developmental
Perspective

- Human development occurs in clearly defined age-graded stages.
- Each stage of life is qualitatively different from all other stages.
- Stages of development are sequential, with each stage building on earlier stages.
- Human development is a complex interaction of biological, psychological, and social factors.
- Moving from one stage to the next involves changes in statuses and roles.

theorists include Daniel Levinson, George Vaillant, Roger Gould, Lawrence Kohlberg, Robert Havighurst, Joan Borysenko, Barbara Newman, and Philip Newman.

Erikson (1963) proposed an *epigenetic model of human development,* in which the psychological unfolding of personality takes place in sequences. Healthy development depends on the mastery of life tasks at the appropriate time in the sequence. Most life span theorists agree with this epigenetic principle. Erikson divided the life cycle into eight stages, each with a special psychosocial crisis:

Stage 1 (birth-1 year): basic trust versus mistrust

Stage 2 (ages 2-3): autonomy versus shame, doubt

Stage 3 (ages 3-5): initiative versus guilt

Stage 4 (ages 6-12): industry versus inferiority

Stage 5 (ages 12-18 or so): identity versus role confusion

Stage 6 (early-late 20s): intimacy versus isolation

Stage 7 (late 20s-50s): generativity versus stagnation

Stage 8 (late adulthood): integrity versus despair

Most life span theorists, including Erikson, see their models of development as universal, applying equally well to all groups of people. This idea has been the target of much criticism, with suggestions that the traditional models are based on the experiences of Anglo, white, heterosexual, middle-class men and do not apply well to members of other groups. This criticism has led to a number of life cycle models for specific groups, such as women (Borysenko, 1996) and gay and lesbian persons (e.g., Troiden, 1989). Life span theories have also been criticized for failing to deal with historical time and the cohort effects on human behavior that arise when groups of persons born in the same historical time share cultural influences and historical events at the same period in their lives.

These criticisms have helped to stimulate development of the *life course perspective* in sociology. This relatively new perspective conceptualizes the life course as a social, rather than psychological, phenomenon that is nonetheless unique for each individual, with some common life course markers, or transitions, related to shared social and historical contexts (George, 1993). Glen Elder Jr. (1998) and Tamara Hareven (2000) have been major forces in the development of the life course perspective. In its current state, there are six major themes in the life course perspective: interplay of human lives and historical time; biological, psychological, and social timing of human lives; linked or interdependent lives; human capacity for choice-making; diversity in life course trajectories;

and developmental risk and protection. As you may recall, the life course perspective is the conceptual framework for the companion volume to this book.

The life course perspective would suggest that Martha Clark's beliefs about what it means to be "old" or to be female have been influenced by the historical time in which she has lived and are probably shared by many other women her age. It would also call attention to the way that changes in the economic institution, relocating factories to developing countries to take advantage of cheap labor, are affecting the midlife development of Betty and Al Clark. The evolving life course model respects the idea of role transition that is so central to the developmental perspective, but it also recognizes the multiplicity of interacting factors that contribute to diversity in the timing and experience of these transitions.

Here is how the criteria for evaluating theories apply to the developmental perspective:

- *Coherence and conceptual clarity.* Classical developmental theory's notion of life stages is internally consistent and conceptually clear. Theorists have been able to build on each other's work in a coherent manner. Still in its early stages, the life course perspective has developed some coherence and beginning clarity about the major concepts. When viewing these two developmental streams together, contradictions appear in terms of universality versus diversity in life span/life course development.

- *Testability and evidence of empirical support.* Many of Erikson's ideas have been employed and verified in empirical research, but until recently, much of developmental research has been based on white, heterosexual, middle-class males. Another concern is that by defining normal as average, developmental research fails to capture the life worlds of groups who deviate even moderately from the average, or even to capture the broad range of behavior considered normal. Thus, empirical support for the developmental perspective is based to some extent on statistical masking of diversity. The life course perspective has offered a glimpse of diversity, however, because it has been developed, in the main, from the results of longitudinal research, which follows the same people over an extended period of time. The benefit of longitudinal research is that it clarifies whether differences between age groups are really based on developmental differences or whether they reflect cohort effects from living in particular cultures at particular historical times.

- *Comprehensiveness.* The developmental perspective, when both theoretical streams are taken together, gets relatively high marks for comprehensiveness. Both the life span and the life course streams recognize human behavior as an outcome of complex interactions of biological, psychological, and social factors, although most theorists in both streams pay little attention to the spiritual dimension. The traditional life span approach pays too little attention to the political, economic, and cultural environments of human behavior. The life course perspective pays too little attention to psychological factors. Both approaches attend to the dimension of time, in terms of linear time, but the life course perspective attends to time in a more comprehensive manner, by emphasizing the role of historical time in human behavior.

■   *Diversity and power.* The early life span models were looking for universal stages of human development and did not attend to issues of diversity. More recent life span models have paid more attention to diversity, and diversity of pathways through life is a major theme in the life course perspective. Likewise, the traditional life span approach did not take account of power relationships, with the possible exception of power dynamics in the parent/child relationship. Moreover, traditional life span models are based on the average white, middle-class, heterosexual, Anglo-Saxon male and ignore the worlds of members of nondominant groups. Newer models of life span development have attempted to correct for that failure. Daniel Levinson's (1996) study of women's lives is noteworthy in that regard; it includes a sample of women diversified by race and social class, and acknowledges the impact of gender power differentials on women's development. The life course perspective recognizes patterns of advantage and disadvantage in life course trajectories.

■   *Usefulness for social work practice.* Erikson's model has often been used for assessment purposes in social work practice, and in a positive sense, the model can aid indirectly in the identification of potential personal and social developmental resources. Traditional life span theories should be applied, however, only with recognition of the ethnocentrism expressed in them. They suggest, for example, that there is one right way to raise a child, one "appropriate" type of relationship with the family of origin, and one "healthy" way to develop intimate relationships in adulthood. Although it is harder to extrapolate practice principles from the more complex, still-emerging life course perspective, it seems more promising for understanding diverse persons in diverse environments. It suggests that individuals must always be assessed within familial, cultural, and historical contexts. Overall, the developmental perspective can be viewed as optimistic. Most people face life crises and challenges at some point, and many people have been reassured to hear that their struggle is "typical." Because the developmental perspective sees individuals as having the possibility to rework their inner experiences, as well as their family relationships, clients may be assisted in finding new strategies for getting their lives back on course. For example, Al Clark could explore new roles that would make him feel more productive.

Social Behavioral Perspective

In your assessment of Martha Clark, you may think that she has developed feelings of incompetence, which may have some relationship to her episodes of depression.

EXHIBIT 2.10

Big Ideas of
the Social Behavioral
Perspective

- Human behavior is learned when individuals interact with the environment.
- Similar learning processes taking place in different environments produce differences in human behavior.
- All human problems can be formulated as undesirable behavior.
- All behavior can be defined and changed.
- Human behavior is learned by association of environmental stimuli, by reinforcement, by imitation, and by personal expectations and meanings.

Perhaps Martha's prior experiences reinforced a sense of incompetence rather than competence. Perhaps certain aspects of her current environment further reinforce this belief. For example, when she moved from a one-story apartment in senior housing to the two-story home of Al and Betty, certain aspects of the new physical environment, such as stairs, complicated her ability to do things for herself. You may also want to learn more about her son's aggressive behavior. When did it begin? How often does it happen? In which kinds of situations and environments? Is he imitating behavior that he saw modeled in his parents' home? Viewing the Clark family's situation from the social behavioral perspective (see Exhibit 2.10) leads you to pursue such questions in your assessment.

Theories in the **social behavioral perspective,** sometimes called the social learning perspective, suggest that human behavior is learned as individuals interact with their environments. But behaviorists disagree among themselves about the processes by which behavior is learned. Over time, three major versions of behavioral theory have been presented, proposing different mechanisms by which learning occurs:

1. **Classical conditioning theory,** also known as respondent conditioning, sees behavior as learned through association, when a naturally satisfying stimulus (unconditioned stimulus) is paired with a neutral stimulus (conditioned stimulus). This approach is usually traced to a classic experiment by Russian physiologist Ivan Pavlov, who showed, first, that dogs naturally salivate (unconditioned response) to meat powder on the tongue (unconditioned stimulus). Then, a ringing bell (conditioned stimulus) was paired with the meat powder a number of times. Eventually, the dog salivated (conditioned response) to the ringing of the bell (conditioned stimulus). This approach looks for antecedents of behavior, stimuli that precede behavior, as the mechanism for learning.

2. **Operant conditioning theory**, sometimes known as instrumental conditioning, sees behavior as the result of reinforcement. It is built on the work of two American psychologists, John B. Watson and B. F. Skinner. In operant conditioning,

behavior is learned as it is strengthened or weakened by the reinforcement (rewards and punishments) it receives or, in other words, by the consequences of the behavior. A classic experiment demonstrated that if a pigeon is given a food pellet each time it touches a lever, over time the pigeon learns to touch the lever to receive a food pellet. This approach looks for consequences of behavior, what comes after the behavior, as the mechanism for learning behavior.

3. **Cognitive social learning theory**, also known as cognitive behavioral theory, with Albert Bandura as its chief contemporary proponent, suggests that behavior is also learned by imitation, observation, beliefs, and expectations. In this view, the "learner" is not passively manipulated by elements of the environment but can use cognitive processes to learn behaviors. Bandura proposes that **self-efficacy**, a sense of personal competence, and **efficacy expectation**, an expectation that one can personally accomplish a goal, play an important role in human behavior (Bandura, 1977a, 1986).

Although the different streams of social behavioral theorizing disagree about the mechanisms by which behavioral learning occurs, there is agreement that differences in behavior occur when the same learning processes occur in different environments. In this perspective, all human problems of living can be defined in terms of undesirable behaviors, and all behaviors can be defined, measured, and changed.

This is how social behavioral perspectives rate on the criteria for evaluating theories:

■ *Coherence and conceptual clarity.* Although there are disagreements about the mechanisms of learning among the various streams of the social behavioral perspective, within each stream, ideas are logically developed in a consistent manner. The social behavioral perspective gets high marks for conceptual clarity; concepts are very clearly defined in each of the streams.

■ *Testability and evidence of empirical support.* Social behavioral concepts are easily measured for empirical investigation because theorizing has been based, in very large part, on laboratory research. This characteristic is also a drawback of the social behavioral perspective, however, because laboratory experiments by design eliminate much of the complexity of person/environment configurations. Furthermore, all versions of the social behavioral perspective have had their "share of confirmations and disconfirmations" (Monte, 1999, p. 863). In general, however, it seems fair to say that all streams of the social behavioral perspective have attained a relatively high degree of empirical support (see Thyer, 1991).

■ *Comprehensiveness.* Overall, the social behavioral perspective sacrifices multi-dimensional understanding to gain logical consistency and testability. Although it accepts biology's impact on learning, almost no attention is paid to biology. However, contemporary research on neurophysiology and the immune system indicate that classical conditioning plays a role in physiological functioning (Pert, 1997). Perhaps the social behavioral perspective will give more attention to biology in the future. Cognition and emotion are not included in theories of classical and operant conditioning, but they do receive attention in cognitive social learning theory. Spiritual factors are considered immeasurable and irrelevant in classical and operant conditioning theories. They would be relevant only to the extent that they reinforce behavior. For this reason, many theorists and social workers see social behaviorism as dehumanizing. Although environment plays a large role in the social behavioral perspective, the view of environment is quite limited. Typically, the social behavioral perspective searches for the *one* environmental factor, or contingency, that has reinforced *one* specific behavior. Thus, a proponent of this perspective might attribute Martha Clark's current depression to her son's abusive behavior and ignore both her previous episodes of depression and the multiple losses that she has faced since her husband's death. The identified contingency is usually in the micro system (such as the family) or sometimes in the meso system (e.g., a school classroom), but these systems are not typically put in social, economic, political, or historical contexts. One exception is Albert Bandura's cognitive social learning theory, which acknowledges broad systemic influences on the development of gender roles. Social work scholars applying behavioral principles have also made notable efforts in recent years to incorporate a broader view of the environments of human behavior (Berlin, 1983; Gambrill, 1987; Reid, 1985). Time is important in this perspective only in terms of the juxtaposition of stimuli and reinforcement. The social behaviorist is careful to analyze antecedents and consequences of behavior.

■ *Diversity and power.* The social behavioral perspective receives low marks in terms of both diversity and power issues. Very little attention has been paid to recognizing diversity in human behaviors, and it is assumed that the same mechanisms of learning work equally well for all groups. Nor does the social behavioral perspective attend to issues of power and oppression. Operant behavioral theory recommends rewards over punishment, but it does not account for the coercion and oppression inherent in power relationships at every system level. It is quite possible, therefore, for the professional behavior modifier to be in service to oppressive forces. In contrast, Bandura (1986) writes specifically about power as related to gender roles. He and other theorists note that persons in nondominant positions are particularly vulnerable to **learned helplessness** (see Mikulincer, 1994; Seligman, 1992), in which a person's prior experience with environmental forces has led to low self-efficacy and expectations of efficacy. You may find the concepts of self-efficacy and learned helplessness particularly useful in thinking about both Martha's and Al's situations. Both have experienced some defeats and changes in their physical functioning that may be leading them to expect less of themselves and to resist measures that might improve their functioning.

■ *Usefulness for social work practice.* A major strength of the social behavioral perspective is the ease with which principles of behavior modification can be extrapolated, and it is probably a rare person who has not used social behavioral principles of action at some point (Thomlison & Thomlison, 1996). Social workers and psychologists, primarily, have used social behavioral methods to modify undesirable behavior of individuals. But these methods have not been used effectively to produce social reform. Richard Stuart (1989) reminds us that behavior modification was once a "social movement" that appealed to young social reformers who were more interested in changing social conditions that produce atypical behaviors than in changing systems for managing atypical behavior. Skinner's *Walden Two* was the impetus for attempts by these young reformers to build nonpunitive communities, which represented significant modification of social conditions (see Kinkade, 1973; Wheeler, 1973).

Humanistic Perspective

In a sense, Martha Clark has shown a lot of strength to persevere through all the losses she has experienced over the past 2 years, even though many of her attempts to cope are not working well for her. You could reason that biology and social circumstances constrain her behavioral choices to some degree but that Martha is making choices and is capable of rethinking those choices. However, your reflections about her situation may be very different from her own, and thus your overarching concern is to get a chance to meet with Martha and hear more about how she sees her situation. Similarly, you applaud Al and Betty's commitment to their mother's care, even though some of their attempts to cope are not currently working well for them. You reason that social circumstances serve as constraints to Al's behavior, but you also think that he has made conscious choices and is capable of reworking those choices. The same can be said for Betty. You are eager to hear how both Al and Betty see their current situation. Your thoughts and planned course of action at this point reflect the humanistic perspective, summarized in Exhibit 2.11.

The humanistic perspective is often called the Third Force of psychology, because it was developed in reaction to the determinism found in early versions of both the psychodynamic (behavior as intrapsychically determined) and behavioral perspectives (behavior as externally determined) (Monte, 1999). We are using the term **humanistic perspective** to include humanistic psychology and existential psychology, both of which emphasize the individual's freedom of action and search for meaning. The term also includes the existential sociology tradition, which counters the tendency

EXHIBIT 2.11

Big Ideas of
the Humanistic
Perspective

- Each person is unique and has value.
- Each person is responsible for the choices he or she makes within the limits of freedom.
- People always have the capacity to change themselves, even to make radical change.
- Human behavior can be understood only from the vantage point of the phenomenal self—from the internal frame of reference of the individual.
- People make psychologically destructive demands on each other, and attempts to meet those demands produce anxiety.
- Human behavior is driven by a desire for growth, personal meaning, and competence, and by a need to experience a bond with others.

of some sociological theories to attribute individual behavior primarily to the social structure and presents as a dominant theme the idea that people are simultaneously free and constrained, both active and passive agents.

Like social constructionism, the humanistic perspective is often traced to the German phenomenological philosopher Edmund Husserl (Krill, 1986). It is also influenced by a host of existential philosophers, beginning with Søren Kierkegaard and including Friedrich Nietzsche, Martin Heidegger, Jean-Paul Sartre, Albert Camus, Simone de Beauvoir, Martin Buber, and Paul Tillich. Other early contributors to existential psychology include Viktor Frankl, Rollo May, Carl Jung, R. D. Laing, Karen Horney, and Erich Fromm. Perhaps the most influential contributions to humanistic psychology were made by Carl Rogers (1951) and Abraham Maslow (1962).

Existential psychology, which developed out of the chaos and despair in Europe during and after World War II, presented four primary themes (Krill, 1996):

1. Each person is unique and has value.

2. Suffering is a necessary part of human growth.

3. Personal growth results from staying in the immediate moment.

4. Personal growth takes a sense of commitment.

It is the emphasis on the necessity for suffering that sets existentialism apart from humanism.

Abraham Maslow (1962), a humanistic psychologist, was drawn to understand "peak experiences," or intense mystical moments of feeling connected to other people, nature, or a divine being. Maslow found peak experiences to occur often among self-actualizing people, or people who were expressing their innate potentials. Maslow developed a theory of **hierarchy of needs**, which suggests that higher needs cannot emerge until lower needs have been satisfied. Physiological needs are at the bottom of the hierarchy and the need for self-actualization at the top:

1. *Physiological needs*: hunger, thirst, sex

2. *Safety needs:* avoidance of pain and anxiety; desire for security

3. *Belongingness and love needs*: affection, intimacy

4. *Esteem needs:* self-respect, adequacy, mastery

5. *Self-actualization:* to be fully what one can be; altruism, beauty, creativity, justice

Carl Rogers (1951), another major humanistic psychologist, was interested in the capacity of humans to change in therapeutic relationships. He began his professional career at the Rochester Child Guidance Center, where he worked with social workers who had been trained at the Philadelphia School of Social Work. He has acknowledged the influence of Otto Rank, Jessie Taft, and the social workers at the Rochester agency on his thinking about the importance of responding to client feelings (Hart, 1970). He came to believe that humans have vast internal resources for self-understanding and self-directed behavior. He emphasized, therefore, the dignity and worth of each individual, and presented the ideal interpersonal conditions under which people come to use their vast internal resources to become "more fully functioning." These conditions have become known as the core conditions of the therapeutic process: empathy, warmth, and genuineness.

This is how the humanistic perspective rates on the criteria for evaluating theories:

- *Coherence and conceptual clarity.* Theories in the humanistic perspective are often criticized for being vague and highly abstract, with concepts such as "being" and "phenomenal self." Indeed, theorists in the humanistic perspective, in general, have not been afraid to sacrifice coherence to gain what they see as a more complete understanding of human behavior.

- *Testability and evidence of empirical support.* As might be expected, empirically minded scholars have not been attracted to the humanistic perspective, and consequently there is little empirical literature to support the perspective. A notable exception is the clinical side of Rogers's theory. Rogers began a rigorous program of empirical investigation of the therapeutic process, and such research has provided strong empirical support for his conceptualization of the necessary conditions for the therapeutic relationship: warmth, empathy, and genuineness (Monte, 1999).

■ *Comprehensiveness.* The internal life of the individual is the focus of the humanistic perspective, and it is strong in consideration of both psychological and spiritual dimensions of the person. With its emphasis on search for meaning, the humanistic perspective is the only perspective presented in this chapter to explicitly recognize the role of spirituality in human behavior. Other theories of spirituality are discussed in Chapter 6. In addition, Maslow recognizes the importance of satisfaction of basic biological needs. As might be expected, most theorists in the humanistic tradition give limited attention to the environments of human behavior. Taking the lead from existential philosophers, R. D. Laing sees humans as interrelated with their worlds and frowns on the word *environment* because it implies a fragmented person. In discussions of human behavior, however, Laing (1967, 1969) emphasizes the insane situations in which human behavior is enacted. Erich Fromm was heavily influenced by Karl Marx and is much more inclusive of environment than other theorists in the humanistic perspective, emphasizing industrialization, Protestant reformation, capitalism, and technological revolution as alienating contexts against which humans search for meaning (Fromm, 1941). Although existential sociologists emphasize the importance of feelings and emotions, they also focus on the problematic nature of social life under modernization (see Fontana, 1984). A dehumanizing world is implicit in the works of Maslow and Rogers, but neither theorist focuses on the environments of human behavior, nor do they acknowledge that some environments are more dehumanizing than others.

■ *Diversity and power.* The humanistic perspective, with its almost singular consideration of an internal frame of reference, devotes more attention to individual differences than to differences between groups. The works of Fromm and Horney are striking exceptions to this statement. Karen Horney identified culturally based gender differences at a time when psychology either ignored gender or took a "biology as destiny" approach. She also lost favor among other psychodynamic theorists by reworking Freud's conceptualization of the Oedipus conflict and of feminine psychology to produce a more gender-sensitive perspective (Horney, 1939, 1967). In general, far too little attention is given in the humanistic tradition to the processes by which institutional oppression influences the **phenomenal self**—the individual's subjectively felt and interpreted experience of "who I am." Like the social constructionist perspective, however, the humanistic perspective is sometimes quite strong in giving voice to experiences of members of nondominant groups. With the emphasis on the phenomenal self, members of nondominant groups are more likely to have preferential input into the telling of their own stories. Your intention to hear and honor the stories of Martha, Al, and Betty may be a novel experience for each of them, and you may, indeed, hear very different stories from what you expect to hear. Erich Fromm and Michael Maccoby (1970) illustrate this emphasis in their identification of the different life worlds of members of groups of different socioeconomic statuses in a Mexican village. Most significantly, Rogers developed his respect for the personal self, and consequently his client-centered approach to therapy, when he realized that his perception of the life worlds of his low-income clients in the Child Guidance Clinic were very different from their own perceptions (Hart, 1970).

■   *Usefulness for social work.* If the social constructionist perspective gives new meaning to the old social work adage "Begin where the client is," it is social work's historical involvement in the development of the humanistic perspective that gave original meaning to the adage. It is limited in terms of providing specific interventions, however. The humanistic perspective suggests that social workers begin by developing an understanding of how the client views the situation and, with its emphasis on the individual drive for growth and competence, recommends a "strengths" rather than "pathology" approach to practice. George Vaillant (2002), a research psychiatrist, recently suggested that this attention to strengths is what distinguishes social workers from other helping professionals. From this perspective, then, you might note the strong commitment to helping one another displayed by the Clark family, which might be the basis for successful intervention. At the organizational level, the humanistic perspective has been used by organizational theorists, such as Douglas McGregor (1960), to prescribe administrative actions that focus on employee well-being as the best route to organizational efficiency and effectiveness. Conflict theorists have criticized the organizational humanists, however, for their failure to take account of the ways in which organizations are instruments of domination (Hearn & Parkin, 1993).

The Merits of Multiple Perspectives

You can see that each of these perspectives puts a different lens on the unfolding story of the Clark family, and that each of them has been used to guide social work practice over time. But do these different ways of thinking make you more effective when you meet with clients like the Clarks? We think so. It was suggested in Chapter 1 that each situation can be examined from several perspectives, and that using a variety of perspectives brings more dimensions of the situation into view. Eileen Gambrill (1990) has suggested that all of us, whether new or experienced social workers, have biases that predispose us to do too little thinking, rather than too much, about the practice situations we confront. We are, she suggests, particularly prone to ignore information that is contrary to our hypotheses about situations. Consequently, we tend to end our search for understanding prematurely. One step we can take to prevent this premature closure is to think about practice situations from multiple theoretical perspectives.

The fields of psychology and sociology offer a variety of patterned ways of thinking about changing person/environment configurations, ways that have been worked out over time to assist in understanding human behavior. They are tools that can help us make sense of the situations we encounter. We do not mean to suggest that all eight of the perspectives discussed in this chapter will be equally useful, or even useful at all, in all situations. But each of these perspectives will be useful in some situations that you encounter as a social worker, and therefore should be in your general knowledge base. We hope that over time you will begin to use these multiple perspectives in an integrated fashion so that you can see the many dimensions, the contradictions as well as the consistencies, in stories like the Clark family's. We remind you, again, however, to use general knowledge only to generate hypotheses to be tested in specific situations.

IMPLICATIONS FOR SOCIAL WORK PRACTICE

The eight perspectives on human behavior discussed in this chapter suggest a variety of principles for social work assessment and intervention:

- In assessment, consider any recent role transitions that may be affecting the client. Assist families and groups to renegotiate unsatisfactory role structures. Develop networks of support for persons experiencing challenging role transitions.

- In assessment, consider power arrangements and forces of oppression, and the alienation that emanates from them. Assist in the development of advocacy efforts to challenge patterns of dominance, when possible. Be aware of the power dynamics in your relationships with clients; when working with nonvoluntary clients, speak directly about the limits and uses of your power.

- In assessment, consider the patterns of exchange in the social support networks of individual clients, families, and organizations, using ecomaps for network mapping when useful. Assist individuals, families, and organizations to renegotiate unsatisfactory patterns of exchange, when possible. Consider how social policy can increase the rewards for prosocial behavior.

- Begin your work by understanding how clients view their situations. Engage clients in thinking about the environments in which these constructions of situations have developed. When working in situations characterized by differences in belief systems, assist members to engage in sincere discussions and to negotiate lines of action.

- Assist clients in expressing emotional conflicts and in understanding how these are related to past events, when appropriate. Assist clients in developing self-awareness and self-control, where needed. Assist clients in locating and using needed environmental resources.

■ In assessment, consider the familial, cultural, and historical contexts in the timing and experience of developmental transitions.

■ In assessment, consider the variety of learning processes by which behavior is learned. Be sensitive to the possibility of learned helplessness when clients lack motivation for change. Consider issues of social justice and fairness before engaging in behavior modification.

■ Be aware of the potential for significant differences between your assessment of the situation and the client's own assessment. Focus on strengths rather than pathology.

KEY TERMS

boundary
chaos theory
classical conditioning theory
cognitive social learning theory
conflict perspective
critical theorists
developmental perspective
ecomaps
efficacy expectation
empowerment theories
feedback mechanism
feminist theories
hierarchy of needs
humanistic perspective

learned helplessness
operant conditioning theory
phenomenal self
pluralistic theory of social conflict
psychodynamic perspective
rational choice perspective
role
self-efficacy
social behavioral perspective
social constructionist perspective
social exchange theory
social network theory
systems perspective

ACTIVE LEARNING

1. Reread the case study of the intergenerational stresses in the Clark family. Next, review the big ideas of the eight theoretical perspectives in Exhibits 2.2, 2.4, 2.5, 2.7, 2.8, 2.9, 2.10, and 2.11. Choose three specific big ideas from these exhibits

that you think are most helpful in thinking about the Clark family. For example, you might choose this big idea from the systems perspective: each part of the system affects all other parts and the system as a whole. You might also choose this big idea from the humanistic perspective: human behavior is driven by a desire for growth, personal meaning, and competence, and by a need to experience a bond with others. And likewise, you might choose another specific idea from any of the perspectives. The point is to the find the three big ideas that you find most useful. Now, in a small group, compare notes with three or four classmates about which big ideas were chosen. How do you understand the similarities and differences in thinking about this?

2.   Choose a story that interests you in a current edition of a daily newspaper. Read the story carefully and then think about which of the eight theoretical perspectives discussed in this chapter are most reflected in the story.

WEB RESOURCES

Humanistic Psychology

www.ahpweb.org/aboutahp/whatis.html
Site maintained by the Association of Humanistic Psychology contains the history of humanistic psychology, information on Carl Rogers, the humanistic view of human behavior, methods of inquiry, and humanistic psychotherapies.

Types of Theories

www.grohol.com/therapy.htm
Site run by Dr. John Grohol, Psy.D., listing four major schools of theory and therapy: psychodynamic, cognitive-behavioral, humanistic, and eclectic.

William Alanson White Institute

wawhite.org
Site presented by the William Alanson White Institute of Psychiatry, Psychoanalysis, and Psychology contains contemporary psychoanalysis journal articles, definition and description of psychoanalysis, issues of transference/countertransference, and links to other psychoanalytic sites.

Sociological Theories and Perspectives

www.pcsw.uva.nl/sociosite/TOPICS/theory.html
Site maintained at the University of Amsterdam contains general information on sociological theory and specific information on a number of theories, including chaos theory, interaction theory, conflict theory, and rational choice theory.

Conflict Theory(ies)

www.umsl.edu/~rkeel/200/conflict.html
Site presented by Robert O. Keel at the University of Missouri at St. Louis contains information on the basic premises of conflict theory as well as specific information on radical conflict theory and pluralistic conflict theory.

Personality Theories

www.ship.edu/~cgboeree/perscontents.html
Site maintained by C. George Boeree at the Psychology Department of Shippensburg University provides an electronic textbook on theories of personality, including the theories of Sigmund Freud, Erik Erikson, Carl Jung, B. F. Skinner, Albert Bandura, Abraham Maslow, Carl Rogers, and Jean Piaget.

A Day in the Life of a School Social Worker

One Person's Multifaceted Social Work Practice

Elizabeth D. Hutchison
Virginia Commonwealth University

Mary Gay Hutcherson has worked in a variety of social work settings, including a state psychiatric hospital, protective services, hospitals, and the Red Cross. Currently, she works in the social work department of a suburban school system. She loves this position because of the variety of roles she gets to play in the course of a day. Mary Gay provides social work services to three schools—two elementary schools and one high school. We are going to follow her through a typical day's work at the high school.

Early morning. Mary Gay arrives at the high school, as usual, at about 7:00 A.M. She feeds the fish in her office and goes immediately to meet with one of the special education teachers and touch base about a student with whom they have both been working.

Earlier in the week, the student had reported to the teacher that his mother had been behaving very strangely for a few weeks—laughing to herself all day, not paying bills, and quitting her job. There was no food in the house, and his mother was not providing care to his younger siblings. The teacher had called Mary Gay to discuss this situation, because she knew that Mary Gay had met with the mother. Mary Gay was concerned and thought that she should go to the home to assess the situation. Because the student knew the teacher well and trusted her, Mary Gay asked the teacher to join her on the home visit.

When they arrived at the home, they found the situation very much as the student had described it. After assessing the situation, Mary Gay returned to her office and called the crisis unit at the county mental health center. She also placed a call to child protective services because of her concern about the care of the children. The crisis worker agreed to see the client if she could be brought to the crisis center. Mary Gay contacted the police department to request assistance in transporting the mother to the crisis center; she met them at the home and persuaded the mother to go for the assessment. The crisis worker recommended that the mother needed to be hospitalized. Mary Gay consulted with the child protection agency to discuss arrangements for the care of the children, and called relatives in another state to let them know what was happening with the family.

This morning, Mary Gay is checking with the teacher to get a report on how the student is coping with this family crisis. She learns that the student and his siblings are being well cared for and seem to be coping adequately with the situation.

Mary Gay goes back to her office and checks her phone messages. She has a message to call Ms. C at home. Mary Gay is well acquainted with Ms. C, because she has been working with her and her daughter, Jan, for several weeks. Jan, a ninth grader, has a seizure disorder and gets severe migraine headaches. She has been refusing to come to school because she does not want the other students to see her while she is having a seizure. She gets very anxious in the mornings when it is about time for the school bus, exacerbating both the seizure disorder and the migraines.

Mary Gay has been working with Jan to help her learn to use relaxation exercises before getting on the school bus. She has been working with Ms. C about making firmer demands that Jan get on the school bus in the mornings. She has been collaborating with teachers and other school personnel to help them be more supportive of Jan's efforts to be in school. She has asked some of Jan's teachers to reach out to her. She has also been trying to get Jan involved in the after-school Bible study group, where she might make connections with other students with similar interests. She has referred Jan to the school psychologist to have the necessary testing completed to qualify Jan for special education services.

This morning, Ms. C is distressed. Jan was scheduled to meet with the psychologist this morning, but she did not want to come to school. She was afraid that the meeting with the psychologist would upset her and precipitate a seizure. Ms. C also reports that her employer has given her a warning that she must become more consistent in arriving at work punctually. She is "at her wit's end" with trying to get Jan on the school bus in the mornings. Mary Gay and Ms. C problem-solve how Ms. C can talk with her employer about her situation. They agree that a top priority is to get Jan tested so that she will be eligible to have a special education plan developed. Mary Gay tells Ms. C that she will see what she can do to facilitate that.

Mary Gay goes to the office of the school psychologist and discusses Jan's situation. She requests that the psychologist go to Jan's home to do the testing. The psychologist, who has never done testing away from the office and is reluctant to do so now, gets called away to a meeting. Mary Gay resolves to take up this issue later.

Midmorning. Mary Gay leaves the school and drives to the nearby shopping mall, where she and prevention staff from the county mental health center are presenting a 2-hour parent training program, Love and Logic. Attendance is good today—15 parents present—and the parents are receptive.

Early afternoon. When Mary Gay arrives back at school, she has a few minutes to finish writing a social history report for tomorrow's meeting of the Special Education Eligibility Team. Then she goes across the hall to attend today's meeting to review three applications. After this meeting, Mary Gay has a few minutes to talk with the psychologist about Jan's evaluation and to return phone calls.

Then she moves on to a meeting with the Student Assistance Team. This team reviews referrals from teachers and parents that involve a variety of student problems. Recently it seems that most of the situations are drug related, and Mary Gay suggests that the Student Assistance Team invite a substance abuse consultant from the county mental health center to meet with them. Other team members like this idea, and Mary Gay volunteers to make the call.

Midafternoon. A teacher from one of the elementary schools calls to consult with Mary Gay about a potential child abuse situation. Mary Gay concludes that the situation needs to be reported, and calls a social worker at protective services because the teacher is uncomfortable about making the call herself.

Mary Gay meets for a few minutes with the social work student for whom she is serving as field instructor, to review the social history report that the student will be presenting at tomorrow's Special Education Eligibility Team meeting. Mary Gay is pleased with the progress the student is making and tells her so.

Late afternoon. Mary Gay makes two home visits to meet with families of students who have been referred for special education eligibility screening. Both students are thought to have undiagnosed learning disabilities. Mary Gay sees these meetings with families as the core of her job as a school social worker. In addition to obtaining social history data, her goal is to get the family on board as active members of the team. She wants to understand how the family feels about learning disabilities, and she wants to make sure that they understand the process of eligibility screening, what to expect at the team meeting, and the criteria used for diagnosing a learning disability. She prefers to have these conversations in the families' homes—on their turf—to get a better understanding of the family's needs and strengths and to allow the family the opportunity to be interviewed in the comfort of familiar surroundings.

In her second visit today, Mary Gay learns that the single mother is facing severe financial problems. As she problem-solves with the mother, she realizes that this family does not qualify for the free lunch program because the mother is employed. She reminds herself to check with the school principal about the possibility of waiving this policy, which is detrimental to families like this one.

Evening. After a quick dinner, Mary Gay is off to the weekly meeting of the Organization for Sexual Minority Youth. Mary Gay was instrumental in forming this group a few years ago when she became aware that these youth were frequent targets of hate crimes. The purpose of the group is twofold: to be supportive to gay and lesbian youth and to work with the community to develop a better understanding of issues facing these youth. Although this is not an official part of Mary Gay's work as a school social worker, she sees it as a part of her professional obligation to actively promote social justice.

Something to Think About

I continue to be impressed with the multifaceted nature of social work practice and challenged by the demands of such work. In the beginning, of course, the demands seemed overwhelming—just as they did when I was first learning to play the piano and to play basketball. The following questions should help you think about your own process of learning to do social work:

- How does this day in the life of Mary Gay Hutcherson fit with the understanding you had about what social work is when you decided you wanted to be a social worker? How is it similar, and how is it different?

- What about the way your family and friends understand social work? Which of Mary Gay's activities fit with their picture of social work? Given this day in Mary Gay's life, how would you answer when Aunt Louise asks, "What is social work anyway?"

- How does this day fit with your experiences, to date, as a social work student? How is it similar, and how is it different?

- As you follow Mary Gay through the day, think about what general information she needs for each of the activities in which she engages. What have you learned already—from experience and education—in each of these knowledge areas? What else do you need to learn to be able to step into Mary Gay's shoes?

■ What dimensions of person and environment seem to be important to Mary Gay's work on this particular day? Do the same dimensions seem important across the different activities of the day, or do you find yourself thinking more about specific dimensions during specific episodes?

■ How might you draw on specific theoretical perspectives to assist in any of the social work roles played by Mary Gay on this day?

PART II

The Multiple Dimensions of Person

The multiple dimensions of person, environment, and time have unity; they are inseparable and embedded. That is the way I think about them and the way I am encouraging you to think about them. However, you will be better able to think about the unity of the three aspects of human behavior when you have developed a clearer understanding of the different dimensions encompassed by each one. A review of theory and research about the different dimensions will help you to sharpen your thinking about what is involved in the changing configurations of persons and environments.

The purpose of the four chapters in Part II is to provide you with an up-to-date understanding of theory and research about the dimensions of person. It begins with a chapter on the biological dimension and ends with one on the spiritual dimension. Because so much has been written about the psychological dimension, it is covered in two chapters: the first one about the basic elements of a person's psychology and the second one about the processes a person uses to maintain psychological balance in a changing environment. The Knowledge Into Practice for Part II illustrates the integration of the biological, psychological, and spiritual dimensions in social work practice.

With a state-of-the-art knowledge base about the multiple dimensions of persons, you will be prepared to consider the interactions between persons and environments, which is the subject of Part III. And then you will be able to think more comprehensively and more clearly about the ways configurations of persons and environments change across the life course. The discussion of the life course in *The Changing Life Course*, the companion volume to this book, attempts to put the dimensions of persons and environments back together and help you think about their embeddedness.

Understanding the Whole Person

What does it mean to be a person? At root, a human being is a biological mass of living tissue: blood, bones, organs, glands, nerves. Social workers often help people detect, adjust to, or adapt to biological conditions that threaten their well-being.

For example, social workers often help people live with diabetes. Although diabetes can be easily detected, many people go years without diagnosis and treatment. The result is a pervasive set of physical problems involving several biological systems. By helping to make sure that testing is available, even for children, social workers can greatly improve people's lives.

Genes predispose people to diabetes, but lifestyle also plays a large role. Social workers can help people become more active in their own health management. Even children with diabetes can learn what to eat and how to administer insulin to lessen the disease's impact on their everyday lives.

Photograph © Emily Niebrand. Used by permission.

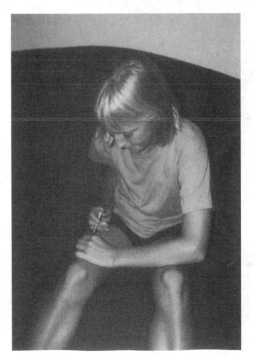

Photograph © Emily Niebrand. Used by permission.

Disease isn't the only aspect of the biological person that is relevant to social workers. Encouraging pregnant women to take care of themselves is a good way to give their babies a healthy start in life.

Exercise and physical conditioning can improve the bones and muscles that nature gave people. Advocating good nutrition, immunizations, and safety precautions like seat belts and protected sex is another way we can influence people's physical health.

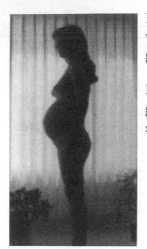

Photograph © Douglas Buerlein. Used by permission.

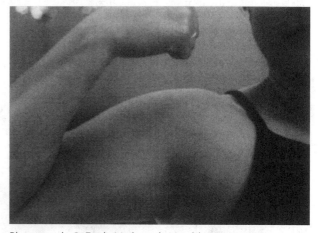

Photograph © Emily Niebrand. Used by permission.

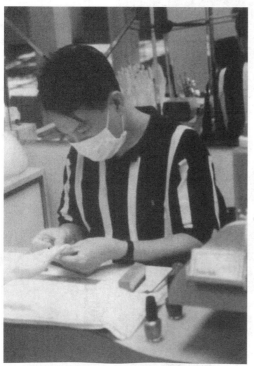

Photograph © Stacey Kowalski. Used by permission.

We also need to acknowledge that the environments people live and work in can negatively affect their bodies. The person who makes other people's hands and nails beautiful by giving manicures risks getting cancer from inhaling the toxic chemicals that are used.

Working with carcinogens, living in a polluted area, and being exposed to high levels of stress all have the potential to do damage. Thus, biological health is not only an individual concern but also a community issue.

The biological person is closely related to the psychological person. Physical makeup and health play an important part in the way a person's brain functions. And cognitive abilities affect the way a person thinks about problems and situations as well as synthesizes and applies information.

Through play, children refine the cognitive skills they need to perform the complex tasks associated with well-paying jobs. Poor children often don't get the stimulus they need to compete in a high-tech world.

© Corbis.

© Corbis.

As adults, they may be limited in their employment opportunities and lifelong earning potential.

But for youngsters fortunate enough to have sufficient time and resources to play, the world is enlarged. This boy plays games at a museum, simultaneously increasing his imagination and his sense of history.

Photograph © Reuter/Corbis-Bettman. Used by permission.

© Image 100/Royalty-Free/Corbis.

That sort of mind expansion is just what it takes to develop the cognitive skills needed to prosper in the information age.

To give all children the opportunity for success, social workers need to be concerned about children's opportunities for play and learning.

Another aspect of the psychological person that concerns social workers is emotion. We must be able to accurately recognize emotions, in ourselves and in our clients. We must also be able to help clients recognize and deal with their emotions. The difficulty is that people respond differently to the events in their lives.

Can you determine which of these two people is most stressed?

The more demonstrative person is not always the one being most affected by stress. In our society, men have traditionally been more stoic than women, but that does not mean that men feel less stress. Cultural factors play a large part in the expression of emotions.

Photograph © Emily Niebrand. Used by permission.   Photograph © Emily Niebrand. Used by permission.

Photograph © Stacey Kowalski. Used by permission.

Everyone experiences some level of stress from time to time. But sometimes that stress becomes overwhelming.

A person who is not able to cope with stress may feel immobilized and on the brink of complete collapse. In these situations, people need to rely on something or someone outside themselves.

Social support is the most common method of coping with stress. Usually people get support by talking with others—friends, family, or a social worker or therapist.

Photograph © Stacey Kowalski. Used by permission.

Another effective way to cope with the stresses of life is to exercise. By working out physically, people can often work out their psychological problems. And if they exercise in a group, they benefit from socializing with others as well.

© Corbis.

Photograph © Stacey Kowalski. Used by permission.

Sometimes, however, the only way to really relieve stress is to change the environment. For example, public transportation that has been adapted for use by people with disabilities offers them a way to get around while reducing their stress levels and expanding their opportunities.

In addition to considering the biological person and the psychological person, social workers should take into account the spiritual aspects of being human. Spirituality is often equated with religious practice. However, religion is more narrow than spirituality.

Photograph © Stacey Kowalski. Used by permission.

Nevertheless, we need to recognize that religious elements may be part of our clients' culture and background, influencing how they behave even when they claim to be "not religious."

© Corbis.

Spirituality may also be expressed as altruism. An act such as helping a person in a wheelchair navigate a busy street gives us a deeper and more profound connection with that person, which is one of the initial steps in expanding spiritual awareness.

Indeed, many social workers choose the profession because it offers spiritual connection.

Others seek to expand spiritual awareness through practices like meditation and prayer.

The contemplation of nature is another way to seek connection with forces beyond ourselves.

Photograph © Emily Niebrand. Used by permission.

Whatever the focus, spirituality is the search for connection. Thus, it helps to link all the dimensions of the person with the environment and the passage of time.

Photograph © Emily Niebrand. Used by permission.

Photograph © Stacey Kowalski. Used by permission.

CHAPTER 3

The Biological Person

Stephen French Gilson

The Biological Person

Stephen French Gilson
University of Maine

What do social workers need to know about human biology?

How does knowledge of biology contribute to important roles that social workers play in individual and community health and illness?

Key Ideas

As you read this chapter, take note of these central ideas:

1. There is strong evidence of relationships among physical health, psychological health, and social experiences. Biological functioning is the result of complex transactions among all biological systems. No biological system operates in isolation from others.

2. The nervous system is responsible for processing and integrating incoming information, and it influences and directs reactions to that information. It is divided into three major subsystems: central nervous system, peripheral nervous system, and autonomic nervous system.

3. The endocrine system plays a crucial role in growth, metabolism, development, learning, and memory.

4. The immune system is made up of organs and cells that work together to defend the body against disease. Autoimmune diseases occur when the immune system mistakenly targets parts of the body.

Acknowledgments: The author wishes to thank Elizabeth DePoy, Ph.D., Elizabeth Hutchison, Ph.D., Andrew S. Levitas, M.D., Michael Godschalk, M.D., and June M. Stapleton, Ph.D., for their helpful comments, insights, and suggestions for this chapter.

5. The cardiovascular system is made up of the heart and the blood circulatory system. The circulatory system supplies cells of the body with the food and oxygen they need for functioning.

6. The musculoskeletal system supports and protects the body and its organs and provides motion. The contraction and relaxation of muscles attached to the skeleton is the basis for all voluntary movements.

7. The reproductive system is comprised of both internal and external structures that are different for males and females.

CASE STUDY 3.1

MAGGIE'S BRAIN INJURY

Maggie is a Japanese American woman whose family had prohibited her from dating men who were not of Japanese descent. While attending college on the West Coast of the United States, she met and fell in love with Sam, a white Anglo-American who had grown up only a few blocks away from Maggie. During their first school vacation, Maggie made arrangements to meet Sam to ride with him on his new motorcycle. Sam had given Maggie a helmet at school for her safety, which she brought home and hid in her closet. Maggie respected her parents and was not prepared to tell them about Sam until she knew if she was serious about a future with him. Therefore, when she went to meet Sam on the first evening she was home, she arranged to meet him in an area close to home but out of view of her parents. However, Maggie's parents questioned her about where she was going, and because they were watching as she left the house, Maggie did not take her helmet. A few hours after Maggie left the house, the police called her parents and informed them that Maggie had been thrown 20 feet from the rear of the motorcycle that Sam was driving. He had swerved onto the shoulder of the road to avoid running into a car. Sam was not hurt, but Maggie sustained multiple fractures and a severe closed head injury. She was in a coma for 3 weeks.

Miraculously, over a 6-month period, all of Maggie's external bodily injuries, including the fractures, healed, and she was able to walk and talk with no apparent residual impairments. Cognitively, Maggie was not so lucky. She was able to read but could not retain what she had just read a minute ago. She lost all of her previous knowledge of math and could not do the simplest addition and subtraction problems. Copying her name from a piece of paper to another page would take her at least 5 minutes. Sometimes she would astound and even hurt her friends with blunt, tactless remarks, and she would occasionally become irritated out of all proportion with the stimulus.

Maggie had just finished her junior year in college when the accident occurred, and everyone expected that she would return to school and finish her degree and live happily ever after. But 2 years after the accident, Maggie's family knows, in their hearts, that she is not going to finish her last year of college. Sam is about to get engaged to another woman, but Maggie thinks that she is still dating Sam and thinks that he is just waiting for her to finish college before they get married. Everyone who knew Maggie before the accident cannot understand why her personality has markedly changed, and they even say, "She's a completely different person!" Helping her will require that you understand what has happened to Maggie's body and how it affects her behavior.

CASE STUDY 3.2

A DIABETES DIAGNOSIS FOR BESS

Bess, a 52-year-old Franco-American woman who lives in rural Maine, was enjoying her empty nest just before you met her. The youngest of her three children had married 6 months ago, and although Bess was proud of what she had accomplished as a single mother, she was now ready to get on with her life. Her first order of business was to get her body back into shape, so she started on a high-carbohydrate, low-fat diet she had read about in a magazine. Drinking the recommended 8 glasses of water or more each day was easy, because it seemed that she was always thirsty. But Bess was losing more weight than she thought possible on a diet, and she was always cheating! Bess had thought that she would have to get more exercise to lose weight, but even walking to and from her car at the grocery store tired her out.

One morning, Bess did not show up at the country store where she worked. Because it was very unusual for her not to call and also not to answer her phone, a coworker went to her house. When there was no response to the knocking, the coworker and one of Bess's neighbors opened the door to Bess's house and walked in. The coworker and neighbor found

CASE STUDY 3.2

Bess sitting on her couch, still in her nightclothes, which were drenched with perspiration. Bess was very confused, unable to answer simple questions with correct responses. Paramedics transported Bess to the local community hospital.

In the emergency room, after some blood work, a doctor diagnosed diabetes mellitus (diabetes). Because diabetes is common among middle-aged and elder Franco-Americans in this poor rural town, you had already established a psychoeducational group for persons with diabetes that Bess now attends.

CASE STUDY 3.3

MELISSA'S HIV DIAGNOSIS

Melissa's "perfect life" has just fallen apart. As a young Jewish, urban, professional who grew up in a middle-class suburb, Melissa had always dreamed of a big wedding at her parents' country club, and now her dreams were coming true. All the plans had been made, invitations sent out, bridesmaids' dresses bought and measured, and her wedding dress selected. All that remained was finalizing the menu and approving the flower arrangements. Because Melissa and her fiancé planned to have children soon after their marriage, she went to her physician for a physical exam 2 months before her wedding. As she does with all of her patients, the doctor asked if Melissa had ever been tested for HIV. Melissa said no, and gave her permission for an AIDS test to be run with all the other routine blood work.

One week after her physical, the doctor's office called and asked Melissa to return for more blood work because of what was thought to be an inaccuracy in the report. Another week passed, but Melissa did not think again about the tests because she was immersed in wedding plans. Her physician called her at home at 8:00 in the morning and asked her to come to her office after work that day. Because she was distracted by the wedding plans and a busy schedule at work, Melissa did not think anything of the doctor's request.

When she arrived at the doctor's office, she was immediately taken to the doctor's private office. The doctor came in, sat down, and told Melissa

CASE STUDY 3.3

that two separate blood tests had confirmed that she was HIV positive. Melissa spent over 3 hours with her physician that evening, and soon thereafter she began to attend your HIV support group.

Melissa has never used illicit drugs, and she has only had two sexual partners. She and her fiancé had decided not to have unprotected intercourse until they were ready for children, and because they used a condom, he was not a prime suspect for passing along the infection. Melissa has remembered that the man with whom she was involved prior to meeting her fiancé would not talk about his past. She has not seen this former lover for the past 3 years, ever since she moved away from New York.

CASE STUDY 3.4

LIFESTYLE CHANGES FOR THOMAS

Thomas is 30 years of age and lives with his parents. Both of his parents are obese, as are his two older sisters. Thomas loves his mom's cooking, but some time ago realized that its high-fat and high-sodium content were contributing to his parents' obesity and high blood pressure.

In contrast, Thomas takes pride in watching his diet (when he isn't eating at home) and is pretty smug about being the only one in the family who is not obese. Being called "the thin man" is, to Thomas, a compliment. He also boasts about being in great physical shape, and exercises to the point of being dizzy.

After one of his dizziness episodes, a friend told him that he should get his blood pressure checked. Although Thomas knew of the high incidence of heart disease among African Americans, he never considered that he would have a problem. After all, he is young and in good physical shape. Out of curiosity, the next time Thomas stopped at his local drug store, he decided to use one of those self-monitoring blood pressure machines to check his blood pressure. To his astonishment, the reading came back 200/105. Thomas will need your help to adopt some major lifestyle changes.

CASE STUDY 3.5

MAX'S POSTPOLIO SYNDROME

Max is a polio survivor from an Eastern European immigrant family that settled in a Midwestern city in the United States. When he was 2 years old, he contracted polio that affected only his legs. He never had any breathing difficulties nor any involvement in his arms. In fact, after 6 months in the hospital and another 6 months of therapy when he returned home, Max appeared to be "cured."

Afterward, as he was growing up, there were no visible signs of previous illness. He clearly could keep up with his friends except he could never run very long distances.

Now, 43 years later, Max has developed the symptoms of postpolio syndrome. He has noticed increasing weakness in his legs, unusual fatigue, and a lot of pain all over his body. A recent evaluation at a university clinic confirmed the diagnosis of postpolio syndrome, and the clinicians who saw him recommended that he consider getting the type of brace that is inserted in his shoes to support both ankles, as well as use forearm crutches for walking long distances. Max has earned his living all his life as a house painter. He needs your help figuring out how to cope with these new developments and how to support his two young children.

CASE STUDY 3.6

JUAN AND BELINDA'S REPRODUCTIVE HEALTH

Juan and Belinda, now both 17 years old, grew up in the same neighborhood and attend the same church, St. Joseph's Catholic Church. They do not attend the same school, however. Belinda has received all of her education at the schools at St. Joseph's; Juan attended J. F. Kennedy Elementary School, John Marshall Junior High, and now attends Cesar Chavez High School. Since seventh grade, Juan has met Belinda after school and walked her home.

They each live in small, well-kept homes in a section of the community that is largely Hispanic with very strong influences from the wide variety of countries of origin represented by community residents: Mexico, Honduras, El Salvador, Nicaragua, among others. The Catholic church is a dominant force in shaping community social, political, economic, and personal values and behaviors.

Both Juan's and Belinda's parents immigrated to the United States from Mexico, seeking to improve the opportunities for their, at that time, yet unborn families. Juan's mother found a job as a housekeeper at a local hotel, where she now manages the housekeeping staff. His father began as a day laborer and construction worker, eventually moving up to becoming foreman of the largest construction company in the area. He anticipates beginning his own construction company within the next year. Belinda's mother was a skilled seamstress and was able to start her own tailoring business shortly after immigrating. Belinda's father, with a background in diesel mechanics, was able to find work at a large trucking company where he continues to work today.

Like many teenagers today, Juan and Belinda face the difficulties of seeking to sort out the complexities and the intricacies of their relationship. They feel very much in love, knowing in their hearts that they want to get married and raise a family. At 17, they are at the crossroads of intimacy, because they face conflicts about their future sexuality with limited information and strong prohibitions against premarital sex. Following many of the teachings of their church and the urgings of their parents, Juan and Belinda have avoided much physical contact except for kissing and holding each other.

Like many communities in the United States, their community struggled with the question of just what information should be given to students about physical health and sexuality. Their community decided to limit the amount and type of information to the basics of female and male sexual anatomy and physiology. The result of this decision for Juan and Belinda was that they learned very little about sexual response and behavior, conception, pregnancy, childbirth, contraception, safe sex practices, or other areas that are critical in today's world. The decision by the school board was based on a belief that it was the family's responsibility to provide this information to their children. As the school social worker at Cesar Chavez High School, you are aware of the Juans and Belindas in your community.

An Integrative Approach for
Understanding Biological Health and Illness

As we think about the stories of Maggie, Bess, Melissa, Thomas, Max, Juan, and Belinda, we can see what an important dimension of their behavior biology is. But despite growing agreement that biology is an important dimension of human behavior and of the work that social workers do, the profession is struggling to articulate exactly what social workers need to know about human biology. Because social workers deal with people, social workers deal with biological phenomena and related issues such as poverty, chronic illness, addictions, violence, reproductive problems, and child abuse. And in the cases of Maggie, Bess, Melissa, Thomas, Max, Juan, and Belinda, their bodies are the central reason they are seeking social work assistance. To be helpful, their social workers must have a working knowledge of the body's systems and the ways these systems interact with each other and with other dimensions of human behavior. Social workers also must be capable of discussing intimate details of biological functioning (Johnson et al., 1990; Saleebey, 1985, 1992; Tangenberg & Kemp, 2002; Weick, 1986).

Systems Perspective   It is important to remember that social work's biopsychosocial-spiritual model of human behavior is an interdependent systems model, a model that sees the biological dimension of human behavior intertwined with and inseparable from psychological, social, and spiritual dimensions. Social work's growing interest in human biology as an integral part of human behavior coincides with an expanding scientific literature about the interactions of biological, psychological, and social dimensions and with heightened attention in the popular culture to "mind-body interactions."

At this point, we have strong conceptual, theoretical, and empirical evidence of relationships among physical health, psychological health, and social experiences (House, Landis, & Umberson, 1988; Levine, Coe, & Wiener, 1989; Weitz, 2000). But this is a rapidly emerging area of study, and it is difficult for social workers to sift through the contradictions and overstatements often found in popular media presentations of "new findings" and "advancements."

In March 2001, the National Institutes of Health sponsored a conference titled Vital Connections: The Science of Mind-Body Interactions (MacArthur Network on Mind-Body Interactions, 2001), bringing together some of the best mind-body researchers in the world to evaluate the state of knowledge in this area. They reported on several topics receiving intense research scrutiny in the past decade: the neurobiology of human emotions, early care and brain development, the biology of social interactions, socioeconomic status and health, neuroendocrinology of stress, and the role of sleep in health and cognition. Presentations at this conference revealed further evidence of the critical connections between the social, biological, and psychological dimensions of human behavior. Throughout the 3-day conference, presenters emphasized the "integrative mechanisms" that link social and psychological dimensions to the brain and the rest of the body. They were clear that we are just beginning to understand these mechanisms and we need to be cautious about overstating what is known. Much of the current evidence is based on animal studies. Yet, most of the scientists who presented at the conference were reporting on decade-long research endeavors, and they were optimistic that they are making real progress in developing knowledge to help medical specialists think of people as biopsychosocial-spiritual wholes.

Although these attempts to understand mind-body connections have led to many important discoveries about health and illness, they may also unintentionally lead us to reduce biological issues to a simple faith in mind over matter. Social workers therefore would be advised to heed Gerald Fischbach's warning that "the march of medicine is having profound effects on how we think of mental life . . . but there is a danger in biologizing complex phenomena and claiming too much too soon" (McArthur Network on Mind-Body Interactions, 2001, p.10). The danger is that we will fail to consider the full range of environmental influences on health, and blame individuals for their illnesses or diagnoses. We cannot forget that health and illness are also influenced by social, political, cultural, and economic experiences (Saleebey, 1994). Political and economic arrangements have an impact not only on resource availability but also on the coping processes used by different groups in society (Banyard & Graham-Bermann, 1993).

Likewise, although social workers need to take physical health into account, we must avoid the temptation to view the social problems of individuals within a disease framework. Efficiency is an advantage of a disease framework, because medical researchers typically develop detailed diagnostic and treatment guidelines for diseases, which can easily be activated (Mechanic, 1995, p. 1209). However, focusing on disease may mask the strengths of individuals who have biological problems and may thus limit our ability to identify the nature of problems, needs, and appropriate interventions to resolve the problems.

The experience of a physical disability, such as paralysis or low vision, receives much of its meaning from political, social, cultural, and economic contexts (Albrecht, Seelman, & Bury, 2001; Barnes, Mercer, & Shakespear, 1999; Barnett & Scotch, 2002; Gilson & DePoy, 2000, 2002; Gilson, Tusler, & Gill, 1997; Thomson, 1996; Wang, 1992). For example, the experience of having low vision is influenced by shared cultural understandings of the "proper roles" for persons with low vision and by actions or inactions of the political institution to secure their access to physical and social environments. We may automatically assume that an individual with low vision is in need of professional intervention, when that person in effect has his or her life well organized and functions well in all chosen living and working environments. Thus, rather than being caused by the biological condition itself, limitation associated with a biological anomaly may be a function of the environment; the characteristics of the task; personal attitude; and available supports, such as assistive technology, personal

---

Humanistic Perspective

Social Constructionist Perspective

assistance services, accessible transportation, and community living options (Mechanic, 1995).

Systems Perspective   Although social workers do not diagnose medical conditions in the scope of our practice, our assessments of individuals help us determine whether referrals to biomedical professionals may be indicated. And in our ongoing work, we should be able to assess what type of advocacy may better ensure that biological needs and issues are addressed. For example, the social work administrator who is developing or operating a shelter, a food kitchen, or an advocacy center may integrate medical and mental health services with employment, housing, financial, and companionship services (Gelberg & Linn, 1988). Jane Lowe (1997) has proposed a social-health model that calls for us to view health not only as an individual experience but within the context of the community, group, and organization. Lowe recommends a model of social work practice that promotes healthy communities as well as empowering individuals, families, and groups to advocate for their own health needs. The delivery of broad-based social-health services may occur in places such as schools, work, community centers, and places of faith, in addition to hospitals and medical clinics.

A Look at Six Systems

Systems Perspective   To adequately integrate the biological dimension into our understanding of human behavior, social workers need a basic understanding of biological systems and their interactions. Six biological systems are discussed in this chapter: the nervous system, the endocrine system, the immune system, the cardiovascular system, the musculoskeletal system, and the reproductive system. All the other biological systems (such as the digestive system, the respiratory system, and the urinary system) also warrant our attention, but the six described here are commonly involved in many of the biologically based issues that social workers encounter, and they can serve as a model for our thinking about other systems.

As you read the individual descriptions of these six systems, keep in mind their connectedness with each other. Just as human behavior is a complex transaction of person and environment, biological functioning is the result of complex transactions among all biological systems (Ader, Felten, & Cohen, 1990). No one system operates in isolation from other systems.

Nervous System

In the first case study, you met Maggie, who is like the more than 230,000 people in the United States hospitalized each year with a **brain injury (BI).** For Maggie, we are referring to what is commonly termed a traumatic brain injury. A *traumatic brain injury*

(TBI) is defined as an insult to the brain caused by an external physical force that may result in a diminished or altered state of consciousness (Brain Injury Association, 2001). Included here are what might be classified as mild brain injuries or concussions. According to the Centers for Disease Control and Prevention (CDC), approximately 1.5 million individuals sustain traumatic brain injury in the United States each year, creating $48.3 billion yearly in hospital and injury-related costs. Traumatic brain injuries include head injuries that result from falls, automobile accidents, infections and viruses, insufficient oxygen, and poisoning. Motorcycle accidents, particularly those in which the rider was not wearing a helmet, have been identified as one of the primary causes of TBI.

Although the symptoms may be similar, *acquired brain injury (ABI)* is a different classification of brain injury. It does not result from traumatic injury to the head, is not hereditary, congenital, or degenerative, and occurs after birth. Included in this category are oxygen deprivation (anoxia), aneurysms, infections to the brain, and stroke (Brain Injury Association, 2001).

Each type of BI may present specific issues and problems for the individual. However, brain injury in general can affect cognitive, physical, and psychological skills. Cognitive problems may present as difficulties with language and communication, information processing, memory, and perception. Maggie's difficulties with writing her name is an example of these problems, as well as a reflection of fine motor skill deficits. Physical limitations often present as difficulty with walking (ambulation), balance and coordination, strength, and endurance. Psychological problems may come from two different sources. They may be *primary* or directly related to the BI, often irritability and judgment errors. Or they may be *reactive* to the adjustments required to live with the BI and its consequences, typically depression and changes in self-esteem. Maggie's difficulty in recognizing that Sam is not going to marry her and her misjudgments in other social situations are symptoms of the psychological consequences of her BI.

The **nervous system** provides the structure and processes for communicating sensory, perceptual, and autonomically generated information throughout the body. Three major subsystems comprise the nervous system:

1. *Central nervous system (CNS)*: the brain and the spinal cord

2. *Peripheral nervous system (PNS)*: spinal and cranial nerves

3. *Autonomic nervous system (ANS)*: nerves controlling cardiovascular, gastrointestinal, genitourinary, and respiratory systems

The brain sends signals to the spinal cord, which in turn relays the message to specific parts of the body by way of the PNS. Messages from the PNS to the brain travel back by way of a similar pathway (Carey, 1990). Note that Maggie's brain injury affects only a part of her nervous system—in fact, only part of the CNS. Damage to other parts of the nervous system can have devastating effects, but I focus on her brain injury because it is so closely linked with behavioral issues.

The human brain, which constitutes only about 2% of total body weight, may contain as many as 10 million neurons. Its three major internal regions are referred to as the forebrain, midbrain, and hindbrain. Viewed from the side (see Exhibit 3.1), the largest structure visible is the cerebral cortex, part of the forebrain. The *cerebral cortex* is the seat of higher mental functions, including thinking, planning, and problem solving. The cerebral cortex is more highly developed in humans than in any other animal. It is divided into two hemispheres—left and right—that are interconnected by nerve fibers. The hemispheres are thought to be specialized, one side for language and the other for processing of spatial information, such as maps and pictures. Each hemisphere controls the opposite side of the body, so that damage to one side of the brain may cause numbness or paralysis of the arm and leg on the opposite side.

The cerebral cortex has four lobes, which are depicted in Exhibit 3.1. As Exhibit 3.2 explains, functions such as vision, hearing, and speech are distributed in specific regions, with some lobes being associated with more than one function. The frontal lobe is the largest, making up nearly one third of the surface of the cerebral cortex. Lesions of any one of the lobes can have a dramatic impact on the functions of that lobe (Carpenter, 1991; Earle, 1987). Other forebrain structures process information from the

EXHIBIT 3.1
Selected Areas
of the Brain

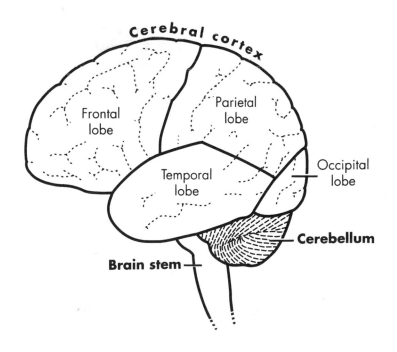

Brain Region	Function
Frontal lobe	Motor behavior
	Expressive language
	Social functioning
	Concentration and ability to attend
	Reasoning and thinking
	Orientation to time, place, and person
Temporal lobe	Language
	Memory
	Emotions
Parietal lobe	Intellectual processing
	Integration of sensory information
Left parietal lobe	Verbal processing
Right parietal lobe	Visual/spatial processing
Occipital lobe	Vision

sensory and perceptual organs and structures and send it to the cortex, or receive orders from cortical centers and relay them on down through central nervous system structures to central and peripheral structures throughout the body. Also in the forebrain are centers for memory and emotion, as well as control of essential functions such as hunger, thirst, and sex drive.

The midbrain is a small area, but it contains important centers for sleep and pain as well as relay centers for sensory information and control of movement.

In Exhibit 3.1, part of the hindbrain, including the cerebellum, can also be seen. The *cerebellum* controls complex motor programming, including maintaining muscle tone and posture. Other hindbrain structures are essential to the regulation of basic physiological functions, including breathing, heart rate, and blood pressure. The brain stem connects the cerebral cortex to the spinal cord.

The basic working unit of all the nervous systems is the **neuron,** or nerve cell. The human body has a great diversity of neuronal types, but all consist of a cell body with a nucleus and a conduction fiber, an **axon**. Extending from the cell body are dendrites, which conduct impulses to the neurons from the axons of other nerve cells. Exhibit 3.3 shows how neurons are linked by axons and dendrites.

The connection between each axon and dendrite is actually a gap called a **synapse.** Synapses use chemical and electrical **neurotransmitters** to communicate. As the inset box in Exhibit 3.3 shows, nerve impulses travel from the cell body to the ends of the

EXHIBIT 3.3
Features of
a Typical Neuron

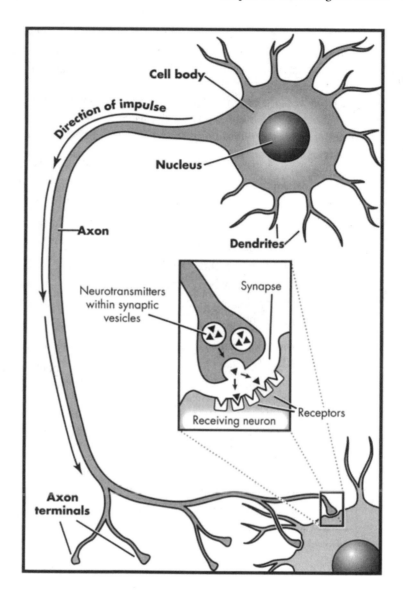

axons, where they trigger the release of neurotransmitters. The adjacent dendrite of another neuron has receptors distinctly shaped to fit particular types of neurotransmitters. When the neurotransmitter fits into a slot, the message is passed along.

Although neurotransmitters are the focus of much current research, scientists are not exactly sure about all that neurotransmitters do. Essentially, they may either excite or inhibit nervous system responses. But we know very little about many of the neurotransmitters, and we may not yet have discovered them all. Here are a few:

- *Acetylcholine (ACh):* The first neurotransmitter identified (nearly 70 years ago) is an excitatory neurotransmitter active in both the CNS and the PNS. Acetylcholine may be critical for intellectual activities such as memory.

- *Dopamine (DA):* This neurotransmitter, which is widely present in the CNS and PNS, is implicated in regulation of the endocrine system. Dopamine is thought to play a role in influencing emotional behavior, cognition, and motor activity.

- *Norepinephrine (NE):* Like dopamine, norepinephrine appears in many parts of the body. It may play a role in learning and memory and is also secreted by the adrenal gland in response to stress or events that produce arousal. Norepinephrine connects the brain stem with the cerebral cortex (Bentley & Walsh, 2001).

- *Serotonin:* Present in blood platelets, the lining of the digestive tract, and in a tract from the midbrain to all brain regions, this neurotransmitter is thought to be a factor in many body functions. Serotonin plays a role in sensory processes, muscular activity, thinking, states of consciousness, mood, depression, and anxiety (Bentley & Walsh, 2001).

- *Amino acids:* Some types of these molecules, which are found in proteins, are distributed throughout the brain and other body tissues. One amino acid, *gamma aminobutyric acid (GABA),* is thought to play a critical role in inhibiting the firing of impulses of some cells. Thus, GABA is believed to play an important role in many functions of the CNS, such as locomotor activity, cardiovascular reactions, pituitary function, and anxiety (Bentley & Walsh, 2001).

- *Peptides:* Amino acids that are joined together have only recently been studied as neurotransmitters. *Opioids,* many of which are peptides, play an important role in activities ranging from moderating pain to causing sleepiness. *Endorphins* help to minimize pain and enhance adaptive behavior (Carey, 1990; Kaplan & Sadock, 1998).

Behavior is affected by not only the levels of a neurotransmitter but also the balance between two or more neurotransmitters. Psychotropic medications affect behaviors and symptoms associated with mental illness by affecting the levels of specific neurotransmitters and altering the balance among neurotransmitters. Social workers would be well advised to possess knowledge about the effects of neurotransmitters on human behavior when working with individuals who are typically referred for medications evaluation and when following up with individuals who have been placed on medication treatment regimens (Long, 1996).

For Maggie, as for many survivors of traumatic brain injury, her skills, abilities, and deficits may be affected by a variety of circumstances—including which parts of the brain were injured, her achievements prior to injury, her social and psychological supports, and the training and education that she is offered following her accident. Tremendous advances are being made in rehabilitation following brain injuries (Horn, 1991). The better the social worker understands brain functions and brain plasticity, the more helpful the intervention is likely to be. We may be able to help with adjustment or adaptation to changes as well as the recovery of functions. Maggie could benefit from cognitive retraining, support in finding and maintaining employment, family counseling, and individual counseling that will help her end her relationship with Sam and repair the damage in her family caused by her secrecy about Sam and his ethnic identity. A key to recovery for many individuals who have experienced similar trauma is an opportunity to interact with peers and other survivors. Such peer networks provide the individual with access to new skills and a key link to psychological and social support. A social worker working with Maggie may fill several roles: case manager, advocate, counselor, resource coordinator, referral source.

Endocrine System

Remember Bess, the middle-aged woman diagnosed with diabetes? If you had first met her in a nonhospital setting, you might have interpreted her behaviors quite differently. Because of the recent rural health initiative in Bess's town, it was not unusual to hear women speaking in both French and English about their diets and exercises, and initially you may have been quite pleased for Bess's success. If Bess had told you that she was tired, you might have suggested that she slow down and get more rest, or perhaps that she include vitamins in her diet. Sitting in the morning, in her nightclothes on her couch, and missing work might suggest alcohol or other drug use. Confusion, switching back and forth between speaking French and English in the same sentence, and inability to answer simple questions could signal stroke, dementia, or a mental illness such as schizophrenia. But only a thorough medical assessment revealed the biological cause of Bess's behaviors: a physical health condition traceable to a malfunction in the endocrine system.

The **endocrine system** plays a crucial role in our growth, metabolism, development, learning, and memory. It is made up of *glands* that secrete hormones into the blood system; those hormones bind to receptors in target organs, much as neurotransmitters do in the brain, and affect the metabolism or function of those organs (Besser & Thorner, 1994; Kapit, Macey, & Meisami, 2000; Mader, 2001; Rosenzweig & Leiman, 1989). Distinguishing differences between hormones and neurotransmitters are often the distance of travel from the point of release to the target, as well as the route of travel. Hormones travel long distances through the bloodstream; neurotransmitters travel shorter distances from cell to cell, across the synaptic cleft.

Endocrine glands include the pineal, pituitary, thyroid, parathyroid, pancreas, and adrenal. Endocrine cells are also found in some organs that have primarily a

EXHIBIT 3.4

Selected Endocrine Glands and Their Effects

Gland	Hormone	Effect
Hypothalamus	Releasing and release-inhibiting factors	■ Targets pituitary gland, which affects many hormonal activities
Pituitary	Adrenocorticotropic (ACTH) Growth (GH, somatotropic) Vasopressin Prolactin	■ Stimulates adrenal cortex ■ Stimulates cell division, protein synthesis, and bone growth ■ Stimulates water reabsorption by kidneys ■ Stimulates milk production in mammary glands
Testes	Androgens (testosterone)	■ Stimulates development of sex organs, skin, muscles, bones, and sperm ■ Stimulates development and maintenance of secondary male sex characteristics
Ovaries	Estrogen and progesterone	■ Stimulates development of sex organs, skin, muscles, bones, and uterine lining ■ Stimulates development and maintenance of secondary female sex characteristics
Adrenal	Epinephrine Adrenal Cortical Steroids	■ Stimulates fight-or-flight reactions in heart and other muscles ■ Raises blood glucose levels ■ Stimulates sex characteristics
Pancreas	Insulin Glucagon	■ Targets liver, muscles, adipose tissues ■ Lowers blood glucose levels ■ Promotes formation of glycogen, proteins, and fats
Thymus	Thymosins	■ Triggers development of T lymphocytes, which orchestrate immune system response
Pineal	Melatonin	■ Maintains circadian rhythms (daily cycles of activity)
Thyroid	Thyroxin	■ Plays role in growth and development ■ Stimulates metabolic rate of all organs

nonendocrine function: the hypothalamus, liver, thymus, heart, kidney, stomach, duodenum, testes, and ovaries. Exhibit 3.4 lists some of the better-known glands and organs, the hormones they produce, and their effects on other body structures.

Systems perspective

The most basic form of hormonal communication is from an endocrine cell through the blood system to a target cell. A more complex form of hormonal communication is directly from an endocrine gland to a target endocrine gland.

EXHIBIT 3.5

An Example of a
Feedback Loop

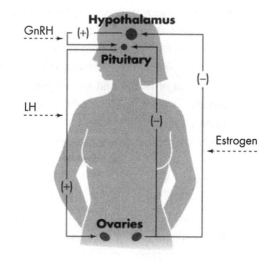

The endocrine system regulates the secretion of hormones through a **feedback control mechanism**. Output consists of hormones released from an endocrine gland; input consists of hormones taken into a target tissue or organ. The system is self-regulating. Similar to neurotransmitters, hormones have specific receptors, so that the hormone released from one gland has a specific target tissue or organ (Mader, 2001).

A good example of a feedback loop is presented in Exhibit 3.5. The hypothalamus secretes the gonadotropin-releasing hormone (GnRH), which binds to receptors in the anterior pituitary and stimulates the secretion of luteinizing hormone (LH). LH binds to receptors in the ovaries to stimulate the production of estrogen. Estrogen has a negative effect on the secretion of LH and GnRH at both the pituitary and hypothalamus, thus completing the loop. Loops like these allow the body to finely control the secretion of hormones.

Another good way to understand the feedback control mechanism is to observe the results when it malfunctions. Consider what has happened to Bess, who has been diagnosed with the most common illness caused by hormonal imbalance: **diabetes mellitus**. Insulin deficiency or resistance to insulin's effects is the basis of diabetes. Insulin and glucagon, which are released by the pancreas, regulate the metabolism of carbohydrates, the source of cell energy. They are essential for the maintenance of blood glucose levels (blood sugar). High blood glucose levels stimulate the release of insulin, which in turn helps to decrease blood sugar by promoting the uptake of glucose by tissues. Low blood sugar stimulates the release of glucagon, which in turn stimulates the liver to release glucose, raising blood sugar. In individuals with insulin deficiency, muscle cells are deprived of glucose. As an alternative, those muscle cells tap fat and protein reserves in muscle tissue as an energy source. The results include wasting of muscles, weakness, weight loss, and *metabolic acidosis,* a chemical imbalance in the blood. The increase in blood acidity suppresses higher nervous system functions, leading to coma. Continued suppression of the respiratory centers in the brain leads to death (Kapit et al., 2000).

Nearly 5% of the population of the United States has diabetes. According to the U.S. Department of Health and Human Services (2000), nearly 800,000 new cases of diabetes are diagnosed each year, or 2,200 per day. The number of persons who have been diagnosed with diabetes has shown a steady increase over the past 10 years. There are currently 10.5 million persons who have been diagnosed with diabetes, with an estimated 5.5 million persons having undiagnosed diabetes (U.S. Department of Health and Human Services, 2000). Juvenile-onset diabetes (Type I) is found in children and young adults; maturity-onset diabetes (Type II) most commonly arises in individuals over the age of 40 who are also obese. Type I diabetes may be an autoimmune disease and does not appear to have genetic or familial traits. Type II diabetes shows a strong familial association.

Rational choice perspective

For Bess, as for many individuals with symptoms indicating the presence of a medical condition, a crucial role for the social worker is to supply information and knowledge about the symptoms and the diagnosed condition. Social workers can also aid in the translation of this information, so clients, such as Bess, whose first language is French and who might not understand medical jargon, can grasp what is happening to them. As with any specialized field, becoming comfortable with the terminology often takes time and is even that much more difficult for people who do not speak English as their primary language. The social worker must also help Bess begin to examine the lifestyle changes that may be suggested by this diagnosis. What might it mean in terms of diet, exercise, home and work responsibilities, and so forth? Bess may need assistance in working with her insurance company to plan how her care will be financed. She may also need counseling as she works to adjust to life with this new condition.

Immune System

Melissa is far from alone in testing positive for HIV. Nearly 1 out of every 250, or about 1 million Americans, are infected with **human immunodeficiency virus** (HIV), the virus that causes AIDS—**acquired immunodeficiency syndrome**. Between 800,000 and 900,000 people in the United States are infected with HIV, and between 200,000 and 250,000 people are not aware of their infection (U.S. Department of Health and Human Services, 2000). The U.S. Department of Health and Human Services (2000) reported that more than 680,000 cases of AIDS had been reported by the end of 1998, and nearly 410,800 people had died from HIV disease or AIDS.

Cumulatively, 83% of AIDS cases reported by the end of 1998 had occurred in males, 16% in females, and 1% in children. Persons of all ages and racial and ethnic groups were affected: 304,094 cases of AIDS among whites, 251,408 cases among

African Americans, and 124,841 cases among Hispanics. Although 55% of the reported cases of AIDS occurred among African Americans and Hispanics, African Americans represent only an estimated 13% and Hispanics only 12% of the total population of the United States.

AIDS is the leading cause of death among men and women 15 to 44 years old in the United States (Novello, 1993). In 1997, for all African Americans aged 25 to 44 years old, AIDS was the leading cause of death; it was the second leading cause of death among African American females and the leading cause among African American males (U.S. Department of Health and Human Services, 2000).

According to the CDC, the fastest growing groups of persons reported with AIDS have been men and women who acquire HIV through heterosexual contact, a group to which Melissa now belongs. Although HIV is more easily transmitted from men to women, it can be transmitted from women to men. Heterosexual transmission occurs mainly through vaginal intercourse.

Once a person is infected with HIV, the disease-fighting immune system gradually weakens. This weakened immune system lets other diseases begin to attack the body. Over the next few years, Melissa will learn a great deal about how her body protects itself against disease and infection. We hope she will also adopt behaviors that will lessen the impact of specific illnesses and help her live longer.

The **immune system** is made up of organs and cells that work together to defend the body against disease (Kennedy, Kiecolt-Glaser, & Glaser, 1988; Sarafino, 2001). When operating in an optimal manner, the immune system is able to distinguish our own cells and organs from foreign elements (Sarafino, 2001). When the body recognizes something as foreign, the immune system mobilizes body resources and attacks. The foreign substance that can trigger an immune response may be a tissue or organ transplant or, more commonly, an antigen. **Antigens** include bacteria, fungi, protozoa, and viruses.

Sometimes, however, the immune system is mistakenly directed at parts of the body it was designed to protect, resulting in **autoimmune diseases**. Examples include rheumatoid arthritis, rheumatic fever, and lupus erythematosus. With rheumatoid arthritis, the immune system is directed against tissues and bones at the joints. In rheumatic fever, the immune system targets the muscles of the heart. With lupus erythematosus, the immune system affects various parts of the body, including the skin and kidneys (Sarafino, 2001).

Organs of the immune system are located throughout the body. They have primary involvement in the development of **lymphocytes**, or white blood cells (Sarafino, 2001). The main lymphatic organs include the following:

■ *Bone marrow:* The largest organ in the body. It is the soft tissue in the core of bones. There are two types of bone marrow, red and yellow. Yellow bone marrow is inactive. In adults, red bone marrow is found in the sternum, ribs, vertebrae, skull, and long bones. The bone marrow produces both red (erythrocytes) and white (leukocytes and lymphocytes) blood cells.

- *Lymph nodes:* Small oval or round spongy masses distributed throughout the body (Sarafino, 2001). Lymph nodes are connected by a network of lymphatic vessels that contain a clear fluid called lymph. As the lymph passes through a lymph node, it is purified of infectious organisms. These vessels ultimately empty into the bloodstream.

- *Spleen:* An organ in the upper left quadrant of the abdomen. The spleen functions much like a very large lymph node, except that instead of lymph, blood passes through it. The spleen filters out antigens and removes ineffective or worn-out red blood cells from the body (Sarafino, 2001). An injured spleen can be removed, but the individual becomes more susceptible to certain infections (Mader, 2001).

- *Thymus:* Located along the trachea in the chest behind the sternum. The thymus secretes thymosins, hormones believed to trigger the development of T cells. *T cells,* white blood cells that mature in the thymus, have the task of slowing down, fighting, and attacking antigens (Mader, 2001).

The immune system's response to antigens occurs in both specific and nonspecific ways (Safyer & Spies-Karotkin, 1988). **Nonspecific immunity** is more general. "Scavenger" cells or phagocytes circulate in the blood and lymph, being attracted by biochemical signals to congregate at the site of a wound and ingest antigens (Safyer & Spies-Karotkin, 1988; Sarafino, 2001). This process, known as *phagocytosis,* is quite effective but has two limitations: (1) certain bacteria and most viruses can survive after they have been engulfed, and (2) because our bodies are under constant attack and our phagocytes are constantly busy, a major assault on the immune system can easily overwhelm the nonspecific response. Thus, specific immunity is essential (Safyer & Spies-Karotkin, 1988).

Specific immunity, or acquired immunity, involves the lymphocytes. They not only respond to an infection, but they develop a memory of that infection and allow the body to make rapid defense against it in subsequent exposure. Certain lymphocytes produce **antibodies**, protein molecules designed to attach to the surface of specific invaders. The antibodies recruit other protein substances that puncture the membrane of invading microorganisms, causing the invaders to explode. The antibodies are assisted in this battle by T cells, which destroy foreign cells directly and orchestrate the immune response. Following the *primary response,* the antibodies remain in the circulatory system at significant levels until they are no longer needed. With reexposure to the same antigen, a *secondary immune response* occurs, characterized by a more rapid rise in antibody levels—a period of hours rather than days. This rapid response is possible because, during initial exposure to the antigen, memory cells were created.

Memory T cells store the information needed to produce specific antibodies. Memory T cells also have very long lives (Safyer & Spies-Karotkin, 1988).

Developmental
Perspective

The immune system becomes increasingly effective throughout childhood and declines in effectiveness in older adulthood. Infants are born with relatively little immune defense, but their immune system gradually becomes more efficient and complex. Thus, as the child develops, the incidence of serious illness declines. During adolescence and most of adulthood, the immune system, for most individuals, functions at a high level of effectiveness. As we age, although the numbers of lymphocytes and antibodies circulating in the lymph and blood do not decrease, their potency diminishes.

The functioning of the immune system can be hampered by a diet low in vitamins A, E, and C and high in fats and cholesterol and by excess weight (Sarafino, 2001). But there are far more serious problems with the immune system, such as HIV, that are life threatening. HIV, like other viruses, infects "normal" cells and "hijacks" their genetic machinery. These infected cells in essence become factories that make copies of the HIV, which then go on to infect other cells. The hijacked cells are destroyed. A favorite target of HIV is the T cells that tell other cells when to start fighting off infections. HIV thus weakens the immune system and makes it increasingly difficult for the body to fight off other diseases and infections. Most of us host organisms such as fungi, viruses, and parasites that live inside us without causing disease. However, for people with HIV, because of the low T cell count, these same organisms can cause serious infection. When such a disease occurs or when the individual's number of T cells drops below a certain level, the person with HIV is considered to have AIDS (Markowitz, 1997).

Melissa's life may undergo significant changes as symptoms of HIV infection begin to emerge. Like other women with HIV, Melissa will be at increased risk of repeated serious yeast infections of the vagina, and she may also be at increased risk for cancer of the cervix and pelvic inflammatory disease. Both men and women are vulnerable to opportunistic diseases and infections such as Kaposi's sarcoma, cytomegalo virus (CMV), AIDS retinopathy, pneumocystis carinii pneumonia (PCP), mycobacterium tuberculosis, and Candida albicans (thrush); cognitive conditions and illnesses such as AIDS dementia, loss of memory, loss of judgment, and depression; and other symptoms such as gastrointestinal dysfunction/distress, joint pain, anemia, and low platelet counts. The social worker can help to educate Melissa about these increased risks. In order to protect her health and the health of others, Melissa will need to take special precautions. She can be supported in staying well by getting early treatment, adopting a healthy lifestyle, and remaining hopeful and informed about new treatments (Novello, 1993).

The social worker also may have a role to play in working with Melissa as she tells her family and fiancé about her diagnosis. Melissa and her fiancé may need advice about how to practice safe sex. Because at present HIV infection inevitably leads to AIDS and death, the social worker should also be available to work with Melissa, her fiancé, and her family as they adjust to her diagnosis and the grief frequently associated with the diagnosis. The social worker may explore reactions and responses of Melissa, her fiancé, and her parents to this health crisis.

Because of the tremendous costs for medications, particularly new medications, the social worker may link Melissa to sources of financial support. This aid will become increasingly critical if she gets sicker, her income declines, and her medical expenses increase. Given recent advances in medical diagnostics and therapeutics, the U.S. Department of Health and Human Services (2000) estimates that the lifetime costs of health care associated with HIV may be more than $155,000 per person. Medications such as *protease inhibitors,* drugs that slow down the spread of HIV, are not a cure, but they allow the individual with HIV to fight off other infections and live longer (Markowitz, 1997). However, side effects of some of the drugs are just as debilitating as the effects of AIDS.

Conflict perspective   In addition to providing Melissa with information about her immune system, HIV, AIDS, and other physical health issues, the social worker can advise Melissa of the protections under the Americans With Disabilities Act of 1990. Melissa has joined an HIV support group, but the social worker may also offer to provide her with or refer her to counseling. The social worker may also have a role to play on behalf of all the Melissas, working to address the issues of social injustice and social intolerance—in part by providing HIV/AIDS education to business groups, schools, civic and volunteer associations, and neighborhood groups.

Cardiovascular System

According to current estimates, 57 million people in the United States, or more than one in five, have one or more types of *cardiovascular disease,* the most common cause of death in this country. An estimated 50 million people in the United States aged 6 and over have high blood pressure, 14 million have a history of coronary heart disease ("heart attack"), and 4 million have a history of having had a stroke (American Heart Association, 1997b).

Each year there are 600,000 strokes in the United States, resulting in about 158,000 deaths; stroke is the third leading cause of death (U.S. Department of Health and Human Services, 2000). In 2000, the rate of stroke for individuals aged 20 years and older was 2.2% for non-Hispanic white males and 1.5% for white females; 2.5% for non-Hispanic black males and 3.2% for black females; and among Mexican Americans, the rates were 2.3% for males and 1.3% for females. For American Indians aged 65 to 74, the rate of stroke was 1.5% for males and 0.8% for females (U.S. Department of Health and Human Services, 2000). In the United States, the death rate from heart disease has been consistently higher in males than in females and higher among African Americans than whites (U.S. Department of Health and Human Services, 2000).

Thomas's cardiovascular diagnosis is **high blood pressure** (hypertension), defined as a systolic blood pressure equal to or greater than (>) 140 mm Hg and/or diastolic blood pressure >90 mm Hg (his was 200/105). Blacks, Puerto Ricans, Cubans, and Mexican Americans are all more likely to suffer from high blood pressure than are Anglo-Americans, and the number of existing cases of high blood pressure is nearly 40% higher among African Americans than among whites. An estimated 6.4 million African Americans have high blood pressure with more frequent and severe effects than in other population subgroups (U.S. Department of Health and Human Services, 2000). In 1993, the death rates related to high blood pressure were 6.5 per 100,000 population for white males and 4.8 for white females versus 30 for black males and 22.6 for black females. High blood pressure also tends to be more common in people with lower education and income levels (American Heart Association, 1997a).

The cost of cardiovascular diseases and strokes in 1997 was estimated at $259.1 billion. This figure includes direct health expenditures (cost of physicians and other health professionals, hospital and nursing home services, medications, home health care, and other medical equipment) and indirect costs (lost productivity associated with illness and death) (American Heart Association, 1997b).

To better understand cardiovascular disease, it is first important to gain insight into the functioning of the **cardiovascular system,** which is made up of the heart and the blood circulatory system (Kapit et al., 2000; Mader, 2001). The heart's walls are made up of specialized muscle. As the muscle shortens and squeezes the hollow cavities of the heart, blood is forced in the directions permitted by the opening or closing of valves. Blood vessels continually carry blood from the heart to the rest of the body's tissues and then return the blood to the heart. Exhibit 3.6 shows the direction of the blood's flow through the heart.

There are three types of blood vessels:

1. *Arteries:* Have thick walls containing elastic and muscular tissues. The elastic tissues allow the arteries to expand and accommodate the increase in blood volume that occurs after each heartbeat. Arterioles are small arteries that branch into smaller vessels called capillaries.

2. *Capillaries:* A critical part of this closed circulation system, as they allow the exchange of nutrients and waste material with the body's cells. Oxygen and nutrients transfer out of a capillary into the tissue fluid surrounding cells and absorb carbon dioxide and other wastes from the cells.

3. *Veins:* Take blood from the capillaries and return it to the heart. Some of the major veins in the arms and legs have valves allowing the blood to flow only toward the heart when they are open and block any backward flow when they are closed (Kapit et al., 2000; Mader, 2001).

EXHIBIT 3.6
The Direction
of Blood Flow
Through the Heart

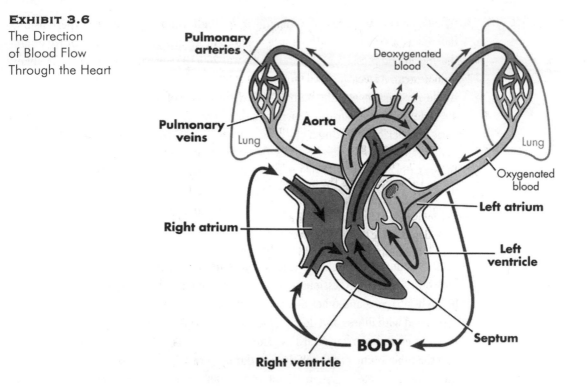

The heart has two sides (right and left) separated by the septum. Each side is divided into an upper and a lower chamber. The two upper, thin-walled chambers are called **atria**. The atria are smaller than the two lower, thick-walled chambers, called **ventricles**. Valves within the heart direct the flow of blood from chamber to chamber, and when closed, prevent its backward flow (Kapit et al., 2000; Mader, 2001).

As Exhibit 3.6 shows, the right side of the heart pumps blood to the lungs, and the left side of the heart pumps blood to the tissues of the body. Blood from body tissues that is low in oxygen and high in carbon dioxide (deoxygenated blood) enters the right atrium. The right atrium then sends blood through a valve to the right ventricle. The right ventricle then sends the blood through another valve and the pulmonary arteries into the lungs. In the lungs, the blood gives up carbon dioxide and takes up oxygen. Pulmonary veins then carry blood that is high in oxygen (oxygenated) from the lungs to the left atrium. From the left atrium, blood is sent through a valve to the left ventricle. The blood is then sent through a valve into the aorta for distribution around the body (Kapit et al., 2000; Mader, 2001).

Contraction and relaxation of the heart moves the blood from the ventricles to the lungs and to the body. The right and left sides of the heart contract together—first the two atria, then the two ventricles. The heart contracts ("beats") about 70 times per minute. The contraction and relaxation cycle is called the cardiac cycle. The sound of the heartbeat, as heard through a stethoscope, is caused by the opening and closing of the heart valves.

Although the heart will beat independently of any nervous system stimulation, regulation of the heart is primarily the responsibility of the ANS. *Parasympathetic activities* of the nervous system, which tend to be thought of as normal or routine activities, slow the heart rate. *Sympathetic activities,* associated with stress, increase the heart rate. As blood is pumped from the aorta into the arteries, their elastic walls swell, followed by an immediate recoiling. The alternating expansion and recoiling of the arterial wall is the pulse. The pulse rate is normally about 70 times per minute, the rate of the heartbeat.

Blood pressure is the measure of the pressure of the blood against the wall of a blood vessel. A sphygmomanometer is used to measure blood pressure. The cuff of the sphygmomanometer is placed around the upper arm over an artery. A pressure gauge is used to measure the *systolic blood pressure,* the highest arterial pressure, which results from ejection of blood from the aorta. *Diastolic blood pressure,* the lowest arterial pressure, occurs while the ventricles of the heart are relaxing. Normal blood pressure for a young adult is 120 mm of mercury systole over 80 mm of mercury diastole, or 120/80 (Kapit et al., 2000; Mader, 2001).

Blood pressure accounts for the movement of blood from the heart to the body by way of arteries and arterioles, but skeletal muscle contraction moves the blood through the venous system. As skeletal muscles contract, they push against the thin or weak walls of the veins, causing the blood to move past valves. Once past the valve, the blood cannot return, forcing it to move toward the heart.

High blood pressure has been called the silent killer, because many people like Thomas have it without noticeable symptoms. It is the leading cause of strokes and is a major risk factor for heart attacks and kidney failure.

Conflict perspective

Suddenly faced with startling information, such as a dramatic change in what was believed to be good health, Thomas might experience a range of responses, including but not limited to denial, questioning, self-reflection, self-critique, and even anger. The social worker can play many critical roles with Thomas. Perceptions of racial discrimination, daily hassles, and stressful life events (Gary, 1995) place him at increased risk for having a stroke or dying as a result of his high blood pressure. Social workers are uniquely positioned to see the links between sociocultural issues—such as vocational and educational opportunities, economics and income, housing, and criminal victimization—and health issues.

On an individual level, it is critical that Thomas has the knowledge to access the benefits of medical examination and treatment. The social worker can supplement the doctor's care by helping Thomas learn the essential elements of effective health practice, including knowledge of what it means to have high blood pressure, the causes, and strategies for decreasing the health risks. If medication is prescribed, the social worker can help to explain the medication regimen and support Thomas's decision about how to follow it.

The social worker also can help Thomas develop a strategy for identifying and deciding on lifestyle changes that can help lower his blood pressure. These may include examination of sources of stress and patterns of coping, what he eats, how much exercise he gets on a regular basis, and his social and economic supports.

Because high blood pressure appears to affect other family members, the social worker can also help Thomas's family understand lifestyle factors that might contribute to high blood pressure, such as exposure to stress, cigarette/tobacco use, a diet high in cholesterol, physical inactivity, and excess weight.

Systems perspective

Because African Americans and some other minorities have been shown to be at increased risk for high blood pressure, the social worker may work with community organizations, community centers, and religious organizations to put in place education and prevention programs as well as a physician and health care provider referral program. Because these health issues are also often tied to experiences of discrimination and prejudice, the social worker will need to pay attention to the sociocultural issues of unemployment and underemployment, differential earnings and low incomes, housing availability, safety, family relationships and supports, and criminal as well as social victimization.

Musculoskeletal System

Today polio, a viral infection of the nerves that control muscles, has been nearly eradicated in industrialized countries. But in the middle of the 20th century, the disease was much more common, and it temporarily or permanently paralyzed both children and adults. Of the 300,000 polio survivors now living in the United States, about 25% may be affected by **postpoliomyelitis syndrome** (PPS), progressive atrophy of muscles in those who once had polio (National Institute of Neurological Disorders and Stroke, 1997). Case Study 3.5 involves Max, who has PPS.

PPS has many causes. Some of the symptoms may be the result of the natural aging of muscles and joints damaged by polio or by overuse of unaffected muscles. Unrelated medical conditions may lead to new symptoms in polio survivors and a progression of earlier weaknesses. Unexplained new muscle atrophy and weakness may also develop. The overuse or repetitive use of weakened muscle fibers and tissues leads to musculoskeletal pain, which in turn leads to the need for increased rest, further atrophy, and possibly an increasing level of impairment (Maynard, 1998).

For Max, as for many survivors of polio, this onset of new symptoms is typically unexpected. It may signal increasing physical impairment, which may require new adjustments and adaptations. A social worker working with Max must first acquire a knowledge base and then work to identify the client's rehabilitation and socioemotional resources.

At the center of PPS is dysfunction in the **musculoskeletal system**, which supports and protects the body and provides motion. The contraction and relaxation of muscles attached to the skeleton is the basis for all voluntary movements. Over 600 skeletal muscles in the body account for about 40% of our body weight.

When a muscle contracts, it shortens; it can only pull, not push. Therefore, for us to be able to extend and to flex at a joint, muscles work in "antagonistic pairs." As an example, when the hamstring group in the back of the leg contracts, the quadriceps in the front relax; this allows the leg to bend at the knee. When the quadriceps contract, the hamstring relaxes, allowing the leg to extend.

The contraction of a muscle occurs as a result of an electrical impulse passed to the muscle by a controlling nerve that releases acetylcholine. When a single stimulus is given to a muscle, it responds with a twitch, a contraction lasting only a fraction of a second. But when there are repeated stimulations close together, the muscle cannot fully relax between impulses. As a result, each contraction benefits from the previous contraction, giving a combined contraction greater than an individual twitch. When stimulation is sufficiently rapid, the twitches cease to be jerky and fuse into a smooth contraction/movement called tetanus. However, tetanus that continues eventually produces muscle fatigue due to depletion of energy reserves.

Skeletal muscles exhibit tone when some muscles are always contracted. Tone is critical if we are to maintain body posture. If all the muscle fibers in the neck, trunk, and legs were to relax, our bodies would collapse. Nerve fibers embedded in the muscles emit nerve impulses that communicate to the CNS the state of particular muscles. This communication allows the CNS to coordinate the contraction of muscles (Kapit et al., 2000; Mader, 2001).

In its entirety, the musculoskeletal system both supports the body and allows it to move. The skeleton, particularly the large heavy bones of the legs, supports the body against the pull of gravity and protects soft body parts. Most essential, the skull protects the brain, the rib cage protects the heart and lungs, and the vertebrae protect and support the spinal cord.

Bones serve as sites for the attachment of muscles. It may not seem so, but bone is a very active tissue, supplied with nerves and blood vessels. Throughout life, bone cells repair, remold, and rejuvenate in response to stresses, strains, and fractures (Kapit et al., 2000).

A typical long bone, such as the arm and leg bones, has a cavity surrounded by a dense area. The dense area contains compact bone. The cavernous area contains blood vessels and nerves surrounded by spongy bone. Far from being weak, spongy bone is designed for strength. It is the site of red marrow, the specialized tissue that produces red and white blood cells. The cavity of a long bone also contains yellow marrow, which is a fat-storage tissue (Kapit et al., 2000; Mader, 2001).

EXHIBIT 3.7
Structure of
the Knee Joint

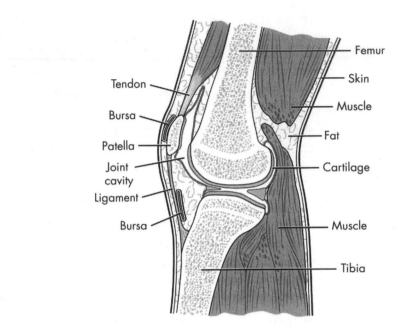

Tendon

Bursa

Patella

Joint
cavity

Ligament

Bursa

Femur

Skin

Muscle

Fat

Cartilage

Muscle

Tibia

Developmental
perspective

Most bones begin as cartilage. In long bones, growth and calcification (hardening) begin in early childhood and continue through adolescence. Growth hormones and thyroid hormones stimulate bone growth during childhood. Androgens, which are responsible for the adolescent growth spurt, stimulate bone growth during puberty. In late adolescence, androgens terminate bone growth.

Bones are joined together at joints. Long bones and their corresponding joints are what permit flexible body movement (Mader, 2001). Joints are classified according to the amount of movement they permit. Bones of the cranium, which are sutured together, are examples of immovable joints. Joints between the vertebrae are slightly movable. Freely movable joints, which connect two bones separated by a cavity, are called *synovial joints.* Synovial joints may be hinge joints (knee and elbow) or ball-and-socket joints (attachment of the femur to the hipbone). Exhibit 3.7 shows the structure of the knee joint. Synovial joints are prone to arthritis because the bones gradually lose their protective covering and grate against each other as they move (Mader, 2001).

The bones in a joint are held together by *ligaments*; *tendons* connect muscle to bone. The ends of the bones are capped by cartilage, which gives added strength and support to the joint. Friction between tendons and ligaments and between tendons and bones is eased by fluid-filled sacs called bursae. Inflammation of bursae is called bursitis.

Although overuse is damaging to the musculoskeletal system, underuse is too. Without a certain amount of use, muscles atrophy and bone density declines. Thus, the advice given to many polio survivors has been to "use it or lose it." Unfortunately, this advice may have inadvertently contributed to Max's postpolio symptoms.

Social workers and other health care professionals have generally believed that the greater the degree of independence, the better. Therefore, they have often discouraged a person with a medical condition from depending on environmental modifications such as ramps, elevators, and electrically operated doors or on assistive devices. **Assistive devices** are those that help a person to communicate, see, hear, or maneuver. Examples that have been used by individuals with activity limitations include manual wheelchairs, motorized wheelchairs, motorized scooters, and other aids that enhance mobility; hearing aids, telephone communication devices for the deaf, assistive listening devices, visual and audible signal systems, and other aids that enhance an individual's ability to hear; and voice-synthesized computer modules, optical scanners, talking software, Braille printers, and other devices that enhance a sight-impaired individual's ability to communicate.

Those who believed that working to overcome challenges was a helpful approach in adjusting to or working with limitation were well meaning. But hidden within this belief system was the impression that being labeled as disabled ascribed deficiency that made an individual less than whole, less than competent, and less than capable. Having attended school before the Rehabilitation Act of 1973, the Individual Education Act of 1975, and the Americans With Disabilities Act of 1990, Max's early years were spent in a world with little understanding or acceptance of disability. For Max, as for many people considered to be disabled, the pressure was and is to overcome or to succeed in spite of a disability. Unfortunately, that pressure may have contributed to Max's current problem. For Max and many other people with limitations, "conserve it to preserve it" is a far better adage than "use it or lose it."

The social worker has many options for working with Max. First, however, Max may choose to receive a thorough examination by a physician knowledgeable about polio and PPS. The social worker would then be able to serve as a resource and referral agent. She or he may work with rehabilitation professionals, such as physical therapists and occupational therapists, in identifying needed adaptations in Max's home and work environment. The social worker can provide counseling but may also refer Max to a PPS peer support group. Because Max may choose to acquire new assistive technology, the social worker may also intervene with insurance companies reluctant to purchase expensive equipment.

Reproductive System

Juan and Belinda are at the age when an understanding of reproduction and sexuality is critical. In the United States, the typical age for the first experience of sexual intercourse is between 16 and 17 years old, with 75% of high school seniors reporting having had sexual intercourse (Caron, 1998). "Most teens do not use contraception the first few times they have sex," and they typically do not visit a family planning clinic until a year after their first sexual intercourse experience (Caron, 1998, p. 194). This contributes to the incidence of teen pregnancy and sexually transmitted disease (STD). Over 1 million teenage girls become pregnant each year, and 3 million teenage boys and girls acquire an STD (Kirby, 1994).

The issue of sex education is very much related to these statistics. As of 2001, 39 states required some education about human sexuality. Twenty-one states required both sexuality and STD education, 17 states required STD education but not sexuality education, and 1 state required sexuality education but not STD education (The Alan Guttmacher Institute, 2001). Many states specifically prohibit teaching "such subjects as intercourse, abortion, masturbation, homosexuality, condoms and safer sex" (Caron, 1998, p. 195). Although the majority of parents, 8 in 10, support sex education in high schools, fewer than 10% of the communities in the United States have initiated inclusive sexuality education.

Social constructionist perspective

If adolescents are to make responsible decisions about their sexuality, they must develop an understanding of the structures and functions of the reproductive system as well as a value base. For some individuals, this information may come from the home, for others their schools or community activity centers, and for others family planning centers. As social workers involved with adolescents, families, community groups, schools, or other related organizations, we have a responsibility to have a fundamental understanding of human sexuality. Although much of the discussion that follows focuses on the biological aspects of sexuality, we remain aware of the ways in which culture may influence beliefs and attitudes about sexuality, as well as sexual behaviors (Rathus, Nevid, & Fichner-Rathus, 1998).

In humans, the reproductive system comprises internal and external structures. After conception, the sex-determining chromosome produced by the father unites with the mother's egg, and it is this configuration that determines the child's sex. At birth, boys and girls are distinguished by the presence of specific genitalia.

As Exhibit 3.8 shows, the external male organs are the penis and scrotum. Internal organs consist of the testes; the tubes and ducts that serve to transfer the sperm through the reproductive system; and the organs that help nourish and activate sperm and neutralize some of the acidity that sperm encounter in the vagina. The penis functions as a conduit for both urine and semen.

Externally, one can view the shaft and the glans (often referred to as the head or tip) of the penis. The shaft contains three cylinders. The two largest are called the corpa cavernosa (singular: corpus cavernosum). During sexual arousal, these become engorged with blood and stiffen. The corpus spongiosum, the third cylinder, contains the urethra. It enlarges at the tip of the penis to form a structure called the glans. The ridge that separates the glans from the shaft of the penis is called the corona. The frenulum is the

EXHIBIT 3.8
The Male
Reproductive System

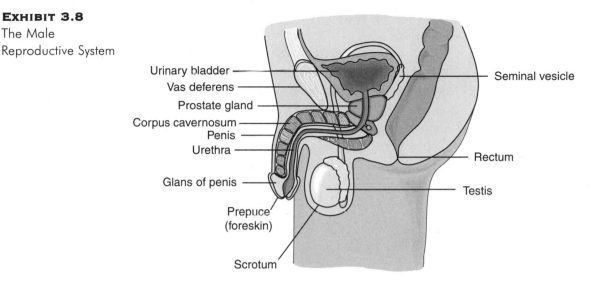

Urinary bladder
Vas deferens
Prostate gland
Corpus cavernosum
Penis
Urethra
Glans of penis
Prepuce
(foreskin)
Scrotum

Seminal vesicle
Rectum
Testis

sensitive strip of tissue connecting the underside of the glans to the shaft. At the base of the penis is the root, which extends into the pelvis.

Three glands are part of the feedback loop that maintains a constant level of male hormones in the bloodstream. The **testes**, or male gonads, are best known for their functions in producing sperm (mature germ cells that fertilize the female egg) and in secreting male hormones called *androgens. Testosterone* is one of the most important hormones in that it stimulates the development of the sex organs in the male fetus and the development of secondary sex characteristics such as facial hair, male muscle mass, and a deep voice. The two other glands in the feedback loop are the hypothalamus and the pituitary gland. Both secrete hormones that serve a regulatory function, primarily retaining a constant testosterone level in the blood.

In the early stages of their development, sperm cells are called spermatocytes. Each contains 46 chromosomes, including both an X and a Y chromosome that determine sex. As the spermatocytes mature and divide, chromosomes are reduced by half, and only one (either the X or Y) sex-determining chromosome is retained. The mature sperm cell is called the spermatozoan. This cell fertilizes the female egg (ovum), which contains only X chromosomes. Thus, the spermatozoan is the determining factor for the child's sex. (Females have two X chromosomes and males have one X and one Y chromosome.)

Before ejaculation, the sperm pass through a number of tubes and glands, beginning with a testis, proceeding through a maze of ducts, and then to an epididymis, which is the convergence of the ducts and serves as the storage facility for sperm in a testicle. Each epididymis empties into the vas deferens, which brings the mature sperm to the seminal vesicles, small glands that lie behind the bladder. In these glands, a nourishing and activating fluid combines with the sperm before the mixture is carried through the urethra to the outside of the penis. The *prostate gland,* through which the urethra passes, produces and introduces the milky fluid that preserves the sperm and neutralizes the alkalinity that is met in the female reproductive system. Cowper's glands also make their contribution to the seminal fluid before it leaves the male.

However, even if there is early ejaculation and the Cowper's glands do not have time to secrete fluid, viable sperm exist in the ejaculate and can fertilize the female egg. Early withdrawal of the penis therefore does not prevent the passage of some viable sperm cells. It is also important to know that sperm only compose about 1% of the ejaculate (3 to 5 ml of fluid total), but that this small percentage contains between 200 million and 400 million sperm. The number of sperm decreases with frequent ejaculation and advancing age.

Exhibit 3.9 shows the external female sex organs. They include the pudendum, also called vulva, which consists of the mons veneris, the fatty tissue below the abdomen

Exhibit 3.9

The Female External Sex Organs

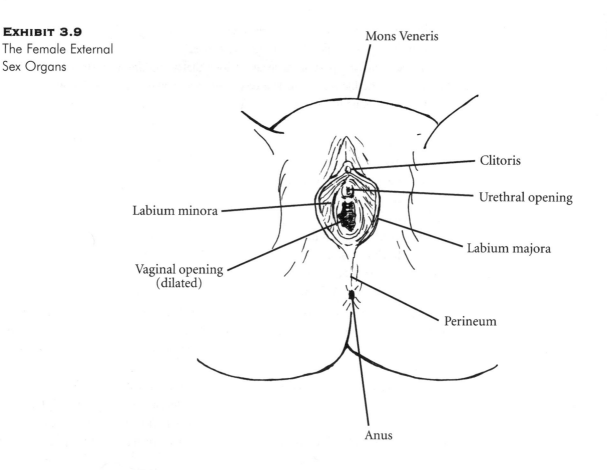

EXHIBIT 3.10
The Female
Internal Sex Organs

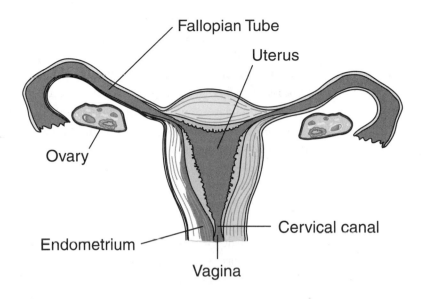

that becomes covered with hair after puberty; the labia majora and minora; the clitoris; and the vaginal opening. Unlike the male, the female has a physical separation between excretion and reproductive organs. Urine passes from the bladder through the urethra to the urethral opening, where it is expelled from the body. The urethra is located immediately before the vaginal opening and is unconnected to the vaginal opening.

The labia majora, large folds of skin, both contain nerve endings that are responsive to stimulation and protect the inner genitalia. Labia minora join the prepuce hood at the top that covers the clitoris. These structures, when stimulated, engorge with blood and darken, indicating sexual arousal. Resembling the male penis and developing from the same embryonic tissue, the clitoris is about 1 inch long and ¼ inch wide. However, unlike the penis, the clitoris is not directly involved in reproduction but serves primarily to produce sexual pleasure. The vestibule located inside the labia minora contains openings to the urethra and the vagina. It is also a site for arousal because it is rich in nerve endings that are sensitive to stimulation.

Internal structures of the female reproductive system, which are shown in Exhibit 3.10, include the vagina, ovaries, fallopian tubes, cervical canal (cervix), and uterus. The vagina is the structure that articulates with the external sexual structures. Composed of three layers and shaped cylindrically, the vagina both receives the penis during intercourse and is the canal through which the child passes from the uterus to the world outside the mother. Because of its multiple functions, the vagina is flexible in size and changes climate from dry to lubricated. The cervix is the lower end of the uterus and protrudes into the vagina. It maintains the chemical balance of the vagina through its secretions.

The **uterus**, also called the womb, serves as the pear-shaped home for the unborn child for the 9 months between implantation and birth. The innermost of its three layers, the endometrium, is the tissue that builds to protect and nourish the developing fetus. If pregnancy does not occur, the endometrium is shed monthly through the process of menstruation. If pregnancy does occur, the well-muscled middle layer of the uterus produces the strong contractions necessary at birth to move the fetus out of the uterus, into the vaginal canal, and then into the world. The external layer protects the uterus within the body.

The fallopian tubes connect the ovaries to the uterus and serve as a conduit for the ova (egg cells) from the ovaries to the uterus. Located on either side of the uterus, the ovaries have two major functions: the production of ova and the production of the female sex hormones, progesterone and estrogen.

Unlike males, who produce an unlimited number of sperm throughout their lives, females are born with the total number of ova that they will ever possess. Less than half of the 2 million ova mature sufficiently to be maintained in the ovaries past puberty. Of the approximately 400,000 that remain, only 400 are released in the monthly cycle.

Estrogen facilitates sexual maturation and regulates the menstrual cycle in premenopausal women. The benefits of estrogen in postmenopausal women, who can only obtain it from taking a supplement, are debatable. Some argue that estrogen maintains cognitive function and cardiac well-being in older women. However, estrogen supplements (also called hormone replacement therapy) have been indicted for increasing breast and uterine cancer risk, among other problems. Progesterone, though less discussed in the popular media, is critically important in preparing the uterus for pregnancy. It also is a regulator of the menstrual cycle.

Women's breasts are considered to be secondary sex characteristics because they do not have a direct function in reproduction. Mammary glands contained in the breast produce milk that is discharged through the nipple. The nipples are surrounded by the aureoles and become erect when touched in a sexual context. The size of the mammary glands is incidental to breast size and milk production. Rather, breast size is a function of the fatty tissue within the breast.

Humanistic perspective

The social worker who is knowledgeable about these mechanisms can clarify the specifics of male and female sexuality for Juan and Belinda. In the school setting or a local community agency, youth may come to talk about their feelings for each other and ask questions regarding sexual and emotional intimacy. Young people in the United States often have inaccurate information about sexuality and the biological aspects of sexual intimacy. Accurate information about sexuality would provide a basis for Juan and Belinda to make informed decisions about exercising their values related to sexuality.

Socioeconomic Status and Health

Research on mind-body connections is beginning to clarify the importance of socioeconomic status (SES) in maintaining health and well-being (Syme, 2001). Low SES is clearly related to disease in all body systems. This finding has not been a surprise to public health experts, who have long noted the association of poor health outcomes with low education, unsanitary housing, inadequate health care, unstable employment, and unsafe physical environments (Auerbach & Krimgold, 2001).

Until recently, however, researchers have made little attempt to understand the reasons behind the connection of SES and health. S. Leonard Syme (2001, p. 14) suggests why:

> Epidemiologists were not interested in studying risk factors about which nothing could be done, short of a revolution. Thus, they turned to issues that they considered amenable to intervention—individual behaviors such as eating habits, physical activity, and smoking.

But by the mid-1990s, researchers in several countries began to try to understand how health is related to SES. In the United States, that research effort became much more focused in 1997, when the MacArthur Foundation established the Network on Socioeconomic Status and Health (Adler, 2001). This network is interdisciplinary, including scholars from the fields of anthropology, biostatistics, clinical epidemiology, economics, medicine, neuroscience, psychoimmunology, psychology, and sociology.

The relationship between SES and health is turning out to involve complex interactions of persons and environments. And the researchers are finding some surprises. For example, it is often assumed that poor people have poorer health because they do not have access to quality health care. Cross-national research indicates, however, that access to health care plays only a small role in health status. Declines in mortality in industrial countries since 1900 have been associated more with improved social and physical environments than with medical advances (Auerbach & Krimgold, 2001). In the United States, a recent study of premature mortality conducted by the CDC indicates that inadequate health care was a factor in only 10% of premature deaths.

Conflict perspective

One of the most consistent, but also most controversial, findings is that the level of income inequality in a country and not purely SES is associated with health (Adler, 2001). Residents in more egalitarian countries, like Sweden and Japan, are healthier on average than residents in countries like Great Britain and the United States, where differences in the incomes of the poor and the rich are larger (Wilkinson, 2001). Likewise, in the United States, residents in states with the greatest levels of inequality are 25% more likely to report their health to be fair or poor than residents in states with less inequality

(Kawachi & Kennedy, 2001). High levels of inequality are particularly associated with heart attack, cancer, homicide, and infant mortality. Of course, individuals in the lowest SES group are those hardest hit with the negative health effects of inequality.

The mechanisms of this health-and-wealth connection are still unclear, but several possibilities are being explored:

■ *Persons with lower incomes engage in riskier health behaviors and lifestyles.* Persons with low income are more likely than higher SES individuals to smoke, use alcohol excessively, be sedentary, and eat high-fat diets. Researchers are noting that persons with low incomes, living in geographic areas with a high concentration of low-income families, are less likely to have access to health-related information, to health clubs and other facilities that foster good health, and to safe places to walk or jog. They are more likely to be targeted by advertisers for fast food restaurants and to work in jobs with less flexibility. For example, one study of health among a sample of bus drivers found that many drivers with hypertension did not take prescribed medications because the diuretics would increase their need to visit a bathroom. Their rigid bus schedules did not allow for bathroom breaks (Ragland, Drause, Greiner, & Fisher, 1998). When discussing health behaviors with clients, social workers need to become familiar with the patterns of their lives.

■ *Persons with lower incomes are more likely to be exposed to carcinogens and pathogens.* There is clear evidence that toxic waste sites are more likely to be located in neighborhoods with a high concentration of low-income residents. Community social workers can collaborate with other groups to promote environmental justice.

■ *Persons with lower incomes are exposed to more stressors, and they also have fewer resources for coping with stress.* Persons with lower incomes have less control over their work situations, a situation that has been found to have a powerful negative impact on health (Wilkinson, 2001). Repeated exposure to threat has also been linked to both SES and health outcomes (McEwen, 1998). It has also been found that "subjective social status," or an individual's evaluation of where she or he stands in the social hierarchy, is strongly related to health status (Adler, 2001). The subjective experience of being disadvantaged has been found to be highly correlated with endocrine response to stressors and with respiratory illness when exposed to a virus. These findings are in line with the emerging idea that the size of the difference in wealth among a population has a greater effect than low SES alone. This gives further impetus to social work's commitment to economic justice.

The research so far clearly indicates that the health care system alone cannot offset the effects of other social forces on health. An important social work role is therefore advocacy in the political arena for an integrative, biopsychosocial-spiritual approach for understanding biological health and illness.

IMPLICATIONS FOR SOCIAL WORK PRACTICE

This discussion of the biological person suggests several principles for social work assessment and intervention.

- Develop a working knowledge of the body's systems, their interconnectedness, and the ways they interact with other dimensions of human behavior.

- In assessments and interventions, recognize that experiences of health and illness are influenced by the social, political, cultural, and economic context.

- Recognize that the meanings attached to health and illness influence not only the physical experience but also the values and socioemotional response assigned to health and illness.

- In assessment and intervention activities, look for the ways that behavior affects biological functions and the ways biological systems affect behaviors.

- In assessment and interventions, evaluate the influence of health status on cognitive performance, emotional comfort, and overall well-being.

- In assessment and intervention, consider the ways in which one person's health status is affecting other people, particularly other family members.

- Where appropriate, incorporate multiple roles into practice related to the health of the biological system, including the roles of clinician, educator, case manager, service coordinator, prevention specialist, and policy advocate.

KEY TERMS

acquired immunodeficiency syndrome (AIDS)
antibodies
antigens
assistive devices

atria
autoimmune disease
axon
blood pressure
brain injury (BI)

cardiovascular system

diabetes mellitus

endocrine system

feedback control mechanism

high blood pressure

human immunodeficiency virus (HIV)

immune system

lymphocytes

musculoskeletal system

nervous system

neuron

neurotransmitters

nonspecific immunity

postpoliomyelitis syndrome (PPS)

specific immunity

synapse

testes

uterus

ventricles

ACTIVE LEARNING

1. You have been asked by the local public middle school to teach youth about the experiences of living with one of the following conditions: brain injury, diabetes, HIV, high blood pressure, or postpolio syndrome. Locate literature and Web resources on your chosen topic, select the material that you wish to present, and prepare a presentation in lay terms that will be accessible to the youth audience.

2. Working in small groups, prepare two arguments, one supporting and one opposing sex education in public school. Give some consideration to content that should and/or should not be included in sex education programs in public school and the ages at which such education should occur. Provide evidence for your arguments.

WEB RESOURCES

National Center for Health Statistics

www.cdc.gov/nchs
Site presented by the National Center for Health Statistics contains FASTATS on a wide range of health topics as well as news releases and publication listing.

Explore the Brain and Spinal Cord

faculty.washington.edu/chudler/introb.html
Site maintained by faculty at the University of Washington presents basic neuroscience information, including brain basics, the spinal cord, the peripheral nervous

system, the neuron, sensory systems, effects of drugs on the nervous system, and neurological and mental disorders.

American Diabetes Association

www.diabetes.org/main/application/commercewf

Site maintained by the American Diabetes Association contains basic diabetes information as well as specific information on Type I diabetes, Type II diabetes, community resources, and healthy living.

Centers for Disease Control and Prevention (CDC) Divisions of HIV/AIDS Prevention

www.cdc.gov/hiv/dhap/htm

Site maintained by the CDC Divisions of HIV/AIDS Prevention contains basic science information on HIV/AIDS, basic statistics, fact sheets, and links to other sites.

American Heart Association

www.americanheart.org

Site maintained by the American Heart Association contains information on diseases and conditions, healthy lifestyle, news, and a heart and stroke encyclopedia.

Postpolio Syndrome Central

www.skally.net/ppsc

Site maintained by a group of volunteers contains a postpolio syndrome (PPS) survey and links to other Web resources about PPS.

The Alan Guttmacher Institute

www.agi-usa.org

Site presented by the Alan Guttmacher Institute, a nonprofit organization that focuses on sexual and reproductive health research, policy analysis, and public education, contains information on abortion, law and public policy, pregnancy and birth, prevention and contraception, sexual behavior, sexually transmitted infections and HIV, and sexuality and youth.

CHAPTER 4

The Psychological Person: Cognition, Emotion, and Self

Joseph Walsh

The Psychological Person
Cognition, Emotion, and Self

Joseph Walsh
Virginia Commonwealth University

How is human behavior influenced by cognitions and emotions?
How do humans develop a sense of self?

Key Ideas

As you read this chapter, take note of these central ideas:

1. Cognition and emotion are different but interrelated internal processes, and the nature of their relationship has long been debated.

2. Cognition includes the conscious thinking processes of taking in relevant information from the environment, synthesizing that information, and formulating a plan of action based on that synthesis. Cognitive theory in social work practice asserts that thinking, not emotion, should be the focus of intervention.

3. Moral development is related to cognitive development, because it proceeds from stages of egocentrism through abstract principles of justice and caring.

4. Emotions can be understood as feeling states characterized by appraisals of a stimulus, changes in bodily sensations, and displays of expressive gestures.

5. The symptoms of psychological problems may be primarily cognitive or emotional, but both cognition and emotion influence the development of problems.

6. The self may be conceptualized as soul, organizing activity, cognitive structure, verbal activity, experience of cohesion, or flow of experience.

CASE STUDY

SHEILA'S DIFFICULT
TRANSITION TO UNIVERSITY LIFE

Sheila, age 22 and in her first semester at the state university, experienced a crisis during the 7th week of classes. It was the midpoint of the semester, when instructors were required to give interim grades so that students would clearly understand their academic status before the final date for course drops passed. Sheila knew that she was having trouble in all four of her courses but was shocked to receive two Cs and two Ds. She realized that she was at risk of failing two courses! Her chronic sense of sadness became worse; she had the occasional thoughts of suicide that she had experienced in the past. Sheila knew that she needed to study that weekend, but instead she made the 5-hour drive to her parents' home, feeling a need to be around familiar faces. She had no close friends at school. Distraught, Sheila considered dropping out, but her parents convinced her to talk to her academic adviser first.

Sheila has told you that she was quiet during her only previous meeting with the adviser, but this time she vented much emotion. Her adviser learned that Sheila had been a troubled young woman for quite some time. In fact, Sheila said that she had felt depressed and inferior to her peers since childhood. The patterns of negative thinking and feeling that influenced Sheila's current crisis had been in place for 10 years. At this moment, Sheila believed that she simply did not have the intelligence to succeed in college. She did, in fact, have a diagnosed learning disability, a type of dyslexia that made it difficult for her to read and write. A special university adviser was helping her manage this problem within her course load, although not all the professors seemed sympathetic to her situation. Neither did Sheila believe that she had the social competence to make friends, male or female, or the strength of will to overcome her negative moods and outlook. She believed her depression was a basic part of her personality. After all, she couldn't recall ever feeling differently.

Sheila's family included her parents and an older sister (by 2 years), Amy. During the previous 2 years, Sheila had commuted from her family home to a nearby community college. She had stayed home and worked for 1 year after high school graduation, without the motivation or direction to continue with schooling. Amy was, in contrast, the "star" child, who attended a major university to pursue a career in commercial art after winning academic awards throughout her high school years. Sheila had watched Amy, so polished and popular, make her way easily and independently into the world. Sheila, by comparison, knew that she could not function so well. Eventually, she decided to enroll in the community college for general education studies. She felt awkward around the other students, as usual, but liked the small size of the school. It was peaceful and kept Sheila near her parents.

When Sheila completed her studies at the community college, she applied for admission to the state university. She decided to major in art preservation, an area of study similar to Amy's. Sheila's adjustment to the state university had been difficult from the beginning. She was intimidated by the grand scale of the institution: the size of the classes, the more distant, formal manner of her professors, the large numbers of students she saw on the campus streets, and the crowds in the student union. The university seemed cold, and the students unfriendly. Sheila was a white middle-class student like the majority at her campus, but she believed that the other students saw her as a misfit. She didn't dress in the latest styles, was not interesting or sophisticated, and was not intelligent enough to stand out in her classes. Even as she sat in the back of her classrooms, she believed that others were thinking of her, in her own words, as a "geek." Sheila even felt out of place in her off-campus living quarters. A cousin had found her a basement apartment in a house in which a married couple resided. The walls were thin, and Sheila felt that she lacked privacy.

Many students experience a difficult transition to college. Sheila's academic adviser, however, was struck by several family themes that seemed to contribute to Sheila's low self-esteem. Sheila's paternal grandmother, a powerful matriarch, had always lived near the family. She disapproved of much of her grandchildren's behavior, and was frequently critical of them to the point of cruelty. She had good social graces, and thus was particularly unhappy with Sheila's lack of social competence. Sheila's mother was always reluctant to disagree with her mother-in-law or defend her children. This passivity made Sheila angry at her mother, as did the fact that her mother argued with her father quite often and was known to have had several affairs.

Sheila was closer to her father, who was also fond of her, but he maintained a strict work ethic and believed that productive people should have no time for play. He felt that his children showed disrespect to him when they "wasted time" with recreation. Amy seemed able to take her father's admonitions in stride, and was closer in spirit and personality to her exuberant mother. Sheila, however, felt guilty when violating her father's wishes. They did have a special relationship, and her father tended to confide in Sheila, but he sometimes did so inappropriately. He told her on several occasions that he was thinking of divorcing his wife, and that in fact Sheila might have been fathered by one of his wife's boyfriends.

Thus, during her transition to the university, Sheila was faced with the task of making her way with a learning disability, a work ethic that did not permit her to enjoy college life and young adulthood, a personal history of being criticized with little balancing support, and even a lack of identity. Now, in her 7th week, Sheila is depressed and vaguely suicidal—an outsider among her peers, without acknowledged strengths, and feeling all alone. She has come to you for help on her academic adviser's suggestion.

Cognition and Emotion

Sheila's difficult transition to college life reflects her personal **psychology,** which can be defined as her mind and her mental processes. Her story illustrates the impact on social functioning of a person's particular patterns of cognition and emotion. **Cognition** can be defined as our conscious or preconscious thinking processes—the mental activities of which we are aware or can become aware with probing. Cognition includes taking in relevant information from the environment, synthesizing that information, and formulating a plan of action based on that synthesis (Beck & Weishaar, 1995). *Beliefs,* key elements of our cognition, are ideas that we hold to be true. Our assessment of any idea as true or false is based on the synthesis of information. Erroneous beliefs, which may result from misinterpretations of perceptions or from conclusions based on insufficient evidence, frequently contribute to social dysfunction.

Emotion can be understood as a feeling state characterized by our appraisal of a stimulus, by changes in bodily sensations, and by displays of expressive gestures (Thoits, 1989). The term *emotion* is often used interchangeably in the study of psychology with the term **affect,** but the latter term refers only to the physiological manifestations of feelings. Affect may be the result of *drives* (innate compulsions to gratify basic needs). It generates both conscious and **unconscious** feelings (those of which we are not aware but which influence our behavior). In contrast, emotion is always consciously experienced. Nor is emotion the same as **mood,** a feeling disposition that is more stable than emotion, less intense, and less tied to a specific situation.

The evolution of psychological thought in this century has consisted largely of a debate about the origins of cognition and emotion, the nature of their influence on behavior, and their influence on each other. The only point of agreement seems to be that cognition and emotion are complex and interactive.

Theories of Cognition

Theories of cognition, which emerged in the 1950s, assume that conscious thinking is the basis for almost all behavior and emotions. Emotions are defined within these theories as the physiological responses that follow our cognitive evaluations of input. In other words, thoughts produce emotions.

Cognitive Theory

Developmental
perspective

Jean Piaget's cognitive theory is the most influential theory of cognition in social work and psychology (Maier, 1978). In his system, our capacity for reasoning develops in stages, from infancy through adolescence and early adulthood. Piaget saw the four stages as sequential and interdependent, evolving from activity without thought to thought with less emphasis on activity—from doing, to doing knowingly, and finally to conceptualizing. He saw physical and neurological development as necessary for cognitive development.

A central concept in Piaget's theory is **schema** (plural: **schemata),** defined as an internalized representation of the world or an ingrained and systematic pattern of thought, action, and problem solving. Our schemata develop through *social learning* (watching and absorbing the experiences of others) or direct learning (our own experiences). Both of these processes may involve **assimilation** (responding to experiences based on existing schemata) or **accommodation** (changing schemata when new situations cannot be incorporated within an existing one). As children, we are motivated to develop schemata as a means of maintaining psychological *equilibrium,* or balance. Any experience that we cannot assimilate creates anxiety, but if our schemata are adjusted to accommodate the new experience, the desired state of equilibrium will be restored. From this perspective, you might interpret Sheila's difficulties in college as an inability to achieve equilibrium by accommodating new experience within her existing schemata. As a shy person, Sheila was accustomed to making friends very slowly in environments where she interacted with relatively small numbers of peers. She could not easily adjust to the challenge of initiating friendships quickly in a much larger and more transient student population.

Another of Piaget's central ideas is that cognitive development unfolds sequentially. Infants are unable to differentiate between "self" and the external world; the primary task in early cognitive development is the gradual reduction of such egocentricity, or self-centeredness. The child gradually learns to perform **cognitive operations**—to use

EXHIBIT 4.1
Piaget's Stages
of Cognitive
Operations

Stage	Description
Sensorimotor stage (birth to 2 years)	The infant is egocentric; he or she gradually learns to coordinate sensory and motor activities and develops a beginning sense of objects existing apart from the self.
Preoperational stage (2 to 7 years)	The child remains primarily egocentric but discovers rules (regularities) that can be applied to new incoming information. The child tends to overgeneralize rules, however, and thus makes many cognitive errors.
Concrete operations stage (7 to 11 years)	The child can solve concrete problems through the application of logical problem-solving strategies.
Formal operations stage (11 to adulthood)	The person becomes able to solve real and hypothetical problems using abstract concepts.

abstract thoughts and ideas that are not tied to sensory and motor information. Piaget's four stages of normal cognitive development are summarized in Exhibit 4.1.

Information Processing Theory

Social behavioral perspective; Systems perspective

Cognitive theory has been very influential but, as you might guess, leaves many aspects of cognitive functioning unexplained. Whereas Piaget sought to explain how cognition develops, **information processing theory** offers details about how our cognitive processes are organized (Granvold, 1994). This theory makes a clear distinction between the thinker and the external environment; each is an independent, objective entity in the processing of inputs and outputs. We receive stimulation from the outside and code it with sensory receptors in the nervous system. The information is first represented in some set of brain activities and then integrated (by accommodation or assimilation) and stored for purposes of present and future adaptation to the environment. All of us develop increasingly sophisticated problem-solving processes through the evolution of our cognitive patterns, which enable us to draw attention to particular inputs as significant.

Information processing is a *sensory theory* in that it depicts information as flowing passively from the external world inward through the senses to the mind. It views the mind as having distinct parts—including the sensory register, short-term memory, and long-term memory—that make unique contributions to thinking in a specific sequence. In contrast, a *motor theory* such as Piaget's sees the mind as playing an active role in processing—not merely recording but actually constructing the nature of the input it receives. In Sheila's case, information processing theory would suggest that she simply has not experienced a situation like her current one and thus lacks the schemata required to adapt. Cognitive theory would suggest that faulty processing somewhere in Sheila's past is making her adjustment difficult.

Social Learning Theory

Social behavioral perspective

According to *social learning theory,* we are motivated by nature to experience pleasure and avoid pain. Social learning theorists acknowledge that thoughts and emotions exist, but understand them as behaviors in need of explaining rather than as primary motivating factors.

Social learning theory relies to a great extent on social behavioral principles of conditioning, which assert that behavior is shaped by its reinforcing or punishing consequences (operant conditioning) and antecedents (classical conditioning). Albert Bandura (1977b) added the principle of vicarious learning, or *modeling,* which asserts that behavior is also acquired by witnessing how the actions of others are reinforced.

Social learning theorists, unlike other social behavioral theorists, do assert that thinking takes place between the occurrence of a stimulus and our response. They call this thought process **cognitive mediation**. The unique patterns we learn for evaluating environmental stimuli explain why each of us may adopt very different behaviors in response to the same stimulus—for example, why Sheila's reaction to the crowds in the student union is very different from the reactions of some of her peers. Bandura (1977b, 1986) takes this idea a step further and asserts that we engage in self-observations and make self-judgments about our competence and mastery. We then act on the basis of these self-judgments. It is clear that Sheila made very negative self-judgments about her competence as she began her studies at the university.

Theory of Multiple Intelligences

Howard Gardner's (1983, 1999) theory of **multiple intelligences** constitutes a major step forward in our understanding of how people come to possess different types of cognitive skills and how the same person is able to effectively use cognitive skills in some areas of life but not others. In this theory, intelligence is defined as a "biopsychosocial potential to process information that can be activated in a cultural setting to solve problems or create products that are of value in a culture" (Gardner, 1999, p. 23). Intelligence includes

- The ability to solve problems that one encounters in life

- The ability to generate new problems to solve

- The ability to make something or offer a service that is valued within one's culture

Systems perspective

In this theory, the brain is understood not as a single cognitive system but as a central unit of neurological functioning that houses relatively separate cognitive faculties. During its evolution the brain has developed *separate* organs, or modules, as information-processing devices. Thus, all people have a unique blend of intelligences derived from these modules. Gardner has delineated seven intelligences, which are overviewed in Exhibit 4.2, although in his ongoing research he is considering additional possibilities.

Two intelligences, the *linguistic* (related to spoken and written language) and the *logical-mathematical* (analytic), are consistent with traditional notions of intelligence. The five others are not, however. Gardner (1999) has considered naturalist, spiritual, and existential intelligences as other possibilities.

Humanistic perspective

One of the most positive implications of the theory of multiple intelligences is that it helps us see strengths in ourselves that lie outside the mainstream. For example, Sheila, so self-critical, might be encouraged to consider that she has a strong spatial intelligence that contributes to her artistic sensibilities. She needs help, however, in further development of both her intrapersonal and interpersonal intelligences.

Theories of Moral Reasoning

Developmental perspective

Morality is our sensitivity to, and knowledge of, what is right and wrong. It develops from our acquired principles of justice and ways of caring for others. Theories of moral reasoning are similar to those of cognitive development in that a sequential process is involved. Familiarity with these theories can help social workers understand how clients make decisions and develop preferences for action in various situations. Both of these issues are important in our efforts to develop goals with clients. The best-known theories of moral reasoning are those of Lawrence Kohlberg and Carol Gilligan.

Kohlberg (1969) formulated six stages of moral development, beginning in childhood and unfolding through adolescence and young adulthood (see Exhibit 4.3). The first two stages represent **preconventional morality,** in which the child's primary motivation is to avoid immediate punishment and receive immediate rewards. **Conventional morality** emphasizes adherence to social rules. A person at this level of morality might be very troubled, as Sheila is, by circumstances that make her or him different from other people. Many people never move beyond this level to **postconventional morality,** which is characterized by a concern with moral principles transcending those of their own society.

Exhibit 4.2

Gardner's Seven Intelligences

Linguistic Intelligence: The capacity to use language to express what is on your mind and to understand other people. Linguistic intelligence includes listening, speaking, reading, and writing skills.

Logical-Mathematical Intelligence: The capacity for mathematical calculation, logical thinking, problem solving, deductive and inductive reasoning, and the discernment of patterns and relationships. Gardner suggests that this is the type of intelligence addressed by Piaget's model of cognitive development, but he does not think Piaget's model fits other types of intelligence.

Visual-Spatial Intelligence: The ability to represent the spatial world internally in your mind. Visual-spatial intelligence involves visual discrimination, recognition, projection, mental imagery, spatial reasoning, and image manipulation.

Bodily Kinesthetic Intelligence: The capacity to use your whole body or parts of your body to solve a problem, make something, or put on some kind of production. Gardner suggests that our tradition of separating body and mind is unfortunate because the mind can be trained to use the body properly and the body trained to respond to the expressive powers of the mind. He notes that some learners rely on tactile and kinesthetic processes, not just visual and auditory processes.

Musical Intelligence: The capacity to think in music, to be able to hear patterns, recognize them, remember them, and perhaps manipulate them.

Intrapersonal Intelligence: The capacity to understand yourself, to know who you are, what you can do, what you want to do, how you react to things, which things to avoid, which things to gravitate toward, and where to go if you need help. Gardner says we are drawn to people who have a good understanding of themselves because those people tend not to make mistakes. They are aware of their range of emotions and can find outlets for expressing feelings and thoughts. They are motivated to pursue goals and live by an ethical value system.

Interpersonal Intelligence: The ability to understand and communicate with others, to note differences in moods, temperaments, motivations, and skills. Interpersonal intelligence includes the ability to form and maintain relationships and to assume various roles within groups, and the ability to adapt behavior to different environments. It also includes the ability to perceive diverse perspectives on social and political issues. Gardner suggests that individuals with this intelligence express an interest in interpersonally oriented careers, such as teaching, social work, and politics.

Source: Based on Gardner, 1999.

Conflict perspective   One limitation of Kohlberg's theory is that it does not take into account gender differences (his subjects were all male). In fact, he claims that women do not advance through all six stages as often as men. Addressing this issue, Gilligan (1982) notes that boys tend to emphasize independence, autonomy, and the rights of others in their moral thinking, using a *justice-oriented* approach. Girls, on the other hand, develop an ethic of care that grows out of a concern for the needs of others rather than the value of independence. To account for this difference, Gilligan proposed the three stages of moral

EXHIBIT 4.3

Kohlberg's Stages of
Moral Development

Stage	Description
Preconventional	
Heteronomous morality	Accepting what the world says is right
Instrumental purpose	Defining the good as whatever is agreeable to the self and those in the immediate environment
Conventional	
Interpersonal experiences	Seeking conformity and consistency in moral action with significant others
The societal point of view	Seeking conformity and consistency with what one perceives to be the opinions of the larger community
Postconventional	
Ethics	Observing individual and group (societal) rights
Conscience and logic	Seeking to apply universal principles of right and wrong

development listed in Exhibit 4.4. Her stages place greater emphasis than Kohlberg does on the ethic of care and are meant to more accurately describe the moral development of females. We see in the next chapter how Gilligan's work has influenced feminist psychology.

The research findings on gender differences in moral reasoning are inconsistent. Some research indicates that boys do tend to emphasize justice principles, whereas girls emphasize caring, but these differences are not great (Gump, Baker, & Roll, 2000). Other researchers find no differences in the ways that males and females reason about moral dilemmas (Al-Ansari, 2002; Wimalasiri, 2001). It is possible that gender differences in moral reasoning, when they do occur, are related to power differences and differences in the typical ethical dilemmas faced by males and females. In one study, a sample of men and women were asked to respond to a set of hypothetical scenarios in which all respondents needed to assume positions of limited power and were required to assume caregiving roles (Galotti, 1989). Under these conditions, the moral responses of men and women were similar. Researchers have also found evidence that culture may have a greater influence on moral reasoning than gender, with Anglo-Americans putting less emphasis on an ethic of care than members of other ethnic groups (Al-Ansari, 2002; Gump et al., 2000).

EXHIBIT 4.4
Gilligan's Three
Stages of Moral
Development

Stage	Description
Survival orientation	Egocentric concerns of emotional and physical survival are primary.
Conventional care	The person defines as right those actions that please significant others.
Integrated care	A person's right actions take into account the needs of others as well as the self.

Both Kohlberg's and Gilligan's stages of moral reasoning, like Piaget's cognitive theory, assume an increasing ability to think abstractly as the person progresses through adolescence. With her great concern about what her parents and grandmother want her to do, Sheila seems to fall in Kohlberg's stage of conventional morality and Gilligan's stage of conventional care.

Theories of Cognition in Social Work Practice

When theories of cognition first emerged, they were mainly a reaction against psychodynamic theories, which focused on the influence of unconscious thought. Many practitioners had come to believe that although some mental processes may be categorized as unconscious, they have only a minor influence on behavior. Rather, conscious thinking is the basis for almost all behavior and emotions (Lantz, 1996).

Piaget's cognitive theory postulates that we develop mental schemata, or general information-processing rules that become enduring, from past experiences. Schemata are the basis for the way individuals screen, discriminate, and code stimuli; categorize and evaluate experiences; and make judgments. Cognition is viewed as active—our minds do not merely receive and process external stimuli but are active in constructing the reality they seek to apprehend. We are "rational" to the extent that our schemata, the basis for our perceptions, accommodate available environmental evidence and our decisions do not rely solely on preconceived notions of the external world.

So long as a person's cognitive style helps to achieve his or her goals, it is considered healthy. However, a person's thinking patterns can become distorted, featuring patterns of bias that dismiss relevant environmental information from judgment, which can lead in turn to the maladaptive emotional responses described in Exhibit 4.5. These *cognitive errors* are habits of thought that lead people to distort input from the environment and experience psychological distress (Granvold, 1994).

Cognitive Error	Description
Absolute thinking	Viewing experience as all good or all bad, and failing to understand that experiences can be a mixture of both
Overgeneralization	Assuming that deficiencies in one area of life necessarily imply deficiencies in other areas
Selective abstraction	Focusing only on the negative aspects of a situation, and consequently overlooking its positive aspects
Arbitrary inference	Reaching a negative conclusion about a situation with insufficient evidence
Magnification	Creating large problems out of small ones
Minimization	Making large problems small, and thus not dealing adequately with them
Personalization	Accepting blame for negative events without sufficient evidence

As a social worker, you could use cognitive theory to surmise that Sheila feels depressed because she subjectively assesses her life situations in a distorted manner. For example, *arbitrary inferences* may lead her to conclude that because the university students do not approach her in the crowded student union, they are not friendly. Because she mistakenly concludes that they are not friendly, she may also conclude that she will continue to be lonely at the university, and this thought produces her emotional response of sadness.

To adjust her emotions and mood, Sheila needs to learn to evaluate her external environment differently. She needs to change some of the beliefs, expectations, and meanings she attaches to events, because they are not objectively true. She might conclude, for example, that the union is simply not an appropriate place to meet people, because it is crowded and students tend to be hurrying through lunch and off to classes. Sheila can either change her perceptions or change the troubling environments by seeking out new situations. In either case, cognitive theorists would make Sheila's thinking the primary target of change activity, assuming that cognitive change will in turn produce changes in her emotional states.

Cognitive theory is a highly rational approach to human behavior. Even though the theory assumes that many of a person's beliefs are irrational and distorted, it also assumes that human beings have great potential to correct these beliefs in light of contradictory evidence. In clinical assessment, the social worker must assess the

EXHIBIT 4.6

Four Behavioral
Change Strategies

Strategy	Description
Desensitization	Confronting a difficult challenge through a step-by-step process of approach and anxiety control
Shaping	Differentially reinforcing approximations of a desired but difficult behavior so as to help the person eventually master the behavior
Behavioral rehearsal	Role-playing a desired behavior after seeing it modeled appropriately and then applying the skill to real-life situations
Extinction	Eliminating a behavior by reinforcing alternative behaviors

client's schemata, identify any faulty thinking patterns, and consider the evidence supporting a client's beliefs. During intervention, the social worker helps the client adjust his or her cognitive process to better facilitate the attainment of goals. As a result, the client will also experience more positive emotions. Sheila's belief that other students in the busy union have critical thoughts about her as she passes by is an arbitrary inference, based on her own inclination to think poorly of herself. To help her overcome this cognitive error, the social worker could review the available evidence, helping Sheila to understand that the other students probably did not notice her at all.

Social learning theory takes the tendency in cognitive theory to deemphasize innate drives and unconscious thinking even further. Some practitioners in the social learning tradition make no attempt to understand internal processes at all and avoid making any inferences about them. Social workers who practice from the behavioral approach conceptualize thoughts and emotions as behaviors subject to *reinforcement contingencies* (Gambrill, 1994; Thyer & Myers, 1998). Thus, behaviors can be modified through the application of specific action-oriented methods, such as those listed in Exhibit 4.6. If Sheila is depressed, the social worker would help to identify the things that reinforce her depressed behavior and adjust them so that her emotional states (as revealed in behaviors) will change in response. Through desensitization and behavioral rehearsal, for example, Sheila could learn step by step to approach a small group of students at a lunch table and ask to join them. Her positive reinforcers might include success in these measured experiences, a new sense of efficacy, reduced anxiety, and the affirmation of her social worker.

Theories of Emotion

Emotion is physiologically programmed into the human brain (see Chapter 3). Its expression is primarily mediated by the hypothalamus, whereas the experience of emotion is a limbic function. But emotion also involves a cognitive labeling of these programmed feelings, which is at least partially a learned process. That is, some emotional experience is an interpretation, and not merely given by our physiological state. For example, two students might feel anxious walking into the classroom on the first day of a semester. The anxiety would be a normal reaction to entering a new and unfamiliar situation. However, one student might interpret the anxiety as a heightened alertness that will serve her well in adjusting to the new students and professor, whereas the other student might interpret the same emotion as evidence that she is not prepared to manage the course material. The first student may become excited, but the second student becomes distressed.

Many theorists distinguish between primary and secondary emotions (Thoits, 1989; Turner, 1996). The **primary emotions** may have evolved as specific reactions with survival value for the human species. They mobilize us, focus our attention, and signal our state of mind to others. There is no consensus on what the primary emotions are, but they are usually limited to anger, fear, sadness, joy, and anticipation (Panksepp, 1991). The **secondary emotions** are more variable among people and are socially acquired. They evolved as humans developed more sophisticated means of learning, controlling, and managing emotions to promote flexible cohesion in social groups. The secondary emotions may result from combinations of the primary emotions (Plutchik, 1991), and their greater numbers also imply that our cognitive processes are significant in labeling them. These emotions include (but are not limited to) envy, jealousy, anxiety, guilt, shame, relief, hope, depression, pride, love, gratitude, and compassion (Lazarus & Lazarus, 1994).

Systems perspective The autonomic nervous system is central to our processing of emotion. This system consists of nerve tracts running from the base of the brain, through the spinal cord, and into the internal organs of the body. It is concerned with maintaining the body's physical homeostasis. Tracts from one branch of this system, the sympathetic division, produce physiological changes that help make us more alert and active. These changes are sustained by the release of hormones from the endocrine glands into the bloodstream. As part of the feedback control mechanism, parasympathetic system nerve tracts produce opposite, or calming, effects in the body. The two systems work together to maintain an appropriate level of physical arousal.

Still, psychologists have debated for more than a century the sources of emotion. Theories range from those that emphasize physiology to those that emphasize the psychological or the purely social context, and they give variable weight to the role of cognition.

Physiological Theories of Emotion

A theory of emotion (James, 1890) developed over a century ago speculated that our bodies produce automatic physiological reactions to any stimulus. We notice these reactions after the fact and then attempt through cognition to make sense of them. This "making sense" involves labeling the emotion. Thus, emotion follows cognition, which itself follows the physiological reaction to a stimulus. The original theory stated that a distinct emotion arises from each physiological reaction.

A few decades later, another theory was developed (Cannon, 1924) that argued that physiological arousal and the experience of emotion are unrelated. Our physiological responses to a stimulus are nonspecific and only prepare us for a general fight-or-flight response (to confront or avoid the stimulus). This response in itself has nothing to do with the experience of emotion, because any particular physiological activity may give rise to different emotional states and may not even involve our emotions at all. Thus, a separate cognitive process produces our feeling of emotion. Emotion derives from the associations we make based on prior attempts to understand the sensation of arousal.

Physiology-based theories of emotion lost favor in the mid-20th century, but recent brain research is once again suggesting a strong link between physiological processes and emotion. The new theory (Magai, 1996) asserts that emotions originate in our neurophysiology and that our personalities are organized around "affective biases." All of us possess five primary human emotions: happiness, sadness, fear, anger, and interest/excitement. These emotions are instinctual, are in a sense hard-wired into our brains, and are the source of our motivations. When our emotions are activated, they have a pervasive influence on our cognition and behavior. A key theme in this theory is that emotions influence cognition, a principle opposite to that stressed in cognitive theory.

For example, Sheila has a persistent bias toward sadness, which may reflect some personal or material loss long before she started college. Her sadness has a temporary physical response: a slowing down and a decrease in general effort. It also leads her to withdraw in situations where her efforts to recover the loss would likely be ineffective. The sadness thus allows Sheila time to reevaluate her needs and regain energy for more focused attempts to reach more achievable goals. It is also a signal for others to provide Sheila with support. The sadness of others promotes our own empathic responses. In contrast, anger tends to increase a person's energy and motivate behavior that is intended to overcome frustration. Furthermore, it is a signal to others to respond with avoidance, compliance, or submission so that the person may resolve the problem.

Social constructionist perspective

Researchers have speculated for decades about the precise locations of emotional processing in the brain. Much has been learned about structures that participate in this process, but many areas of the brain have a role (LeDoux & Phelps, 2000). Furthermore, it is now widely accepted that cultural patterns shape the ways in which environmental input is coded in the brain (McNeal, 1999).

As suggested in Chapter 3, the brain may be conceived as having three sections: hindbrain, midbrain, and forebrain. The hindbrain is the oldest of these, and is sometimes called the reptilian brain. It consists of the brain stem and cerebellum and is responsible for involuntary life support functions. The *midbrain* is located just above the brain stem. It represents a second level of brain evolution, more advanced than the hindbrain. It includes the limbic system, a group of cell structures and the center of activities that create emotions. The *forebrain* is more focused on the external environment and on "rational" functions. It is the center of emotion, memory, reasoning, abstract thought, and judgment, and integrates diverse brain activities. All of these sections have a role in the processing of emotion that researchers are only beginning to understand in depth.

The physiology of emotion begins in the *thalamus,* a major integrating center of the brain. Located in the forebrain, the thalamus is the site that receives and relays sensory information from the body and from the environment to other parts of the brain. Any perceived environmental event travels first to the thalamus and then to the sensory cortex (for thought), the basal ganglia (for movement), and the hypothalamus (for feeling). The *amygdala,* part of the limbic system, is key in the production of emotional states. There are in fact two routes to the amygdala from the thalamus. Sensations that produce the primary emotions described above may travel there directly from the thalamus, bypassing any cognitive apparatus, to produce an immediate reaction that is key to survival. Other inputs first travel through the cortex, where they are cognitively evaluated prior to moving on to the limbic system and amygdala to be processed as the secondary emotions.

Systems perspective   Culture and the characteristics of the individual may influence the processing of stimulation because the cognitive structures (schema) that interpret this stimulation may, through feedback loops to the thalamus, actually shape the neural pathways that will be followed by future stimuli. In other words, neural schemata tend to become rigid patterns of information processing, shaping subsequent patterns for making sense of the external world.

Psychological Theories of Emotion

Perhaps the most contentious debates about the role of cognition in emotion have taken place among psychological theorists. As Exhibit 4.7 shows, some psychologists have considered emotion as primary and others have considered cognition as primary; psychological theories in the social behavioral perspective, somewhat like physiology-based theories, assume an automatic, programmed response that is then interpreted as emotion.

Exhibit 4.7

Psychological Views of the Source of Emotion

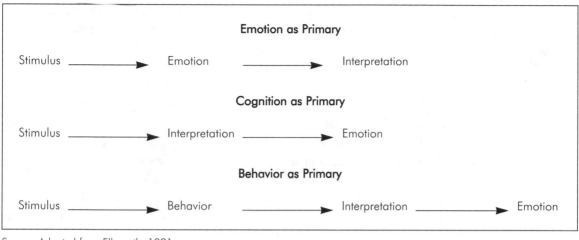

Emotion as Primary

Stimulus ⟶ Emotion ⟶ Interpretation

Cognition as Primary

Stimulus ⟶ Interpretation ⟶ Emotion

Behavior as Primary

Stimulus ⟶ Behavior ⟶ Interpretation ⟶ Emotion

Source: Adapted from Ellsworth, 1991.

Psychodynamic perspective

Psychoanalytic Theory. Freud's landmark work *The Interpretation of Dreams,* first published in 1899, signaled the arrival of **psychoanalytic theory**. Freud's theories became prominent in the United States by the early 1900s, immediately influencing the young profession of social work, and were a dominant force through the 1950s. Psychoanalytic thinking continues to be influential in social work today, through the theories of ego psychology and self psychology.

The basis of psychoanalytic theory is the primacy of internal drives and unconscious mental activity in human behavior. Sexual and aggressive drives are not "feelings" in themselves, but they motivate behavior that will presumably gratify our impulses. We experience positive emotions when our drives are gratified and negative emotions when they are frustrated.

Our conscious mental functioning takes place within the **ego**, that part of the personality responsible for negotiating between internal drives and the outside world. It is here that cognition occurs, but it is driven by those unconscious thoughts that are focused on drive satisfaction.

In psychoanalytic thought, then, conscious thinking is a product of the drives from which our emotions also spring. By nature, we are pleasure seekers and "feelers," not thinkers. Thoughts are our means of deciding how to gratify our drives. Defense mechanisms result from our need to indirectly manage drives when we become frustrated, as we frequently do in the social world, where we must negotiate acceptable behaviors with others. The need to manage drives also contributes to the development of our unconscious mental processes. According to psychoanalytic theory, personal growth cannot be achieved by attending only to conscious processes. We need to explore all of our thoughts and feelings to understand our essential drives. Change requires that we uncover unconscious material and the accompanying feelings that are repressed, or kept out of consciousness.

Let us grant, for example, that Sheila has a normal, healthy drive for pleasure. She may thus be angry with her father for the manner in which he discourages her from developing a social life and also burdens her with his personal problems. This feeling of anger might be repressed into unconsciousness, however, because Sheila is close to her father in many ways and may believe that it is not permissible for a daughter to be angry with a well-meaning parent. Sheila's unconscious anger, having been turned onto herself, may be contributing to her depression. A psychoanalytically oriented social worker might suspect from Sheila's presentation that she experiences this anger. The social worker might try to help Sheila uncover this by reflecting on her feelings about her father in detail, in a safe clinical environment. With the insights that might result from this reflection, Sheila's feeling may become conscious and she can then take direct measures to work through her anger.

Psychodynamic perspective

Ego Psychology. **Ego psychology**, which emerged in the 1930s (Goldstein, 1995), shifted to a more balanced perspective on the influences of cognition and emotion in social functioning. As an adaptation of psychoanalytic theory, it signaled a reaction against Freud's heavy emphasis on drives and highlighted the ego's role in promoting healthy social functioning. Ego psychology represents an effort to build a holistic psychology of normal development.

In ego psychology, the ego is conceived of as present from birth, and not as derived from the need to reconcile drives within the constraints of social living, as psychoanalytic theory would say. The ego is the source of our attention, concentration, learning, memory, will, and perception. Both past and present experiences are relevant in influencing social functioning. The influence of the drives on emotions and thoughts is not dismissed, but the autonomy of the ego, and thus conscious thought processes, receives greater emphasis than in psychoanalytic theory. The ego moderates internal conflicts, which may relate to drive frustration, but it also mediates the interactions of a healthy person with stressful environmental conditions.

If we experience sadness, then, it is possible that we are having conflicts related to drive frustration that are internal in origin. However, it is also possible that we are experiencing person/environment conflicts in which our coping efforts are not effective; the negative emotion may result from a frustration of our ability to manage an environmental stressor and thus arise from cognitive activities. Sheila may be experiencing both types of conflict. Her anger at the lack of adequate nurturance in her early family history may have been turned inward to produce a depression that has persisted in all of her environments. At the same time, the mismatch between her personal needs for mastery and the demands of this particular academic environment may be contributing to her frustration and depression.

Social behavioral
perspective

Attribution Theory. Attribution theory was the first of the psychological theories of emotion to give clear primacy to cognition as a producer of emotions (Schacter & Singer, 1962). **Attribution theory** holds that our experience of emotion is based on conscious evaluations we make about physiological sensations in particular social settings. We respond to situations as we understand them cognitively, which leads directly to our experience of a particular emotion. For example, Sheila has often experienced anxiety, but she interprets it differently in dealing with her strict father (who makes her feel guilty about enjoying life) and her fellow students (who make her feel ashamed of who she is). Attribution theory also notes that the social setting determines the type of emotion experienced; the physiological response determines the strength of the reaction. In other words, the nature of the social setting is key to the process of emotional experience.

A further refinement of attribution theory states that our initial reactions to any stimulus are limited to the sense of whether it will have positive or negative consequences for us (Weiner, 1985). Afterward, we consider what has caused the event, which leads to modification of the emotion we feel. The less we understand about the physiological nature of a sensation, the less likely we are to perceive it as physiological, and the more likely it is that we will be influenced by external cues in determining its cause and labeling the emotion. Thus, our perceptions of internal versus external cause determine in part the type of emotion that we experience. For example, if we experience frustration, the emotion of shame may emerge if we decide that it is due to our own behavior. However, we may experience anger if we decide that the frustration is due to the actions of someone else.

Richard Lazarus (1980) has proposed a three-part psychological theory of emotion based on appraisals of situations. He suggests that emotion develops when we assess a situation as somehow relevant to a personal value or life concern. First, we make an unconscious appraisal of whether a situation constitutes a threat. This appraisal is followed by coping responses, which may be cognitive, physiological, or both, and may be conscious or unconscious. Once these coping mechanisms are in place, we reappraise the situation and label our associated emotion. This process implies that our feelings originate with an automatic evaluative judgment. We decide whether there is a threat, take immediate coping action to deal with it, and then take a closer look to see exactly what was involved in the situation. At the end of this process, we experience a specific emotion.

A major life concern for Sheila is feeling secure in her interpersonal environments. She feels secure in familiar environments (such as her hometown) but feels threatened in unfamiliar places. When she walks into a new classroom, she experiences anxiety. The feeling seems to Sheila to be automatic, because her need for security is threatened in the situation. Her means of coping is to ignore the other students, neither speaking to nor making eye contact with them, and to sit in a relatively isolated area of the room.

Sheila then makes at least a partly conscious appraisal that the room is not only occupied with strangers, but that they will quickly judge her in negative ways. Sheila labels her emotion as shame, because she concludes (erroneously, we would think) that her classmates are correct in perceiving her as socially inferior.

Systems perspective

Theory of Emotional Intelligence. **Emotional intelligence** is a person's ability to process information about emotions accurately and effectively, and consequently to regulate emotions in an optimal manner (Goleman, 1998). It includes self-control, zest and persistence, ability to motivate oneself, ability to understand and regulate one's own emotions, and ability to read and deal effectively with other people's feelings. This is a relatively new concept in psychology. The idea of integrating the emotional and intellectual systems was considered contradictory for many years. Emotions deal with narrow informational content and specific events that are seen as changeable and unique. The intellect is related to patterns and regularities. But recently psychologists have determined that emotional stimulation is necessary for activating certain schematic thought patterns.

Emotional intelligence involves *recognizing* and *regulating* emotions in ourselves and other people. It requires emotional sensitivity, or the ability to evaluate emotions within a variety of social circumstances. A person who is angry but knows that certain expressions of anger will be counterproductive in a particular situation, and as a result constrains his or her expressions of anger, is emotionally intelligent. On the other hand, a person with this same knowledge who behaves angrily in spite of this awareness is emotionally unintelligent.

People are not necessarily equally emotionally intelligent about themselves and other people. We may be more emotionally intelligent about other people than we are about ourselves, and vice versa. The first possibility helps to explain why some people, social workers included, seem to be better at giving advice to others than they are to themselves.

Emotional intelligence requires an integration of intellectual and emotional abilities. Recognizing and regulating emotions requires emotional self-awareness and empathy, but it also requires the intellectual ability to calculate the various implications of different behavioral alternatives. To understand how and why we feel like we do, and other people feel like they do, requires emotional acquaintance and intellectual reasoning. Emotional intelligence is more important to excellence in many aspects of life than pure intellect because it includes intellect *plus* other capacities.

There is not a necessary relationship between emotional intelligence and emotional intensity. Emotional intelligence includes the capacity to regulate and use emotions, which may in fact favor a type of detachment that is not typical of emotionally expressive people.

For example, one of Sheila's great assets, and one that she herself can "own," is her sensitivity to preadolescent children. She likes them and is always attuned to the nuances of their thoughts and emotions. Sheila functions exceptionally well as a sitter for her friends and neighbors because children pick up on her sensitivity and reciprocate those positive feelings. On the other hand, as we have already seen, Sheila generally lacks emotional self-awareness and intensity. It seems that her negative moods and attitudes contribute to her generally flat emotional style with most people. In fact, her wariness of others may contribute in an odd way to her sensitivity to their emotional states. She is able to engage emotionally with children because, unlike her peers and older persons, they do not constitute any kind of threat to her.

Social Theories of Emotion

Social constructionist perspective

Social theories of emotion also take the view that cognition precedes emotion. But they emphasize the purpose of emotion, which is to sustain shared interpersonal norms and social cohesion. Two social theories are considered here.

James Averill's (1980) theory states that emotions can be understood as socially constructed, transitory roles. They can be considered socially constructed because they originate in our appraisals of situations. They are transitory in that they are time limited. Finally, emotions are roles because they include a range of socially acceptable actions that may be performed in a certain social context. We organize and interpret our physiological reactions to stimuli with regard to the social norms involved in the particular situations where these reactions occur. Emotions permit us, in response to these stimuli, to step out of the conventional social roles to which people not experiencing the emotion are held. For example, in our culture, we generally would not say that we wish to harm someone unless we were feeling anger. We would generally not lash out verbally at a friend or spouse unless we felt frustrated. We would generally not withdraw from certain personal responsibilities and ask others for comfort unless we felt sad. Because of the social function of emotions, we often experience them as passions, or feelings not under our control. Experiencing passion permits unconventional behavior because we assume that we are somehow not "ourselves," not able to control what we do at that moment. Our society has adopted this mode of thinking about emotions because it allows us to distance ourselves from some of our actions. Emotions are thus legitimized social roles, or permissible behaviors for persons when in particular emotional states.

George Herbert Mead (1934), the originator of symbolic interaction theory, took a somewhat different view. He suggested that emotions develop as symbols for communication (Franks, 1991). He also believed that humans are by nature more sensitive to visual than to verbal cues. Emotional expressions are thus particularly powerful in that they are apprehended visually rather than verbally. Our emotional expression is a signal about how we are inclined to act in a situation, and others can adjust their own behavior in response to our perceived inclinations. Sheila's lack of eye contact, tendency to look down, and physical distancing from others are manifestations of her sadness.

Other persons, in response, may choose either to offer her support or, more likely in a classroom setting, to avoid her if they interpret her expressions as a desire for distance.

Theories of Emotion in Social Work Practice

The preceding theories are useful in assessment and intervention with clients because they enhance the social worker's understanding of the origins of emotional experiences and describe how negative emotional states may emerge and influence behavior. The social worker can help the client develop more positive emotional responses by providing insight or corrective experiences. What follows, however, is a theory that is even more precise in identifying the processes of emotional experience.

J. S. Greenberg (1996) has offered an emotion-focused practice theory, similar to psychoanalytic theory, that promises to help in social work interventions. Greenberg asserts that all primary emotions—those that originate as biologically based rapid responses—are adaptive. Every primary emotion we experience has the purpose of helping us adjust our relationship with an environmental situation to enhance coping. Secondary emotions emerge from these primary emotions as a result of cognitive mediation. Problems in social functioning may occur in one of four scenarios, summarized in Exhibit 4.8.

From this perspective, it is the **preconscious** (mental activity that is out of awareness but can be brought into awareness with prompting) appraisal of situations in relation to our needs that creates emotions. Furthermore, as Mead (1934) pointed out, we experience our emotions as images, not as verbal thoughts. Emotions are difficult to apprehend cognitively, and in our attempts to do so, we may mistake their essence. The bad feelings that trouble us come not from those primary emotional responses, which, if experienced directly, would tend to dissipate, but from cognitive distortions of those responses. We tend to appraise situations accurately with our primary emotions, but

EXHIBIT 4.8
Four Sources of Emotion-Based Problems in Social Functioning

1. A primary emotion may not achieve its aim of changing our relationship with the environment to facilitate adaptation.
2. We may, prior to awareness of a primary emotion, deny, distort, avoid, or repress it and thus become unable to constructively address our person/environment challenge.
3. We may develop cognitive distortions, or irrational "meaning construction" processes, that produce negative secondary emotions.
4. We may regulate our appropriate emotional experiences poorly, by either minimizing or not maintaining control over them.

our frustration in achieving affective goals can produce cognitive distortions. Thus, in contrast to the assumptions of cognitive theory, distortions of thought may be the result of emotional phenomena rather than their cause.

Consider Sheila's depression as an example. Perhaps she is interpersonally sensitive by nature and accurately perceives aloofness in others. Her affective goals of closeness are threatened by this appraisal, and the intensity of her reaction to this frustration becomes problematic. Her emotional patterns evoke tendencies to withdraw temporarily and to become less active in response to discouragement or sadness. To this point, the process may be adaptive, as she may be able to rest and regain energy during her temporary withdrawal. This particular feeling state, however, may become a cue for negative thoughts about herself, which then prevent her from actively addressing her frustrations.

Personal reality, then, may be as much a product of emotion as cognition. In any situation, the meaning we construct may automatically determine our conscious cognitive responses. It is when we directly experience primary emotions that we are functioning in an adaptive manner.

In emotion-focused practice, the social worker would attempt to activate the person's primary emotional reactions, making them more available to awareness within the safety of the social worker/client relationship and making secondary emotional reactions amenable to change when necessary. Emotional reactions, cognitive appraisals, and action tendencies may then be identified more clearly by the client. Affective needs can be identified, the sequencing of the emotional/cognitive process can be clarified, and a new sense of self may emerge along with an improved capacity for self-direction.

From this perspective, a social worker could help Sheila understand that she carries much anger at her family because of their long-term lack of adequate support for her emotional development. Sheila could be encouraged within the safety of the social worker/client relationship to experience and ventilate that anger. Once Sheila can consciously identify and experience that negative emotion, she may be less incapacitated by the depression, which is a secondary emotion resulting from her suppression of anger. She would then have more energy to devote to her own social and academic goals.

Cognitive/Emotional "Disorders"

As social workers, we are reluctant to label people as having cognitive or emotional "disorders." Instead, we conceptualize problems in social functioning as mismatches in the fit between person and environment. Still, in our study of the psychological person, we can consider how problems are manifested in the client's cognitive and emotional patterns.

Many social workers are employed in mental health agencies and use the *Diagnostic and Statistical Manual of Mental Disorders* (DSM-IV-TR) (American Psychiatric Association, 2000) to make diagnoses as part of a comprehensive client assessment. Four examples of disorders selected from the DSM can illustrate how either cognitive or emotional characteristics may predominate in a client's symptom profile, even though both aspects of the psychological person are always present:

- Two disorders that feature cognitive symptoms are obsessive-compulsive disorder and anorexia nervosa. Obsessive-compulsive disorder is an anxiety disorder that, when featuring obsessions, is characterized by persistent thoughts that are experienced as intrusive, inappropriate, unwelcome, and distressful. The thoughts are more than excessive worries about real problems, and the person is unable to ignore or suppress them. In anorexia nervosa, an eating disorder, the person becomes obsessional about food, thinking about it almost constantly. The person refuses to maintain a reasonable body weight because of distorted beliefs about physical appearance and the effects of food on the body.

- Two disorders that feature emotional symptoms are dysthymia and agoraphobia. Dysthymia, a mood disorder, is characterized by a lengthy period of depression. It features the emotion of sadness, which persists regardless of external events. Agoraphobia is an anxiety disorder characterized by fear. The person is afraid to be in situations (such as crowds) or places (such as large open areas) from which escape might be difficult or embarrassing. The person must restrict his or her range of social mobility out of fear of having a panic attack (being overwhelmed by anxiety) for reasons that are not consciously clear.

As a social worker, you might note that Sheila is depressed and also has a mild form of agoraphobia. She feels uncomfortable and insecure on the large, crowded campus, and developed fears of having panic attacks when in the student union. This building includes several large open areas that are highly congested at certain times of the day. Sheila is concerned that people there look at her critically. You might conclude that Sheila's problems are primarily emotional. However, Sheila's cognitive patterns have contributed to the development of her negative emotions. Her overall negative self-assessment sustains her depression, and her distorted beliefs about the attitudes of others contribute to her fears of being in the crowded union. It is rarely the case that only cognitive factors or only emotional factors are behind a client's problems.

The Self

It remains for us to integrate cognition and emotion into a cohesive notion of the self. This is a difficult task—one that may, in fact, be impossible to achieve. All of us possess

Exhibit 4.9
Six Concepts of
the Sense of Self

Concept	Definition
The self as	
Soul	A constant, unchanging self, existing apart from its material environment and material body, perhaps transcending the life of the physical body
Organizing activity	The initiator of activity, organizer of drives, and mediator of both internal and person/environment conflicts; an evolving entity in the synthesizing of experiences
Cognitive structure	The thinker and definer of reality through conscious activities that support the primacy of thought
Verbal activity	The product of internal monologues (self-talk) and shared conversation with others; the product of what we tell ourselves about who we are
Experiences of cohesion	The sense of cohesion achieved through action and reflection; the three-part self (grandiose, idealized, and twinship components)
Flow of experience	The self-in-process, the changing self

a sense of self, but it is difficult to articulate. How would you define self? Most of us tend to think of it as incorporating an essence that is more or less enduring. But beyond that, what would you say? Thinkers from the fields of philosophy, theology, sociology, psychology, and social work have struggled to identify the essence of the **self,** and they offer us a range of perspectives: self as a soul, as an organizing activity, as a cognitive structure, as a verbal activity, as an experience of cohesion, or as a flow of experience (Levin, 1992). See Exhibit 4.9 for a summary of these perspectives.

The Self as Soul

Understanding the self as a soul appeals to those who see their essence as constant throughout life and perhaps transcending their physical lives. The soul may be identical with the conscious self, or the soul may be separate from (but intimately connected with) the self. This idea is based on certain spiritual traditions (see Chapter 6), and though widely shared, it does not easily lend itself to examination in terms of changing configurations of person and environment. If the self as soul is constant, that is, it may not be substantively influenced by interactions with the environment. This self can be conceived as existing apart from its material environment.

The Self as Organizing Activity

The notion of self as an organizing activity incorporates the notions of action, initiative, and organization. We certainly experience ourselves as capable of initiating action, and the sense of organization emerges as we synthesize our activities and experiences.

Psychodynamic perspectives

Psychoanalytic theory and ego psychology are consistent with these ideas, as they conceptualize the ego as the organizer of drives and mediator of internal and external conflicts. In both theories, the ego organizes the drives in response to external restrictions on their satisfaction. The ego is neither thought nor emotion, but a coordinator of both. In ego psychology, this self is present from birth and includes a drive to mastery and competence. In traditional psychoanalytic theory, the ego is not present from birth and must develop, and the drives thought to motivate human behavior do not include mastery and competence. In both theories, the ego is responsible for defensive functions, judgment, rational thinking, and reality awareness.

The ego is largely, although not entirely, conscious, whereas the other portions of the mind—including the id (the source of drives) and the superego (our sense of ideal behavior)—remain outside awareness and thus cannot be apprehended as part of our sense of self. Healthy human behavior is enhanced by bringing unconscious mental activity into conscious awareness, so we can have more choices and solve problems more rationally.

The Self as Cognitive Structure

The self as a cognitive structure is accepted as at least a part of most accounts of the self. All of us are in touch (although to varying degrees) with our conscious thinking processes and may come to accept them as representing our essence. This cognitive structure includes self-representations that develop within our schemata. The self as thinker implies that action and emotion originate in thought.

Humanistic perspective

This self may be consistent with the view of reality as a human construction. As thinkers, our sense of self evolves as we actively participate in processing stimuli and define our realities in accordance with our perceptions. The cognitive self is thus interactional and dynamic, not static.

The Self as Verbal Activity: Symbolic Interactionism

The self can be understood as the product of the stories we tell ourselves about who we are, who we were, and how we became who we are. We change by changing the stories we tell ourselves, according to the theory of symbolic interactionism.

Social constructionist perspective

Symbolic interactionism seeks a resolution to the idea that person and environment are separate and opposite (Blumer, 1969; Gergen & Davis, 1985; Mead, 1934). It stresses that we develop a sense of meaning in the world through interaction with our physical and social environments, which include other people but also all manifestations of cultural life. The mind represents our capacity to respond subjectively to external stimuli through conceptualizing, defining, symbolizing, valuing, and reflecting. This activity is not mechanical, but a creative and selective construction. Through social interaction, interpretation of symbols (objects and ideas with shared cultural meanings), and the filtering processes of the mind, we acquire meaning about ourselves and the world. The sense of self develops from our perceptions of how others perceive us. It is a role-taking process at odds with the psychoanalytic view that self involves internal drives. Symbolic interactionism suggests that we define ourselves through the attitudes and behavior of others toward us and ultimately from the standards of our society. Our sense of self changes with the changing expectations of others about how we should behave, think, and feel.

The medium through which these processes occur is language. Words are symbols, and language is a product of the shared understandings of people within a culture. Thus, social interaction involves an ongoing negotiation of the meanings of words among persons. Consciousness and the sense of self become possible through language as we learn to talk to ourselves, or think, using these symbols (Wood & Wardell, 1983).

Communicators must share an understanding of the cultural norms and rules governing conduct for their interaction to proceed coherently. Symbolic interactionism suggests that socialization is a highly dynamic process that continues throughout life and consists of the creation of new meanings, understandings, and definitions of situations through social interaction (Mortimer & Simmons, 1978). We change as we bring structure to ambiguous social situations to solve problems.

This concept of self includes both the *I* and the *me* (Lane, 1984). The *I* is the conscious self—what we are aware of in self-reflection and what actively processes information and solves problems. This self emerges as we become objects of our own thoughts. It develops through the influence of *significant others*—persons who have immediate influence on our self-definitions. The *me,* on the other hand, incorporates the thoughts, feelings, and attitudes that we have internalized over time and that are beneath the level of ready awareness. The *me* is influenced by *generalized others*—the types of people whose expectations have come to guide our behavior over time.

Significant others can shape our sense of self (the *I*), even if other acquaintances (family and friends) have already made their mark on us. Sheila's sense of herself as unattractive, unintelligent, and socially incompetent may have originated in critical messages she received from her family, neighbors, teachers, and peers early in life. They may have acted toward her in ways that encouraged her to assume dependent and subservient roles. But interacting with other people who have more positive expectations for Sheila might influence her to enact different behaviors and lead eventually to greater social competence. If these alternative social actions became prevalent in her life,

Sheila's *me* would experience change as well. She might come to think of herself as more independent and attractive. By guidance and example, an individual may become involved in a community of supportive individuals whose role expectations strengthen the self-concept. The sense of self as competent in specific situations may improve, and the sense of having a substantial role as a member of a social group may develop.

The Self as the Experience of Cohesion: Self Psychology

Psychodynamic
perspective

Self psychology, which derives from psychoanalytic theory, conceives of the self as experienced cohesion through action and reflection (Flanagan, 1996). Essentially, the self is the self-image, or what each of us perceives when we look into the mirror. It is not fundamentally cognitive or affective, but a mixture of both elements of the psychological self.

Self psychology proposes that the self has three parts, and our sense of cohesion results from their mutual development:

1. *Grandiose self* arises from the positive affirmations we internalize from others; it gives rise to our ambitions and enthusiasm.

2. *Idealized parent image* represents guidance from others, which results in our ability to be self-directed and to set goals.

3. *Twinship* represents our natural social propensities to connect with others and, through this process, to develop our individual talents and skills.

Significant others are essential parts of the self in this view. They provide us with emotional stability, energy, and an internal sense of cohesion. We all require the affirmation and support of others to feel competent and internally cohesive. We always try to achieve higher levels of coherence, improve our capacity to regulate self-esteem, and integrate new relationships with our older ones. Our psychological growth occurs primarily through empathic understanding from others.

Persons who experience problems in functioning may be experiencing situational stress or "disorders" of the self. Such problematic self-states may be characterized by understimulation or overstimulation in transactions with the environment, excessive external stress, or fragmentation (a feeling of incompleteness due to insufficient affirmation, idealization, or twinship experiences). Change is contingent on restoring self-esteem through corrective interpersonal experiences.

Consider Sheila's case. She is depressed and has a poor self-image. Perhaps she did not receive adequate affirmations from her family while she was growing up, did not receive sufficient direction from other adults and mentors to develop mature self-direction, or did not develop the social skills required to form and maintain the relationships that would help her mature in age-appropriate ways. Her self may thus be incomplete, or fragmented, which would be the source of her negative affect. Corrective experience in any of these three areas—perhaps through supportive relationships with her academic adviser (affirmation), teachers and employers (idealized parent image), and student peers on campus (twinship)—might enhance her sense of self.

The Self as a Flow of Experience

Humanistic perspective

The concept of self as an ongoing process of experience may be closer to what we actually live than any of the other concepts. The sense that the flow is the actuality is incorporated in the philosophy and practice theory of *existentialism* (Krill, 1996). Persons who assume the existential viewpoint hold that there is no standard or "correct" human nature; we are all unique, alone, and unable to be categorized. What we are is a subjective and ever-changing notion. The self is never any "thing" at a single point in time, because we are defined by the process of becoming, a process to which there is no end point. The self is always in process. Our essence is defined by our freedom to make choices and our need to discover or create meaning (sometimes called *will* or *drive*) for ourselves. The self unfolds as we make commitments to ideals outside ourselves (Frankl, 1988).

Existential philosophy is often seen as a pessimistic view of reality because it emphasizes human loneliness, but it does remind us of our uniqueness and the idea that we can always make choices about the directions our lives will take. However negatively Sheila sees herself, for example, she need not necessarily maintain that self-image. She can and will always make choices that will make her a different person—that is, a different self. If Sheila can be helped to recognize her free will, she can perhaps make those choices that will enable her to define herself differently.

IMPLICATIONS FOR SOCIAL WORK PRACTICE

The study of the psychological person as a thinking and feeling being and as a self has many implications for social work practice:

- Be alert to the possibility that practice interventions may need to focus on any of several systems, including family, small groups, organizations, and communities. The person's transactions with all of these systems affect psychological functioning.

- Where appropriate, help individual clients to develop a stronger sense of competence through both ego-supportive and ego-modifying interventions.

- Where appropriate, help individual clients to enhance problem-solving skills through techniques directed at both cognitive reorganization and behavioral change.

- Where appropriate, help individual clients strengthen the sense of self by bringing balance to emotional and cognitive experiences.

- Help clients consider their strengths in terms of the unique sets of intelligences they may have, and show how these intelligences may help them address their challenges in unique ways.

- Where appropriate, encourage clients to become involved in small group experiences that assist them to understand and change their thoughts, emotions, and behaviors.

- Help clients assess their transactions with formal organizations and the effects of these transactions on their psychological functioning.

- Help clients assess and make necessary changes in their transactions with the community. A person's perspective on his or her community may be influenced by its spatial organization, the conflicts between different groups, the relative harmony of the overall social system, the potential for bonding and meeting spiritual needs, and the community's networks of organizations.

KEY TERMS

accommodation
affect
assimilation
attribution theory
cognition
cognitive mediation
cognitive operations
conventional morality
ego
ego psychology
emotion
emotional intelligence
information processing theory

mood
multiple intelligences
postconventional morality
preconscious
preconventional morality
primary emotions
psychoanalytic theory
psychology
schema (schemata)
secondary emotions
self
self psychology
unconscious

ACTIVE LEARNING

1.   Reread the case study at the beginning of this chapter. As you read, what do you see as the driving force of Sheila's behavior as she makes the transition to the university? Is it cognition? Is it emotion? What theories presented in the chapter are most helpful to you in thinking about this?

2.   Howard Gardner has proposed a theory of multiple intelligences and suggests that each profession must decide which intelligences are most important to the work of the profession. Working in small groups, discuss which of Gardner's seven intelligences are most important for doing social work. Are some intelligences more important in some social work settings than in others?

WEB RESOURCES

The Emotion Home Page

emotion.salk.edu/emotion.html
Site presented by the Salk Institute contains information on emotion research from the psychological, neuroscience, and cognitive science perspectives and provides a historical perspective on emotion and links to other Internet resources on emotion.

Piaget's Developmental Psychology

www.dmu.ac/uk/~james/learning/piaget.htm
Site maintained by James Atherton of the United Kingdom overviews Jean Piaget's key ideas and developmental stages.

Information Processing Theory

www.educationau.edu.au/archives/cp/04.htm
Site maintained by the Open Learning Technology Corporation Limited overviews information process theory and provides applications and examples.

Multiple Intelligences for Adult Literacy and Education

literacyworks.org/mi/home.html
Site presented by Literacyworks contains a visual overview of Howard Gardner's theory of multiple intelligences, guidelines for assessment, and suggestions for putting the theory to practice in adult literacy programs.

Lawrence Kohlberg's Stages of Moral Development

www.xenodocy.org/ex/lists/moraldev.html

Site maintained by Ralph Kenyon contains an overview and critique of Kohlberg's stage theory of moral development.

The Consortium for Research on Emotional Intelligence in Organizations

www.eiconsortium.org

Site maintained by The Consortium for Research on Emotional Intelligence in Organizations contains recent research and model programs for promoting the development of emotional intelligence in the work setting.

Self Psychology Page

www.selfpsychology.org

Site maintained by Martin Gossmann and David Wolf contains a definition of the self psychology of Heinz Kohut, bibliography, papers, discussion groups on self psychology, and links to other Internet sites.

CHAPTER 5

The Psychosocial Person: Relationships, Stress, and Coping

Joseph Walsh

Key Ideas

CASE STUDY: ■ *Sheila's Coping Strategies for College*

The Self in Relationships
Object Relations Theory
Feminist Theories of Relationships
Afrocentric Relational Theory
Social Identity Theory
The Impact of Early Nurturing

The Concept of Stress
Three Categories of Psychological Stress
Stress and Crisis
Traumatic Stress
Vulnerability to Stress

Coping and Adaptation
Biological Coping
Psychological Coping
Coping Styles
Coping and Traumatic Stress
Social Support
How Social Support Aids Coping
How Social Workers Evaluate Social Support

Normal and Abnormal Coping
The Medical (Psychiatric) Perspective
Psychological Perspectives
The Sociological Approach: Deviance
The Social Work Perspective: Social Functioning

Implications for Social Work Practice

Key Terms

Active Learning

Web Resources

The Psychosocial Person

Relationships, Stress, and Coping

Joseph Walsh
Virginia Commonwealth University

How do relationships help us cope with stress?
What are some different approaches to coping with stress?

Key Ideas

As you read this chapter, take note of these central ideas:

1. Understanding the nature of a person's relationship patterns is important for evaluating her or his susceptibility to stress and potential for coping and adaptation. A variety of psychological (object relations, feminist) and social (Afrocentric, social identity development) theories are useful toward this end.

2. The quality of one's relationships with primary caregivers in infancy and childhood affects neurological development and has lasting effects on the capacity for mental and physical health in later life.

3. Stress, an event that taxes adaptive resources, may be biological, psychological, or social in origin; psychological stress can be categorized as harm, threat, and challenge.

4. Traumatic stress refers to events that are so overwhelming that almost anyone would be affected—events such as natural and technological disasters, war, and physical assault.

5. Our efforts to master the demands of stress are known as coping.

6. All people rely on social supports as means of dealing with stress.

7. Classification of human behavior as normal or abnormal differs among the helping professions. Psychiatry focuses on personal inadequacy in goal attainment and in social presentation, from a context of disease or disorder. Psychology focuses on personal inadequacy in a developmental context and often deemphasizes the idea of disease. Sociology considers abnormality, or deviance, as an inability to fulfill a significant social role within a range of accepted behaviors as assessed by significant others in the community. Social work is reluctant to label persons as abnormal, because all behavior is conceptualized as interactional and related to the nature of the social context.

CASE STUDY

SHEILA'S COPING STRATEGIES FOR COLLEGE

Midway through her first semester at the state university, Sheila (whom you met in Chapter 4) had reached a crisis point. It was bad enough that she was having trouble academically. But even worse, she was feeling isolated from her fellow students and thinking of herself as hopelessly incompetent at making friends. She was depressed, and expected no better for the foreseeable future. Fortunately, Sheila's parents convinced her to talk with her academic adviser. The adviser immediately became more involved in helping Sheila manage her dyslexia. Sheila learned to become more assertive with her instructors so that they understood her special challenges with the course work.

The academic adviser also encouraged Sheila to begin seeing a counselor. Over several months, you have helped Sheila focus her thoughts and feelings in ways that were productive for her problem solving. First, Sheila found an apartment that afforded her some privacy and personal space. Then she got a part-time job at a shop on the campus perimeter to help keep busy and involved with people. With your encouragement, Sheila also joined some small university clubs focused on academic topics as a way for her to feel more comfortable on campus and begin interacting with other students. She made a couple of good friends whose attention helped her believe that she was a person of worth. You also helped her learn not to bury her emotions by escaping to her apartment, into her work, or back to her parents' home; rather, Sheila learned to experience her emotions as valid indicators that she was feeling threatened. This new way of coping was frightening to Sheila, but your support is helping her develop a greater sense of competence to manage stress.

> **CASE STUDY**
>
> By the end of her 1st year at the university, Sheila was still mildly depressed but feeling significantly better than she had been a few months before. She felt more sure of herself, had more friends, and was looking forward to her 2nd year at the university.

The Self in Relationships

In this chapter, we focus on how the psychological person manages challenges to social functioning, particularly stress. Sheila was fortunate: in addition to her personal strengths, she had access to support systems that helped her confront and begin to overcome the stress she was experiencing. We look at the common processes by which we all try to cope with the stresses we experience in life. As Sheila learned, the ability to form, sustain, and use significant relationships with other people is a key to the process of successful coping and adaptation. With this theme in mind, we begin by considering several theories that address the issue of how we exist in the context of relationships, including object relations theory, feminist and Afrocentric theories, social identity theory, and evidence demonstrating the importance of early nurturing in the ability to build relationships throughout life.

Object Relations Theory

The basic assumption of object relations theory is that all people naturally seek relationships with other people. The question is how well an individual forms interpersonal relationships and how any deficiencies in social functioning might have arisen. The term *object relations* is synonymous with *interpersonal relations*. An "object" is another person but may also be the mental image of a person that we have incorporated into our psychological selves.

Psychodynamic
Perspective

Object relations theory is a psychodynamic theory of human development that considers our ability to form lasting attachments with others to be based on early experiences of separation from and connection with our primary caregivers. We internalize our early relationship patterns, meaning that our first relationships make such an impression on us that they determine how we approach relationships from that point on. These early relationships are a primary determinant of our personality and the quality of our interpersonal functioning (St. Clair, 1999).

The ideal is to be raised by caregivers who help us gradually and appropriately move away from their physical and emotional supervision while communicating their availability for support. In such conditions, we acquire the capacity to form trusting attachments with others. This is known as *object constancy*. If, on the other hand, we learn (because of loss or negative caregiver behavior) that we cannot count on others for support as we take risks to move away, we might "internalize" a schema that other people cannot be counted on. Stable object relations result in our ability to form stable relationships, to trust others, and to persist with positive relationships during times of conflict. This idea of internalization is very important, as it implies that we carry our attachments with us. Those significant others in our lives do not only exist as memories, but are part of our psychological makeup—they are a part of who we are.

Object relations theorists have suggested a variety of stages in this process of developing object constancy, but we need not get into that level of detail. Suffice it to say that, in addition to the process of developing object relations in early childhood, we also experience a second such process in early adolescence. At that time (at least in Anglo-American society), we begin to move away from the pervasive influence of our families and test our abilities to develop our own identities. This is another time of life in which we need to feel that we can trust our primary caregivers as we experiment with independence.

If you are concerned that your own early relationships might have been problematic, don't worry. Object relations theorists do not assert that caregivers need to be perfect (whatever that might be), only that they communicate a sense of caring and permit the child to develop a sense of self. Even if early object relations are problematic, a person's ability to develop trusting relationships can always be improved, sometimes with therapy.

Feminist Theories of Relationships

Conflict
perspective

The term *feminism* does not refer to any single body of thought. It refers to a wide-ranging system of ideas about human experience developed from a woman-centered perspective. Feminist theories may be classified as liberal, radical, Marxist, socialist, existential, postmodern, multicultural, and ecofeminist (Lengermann & Niebrugge-Brantley, 2000). Among the psychological theories are psychoanalytic feminism and gender feminism (Tong, 1998). We focus on these two as we consider how feminism has deepened our capacity for understanding human behavior and interaction. All of these theorists begin from the position that women and men approach relationships differently, and that patriarchal societies consider male attributes to be superior.

Psychodynamic
Perspective

Psychoanalytic feminists assert that women's ways of acting are rooted deeply in women's unique ways of thinking. These differences may be biological, but they are certainly influenced by cultural and psychosocial conditions. Feminine behavior features gentleness, modesty, humility, supportiveness, empathy, compassion, tenderness, nurturance, intuitiveness, sensitivity, and unselfishness. Masculine behavior is characterized by strength of will, ambition, courage, independence, assertiveness, hardiness, rationality, and emotional control. Psychoanalytic feminists assert that these differences are largely rooted in early childhood relationships. Because women are the primary caretakers in our society, young girls tend to develop and enjoy an ongoing relationship with their mothers that promotes their valuing of relatedness as well as the other feminine behaviors. For young boys, on the other hand, the mother is eventually perceived as fundamentally different, particularly as they face social pressures to begin fulfilling male roles. The need to separate from the mother figure has long-range implications for boys: they tend to lose what could otherwise become a learned capacity for intimacy and relatedness.

Gender feminists tend to be concerned with values of separateness (for men) and connectedness (for women) and how these lead to a different morality for women. Carol Gilligan (1982) (also discussed in Chapter 4) is a leading thinker in this area. She elucidated a process by which women develop an ethic of care rather than an ethic of justice based on the value they place on relationships. Gender feminists believe that these female ethics are equal to male ethics, although they have tended in patriarchal societies to be considered inferior. Gilligan asserts that all of humanity would be best served if both ethics could be valued equally. Other gender feminists go further, however, arguing for the superiority of women's ethics. For example, Nel Noddings (1982, 1989) asserts that war will never be discarded in favor of the sustained pursuit of peace until the female ethic of caring, aimed at unification, replaces the male ethic of strenuous striving, aimed at dividing people.

All psychological feminist theories promote the value of relationships and the importance of reciprocal interpersonal supports. They encourage us to note that Sheila's father raised her to be achievement- and task-oriented. These are admirable characteristics, but they represent male perspectives. Sheila's inclinations for interpersonal experience may have been discouraged, which was harmful to her overall development.

Afrocentric Relational Theory

Humanistic perspective

The origins of Afrocentric relational theory are in traditional Africa, before the arrival of European and Arabian influences. The Afrocentric worldview values cultural pluralism and, in fact, values difference in all of its forms. It does not accept hierarchies based on social differences, however. Eurocentric thinking, emphasizing mastery rather than harmony with the environment, is seen as oppressive. The three major objectives of Afrocentric theory are to provide an alternative perspective that reflects African cultures, to dispel negative distortions about African people held by other cultures, and to promote social transformations that are spiritual, moral, and humanistic.

Afrocentric relational theory assumes a collective identity for people rather than valuing individuality (Akbar, 1984; Bell, Bouie, & Baldwin, 1990; Schiele, 1996). It places great value on the spiritual or nonmaterial aspects of life, understood broadly as an "invisible substance" that connects all people. It values an affective approach to knowledge, conceptualizing emotion as the most direct experience of the self. This is of course in contrast to the Western emphasis on cognition and rationality. In its emphasis on the collective, Afrocentrism does not distinguish between things that affect the individual and things that affect larger groups of people, and it sees all social problems as related to practices of oppression and alienation. Personal connection and reciprocity are emphasized in helping relationships. Like feminism, Afrocentrism counters the object relations emphasis on individuality and independence with attention to collective identity and human connectedness.

Social Identity Theory

Developmental
Perspective

Social identity theory is a stage theory of socialization that articulates the process by which we come to identify with some social groups and develop a sense of difference from other social groups (Hardiman & Jackson, 1997). Social identity development can be an affirming process that provides us with a lifelong sense of belonging and support. I might feel good to have membership with a Roman Catholic or Irish American community. Because social identity can be exclusionary, however, it can also give rise to prejudice and oppression. I may believe that my race is more intelligent than another, or that persons of my cultural background are entitled to more benefits than those of another.

Social identity development proceeds in five stages. These stages are not truly distinct or sequential, however; people often experience several stages simultaneously.

1. *Naïveté.* During early childhood we have no social consciousness. We are not aware of particular codes of behavior for members of our group or any other social group. Our parents or other primary caregivers are our most significant influences, and we accept that socialization without question. As young children we do, however, begin to distinguish between ourselves and other groups of people. We may not feel completely comfortable with the racial, ethnic, or religious differences we observe, but neither do we feel fearful, superior, or inferior. Children at this stage are mainly curious about differences.

2. *Acceptance.* Older children and young adolescents learn the distinct ideologies and belief systems of their own and other social groups. During this stage, we learn that the world's institutions and authority figures have rules that encourage certain behaviors and prohibit others, and we internalize these dominant cultural beliefs and make

them a part of our everyday lives. Those questions that emerged during the stage of naïveté are submerged. We come to believe that the way *our* group does things is normal, makes more sense, and is better. We regard the cultures of people who are different from us as strange, marginal, and perhaps inferior. We may passively accept these differences or actively do so by joining organizations that highlight our own identity and (perhaps) devalue others.

3. *Resistance.* In adolescence, or even later, we become aware of the harmful effects of acting on social differences. We have new experiences with members of other social groups that challenge our prior assumptions. We begin to reevaluate those assumptions and investigate our own role in perpetuating harmful differences. We may feel anger at others within our own social group who foster these irrational differences. We begin to move toward a new definition of social identity that is broader than our previous definition. We may work to end our newly perceived patterns of collusion and oppression.

4. *Redefinition.* Redefinition is a process of creating a new social identity that preserves our pride in our origins while perceiving differences with others as positive representations of diversity. We may isolate from some members of our social group and shift toward interactions with others from our social group who share our level of awareness. We see all groups as being rich in strengths and values. We may reclaim our own group heritage but broaden our definition of that heritage as one of many varieties of constructive living.

5. *Internalization.* In the final stage of social identity development, we become comfortable with our revised identity and are able to incorporate it into all aspects of our life. We act unconsciously without external controls. Life continues as an ongoing process of discovering vestiges of our old biases, but now we test our integrated new identities in wider contexts than our limited reference group. Our appreciation of the plight of all oppressed people, and enhanced empathy for others, is a part of this process. For many people, the internalization stage is an ongoing challenge rather than an end state.

The Impact of Early Nurturing

Psychodynamic perspective, Developmental perspective

We have been looking at theories that deem relationships to be important throughout our lives. Turning to the empirical research, we can find evidence that, as suggested by object relations theory, the quality of our *early* relationships is crucial to our lifelong capacity to engage in healthy relationships, and even to enjoy basic physical health.

There is a large body of research devoted to studying the links between early life experiences and physical and mental health risks (e.g., Gunnar, Broderson, Nachimas,

Buss, & Rigatuso,1996; Hertsgaard, Gunnar, Erickson, & Nachimas, 1995; Nachimas, Gunnar, Mangelsdorf, Parritz, & Buss, 1996). This work demonstrates that negative infant experiences such as child abuse, family strife, poverty, and emotional neglect correlate with later health problems ranging from depression to drug abuse and heart disease. Relational elements of our early environments appear to permanently alter the development of central nervous system structures that govern our autonomic, cognitive, behavioral, and emotional responses to stress.

Animal models are common in this research, tracing the physiological aspects of rat and monkey stress responses all the way to the level of gene expression (Ainsman, Zaharia, Meaney, & Merali, 1998; Bredy, Weaver, Champagne, & Meaney, 2001; Lupien, King, Meaney, & McEwen, 2000). It has been found that highly groomed young rats (pups) develop more receptors in their brains for the substances that inhibit the production of corticotropin-releasing hormone (CRH), the master regulator of the stress response. As a result of the tactile stimulation they received from mothers, the pups' brains developed in a way that lowered their stress response—not only while being groomed, but also throughout life! When the rats are switched at birth to different mothers, the pups' brain development matched the behavior of the mother who reared them, not their biological mothers. Furthermore, high-licking and high-grooming (nurturing) mother rats change their behavior significantly when given a substance that stimulates the hormonal effects of chronic stress, raising their CRH and lowering oxytocin, a hormone related to the equanimity many human mothers feel after giving birth. That is, under the influence of these stress hormones, the high nurturing mothers behaved like the low nurturing mothers, and their offspring grew up the same way.

Some of you may be familiar with the tradition of research on the nurturing practices of rhesus monkeys. Research continues in this area (Nelson & Carver, 1998; Webb, Monk, & Nelson, 2001). In some of these experiments, monkeys are separated from their mothers at age intervals of 1 week, 1 month, 3 months, and 6 months and raised in a group of other monkeys that includes a different mother monkey. The infants who are separated later (3 or 6 months) exhibit normal behavior in the new setting. Those separated earlier, however, show a variety of abnormalities. The monkeys separated at 1 month initially exhibit a profound depression and refusal to eat. Once they recover, they show a deep need for attachments with other monkeys and also show great anxiety during social separation whenever they feel threatened. The monkeys separated at 1 week showed no interest in social contact with other monkeys, and this behavior did not change as they grew older. Autopsies of these monkeys show changes in brain development. The timing of separation from the primary caregiver seems to be significant to their later development. These findings in monkeys may have a sad counterpart in human children who are separated at early ages from their mothers.

Although much of this research is being conducted on rats, monkeys, and other animals, it has clear implications for human development. The concept of **neural plasticity,** which refers to the capacity of the nervous system to be modified by experience, is significant here (Nelson, 2000). Humans may have a window of opportunity or a critical period for altering neurological development, but this window varies, depending on the area of the nervous system. Even through the 2nd decade of life, for example, neurotransmitter and synapse changes are influenced by internal biology but perhaps by external signals as well.

Stress can clearly affect brain development, but there is little evidence to assume that the first 3 years of life are all-important (Nelson, 1999). A study of 2,600 undergraduate students found that even in late adolescence and early adulthood, satisfying social relationships were associated with greater autonomic activity and restorative behaviors when confronting acute stress (Cacioppo, Bernston, Sheridan, & McClintock, 2000). Higher CRH levels characterized chronically lonely individuals.

In summary, the research evidence indicates that secure attachments play a critical role in shaping the systems that underlie our reactivity to stressful situations. At the time when infants begin to form specific attachments to adults, the presence of caregivers who are warm and responsive begins to buffer or prevent elevations in stress hormones, even in situations that distress the infant. In contrast, insecure relationships are associated with higher CRH levels in potentially threatening situations. Secure emotional relationships with adults appear to be at least as critical as individual differences in temperament in determining stress reactivity and regulation.

Still, there is much to be learned in this area. Many people who have been subjected to serious early life traumas become effective, high functioning adolescents and adults. Infants and children are resilient and have many strengths that can help them overcome these early-life stresses. Researchers are challenged to determine whether interventions such as foster care can remedy the physical, emotional, and social problems seen in children who have experienced poor nurturing and early problems in separation.

The Concept of Stress

One of the main benefits of good nurturing is, as you have seen, the way it strengthens the ability to cope with stress. **Stress** can be defined as any event in which environmental or internal demands tax the adaptive resources of an individual. Stress may be biological (a disturbance in bodily systems), psychological (cognitive and emotional factors involved in the evaluation of a threat), and even social (the disruption of a social unit). Sheila experienced psychological stress, of course, as evidenced by her troublesome thoughts and feelings of depression, but she also experienced other types of stress. She experienced biological stress because, in an effort to attend classes, study, and work, she did not give her body adequate rest. As a result, she was susceptible to colds and the flu, which kept her in bed for several days each month and compounded her worries about managing course work. Sheila also experienced social stress, because she had left the slow-paced, interpersonally comfortable environments of her home and community college to attend the university.

Three Categories of Psychological Stress

Psychological stress, about which we are primarily concerned in this chapter, can be broken down into three categories (Lazarus & Lazarus, 1994):

1. *Harm*: A damaging event that has already occurred. Sheila avoided interaction with her classmates during much of the first semester, which may have led them to decide that she is aloof and that they should not try to approach her socially. Sheila has to accept that this rejection happened and that some harm has been done to her as a result, although she can learn from the experience and try to change in the future.

2. *Threat:* A perceived potential for harm that has not yet happened. This is probably the most common form of psychological stress. We feel stress because we are apprehensive about the possibility of the negative event. Sheila felt threatened when she walked into a classroom during the first semester, because she anticipated rejection from her classmates. We can be proactive in managing threats to ensure that they do not in fact occur and result in harm to us.

3. *Challenge*: An event we appraise as an opportunity rather than an occasion for alarm. We are mobilized to struggle against the obstacle, as with a threat, but our attitude is quite different. Faced with a threat, we are likely to act defensively to protect ourselves. Our defensiveness sends a negative message to the environment: we don't want to change; we want to be left alone. In a state of challenge, however, we are excited, expansive, and confident about the task to be undertaken. The challenge may be an exciting and productive experience for us. In her 2nd year at the university, Sheila may feel more excited than before about entering a classroom full of strangers at the beginning of a semester. She may look forward with more confidence to meeting some persons who may become friends.

Stress has been measured in several ways (Aldwin, 1994; Lazarus & Lazarus, 1994). One of the earliest attempts to measure stress consisted of a list of *life events*, uncommon events that bring about some change in our lives—experiencing the death of a loved one, getting married, becoming a parent, and so forth. The use of life events to measure stress is based on the assumption that major changes involve losses and disrupt our behavioral patterns.

More recently, stress has also been measured as **daily hassles,** common occurrences that are taxing—standing in line waiting, misplacing or losing things, dealing with troublesome coworkers, worrying about money, and many more. It is thought that an accumulation of daily hassles takes a greater toll on our coping capacities than do relatively rare life events.

Sociologists and community psychologists also study stress by measuring **role strain**—problems experienced in the performance of specific roles, such as romantic partner, caregiver, or worker. Research on caregiver burden is one example of measuring stress as role strain (Aldwin, 1994).

Stress and Crisis

A **crisis** is a major upset in our psychological equilibrium due to some harm, threat, or challenge with which we cannot cope (Hepworth, Rooney, & Larsen, 1997). The crisis poses an obstacle to achieving a personal goal, but we cannot overcome the obstacle through our usual methods of problem solving. We temporarily lack either the necessary knowledge for coping or the ability to focus on the problem, because we feel overwhelmed. A crisis episode often results when we face a serious stressor with which we have had no prior experience. It may be biological (major illness), interpersonal (the sudden loss of a loved one), or environmental (unemployment or a natural disaster such as flood or fire). We can regard anxiety, guilt, shame, sadness, envy, jealousy, and disgust as stress emotions (Lazarus, 1993). They are the emotions most likely to emerge in a person experiencing crisis.

Crisis episodes occur in three stages:

1. Our level of tension increases sharply.

2. We try and fail to cope with the stress, which further increases our tension and contributes to our sense of being overwhelmed. We are particularly receptive to receiving help from others at this time.

3. The crisis episode ends, either negatively (unhealthy coping) or positively (successful management of the crisis).

Sheila's poor midterm grades during her first semester illustrate some of these points. First, she was overwhelmed by the negative emotions of shame and sadness. Then she retreated to her parents' home, where she received much-needed support from her family. With their encouragement, she sought additional support from her academic adviser and a counselor. Finally, as the crisis situation stabilized, Sheila concluded that she could take some actions to relieve her feelings of loneliness and incompetence (a positive outcome).

Traumatic Stress

Although a single event may pose a crisis for one person but not another, some stressors are so severe that they are almost universally experienced as crisis. The stress is so overwhelming that almost anyone would be affected. The term **traumatic stress** is used to refer to events that involve actual or threatened severe injury or death, of oneself or significant others (American Psychiatric Association, 1994). Three types of traumatic stress have been identified: natural (such as flood, tornado, earthquake) and technological (such as nuclear) disasters; war and related problems, such as concentration camps; and individual trauma, such as being raped, assaulted, or tortured (Aldwin, 1994). People respond to traumatic stress with helplessness, terror, and horror (American Psychiatric Association, 1994).

Some occupations—particularly those of emergency workers such as police officers, firefighters, and disaster relief workers—involve regular exposure to traumatic events that most people do not experience in a lifetime. The literature about the stress faced by emergency workers refers to these traumatic events as critical incidents (CIs) and the reaction to them as critical incident stress (Prichard, 1996). Emergency workers, particularly police officers and firefighters, may experience threats to their own lives and the lives of their colleagues, as well as encountering "mass casualties of a gory and grotesque nature" (Prichard, 1996, p. 19). Emergency workers may also experience compassion stress, a "feeling of deep sympathy and sorrow for another who is stricken by suffering or misfortune, accompanied by a strong desire to alleviate the pain or remove its cause" (Figley, 1995, p. 299). Any professionals who work regularly with trauma survivors are susceptible to compassion stress. Many social workers fall into this category.

Vulnerability to Stress

Systems
perspective

Our experience of stress is in part related to our individual biological constitutions and our previous experiences with stress. Research from the field of mental illness underscores this point. In an attempt to understand the causes of schizophrenia and other disorders, several researchers have postulated **stress/diathesis models** of mental illness (Gottesman, 1991). These models are based on empirical data indicating that schizophrenia develops from the interaction of environmental stresses and a diathesis, or vulnerability, to schizophrenia. The diathesis may be biological (a genetic or biochemical predisposition), environmental (history of severe stressors), or both (Kaplan & Sadock, 1998). Most models, however, emphasize biological factors.

Stress/diathesis models suggest that all persons do not have an equal chance of developing schizophrenia, because it depends in part on one's chemical makeup. A person at risk may have an innate inability to manage high levels of stimulation from the outside world. One model postulates that the onset of schizophrenia is 70% related to innate predisposition and 30% related to external stress (Gottesman, 1991).

The stress/diathesis view highlights a probable interaction between constitutional and environmental factors in our experience and tolerance of stress. It suggests that a single event may pose a crisis for one person but not another. In its broadest versions, it also suggests that vulnerability to stress is related to one's position in the social structure, with some social positions exposed to a greater number of adverse situations—such as poverty, racism, and blocked opportunities—than others (Aldwin, 1994).

Coping and Adaptation

Our efforts to master the demands of stress are referred to as **coping.** Coping includes the thoughts, feelings, and actions that constitute these efforts. One method of coping is **adaptation,** which may involve adjustments in our biological responses, in our perceptions, or in our lifestyle.

Biological Coping

The traditional biological view of stress and coping, developed in the 1950s, emphasizes the body's attempts to maintain physical equilibrium, or **homeostasis,** which is a steady state of functioning (Selye, 1991). Stress is considered the result of any demand on the body (specifically, the nervous and hormonal systems) during perceived emergencies to prepare for fight (confrontation) or flight (escape). A stressor may be any biological process, emotion, or thought.

In this view, the body's response to a stressor is called the **general adaptation syndrome.** It occurs in three stages:

1. *Alarm.* The body first becomes aware of a threat.

2. *Resistance.* The body attempts to restore homeostasis.

3. *Exhaustion.* The body terminates coping efforts because of its inability to physically sustain the state of disequilibrium.

The general adaptation syndrome is explained in Exhibit 5.1.

In this context, *resistance* has a different meaning than is generally used in social work: an active, positive response of the body in which endorphins and specialized cells of the immune system fight off stress and infection. Our immune systems are constructed for adaptation to stress, but cumulative wear and tear of multiple stress episodes can gradually deplete our body's resources. Common outcomes of chronic

Exhibit 5.1

The General Adaptation Syndrome

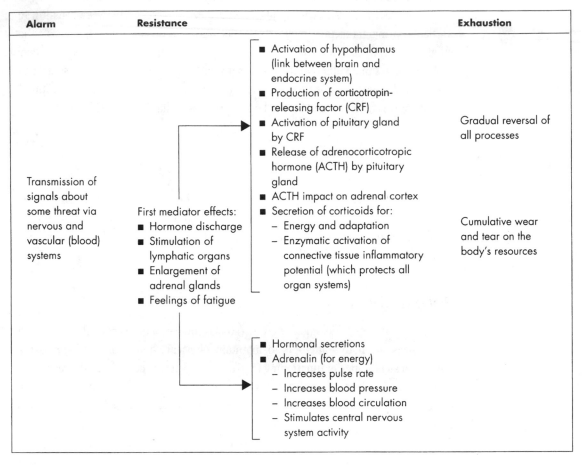

stress include stomach and intestinal disorders, high blood pressure, heart problems, and emotional problems. If only to preserve healthy physical functioning, we must combat and prevent stress.

This traditional view of biological coping with stress came from research that focused on males, either male rodents or human males. Since 1995, the federal government has required federally funded researchers to include a broad representation of both men and women in their study samples. Consequently, recent research on stress has included female as well as male participants, and gender differences in responses to stress have been found.

Recent research by Shelley Taylor and colleagues (Taylor, Klein, et al., 2000; Taylor, Lewis, et al., 2002) found that females of many species, including humans, respond to stress with "tend-and-befriend" rather than the "fight-or-flight" behavior described in the general adaptation syndrome. Under stressful conditions, females have been found to turn to protecting and nurturing their offspring and to seek social contact. The researchers suggest a possible biological basis for this gender difference in the coping response. More specifically, they note a large role for the hormone oxytocin, which plays a role in childbirth but also is secreted in both males and females in response to stress. High levels of oxytocin in animals are associated with calmness and increased sociability. Although males as well as females secrete oxytocin in response to stress, there is evidence that male hormones reduce the effects of oxytocin. Taylor and colleagues believe this explains the gender differences in response to stress.

Psychological Coping

Psychodynamic Perspective

The psychological aspect of managing stress can be viewed in two different ways. Some theorists consider coping ability to be a stable personality characteristic, or **trait**; others see it instead as a transient **state**—a process that changes over time depending on the context (Lazarus, 1993).

Those who consider coping to be a *trait* see it as an acquired defensive style. **Defense mechanisms** are unconscious, automatic responses that enable us to minimize perceived threats or keep them out of our awareness entirely. Exhibit 5.2 lists the common defense mechanisms identified by ego psychology (discussed in Chapter 4). Some defense mechanisms are considered healthier, or more adaptive, than others. Sheila's denial of her need for intimacy, for example, did not help her meet her goal of developing relationships with peers. But through the defense of sublimation (channeling the need for intimacy into alternative and socially acceptable outlets), she has become an excellent caregiver to a friend's child.

Those who see coping as a *state,* or process, observe that our coping strategies change in different situations. After all, our perceptions of threats, and what we focus on in a situation, change. The context also has an impact on our perceived and actual abilities to apply effective coping mechanisms. From this perspective, Sheila's use of denial would be adaptive at some times and maladaptive at others. Perhaps her denial of loneliness during the first academic semester helped her focus on her studies, which would help her achieve her goal of receiving an education. During the summer, however, when classes are out of session, she might become aware that her avoidance of relationships has prevented her from attaining interpersonal goals. Her efforts to cope with loneliness might also change when she can afford more energy to confront the issue.

Systems perspective

The trait and state approaches can usefully be combined. We can think of coping as a general pattern of managing stress that allows flexibility across diverse contexts. This perspective is consistent with the idea that cognitive schemata develop through the dual processes of assimilation and accommodation, described in Chapter 4.

EXHIBIT 5.2

Common Defense Mechanisms

Defense Mechanism	Definition	Example
Denial	Negating an important aspect of reality that one may actually perceive.	A woman with anorexia acknowledges her actual weight and strict dieting practices, but firmly believes that she is maintaining good self-care by dieting.
Displacement	Shifting feelings about one person or situation onto another.	A student's anger at her professor, who is threatening as an authority figure, is transposed into anger at her boyfriend, a safer target.
Intellectualization	Avoiding unacceptable emotions by thinking or talking about them rather than experiencing them directly.	A person talks to her counselor about the fact that she is sad but shows no emotional evidence of sadness, which makes it harder for her to understand its effects on her life.
Introjection	Taking characteristics of another person into the self in order to avoid a direct expression of emotions. The emotions originally felt about the other person are now felt toward the self.	An abused woman feels angry with herself rather than her abusing partner, because she has taken on his belief that she is an inadequate caregiver. Believing otherwise would make her more fearful that the desired relationship might end.
Isolation of affect	Consciously experiencing an emotion in a "safe" context rather than the threatening context in which it was first unconsciously experienced.	A person does not experience sadness at the funeral of a family member, but the following week weeps uncontrollably at the death of a pet hamster.
Projection	Attributing unacceptable thoughts and feelings to others.	A man does not want to be angry at his girlfriend, so when he is upset with her, he avoids owning that emotion by assuming that she is angry at him.
Rationalization	Using convincing reasons to justify ideas, feelings, or actions so as to avoid recognizing true motives.	A student copes with the guilt normally associated with cheating on an exam by reasoning that he was too ill the previous week to prepare as well as he wanted.
Reaction formation	Replacing an unwanted unconscious impulse with its opposite in conscious behavior.	A person cannot bear to be angry with his boss, so after a conflict he convinces himself that the boss is worthy of loyalty and demonstrates this by volunteering to work overtime.

(continued)

EXHIBIT 5.2

Common Defense Mechanisms (*continued*)

Defense Mechanism	Definition	Example
Regression	Resuming behaviors associated with an earlier developmental stage or level of functioning in order to avoid present anxiety. The behavior may or may not help to resolve the anxiety.	A young man throws a temper tantrum as a means of discharging his frustration when he cannot master a task on his computer. The startled computer technician, who had been reluctant to attend to the situation, now comes forth to provide assistance.
Repression	Keeping unwanted thoughts and feelings entirely out of awareness.	A son may begin to generate an impulse of hatred for his father, but because the impulse would be consciously unacceptable, he represses the hatred and does not become aware of it.
Somatization	Converting intolerable impulses into somatic symptoms.	A person who is unable to express his negative emotions develops frequent stomachaches as a result.
Sublimation	Converting an impulse from a socially unacceptable aim to a socially acceptable one.	An angry, aggressive young man becomes a star on his school's debate team.
Undoing	Nullifying an undesired impulse with an act of reparation.	A man who feels guilty about having lustful thoughts about a coworker tries to make amends to his wife by purchasing a special gift for her.

Source: Adapted from Goldstein, 1995.

Coping Styles

Another way to look at coping is by the way the person responds to crisis. Coping efforts may be problem-focused or emotion-focused. The function of **problem-focused coping** is to change the situation by acting on the environment. This method tends to dominate whenever we view situations as controllable by action. For example, Sheila was concerned about her professors' insensitivity to her learning disability. When she took action to educate them about it and explain more clearly how she learns best in a classroom setting, she was using problem-focused coping. In contrast, the function of **emotion-focused coping** is to change either the way the stressful situation is attended to (by vigilance or avoidance) or the meaning to oneself of what is happening.

The external situation does not change, but our behaviors or attitudes change with respect to it, and we may thus effectively manage the stressor. When we view stressful conditions as unchangeable, emotion-focused coping may dominate. If Sheila learns that one of her professors has no empathy for students with learning disabilities, she might avoid taking that professor's courses in the future, or decide that getting a good grade in that course is not as important as being exposed to the course material.

Conflict Perspective

U.S. culture tends to venerate problem-focused coping and the independently functioning self and to distrust emotion-focused coping and what may be called relational coping. **Relational coping** takes into account actions that maximize the survival of others—such as our families, children, and friends—as well as ourselves (Banyard & Graham-Bermann, 1993). Feminist theorists propose that women are more likely than men to employ the relational coping strategies of negotiation and forbearance, and Taylor's recent research (Taylor, Klein et al., 2000; Taylor, Lewis et al., 2002), cited above, gives credence to the idea that women are more likely than men to use relational coping. As social workers, we must be careful not to assume that one type of coping is superior to the other. Power imbalances and social forces such as racism and sexism affect the coping strategies of individuals (Banyard & Graham-Bermann, 1993). We need to give clients credit for the extraordinary coping efforts they may make in hostile environments.

Richard Lazarus (1993) has identified some particular behaviors typical of each coping style:

- *Problem-focused coping:* confrontation, problem solving

- *Emotion-focused coping:* distancing, escape or avoidance, positive reappraisal

- *Problem- or emotion-focused coping (depending on context):* self-control, search for social support, acceptance of responsibility

Lazarus emphasizes that all of us use any or several of these mechanisms at different times. None of them is any person's sole means of managing stress.

Using Lazarus's model, we might note that Sheila did not initially employ many problem-focused coping strategies to manage stressors at the university, and she overused emotion-focused methods. For example, she accepted responsibility (that is, blamed herself) for her difficulties at first and tried without success to control her moods through force of will. Later, she distanced herself from her emotions and avoided stressors by spending more time away from campus working, and she was in fact quite skilled at this job. When she began seeking social support, she became more problem-focused.

I probably don't need to tell you that college students face many predictable stressors when attending to the demands of academic work. A few years ago, I wanted to learn more about how students use both problem- and emotion-focused coping strategies in response to stress. I surveyed social work students in two Human Behavior in the Social Environment courses at a large urban university at the beginning of an academic year about their anticipated stressors and the ways they might cope with them. The results of this informal survey are outlined in Exhibit 5.3. The students chose problem- and emotion-focused coping strategies almost equally—a healthy mix.

Coping and Traumatic Stress

People exhibit some similarities between the way they cope with traumatic stress and the way they cope with everyday stress. For both types of stress, they use "problem-focused action, social support, negotiation skills, humor, altruism, and prayer" (Aldwin, 1994, p. 188). However, coping with traumatic stress differs from coping with everyday stress in several ways (Aldwin, 1994, pp. 188-190):

- Because people tend to have much less control in traumatic situations, their primary emotion-focused coping strategy is emotional numbing, or the constriction of emotional expression. They also make greater use of the defense mechanism of denial.

- Confiding in others takes on greater importance.

- The process of coping tends to take a much longer time. Reactions can be delayed, for months or even years.

- Search for meaning takes on greater importance, and transformation in personal identity is more common.

Although there is evidence of long-term negative consequences of traumatic stress, trauma survivors sometimes report positive outcomes as well. Studies have found that 34% of Holocaust survivors and 50% of rape survivors report positive personal changes following their experiences with traumatic stress (Burt & Katz, 1987; Kahana, 1992).

However, many trauma survivors experience a set of symptoms known as **post-traumatic stress disorder** (American Psychiatric Association, 1994). These symptoms include the following:

- *Persistent reliving of the traumatic event.* Intrusive, distressing recollections of the event; distressing dreams of the event; a sense of reliving the event; intense distress when exposed to cues of the event

- *Persistent avoidance of stimuli associated with the traumatic event.* Avoidance of thoughts or feelings connected to the event; avoidance of places, activities, and

EXHIBIT 5.3
Coping Styles
Among Social
Work Students

Problem-Focused Coping

Confrontation
- Learn to say no.

Problem Solving
- Exercise.
- Work with other students.
- Talk with professors.
- Go to the beach (for relaxation).
- Manage time.
- Undertake self-care.
- Reserve time for oneself.
- Stay ahead.
- Use relaxation techniques.
- Walk.
- Clean the house.
- Carry own lunch (save money).
- Aim for good nutrition.
- Take breaks.
- Look for "free" social activities.
- Pursue art interest.
- Organize tasks.
- Carefully budget finances.
- Plan for a job search.

Self-Control
- Bear down and "gut it out."
- Take on a job.

Search for Social Support
- Talk.
- Network with others.
- Demand support from others.
- Reserve time with family.

Emotion-Focused Coping

Distancing
- Deny that problem exists.
- Procrastinate.

Escape or Avoidance
- Drink.
- Smoke.
- Drink too much caffeine.
- Overeat, undereat.
- Give up.
- Vent on others.
- Curse other drivers.
- Neglect others.
- Watch too much television.
- Neglect other important concerns.
- Use charge cards.

Positive Reappraisal
- Think of money produced by job.
- Maintain perspective.
- Maintain flexibility.
- Reframe frustrations as growth opportunities.

Self-Control
- Push too hard.
- Study all night.

Search for Social Support
- Seek intimacy.
- Engage in sex.
- Participate in therapy.

Acceptance of Responsibility
- Cry.

people connected to the event; inability to recall aspects of the trauma; loss of interest in activities; feeling detached from others; emotional numbing; no sense of a future

- *Persistent high state of arousal.* Difficulty sleeping; irritability; difficulty concentrating; excessive attention to stimuli; exaggerated startle response

Symptoms of post-traumatic stress disorder have been noted as soon as 1 week following the traumatic event, or as long as 30 years after (Kaplan & Sadock, 1998). Complete recovery from symptoms occurs in 30% of the cases, mild symptoms continue over time in 40%, moderate symptoms continue in 20%, and symptoms persist or get worse in about 10% (Kaplan & Sadock, 1998). Children and older adults have the most trouble coping with traumatic events. A strong system of social support helps to prevent or to foster recovery from post-traumatic stress disorder. Besides providing support, social workers may be helpful by encouraging the person to discuss the traumatic event and by providing education about a variety of coping mechanisms (Kaplan & Sadock, 1998).

Social Support

In coping with the demands of daily life, our social supports—the people we rely on to enrich our lives—can be invaluable. **Social support** can be formally defined as the interpersonal interactions and relationships that provide us with assistance or feelings of attachment to persons we perceive as caring (Hobfoll, Freedy, Lane, & Geller, 1990). Three types of social support resources are available (Walsh & Connelly, 1996):

1. *Material support*: food, clothing, shelter, and other concrete items

2. *Emotional support*: interpersonal support

3. *Instrumental support*: services provided by casual contacts, such as grocers, hairstylists, and landlords

Our **social network** includes not just our social support but all the people with whom we regularly interact and the patterns of interaction that result from exchanging resources with them (Specht, 1986). Network relationships often occur in *clusters* (distinct categories such as nuclear family, extended family, friends, neighbors, community relations, school, work, church, recreational groups, and professional associations). Network relationships are not synonymous with support; they may be negative or positive. But the scope of the network does tend to indicate our potential for obtaining social support (Vaux, 1990). Having supportive others in a variety of clusters indicates

EXHIBIT 5.4
Sheila's Social
Network

Network Cluster	Network Member*	Type of Support
Family of origin	Mother*	Material and emotional
	Father*	Material and emotional
	Sister*	Emotional
Extended family	Grandmother*	Emotional
Intimate friends	Christine*	Emotional
	Tiffany*	Emotional
	Ben*	Emotional
Neighborhood	Landlord	Instrumental
Informal community relations	None	
School	Barbara	Instrumental
	Terri	Instrumental
	Academic adviser	Instrumental
	Instructor	Instrumental
	Paul* (counselor)	Emotional
Work	Kim	Instrumental
	Thomas	Instrumental
	Laura	Instrumental
Church/religion	None	
Recreation	None	
Associations	None	

that we are supported in many areas of our lives, rather than being limited to relatively few sources. Our **personal network** includes those from the social network who, in our view, provide us with our most essential supports.

Exhibit 5.4 displays Sheila's social network. She now has two close friends at the university with whom she spends much time. She met both Christine and Ben in her classes. Christine has a young child, Tiffany, for whom Sheila frequently baby-sits. Sheila feels a special closeness to the infant, who makes her feel unconditionally accepted and worthwhile. Ironically, Sheila finds herself doing much advice-giving and caregiving for these friends while wanting (but lacking) nurturing for herself. Still, Sheila feels good about the nature of these relationships, because she does not want to confide too much in her friends. She is concerned that they might reject her if they get to know her too well. Sheila feels some instrumental connection with several coworkers because they represent consistency in her life and affirm her competence as a worker. She is also supported emotionally as well as materially by her family members, with whom she keeps in regular contact. Sheila particularly looks to her sister for understanding and emotional support, and uses her sister as a model in many ways. She has always enjoyed seeing her parents and, ironically, even the grandmother who can be so critical of her. They make her feel more "whole" and reinforce her sense of identity, even though, like many young adults working toward independence, she has mixed feelings about spending more than a few days at a time with them. At school, Sheila has casual relationships with two classmates, her academic adviser, and a couple of faculty members, although she does not identify them as significant. They qualify as instrumental resources for her.

Systems perspective, Psychodynamic perspective

In total, Sheila has 16 persons in her social support system, representing 6 of a possible 10 clusters. She identifies eight of these people as personal, or primary, supports. It is noteworthy that half of her network members (eight) provide only instrumental support, which is an important type but the most limited. Because persons in the general population tend to identify about 25 network members (Vaux, 1988), we can see that Sheila's support system, on which she relies to cope with stress, is still probably not adequate for her needs at this time in her life.

How Social Support Aids Coping. The experience of stress creates a physiological state of emotional arousal, which reduces the efficiency of cognitive functions (Caplan, 1990). When we experience stress, we become less effective at focusing our attention and scanning the environment for relevant information. We cannot access the memories that normally bring meaning to our perceptions, judgment, planning, and integration of feedback from others. These memory impairments reduce our ability to maintain a consistent sense of identity.

Social support helps in these situations by acting as an "auxiliary ego." Our social support, particularly our personal network, compensates for our perceptual deficits, reminds us of our sense of self, and monitors the adequacy of our functioning. Here are ten characteristics of effective support (Caplan, 1990):

1. Nurtures and promotes an ordered worldview

2. Promotes hope

3. Promotes timely withdrawal and initiative

4. Provides guidance

5. Provides a communication channel with the social world

6. Affirms one's personal identity

7. Provides material help

8. Contains distress through reassurance and affirmation

9. Ensures adequate rest

10. Mobilizes other personal supports

Systems Perspective

Some of these support systems are formal (service organizations), and some are informal (such as friends and neighbors) (Caplan, 1990). Religion, which attends to the spiritual realm, also plays a distinctive support role (Caplan, 1990). This topic is explored in Chapter 6.

Two schools of thought have emerged around the question of how we internalize social support (Cohen & Wills, 1985):

Systems perspective, Social constructionist perspective

1.   *Main effect model.* Support is seen as related to our overall sense of well-being. Social networks provide us with regular positive experiences, and within the network a set of stable roles (expectations for our behavior) enables us to enjoy stability of mood, predictability in life situations, and recognition of self-worth. We simply don't experience many potential stressors as such, because with our built-in sense of support, we do not perceive situations as threats.

Psychodynamic perspective

2.   *Buffering model.* Support is seen as a factor that intervenes between a stressful event and our reaction. Recognizing our supports helps us to diminish or prevent a stress response. We recognize a potential stressor, but our perception that we have resources available redefines the potential for harm or reduces the stress reaction by influencing our cognitive, emotional, and physiological processes.

Most research on social support focuses on its buffering effects, in part because these effects are more accessible to measurement. Social support as a main effect is difficult to isolate, because it is influenced by, and may be an outcome of, our psychological development and ability to form attachments. The main effect model has its roots in sociology, particularly symbolic interaction theory, in which our sense of self is said to be shaped by behavioral expectations acquired through our interactions with others. The buffering model, more a product of ego psychology, conceptualizes social support as an external source of emotional, informational, and instrumental aid (Auslander & Litwin, 1987).

How Social Workers Evaluate Social Support. There is no consensus about how social workers can evaluate a client's level of social support. The simplest procedure is to ask for the client's subjective perceptions of support from family and friends (Procidano & Heller, 1983). One of the most complex procedures uses eight indicators of social support: available listening, task appreciation, task challenge, emotional support, emotional challenge, reality confirmation, tangible assistance, and personal assistance (Richman, Rosenfeld, & Hardy, 1993). One particularly useful model includes three social support indicators (Vaux, 1988):

1.   *Listing of social network resources.* The client lists all the people with whom he or she regularly interacts.

2. *Accounts of supportive behavior.* The client identifies specific episodes of receiving support from others in the recent past.

3. *Perceptions of support.* The client subjectively assesses the adequacy of the support received from various sources.

In assessing a client's social supports from this perspective, the social worker first asks the client to list all persons with whom he or she has interacted in the past 1 or 2 weeks. Next, the social worker asks the client to draw from that list the persons he or she perceives to be supportive in significant ways (significance is intended to be open to the client's interpretation). The client is asked to describe specific recent acts of support provided by those significant others. Finally, the social worker asks the client to evaluate the adequacy of the support received from specific sources, and in general. On the basis of this assessment, the social worker can identify both subjective and objective support indicators with the client and target underused clusters for the development of additional social support.

Sheila's support network is outlined in Exhibit 5.4. From a full assessment of her social supports, a social worker might conclude that her personal network is rather small, consisting only of her sister, counselor, and three friends. Sheila might report to the social worker that she does not perceive many of her interactions to be supportive. The social worker might explore with Sheila her school, neighborhood, and work clusters for the possibility of developing new supports.

Normal and Abnormal Coping

Most people readily assess the coping behaviors they observe in others as "normal" or "abnormal." But what does "normal" mean? We all apply different criteria. The standards we use to classify coping thoughts and feelings as normal or abnormal are important, however, because they have implications for how we view ourselves and how we behave toward those different from us. For example, Sheila was concerned that other students at the university perceived her as abnormal because of her social isolation and her inadequacy. Most likely, other students did not notice her at all. It is interesting that, in Sheila's view, her physical appearance and her demeanor revealed her as abnormal. However, her appearance did not stand out, and her feelings were not as evident to others as she thought.

Social workers struggle just as much to define *normal* and *abnormal* as anybody else. And their definitions may have greater consequences. Misidentifying someone as normal may forestall needed interventions; misidentifying someone as abnormal may create a stigma or become a self-fulfilling prophecy. To avoid such problems, social workers may profitably consider how four different disciplines define normal.

The Medical (Psychiatric) Perspective

One definition from psychiatry, a branch of medicine, states that we are normal when we are in harmony with ourselves and our environment. Normality is characterized by conformity with our community and culture. We can be deviant from some social norms, so long as our deviance does not impair our reasoning, judgment, intellectual capacity, and ability to make personal and social adaptations (Campbell, 1996).

The current definition of *mental disorder* used by the American Psychiatric Association (1994), which is intended to help psychiatrists and many other professionals distinguish between normality and abnormality, is a "significant behavioral or psychological syndrome or pattern that occurs in an individual and that is associated with present distress (e.g., a painful symptom) or disability (i.e., impairment in one or more important areas of functioning) or with significantly increased risk of suffering death, pain, disability, or an important loss of freedom" (p. xxiii). The syndrome or pattern "must not be an expectable and culturally sanctioned response to a particular event" (p. xxiii). Whatever its cause, "it must currently be considered a manifestation of behavioral, psychological, or biological dysfunction in the individual" (p. xxiii). Neither deviant behavior nor conflicts between an individual and society are to be considered mental disorders unless they are symptomatic of problems within the individual.

In summary, the medical model of abnormality focuses on underlying disturbances within the person. An assessment of the disturbance results in a diagnosis based on a cluster of observable symptoms. This is sometimes referred to as the disease model of abnormality. Interventions, or treatments, focus on changing the individual. The abnormal person must experience internal, personal changes (rather than induce environmental change) in order to be considered normal again. Exhibit 5.5 summarizes the format for diagnosing mental disorders as developed by psychiatry in the United States and published in the *Diagnostic and Statistical Manual of Mental Disorders* (American Psychiatric Association, 2000), generally referred to as DSM-IV-TR. Many people in the helping professions follow this format, including social workers in some service settings.

Psychological Perspectives

One major difference between psychiatry and psychology is that psychiatry tends to emphasize biological and somatic interventions to return the person to a state of normalcy, whereas psychology emphasizes various cognitive, behavioral, or reflective interventions.

Developmental perspective

The field of psychological theory is quite broad, but some theories are distinctive in that they postulate that people normally progress through a sequence of life stages. The time context thus becomes important. Each new stage of personality development

Exhibit 5.5
DSM-IV
Classification of
Mental Disorders

Axis I	Clinical or mental disorders	
	Other conditions that may be a focus of clinical attention	
Axis II	Personality disorders	
	Mental retardation	
Axis III	General medical conditions	
Axis IV	Psychosocial and environmental problems	
	Primary support group	Economic
	Social environment	Access to health care services
	Educational	Interaction with the legal system
	Occupational	Other psychosocial and
	Housing	environmental problems
Axis V	Global assessment of functioning (based on the clinician's judgment):	
	90–100 Superior functioning in a wide range of activities	
	0–10 Persistent danger of severely hurting self or others, persistent inability to maintain personal hygiene, or serious suicidal acts with clear expectation of death	

Source: Adapted from American Psychiatric Association, 2000.

builds on previous stages, and any unsuccessful transitions can result in abnormal behavior—that is, a deviant pattern of coping with threats and challenges. An unsuccessful struggle through one stage implies that the person will experience difficulties in mastering subsequent stages.

One life-stage view of normality very well known in social work is that of Erik Erikson (1968), who proposed eight stages of normal *psychosocial development* (see Exhibit 5.6). Sheila, although 22 years old, is still struggling with the two developmental stages of adolescence (in which the issue is identity vs. diffusion) and young adulthood (in which the issue is intimacy vs. isolation). Common challenges in adolescence include developing a sense of one's potential and place in society by negotiating issues of self-certainty versus apathy, role experimentation versus negative identity, and anticipation of achievement versus work paralysis. Challenges in young adulthood include developing a capacity for interpersonal intimacy as opposed to feeling socially empty or isolated within the family unit. According to Erikson's theory, Sheila's difficulties are related to her lack of success in negotiating one or more of the four preceding developmental phases.

EXHIBIT 5.6
Erikson's Stages of Psychosocial Development

Life Stage	Psychosocial Challenge	Significant Others
Infancy	Trust versus mistrust	Maternal person
Early childhood	Autonomy versus shame and doubt	Parental persons
Play age	Initiative versus guilt	Family
School age	Industry versus inferiority	Neighborhood
Adolescence	Identity versus identity diffusion	Peers
Young adulthood	Intimacy versus isolation	Partners
Adulthood	Generativity versus self-absorption	Household
Mature age	Integrity versus disgust and despair	Humanity

From this perspective, Sheila's experience of stress would not be seen as abnormal, but her inability to make coping choices that promote positive personal adaptation would signal psychological abnormality. For example, in her first semester at the university, she was having difficulty with role experimentation (identity vs. identity diffusion). She lacked the necessary sense of competence and self-efficacy to allow herself to try out various social roles. She avoided social situations such as study groups, recreational activities, and university organizations in which she might learn more about what kinds of people she likes, what her main social interests are, and what range of careers she might enjoy. Instead, she was stuck with a negative identity, or self-image, and could not readily advance in her social development. From a stage theory perspective, her means of coping with the challenge of identity development would be seen as maladaptive, or abnormal.

The Sociological Approach: Deviance

Social constructionist perspective

The field of sociology offers a variety of approaches to the study of abnormality, or deviance. As an example, consider one sociological perspective on deviance derived from symbolic interactionism. It states that those who cannot constrain their behaviors within role limitations acceptable to others become labeled as deviant. Thus, *deviance* is a negative labeling that is assigned when one is considered by a majority of significant others to be in violation of the prescribed social order (Hewitt, 1994). Put more simply, we are unable to grasp the perspective from which the deviant person thinks and acts; the person's behavior does not make sense to us. We conclude that our inability to understand the other person's perspective is due to that person's shortcomings rather than to our own rigidity, and we label the behavior as deviant. The deviance label may be mitigated if the individual accepts that he or she should think or behave otherwise and tries to conform to the social order (Anderson, 1994).

From this viewpoint, Sheila would be perceived as abnormal, or deviant, only by those who had sufficient knowledge of her thoughts and feelings to form an opinion about her allegiance to their ideas of appropriate social behavior. Those who knew Sheila well might understand the basis for her negative thoughts and emotions, and in that context continue to view her as normal in her coping efforts. However, it is significant that Sheila was trying to avoid intimacy with her university classmates and work peers so that she would not become well known to them. Because she still views herself as somewhat deviant, she wants to avoid being seen as deviant (or abnormal) by others, which in her view would lead to their rejection of her. This circular reasoning poorly serves Sheila's efforts to cope with stress in ways that promote her personal goals.

The Social Work Perspective: Social Functioning

Social behavioral perspective

The profession of social work is characterized by the consideration of systems and the reciprocal impact of persons and their environments (the bio-psycho-social-spiritual perspective) on human behavior. Social workers tend not to classify individuals as abnormal. Instead, they consider the person-in-environment as an ongoing process that facilitates or blocks one's ability to experience satisfactory social functioning. In fact, in clinical social work, the term *normalization* refers to helping clients realize that their thoughts and feelings are shared by many other individuals in similar circumstances (Hepworth et al., 1997).

Three types of situations are most likely to produce problems in social functioning: stressful life transitions, relationship difficulties, and environmental unresponsiveness (Germain & Gitterman, 1996). Note that all three are related to transitory interactions of the person with other persons or the environment and do not rely on evaluating the client as normal or abnormal.

Social work's **person-in-environment (PIE) classification system** formally organizes the assessment of individuals' ability to cope with stress around the four factors shown in Exhibit 5.7: social functioning problems, environmental problems, mental health problems, and physical health problems. Such a broad classification scheme helps ensure that Sheila's range of needs will be addressed. James Karls and Karin Wandrei (1994), the authors of the PIE system, state that it "underlines the importance of conceptualizing a person in an interactive context" and that "pathological and psychological limitations are accounted for but are not accorded extraordinary attention" (p. x). Thus, the system avoids labeling a client as abnormal. At the same time, however, it offers no way to assess the client's strengths and resources.

With the exception of its neglect of strengths and resources, the PIE assessment system is appropriate for social work because it was specifically developed to promote

Exhibit 5.7

The Person-in-Environment (PIE) Classification System

Factor I: Social Functioning Problems

A. Social role in which each problem is identified
    1. Family (parent, spouse, child, sibling, other, significant other)
    2. Other interpersonal (lover, friend, neighbor, member, other)
    3. Occupational (worker/paid, worker/home, worker/volunteer, student, other)

B. Type of problem in social role

1. Power	4. Dependency	7. Victimization
2. Ambivalence	5. Loss	8. Mixed
3. Responsibility	6. Isolation	9. Other

C. Severity of problem

1. No problem	4. High severity
2. Low severity	5. Very high severity
3. Moderate severity	6. Catastrophic

D. Duration of problem

1. More than five years	4. Two to four weeks
2. One to five years	5. Two weeks or less
3. Six months to one year	

E. Ability of client to cope with problem

1. Outstanding coping skills	4. Somewhat inadequate
2. Above average	5. Inadequate
3. Adequate	6. No coping skills

Factor II: Environmental Problems

A. Social system where each problem is identified

1. Economic/basic need	4. Health, safety, social services
2. Education/training	5. Voluntary association
3. Judicial/legal	6. Affectional support

B. Specific type of problem within each social system

C. Severity of problem

D. Duration of problem

Factor III: Mental Health Problems

A. Clinical syndromes (Axis I of DSM)

B. Personality and developmental disorders (Axis II of DSM)

Factor IV: Physical Health Problems

A. Disease diagnosed by a physician

B. Other health problems reported by client and others

a holistic biopsychosocial perspective on human behavior. For example, at a mental health center that subscribed to psychiatry's DSM-IV classification system, Sheila might be given an Axis I diagnosis of adjustment disorder or dysthymic disorder, and her dyslexia might be diagnosed on Axis III. In addition, some clinicians might use Axis IV to note that Sheila has some school adjustment problems. With the PIE, the social worker would, in addition to her mental and physical health concerns, assess Sheila's overall social and occupational functioning, as well as any specific environmental problems. For example, her problems with the student role that might be highlighted on PIE Factor I include her ambivalence and isolation, the high severity of her impairment, its 6 months' to 1 year's duration, and the inadequacy of her coping skills. Her environmental stressors on Factor II might include a deficiency in affectional support, of high severity, with a duration of 6 months to 1 year. Assessment with PIE provides Sheila and the social worker with more avenues for intervention, which might include personal interventions, interpersonal interventions, and environmental interventions.

IMPLICATIONS FOR SOCIAL WORK PRACTICE

Theory and research about the psychosocial person have a number of implications for social work practice, including the following:

- Always assess the nature, range, and intensity of a client's interpersonal relationships.

- Help clients identify their sources of stress and patterns of coping. Recognize the possibility of particular vulnerabilities to stress.

- Help clients assess the effectiveness of particular coping strategies for specific situations.

- Where appropriate, help clients develop a stronger sense of competence in problem solving and coping. Identify specific problems and related skill-building needs, teach and rehearse skills, and implement graduated applications to real-life situations.

- Where appropriate, use case management activities focused on developing a client's social supports through linkages with potentially supportive others in a variety of social network clusters.

- Recognize families as possible sources of stress as well as support.

- Recognize the benefits that psychoeducational groups, therapy groups, and mutual aid groups may have for helping clients cope with stress.

- Where appropriate, take the roles of mediator and advocate to attempt to influence organizations to be more responsive to the needs of staff and clients. When appropriate, take the roles of planner and administrator to introduce flexibility into organizational policies and procedures so that agency/environment transactions become mutually responsive.

- Link clients who experience stress related to inadequate community ties to an array of formal and informal organizations that provide them with a greater sense of belonging in their communities.

- When working with persons in crisis, attempt to alleviate distress and facilitate a return to the previous level of functioning.

- Assess with clients the meaning of hazardous events, the precipitating factors, and potential and actual support systems. When working with persons in crisis, use a here-and-now orientation, and use tasks to enhance support systems. Help clients connect current stress with patterns of past functioning and to initiate improved coping methods. As the crisis phase terminates, review tasks accomplished, including new coping skills and social supports developed.

KEY TERMS

adaptation
Afrocentric relational
  theory
coping
crisis
daily hassles
defense mechanisms
emotion-focused coping
general adaptation
  syndrome
homeostasis
neural plasticity
object relations theory
personal network

person-in-environment (PIE)
  classification system
post-traumatic stress disorder
problem-focused coping
relational coping
role strain
social identity theory
social network
social support
state
stress
stress/diathesis models
trait
traumatic stress

ACTIVE LEARNING

1. You have been introduced to four ways of conceptualizing normal and abnormal coping: mental disorder, psychosocial development, deviance, and social functioning. Which of these ways of thinking about normality and abnormality are the most helpful to you in thinking about Sheila's situation? For what reasons?

2. Think of your own social support network. List all persons you have interacted with in the past month. Next, circle those persons on the list who you perceive to be supportive in significant ways. Describe specific recent acts of support provided by these significant others. Finally, evaluate the adequacy of the support you receive from specific sources, and in general. What can you do to increase the support you receive from your social network?

WEB RESOURCES

Object Relations Theory and Psychopathology

www.objectrelations.org

Site maintained by Thomas Klee, Ph.D., clinical psychologist, contains information on object relations theory, a method of object relations psychotherapy, and current articles on object relations theory and therapy.

Stone Center

www.wcwonline.org/w-stone.html

Site presented by the Stone Center of the Wellesley Centers for Women, the largest women's research center in the United States, contains theoretical work on women's psychological development and model programs for the prevention of psychological problems.

MEDLINEplus: Stress

www.nlm.nih.gov/medlineplus/stress.html

Site presented by the National Institute of Mental Health presents links to latest news about stress research, coping, disease management, specific conditions, and stress in children, seniors, teenagers, and women.

Stress Management: A Review of Principles

www.unl.edu/stress/mgmt

Site presented by Wesley Sime at the Department of Health and Human Performance at the University of Nebraska—Lincoln site contains information on stressors and stress responses, the psychophysiology of stress, physiology of stress, and stress-related disorders.

National Center for Post-Traumatic Stress Disorder

www.ncptsd.org

Site presented by the National Center for PTSD, a program of the U.S. Department of Veterans Affairs, contains facts about PTSD, information about how to manage the traumatic stress of terrorism, and recent research.

CHAPTER 6

The Spiritual Person

Michael J. Sheridan

Key Ideas

CASE STUDY: ■ *Sean's Search for Meaning and Connection*

CHAPTER 6

The Spiritual Person

Michael J. Sheridan
Virginia Commonwealth University

How does the inclusion of the spiritual dimension in the existing biopsychosocial framework expand and enhance our understanding of human behavior? What challenges does it bring to this understanding?

How can social workers effectively tap into the universals (e.g., love, compassion, service, justice) found in most spiritual perspectives—both religious and nonreligious—while recognizing and honoring diversity among various spiritual paths?

Key Ideas

As you read this chapter, take note of these central ideas:

1. Spirituality, a universal and fundamental aspect of human existence, is a broad concept that includes a search for purpose, meaning, and connection between oneself, other people, the universe, and the ultimate reality. It may be experienced within either a religious or nonreligious framework.

2. Religion refers to a set of beliefs, practices, and traditions experienced within a specific social institution over time.

3. There is a rich diversity of religious and spiritual beliefs and expression in the United States and the world that needs to be understood and taken into account in the current climate of globalization.

4. Spiritual development can be conceptualized as moving through a series of stages—each with its own particular characteristics—similar to physical, cognitive, or psychosocial development.

5. Two popular theories of spiritual development are Fowler's theory of stages of faith and Wilber's full-spectrum model of consciousness; both models envision an

endpoint in human development that is beyond a mature ego and self-actualization, allowing humans to transcend the body and the ego and to experience a wider and deeper connection with all beings and the universe.

6. Social work's relationship to religion and spirituality has changed over time—beginning with strong religious or moral foundations, then moving to increased professionalization and secularization, and more recently experiencing a resurgence of interest and attention.

7. A growing body of literature explores the relevance of spirituality to both human diversity and the human condition, with implications for all levels of practice.

CASE STUDY

SEAN'S SEARCH FOR
MEANING AND CONNECTION

Sean was born into a large Irish American, Catholic family on a cold day in February 1950. His birth was followed within a span of 10 years by the births of his two sisters and two brothers. Sean's parents, Joseph and Mary Cassidy, lived in Boston, Massachusetts, where their families had first immigrated during the late 1800s. The Cassidy clan consisted of numerous aunts, uncles, and cousins, plus Mary's mother and father; Joseph's parents were both deceased.

Joseph and his brothers, Sam and Elliot, ran a small trucking business, which specialized in carrying produce to various markets in New England. Joseph was the head of the company, but he still took his turn hauling produce. Although the business had struggled in the beginning, it eventually grew into a fairly stable source of income for the three brothers' families. Mary was a full-time homemaker who spent her days caring for her growing family.

The Catholic religion was an important facet of the Cassidy household. All the children were enrolled in Catholic schools, and weekends were dedicated to church activities. Mary was particularly active in their church and made sure that the children were involved either as acolytes or as members of the choir. Although Joseph accompanied Mary to church, his personal connection to the Catholic faith was not as strong as hers—a difference that sometimes caused difficulties between them.

Sean remembers his early childhood with fondness—especially the strong sense of belonging that came from his large extended family, his school, and the church. He felt close to his mother and nurtured by her. He was in awe of his father, who would swoop into the house after being gone for several days and entertain them with colorful stories of his trips on the road.

The tenor of the household changed dramatically in Sean's 10th year, however, when his Uncle Elliot was killed in a trucking accident on his way home from a trip to Maine. The entire Cassidy clan was devastated, but Sean's father was particularly hard hit. Most of the family found solace in the teachings and rituals of their faith, but Joseph became increasingly morose and seemed to find comfort only in the company of a whiskey bottle—a practice he had previously avoided because of his own father's alcoholism. He felt responsible for his brother's family following Elliot's death and worried about how he could support both families financially. He became more and more withdrawn and tense, and Mary and the children learned to tip-toe around him when he was at home so as not to "upset him."

The situation went from bad to worse. Sean's parents argued more and more as his father's drinking increased and he began to miss work. The children were fearful and felt that things were out of control. Several of them, including Sean, started to have problems in school with falling grades and fights with other kids. Sean's feelings about his father began to change. Once he had been proud of him, but now he was both frightened and ashamed of him. He no longer felt close to his mother, who seemed constantly preoccupied with either arguing with his father or praying to God to save her husband.

The family tension ended when Sean's father was killed in a trucking accident similar to the one that had taken the life of his brother. Joseph had been drinking on a late night run and lost control of the truck, which went off the road, smashed into a tree, and caught fire. Sean went with his Uncle Sam to identify his father's charred remains—an experience that haunted him for many years. The family quietly buried Joseph and never voiced their fears that his death had perhaps not been "accidental." Sean was 15 years old at the time.

The remainder of Sean's growing up years were spent trying to help his mother keep the family together while growing increasingly distant and angry with her and the rest of his family. He found himself rebelling against everything—his family, school, the church—and all that they stood for. When he graduated from high school in 1968, the world around him was in turmoil, and so was he.

Although he was able to go off to college, thanks to a small college fund, financial aid, and money saved from part-time jobs, Sean found it difficult to concentrate on his studies. There was too much else going on. Civil rights, the Vietnam war, free love, and the drug culture were vastly more interesting than his courses in English literature, and he was exposed to ideas that were radically different from the perspectives he had been taught at home. He found himself particularly enjoying long discussions with other students about the hypocrisy of religion and mainstream politics and the need to break away from all of the values of the "establishment." He felt a sense of belonging and connection in his group of counterculture friends that he had not experienced since early childhood.

One of these friends was a free spirit named Molly, who was different from any girl he had known in Boston. She taught him the art of smoking dope and dropping acid and the pleasures of lovemaking while stoned out of his mind. On a whim one weekend, they decided to drop out of college and go join a commune in the country where they could live their lives free from the "shackles of society." Initially, Sean felt at home in this new environment and believed that he had finally found his true purpose in life. However, as time went by, Sean's drug and alcohol use grew more intense, until finally even Molly was complaining to him about it. One morning, after a particularly upsetting fight with Molly, Sean went off to his favorite place in the woods to be alone and think about things. He recognized how desperately unhappy and alone he felt and how scared he was about his substance use, which he knew was out of control. He wondered whether his father's death had been a suicide and realized that he felt somewhat suicidal himself. He missed his family and felt guilty about his distance from them.

A sense of panic grew inside Sean, and he began to do something he had not done in a very long time—he began to pray. As he prayed, tears started to stream down his face as he allowed himself to feel the pain of his father's death and despair about the changes in his family—feelings he had kept bottled up inside for years. His tears turned to deep sobs, and he thought he was going to drown in the depths of his sorrow. Suddenly, he felt a warm presence, as if someone had his arms around him, and he heard his father's voice say quietly in his ear, "It will be all right, son, it will be all right." The power and comfort of this experience was incredibly intense, although Sean began to doubt it as quickly as he experienced it. It seemed so bizarre to him, and yet so real and natural, to feel his father's presence and to hear his voice at the very moment that he finally let himself grieve for him.

This experience was a turning point for Sean, although he still struggled to make sense of it and told no one about it. He went home to his family

and had long talks with his mother about his father and the family.
He stopped his use of alcohol and drugs, started attending Alcoholics
Anonymous (AA) and Narcotics Anonymous (NA) meetings, and got
some counseling. Eventually, Sean reenrolled in college and at the age of
27 completed his degree in English, with a focus on journalism. He then
found work with an environmental group writing brochures and advocacy
materials, which fit with his sense of social consciousness. He had made
peace with his mother, was reunited with his family, and felt like he was on
track again.

On his 28th birthday, he met Nancy, a young woman who came to a
birthday celebration his friends threw for him. He was immediately taken by
her, and after a year of dating, they married and settled in the Boston area.
Nancy was a social worker who worked in a youth program in the inner city
and was very committed to her work. She had also had family difficulties—her
mother was an alcoholic—and Sean found it easy to talk with her about his
own life. He finally told her of his experience in the woods when it seemed
that his father had come to comfort him. He told her that he still did not know
whether it had really happened or was a "figment of my imagination," but
that it clearly had helped him make an important decision in his life.

Nancy and Sean began to talk more and more about their early
experiences with religion, both positive and negative, and about their current
beliefs. Sean shared with his wife the concepts of a "higher power" that he
had gained from AA and NA and his growing sense that there was
"something more" to life than the everyday reality. They began to read books
on different faith traditions and began to practice meditation and study
Celtic shamanism together. They talked about the core themes of love and
compassion that seemed to be central to many of the religions they were
studying. Although neither had a desire to return to the faiths of their
childhood, both Sean and Nancy recognized that they would like to be a
part of some spiritual community.

But the decision to actually join a church did not come until after
the birth of their first child, when they joined a Unitarian Universalist
congregation. Over the years, Sean and Nancy have felt that this community
has provided a good spiritual foundation for both themselves and their two
boys. They have found personal meaning in the worship services and a
sense of social responsibility and connectedness in the church's outreach
programs. They have been members for 15 years.

Sean still reads a lot of different religious writings and feels that there is
a good fit between the practices of meditation and shamanism and the

teachings of his adopted faith. He sees his involvement in the Unitarian church and his personal practices as different but equally important expressions of his spiritual life, and he is becoming more and more aware of the "sacred in everyday life." He is very conscious of trying to transmit this sense of spirituality to his sons as they move into adolescence and young adulthood. Both personal faith and a spiritual community are especially important to both Sean and Nancy these days, as they have just learned that Nancy has advanced-stage breast cancer.

The Spiritual Dimension

Systems
perspective

Sean's story could be viewed through many different lenses. Social work's biopsycho-social framework would be helpful in understanding many facets of his life. Knowledge of the biological influences on behavior would be useful in understanding the inter-generational pattern of substance abuse and biochemical depression in the Cassidy family. Psychological perspectives would shed light on Sean's struggles during adoles-cence and young adulthood, as well as help us understand the crisis that he and his wife currently face. Social theories on family dynamics, ethnicity and culture, social move-ments, socioeconomic class, and social institutions would provide invaluable informa-tion about the various interacting systems in which Sean's life is embedded. This use of multiple perspectives to understand human behavior is consistent with social work's focus on changing configurations of person and environment.

However, the biopsychosocial framework omits an important dimension of human existence: spirituality. This omission seems antithetical to social work's commitment to holistic practice. What would be gained if we added a spiritual lens to our attempt to understand Sean's life? And how would this perspective help you as a social worker in working with Sean and his wife in their current life situation?

The Meaning of Spirituality

The concept of spirituality is often confused with religion. But recent social work literature includes a number of attempts to delineate these terms and distinguish them from one another. Edward Canda (1997) has analyzed the major themes in these various writings and proposes the following definitions:

■ **Spirituality** "relates to the person's search for a sense of meaning and morally fulfilling relationships between oneself, other people, the encompassing universe, and the ontological [metaphysical] ground of existence, whether a person understands this in terms that are theistic, atheistic, nontheistic, or any combination of these" (p. 302).

■ **Religion** "involves the patterning of spiritual beliefs and practices into social institutions, with community support and traditions maintained over time" (p. 303).

Thus, spirituality is a broader concept than religion, and spiritual expression may or may not involve a particular religious faith or religious institution. As we can see in Sean's story, his involvement in both the Catholic and Unitarian churches is only part of a larger spiritual journey that has included many different experiences and influences.

Regardless of the precise words that are used to capture the meaning of spirituality, it brings to mind many related themes. Exhibit 6.1 lists 20 symbolic themes of spirituality identified by Patrick O'Brien (1992). Sean's life story reveals a number of these themes or bridges to spiritual understanding: the nature and meaning of self and the

EXHIBIT 6.1

Symbolic Themes of Spirituality

1. Morality, ethics, justice, and right effort
2. The nature and meaning of self and the intention and purpose of human existence
3. Interconnection, wholeness, alignment, and integration of persons, place, time, and events
4. Creativity, inspiration, and intuition
5. Altruistic service for the benefit of others
6. The mystery and wonder that are woven into nature, the universe, and the unknown
7. Sociocultural-historical traditions, rituals, and myths
8. Virtues (such as compassion, universal love, peace, patience, forgiveness, hope, honesty, trust, faith)
9. Mystical, altered states of consciousness
10. Sexuality
11. Openness, willingness, surrender, and receptivity
12. The power of choice, freedom, and responsibility
13. Special wisdom or revealed knowledge
14. Prayer, meditation, and quiet contemplation
15. Answers to pain, suffering, and death
16. Identity and relation to the metaphysical ground of existence, ultimate reality, and life force
17. The relationship of cause and effect regarding prosperity and/or poverty
18. Beliefs or experiences related to intangible reality or the unobstructed universe
19. The path to enlightenment or salvation
20. Sensitive awareness of the earth and the nonhuman world

Source: Adapted from O'Brien, 1992.

intention and purpose of human existence; mystical, altered states of consciousness; prayer, meditation, and quiet contemplation; and answers to pain, suffering, and death.

Spirituality in the United States

The current spiritual landscape in the United States reveals both common threads and a colorful array of unique patterns. A number of polls have consistently reported that between 92% and 97% of Americans say they believe in God or a higher power, and 87% report that religion is either "very" or "fairly important" in life (Gallup & Lindsay, 1999). These statistics indicate a strong thread of spirituality in the United States. However, expressions of both religious and nonreligious spirituality have become increasingly diverse in the United States.

This diversity is due, in part, to ongoing schisms and divisions among many of the organized religions historically present within the United States. For example, the number of Christian denominations alone grew from 20 to more than 900 from 1800 to 1988 (Melton, 1993). In addition, there has been a significant rise in other spiritual traditions with each new influx of immigrants from other parts of the world. They have brought their faith in not only those traditions recognized as major religions (e.g., Islam, Buddhism, Confucianism, Hinduism) but also various forms of spiritualism, folk healing, and shamanism (e.g., Santeria, *espiritismo,* vodoun, *cuanderismo, krou kmer, mudang*). This trend is further augmented by a growing interest among European Americans in Middle Eastern and Eastern religions (e.g., Islam, Buddhism, and Hinduism) and earth-based spiritualities (e.g., Neopaganism, Goddess worship, and deep ecology). There has also been a revived or more visible involvement in traditional spiritual paths among indigenous American people, as increasing numbers of Native Americans explore their tribal traditions or combine these traditions with faith in Christianity. Many of these "new" religions are among the fastest growing in the United States, although their overall numbers are still relatively small. Exhibit 6.2 shows the top 10 religions in the United States, along with their growth rates since 1990.

It should be noted that estimates of members of any particular religious group vary widely depending on the source, data collection methods, and definition of "adherents" (e.g., self-identified, formal membership, regular participant). For example, figures for adherents of Islam groups range from 1 million to 8 million; adherents of Judaism from 1 million to 5 million; adherents of Buddhism from 1 million to 5 million; and adherents to Neopagan groups from 10,000 to 770,000 (Canda & Furman, 1999; *Major Branches of Religion,* 2001).

As tempting as it is to make overarching statements based on statistics on belief in God and religious identification—for example, that Americans are highly religious—we must be cautious in drawing specific conclusions, as the picture changes depending on

EXHIBIT 6.2

Top 10 Religions in the United States

Religion	1990 Estimates	2001 Estimates	% of U.S. Population in 2000	% Change 1990-2000
Christianity	151,225,000	159,030,000	76.5%	+ 5%
Judaism	3,137,000	2,831,000	1.3%	− 10%
Islam	527,000	1,104,000	0.5%	+ 109%
Buddhism	401,000	1,082,000	0.5%	+ 170%
Hinduism	227,000	766,000	0.4%	+ 237%
Unitarian-Universalist	502,000	629,000	0.3%	+ 25%
Wiccan/Pagan/Druid		307,000	0.1%	
Spiritualist		116,000	< 0.1%	
Native American Religion	47,000	103,000	< 0.1%	+ 119%
Baha'i	28,000	84,000	< 0.1%	+ 200%

Source: Based on data drawn from the 1990 National Survey of Religious Identification (NSRI) and the 2001 American Religious Identity Survey (ARIS). These data are published online at www.gc/cuny.edu/studies/aris_index.htm.

the particular indicator. During the same period, 1991 to 1996, those self-identifying as "nonreligious or secular" increased 13.2% (*Major Branches of Religion,* 2001), and American adults who regularly attend religious services decreased from 49% to 36%, reflecting a worldwide trend among industrialized countries (Reeves, 1998). Other research findings report a rise of 4 percentage points (from 27% to 31%) in "unchurched" Americans (persons who have not gone to a religious service during the previous 6 months, excluding special events like weddings, funerals, and holidays). This rise does not seem remarkable except that it occurred in only 18 months, from January 1997 to July 1998 (Barma Research Group, n.d.). In another 1993 in-depth survey of about 4,000 American adults, 30% were totally secular in outlook, 29% were barely or nominally religious, 22% were modestly religious, and only 19% regularly practiced their religion (Reeves, 1998).

Interestingly, these figures emerge at a time when Americans are expressing an unprecedented interest in spirituality. In 1994, just 58% of Americans said they "feel the need in their lives to experience spiritual growth," but 82% made the same claim in 1998, 4 years later (Gallup & Lindsey, 1999, p. 1). It is apparent that this interest in spiritual growth may or may not be expressed within traditional religious institutions. Indeed, we seem to be witnessing a tremendous variety of spiritual paths evidenced by increased interest "in Eastern religions, in evangelical and fundamentalist teachings, in mysticism and New Age movements, in Goddess worship and other ancient religious rituals, in the mainline churches and synagogues, in Twelve-Step recovery groups, in concern about the environment, in holistic health, and in personal and social transformation" (Roof, 1993, p. 5).

Given this diversity, social workers may gain very little real understanding of a person by knowing her or his primary religious affiliation. First, religious affiliation may or may not hold great significance for the person, and identification with a religion alone does not indicate depth of involvement. Second, belief, practice, and involvement can be quite varied, even among adherents of the same spiritual tradition or among members of the same family, kinship group, or faith community—even if they all self-identify as Methodist or Muslim or Wiccan. Third, some people feel connected to multiple spiritual perspectives simultaneously, such as combining Judaism and Buddhism or traditional indigenous spiritual beliefs with Christianity. And finally, the meaning of religious or spiritual affiliation may change across the life span; a person may feel more or less connected to a spiritual tradition at different points in his or her life. As in Sean's case, it is important to understand the range of spiritual influences (both religious and nonreligious) that may contribute to anyone's life story at any particular time.

Transpersonal Theories of Human Development

The idea that spirituality is an important dimension of human behavior is not a new one in social work or in the other helping professions. Although Sigmund Freud (1928) asserted that all religious and spiritual beliefs were either illusions or projections of unconscious wishes, many other early behavioral science theorists viewed the role of spirituality differently.

Psychodynamic perspective, Developmental perspective

Notably, Carl Jung, a student of Freud's, differed with his former teacher and mentor in regard to the topic of spirituality. Jung's (1933) theory of personality includes physical, mental, and spiritual selves, which all strive for unity and wholeness within each person. In Jung's view, an important archetype (a universal unconscious idea) is the Spirit (1959, p. 214). Jung further proposed that the evolution of consciousness and the struggle to find a spiritual outlook on life were the primary developmental tasks in midlife. If successfully accomplished, the result was *individuation,* which he defined as "the moment when the finite mind realizes it is rooted in the infinite" (Keutzer, 1982, p. 76).

Psychodynamic perspective

Robert Assagioli (1965, 1973), in an approach known as *psychosynthesis,* also emphasized the spiritual dimension. His view of the human psyche includes the constructs of "higher unconscious" or "superconscious" as the source of creativity and spirituality. In Assagioli's view, some psychological disturbances are best understood as crises of spiritual awakening rather than symptoms of psychopathology. In such cases, the responsibility of the therapist is to facilitate the client's exploration of spiritual possibilities while dealing with the difficulties that such awakenings can engender. As Assagioli defined it, "'spiritual' refers not only to experiences traditionally considered religious but to *all* the states of awareness, all the human functions and activities which have as their common denominator the possession of *values* higher than average" (1989, p. 30).

Humanistic
perspective

A third major contributor to early formulations on spirituality and human behavior was Abraham Maslow, founding father of humanistic psychology. Maslow described spirituality as innate and a key element in human nature (1971). In his study of optimally functioning people, he characterized people at the top of his hierarchy as "transcendent self-actualizers" and described them as having (among other traits) a more holistic view of life; a natural tendency toward cooperative action; a tendency to be motivated by truth, goodness, and unity; a greater appreciation for peak experiences; an ability to go beyond their ego self to higher levels of identity; and more awareness of the sacredness of every person and of every living thing. Maslow later came to believe that even this definition was not adequate to explain the highest levels of human potential. Near the end of his life, he predicted the emergence of a more expansive understanding of human behavior: "a still 'higher' Fourth psychology, transpersonal, trans-human, centered in the cosmos, rather than in human needs and interests, going beyond humanness, identity, self-actualization, and the like" (Wittine, 1987, p. 53).

Describing this evolution of forces within psychology, Au-Deane Cowley (1993, 1996) delineates four major therapeutic approaches that have emerged over the past century, each developed in response to our understanding of human behavior and human needs at the time:

Psychodynamic
perspective

1. **First Force therapies** are based on dynamic theories of human behavior. The prime concern of these therapies is dealing with repression and resolving instinctual conflicts by developing insight.

Social behavioral
perspective

2. **Second Force therapies** evolved from behavioral theories. These therapies focus on learned habits and seek to remove symptoms through various processes of direct learning.

Humanistic perspective

3. **Third Force therapies** are rooted in experiential/humanistic/existential theories. They help the person deal with existential despair and seek the actualization of the person's potential through techniques grounded in immediate experiencing.

4. **Fourth Force therapies**, based on transpersonal theories, specifically target the spiritual dimension. They focus on helping the person let go of ego attachments—external identifications with the mind and body—and transcend the self through various spiritually based practices (Cowley, 1996).

The Fourth Force builds upon the previous three forces and thus incorporates existing knowledge concerning human behavior within its framework. What differentiates the Fourth Force—the **transpersonal approach**—from other theoretical orientations is the premise that some states of human consciousness and potential go beyond our traditional views of health and normality. These states explicitly address the spiritual dimension of human existence (Cowley & Derezotes, 1994).

The term *transpersonal* literally means "beyond" or "through" the "persona" or "mask" (Wittine, 1987). When applied to theories of human behavior, *transpersonal* means going beyond identity rooted in the individual body or ego to include spiritual experience or higher levels of consciousness. A major objective of transpersonal theories is to integrate spirituality within a larger framework of human behavior.

Two theorists who have developed comprehensive perspectives on spiritual development are James Fowler and Ken Wilber. Although these two theorists are certainly not the only writers in this area, they have produced two of the best-known and most widely used models of spiritual development in the field today. The following sections provide an overview of these two transpersonal theories of human behavior and a consideration of Sean's search for purpose, connection, and meaning from each perspective.

Fowler's Stages of Faith Development

Developmental perspective

James Fowler's (1981) theory of faith development grew out of 359 in-depth interviews conducted between 1972 and 1981 in Boston, Chicago, and Toronto. The sample was overwhelmingly white (97.8%), largely Christian (over 85%), evenly divided by gender, and widely distributed in terms of age (3.5 years to 84 years). Each semistructured interview consisted of more than 30 questions about life-shaping experiences and relationships, present values and commitments, and religion. After the responses were analyzed, interviewees were placed in one of six **faith stages** (see Exhibit 6.3). Fowler found a generally positive relationship between age and stage development; as age increased, so did the tendency for persons to be in higher stages. However, only a minority of persons revealed characteristics of Stages 5 or 6, regardless of age.

To Fowler, **faith** is broader than religious faith, creed, or belief. It can, in fact, be expressed even by people who do not believe in God. Instead, faith is a universal aspect of human existence, "an integral, centering process, underlying the formation of beliefs, values, and meanings that (1) gives coherence and direction to people's lives, (2) links them in shared trusts and loyalties with others, (3) grounds their personal stances and communal loyalties in a sense of relatedness to a larger frame of reference, and (4) enables them to face and deal with the limited conditions of life, relying upon that which has the quality of ultimacy in their lives" (Fowler, 1996, p. 56). Faith as defined by Fowler is similar to the definition of spirituality given at the beginning of this chapter and is clearly distinguished from more particular notions of belief or religion.

Another important concept in Fowler's theory is the **ultimate environment** (also known as the ultimate reality or simply the ultimate)—the highest level of

(text continued on page 238)

EXHIBIT 6.3
Fowler's Faith Stages

Faith Stage	Life Stage	Major Characteristics	Form of Logic (Piaget)	Form of Moral Judgment (Kohlberg)
Prestage: Primal faith	Infancy	Learn to trust (or not trust) immediate environment, develop sense of object permanence, and form first preimages or sense of the ultimate. If consistent nurturance is experienced, develop a sense of trust and safety about the universe and the divine. Conversely, negative experiences produce images of the ultimate as untrustworthy, punitive, or arbitrary. Sets the stage for further faith development. Transition to next stage begins with integration of thought and languages, which facilitates use of symbols in speech and play.		
Stage 1: Intuitive-projective faith	Early childhood	Generally emerges in children aged 2 to 7, who have new tools of speech and symbolic representation. Thought patterns are generally fluid and magical, and ways of knowing are based in intuition and imagination. Awareness of self is egocentric, with little ability to take the perspective of others. Have first awareness of death and sex and learn familial and cultural taboos. Faith is fantasy-filled and imitative and can be powerfully influenced by examples, modes, actions, and stories of significant others. Because faith images at this stage can be long-lasting, it is important to honor the child's own process of faith development. Stage normally ends at age 6 or 7, but may be found in adolescents or adults experiencing psychological difficulties. Transition to next stage is facilitated by emergence of concrete operational thinking and resolution of Oedipal issues.	Preoperational	Punishment/ reward

(continued)

EXHIBIT 6.3
Fowler's Faith Stages *(continued)*

Faith Stage	Life Stage	Major Characteristics	Form of Logic (Piaget)	Form of Moral Judgment (Kohlberg)
Stage 2: Mythic-literal faith	Middle childhood and beyond	Generally begins between ages 7 and 8, when child takes or stories, beliefs, and practices that symbolize belonging to his or her community. High level of conformity (reciprocal fairness) to community beliefs and practices, and symbols are seen as one-dimensional and literal in meaning. Authority and tradition very powerful influences as child incorporates moral rules and attitudes of community. Ability to engage in concrete operations allows distinction between fantasy and reality, which reorders imaginative picture of the world developed in Stage 1. Narrative and story are very important as the major way of gaining coherence and meaning of experiences; thus, child can be deeply affected by symbolic and dramatic presentations concerning the ultimate reality. Increased capacity to take perspective of others and ideas about reciprocity and fairness become central. Majority of persons in this stage are in elementary school, but can be found in some adolescents and adults. Transition to next stage occurs with breakdown of literalism, disillusionment with previous teachers, and clashes or conflicts between accounts by various authority figures (e.g., creation story vs. theory of evolution). Movement into Piaget's formal operational thought and development of capacity for mutual perspective taking allows for deeper reflection and creates need for more personal relationship with the ultimate in the next stage.	Concrete operational	Instrumental hedonism (reciprocal fairness)

(continued)

EXHIBIT 6.3

Fowler's Faith Stages (continued)

Faith Stage	Life Stage	Major Characteristics	Form of Logic (Piaget)	Form of Moral Judgment (Kohlberg)
Stage 3: Synthetic-conventional faith	Adolescence and beyond	Capacity for abstract thinking and manipulation of concepts affects process of developing both identity and faith. Environment broadens and increased influence of peers, school and work associates, and media and popular culture. Authority perceived as external and is found in traditional authority figures (parents, teachers) or valued groups (peers). Images of the ultimate reflect qualities experienced in personal relationships (e.g., compassion exhibited by parent or teacher). Beliefs and values often deeply felt, but are primarily tacit rather than critically examined. Person has an ideology, or outlook, but has not systematically reflected on it and is largely unaware of having it. Differences in outlook between people understood as differences in "kinds" of people. Symbols are not perceived as literally as in Stage 2, but symbols that evoke deep meaning and loyalty are not seen as separate from what they represent. Although this stage is most evident in adolescence, a considerable number of adults also fall within this stage, and it can become long-lasting or permanent. Factors leading to transition to next stage include serious clashes or contradictions between authority figures, changes in previously sanctioned religious practices or policies, experiences that lead to critical reflection about one's own beliefs and values, or experience of "leaving home"—physically or emotionally.	Early formal operations	Interpersonal expectations and concordance
Stage 4: Individuative-Reflective faith	Young adulthood and beyond	Stage of increased responsibility for one's commitments, lifestyle, beliefs, and attitudes. Constructs an individual self (identity) and outlook (ideology) from previously held	Formal operations (dichotomizing)	Societal perspective: reflective

(continued)

EXHIBIT 6.3

Fowler's Faith Stages (continued)

Faith Stage	Life Stage	Major Characteristics	Form of Logic (Piaget)	Form of Moral Judgment (Kohlberg)
		conventional faith. Requires struggling with unavoidable tensions (e.g., individuality vs. being defined by group membership; subjectivity and unexamined feelings vs. objectivity and critical reflection; self-fulfillment and self-actualization vs. service to and being for others; commitment to the relative vs. struggle with the possibility of an absolute). Previously held creeds, symbols, and stories are demythologized through critical analysis. The ultimate becomes more explicit and personally meaningful, and symbols are reshaped into more powerful conceptualizations. Goal is to create a rational, workable, and personal worldview or faith. Ideal time for movement into Stage 4 is early to mid-20s, but for many this transition occurs during the 30s or 40s (if at all). Process creates significant upheaval and can last for 5 to 7 years or longer. Transition to the next stage begins with a growing awareness of the paradoxes and complexities of life and increased attention to inner voices and images that have previously been submerged or set aside.		relativism or class-biased universalism
Stage 5: Conjunctive faith	Midlife and beyond	Most people do not reach Stage 5; only one of six interviewees in Fowler's sample fit the characteristics of this stage, and no one prior to midlife. Involves the integration of what has been suppressed or unrecognized during rational certainty of Stage 4. Must rework the past and be open to "voices of the "deeper self." Requires capacity for "both/and" vs. "either/or" thinking; polarities are not seen as problems but as realities to be accepted (e.g., both determinism and free will play a role in life;	Formal operations (dialectical)	Prior to society: principled higher law (universal and critical)

(continued)

EXHIBIT 6.3

Fowler's Faith Stages (continued)

Faith Stage	Life Stage	Major Characteristics	Form of Logic (Piaget)	Form of Moral Judgment (Kohlberg)
		the ultimate is experienced as both personal and abstract; humanity is understood as both good and evil). Symbolic power reunited with conceptual meaning at deeper level (e.g., cross is both a symbol of the crucifixion of Christ and representation of sacrifice or death and rebirth). Person strives to unify opposites in mind and in experience. Increased openness to the truths of those who are "other" and critical examination of one's social constructions (e.g., myths, ideal images, and prejudices internalized as a result of membership in certain social class, religious tradition, ethnic group, etc.). Definition of "community" expands beyond own immediate environment and faith community to encompass all human beings. Recognition that one's personal faith, however defined, is of supreme value and commitments based on this faith must be carried out despite consequences. Ready to expend energies in service of generating identity and meaning within the lives of others. Transition to next stage (experienced by very few) comes when person can no longer live with the paradoxical and divided world of Stage 5 and is willing to make sacrifices required of Universalizing faith.		
Stage 6: Universalizing faith		Able to confront dilemmas faced in Stage 5 because of ability to truly embrace paradox. Injustice seen more clearly because of enlarged awareness of demands of justice. Partial truths recognized because of expanded vision of truth. Symbols, myths, and rituals appreciated and cherished at deeper level because of knowledge	Formal operations (synthetic)	Loyalty to being

(continued)

EXHIBIT 6.3

Fowler's Faith Stages (continued)

Faith Stage	Life Stage	Major Characteristics	Form of Logic (Piaget)	Form of Moral Judgment (Kohlberg)
		of depth of reality that symbols, myths, and rituals reflect. Divisions within human family felt with vivid pain because of recognition of possibility of inclusive union of all beings. Stage 6 persons move beyond these universalizing understandings to action, regardless of threats to self, to primary groups, or to institutional arrangements of society. Become disciplined, activist embodiment of imperatives of love and justice. Live sacrificial life aimed at transformation of humankind. Very few persons reach this stage; Fowler identifies Gandhi, Mother Teresa, and Martin Luther King Jr. Although Universalizers are not "perfect," they shake up notions of normalcy and call into question the compromise arrangements that most people accept. As such, Universalizers "lean into the future of God for all being" (p. 211).		

Source: Fowler, 1981.

reality. Faith is not only your internal image of the ultimate environment, but also your relationship with that image. Your view of the ultimate environment—as personal or impersonal, trustworthy or not dependable, capable of dialogue or silent, purposeful or based on chance—and your relationship with it is an evolving, dynamic process that is strongly influenced by your experiences throughout the life course.

Fowler's stages of faith development should not be viewed as goals to be achieved or as steps necessary for "salvation." Rather, they help us understand a person's values, beliefs, and sense of meaning and help us better appreciate the tasks, tensions, and challenges at various points in life. They also reveal increasing capacity in terms of cognitive functioning; moral reasoning; perspective taking; critical reflection and dialectical thought; understanding of symbols, myths, and rituals; deeper faith commitments; and openness and acceptance of difference.

Now let us consider Sean's story through the lens of Fowler's faith stages, based on both Fowler's early research and later theoretical refinements. As you read through these descriptions, refer to Exhibit 6.3, which summarizes some of the features of each faith stage and correlates Fowler's stages with Piaget's stages of cognitive development and Kohlberg's stages of moral development (both described in Chapter 4).

In Fowler's model, our early experiences set the stage for later faith development. Given what we know about Sean's family at the time of his birth, it is probably safe to assume that Sean was able to develop at least a "good enough" fund of basic trust and mutuality during the *Prestage: Primal faith* for later development of a relationship with the ultimate.

Sean's story does not tell us much about the development of his early images of the ultimate environment during *Stage 1: Intuitive-projective faith.* However, we can speculate that many of these images were drawn from his family's Catholic faith. In working with Sean, we would want to understand how this process of image making was handled by his family and others in his life, and how much support he was given for his own intuition and imagination during this time.

If Fowler had interviewed Sean at age 10 before his uncle's death, Sean more than likely would have reflected many of the aspects of *Stage 2: Mythic-literal faith.* As you remember from Sean's story, the Catholic church was a central force in both his family and his community. Sean had learned much about the world and his place in it from the rich narratives and symbols of the Catholic religion, and they helped create a sense of order and meaning in his life. He felt a strong sense of guidance and belonging in this faith community. It would be useful to know what meaning Sean made of the deaths of both his uncle and father, based on the narratives and practices he was exposed to in his faith community. These early losses, and his family's responses to them, were undoubtedly major factors in Sean's continuing faith development as he moved into adolescence.

The events that occurred in Sean's life prior to and during his adolescence probably had a profound effect on his faith development during *Stage 3: Synthetic-conventional faith.* Not only did he lose his uncle and his father, but these losses strongly affected his family system for some time. It is easy to imagine that Sean experienced this period as a series of betrayals—betrayed by his father for leaving him (emotionally after Uncle Elliott's death and then physically by dying himself); betrayed by his mother for becoming so engrossed in her own concerns that she grew distant with her son; betrayed by the church and its teachings for not being able to bring real comfort to his family during these crises; and even betrayed by God, with whom he could not seem to connect during this time. This sense of betrayal at many levels probably led him to reject his earlier faith conceptualizations somewhat prematurely and created difficulties for him as he moved into young adulthood.

If we look at Sean's life during his late adolescence and early 20s (*Stage 4: Individual-reflective faith*), we see a young man in turmoil. Having rejected the faith structures of his childhood, he is drawn to the worldview of the people he meets at college and the new and unorthodox ideas circulating during the late 1960s and early 1970s. He sets his heart on resistance to the old structures, and he buries his pain in mind-altering substances. He finds passion and purpose in politics and in personal relationships. He is indeed critical of the values, beliefs, and symbols of his past, but is this really a process of critical examination? He is certainly trying to express his individuality, but is he really developing a personal self (identity) and outlook (**ideology**)?

Using Fowler's framework as a guide, it could be argued that Sean does not truly move into Stage 4 until after his experience in the woods, when he feels his father's presence and decides to go home and work things out with his family. It is only after he deals with the pain and unresolved losses of his childhood and his own self-destructive behaviors that he truly begins to critically examine his past beliefs and construct his own worldview. He is assisted in this process by his relationship with his wife, Nancy, who also appears to be engaged in her own evolving faith identity. As they both move into their 30s, they take on the serious responsibility of defining their own commitments, lifestyle, values, and beliefs.

We see glimpses of emerging *Stage 5: Conjunctive faith* in Sean's story as he moves into midlife. We know that with his wife, Sean purposefully studied different religious and spiritual traditions and was able to identify and appreciate common truths from various paths. Sean has also integrated different spiritual practices into his daily life as part of his spiritual journey. Both Sean and Nancy have developed a broad social consciousness and embrace a sense of community that is larger than their own immediate network. There are also signs of commitment to faith generativity, not only with their own sons but with a wider circle of persons as well. Further clarity about how far Sean has moved into Conjunctive faith would be helpful in order to understand how well he will be able to deal with the paradox of both crisis and opportunity inherent in his wife's current illness. An understanding of faith stage development would also be useful in helping both Sean and Nancy garner the supports they will need in the weeks and months ahead.

Finally, it is clear that Sean is not at *Stage 6: Universalizing faith.* Given the rarity of such persons, it is unlikely that he will develop into this stage. Sean is probably best characterized as in transition from Stage 4 (Individuative-reflective faith) to Stage 5 (Conjunctive faith).

Wilber's Full-Spectrum Model of Consciousness

Developmental perspective

Ken Wilber first published his transpersonal theory of development in *The Spectrum of Consciousness* in 1977, but continues to develop and refine the model in numerous writings. His work reflects a unique integration of biology, history, psychology, sociology, philosophy, and religion. It is rooted in both conventional Western approaches and Eastern contemplative traditions. Wilber's overall model is comprehensive and complex, addressing development at both the individual and collective (or social) levels. Wilber's most recent ideas about individual development (see Wilber, 1995, 1996, 1997; Wilber, Engler, & Brown, 1986) are summarized here.

Wilber's full-spectrum model of consciousness has three major components:

1. **Basic structures** are those deep and inherent levels of consciousness that, once they emerge during development, tend to remain in existence throughout the life of the individual. Wilber posits 10 major structures or levels of consciousness, all of which are potentially present at the onset of development, but each of which emerges sequentially, one level at a time. Levels cannot be skipped over, and each level incorporates the capacities of earlier levels. This process of incorporation is rooted in the concept of *holons,* or "that which, being a *whole* in one context, is simultaneously a *part* in another" (Wilber, 1995, p. 18). Thus, Wilber refers to his spectrum of consciousness as a *holarchy* (rather than a hierarchy), because it reflects an ordering of holons (or increasing levels of complexity and wholeness) throughout the developmental process.

2. **Transitional structures** are temporary or stage-specific perspectives or worldviews. In describing how human beings move through the basic structures or levels of consciousness, Wilber uses the metaphor of a ladder. The basic structures themselves he likens to the rungs of the ladder. When a person moves from one rung to the next, he or she temporarily gains a different perspective or worldview, including a different *self-identity,* a different *self-need,* and a different *moral stance.* New perspectives eventually replace these transitional structures, but the actual rungs (or basic structures) remain in existence and are an enduring part of the person. To illustrate the distinction between basic and transitional structures, Wilber points to the differences between Piaget's stages of cognitive development and Kohlberg's stages of moral development. In cognition, when a person moves to Level 4 (formal operations), the cognitive structures of earlier stages (sensorimotor, preoperational, concrete operational) are not lost, but are

still accessible to the person; they remain as basic structures. In moral development, however, higher stages replace lower stages, in that a person does not simultaneously act from Stage 1 (preconventional) and Stage 5 (postconventional) morality; thus, these stages are transitional structures.

3. **Self system** refers to the person climbing the ladder of spiritual development. The self system (or self) mediates between the basic structures and the transitional stages. It is also the locus of several crucial capacities and operations: *identification,* or the locus of self-identity; *organization,* or that which gives cohesiveness to the psyche; *will,* or the locus of choice within the constraints of the present developmental level; *defense,* or the locus of phase-specific and phase-appropriate defense mechanisms; *metabolism,* or the ability to metabolize or "digest" experience; and *navigation,* or the capacity to make developmental choices by moving up or down the developmental ladder or staying at a particular level.

As a person negotiates each unfolding basic structure, he or she moves from a narrower to a wider self-identity. At each point, the self goes though a **fulcrum,** or switch point, in its development. Specifically, each time the self steps up to a new rung on the developmental ladder, it goes through a three-step process. First, the self becomes comfortable and eventually identifies with the basic functioning of that level. Second, new experiences begin to challenge the way of being at this level, and the self begins to differentiate or "disidentify" with it. Third, the self begins to move toward and identify with the next level while integrating the functioning of the previous basic structure into the new organization. If the person is able to negotiate these fulcrum points successfully, development is largely nonproblematic. However, disturbances at the different fulcrum points produce various pathologies. Although Wilber lists specific types of pathology at each level, he also states that we must take into account "the standard cautions and qualifications . . . [of] no pure cases, the influence of cultural influences, genetic predispositions, genetic and traumatic arrests, and blended cases" (1996, p. 107).

Wilber has an additional caveat: although the process of development in his model is hierarchical (or "holarchical"), it is not strictly linear. Rather, it involves "all sorts of regressions, spirals, temporary leaps forward, peak experiences, and so on" (Wilber, 1996, p. 148). A person does not have to master all the competencies of one level to move into the next; in fact, the self at any given level will often respond about 50% from one level, 25% from the level above, and 25% from the level below. Furthermore, people can have a spiritual or peak experience at any level, but they will have to make sense of this experience within their current stage and may have to grow and develop further to really accommodate the full depth or meaning of that experience. As Wilber puts it, "They still have to go from acorn to oak if they are going to become one with the forest" (1996, p. 152).

Exhibit 6.4 depicts Wilber's 10 basic structures or stages of consciousness, along with their corresponding fulcrums, pathologies, and treatment modalities. His model is rooted in the "perennial philosophy," which he states is evident across all cultures and across all ages. Also referred to as the Great Chain of Being, this philosophy proposes that reality or consciousness moves from matter to body to mind to soul to spirit. Wilber's spectrum of consciousness can be further categorized into the three phases of development: the Prepersonal or Preegoic Phase, the Personal or Egoic Phase, and the Transpersonal or Transegoic Phase.

The specific stages of consciousness at both the Prepersonal and Personal phases in Wilber's theory are very similar to the first five stages of Fowler's faith stages, and will not be presented in detail here. (See Wilber, 1995, 1996, 1997, and Wilber et al., 1986, for a detailed discussion of these phases.) A review of the stages of the Prepersonal and Personal phases of consciousness should sound familiar to students of conventional approaches to human development. In contrast, the stages of the Transpersonal phase (and the language used to describe them) are most likely unfamiliar to those who are not well versed in contemplative Eastern ideas about human development. However, this synthesis of both conventional and contemplative approaches and the inclusion of "higher-order" levels of development is Wilber's primary contribution to our attempts to understand human behavior.

As a prelude to the transpersonal or transegoic phase, the observing self becomes aware of both the mind and the body as *experiences* and thus has the capacity to *transcend* ego-based reality. Thus, the person can move beyond egocentrism and ethnocentrism to embrace a worldcentric awareness of the complete interdependence of all things in the cosmos. The person retains all the capacities developed during previous levels but is able to incorporate these functions into new levels of consciousness at the Transpersonal phase. The transformation occurs in three stages, which are Wilber's Stages 7, 8, and 9:

- *Stage 7: Psychic stage* is characterized by a continuing evolution of consciousness as the observing self develops more and more depth. Wilber refers to this evolving inner sense as the Witness, because it represents an awareness that moves beyond ordinary reality (sensorimotor, rational, existential) into the transpersonal (beyond ego) levels. A distinguishing spiritual experience at this stage is a strong interconnectedness of self with nature. For example, a person may temporarily "become one" with a mountain or bird or tree. This type of experience is not psychotic fusion—the person is still very clear about his or her own personal boundaries—but it is a strong awareness of communion with the natural world. At this point, one's higher self becomes a World Soul and experiences *nature mysticism*. Because of this powerful experience of connection and identification, there is a natural deepening of compassion for all living things, including nature itself.

EXHIBIT 6.4
Wilber's Full Spectrum of Consciousness

Phase of Development	Stage	Basic Structures of Consciousness	Corresponding Fulcrums	Characteristic Pathologies	Treatment Modalities
				Nondual	**Nondual**
Transpersonal or Trans-egoic	9	Causal	F-9	Causal pathology	Formless mysticism
	8	Subtle	F-8	Subtle pathology	Deity mysticism
	7	Psychic	F-7	Psychic disorders	Nature mysticism
Personal or Egoic	6	Centauric or Vision-Logic	F-6	Existential pathology	Existential therapy
	5	Formal-Reflexive Mind (formal operations)	F-5	Identity neuroses	Introspection
	4	Rule/Role Mind (concrete operations)	F-4	Script pathology (problems with roles or rules)	Script analysis
Prepersonal or Pre-egoic	3	Representational-Mind	F-3	Psychoneuroses	Uncovering techniques
	2	Phantasmic-Emotional	F-2	Narcissistic-borderline	Structuring/building techniques
	1	Sensoriphysical	F-1	Psychoses	Physiological/pacification techniques
	0	Primary Matrix	F-0	Perinatal pathology	Intense regressive therapies

Source: Wilber, 1996; Robbins, Chatterjee, & Canda, 1998a.

■ *Stage 8 (Subtle stage)* is characterized by an awareness of more subtle processes than are commonly experienced in gross, ordinary states of waking consciousness. Examples of such processes are interior light and sounds; awareness of transpersonal archetypes; and extreme states of bliss, love, and compassion. At this point, even nature is transcended, yet understood as a manifest expression of the ultimate. One's sense of connection and identification is extended to communion with the Deity, or union with God, by whatever name. Thus, consciousness at this level is not just nature mysticism—union with the natural world—but gives way to *deity mysticism.* This level of consciousness can be experienced in many forms, often rooted in the person's personal or cultural history. For example, a Christian may feel union with Christ, and a Buddhist might experience connection with the Buddha.

■ *Stage 9 (Causal stage)* transcends all distinctions between subject and object (even self and God). The Witness is experienced as pure consciousness, pure awareness, and prior to the manifestation of anything. Thus, this state is said to be timeless, spaceless, and objectless. As Wilber describes it, "Space, time, objects—all of those merely parade by. But you are the Witness, the pure Seer that is itself pure Emptiness, pure Freedom, pure Openness, the great Emptiness through which the entire parade passes, never touching you, never tempting you, never hurting you, never consoling you" (1996, p. 224). This state is pure *formless mysticism,* in that all objects, even God as a perceived form, vanish into pure consciousness. This stage of consciousness is sometimes referred to as the "full Enlightenment, ultimate release, pure nirvana" (1996, p. 226). But it is still not the final story.

Wilber also proposes a *Stage 10 (Nondual),* so to speak, which is characterized by disidentification with even the Witness. (This stage is represented in Exhibit 6.4 by the word "Nondual" in the space surrounding the other stages.) The interior sense of *being* a Witness disappears, and the Witness turns out to be everything that is witnessed. Emptiness is a level of awareness at that particular state (awareness of pure consciousness without form) in the causal stage. But in the Nondual stage, Emptiness becomes pure Consciousness itself. There is no sense of "two," there is only "one" (hence the name Nondual). Essentially, the person's awareness has moved beyond nature, Deity, and formless mysticism to *nondual mysticism.* Furthermore, it is not really a stage among other stages but is rather the condition or reality of *all* stages. It is simultaneously the source, the process, and the realization of consciousness. Wilber describes it as "the Ground or Suchness or Isness of *all* stages, at all times, in all dimensions: the Being of all beings, the Condition of all conditions, the Nature of all Natures" (1995, p. 301). Wilber does not depict the Nondual as a separate stage in his illustration of the structures of consciousness, because it represents the ground or origin of all the other stages—the paper on which the figure is drawn.

With this model, Wilber is proposing that the personal level of development, with its achievement of strong ego development and self-actualization, is not the highest potential of human existence. Rather, the ultimate goal of human development is the transpersonal or "spirit" level—beyond ego or self to self-transcendence and unity with the ultimate reality. The capacity for attaining the highest levels of consciousness is innate within each human being, although Wilber acknowledges that very few people reach the higher transpersonal levels. He describes these individuals as "a rather small pool of daring men and women—both yesterday and today—who have bucked the system, fought the average and the normal, and struck out toward the new and higher spheres of awareness" (Wilber, 1996, p. 198).

As for the characteristic pathologies, or problems in development at each stage, all the disorders or conditions listed in Exhibit 6.4 for the lower phases of development are well recognized within conventional diagnostic approaches (albeit with different labels). It is again at the Transpersonal level that Wilber strikes new ground, by including what he calls psychic disorders and subtle or causal pathologies. Examples of such problems in living include unsought spiritual awakenings, psychic inflation, split life-goals, integration/identification failure, pseudo nirvana, and failure to differentiate or integrate. Wilber states that although these conditions are not well known, because most people do not reach these higher levels of development, they must be understood in order to be treated properly when they do occur.

Again, the treatment modalities listed in Exhibit 6.4 at the Prepersonal and Personal levels are well known to most social workers. However, the approaches that Wilber proposes for Transpersonal level disorders—nature mysticism, deity mysticism, and formless mysticism—are largely unknown (and sound a bit strange) to the majority of helping professionals. But they have been used in non-Western cultures for centuries. Furthermore, they are becoming more widely accepted in this country as effective, alternative treatment approaches (as in meditation/yoga, visualization, dreamwork, disidentification techniques, body work, acupuncture, journaling, intuition techniques, and the like). Wilber stresses that practitioners should be able to correctly identify the level of development in order to provide the most appropriate treatment. If not, a problem at the Transpersonal level (such as a spiritual awakening) may be treated as if it were a Prepersonal or Personal disorder (a psychotic episode or existential crisis), or vice versa.

How do Wilber's ideas about the Transpersonal or Transegoic phase help us work with someone like Sean, who may be at a fulcrum point? We would have to talk with Sean more about his contemplative practices (meditation and shamanism) to see if he has begun to develop any of the capacities at the Psychic level (Stage 7) other than the one "inner vision" that he experienced when he was younger. It is quite possible that this early event represented a "peak experience" or a "peek" into transpersonal consciousness for Sean, although he was clearly not in a transpersonal level of development at the time.

Thus, he had to interpret this experience initially within his existing developmental stage (probably the beginning phase of the Formal-Reflexive Mind) and continue to revisit and "make meaning" of the experience as he moved into higher stages of consciousness. It is unlikely that Sean will move significantly into the Transpersonal phase of Wilber's developmental spectrum unless he makes deliberate and consistent efforts to engage in the extensive practices usually required to reach these higher stages of consciousness. Thus, we could support Sean's spiritual practices during this time while watching for signs of possible difficulties at the Transpersonal level.

A Critique of Fowler's and Wilber's Theories

Both Fowler's and Wilber's models of spiritual development reflect Fourth Force theory in that they incorporate the first three forces (dynamic, behavior, and experiential/humanistic/existential theories). In fact, both Fowler and Wilber use many of the same theorists as foundations for their own work (e.g., Piaget, Kohlberg, Maslow). And both are clearly proposing higher and more transcendent levels of human development than have been previously proposed by conventional theorists.

Conflict perspective

As developmental models, Fowler's and Wilber's models are open to the criticisms of all developmental perspectives, including charges of dominant group bias. Such perspectives do not pay enough attention to social, economic, political, and historical factors and the role of power dynamics and oppression in human development. Developmental perspectives are also said to convey the idea that there is only one "right" way to proceed down the developmental path, and thus display an ethnocentrism often rooted in middle-class, heterosexual, Anglo-Saxon male life experience.

Both Fowler and Wilber might counter by pointing out that familial, cultural, and historical contexts are considered in their models. Wilber, in particular, would highlight the extensive use of cross-cultural knowledge in the development of his theory and point to the cessation of ethnocentrism as a major characteristic of his later stages of consciousness. Both would also support the notion of "many paths" in spiritual development, although they would say that these many paths have common features in their evolution.

Although Fowler's model was developed through an inductive research process and Wilber's formulations are grounded in multiple areas of research, there has been little attempt at empirical verification of either model. However, limited empirical exploration of Fowler's faith stages has provided partial support for his framework (Das & Harries, 1996; Furushima, 1983; Mischey, 1981; Swenson, Fuller, & Clements, 1993). The paucity of research is somewhat understandable, given the difficulties of empirical investigation in such an abstract realm. It is difficult enough to operationalize and measure such concepts as formal operational cognition or self-esteem; the challenge of investigating transcendence or a World Soul is even more daunting. Nonetheless, strategies from both positivist and constructivist research approaches are currently available to study interior states and subjective experiences of meaning, as well as biophysical manifestations of different states of consciousness. (See Chapters 1 and 2 for a review of positivist and constructivist research approaches.) As is true for all theories of human behavior, transpersonal models such as Fowler's and Wilber's need to be specifically tested and refined through the research process. Furthermore, this research must be replicated with different groups (defined by sex and gender, age, race, ethnicity, socioeconomic status, geopolitical membership, and the like) in order to explore the universality of the models.

The most obvious difference between the two models is that Wilber provides more substance and specification than Fowler does about what transpersonal levels of development look like and how they evolve. Wilber also provides much more detailed descriptions of the potential pitfalls of spiritual development than Fowler, who provides only a general overview of the possible dangers or deficits of development at each of his faith stages. However, Fowler provides more specification about the content and process of spiritual development at the prepersonal and personal levels. In terms of their utility for social work practice, we could say that Fowler's model is more descriptive and Wilber's more prescriptive.

Although only formulations concerning individual development have been presented here, Wilber has also developed stages of consciousness for larger systems. These sociocultural stages parallel the first six individual stages of consciousness and are referred to as Archaic, Magical, Mythic, Mythic-Rational, Rational, and Vision-Logic or Centauric (Wilber, 1995, 1996). These stages reflect changes in human evolution over time, including shifts in such areas as technological/economic production, gender roles, family and social organization, worldviews, and conceptualizations of religion and spirituality. Each era has a typical mode of consciousness, although some individuals are always at the cutting edge of spiritual development, helping to move humanity forward. Wilber states that we have moved as a human species to the beginning phases of the Vision-Logic or Centauric stage, as evidenced by an increase in global awareness and the beginnings of a transrational, transcultural, and worldcentric vision.

Although Fowler does not explicitly include sociocultural stages in his theory, his most recent writings also address the application of faith stages to larger systems (1996). He describes our current political and social landscape as a standoff between those with "orthodox" and "progressive" worldviews, each with their own different assessments of social, political, and economic reality. The orthodox worldview reflects the Synthetic-Conventional stage of faith development; the progressive perspective is grounded in the Individual-Reflective stage. Because of the standoff, Fowler states that we are locked in the either/or thinking of the "culture wars." He proposes that until we move as a society beyond orthodox and progressive paradigms to the Conjunctive faith stage (with its capacity for integrated, both/and thinking), we will not be able to effectively address the serious problems of our times. Such movement will require a different level of dialogue and debate about the role of spirituality in both our private and public lives. Although the level of specificity regarding spiritual development at the sociocultural level is very different for Fowler and Wilbur, both theorists are making connections between the individual and institutional levels of spiritual development.

In conclusion, both Fowler and Wilber provide perspectives beyond our traditional biopsychosocial framework that allow us to better understand people like Sean and suggest a direction for working with them in their life situations. However, we still need viable practice theories that explicitly address the spiritual dimension. An example of such a practice theory is Elizabeth Smith's "Trans-egoic Model" of intervention, originally developed for work with cancer patients and later expanded to apply to other issues of loss, such as divorce (Smith, 1995; Smith & Gray, 1995). This model outlines four therapeutic stages and specific techniques that could be quite useful in working with Sean and his family. However, it too must be tested and revised to determine its utility and applicability to a wide range of client situations.

The Role of Spirituality in Social Work

Interest in spirituality within the social work profession has progressed through three broad stages (Canda, 1997; Canda & Furman, 1999):

1. *Sectarian origins* (began with the colonial period and lasted through the early 20th century). Early human services and institutions were primarily influenced by Judeo-Christian worldviews on charity, communal responsibility, and justice (Fauri, 1988; Leiby, 1985; Lowenberg, 1988; Marty, 1980; Niebuhr, 1932; Popple & Leighninger, 1990). This period witnessed competing explanations of human behavior: an emphasis on distinguishing between moral blame and merit (e.g., the worthy and unworthy poor) versus a focus on social reform and social justice (e.g., Jewish communal service and the settlement house movement).

2. *Professionalization and secularization* (1920s through 1970s). Social work began to distance itself from its early sectarian roots. This movement mirrored a shift within the larger society, which began to replace moral explanations of human problems with a scientific, rational understanding. The social work profession increasingly relied on empiricism, secular humanism, and libertarian morality as the major foundation for its values, ethics, and practice approaches (Imre, 1984; Siporin, 1986). As this stage has been described, "Religion and spirituality were increasingly viewed, at best, as unnecessary and irrelevant, and, at worst, as illogical and pathological" (Russel, 1998, p. 17).

3. *Resurgence of interest in spirituality* (beginning in the 1980s and continuing through the present) (Canda, 1997; Russel, 1998). Indicators of this new phase within the profession include a marked increase in the numbers of publications and presentations on the topic, the development of a national Society for Spirituality and Social Work, and the reintroduction of references to religion and spirituality in the Council on Social Work Education's 1994 Curriculum Policy Statement and 2000 Educational Policy and Accreditation Standards after an absence of more than 20 years. Although the inclusion of spirituality within the profession is still somewhat controversial, discussion has largely shifted from whether the topic should be included to how to integrate spirituality within the profession in an ethical, effective, and spiritually sensitive manner (Canda & Furman, 1999; Sheridan, 2002). This trend toward reexamination and reintegration of spirituality within the profession reflects similar developments within the larger culture (Gallup & Lindsay, 1999).

Recent empirical studies reveal how social work is currently addressing the inclusion of spirituality in the profession. Several studies of social work practitioners have shown generally favorable attitudes toward the role of spirituality in practice and an understanding of the importance of spirituality in the lives of clients (Canda, 1988; Derezotes, 1995; Derezotes & Evans, 1995; Joseph, 1988; Sheridan, 2000; Sheridan & Bullis, 1991; Sheridan, Bullis, Adcock, Berlin, & Miller, 1992). Studies also report that the majority of social work educators and students favor inclusion of content on religion and spirituality in the social work curriculum either through electives, required courses, or infusion of material into existing courses (Dudley & Helfgott, 1990; Kaplan & Dziegielewski, 1999; Sheridan, Wilmer, & Atcheson, 1994; Sheridan & Amato-von Hemert, 1999). Others report steady increases in the number of courses on the topic in schools of social work across the country (Russel, 1998). Moreover, practitioners and students are already using several religiously oriented or spiritually sensitive intervention techniques with clients in their work settings or field placements (such as gathering information on clients' religious or spiritual backgrounds, using religious or spiritual language and concepts, recommending religious or spiritual programs, discussing religious beliefs, and praying for or with clients) (Bullis, 1996; Canda & Furman, 1999; Mattison, Jayaratne, & Croxton, 2000; Sheridan, 2000; Sheridan et al., 1992; Sheridan & Amato-von Hemert, 1999).

These results contrast with consistent findings that social workers report receiving very little education and training on religious or spiritual matters during their social work studies. Specifically, from 73% to more than 88% report "little or no" exposure to such material (Derezotes, 1995; Kaplan & Dziegielewski, 1999; Joseph, 1988; Sheridan, 2000; Sheridan & Amato-von Hemert, 1999; Sheridan et al., 1992; Sheridan et al., 1994). These findings raise concerns about how well social workers can address spiritual issues with clients.

Currently, two of the most often proposed rationales for including content on spirituality within social work education are the important roles it plays in both human diversity and overall human experience. Studies of social work educators (Sheridan et al., 1994) and students (Sheridan & Amato-von Hemert, 1999) reveal general endorsement of these two rationales, as reflected in the following statements:

- Religious and spiritual beliefs and practices are part of multicultural diversity. Social workers should have knowledge and skills in this area in order to work effectively with diverse client groups (90% of educators "strongly agree/agree"; 93% of students "strongly agree/agree").

- There is another dimension of human existence beyond the biopsychosocial framework that can be used to understand human behavior. Social work education should expand this framework to include the spiritual dimension (61% of educators "strongly agree/agree"; 72% of students "strongly agree/agree").

A growing body of literature reflects the relevance of spirituality for the profession in these two domains. The following sections provide a brief overview of this literature.

Spirituality and Human Diversity

Conflict
perspective

Commitment to issues of human diversity and to oppressed populations is a hallmark of the social work profession. At various times in history, some branches of organized religion have played a negative or impeding role in the attainment of social justice for various groups. Examples include the use of religious texts, policies, and practices to deny the full human rights of persons of color; women; and gay, lesbian, bisexual, and transgendered persons. At the same time, organized religion has a rich heritage of involvement in myriad social justice movements and causes, including the civil rights movement, the peace movement, the women's movement, the gay rights movement, abolition of the death penalty, and the deep ecology movement.

It is beyond the scope of this chapter to do an overall analysis of the role of religion in the struggle for social and economic justice. However, the following sections provide examples of the impact of both religious and nonreligious spirituality in the lives of oppressed groups as defined by race and ethnicity, sex and gender, and sexual orientation.

Race and Ethnicity. Spirituality expressed in both religious and nonreligious forms has been pivotal in the lives of many persons of color and other marginalized ethnic groups. This brief discussion of spirituality and race/ethnicity emphasizes common experiences and themes in order to provide a general overview. However, remember that a great deal of diversity exists within these groups and that every person's story will be unique.

1. *African Americans.* Religious affiliation for African Americans is generally high. Most African Americans today are Protestant (80%), 10% are Catholic, less than 1% are Jewish, and 5% report no or some other religious preference, including Islam (Corbett, 1997). African Americans compose about one third of the adherents to Islam in the United States, whether they are members of Sunni Islam or other mainstream Islamic denominations, the Nation of Islam, or smaller Black Muslim sects (Haddad, 1997). Black churches, in particular, have historically been a safe haven for African Americans facing racism and oppression, as well as an important source of social support, race consciousness and inspiration, leadership training, human services, and empowerment and social change (Bell & Bell, 1999; Eugene, 1995; Franklin, 1994; Logan, 1996; Moore, 1992; Taylor, Ellison, Chatters, Levin, & Lincoln, 2000). The legacy of slavery and the integrated heritage of African and African American spiritual values has emphasized collective unity and the connection of all beings: "I am because we are, and because we are, therefore, I am" (Nobles, 1980, p. 29). Afrocentric spirituality stresses the interdependence between God, community, family, and the individual. Its central virtues include beneficence to the community, forbearance through tragedy, wisdom applied to action, creative improvisation, forgiveness of wrongs and oppression, and social justice (Paris, 1995). Kwanzaa is an important nonsectarian Afrocentric spiritual tradition, which was developed by Maulana Karenga in the 1960s as a mechanism for celebrating and supporting African and African American strengths and empowerment. Seven principles represent the core values of Kwanzaa: *Umoja* (Unity), *Kujichagulia* (Self-determination), *Ujima* (Collective Work and Responsibility), *Ujamaa* (Collective Economics), *Nia* (Purpose), *Kuumba* (Creativity), and *Imani* (Faith) (Karenga, 1995). Many writers stress the importance of paying attention to the role of spirituality in its various forms when working with African American clients and communities (Eng & Hatch, 1992; Frame & Williams, 1996; Logan, Freeman, & McRoy, 1990; Richardson, 1991).

2. *Hispanic and Latino(a) Americans.* The majority (72%) are Roman Catholic (Curiel, 1995), but there is also a large and growing number (23%) of Protestants among this group (Castex, 1994). In addition, many Latino(a) people follow beliefs and practices that represent a blending of Christian, African, and indigenous spiritual traditions (Canda & Furman, 1999). Latino(a) American spirituality has been strongly affected by factors related to colonialism (Costas, 1991). This history includes military, political, economic, cultural, and religious conquest, forcing many indigenous peoples to take on the Catholicism of their conquerors. Many traditional places of worship, spiritual texts, beliefs, and practices were destroyed, repressed, or blended with Catholic traditions (Canda & Furman, 1999). Today, Christian Hispanic faith has these central features: a personal relationship with God that encompasses love and reverence as well as fear and dread; an emphasis on both faith and ritual behavior; belief in the holiness

of Jesus Christ as savior, king, and infant God; special reverence shown to Mary as the mother of God; recognition of saints as models of behavior and as benefactors; significance of sacred objects as both symbols of faith and transmitters of luck or magic; and special events and celebrations, such as saints' feast days, Holy Week, Christmas Eve, feasts of the Virgin, and life passages (e.g., baptisms, first communions, confirmations, coming-of-age ceremonies, weddings, and funerals) (Ramirez, 1985). In addition to mainstream religions, a number of African and indigenous spiritual healing traditions continue to be practiced by some Latino(a) groups today, including *curanderismo, santiguando, espiritismo,* Santeria, and vodoun (de la Rosa, 1988; Delgado, 1988; Paulino, 1995a, 1995b; Torrez, 1984). Social workers thus need to understand the importance of both religious institutions and folk healing traditions when working with Latino(a) populations. Their positive contributions include social support, coping strategies, means of healing, socialization and maintenance of culture, and resources for human services and social justice efforts (Berthold, 1989; de la Rosa, 1988; Delgado, 1988; Delgado & Barton, 1998; Delgado & Humm-Delgado, 1982; Gallego, 1988).

3. *Asian Americans and Pacific Islanders.* This population represents many different cultures, including Chinese, Filipino, Japanese, Korean, Asian Indian, Vietnamese, Hawaiian, Cambodian, Laotian, Thai, Hmong, Pakistani, Samoan, Guamanian, Indonesian, and others (Healey, 1995). These different peoples are affiliated with a wide range of spiritual traditions, including Hinduism, Buddhism, Islam, Confucianism, Sikhism, Zoroastrianism, Jainism, Shinto, Taoism, and Christianity (Tweed, 1997). There is much diversity within these various religious traditions as well, making it particularly difficult to discuss common elements of spiritual beliefs or practices. However, several themes can be discerned: the connection between and the divinity of all beings; the need to transcend suffering and the material world; the importance of displaying compassion, selflessness, and cooperation; the honoring of ancestors; a disciplined approach to life and spiritual development; and a holistic understanding of existence (Canda & Furman, 1999; Chung, 2001; Singh, 2001). Both religious institutions and traditional practices have been helpful to a variety of Asian and Pacific Islander immigrants and refugees and their descendants. For example, many Southeast Asian refugee communities have established Buddhist temples and mutual assistance associations, which provide social, physical, mental, and spiritual resources (Canda & Phaobtong, 1992; Morreale, 1998; Timberlake & Cook, 1984), and the Korean church has been an essential provider of social services (Choi & Tirrito, 1999). Some Asian Americans and Pacific Islanders also use indigenous healers, such as the Cambodian *kro kmer,* the Korean *mudang,* the Hmong spirit medium, and the Hawaiian kahuna (Canda & Furman, 1999; Canda, Shin, & Canda, 1993; Hurdle, 2002). As with other groups, there is an emerging literature stressing the importance of attending to spirituality in practice with clients from this large and diverse cultural population (Canda, 2001; Chu & Carew, 1990; Chung,

2001; Das, 1987; Fukuyama & Sevig, 1999; Furuto, Biswas, Chung, Murase, & Ross-Sherif, 1992; Hurdle, 2002; Singh, 2001). In addition, several writers have proposed incorporating concepts and practices from Asian spiritual traditions into mainstream social work practice, including meditation (Keefe, 1996; Logan, 1997), Zen-oriented practice (Brandon, 1976), and yoga (Fukuyama & Sevig, 1999).

4. *Native Americans.* First Nations people originally numbered in the millions and were members of hundreds of distinct tribes or nations, each with its own language, heritage, and spiritual traditions (Healey, 1995; Swift, 1998). As part of the effort to "humanize and civilize" First Nations people, Congress regularly appropriated funds for Christian missionary efforts beginning in 1819 (U.S. Commission of Human Rights, 1998). American Indian boarding schools were a major component of these efforts, where children were forbidden to wear their native attire, eat their native foods, speak their native language, or practice their traditional religion, and were often severely punished for failure to adhere to these prohibitions (Hag-Brown, 1988; Snipp, 1998). Through a long history of resistance and renewal, however, indigenous spiritual traditions have persisted and are today being restored and revitalized (Swift, 1998). Various expressions of First Nations spirituality have several common themes: the inseparability of spirituality from the rest of life; connection to and responsibility for the Earth and all her creatures; the sacredness of all things, including animals, plants, minerals, and natural forces; the values of balance, harmony, and connectedness; the importance of extended family and community; and the use of myth, ritual, and storytelling as spiritual practices (Duran & Duran, 1995; Garrett & Garrett, 1994; Matheson, 1996; Yellow Bird, 1995). Many of these values are of increasing appeal to nonindigenous people, producing great concern among First Nations people regarding the cultural appropriation of their customs, ceremonies, rituals, and healing practices (Kasee, 1995; LaDue, 1994). This cross-tradition borrowing of spiritual practices requires sensitivity, respect, competence, and permission in such matters (Canda & Yellow Bird, 1996). Many service providers also call for sensitivity and awareness of the effects of historical trauma on Native Americans and recommend the integration of traditional practices for more effective service delivery (Brave Heart, 2001a, 2001b; Garrett & Garret, 1994; Garrett & Myers, 1996; Hurdle, 1998; Matheson, 1996; Voss, Douville, Little-Soldier, & White Hat, 1999; Weaver, 1999, 2000). Of course, indigenous worldviews and spiritual practices also have application to social work (Canda, 1983; Voss, Douvill, Little-Solder, & Twiss, 1999).

It is important to remember the experience of other groups that have been more extensively assimilated into the dominant culture of the United States (e.g., Irish, Italian, and Jewish Americans). Many of these groups also have histories of discrimination and religious intolerance. In the aftermath of the terrorist attacks on September 11, 2001, we have witnessed oppressive acts against Muslim Americans, especially those of

Middle Eastern descent. Social workers must be sensitive to the particular history and spiritual traditions of all racial and ethnic groups.

Sex and Gender. Women are more likely than men to report that they consider themselves to be religious, church-affiliated, and frequent users of prayer; that they feel close to God; and that they hold a positive view of their church (Cornwall, 1989; de Vaus & McAllister, 1987; Felty & Poloma, 1991). Women also are the majority of members in most religious bodies in the United States and play important roles in the life of many religious communities (Braude, 1997).

However, in several denominations, women's participation has been significantly restricted, prohibiting them from holding leadership positions or performing certain religious rites and ceremonies (Baer, 1993; Holm & Bowker, 1994; Reilly, 1995). In addition, women members of traditional Judeo-Christian-Islamic faiths generally experience conceptualizations and symbols of the divine as masculine, suggesting that men are closer to (and thus more like) God than women (Reuther, 1983).

Although most women who belong to mainstream denominations report being generally satisfied with their affiliations (Corbett, 1997), some do struggle with the patriarchal aspects of their faith. One study conducted in-depth interviews of 61 women between the ages of 18 and 71 who were affiliated with either Catholic, United Methodist, Unitarian Universalist, or Jewish congregations (Ozorak, 1996). Most (93%) perceived gender inequality within their religions. Sixteen percent viewed these inequalities as appropriate, and thus accepted them; 8% left their faith in reaction to this issue and others. The remainder coped by using either behavioral strategies (e.g., requesting equal treatment; requesting gender-inclusive language; substituting feminine words, images, or interpretations; participating in feminist activities), cognitive strategies (e.g., focusing on positive aspects of the religion; comparing their faith favorably to others; emphasizing signs of positive change), or a combination of both behavioral and cognitive mechanisms.

Christian and Jewish feminist theologians have made efforts to emphasize the feminine heritage of conventional faiths, and some Christian and Jewish denominations have increased opportunities for women in both lay leadership roles and clerical positions (Canda & Furman, 1999). There also has been a movement toward alternative women's spiritualities. Some women have become involved in spiritual support groups or explored other religious traditions, such as Buddhism (Carnes & Craig, 1998; Holm & Bowker, 1994). Others have pursued feminist-identified theology, such as Goddess worship (Bolen, 1984; Christ, 1995; Kruel, 1995), Wicca (Starhawk, 1979; Warwick, 1995), Jewish feminism (Breitman, 1995), or Christian womanist spirituality (Jackson, 2002). These spiritual traditions emphasize the feminine aspect of the divine; the sacredness of women's bodies, rhythms, and life cycles; the power and creativity of women's spirituality; a connection to earth-centered practices; and the care of all people and the planet (Gray, 1988; Harris, 1989; Martin, 1993; Starhawk, 1979; Walker,

1990; Warwick, 1995). Some men are also turning to alternative spiritual traditions to overcome religious experiences and conceptions of God and masculinity that they feel have been detrimental to them (Kivel, 1991; Warwick, 1995).

Sexual Orientation. Nonheterosexual persons are often linked together as the GLBT community (gay men, lesbian women, bisexual persons, and transgendered persons). It should be noted, however, that transgendered persons may identify themselves as heterosexual, bisexual, or homosexual; therefore, transgendered status is most accurately a matter of sex and gender, not sexual orientation. However, as a group, transgendered persons have much in common with gay men, lesbians, and bisexual persons when it comes to experiences with oppression and thus will be included with these groups in this discussion of spirituality.

As an oppressed population, GLBT persons have suffered greatly at the hands of some groups affiliated with organized religion. Some egregious examples are the pronouncement by certain religious leaders that AIDS is a "punishment for the sins" of GLBT persons and the picketing of Matthew Shephard's funeral by religiously identified individuals. More pervasively, many GLBT members of various faiths have had to struggle with religious teachings that tell them their feelings and behaviors are immoral or sinful.

Many GLBT persons who grew up in conventionally religious families and communities experience tension between their faith and their sexuality. They, and others close to them, may resolve this tension in four possible ways (Canda & Furman, 1999):

1. Support traditional religious beliefs and condemn homosexuality and homosexual persons.

2. Accept homosexual persons but condemn homosexual behavior.

3. Critique and transform traditional ideology.

4. Reject the traditional position and depart from the faith.

The first two positions are most likely to foster self-loathing and remaining closeted, whereas the third and fourth positions are more supportive of self-acceptance and self-affirmation.

It is important to respect the diverse spiritual journeys that individual GLBT persons may take. One narrative describes the pain and joy of a man who "did not believe anyone, including God, could love me for myself" but who was able to grow into self-acceptance through a process that began during a spiritual retreat (McNeill, 1995, p. 35). Some remain with their original faith communities and deal with whatever dissonance or challenges that entails. Others leave the faith of their childhood to become active in religious bodies that minister specifically to the GLBT community (e.g., Metropolitan Community Church, Dignity). Some have found acceptance and affirmation among more progressive denominations or branches of organized religion (e.g., the Society of Friends, or Quakers, Unitarian Universalist). Still others disaffiliate with any form of organized religion. For most, regardless of their decision regarding religion, the process of self-acceptance is a spiritual journey unto itself (Barret & Barzan, 1996).

Other Aspects of Diversity. The issues and implications relative to spirituality that pertain to race and ethnicity, sex and gender, and sexual orientation apply to other forms of human diversity as well. For example, some religious teachings have interpreted disability as a punishment for the sins of the person or family (Miles, 1995) or as a means for nondisabled persons to acquire spiritual status through pity and charity (Fitzgerald, 1997). Conversely, spirituality has been noted as both a significant means of coping and a vehicle toward positive self-definition for persons with disabilities (Delgado, 1996b; DoRozario, 1997; Fitzgerald, 1997; Gourgey, 1994; Horsburgh, 1997; Swinton, 1997).

Spirituality and age is another area that has been widely addressed. Both religious and nonreligious forms of spirituality are an important source of social support for older persons and a pathway for coping, ongoing development, and successful aging (Abramowitz, 1993; Kimble, McFadden, Ellor, & Seeber, 1995; Moberg, 1990; Payne, 1990). In addition, spirituality is an essential foundation for healthy development among young people (Bradford,1995; Coles, 1990; Garbarino, 1999; Myers, 1997). Research has shown spirituality to be a significant protective factor against substance abuse, early sexual activity, and delinquency for children and adolescents (Holder et al., 2000; Johnson, Jang, Larsen, & De Li, 2001; Miller, Davies, & Greenwald, 2000). As our understanding of the interaction between spirituality and various forms of human diversity increases, social work will be in a better position to work sensitively, competently, and ethically with many diverse groups and communities.

Spirituality and the Human Experience

Social workers deal with every aspect of the human experience. They simultaneously focus on solving problems in living while supporting optimal human functioning and quality of life. The literature regarding spirituality in these two areas is immense, with significant development in social work, psychology, nursing, medicine, rehabilitation counseling, pastoral counseling, marital and family counseling, and other helping disciplines. The following is a brief overview of this continually evolving knowledge base.

Problems in Living. It is difficult to find an area related to problems in living in which spirituality is not being explored. For example, much has been written about the link between spirituality and mental health. Various indicators of spirituality—such as religious commitment, involvement in spiritual or religious practices, level of religiosity or spirituality—have been negatively related with depression, anxiety, hopelessness, suicide, and other mental health problems while showing a positive relationship with self-esteem, self-efficacy, hope, optimism, life satisfaction, and general well-being (Koenig, 2001a; Koenig, Larson, & Weaver, 1998; Krause, 1995; Mueller, Plevak, & Rummans, 2001; Pargament, 1997).

Similar influences are found between spirituality and physical health, with spirituality linked to a variety of better health outcomes (Ellison & Levin, 1998; Koenig, 2001b; Matthews et al., 1998). Perhaps religion and spirituality benefit physical health through their support of health-promoting behaviors and discouragement of risk behaviors; they may also have a positive effect on the immune system (Koenig, 1999; Mitka, 1998; Mueller et al., 2001; Perry, 1998).

For both mental and physical health problems, religion and spirituality have been noted as major means of coping (Koenig, Larson, & Larson, 2001; Pargament, 1997). The specific benefits of spiritually based coping include relieving stress, retaining a sense of control, maintaining hope, and providing a sense of meaning and purpose in life (Koenig et al., 2001). Higher levels of social support through religious and spiritual networks also play a significant role in positive coping with health issues (Ellison & Levin, 1998; Perry, 1998; Reese & Kaplan, 2000). Both religious and nonreligious forms of spirituality have also been shown as helpful to persons coping with caregiving demands related to health problems of family members (Poindexter & Linsk, 1999; Sistler & Washington, 1999; Tolliver, 2001).

Similar effects are noted for coping with poverty (Barusch, 1999; Black, 1999) and homelessness (Lindsey, Kurtz, Jarvis, Williams, & Nackerud, 2000; Montgomery, 1994).

Still another body of scholarship explores spirituality and substance abuse. Both religiosity and spirituality have been noted as protective factors in this area (Benson, 1992; Benson & Donahue, 1989; Francis, 1997; Hodge, Cardenas, & Montoya, 2001). In addition, the spiritual dimension has been long recognized in self-help groups such as Alcoholics Anonymous and Narcotics Anonymous and in other treatment approaches (Davis & Jansen, 1998; Hopson, 1996; May, 1988; Miller, 1998). However, cultural and gender sensitivity is necessary in applying spiritual principles to substance abuse treatment (Covington, 1994; Hooks, 1993; Lowery, 1998; Potts, 1991; Tangenberg, 2001; Thomason, 2001).

There is also a growing literature addressing the role of spirituality in understanding and dealing with the effects of various types of trauma—including sexual abuse and sexual assault (Kennedy, Davis, & Taylor, 1998; Robinson, 2000), violence (Garbarino & Bedard, 1997; Parappully, Rosenbaum, van den Daele, & Nzewi, 2002; Ryan, 1998), incarceration (O'Brien, 2001; Sheridan, 1995); and ethnic trauma, war, and terrorism (Mulcahy & Lunham-Armstrong, 1998; Norrell & Walz, 1994; Rothberg, 1992; Schuster et al., 2001). Specific spiritually oriented interventions, such as the use of ceremony and ritual, appear to have particular utility in helping persons recover from trauma and loss (Barrett, 1999; Graham-Poole, 1996; Lubin & Johnson, 1998).

Finally, an area where spirituality has long been viewed as relevant is the area of death and dying. Religious and spiritual issues often arise at the end of life, and thus practitioners need to be able to deal with these issues effectively (Cox, 2000; Doka & Morgan, 1993; Leh & Corless, 1988; Millison & Dudley, 1990; Morgan, 2002; Smith, 1993). Spiritual sensitivity and competence are also needed in work with those who are grieving the loss of loved ones (Angell, Dennis, & Dumain, 1998; Dershimer, 1990; Golsworthy & Coyle, 1999; Richards & Folkman, 1997) or facing other kinds of losses, such as divorce (Carmody, 1991; Nathanson, 1995; Smith & Gray, 1995).

Individual and Community Well-Being. Spirituality also has a role to play in regard to the second major focus of social work: supporting and enhancing optimal human functioning and quality of life. For example, interest in wellness, holistic health, and the body-mind connection has exploded in recent years, as evidenced by increasing numbers of workshops and retreats, weekly groups, self-help books, and media reports on the topic. Furthermore, there has been a marked increase in the use of complementary and alternative medical approaches, such as massage and other relaxation techniques, acupuncture and acupressure, chiropractic, herbal therapy, homeopathy, and reflexology. Over 42% of Americans used some form of complementary and alternative medicine in 1997 compared to 34% in 1990 (Williamson & Wyandt, 2001). In a study of social work practitioners, over 75% of the sample reported either direct use or referral to mind-body techniques or community health alternatives in work with their clients (Henderson, 2000).

A growing number of articles in the professional literature also promote the use of wellness or body-mind approaches for both clients and practitioners. Examples include the development of specialized wellness programs (Clark, 2002; Jones & Kilpatrick 1996; Neufeld & Knipemann, 2001; Scott et al., 2001), the use of stress management and relaxation techniques (de Ande, 1998; Payne, 2000; Sheils & Butler, 1992; Starkey, Deleone, & Flannery, 1995), and the use of meditation and yoga (Derezotes, 2000; Kaye, 1985; Kessell, 1994; Logan, 1997). Many of these approaches are rooted in spiritual traditions, especially Eastern traditions.

There also has been a great deal of recent development concerning spirituality and work. Much of this literature focuses on the search for "right livelihood," or the conscious choice of work that is consistent with one's spiritual values and that facilitates ongoing spiritual growth (Bloch & Richmond, 1998; Fox, 1994; Hansen, 1997; Pulley, 1997; Sinetar, 1989). Other writers exploring the role of spirituality in the workplace discuss such issues as use of power, management style, and workplace environment (Briskin, 1996; DePree, 1997; Marcic, 1997; Natale & Neher, 1997).

The social work enterprise itself has been the subject of such interest. Edward Canda and Leola Furman (1999) identify eleven principles for spiritually sensitive administration of human service organizations. They include such activities as limiting the size and complexity of the organization in order to maintain a "human scale"; supporting the "satisfaction of personal aspirations" of employees; ensuring "participatory decision making" by members of the staff and clients; paying attention to "work environment aesthetics"; and building "social and cultural environmental rapport" within the community, which includes collaboration with religious and spiritual leaders and helpers (pp. 211-212).

The connection between spirituality and creativity is another area being addressed by a variety of writers. Much of this writing emphasizes that linking spirituality and creativity can heal as well as nurture self-expression and optimal development. Examples include the use of the visual arts (Allen, 1995; Cohn, 1997; McNiff, 1992); journaling, poetry, and creative writing (Cameron, 1992; Fox, 1997; Goldberg, 1990; Strand, 1997); music and sound (Campbell, 1997; Gardner, 1990; Goldman, 1996; Newham, 1994); and movement and dance, drama, and other performing arts (Adler, 1995; Chodorow, 1991; Pearson, 1996). Engaging in the creative process seems to facilitate spiritual growth and well-being by encouraging the person to go beyond ego limitations, surrender to process, and tap into spiritual sources of strength and self-expression (Fukuyama & Sevig, 1999).

Finally, spirituality is emerging as an important factor in the optimal functioning of families and communities. Spirituality appears to be relevant in work with both religious and nonreligious couples and families experiencing problems (Cowley, 1999; Denton, 1990; Dosser, Smith, Markowski, & Cain, 2001; Nakhaima & Dicks, 1995; Prest & Keller, 1993; Rey, 1997; Walsh, 1999b). But it also plays a role in supporting family strengths and helping families move through the normal transitions of family life (Carolan & Allen, 1999; Pellebon & Anderson, 1999; Prest & Keller, 1993; Walsh, 1999b; Westbrooks, 1997).

Attention to religious and spiritual resources is also being identified in community work. Examples include community health-promotion programs (Brown, Jemmott, Mitchell, & Walton, 1998; Clark, 2002; Maton & Wells, 1995), collective action and social justice efforts (Arp & Boeckelman, 1997; Breton, 1989; Staral, 2000), services to rural communities (Carter, 1984; Furman & Chandy, 1994; Johnson, 1997; Meystedt, 1984), and other types of community-involved practice (Canda & Furman, 1999). In addition, social work is currently exploring (and debating) the potential benefits and pitfalls of the "Charitable Choice" provisions of the 1996 federal welfare reform legislation. This legislation allows governmental funding for services provided by faith-based organizations. This policy represents both an opportunity and a challenge for social workers in developing effective collaboration with religious groups and organizations.

It is interesting to note that the "search for community and spiritual fulfillment" has been identified as one of the six major issues related to quality of life issues as we move into the coming decades (Schwartz, 1999). Spirituality, in both its religious and nonreligious forms, holds much potential for promoting quality of life, as well as for helping the profession address the problems and possibilities inherent to the human condition.

Spiritually Sensitive Social Work

Increased understanding of the role of spirituality in the lives of the people we serve has implications for many aspects of social work practice. Sheridan (2002) has identified eight areas that should be addressed in spiritually sensitive and competent practice:

1. *Use of theory.* This chapter has described two major transpersonal human behavior theories (Fowler's stages of faith development and Wilber's full-spectrum model of consciousness) and noted one practice theory (Elizabeth Smith's Trans-egoic Model). Other spirituality-related human behavior and practice theories exist as well—regarding, for example, the spiritual development of children (Bradford, 1995), women's spirituality (Hickson & Phelps, 1997), and childhood trauma (Sheridan, 1995). All of these theories provide a more comprehensive view of human behavior by explicitly addressing spirituality as a fundamental part of the human experience. However, all of these theories need empirical testing to determine their utility and relevance for various populations.

2. *Goals of practice.* A focus on spirituality offers a different vantage point from which to make meaning of life challenges and opens up a wider range of possible supports and resources for the client facing such challenges. Spirituality and a transpersonal perspective also support optimal development through their expanded view of human potential. In Sean's case, for example, the goals for practice could incorporate both his personal spirituality and his religious connections within the community to deal with the problem at hand (such as development of a "care circle" among Sean's church community) while facilitating his own continued growth and development (through support for ongoing spiritual reflection and exploration).

3. *Context for practice.* Creating a spiritually sensitive and competent context includes paying attention to several aspects of the practice environment. The first is preparing oneself prior to meeting with clients in order to be fully present and receptive—perhaps through the use of a particular meditation, prayer, or saying that has meaning for the worker or through the simple act of taking a few deep breaths and centering oneself. A second aspect is to realize the impact of the physical setting, especially if services are provided through a faith-affiliated agency. The physical space should be furnished and decorated in a spiritually diverse or neutral manner so clients of various spiritual backgrounds feel welcomed and comfortable. Finally, the practitioner needs to attend to the quality of presence he or she brings to work with clients. Joleen Benedict (1995) calls this aspect "creating sacred space" and discusses ways of staying mindful and interacting with an attitude of honor and respect. All of these aspects would be important in working with Sean.

4. *Nature of the helping relationship.* Deliberate attention to the spiritual dimension also influences the relationship between client and social worker. When clients share their religious or spiritual lives, social workers must accept these offerings with respect, openness, and a willingness to learn. Social workers must be able to critically examine their own biases and prejudices with regard to religion and spirituality, just as they are expected to do with regard to other areas of difference (race, sex, sexual orientation, etc.). They must also feel comfortable being in the student role at times. In Sean's case, the social worker must be willing to learn about Sean's religious and spiritual beliefs *from Sean,* rather than be the "expert" in this area. Furthermore, social workers need to be actively engaged with issues of purpose, meaning, and connection in their own lives through continual self-reflection and disciplined efforts toward personal growth. It would be extremely difficult (if not impossible) for someone without a similar interest in such issues to help Sean work through his current struggle with meaning and connection. All of these dynamics tend to create a more egalitarian partnership between social worker and client, with the social worker acting in the role of guide, midwife, or cocreator rather than interpreter, director, or adviser (Cowley, 1996).

5. *Assessment.* Gathering information about a client's religious or spiritual history and assessing spiritual development and current interests are as important as learning about biopsychosocial factors. Assessment needs to go beyond the surface features of faith affiliation (such as Protestant, Catholic, Jewish, or Muslim) to include deeper facets of a person's spiritual life. Social workers also need to assess both the positive and negative aspects of clients' religious or spiritual beliefs and practices (Joseph, 1987, 1988; Lewandowski & Canda, 1995; Sheridan & Bullis, 1991). For example, Sean's understanding of the meaning of suffering or the issue of guilt might be either helpful or harmful in dealing with his wife's illness and his own midlife experiences. A growing number of assessment instruments and approaches are available to help social workers. Among them are a spiritual history that includes questions about clients, their parents or guardians, and their spouses or significant others (Bullis, 1996); a discussion guide for assessing spiritual propensity that covers spiritual group membership and participation, involvement in spiritual activities, inspirational sources of support, and styles of spirituality (Canda & Furman, 1999); and a set of questions for both assessment and relationship building (Titone, 1991; see Exhibit 6.5). A number of other creative strategies for gathering such information have also been described, including spiritual time lines (Bullis, 1996; Canda & Furman, 1999), spiritual ecomaps and genograms (Hodge, 2000, 2001), and spiritual trees (Raines, 1997). Assessment must also be able to distinguish between a religious/spiritual problem and a mental disorder. Recent changes to the *Diagnostic and Statistical Manual of Mental Disorders* (DSM-IV) provide guidance in this area. "Religious or spiritual problem" is now included as a condition (*not* a mental disorder) that is appropriate for clinical attention. Types of religious

EXHIBIT 6.5

Questions for Spiritual Assessment

1. What nourishes you spiritually? For example: music, nature, intimacy, witnessing heroism, meditation, creative expression, sharing another's joy?
2. What is the difference between shame and guilt? What is healthy and unhealthy shame and guilt?
3. Do you believe there is a supreme being?
4. If yes, what is that being like? What does he/she look like?
5. What were some of the important faith or religious issues in your family background?
6. What do you mean when you say your spirits are low? Is that different from being sad or depressed?
7. What are the areas of compatibility and conflict between you and your spouse (or other significant persons) regarding spirituality?
8. What is an incident in your life that precipitated a change in your belief about the meaning of life?
9. What helps you maintain a sense of hope when there is no immediate apparent basis for it?
10. How and when have you prayed or meditated? What is the difference?
11. What does God think about your feeling angry, inadequate, guilty?
12. Do you need forgiveness from yourself or someone else?
13. How long do you think God wants you to feel guilty?
14. How is your spirituality a rebellion against your parents, a conformity to your parents (or one of them)?
15. Which is the most sensitive subject between you and your spouse (or other significant persons): money, sex, spirituality, children's discipline?
16. What is most frightening to you about death? What do you think would help you have a peaceful death?
17. What is your opinion about the meaning of suffering?
18. Do you have rituals in your family? Have they diminished or stabilized or increased recently?

Source: Titone, 1991.

problems under this new category include difficulties resulting from a change in one's denomination or conversion to a new religion, intensified adherence to beliefs or practices, loss or questioning of faith, guilt, or cult involvement. Spiritual problems may include distress due to mystical experiences, near-death experiences, spiritual emergence/emergency, meditation, or separation from a spiritual teacher (Turner, Lukoff, Barnhouse, & Lu, 1995). This framework would be helpful in understanding Sean's mystical experience as a young adult. Accurate assessment of such an occurrence can help determine whether the experience needs to be integrated and used as a stimulus for personal growth or whether it should be recognized as a sign of mental instability.

6. *Practice interventions.* Studies show that practitioners are already using a wide range of spiritually oriented interventions (Bullis, 1996; Canda & Furman, 1999; Mattison, Jayaratne, & Croxton, 2000; Sheridan, 2000; Sheridan et al., 1992). Examples include use of religious or spiritual language or concepts; use of religious or spiritual writings; use of prayer or meditation; use of self-reflective diaries and journals; exploration of beliefs about loss or other difficult life situations; explorations of whether religious/spiritual beliefs and practices are helpful or harmful; and exploration of the role of religious/spiritual beliefs in relation to significant others. There is also increased interest in using body/mind approaches and techniques from various spiritual traditions. Examples include dream work, visualization or guided imagery, expressive therapies, meditation, breathing techniques, energy work, journeying, use of ceremony and ritual, and yoga and t'ai chi (Achterberg, 1985; Becvar, 1997; Cowley, 1996; Grof, 1988; Hendricks & Weinhold, 1982; Hutton, 1994; Keefe, 1996; Laird, 1984; Muff, 1996; Simpkinson & Simpkinson, 1998). In conjunction with conventional therapeutic approaches, spiritually based interventions hold much promise. However, they also hold the potential for harm if used by untrained practitioners. Thus, social workers must carefully consider the therapeutic benefit of using such approaches with their clients, develop the necessary knowledge and skills required for effective use, and engage in ongoing supervision when necessary to ensure competent practice.

7. *Ethical issues.* Developing the necessary knowledge and skills is a minimal ethical obligation for all social workers using spiritually derived interventions. In addition, workers need to be aware of five general ethical considerations to take into account when integrating spirituality and practice: premature spiritual interventions, blurring of boundaries, countertransference issues, referral to religious professionals, and lack of training (Ganje-Fling & McCarthy, 1996). Other potential ethical problems and complications include misuse of power, inadequate limit setting, and worker discomfort with religious/spiritual material (Benningfield, 1997). One ethical framework that is helpful in determining the appropriate use of spiritually based activities requires consideration of various conditions of the helping situation (e.g., expression of interest by the client, the establishment of a spiritually sensitive relationship between worker and client, and possession of relevant worker qualifications) prior to using any such intervention (Canda & Furman, 1999). Finally, social workers should ensure that their work in this area is consistent with the overall code of ethics of the profession.

8. *Referral and collaboration.* This practice issue first entails developing a working knowledge of the religious and spiritual resources within the community that are most germane to one's work with clients, which requires a good knowledge of the religious and spiritual traditions that are most important to the clients and communities served. Second, the worker should develop an effective referral system to relevant religious/spiritual leaders and helpers, institutions, and support systems, including

both formal and informal resources. Finally, effective collaborative relationships should be developed with such resources, with the goal of developing good working relationships based on understanding of and respect for each partner's role and expertise. Effective referral and collaboration have the potential to expand and strengthen service delivery to clients dealing with religious or spiritual issues (Bilich & Carlson, 1994; Holcomb, 1987; Nakhaima & Dicks, 1995).

IMPLICATIONS FOR SOCIAL WORK PRACTICE

In addition to the preceding discussion of the components of spiritually sensitive and competent practice, the following practice principles are offered as guidelines for effective and ethical social work practice.

- Be respectful of different religious or spiritual paths and be willing to learn about the role and meaning of various beliefs, practices, and experiences for various client systems (individuals, groups, communities).

- Inform yourself about both the positive and negative role of religion and spirituality in the fight for social justice by various groups and be sensitive to this history in working with members of oppressed populations.

- Critically examine your own values, beliefs, and biases concerning religion and spirituality and be willing to work through any unresolved or negative feelings or experiences in this area that may adversely affect your work with clients.

- Develop a working knowledge of the beliefs and practices frequently encountered in your work with clients, especially those of newly arriving immigrants/refugees or nondominant groups (for example, Buddhist beliefs of Southeast Asian refugees, spiritual traditions of First Nations peoples).

- Engage in ongoing self-reflection about what brings purpose, meaning, and connection in your own life and make disciplined efforts toward your own spiritual development, however you define this process.

- Conduct comprehensive spiritual assessments with clients at all levels and use this information in service planning and delivery.

- Acquire the knowledge and skills necessary to employ spiritually based intervention techniques appropriately and effectively.

- Seek information about the various religious and spiritual organizations, services, and leaders pertinent to your practice and develop good working relationships with these resources for purposes of referral and collaboration.

KEY TERMS

basic structures	Second Force therapies
faith	self system
faith stages	spirituality
First Force therapies	Third Force therapies
Fourth Force therapies	transitional structures
fulcrum	transpersonal approach
ideology	ultimate environment
religion	

ACTIVE LEARNING

1. Consider Sean's case study at the beginning of the chapter. Using either Fowler's stages of faith development or Wilber's full-spectrum model of consciousness as the conceptual framework, construct a time line of Sean's spiritual development. Trace the overall growth patterns through the different stages, including any ups and downs, as well as plateau periods. Identify the significant points or transitions that you consider as pivotal in Sean's spiritual development.

- How would this information help you to better understand Sean's story and overall development? How would this information help you work with him as a social worker at various points in his life? For example, as a child following his uncle's death; as an adolescent during his father's alcoholism and subsequent death; as a young man questioning the meaning of life and his place in it; as a young husband and father; as a man in middle-age coping with his wife's illness.

- How might you best incorporate the eight areas of spiritually sensitive social work in your work with Sean?

2.   Select a partner for this exercise. This chapter provides a brief overview of the spiritual diversity present within the United States. Given both your knowledge and experiences with different spiritual traditions—both religious and nonreligious— address the following questions. Take a few moments to reflect on each question before answering it. Partners should take turns answering the questions.

■ For which spiritual perspectives do you have the most *positive reactions* (e.g., are in the most agreement with, feel an appreciation or attraction toward, are the most comfortable with, find it easiest to keep an open mind and heart about)? What is it about you that contributes to these reactions (e.g., previous knowledge, personal experiences, messages from family or larger culture)?

■ For which perspective do you have the most *negative reactions* (e.g., are in the most disagreement with, feel a repulsion or fear about, are the most uncomfortable with, find it most difficult to keep an open mind and heart about)? What is it about you that contributes to these reactions (e.g., previous knowledge, personal experiences, messages from family or larger culture)?

■ What impact(s) might your reactions (both positive and negative) have on work with clients (especially with those who may hold these different spiritual perspectives)? What personal and professional "work" on yourself is suggested by your positive and/or negative reactions?

WEB RESOURCES

Adherents.com

www.adherents.com

Site not affiliated with any religious, political, educational, or commercial organization contains a comprehensive collection of over 41,000 adherent statistics and geography citations and links to other major sites on diverse religious and spiritual traditions.

Religious Tolerance

religioustolerance.org

Site presented by the Ontario Consultants on Religious Tolerance, an agency that promotes religious tolerance as a human right, contains comparative descriptions of world religions and diverse spiritual paths from Asatru to Zoroastrianism and links to other related sites.

Virtual Religion Index

religion.rutgers.edu/vri

Site presented by the Religion Department at Rutgers University contains analysis and highlights of religion-related Web sites and provides links to major sites for specific religious groups and topics.

**E-mail address for the Society
for Spirituality and Social Work:**

sssw@binghamton.edu

An Interview With John

Social Work Practice That Integrates Biological, Psychological, and Spiritual Person

Martin Schwartz
Virginia Commonwealth University

John is a 35-year-old white gay male who sought therapy when his relationship of 10 years ended because of his partner's infidelities. John grew up in an intact blue-collar family from the U.S. Midwest. He described his family as cold, rigid, and very religious. John secured affection and adulation through church activities that he began at an early age when he became a child preacher. He did well in school and was able to secure a full scholarship at a local religious college. Although aware of his homosexual yearnings, which were totally unacceptable to his religion, John married a woman when he was 21. The marriage ended 3 years later when John was able to discuss his homosexuality with his wife.

Following the dissolution of the marriage, John moved to the South and lived openly as a gay male. Although he had been able to come out to himself and enter a gay relationship, he maintained an internal homophobia fueled by his devout religious attitude about homosexuality. John just about severed any relationship with his family, and this estrangement caused a great deal of emotional pain when his mother died suddenly. Following her death, he maintained a rather superficial contact with his father and brother. The ending of his gay relationship reawakened earlier doubts of adequacy as well as guilt and shame about acting on his sexual orientation.

During therapy, John was diagnosed with AIDS after a sudden hospitalization for meningitis. Within a few months, John had quickly moved to the terminal stage of AIDS, manifested by numerous opportunistic diseases and frequent hospitalizations. At the time of this interview, he was totally isolated because he had little strength to venture outside his apartment except for visits to his physicians. His conversations about his illness and impending death often focused on not having his religion to help him through this painful journey. John was clinically depressed and could not find the inner resources to cope with his situation.

As I entered the apartment, I immediately noticed that the lights were on and the window blinds were open to allow the sunlight into the apartment. John was sitting in the living room listening to a recording of a Beethoven symphony.

J.   Marty, do you hear how beautiful it is? God, I haven't listened to this recording for months. I've missed my music.

M.   Yes, it is beautiful. More than that, it's beautiful to hear you talk about your music.

J.   I got so much to talk to you about. Sit down and listen—don't say anything. I haven't figured it all out, but something happened to me that has changed—I'm going to cry—but Marty, it's not like the other times. Inside I feel good—no— I feel at rest—shit—I just know I'm different from last week.

M.   Okay, okay—slow—I'm here and I'm listening. Just talk—let it out.

J.   After our session last week, Mike called me. Remember him? Twenty-year-old kid I met at our group 4 or 5 months ago. You know he was pretty sick—worse than me. Well, he was alone, and it sounded like he was in bad shape. So I called my cab driver and he came up to the apartment and drove me over to Mike's place. Mike was in bed—crap and urine all over him. I don't know how, but I washed him, changed his clothes. I knew he was going—told him that he needed to be in the hospital. He pleaded with me not to call anybody—he wanted to end in his own bed. Marty, I was scared shitless—I didn't know what to do. Christ, I was just about able to stand, but all I could hear was his crying not to leave him. So I stayed with him all day and all night. [Tears are running down John's face. I give him some tissue.] I held him; I talked to him; and Marty, this is going to blow you out of the water—I prayed with him. [Lots of tears; lots of tissue. This time John really let go. I got up from my chair and I held him in my arms—saying nothing, saying a lot—till he was able to go on.] I told Mike that it was okay to go—he had had enough pain—and he died in my arms.

M.   John, are you okay? Sounds like a difficult experience. You really were a friend. But yet it sounds like something else happened to you.

J.   Yeah, that's what I'm talking about. It was. I know this sounds crazy, but it was beautiful. Mike was so calm at the end, and I felt something inside that I haven't felt in years. I was at peace. There was something about helping Mike that helped me. When I was saying the prayer, I was back home again—not home—back. Marty, I know I'm going to die soon, but I'm okay about it. I'm going to spend the time I have left to enjoy whatever I have—my music—but Marty, I can hear every note now. I'm going to smell every rose now—I'm okay with who I am—and I know now that God loves me. [More tears, more tissue, more holding.] Does it make sense? You must think I'm crazy.

M. No, no, far from it. Maybe we don't have to understand everything. What is important is that you've turned a corner and you are feeling—what did you say—more at peace? That's what is important. I'm happy for you and your feelings.

J. Marty, I'm exhausted.

M. I can understand. Why don't we just sit here and listen to the music. Any special CD?

J. No—they're all special. [John smiles.]

John died 4 weeks later in the hospital with his father and brother by his bed, and he asked me to be there too. John asked me to say some words at the cemetery. He had chosen a sonnet by Shakespeare.

Something to Think About

This interview is one event in Marty's social work practice with John. I think you can see how important it is for Marty to be responsive to John as a biological person, a psychological person, and a spiritual person. These questions will help you think about how you might use what you have been learning to be helpful to someone like John:

■ What have you learned about the immune system, T cells, HIV, and AIDS that might be helpful to you in your work with John? How might you use this information? What else would you want to know about the biology of AIDS or about John's biological system?

■ What do you know about John's cognitive and emotional life? Do any psychological theories seem particularly useful in understanding John's situation? What could you say about John's sense of self?

■ Do you think of the stress in John's life as biological, psychological, or social in nature? Describe the nature of this stress. What coping methods do you see John using? What types of social support does he need? How does this change as he moves into the terminal stage of AIDS?

■ What influence—both negative and positive—did religion and spirituality play in John's adjustment to AIDS? Which of Patrick O'Brien's themes of spirituality seem the most pertinent to John's life, and why? John's assistance to Mike while he was dying seemed to transform John. What about this episode seemed so powerful?

■ How do you think about John's depression? Is it biological? Is it psychological (cognitive? emotional?)? Is it spiritual? Is it some interplay of biology, psychology, and spirit?

PART III

The Multiple Dimensions of Environment

Social workers have always recognized the important role the environment plays in human behavior and, equally important, have always understood the environment as multidimensional. The social work literature has not been consistent in identifying the important dimensions of environment, however. Although all dimensions of environment are intertwined and inseparable, social scientists have developed specialized literature on several specific dimensions. Both the environment, and the study of it, become more complex with each new era of technological development, making our efforts to understand the environment ever more challenging.

The purpose of the eight chapters in Part III is to provide you with an up-to-date understanding of the multidisciplinary theory and research about dimensions of environment. It begins with Chapter 7 on an important dimension that is often overlooked in the social work literature, the physical environment. Next comes Chapter 8, which reviews our historical attempts to understand culture and presents a contemporary framework to help us become more competent social workers in a multicultural world. Chapter 9 explores contemporary trends in social institutions and social structure. Chapters 10 and 11 cover the smaller-scale configurations of families and small groups. Part III ends with Chapters 12, 13, and 14 on the large-scale configurations of formal organizations, communities, and social movements. The Knowledge Into Practice story for Part III illustrates one social worker's activities with a multidimensional environment. In Part II, you learned about the multiple dimensions of persons. When you put that knowledge together with the knowledge gained about multiple dimensions of environments, you will be better prepared to understand the situations you encounter in social work practice. This prepares you well to think about the changing configurations of persons and environments across the life course—the subject of the companion volume, *The Changing Life Course*, to this book.

Being in the World

Think for a moment of the environment in which you are reading this book. Did you think immediately of the room you're in? Or did you think of the building in which it is contained, the culture and institutions that determine the features of the room, or the people within the room? Maybe you thought of all these and more. Environment has many dimensions.

The physical environment, which is one such dimension, has a significant effect on people. Consider the quiet serenity of this sunlit bedroom. This is a physical environment that provides positive stimulation and allows for relaxation.

Photograph © Stacey Kowalski. Used by permission.

Not all environments are so conducive to well-being, however. Physical environments like this overcrowded women's shelter keep inhabitants on edge and make it more difficult for them to gain control over their lives.

Photograph © Reuter/Corbis-Bettman. Used by permission.

This office environment reflects the bureaucratic nature of the formal organization housed within it. Not only do the pathways created by desks and partitions channel people's physical movements, but they also create invisible hallways for people's activities and relationships.

Photograph from FotoSearch. Used by permission.

Despite the inadequacies of some settings, people can often inhabit them comfortably if other aspects of the environment are positive. These children find rest in the stark but nurturing environment of their low-income day care center.

Photograph © Reuter/Corbis-Bettman. Used by permission.

When we think of environment, we readily notice buildings and landscapes and even organizations. But less direct and more pervasive forces are part of the environment too. For instance, the culture we live in influences our behavior in ways large and small.

In this procession of New Mexico children, you can see the far-reaching effects of Hispanic and Catholic values, norms, and beliefs. Dress, behavior, social relationships, and demeanor are just some of the aspects of culture that shape people's lives.

The social institutions with which we interact—the education system, the government, and so on—also may affect our lives profoundly, even though they too are less visible to us than the physical environment.

Photograph © Annie Popkins. Used by permission.

Institutions have both a physical aspect and an ethos, or a way of being within the institution, which are closely linked. At Ellis Island, for instance, new immigrants immediately encountered some of the symbols and structures of the U.S. government. The immigrants' socialization into the mainstream U.S. culture thus started almost immediately on their arrival.

Photograph © AP/Wide World Photos. Used by permission.

Institutions are also the source of the numerous policies that influence who gets what kind of help and where they get it. Whether people convicted of drug abuse are given help with their addictions or merely punished is determined by institutional programs and policies. Without access to greater social resources, this woman sentenced to a work crew may have trouble overcoming her drug problems and becoming reintegrated into society.

Photograph © Stacey Kowalski. Used by permission.

Social policy and the physical environment often intersect. People can easily be displaced from their homes and customary way of life through natural disaster, and many live one paycheck away from poverty. During crises like these, social workers may be called on to deal not only with the emotional distress of individuals but also with the logistics of housing and caring for an entire community.

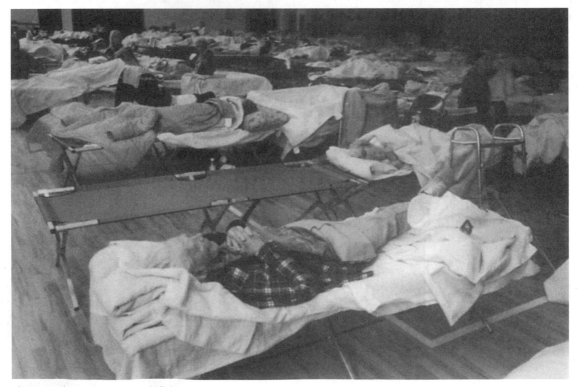

Photograph © Rick Bowner/AP. Used by permission.

Just as social workers need to pay attention to the physical and societal aspects of clients' environments, they also need to understand who their clients interact with. Families are the first and, for many people, most significant element of the social environment. But social workers need to recognize that families vary widely in form. There is no single best style of family.

Photograph © Emily Niebrand. Used by permission.

Photograph © Reuter/ Corbis-Bettman. Used by permission.

Many clients are also part of a small informal group that provides social support, like this group of neighborhood women. Social workers can establish therapy groups that serve the same purpose.

Photograph © Annie Popkins. Used by permission.

Groups like these develop a sense of community, born of closeness and camaraderie. Community appears in various guises. Often it is geographic, but more and more, with developments in transportation and communication technologies, people who are physically far apart may develop a sense of community built around common interests and viewpoints.

The chess matches in the park promote a geographic sense of community, but people who play competitive chess on the Internet develop a similar feeling of psychological closeness.

Photograph © AP/Wide World Photos. Used by permission.

Many of the same forces that create community are behind social movements, although movements usually have a historical sweep and political or economic intent as well.

Many social movements are focused on the very same issues that are important to social workers. Here a large group has gathered to protest, in dramatic fashion, their concerns about global environmental degradation. Social workers have a similar interest in creating and maintaining the conditions that allow society's least advantaged, not just the well-to-do, to live long and healthy lives.

© Corbis.

© Corbis.

Social movements have their greatest impact when ordinary people join the cause and take local action. The multiple aspects of environment, and the myriad forms they may take, make every situation we encounter in practice a unique one. By carefully considering each client's physical, societal, and social environment, we become better able to support their growth.

CHAPTER 7

The Physical Environment

Elizabeth D. Hutchison

Implications for Social Work Practice

Key Terms

Active Learning

Web Resources

The Physical Environment

Elizabeth D. Hutchison
Virginia Commonwealth University

What is the relationship between the physical environment and human behavior?
What are some implications of the research on the relationship between the physical
environment and human behavior for social work practice?

Key Ideas

As you read this chapter, take note of these central ideas:

1. To better understand the relationship between the physical environment and human behavior, social workers can draw on multidisciplinary research from the social sciences and design disciplines.

2. Eleven key concepts for the study of the physical environment and human behavior are accessibility, activity, adaptability, comfort, control, crowding, legibility, meaning, privacy, sensory stimulation, and sociality.

3. Three broad categories of theories about human behavior and the physical environment are stimulation theories, control theories, and behavior settings theories.

4. Researchers have found a strong human preference for elements of the natural environment and positive outcomes of time spent in the natural environment.

5. Built environments may be sociofugal spaces, which discourage social interaction, or sociopetal spaces, which encourage social interaction.

6. A recent recognition that physical environments can be disabling has led to legislation to protect the civil rights of persons with disabilities.

7. Children, adolescents, and elderly adults have special needs with respect to the built environment, particularly for control, privacy, and stimulation.

CASE STUDY

CHERYL GETS A PLACE OF HER OWN

The following story of human strength and triumph is told by Cheryl Davis, a disabled white woman, and her coauthor, Raymond Lifchez (Lifchez & Davis, 1987, pp. 68-71). It is the type of story you might hear as a social worker serving any young client with disabilities.

I left home when I was twenty-two years old. I would like to say that my reasons for leaving were the same as anyone of my age, but it wouldn't be true. "I want my independence," everyone says when moving out on their own, but what it meant for me as a disabled person was not quite what it meant for an able-bodied woman. It was not merely that I wanted to be closer to my job, or that my parents were putting a damper on their daughter's sexual activity (the absence of which was then so total that I regarded myself as nearly neutered). I left because I envisioned myself living with aging parents possibly for the rest of my life, simply because I feared to find out whether or not I could take care of myself.

I lived and quarreled with my parents in an inaccessible home, unable to get in and out unaided. I couldn't afford a car: Father was always reminding me how expensive "under-25" insurance was and expressing doubts that I could get a wheelchair in and out of a car myself, despite my telling him that I had, in fact, done it. (It never occurred to anyone to equip the family car with hand controls.) Taxis were financially disastrous alternatives, and obviously, I couldn't get a wheelchair on a bus. I went places if and when my parents were willing to drive me; they drove me everywhere I wanted, as long as I wanted what they wanted.

My mother believed that I couldn't minister to my own bowel care needs without her; she had convinced me, too, for a long time, but I was beginning to question this. The idea that she might be mistaken was intensely disturbing. It seemed as if she needed to feel needed so badly that my independence would be sacrificed. I was coming to resent her participation in my care as a gross and humiliating intrusion on my body, as an assault to my spirit. In the most basic physical sense, I had no privacy and I felt as if I were being repeatedly violated.

Suffice it to say we did not get along. Our household was perpetually engaged in an undeclared civil war. The only way to break the Gordian knot of our conflict was for someone to leave or die. Until I convinced myself that I might be able to live on my own, the only way out I could see was suicide. I was beginning to think of it continually, and it terrified me. When I realized that anything had to be better than this, I finally found the courage to plan the move.

Eventually, my parents realized that I was right; I had to go. My relatives were astonished that they would "let me go," as if it were their duty to compel me to stay. In reminding them that I was a reasonably intelligent adult, my mother reminded herself. Before too long, my parents (with who knows what internal conflicts) were helping me to look for an apartment.

As a low-income wheelchair user (salary of a junior secretary), my requirements for a dwelling were quite specific. The rent had to be $125 or less. The place had to be within a few blocks of Boston University, where I worked, since I was determined to push to the office, except in bad weather, when I would have to pay for a cab. (Incidentally, cabs were very hard to get for such short runs, since the drivers thought the effort of getting my wheelchair in and out was not adequately offset by the low fare. In winter, I would wait for up to an hour.) I had to be able to enter the apartment unaided and be able to maneuver in the kitchen and bathroom. Realtors told us only the size, the location, and the rent; therefore, we had to run around to all prospective apartments, a colossal waste of time.

This was 1967, and most of the buildings in Boston's Back Bay were hopeless. None of them had accessible front entrances. Most landlords refused to rent to me, saying, "What the hell do you think I'm running, a nursing home?" Finally, Mr. Greenblatt rented me a basement studio near Kenmore Square and let my parents pay to have the back door ramped, "conditional upon the approval of the other tenants." Success! Let me describe this palatial abode.

To get to the rear entry, I had to push down an alley running between a nightclub-disco-bar and a movie theater. The alley, which had about a one-in-eight gradient, culminated in an expanse of fractured blacktop and loose dirt, which was deeply rutted and pocked by water-filled holes. I would never lose my fear of falling into them. I wasn't afraid of getting wet; I was petrified of being unable to get back into my chair in such a lonely spot, since the place was alive with rats. These weren't just any rats; they were Back Bay rats, enormous, sleek, and fearless. In daylight they stood in your path and watched you approach, as if appraising your edibility. The route disgusted me, but it led to the only semi-affordable, partially accessible place I could find in the area; therefore, in the absence of choice, I suspended judgment.

Inside, the studio was wood-paneled and dim. Some of the darkness was caused by the filth on the windows, the outside of which were uncleanable, because the burglar screens bolted onto the frames. A front

CASE STUDY

burner on the stove didn't work, and since I couldn't reach the rear
burners, it necessitated my cooking one-dish meals until I bought a hotplate
(Mr. Greenblatt never did repair the stove). Although the bathroom door was
wide enough, I had to remove it, since it blocked access to the tub; this was
all right for me, but I thought it would disconcert any company I might have.

My parents let me take several pieces of furniture, some dishes and
glassware, and their apprehensive blessings for the new venture. They moved
the furniture in for me, cleaned the place up, and got a carpenter to build a
ramp, under which the rats subsequently made a fine home of their own.
I could see that my parents were far from pleased with the place. I wondered
if they thought I liked it or hated it. This, my first apartment, was small, dark,
roach-infested, hard to get around in, and surrounded by an army of
vermin, but I loved it. It was mine. The door had a dead-bolt lock, and
I could have all the privacy I wanted.

That first night, as my parents left me at my apartment, they assured me
that I could call them any time of day or night; I had only to say the word
and I could come home. I thought they were hoping my independence
would be temporary, but I realize now how anxious they must have been.
I've seen the same pattern when disabled friends leave home. . . .

The next morning was Sunday. I awoke at nine and lay there in bed,
blissfully surveying my books, clothes, couch, walls, floor, ceiling, and door,
luxuriating in my splendid squalor. I could let people in or not. I could
buy the food I wanted, eat when I wanted to, go to bed or stay up when
I wanted, go out when I wanted . . . I would choose. I didn't have to come
home early because my parents didn't like to stay up late. I didn't have to
ask my father to drive me anywhere. I could experience whatever presented
itself, without asking my parents if it was all right with them. That was real
independence. I thought of all that freedom and the new life I had begun.
As I threw back the covers—I remember as if it were this morning—an
incredibly wide grin stole across my face.

The Relationship Between the
Physical Environment and Human Behavior

Systems perspective

As with most stories we hear as social workers, Cheryl's story provides multidimensional information about changing configurations of person and environment. It presents issues of life course development, family conflict, physical disability, and

EXHIBIT 7.1

Key Concepts
for Understanding
Physical
Environment-Behavior
Relationships

Concept	Definition
Accessibility	Ease in movement through and use of an environment
Activity	Perceived intensity of ongoing behavior within an environment
Adaptability	Extent to which an environment and its components can be reorganized to accommodate new or different patterns of behavior
Comfort	Extent to which an environment provides sensory and mobility fit and facilitates task performance
Control	Extent to which an environment facilitates personalization and conveys territorial claims to space
Crowding	Unpleasant experience of being spatially cramped
Legibility	Ease with which people can conceptualize key elements and spatial relationships within an environment and effectively find their way
Meaning	Extent to which an environment holds individual or cultural meaning(s) for people (e.g., attachment, challenge, beauty)
Privacy	Selective control of access to the self or to one's group
Sensory stimulation	Quality and intensity of stimulation as experienced by the various sensory modalities
Sociality	Degree to which an environment facilitates or inhibits social interaction among people

Source: Adapted from Weisman, 1981. Reproduced with permission of the author.

a struggle for emotional well-being. And, of course, a supremely important dimension of this unfolding story is the physical environment.

Perhaps the most obvious aspect of Cheryl's relationship with her physical environment is *accessibility*—the ease with which Cheryl can act in her environment. But accessibility is only one relevant aspect. Gerald Weisman (1981) has identified 11 key concepts that unify the multidisciplinary study of the relationship between human behavior and the physical environment. A slightly revised version of these concepts appears in Exhibit 7.1. In addition to accessibility, Cheryl's story addresses another 6 of Weisman's 11 concepts: *adaptability* (a ramp added, a door removed); *comfort* ("small, dark, roach-infested, hard to get around in, and surrounded by an army of vermin"); *control* ("It was *mine*"); *crowding* (Can friends be entertained without feeling crowded?); *privacy* ("The door had a dead-bolt lock, and I could have all the privacy I wanted"); and *sensory stimulation* (lack of sunlight). We are also aware that the physical environment of the new apartment may hold very different *meanings* for the storyteller, for her parents, and for friends who visit. Three other concepts—activity, legibility, and sociality—will be discussed later in the chapter.

When we as social workers make person-in-environment assessments, we ought to pay attention to the physical environment, which has an inescapable influence on human behavior. Unfortunately, the social work literature includes only scant coverage of the physical environment. A handful of social work scholars (Germain, 1978, 1981; Gutheil, 1991, 1992; Resnick & Jaffee, 1982; Seabury, 1971) have provided most of the existing analyses of the implications for social work of recent theory and research. The relationship between human behavior and the physical environment is a multidisciplinary study that includes contributions from the social and behavioral sciences of psychology, sociology, geography, and anthropology as well as from the design disciplines of architecture, landscape architecture, interior design, and urban and regional planning.

The empirical research on these issues is sometimes contradictory, as you might expect in a multidisciplinary field at such an early stage of analysis. This chapter gives you some ways of thinking about the relationship between human behavior and the physical environment as you begin to consider the role it plays in the stories of the people you encounter in practice.

Systems perspective

Most theorists start from an assumption that person and physical environment are separate entities and emphasize the ways in which the physical environment influences behavior. Some theorists, however, start from an assumption of person/environment unity and propose interlocking and ongoing processes of coexistence between people and physical environments—people shape their environment just as the physical environment influences them—an approach called **transactionalism** (see Minami & Tanaka, 1995; Wapner, 1995; Werner & Altman, 2000). This transactional approach is consistent with the assumption of person/environment unity of this book.

Three broad categories of theory about human behavior and the physical environment are introduced in this chapter: stimulation theories, control theories, and behavior settings theories. The first two categories, stimulation theories and control theories, originated in the theoretical approach that assumes separation of person and physical environment, but they have increasingly recognized the interrelatedness of person and physical environment. Behavior settings theories have always been based in transactionalism. Each of these categories of theory, and the research they have stimulated, provide useful possibilities for social workers to consider as they participate in person/environment assessments, although stimulation theories and control theories have been more widely used than behavior settings theories. Exhibit 7.2 presents the key ideas and important concepts of these three types of theories.

EXHIBIT 7.2

Three Categories of Theories About the Relationship Between the Physical Environment and Human Behavior

Theories	Key Ideas	Important Concepts
Stimulation theories	The physical environment is a source of sensory information essential for human well-being. Patterns of stimulation influence thinking, emotions, social interaction, and health.	Stimulus overload Stimulus deprivation
Control theories	Humans desire control over their physical environments. Some person/environment configurations provide more control over the physical environment than others.	Personal space Territoriality Crowding Privacy
Behavior settings theories	Consistent, uniform patterns of behavior occur in particular settings. Behaviors of different persons in the same setting are more similar than the behaviors of the same person in different settings.	Behavior settings Programs Staffing

Stimulation Theories

Have you thought about how you would react to the lack of light in Cheryl's new apartment? That concern is consistent with stimulation theories. **Stimulation theories** focus on the physical environment as a source of sensory information that is essential for human well-being. The stimulation may be light, color, heat, texture, or scent, or it may be buildings, streets, and parks. Stimulation theorists propose that patterns of stimulation influence thinking, feelings, social interaction, and health.

Stimulation varies by amount—intensity, frequency, duration, number of sources—as well as by type. Stimulation theories that are based on theories of psycho-physiological arousal assume that moderate levels of stimulation are optimum for human behavior (Sundstrom, Bell, Busby, & Asmus, 1996). Thus, both *stimulus overload* (too much stimulation) and *stimulus deprivation* (too little stimulation) have a negative effect on human behavior. Theorists interested in the behavioral and health effects of stimulus overload have built on Han Selye's work regarding stress (see Chapter 5).

Social behavioral perspective, Social constructionist perspective

Some stimulation theories focus on the direct, concrete effect of stimulation on behavior; others focus on the meanings people construct regarding particular stimuli (Gutheil, 1992). In fact, people respond to both the concrete and the symbolic aspects of their physical environments. A doorway too narrow to accommodate a wheelchair has a concrete effect on the behavior of a person in a wheelchair; it will also have a symbolic effect, contributing to the person's feelings of exclusion and stigma. You probably will have a very different emotional reaction to a loud bang if it occurs during a street riot or at a New Year's Eve party; your understanding of the meaning of the noise has a strong influence on your reactions. In this case, your response is primarily symbolic. Stimulation theories alert social workers to consider the quality and intensity of sensory stimulation in the environments where their clients live and work.

Control Theories

Psychodynamic perspective, Social behavioral perspective

The ability to gain control over her physical environment is the central theme of Cheryl's story. In that way, the story is a powerful demonstration of the ideas found in control theories. **Control theories** focus on the issue of how much control we have over our physical environments and the attempts we make to gain control (Gifford, 1987). Four concepts are central to the work of control theorists: personal space, territoriality, crowding, and privacy. Personal space and territoriality are **boundary regulating mechanisms** that we use to gain greater control over our physical environments. (See Chapter 11 for discussion of personal space, territoriality, density, and crowding in relation to small groups.)

Personal Space. **Personal space**, also known as interpersonal distance, is the physical distance we choose to maintain in interpersonal relationships. Robert Sommer (1969, p. 26) has defined it as "an area with invisible boundaries surrounding a person's body into which intruders may not come." More recent formulations (Gifford, 1987) emphasize that personal space is not stable, but contracts and expands with changing interpersonal circumstances and with variations in physical settings. The distance you desire when talking with your best friend is likely to be different from the distance you prefer when talking with a stranger, or even with a known authority figure like your social work professor. The desired distance for any of these interpersonal situations is likely to expand in small spaces (Sinha & Mukherjee, 1996). We will want to recognize our own personal space requirements in different work situations and be sensitive to the personal space requirements of our coworkers and clients.

Social constructionist perspective, Developmental perspective

Variations in personal space are also thought to be related to age, gender, and culture. Personal space increases with age until about age 12 (Evans & Howard, 1973; Hayduk, 1983; Sinha, Nayyar, & Mukherjee, 1995). Males have generally been found to require greater personal space than females, but research indicates that the largest interpersonal distances are kept in male/male pairs, followed by female/female pairs, with the smallest interpersonal distances kept in male/female pairs (Akande, 1997; Kilbury, Bordieri, & Wong, 1996). In *The Hidden Dimensions,* Edward Hall (1966) reported that his field research indicated that members of contact-oriented, collectivist cultures (e.g., Latin, Asian, Arab) prefer closer interpersonal distances than members of noncontact-oriented, individualist cultures (e.g., Northern European, North American). More recent research has supported this suggestion (Evans, Lepore, & Allen, 2000). Hirofumi Minami and Takiji Yamamoto (2000) recently suggested that communal space is more important than personal space in Japan and other Asian cultures that value intimate community life, a preference that should be considered when designing built environments.

Previous research (Langer, Fiske, Taylor, & Chanowitz, 1976; Stephens & Clark, 1987) found that people maintain larger interpersonal distances when interacting with people with disabilities. However, a more recent study found that research participants sat closer to a research assistant in a wheelchair than to one without a visible disability (Kilbury et al., 1996). These researchers conjectured that recent legislation is reducing the stigma of disability. Some of this legislation will be discussed later in this chapter.

Territoriality. Personal space is a concept about individual behavior and about the use of space to control the interpersonal environment. **Territoriality** refers primarily to the behavior of small groups, or individuals in those groups, as they seek control over physical as well as interpersonal space (Taylor, 1988). Territoriality is "a pattern of behavior and attitudes held by an individual or group that is based on perceived, attempted, or actual control of a definable physical space" (Gifford, 1987, p. 137). Territoriality leads us to mark, or personalize, our territory to signify our "ownership," and to engage in a variety of behaviors to protect it from invasion. The study of animal territoriality has a longer history than the study of human territorial behavior.

Irwin Altman (1975) classifies our territories as primary, secondary, and public. A **primary territory** is one that evokes feelings of ownership that we control on a relatively permanent basis and that is vital to our daily lives. For most of us, our primary territory would include our home and place of work. **Secondary territories** are less important to us than primary territories, and control of them does not seem as essential to us; examples might be our favorite table at Starbucks or our favorite stair machine at the health center. **Public territories** are open to anyone in the community, and we generally make no attempt to control access to them—places such as public parks, public beaches, sidewalks, and stores. For people who are homeless and lack access to typical primary territories, however, public territories may serve as primary territories.

Systems perspective, Conflict perspective

Much of the literature on territoriality draws on the functionalist sociological tradition (discussed in Chapter 2), emphasizing the positive value of territorial behavior to provide order to the social world and a sense of security to individuals (Taylor, 1988). We know, however, that territorial behavior can also be the source of conflict, domination, and oppression.

Crowding. Crowding has sometimes been used interchangeably with density, but environmental psychologists make important distinctions between these terms. **Density** is the ratio of persons per unit area of a space. **Crowding** is "the unpleasant experience of spatial restriction" (Gifford, 1987, p. 168). Crowding is not always correlated with density; the feeling of being crowded seems to be influenced by an interaction of personal, social, and cultural, as well as physical, factors. Researchers (Evans et al., 2000) have compared different ethnic groups that live in high-density housing in the United States. They found that Latin American and Asian American residents tolerate more density before feeling crowded than Anglo-Americans and African Americans.

These researchers also found, however, that all four ethnic groups experienced similar psychological distress from crowding. Crowding has also been associated with elevated blood pressure and neuroendocrine hormone activity (Evans & Saegert, 2000).

Psychodynamic perspective

Social constructionist perspective

Privacy. Altman (1975, p. 18) defines *privacy* as "selective control of access to the self or to one's group." This definition contains two important elements: privacy involves control over information about oneself, as well as control over interactions with others.

Some of us require more privacy than others, and some situations stimulate privacy needs more than other situations. Cheryl suspects that future visitors to her apartment will be disconcerted by the lack of privacy allowed for bathroom activities; not surprisingly, she makes no note of the lack of privacy for kitchen activities.

It appears that people in different cultures use space differently to create privacy. Susan Kent (1991) theorizes that the use of partitions, such as walls or screens, to create private spaces increases as societies become more complex. She particularly notes the strong emphasis that European American culture places on partitioned space, both at home and at work (see Duvall-Early & Benedict, 1992).

Have you given much thought to your need for private space? Do the clients at your field agency have private space?

Behavior Settings Theories

Social behavioral perspective, Systems perspective

Would you expect to observe the same behaviors if you were observing Cheryl in different settings—for example, her parents' home, her new apartment, at work, or at a social event with friends? My guess is that you would not. A third major category of theories about the relationship between human behavior and the physical environment is **behavior settings theories.** According to these theories, consistent, uniform patterns of behavior occur in particular places, or **behavior settings**. Behavior is *always* tied to a specific place (Bechtel, 2000).

Behavior settings theory was developed by Roger Barker (1968), who was searching for the factors that influence different individuals to behave differently in the same environment. He and his colleagues studied human behavior in public settings, rather than in the laboratory, where individual differences were usually studied. They unexpectedly noted that observations of different persons in the same setting, even when substantial time elapsed between the observations, were more similar than observations of the same person in different settings, even when there was only a short time between observations. For example, your behavior at a musical festival is more similar to the behavior of other festival attendees than it is to your own behavior in the classroom.

Barker suggested that **programs**—consistent, prescribed patterns of behavior—develop and are maintained in many specific settings. You might argue that behavior settings theory is more about the social environment than the physical environment—that behavioral programs are socially constructed, developed by people in interaction, and not determined by the physical environment. As suggested earlier, however, Barker takes a transactional approach to person in environment (Minami & Tanaka, 1995; Wapner, 1995). In his view, "the behavior pattern and the milieu are dynamically inseparable" (Schoggen, 1989, p. 47). Behavioral programs are created conjointly by individuals and their inanimate surroundings, and behavior settings are distinctive in their physical-spatial features as well as their social rules. The relationships of the social and physical environments to behavior can be summarized in these words: "*[I]t is the social situation that influences people's behavior, but it is the physical environment that provides the cues*" (emphasis in original) (Rapoport, 1990, p. 57).

Behavior settings as conceptualized by Barker had a static quality, but Allan Wicker (1987) has more recently written about the changing nature—the life histories—of behavior settings. In other words, behavior settings themselves are now seen as changing configurations of person and environment. Some settings disappear (have you been to a barn raising lately?), and some become radically altered. The high school prom that my neighbor attended in 2002 was a different setting, with a very different behavioral program, from the high school prom that I attended in 1963.

Behavior settings theory has implications for social work assessment and intervention. It suggests that patterns of behavior are specific to a setting and, therefore, that we must assess settings as well as individuals when problematic behavior occurs. Cheryl was feeling depressed and suicidal at the beginning of the story, but we do not see behaviors that suggest she was feeling the same way at the end of the story. The behavioral setting may not be the only factor involved in this change, but it should be considered as one possible factor. Behavior settings theory also suggests that "the place in which we first master information helps recreate the state necessary to retrieve it" (Gallagher, 1993, p. 132). When we are assisting clients in skill development, we should pay particular attention to the discontinuities between the settings where the skills are being "learned" and the settings where those skills must be used.

Another key concept in behavior settings theory is the level of **staffing** (Barker, 1968; Wicker, 1979). Different behavior settings attract different numbers of participants, or staff. It is important to have a good fit between the number of participants and the behavioral program for the setting. Overstaffing occurs when there are too many participants for the behavioral program of a given setting; understaffing occurs when there are too few participants. Roger Barker and Paul Gump's (1964) study of the optimal high school size is a classic piece of research about optimal staffing for particular behavior settings. This research will be addressed later in the chapter, when we discuss the physical environment and the life course. A growing body of research also suggests that larger settings tend to exclude more people from action, and smaller settings put pressure on more people to perform (Bechtel, 2000). The issue of appropriate staffing, in terms of number of participants, for particular behavioral programs in particular behavior settings has great relevance for the planning of social work programs.

The Natural Environment

Do you find that you feel refreshed from being in the natural environment—walking along the beach, hiking in the mountains, or even walking in your neighborhood? Research findings suggest that you may, and that you should consider the benefits of time spent in the **natural environment**—the portion of the environment influenced primarily by geological and nonhuman biological forces—for both you and your clients. Most of the research on the relationship between human behavior and the natural environment has been in the stimulation theory tradition—looking for ways in which aspects of the natural environment affect our thinking, feeling, social interaction, and health. In general, this research identifies a strong human preference for elements of the natural world and finds many positive outcomes of time spent in the natural environment (Kahn, 1999; Kaplan & Kaplan, 1989). These benefits are summarized in Exhibit 7.3. The findings are not surprising, given the distinctive place accorded to the natural environment in the cultural artifacts—music, art, literature—of all societies. Sociobiologists argue that humans have a genetically based need to affiliate with nature; they call it **biophilia** (Kellert & Wilson, 1993; Wilson, 1984).

In a study of Israeli adults and children, Rachel Sebba (1991) found that almost all the adults retrospectively identified an outdoor setting as the most significant place in their childhood. This finding held for both men and women and for adults from different historical periods and different environmental and social backgrounds. Similarly, a recent cross-cultural study of adults from Senegal, Ireland, and the United States found that 61% of the participants named a setting in the natural environment as their favorite place (Newell, 1997). Sebba also found features of the natural environment to be more effective than features of the built environment in engaging children's interest and stimulating their imaginations. Natural features also stimulated them to action, an outcome related to the concept of *activity,* as defined in Exhibit 7.1.

In recent years, practitioners in various disciplines have taken the age-old advice of poets, novelists, and philosophers that natural settings are good for body, mind, and spirit and have developed programs that center on activities in both wilderness and

EXHIBIT 7.3

Benefits of Time
Spent in the Natural
Environment
(Based on Stimulation
Theory Research)

- Engaging children's interest
- Stimulating children's imagination
- Stimulating activity and physical fitness
- Increasing productivity
- Enhancing creativity
- Providing intellectual stimulation
- Aiding recovery from mental fatigue
- Enhancing group cohesiveness and community cooperation
- Fostering serenity
- Fostering a sense of oneness or wholeness
- Fostering a sense of control
- Improving physical health
- Improving emotional state

urban natural settings. Researchers who have studied the effects of such programs have found some positive gain and no evidence of negative effects (see Burton, 1981; Kahn, 1999; Kaplan & Kaplan, 1989). Studies on the impact of wilderness programs have reported two positive outcomes: recovery from mental fatigue with improved attention (Hartig, Mang, & Evans, 1991; Kaplan & Kaplan, 1989) and enhanced group cohesiveness (Ewert & Heywood, 1991). Ten years of research conducted for the U.S. Forest Service suggest strong spiritual benefits as well (Kaplan & Kaplan, 1989), with participants reporting serenity and a sense of oneness or wholeness as outcomes of their wilderness experiences (see the discussion of spirituality in Chapter 6). But it may not be necessary to travel to wilderness areas to benefit from activity in natural settings. Urban community gardening projects have been found to contribute to the development of cooperation and to improved self-esteem among the participants (Lewis, 1972, 1979). Research with individuals involved in both community gardening and backyard gardening indicates benefits that include a sense of tranquility, sense of control, and improved physical health (Kaplan, 1983; Kaplan & Kaplan, 1987).

One does not have to be active in the natural environment to derive benefits from it. One study found that surgery patients with views of nature from their hospital windows recovered more quickly than did patients whose window views had no nature content (Ulrich, 1984). Two studies in prison settings found that inmates who had views of nature from their cells sought health care less often than those without nature in view from their cells (Moore, 1981; West, 1986). In a psychiatric ward renovation project that included changes in or additions of paint, wallpaper, carpet, lighting, furniture, curtains, plants, and bathtubs, staff rated the addition of plants to be the most positive change (Devlin, 1992). Patients in a short-term psychiatric hospital were found to respond favorably to wall art that involved nature but negatively to abstract wall art (Ulrich, 1993).

Three features of the natural environment have been found to be particularly influential on emotional states:

1. *Water.* A cross-cultural comparison of preferences for landscape elements found water to be the preferred element among both Korean and Western participants (Yang & Brown, 1992).

2. *Trees.* When viewing line drawings and slides of urban streets with and without trees and shrubs, the participants in one study reported more positive feelings when viewing the tree-lined streets (Sheets & Manzer, 1991). They reported feeling friendlier, more cooperative, less sad, and less depressed. Another study found that having well-maintained trees and grass increased the sense of safety of residents of a large inner-city housing project (Kuo, Bacaicoa, & Sullivan, 1998). Another study found that children in inner-city neighborhoods engage in more creative play in settings with trees than in settings without trees (Taylor, Wiley, Kuo, & Sullivan, 1998).

3. *Sunlight.* The relationship between sunlight and human behavior is curvilinear, with benefit coming from increasing amounts until a certain optimum point is reached, after which increasing amounts damage rather than benefit. Excessive sunlight can have negative impacts, such as glare and overheating, and inadequate sunlight has been identified as a contributor to depression, sometimes referred to as seasonal affective disorder (SAD), in some persons (Kaplan & Sadock, 1998). One research team found that sunlight penetration in indoor spaces was related to feelings of relaxation, with patches of sunlight as the optimum situation and both too little and too much penetration decreasing the feeling of relaxation (Boubekri, Hull, & Boyer, 1991).

Although the natural environment can be a positive force, it also has the potential to damage mental, social, and physical well-being. The relationship between sunlight and human behavior provides a clue. The natural environment provides sensory stimulation in an uncontrolled strength, and the patterns of stimulation are quite unstable. Extremely stimulating natural events are known as natural disasters. The Federal Emergency Management Agency (n.d.) includes the following events in its definition of natural disaster: hurricane, tornado, flood, earthquake, volcanic eruption, and fire. Others have included these natural disasters in their discussion of cataclysmic events—a class of stressors with great force, sudden onset, excessive demands on human coping, and large scope (Lazarus & Cohen, 1977). These events are considered to be almost universally stressful (Kobayashi & Miura, 2000), and social workers often play an active role in services to communities that have experienced natural disasters.

The Built Environment

It is exactly this uncontrollable quality of the natural environment that humans try to overcome in constructing the **built environment**—the portion of the physical environment attributable solely to human effort. The built environment is intended to create comfort and controllability, but unfortunately, technological developments often have negative impacts as well. The toxic waste problem is but one example of the risks we have created but not yet learned to control. Social workers have called attention to the fact that the risks of environmental hazards are falling disproportionately on minority and low socioeconomic communities (Rogge, 1993).

Research on the relationship between human behavior and the built environment draws heavily on control theories as well as stimulation theories. Some researchers study stimulation exclusively, others study control exclusively, but most researchers study both—providing a good example of research that attempts to integrate ideas from different theoretical perspectives to achieve a more comprehensive understanding of changing person/environment configurations. That is increasingly the case.

Institutional Design

The ideas of Humphry Osmond (1957, 1959, 1966) about the importance of architecture for the therapeutic functions of mental hospitals stimulated a line of inquiry in different institutional settings, including psychiatric hospitals, state schools for mentally retarded persons, college dormitories, and correctional facilites. This work reflects both stimulation and control theories. These studies have had some impact on institutional design, and probably contributed to the deinstitutionalization movement in mental health and mental retardation services during the 1970s. Too often, however, what is known about the therapeutic use of architecture (see Exhibit 7.4) gets lost in the sociopolitical processes by which design decisions are made. In other words, we know more than we use. The following discussion draws heavily on Paul Cherulnik's (1993) review of 13 of the best research projects on human behavior and the built environment.

Therapeutic Institutions. Osmond noted that mental hospital patients have disturbances of perception (hallucinations and delusions), mood, and thinking that cause them significant difficulties in social relationships. He proposed that the mental hospitals of his era (1950s and 1960s) were designed in such a way as to aggravate these difficulties, with spaces of massive size, large rooms, high ceilings, hard surfaces, and long corridors. Osmond thought that these massive spaces complicated visual and auditory discrimination and discouraged social interaction. He also noted patients' lack of privacy. They shared large sleeping rooms and large, open dayrooms; had no access to spaces where they could not be observed; and were allowed no personal items. According to Osmond, this lack of privacy damaged the patients' already fragile

EXHIBIT 7.4

Selected Research Findings About the Therapeutic Use of Architecture

Therapeutic Design Features	Positive Behaviors
Tables with chairs instead of shoulder-to-shoulder and back-to-back seating Large spaces broken into smaller spaces Flowers and magazines placed on tables	Increase in both brief and sustained interaction
Special activity centers with partitions Sleeping dormitories divided into two-bed rooms with table and chairs Long hallways broken up Sound baffles added to high ceilings Improved lighting, bright colors, and large signs added	Increase in social interaction Decrease in passive and inactive behavior
Painted walls replacing bars Carpeted floors Conventional furniture with fabric upholstery Visually interesting public areas Private rooms with outside windows Solarium with exercise equipment	Decrease in violent behavior in correctional facilities
Open sleeping wards and dayroom turned into personal living spaces and a lounge Places for personal belongings provided Personalized decorations Institutional furniture replaced with noninstitutional furniture Rugs, lamps, and draperies added Control over lighting	Increase in social interaction Decrease in stereotypical behavior Increase in alert, purposive behavior Decrease in intrusive behaviors Increase in use of personal space
Suite-design rooms versus corridor-design rooms Short corridors versus long corridors	Less crowding stress Less social withdrawal Less learned helplessness

self-concepts. He described physical designs that discourage social interaction as **sociofugal spaces**. **Sociopetal spaces**, on the other hand, encourage social interaction; Osmond thought that these spaces would be characterized by small rooms and personalized, noninstitutionalized spaces. In Exhibit 7.1, Weisman refers to this social interaction aspect of the physical environment as *sociality*. Despite much empirical support for the idea that sociopetal design features encourage social interaction, there is some evidence that defensive people are more sociable in sociofugal spaces than in sociopetal spaces (Gifford & Gallagher, 1985).

Sommer (1969) refined Osmond's ideas in his redesign of a sociofugal dayroom in a geriatric ward in which, despite its attractiveness, little social interaction occurred. He focused on the arrangement of the furniture. Chairs and couches were arranged shoulder-to-shoulder along the walls in rows facing each other at a distance too great for conversation; some chairs were clustered back-to-back. Sommer and a colleague (Sommer & Ross, 1958) conducted a 6-week experiment with a new arrangement of furniture to see if social interaction increased. The new, more sociopetal arrangement eliminated shoulder-to-shoulder and back-to-back seating, substituting tables with four chairs around them to encourage face-to-face interaction and to break up the large space into smaller spaces. Flowers and magazines were placed on the tables to encourage the residents to sit at them. The research indicated a substantial increase in both brief and sustained social interaction in the dayroom.

Osmond and Sommer were focusing on one specific type of behavior: social interaction. Other researchers have broadened the focus to include other behaviors. More than a decade after the Sommer and Ross experiment, a group of behaviorally oriented architects redesigned a locked ward for 50 long-term psychiatric patients at Cleveland State Hospital (Cherulnik, 1993). The researchers were interested in increasing the level of social interaction, but the primary behavioral target was the lack of purposeful activity. The redesign was intended to create both sociopetal spaces (to foster social interaction) and private spaces. To encourage social interaction and increase residents' options, activity spaces were created in the dayroom on raised platforms that were circular or semicircular, defined by partitions. To provide privacy, partitions were built to divide the sleeping dormitories into two-bed modules, which also included table and chairs. This redesign also broke up the long hallways. Sound baffles were added below the ceilings to reduce sound reflection and facilitate conversation. Lighting was improved, bright colors added, and large signs provided to assist in orientation to place. This aspect of the physical environment addresses the concept known as *legibility* (see Exhibit 7.1). The researchers found that the overall incidence of social interaction doubled and the incidence of passive or inactive behavior declined. Another group of researchers replicated these physical design elements, comparing a traditional with a redesigned psychiatric admissions ward in a large municipal hospital, and reported similar findings of increased social interaction and decreased passive or inactive behavior (Holahan & Saegert, 1973).

Correctional Settings. Similar design elements also have been tested in correctional settings, with different goals: prevention of violence and brutalization among inmates, and safety of the professional staff. The physical designs include painted walls (replacing bars), carpeted floors, conventional furniture with fabric upholstery, visually interesting public areas, private rooms with outside windows, and a solarium with exercise equipment. In spite of overcrowding in some of the experimental facilities, the redesign resulted in impressive reductions in violent behaviors (Wener, Frazier, & Farbstein, 1985). Despite these research findings, for sociopolitical reasons the results are not being used.

Institutions for Persons With Mental Retardation. The *normalization principle*—which drove policy regarding programs for persons with mental retardation during the 1970s and 1980s, emphasizing the importance of a homelike physical environment (Wolfensberger, 1973)—is based on stimulation theory. One team of interdisciplinary researchers used a sophisticated experimental design to test whether certain behaviors of institutionalized persons with profound mental retardation and organic anomalies would be more positively influenced by increasing privacy and control (control theory) or by improving the homelike appearance of the ward (stimulation theory). The targeted behaviors were social withdrawal, stereotypical behavior such as rocking or repeated vocalizations, alert purposeful behavior such as alert observation of events, use of personal space, intrusion into others' space, and frequency of social interaction.

The researchers found positive changes in the targeted behaviors in both the homelike renovation and the renovation based on privacy and control, as compared to the prerenovation, traditional institutional environment. However, increased privacy and control had a greater positive impact on the targeted behaviors than did improved homelike appearance (Friedman, 1976). These findings are consistent with those of another study, in which clients with physical disabilities were asked about preferred aspects of the physical environment (Cooper & Hasselkus, 1992); the central theme of their responses was control. It is also consistent with the joy with which Cheryl embraced her "small, dark, roach-infested" first apartment.

This is not to say that physical attractiveness is unimportant to persons with mental retardation and physical disabilities. Remember that targeted behaviors also improved with homelike renovations. But it does suggest that control of the physical environment may well be a higher value to them.

College Dormitories. Some of you have had the experience of moving from home to a college dormitory in recent years, and you may have wondered about some changes in your behavior at the time. Control theorists have speculated that the lack of private areas other than the student's room, large public bathrooms, and long corridors force students into more social interaction than they desire and lead to crowding stress, social withdrawal, and learned helplessness. (See Chapter 2 for a discussion of learned helplessness.) Experimental research does indeed provide evidence that suite-design rooms in college dormitories, rather than corridor-design rooms, and short corridors rather than long corridors result in less crowding stress, social withdrawal, and learned helplessness (Aiello, Baum, & Gormley, 1981; Baum & Davis, 1980; Baum & Valins, 1977).

Large Hospitals. Have you had the experience of feeling lost and disoriented when visiting a family member in a large hospital, even when you were there the day before? Large, complex institutional buildings, such as large hospitals, offer examples of another way to improve human control over the physical environment: providing adequate and clear signs to help people find their way. During the planning of the new hospital complex at the University of Michigan in Ann Arbor, a team of researchers invited input from patients and visitors as well as from staff. Some of these studies had to do with the use of signs. The researchers discovered that patients and visitors often differed from staff in their recommendations about what kind of signage would be helpful (Carpman, Grant, & Simmons, 1984). Findings such as these remind us of the importance of getting consumer input into environmental designs.

Recent research in Japan suggests that hospital designers still do not pay enough attention to signage legibility from the patient's perspective, however (Nagasawa, 2000). This researcher also suggests that hospital designers pay too little attention to how to provide a better "healing environment" in hospitals.

Defensible Space and Crime Prevention

Applying the concept of territoriality to crime prevention, Oscar Newman (1972, 1980) developed his theory of **defensible space**. This theory suggests that residential crime and fear of crime can be decreased by means of certain design features that increase residents' sense of territoriality and, consequently, their motivation to "watch out" for the neighborhood. A recent article in the *Yale Law Review* argued that in the United States, we spend too much of scarce resources on law enforcement and too little on the use of architecture to prevent crime (Katyal, 2002). The author provides evidence that some European countries are making better use of what is known about architectural control of crime. The recommended design features are listed in Exhibit 7.5.

Much of the research about defensible space has been conducted in public low-income housing, and the findings from these settings provide strong support for the theory (F. Fowler Jr., 1981; Fowler, McCalla, & Mangione, 1979; Newman, 1972; Perkins, Wandersman, Rich, & Taylor, 1993; Sampson, 1983). The findings suggest that design features help reduce crime and the fear of crime because criminals, as well as residents, perceive the redesigned spaces to be under greater control of the residents.

Research findings that have been used to challenge the defensible space theory have studied crime deterrence in public spaces, such as buses, telephone booths, or business districts, rather than in residential areas (Baldwin, 1975; Mayhew, Clarke, Hough, & Winchester, 1980; Sturman, 1980). This research cannot be interpreted as

EXHIBIT 7.5
Design Features
to Create
Defensible Space

- Real and symbolic barriers, such as fences, walls, or shrubs, to divide the residential environment into smaller, more manageable sections
- Opportunities for surveillance of both interior spaces and exterior spaces by residents
- Opportunities for personalizing both interior and exterior spaces
- Spaces that encourage social interaction and community building
- Strengthening of potential targets of crime, such as raising fire escapes to get them out of reach and having doors in vulnerable spots open outward

Source: Based on Newman, 1972, 1980, and Katyal, 2002.

contradicting the defensible space theory, however, because Newman never suggested that public territories were defensible space. In fact, Newman looked for ways to carve up expansive public spaces near public housing, turning those spaces into primary and secondary territories (Altman, 1975) that residents would be more likely to view as defensible spaces.

Behavior Settings and Addictions

An emerging line of research suggests that behavior settings are an important element in substance addiction. For instance, Winifred Gallagher (1993) reports that large numbers of American soldiers who used heroin during the Vietnam conflict left the drug behind when they returned to an environment that they did not associate with heroin.

Social behavioral perspective

Shepard Siegel's research (Kim, Siegel, & Patenall, 1999; Siegel, 1991; Siegel & Allan, 1998; Siegel, Hinson, Krank, & McCully, 1982) also supports the idea that behavior settings play an important role in substance addiction. Siegel found that when a person with a heroin addiction takes a customary dose of heroin in an environment where he or she does not usually take the drug, the reaction is much more intense, and an overdose may even occur. This consistent finding over time has led Siegel to suggest that *tolerance*—the ability to take increasing amounts of the drug without feeling increased effects—is embedded in the environment in which the drug is usually taken. He has also found that behavior settings stimulate craving, even when the person has been in recovery for some time. Siegel recommends that treatment include systematic exposure to cues from the behavior setting, with no reinforcement of drug ingestion, to provide environmental deconditioning. You may recognize that this approach to treatment comes from classical conditioning.

Maybe the concept of behavior setting also explains why many people with addictions attempt to shake their addictions by moving to a new environment. Siegel reports that "studies from all over the world show that after a year, most of those who don't relapse after drug treatment have relocated" (cited in Gallagher, 1993, p. 138).

Place Attachment

Have you ever been strongly attached to a specific place—a beloved home, a particular beach or mountain spot, or a house of worship? **Place attachment**—the process in which people and groups form bonds with places—is the subject of a growing literature (Low & Altman, 1992; Mesch & Manor, 1998). Although place attachment is usually discussed in terms of emotional bonding, an interplay of emotions, cognitions, and behaviors and actions is what forges the people/place bond (Low & Altman, 1992). Consider the role of behaviors and actions, laboring and sweating, in the attachment to the lost home described by a survivor of the 1972 Buffalo Creek flood:

> I have a new home right now, and I would say that it is a much nicer home than what I had before. But it is a house, it is not a home. Before, I had a home. And what I mean by that, I built the other home. I took a coal company house, I remodeled it, I did the work on it myself. I put many a drop of sweat and drove many a nail into it, and I labored and sweated and worried over it. And it was gone. I left home Saturday morning and I had a home. On Saturday evening I didn't have nothing. (Quoted in Erikson, 1976, p. 175)

This example focuses on attachment to home, but researchers have looked at attachment to places of different scale. We run into the concept of place attachment again in Chapter 13 when we discuss community as a dimension of environment.

In the context of place attachment, *place* is defined as a "space that has been given meaning through personal, group, or cultural processes" (Low & Altman, 1992, p. 5). The literature on place attachment emphasizes emotional bonding to environmental settings that are satisfying in terms of one or more of the aspects of physical environment/ behavior relationships presented in Exhibit 7.1, with different researchers focusing on different aspects. Those who focus on sociality remind us that attachment to places may be based largely on our satisfying relationships with people in those places—once again reminding us of the inseparability of people and environments.

Psychodynamic perspective, Social behavioral perspective

When a strong place attachment develops, it has been suggested that "the meaning of place and the meaning of self begin to merge" (Gifford, 1987, p. 62). When a particular place becomes an important part of our self-identity, this merger of place and self is known as **place identity**. Social psychologists (e.g., Bonaiuto & Bonnes, 2000) have recently suggested that place identity can be studied within the framework of social identity theory (see Chapter 4 for a discussion of social identity theory). In their research on place identity, they define it as *physical rootedness* ("I feel at home here"), *place identification* ("This place has become a part of me"), and *social place identification* ("I feel like a real New Englander"). Place identity can develop where there is strong negative, as well as positive, place attachment, as a boy named Kareem observes:

It's strange, but I really like when the lights go off in the movies because then I'm no longer a "homeless kid." I'm just a person watching the movie like everyone else. A lot of the children at the hotel believe that they are "hotel kids." They've been told by so many people for so long that they are not important, that they live up to what is expected of them. It gets so some children have no dreams and live in a nightmare because they believe that they are "hotel kids." It's worse than being in jail. In jail you can see the bars and you know when you're getting out. In the hotel you can't see the bars because they're inside of you and you don't know when you're getting out. (Quoted in Berck, 1992, p. 105)

Home and work settings are most likely to become merged with our sense of self (Altman, 1993). Place attachment can also play a strong role in group and cultural identity (Low & Altman, 1992). One recent study found that many Cambodian American and Filipino American older adults expressed a desire to die in their homelands (Becker, 2002).

Researchers have been particularly interested in what happens to people when a place of identity is lost. Certainly, we should pay attention to issues of place identity when we encounter people who have relocated, particularly when working with immigrant and refugee families. We should also consider the long-term consequences of early experiences, such as homelessness or frequent movement between foster homes, in which no stable place attachment forms, or that result in a negative place attachment.

Probably the best-known research on place identity is Fried and Gleicher's (1961) study of people relocated as a result of urban redevelopment projects. Planners assumed that people would be pleased to be moved from old, physically run-down neighborhoods into new apartments, but Fried and Gleicher found that relocated residents often sat in their new apartments and grieved for their lost homes. William Yancey (1971) later suggested that planners had undervalued the informal networks that were embedded in the deteriorating neighborhoods. He also argued that the architectural designs of the new apartments—designs that had received high praise in architectural journals—provided no spaces for building new networks; the new apartments were sociofugal spaces, low in sociality. Yancey, therefore, reminds us that attachment to place is often intertwined with attachment to people. He also reminds us that professionals often differ from consumer groups in their ideas about what makes good environments. Social workers, as well as architects and urban planners, need continual reminders to maximize client input when planning services and programs.

Homelessness

As suggested above, place attachment can be quite problematic for people without homes. Exhibit 7.6 shows the federal definition of homelessness. The National Coalition for the Homeless (NCH) (1997b) points out that this definition does not apply as well in rural areas as it does in urban areas, because there are few shelters in rural areas. Many homeless rural people live in crowded situations with relatives, or in substandard housing.

Although it is difficult to count the number of people who are homeless, there is general agreement that homelessness has increased in the past 15 to 20 years. On the basis of a 1996 National Survey of Homeless Assistance Providers and Clients (NSHAPC), researchers at the Urban Institute (2000) estimated that 2.3 million adults and children, almost 1% of the U.S. population, will experience homelessness at least once during a year. About 6.3% of persons living in poverty will experience a spell of homelessness during a year. According to a 2001 survey of 27 major cities conducted by the U.S. Conference of Mayors, single men constitute 40% of homeless persons and families with children constitute another 40%. Half are African American, 35% are white, and 12% are Hispanic. Twenty percent of homeless persons are employed. Homeless persons in rural areas are much more likely to be European Americans (NCH, 1997b).

Poverty and a shortage of affordable housing appear to be the primary factors involved in the rising rate of homelessness (NCH, 1997a). As the housing market tightens, some groups are more likely than others to become homeless at some point. Groups particularly vulnerable to homelessness include people who are unemployed or working in low-wage jobs, women and children who are the victims of domestic

EXHIBIT 7.6
Federal Definition of Homelessness

A person is considered homeless when he or she

1. Lacks a fixed, regular, and adequate nighttime residence or
2. Has a nighttime residence that is
   - A supervised publicly or privately operated shelter designed to provide temporary living accommodations (including welfare hotels, congregate shelters, and transitional housing for the mentally ill);
   - An institution that provides temporary residence for individuals intended to be institutionalized; or
   - A public or private place not designed for, or ordinarily used as, a regular sleeping accommodation for human beings

Source: Stewart B. Mckinney Act, 1994.

violence, veterans, persons with mental illness, and persons with substance abuse disorders (NCH, 1997b). Many people move in and out of homelessness but remain vulnerable to becoming homeless again even when they have homes. NSHAPC found that 49% of homeless clients are in their first episode of homelessness, and 34% have been homeless three or more times (U.S. Department of Housing & Urban Development, n.d.).

Accessible Environments for Persons With Disabilities

Accessibility is one of the key concepts for the study of human behavior and the physical environment (see Exhibit 7.1). In recent years, we have been reminded that environments, particularly built environments, can be disabling because of their inaccessibility to many persons, including most people with disabilities. An emerging model of thinking about disability emphasizes that it is primarily a "problem in the relationship between the individual and the environment" (Law & Dunn, 1993, p. 2).

Conflict Perspective

This way of thinking about disability was the impetus for legislation at all levels of government during the 1970s and 1980s, most notably two pieces of federal legislation (Gilson, 1996). The Rehabilitation Act of 1973 (Public Law 93-112) was the first federal act to recognize the need for civil rights protection for persons with disabilities. It required all organizations receiving federal assistance to have an affirmative action plan to ensure accessibility of employment to persons with disabilities. The Americans With Disabilities Act of 1990 (ADA) (Public Law 101-336) extended the civil rights of persons with disabilities to the private sector. It seeks to end discrimination against persons with disabilities and promote their full participation in society.

The five titles of the ADA seek to eliminate environmental barriers to the full participation of persons with disabilities. You will want to be aware of the legal rights of your clients with disabilities.

■ *Title I* addresses discrimination in the workplace. It requires reasonable accommodations, including architectural modification, for disabled workers.

■ *Title II* requires that all public services, programs, and facilities, including public transportation, be accessible to persons with disabilities.

■ *Title III* requires all public accommodations and services operated by private organizations to be accessible to persons with disabilities. It specifically lists 12 categories of accommodations: hotels and places of lodging; restaurants; movies and theaters; auditoriums and places of public gathering; stores and banks; health care service providers, hospitals, and pharmacies; terminals for public transportation; museums and libraries; parks and zoos; schools; senior centers and social service centers; and places of recreation.

■ *Title IV* requires all intrastate and interstate phone companies to develop telecommunication relay services and devices for persons with speech or hearing impairments, to allow them to communicate in a manner similar to persons without impairments.

■ *Title V* covers technical guidelines for enforcing the ADA.

Under industrial capitalism, wages are the primary source of livelihood. People who cannot earn wages, therefore, tend to be poor. Research by staff at the World Bank indicates that, around the world, poverty and disability are inextricably linked (Elwan, 1999). People with disabilities who lobbied for passage of the ADA argued that government was spending vast sums of money for what they called "dependency programs" but was failing to make the investments required to make environments accessible so that people with disabilities could become employed (Johnson, 1992).

Social workers need to keep in mind the high prevalence of disabilities among older persons, the fastest growing group in the United States (Bachelder & Hilton, 1994). More accessible environments may be an important way to buffer the expected deleterious effects of a large elderly population. As the baby boomers age, they will benefit from the earlier activism of the disability community.

Exhibit 7.7 lists some of the elements of environmental design that improve accessibility for persons with disabilities. It is important to remember, however, that rapid developments in assistive technology are likely to alter current guidelines about what is optimal environmental design. For example, the minimum space requirements in the ADA's guidelines for wheelchairs are already too tight for the new styles of motorized wheelchairs.

The Physical Environment and Human Behavior Across the Life Course

Developmental perspective

People have different physical environment needs at different ages, and may respond to features of the physical environment in different ways as they progress through the life course. Some of these differences have been discussed earlier in this chapter. Because the built environment has been designed, for the most part, to accommodate the needs and responses of adults, this section calls attention to some of the special needs and responses of children, adolescents, and elderly adults.

EXHIBIT 7.7
Elements of
Accessible
Environments for
Persons With
Disabilities

- Create some close-in parking spaces widened to 8 feet to accommodate unloading of wheelchairs (1 accessible space for every 25 spaces).
- Create curb cuts or ramping for curbs, with 12 inches of slope for every inch of drop in the curb.
- Make ramps at least 3 feet wide to accommodate wheelchairs and provide a 5-foot-by-5-foot square area at the top of ramps to entrances to allow space for door opening.
- Remove high-pile carpeting, low-density carpeting, and plush carpeting, at least in the path of travel. Put nonslip material on slippery floors.
- Avoid phone-in security systems in entrances (barriers for persons who are deaf).
- Make all doorways at least 32 inches wide (36 is better).
- Use automatic doors or doors that take no more than 5 pounds of force to open.
- Use door levers instead of doorknobs.
- Create aisles that are at least 3 feet wide (wider is better). Keep the path of travel clear.
- Connect different levels in buildings with ramps (for small level changes) or a wheelchair-accessible elevator.
- Place public phones no higher than 48 inches (35-42 is optimal).
- Place other things that need to be reached at this optimal height.
- Brightly light foyers and areas with directories to assist persons with low vision. Use 3-inch-high lettering in directories.
- Install braille signs about 5 feet off the ground.
- Make restroom stalls at least 3 feet deep by 4 feet wide (5 feet by 5 feet is optimal).
- Install toilets that are 17-19 inches in height.
- Hang restroom sinks with no vanity underneath, so that persons in wheelchairs can pull up to them.
- Use both visual and audible emergency warning systems.

Source: Based on Johnson, 1992.

Children

In infancy and early childhood, home is the primary physical environment, but day care centers constitute a major environment for increasing numbers of young children. As children grow older, neighborhood and school become important environments.

Research indicates that the physical environment can have both positive and negative effects on child development. Thomas David and Carol Weinstein (1987) suggest that the physical environments of children should be designed to serve five common functions of child development:

1. *Personal identity.* Children need "personalized furnishings and individual territories" (David & Weinstein, 1987, p. 8) to assist in the development of personal identity. Place identity is essential to the development of personal identity.

2. *Sense of competence.* A sense of competence is supported when children have physical spaces and furnishings of a size and scale that allow them to meet their personal needs with minimal assistance. Thus, storage areas, furniture, and fixtures should be at the appropriate height and of the appropriate size for children.

3. *Intellectual, social, and motor development.* Development of intellectual, social, and motor skills is supported by the opportunity to move, explore, and play with interesting materials. Environments that restrict movement inhibit development in all domains.

4. *Security and trust.* Familiar, comfortable, and safe physical environments support the development of security and trust.

5. *A balance of social interaction and privacy.* Physical environments should support social interaction but also provide private spaces that allow children the opportunity to retreat from overstimulating situations. Crowding, clutter, and high noise levels have been found to have negative effects on child development. One study found that children who come from crowded homes and attend crowded day care centers are more likely to exhibit withdrawal, aggression, competitiveness, and hyperactivity than children where crowding is present in neither or only one of these environments (Maxwell, 1996). Constant exposure to high noise levels has been found to have a negative effect on language development (Evans & Maxwell, 1997). Recent research found that the negative effects of residential crowding are greatest for children who live in families where there is a lot of interpersonal turmoil (Evans & Saegert, 2000). This is a reminder that the physical environment interacts with the social environment to influence behavior.

Adolescents

After the rapid physical growth of puberty, adolescents have outgrown the need for physical environments with reduced scale and size. They have not outgrown the need for personalized furnishings and individual territories, however. Research indicates that privacy needs increase in adolescence (Sinha et al., 1995). At the same time, with the increased emphasis on peer relationships, adolescents have a special need for safe gathering places and recreational opportunities.

Since the 1964 publication of Barker and Gump's *Big School, Small School: High School Size and Student Behavior,* considerable attention has been given to the question of optimal high school size. As Paul Gump (1987) suggests, high schools need to be larger than elementary schools. First, high schools provide more varied curricular offerings than elementary schools to assist students to sort out their interests and competencies, which requires a larger and more specialized faculty. Second, high schools offer a varied set of extracurricular activities to meet the need for safe gathering places and recreational opportunities, which requires sufficient numbers of students to "staff" each activity and sufficient numbers of faculty sponsors. There is some agreement that high schools of fewer than 500 students will result in "understaffing." On the other hand, as high schools grow larger, they lose some of the continuity and intimacy of small schools, and very large student populations result in "overstaffing," with meaningful opportunities for participation unavailable to many students.

Elderly Adults

The special needs of elderly adults in relation to the physical environment have not been studied as extensively as the special needs of children. There is general agreement, however, that home and neighborhood are the primary physical environments for elderly adults (Carp, 1987). Housing of elderly adults has become a major social policy issue.

Because there are more differences among elderly adults than among children and adolescents, it is difficult to make definitive statements about their needs in relation to the physical environment. To assist in assessing the needs of individual clients who are elderly, however, you may find it helpful to adapt the previous list of five ways that the physical environment supports child development:

1. *Personal identity.* As they attempt to hold on to personal identity in the midst of multiple losses, elderly adults will benefit from personalized furnishings and personal territories.

2. *Sense of competence.* Elderly adults are more likely to maintain a sense of competence when the demands of the physical environment match the capabilities of the person. Few modifications are needed for those elderly adults with no disabilities, but it may be necessary to intensify the level of sensory stimulation to accommodate losses in the sensory system. For those elderly adults with one or more disabilities, however, modifications such as the ones listed in Exhibit 7.7 may be appropriate. Researchers have found that only about 10% of elderly adults who need modifications in the home environment because of disabilities actually make those modifications (Gilderbloom & Markham, 1996).

3. *Intellectual, social, and motor skills.* Maintenance and development of intellectual, social, and motor skills will be supported by opportunities to read, think, reflect, explore, and work with interesting materials, by opportunities for social interaction, and by opportunities for movement.

4. *Security and trust.* Safe homes and neighborhoods are essential for a sense of security and trust.

5. *A balance of social interaction and privacy.* Home environments, private or institutional, should provide private spaces as well as opportunities for social interaction.

IMPLICATIONS FOR SOCIAL WORK PRACTICE

This discussion of the relationship between human behavior and the physical environment suggests several practice principles:

- Where appropriate, collaborate with design professionals to ensure that specific built environments are accessible, adaptable, and comfortable; provide adequate privacy and control; provide an optimal quality and intensity of stimulation; and facilitate social interaction.

- Assess the physical environment of your social service setting. Do clients find it accessible, legible, and comfortable? Do they find that it provides adequate privacy and control? Does it provide optimal quality and intensity of sensory stimulation? If it is a residential setting, does it promote social interaction?

- Routinely evaluate the physical environments of clients—particularly those environments where problem behaviors occur—for accessibility, legibility, comfort, privacy and control, and sensory stimulation. Check your evaluation against the clients' perceptions. If you have no opportunity to see these environments, have the clients evaluate them for you. Provide space on the intake form for assessing the physical environments of clients.

- Know the physical environments of the organizations to which you refer clients. Assist referral agencies and clients in planning how to overcome any existing environmental barriers. Maximize opportunities for client input into design of their built environments.

- Be alert to the meanings that particular environments hold for clients. Recognize that people have attachments to places as well as to people.

- When assisting clients to learn new skills, pay attention to the discontinuities between the setting where the skills are learned and the settings where they will be used.

- When designing social service programs, consider issues of optimal staffing, of both staff and clients, for particular behavior settings.

- When planning group activities, ensure the best possible fit between the spatial needs of the activity and the physical environment where the activity will occur.

- Keep the benefits of the natural environment in mind when planning both prevention and remediation programs. When possible, help clients gain access to elements of the natural environment, and where appropriate, help them plan activities in the natural environment.

- Assist clients to use cues from the physical environment (such as neighborhood landmarks, or carpet color in institutions) to simplify negotiation of that environment.

- Become familiar with technology for adapting environments to make them more accessible.

KEY TERMS

behavior settings
behavior settings theories
biophilia
boundary regulating mechanisms
built environment
control theories
crowding
defensible space
density
natural environment
personal space
place attachment

place identity
primary territory
programs
public territory
secondary territory
sociofugal spaces
sociopetal spaces
staffing
stimulation theories
territoriality
transactionalism

ACTIVE LEARNING

1. Compare and contrast Cheryl's place of her own with your own living space using the 11 concepts found in Exhibit 7.1.

2. Take a walking tour of your neighborhood. Does the neighborhood include defensible space design characteristics found in Exhibit 7.5? Do you note any of the design features to improve accessibility for persons with disabilities noted in Exhibit 7.7? What effects do you think the physical environment of the neighborhood might have on children, adolescents, and elderly adults?

3. Work with a small group of classmates to develop examples of primary territories, secondary territories, and public territories in your lives. What attempts do you make to protect each of these territories?

WEB RESOURCES

Environmental Justice in Waste Programs

www.epa.gov/swerosps/ej

Site maintained by the U.S. Environmental Protection Agency contains special topics in environment justice, action agenda, resources, laws and regulations, and news and events.

National Coalition for the Homeless

www.nationalhomeless.org

Site maintained by the National Coalition for the Homeless contains facts about homelessness, legislation and policy, research, housing and poverty issues, and other Internet resources.

Job Accommodation Network

www.jan.wvu.edu

Site maintained by the Job Accommodation Network of the Office of Disability Employment Policy of the U.S. Department of Labor contains ADA statutes, regulations, guidelines, technical sheets, and other assistance documents.

American Association of People With Disabilities

www.aapd.com

Site maintained by the American Association of People With Disabilities, a national nonprofit cross-disability organization, contains information on benefits, information on disability rights, news, and links to other disability-related sites.

Eldercare Web: Residential Living options

www.elderweb.com/liveopt.htm

Site maintained by Karen Stevenson Brown, CPA, contains links for assisted living, assistive devices, home and day care, home adaptation, housing options, nursing homes, shared housing, and transportation.

CHAPTER 8

Culture

Linwood Cousins

Culture

Linwood Cousins
University of North Carolina—Charlotte

How does culture produce variations in human behavior?
How does culture produce and maintain social inequality?
How do members of nondominant groups respond to the dominant culture?

Key Ideas

As you read this chapter, take note of these central ideas:

1. In contemporary society, culture refers to the ethos and worldview of a particular people, how they construct and employ meanings that guide their perceptions and behavior in multiple contexts.

2. Features of life such as ethnic customs, traditions, values, beliefs, and notions of common sense are not static entities, but neither are they changing very rapidly.

3. Our understandings of others are always in terms of the understandings we have constructed both about ourselves and about how the world does and should operate. We can easily misunderstand others by using our own categories and rankings to order such realities.

4. A practice orientation is a contemporary approach to understanding culture that attempts to understand cultural processes by thinking of human behavior as both a product and producer of history and social structure and a participant in the transformation of social structure.

5. Members of nondominant groups may respond to the dominant culture with different processes, including assimilation, accommodation, acculturation, and bicultural socialization.

6. A multidimensional understanding of culture is necessary to grasp the increasing complexity of the construction and employment of meaning regarding identities and the distribution of resources in a world based on political, social, and economic structures and processes.

CASE STUDY

STAN AND TINA AT COMMUNITY HIGH SCHOOL

Community High School in Newark, New Jersey, has approximately 1,300 students, the majority of whom are black (African American, Afro-Caribbean, and West African). Most of the students live in the community of Village Park, which has a total population of approximately 58,000 people, also predominantly black. Village Park has a distinct social history and identity as well as distinct physical boundaries that distinguish it from less prosperous communities and schools in Newark.

Village Park evolved from a middle- and working-class Jewish community that centered around its academic institutions, such as Community High. The school generated a national reputation for academic excellence as measured by the number of graduates who went on to become doctors, lawyers, scientists, professors, and the like. But after the Newark riots of the late 1960s, Jews and other whites started moving out. By the early 1970s, upwardly mobile middle- and working-class black families had become the majority in Village Park. The same process has occurred in other communities, but what's interesting about Village Park is that its black residents, like the Jewish residents who preceded them, continued to believe in the ethic of upward mobility through schooling at Community High.

Since the mid-1980s, however, Village Park and Community High have undergone another transformation. Slumps in the economy and ongoing patterns of racial discrimination in employment have reduced the income base of the community's families. Many families who were able to maintain a middle-class income moved to the suburbs as crime and economic blight encroached on the community. Increasingly, Village Park was taken over by renters and absentee landlords, along with the social problems—drug abuse, crime, school dropout—that accompany economically driven social despair.

In 1993, the population profile of Newark reflected an ethnic mix that remains: the city is simultaneously black and multiethnic. The majority of Newark's residents are African American, but the city has a considerable population of other ethnic groups: Hispanics (Puerto Ricans, Colombians, Mexicans, Dominicans, etc.), Italians, Portuguese, Africans (from Nigeria, Sierra Leone, Liberia, Ghana, and other countries), Polish, and small groups of others. At the same time, the governing bodies of the city, the school system, and Community High in particular are predominantly composed of black people.

The intermingling of such history and traditions has had an interesting impact on the students at Community High. Like many urban high schools all over the nation, Community High has suffered disproportionate levels of dropout, low attendance, and violence. Yet, a few parents, teachers, school staff, and community officials have tried hard to rekindle the spirit of academic excellence and social competence that are the school's tradition.

In this context, many of the students resist traditional definitions of academic success but value success nonetheless. Consider the behaviors of Stan and Tina, both students at Community High. Stan is the more troubled and more academically marginal of the two students. He is 17 years old, lives with his girlfriend who has recently had a baby, and has made a living selling drugs (which he is now trying to discontinue). Stan was arrested (and released) for selling drugs some time ago. He is also under questioning for the drug-related murder of his cousin, because the police want him to identify the perpetrator. But Stan has considerable social prestige at school and is academically successful when he attends school and is on focus. Stan's mother—who has hammered into his head the importance of education—is a clerical supervisor, his stepfather works in a meat factory, and his biological father sells drugs. Stan has three brothers, and his mother and biological father were never married.

Among his male and female peers, Stan is considered the epitome of urban maleness and style. Stan is an innovator. He mixes and matches the square-toe motorcycle boots normally associated with white bikers with the brand-name shirts and jeans commonly associated with urban, rap-oriented young people of color. At the same time, Stan is respected by teachers and administrators because he understands and observes the rules of conduct preferred in the classroom and because he can do his work at a level reflecting high intelligence. A couple of months ago, Stan visited Howard University in Washington, D.C., and was smitten by the idea that young black men and women were participating in university life. He says he will try very hard to go to that school after he graduates, but the odds are against him.

CASE STUDY

Tina is also 17 years old, but is more academically successful than Stan is. She ranks in the top 25 of her senior class and has been accepted into the premed program of a historically black university. Tina talks about the lower academic performance of some of her black peers. She sees it as a manifestation of the social distractions that seem to preoccupy black youths—being popular and cool. On the other hand, Tina sees her successful academic performance, level of motivation, and assertive style of interacting in the classroom as part of being black too—taking care of business and trying to make it in this world.

Tina is an only child. Her father is an engineer, and her stepmother is a restaurant manager. Tina has never known her biological mother, and she was raised primarily by her father until about 6 years ago. They moved to Village Park from Brooklyn, New York, around that time. Tina's is the kind of family that is likely to leave Village Park not for the suburbs but for a more productive and less hostile urban community. Tina has been raised in a community that, despite its ills, centers around black identity and culture.

Like Stan, Tina is an innovator. She has been allowed to adopt modes of language, demeanor, and clothing that are seen by some as decidedly mainstream in their origins. In fact, however, Tina mixes the aesthetics of black and mainstream white culture as well as the contemporary urban flavor that textures the lives of many youths today. Perhaps the results are most apparent in the way Tina mixes and matches hip-hop-influenced clothing, attitudes, and hairstyles with mainstream clothing styles and the mannerisms associated with the norms and standards of professional, middle-class occupations.

Anyone who would approach Tina as an ally of *the system*—defining the system as the white establishment—would meet with disappointment, however. They would discover that in Tina's view, and perhaps in Stan's, there is nothing generally wrong with black people and their behavior. However, there is something wrong with black individuals who do things that are not in their own best interest and consequently not in the best interest of the black community.

Furthermore, they would hear Tina, Stan, and other students at Community High describe academic success and failure not just in terms of students' actions. These students also indict uninterested and complacent teachers and staff and schools that do not understand "how to educate black people." (Based on an ethnographic study of culture, race, and class during the 1992-1993 academic year.) (Cousins, 1994).

The Challenge of Defining Culture

The U.S. Census Bureau tells us that there are now over 6 billion people in the world (U.S. Census Bureau, 2000b). Roughly 285 million of them live in the United States. The U.S. is the third most populated country, behind China (just over 1.2 billion) and India (just over 1 billion). The U.S. population includes 211 million white people of various ancestries, just over 35 million Hispanics/Latinos, just under 35 million African Americans/blacks, more than 10 million Asians, 2 million American Indians and Alaskan Natives, with Native Hawaiian and other Pacific Islanders and other peoples constituting the rest. Finally, approximately 10.4% of U.S. residents are foreign born.

Much diversity is concealed in this numerical portrait, but it is a good place to begin our discussion of the diverse society we live in. Given this scenario, how should we as social workers interpret the multifaceted context of Tina's and Stan's lives? Economics, race/ethnicity, traditions and customs, gender, political processes, psychology, academic processes, and a host of other factors are all involved. All this and more must be considered in our discussion of culture.

Social constructionist perspective

Over 30 years ago, Peter Berger and Thomas Luckmann stated the following: "Society is a human product. Society is an objective reality. Man is a social product" (Berger & Luckmann, 1966, p. 61). If you replace "society" with "culture," you get the following: Culture is a human product, culture is an objective reality, and humankind is a cultural product. These restatements suggest the enormous span of human behavior we try to make intelligible through the concept of culture.

In this chapter you learn how the concept of culture evolved and applies to the puzzle of human diversity that is so dominant in public discussions today about our multicultural society. Understanding culture as a concept and a process can help you interpret changes in what people believe and value within families, and help you deal with communities with large immigrant populations.

But let me caution you. Defining culture is an arbitrary game. Alfred Kroeber and Clyde Kluckhohn (1963, 1952/1978), two renowned anthropologists, have cataloged more than 100 definitions of culture (see Exhibit 8.1). Definitions and discussions of culture tend to reflect the theoretical perspectives and purposes of the definers.

Like other views of culture, the one I present here has its biases. In keeping with the emphasis in this book on power arrangements, I intend to present a view of culture that will expose not only social differences or human variation but also the cultural bases of various forms of inequality. This chapter looks at the ways in which variations in human behavior have led to subjugation and have become the basis of, among other things, racial, ethnic, economic, and gender oppression and inequality.

EXHIBIT 8.1
Categorical Definitions of Culture

Enumeration of Social Content

- That complex whole that includes knowledge, belief, art, morals, law, custom, and any other capabilities and habits acquired by humans as members of society; the sum total of human achievement

Social Heritage/Tradition

- The learned repertory of thoughts and actions exhibited by members of a social group, independently of genetic heredity from one generation to the next
- The sum total and organization of social heritages that have acquired social meaning because of racial temperament and the historical life of the group

Rule or Way of Life

- The sum total of ways of doing and thinking, past and present, of a social group
- The distinctive way of life of a group of people; their complete design for living

Psychological and Social Adjustment and Learning

- The total equipment of technique—mechanical, mental, and moral—by use of which the people of a given period try to attain their ends
- The sum total of the material and intellectual equipment whereby people satisfy their biological and social needs and adapt themselves to their environment
- Learned modes of behavior that are socially transmitted from one generation to another within a particular society and that may be diffused from one society to another

Ideas and Values

- An organized group of ideas, habits, and conditioned emotional responses shared by members of a society
- Acquired or cultivated behavior and thought of individuals; the material and social values of any group of people

Patterning and Symbols

- A system of interrelated and interdependent habit patterns of response
- Organization of conventional understandings, manifest in act and artifact, that, persisting through tradition, characterizes a human group
- Semiotics—those webs of public meaning that people have spun and by which they are suspended
- A distinct order or class of phenomena—namely, those things and events that are dependent upon the exercise of a mental ability peculiar to the human species—that we have termed *symboling*; or material objects (such as tools, utensils, ornaments, amulets), acts, beliefs, and attitudes that function in contexts characterized by symboling

---

Source: Adapted from Kroeber and Kluckhohn, 1952/1978, pp. 40-79.

A Preliminary Definition of Culture

Culture as we have come to know it today is rooted in definitions based on behavioral and material inventions and accomplishments. The late 19th-century German intellectual tradition, for example, distinguished between peoples who had or did not have art, science, knowledge, and social refinement (Stocking, 1968). These aspects of culture were thought to free humans from the control of nature and give them control over nature. The word *culture* also derives from the Latin verb *colere*—to cultivate. Note that this sense of the concept is associated with tilling the soil and our agricultural origins (Wagner, 1981, p. 21)—another way of controlling nature.

But is culture simply the opposite of nature? According to Raymond Williams (1983, p. 87), "Culture is one of the two or three most complicated words in the English language"—partly because of its intricate historical development in several European languages, but also because it is used as a concept that sometimes has quite different meanings in several incompatible systems of thought. For example, early German intellectual traditions merged with English traditions to define culture as general processes of intellectual, spiritual, and aesthetic development. A modified version of this usage is found in the contemporary field of arts and humanities, which describes culture in terms of music, literature, painting, sculpture, and the like. By contrast, U.S. tradition has produced the use of culture as we know it in contemporary social sciences to describe a particular way of life of a people, a period of time, or humanity in general. But even in this tradition, anthropologists have used the concept to refer to the material production of a people, whereas historians and cultural studies have used it to refer to symbolic systems such as language, stories, and rituals. Currently, these uses of the concept overlap considerably.

Systems perspective, Psychodynamic perspective

A more useful definition for a multidimensional approach to human behavior sees culture as "a set of common understandings, manifest in act and artifact. It is in two places at once: inside somebody's head as understandings and in the external environment as act and artifact. If it isn't truly present in both spheres, it is only incomplete culture" (Bohannan, 1995, p. 47). **Culture**, in other words, includes both behavior (act or actions) and the material outcomes of that behavior (artifact or the things we construct from the material world around us). It both constrains and is constrained by nature, biology, social conditions, and other realities of human existence. But at the same time, it is "inside our heads," or part of our thoughts and feelings. It is expressed through our emotions and thought processes, our motivation, intention, and meaning as we live out our lives.

Social constructionist perspective

It is through culture that we construct, or give and take, meanings associated with the social and material world. Art, shelter, transportation, music, food, or clothing are material examples. The meanings we give these products influence how we use them. In interaction with the social world of things around us, we construct religion, race and ethnicity, family and kinship, gender roles, and complex modern organizations and institutions.

Here's an example of how human beings construct meaning in a cultural context. Slaves of African descent were remarkable for interpreting their plight and quest for freedom in terms of Judeo-Christian religious beliefs. They likened their suffering to that of the crucifixion and resurrection of Jesus Christ. And just like the children of Israel who had to make it to the promised land, so it was that slaves had to find freedom in the promised land of northern cities in the United States and Canada. Associations of the plight of Christians and Jews in the Bible with racial oppression live on today in the lives of many African Americans.

You may encounter clients who believe that their social, economic, and psychological difficulties are the result of God's will rather than of the biopsychosocial causes we study and apply as social workers. How would you apply a multidimensional approach to human behavior in this context? Should a social work assessment include the various meanings that people construct about their circumstances? Applying a cultural perspective that considers these questions will help you find more empowering interpretations and solutions to issues you face as a social worker, especially when working with members of oppressed communities.

Here is another example. Disability in our culture seems to be about its opposite: being normal, competent, "properly human" (Jenkins, 1998, p. 2). It is also about the "assumption or desirability of equality"—that is, sameness or similarity (Ingstad & Whyte, 1995, pp. 7-8). But deciding what is normal is embedded in culture. We may think that physical, mental, or cognitive disabilities are purely biological or psychological and therefore real in a scientific sense. But like race and gender, what they mean to the person possessing them and to those looking on and judging is a matter of the meanings that individuals assign to differing abilities (Ingstad & Whyte, 1995; Jenkins, 1998; Thomson, 1997). These meanings play out in social, economic, and political relations, which generate various types of inequality.

What are your emotional responses to seeing a child in a wheelchair? How do you suppose that child feels? Can you imagine the sexual attractiveness of a woman or man whose legs dangle freely below them as they walk with metal crutches? Do you suppose that person sees herself or himself as a sexual being? What are the bodily images we hold for being "handsome" or "beautiful"? Do they correspond with the images that others hold? The point is that if the culturally diverse people who reside in the United States see life in various ways, we must expect no less regarding those with different types and levels of ability. Here again, social workers must use a multidimensional conceptualization of culture to guide our actions.

The above examples about African Americans and disability occur in a historical context. But culture is about more than dates, names, inventions, and records of events of which history is composed. Rather, culture is an ongoing story about the connections between ideas, communities, peoples, nations, and social transformations within the constraints of the natural world (Roseberry, 1989). Think about how the historical plight of African Americans in the United States influences how they perceive their lives today. Think about the historical development of the terms and ideas associated with disability: "crippled," "handicapped," "disabled," "differently abled," and so on.

Think about the history of social work. It is about more than mere dates and events. Think of the people involved in social work, such as Mary Richmond—a leader in the early charity movement. Think about the philosophy and social practices she espoused in working with the disadvantaged people of her time. What do you know about her ethnic identity, socioeconomic status, gender, and living conditions? What about the dominant thinking and political, social, and economic trends of her time? What do you know about what may have influenced her conception of social work and how those influences connect to the ideas and practices of contemporary social work? This line of thought reveals a lot about U.S. culture and how it has interacted with the development of social work.

To sum up, culture includes multiple levels of traditions, values, and beliefs, as well as social, biological, and natural acts. These processes are driven by the meanings we give to and take from them. These meanings are fortified or changed in relations between people, as history unfolds. Culture so defined is therefore not limited to the elite. It affects all of us.

Conflict perspective

Among those who are affected by culture are the students and staff at Community High School. Culture affects the social and academic process of schooling by influencing what is delivered, how, and by whom. A cultural interpretation would reveal competition and strain, or unequal power relations in this process. For example, many Village Park residents and Community High students have cultural frames of reference that give adversarial meanings to some aspects of schooling and other forms of institutional participation. These individuals do not necessarily dismiss education, but they may see education as part of a system of mainstream institutions that have been oppressive and insensitive toward blacks. They see schools as dismissing their points of view. And the power to change things eludes them. When a teacher at Community High asks black students like Stan and Tina to stop talking out of turn in class, these students hear more than an impartial and benign request. Of course, any adolescent student might resent being told to stop talking by an adult authority. But the interpretation of that request by black students is likely to reflect their understanding about what it means to be put down in front of one's peers by an "outsider" who represents the dominant white society and does not respect the black community.

These are complex issues, but they are part of the everyday problems social workers encounter. Further examination of what culture is and how its meaning has varied over time helps in our quest for multidimensional knowledge and skills.

EXHIBIT 8.2
Ideas and Processes
Influencing the
Evolution of Culture
as a Concept

Time Period	Ideas and Human Processes
18th & 19th centuries: Enlightenment and Romanticism	Rankings of logic, reason, art, technology Culture seizing nature Psychic unity of humankind
19th & 20th centuries: Variation in human behavior and development	Cultural relativism Culture as patterns and structures Culture and personality Symbols as vehicles of culture

Contemporary
  understandings:
Integration and synthesis of
  processes of human
  development and variation
  since 1950s
	Cultural psychology (cognitive psychology and
	  anthropology)
	Meaning, ecology, and culture
	Political and economic systems and culture
	Culture as private and public
	Physical environment, biology, and culture
	Ideology, history, common sense, tradition as
	  cultural systems

Traditional Understandings of Culture and Variation in Human Behavior

Ideas about culture have changed over time, in step with intellectual, social, economic, and political trends. Understanding these changes is integral to understanding current definitions of culture. As you learned earlier, the concept of culture has a lengthy history. But for our purposes, we will summarize some of the ideas and concepts that have become a part of our understanding of culture today. Exhibit 8.2 provides an overview of the evolution of culture as a concept since the 18th century.

The Enlightenment and Romantic intellectual traditions, dating back to the 18th century, have provided influential, but very different, definitions of culture that live on today. The Enlightenment was concerned with, among other things, the universal application of a rational and scientific thought process. Enlightenment thinking also espoused the "psychic unity of humankind," a search for similarities across human cultures to demonstrate the universality of laws of behavior and reasoning for all people.

One result of such thinking was the idea that cultures and civilizations could be ranked according to their developed logic, reason, and technology (or mastery and use of the physical environment). Africans, for example, were seen as less civilized than Europeans because their technology was not on the same scale as some European countries and they apparently lacked written languages. Can you think of situations that demonstrate Enlightenment biases today? Is this the same framework that justifies interpreting the actions of Tina and Stan as less developed, less mature, and less rational than the actions of more mainstream students?

The other side of the coin is a Romantic orientation dating from the late 18th century. This orientation reflects the idea that all people and their cultures are relatively equal in value. The valuation of human culture and its outcomes extends beyond the measuring rod of reason, rationality, and logic. Differences in culture reflect different frameworks of meaning and understanding and thus result in different lifestyles and ways of living (Benedict, 1946, 1934/1989). Unlike the Enlightenment approach, the Romantic orientation makes few rankings of inferiority and superiority (Shweder, 1984/1995, p. 28).

Conflict perspective

This is the idea of **cultural relativism** that frames contemporary multiculturalism. For example, today it would be considered inappropriate to ask which is superior, Islam or Christianity, black culture or white culture, African culture or European culture. They differ in content and meaning, but is one better than the other? If so, what is the standard of measure, and in whose interest is it developed and enforced?

Some today dismiss cultural relativism as "politically correct" thinking. But it does have practical value. For instance, as a social worker, you could contrast the behavior of Tina and Stan with that of successful white students to identify differences between them. How will doing so help Tina, Stan, or the successful white students—or any other students, for that matter? Perhaps it is more productive to measure all of them against some mutually relevant standard, such as how well the students will be able to succeed in their own communities. The point here is not that we should apply different standards to different people. Rather, in social work at least, to start where a person is has been an effective method of moving them to where society wants them to be.

Despite the usefulness of Romanticism and cultural relativism, the premises of Enlightenment thinking have a great influence on our everyday understanding of culture. Consider recent public debates over crime, welfare, and other issues that associate chronic social problems with people's race/ethnicity and socioeconomic status. Some social scientists and the popular media frequently express mainstream, Enlightenment-oriented values, attitudes, and morals in examining these issues, assigning more value to some things than to others (Murray, 1984; Murray & Herrnstein, 1994; Wilson, 1995).

One outcome of such thinking is **biological determinism**—the attempt to differentiate social behavior on the basis of biological and genetic endowment. One form of biological determinism is based on racial identity. A person's intellectual performance is associated with brown skin and other physical differences believed to be related to race. Race, however, is more a social construction than a biological reality. No relationship between differences in racial identity and differences in cognitive and intellectual capacities has been proved. There is no verifiable evidence that the composition and functioning of the brain differs between blacks and whites, Asians and Hispanics, or

EXHIBIT 8.3

Basic Axioms
About Culture

- Culture is learned through social interaction.
- A society may have customary practices, but not all members have the same knowledge of them or attach the same significance to them.
- Culture seizes nature. That is, humans seek to control nature (in the form of climate, oceans and rivers, etc.) and shape it according to their own needs and interests.
- Culture is patterned; culture is symbolic; and culture is adaptive and maladaptive.

Source: Based on Kottak, 1994.

whatever so-called racial groups you can identify and compare (Gould, 1981; Shanklin, 1994). Yet, many still believe that race makes a difference. Such false associations are a vestige of Enlightenment thinking.

As a social work student, you can recognize the malign power and influence of such tendencies. Thinking in terms of natural, ordained, and inevitable differences based on race reinforces the social tendency to think in terms of "we-ness" and "they-ness," which often has unfortunate effects (Ringer & Lawless, 1989). In your personal and professional lives, pay attention to the images and thoughts you use to make sense of the economic, social, and behavioral difficulties of black people or other ethnic groups.

Contemporary Understandings of Culture and Variation in Human Behavior

Social
constructionist
perspective, Social
behavioral perspective

Twentieth-century scholars of culture inherited both advances and limitations in thought from scholars of previous centuries. With these problems in mind, anthropologist Franz Boas encouraged us to understand cultural differences as environmental differences interacting with the accidents of history (Boas, 1940/1948). Boas's ideas, along with those developed by others, have led to the basic axioms about culture found in Exhibit 8.3 (Kottak, 1994).

Why are these axioms important for social workers? Three things come to mind if we are going to work effectively and sensitively with people like Stan and Tina and communities like theirs, whose norms vary from mainstream norms:

1. We must be able to understand how mainstream beliefs, customs, traditions, values, and social institutions, comprising "normal" social behavior, fit into the lives of our clients.

2. We must recognize that beliefs, customs, values, traditions, and social institutions vary in degrees of complexity from one society to another. People have a tendency to consider cultures other than their own to be aberrations from a "universal" norm or standard that all people should meet. Two questions evolve from this point: Which norms and values are acceptable as universal, and based on what criteria? Are these universals adaptive or functional under all social, economic, political, and environmental conditions?

3. Finally, we must pay attention to the development of emotional and cognitive frameworks as elements of society and culture. We must avoid the trap of confounding emotional and cognitive capacities with hierarchies of race and other ways of ranking humankind.

A few additional concepts help round out our discussion of past and present conceptions of culture:

Conflict perspective

- *Ideology.* Ideology is the dominant ideas about the way things are and should work. Problems of inequality and discrimination arise when ideological aspects of the social, economic, and political structures of society support the exploitation and subjugation of people. Institutionalized gender bias, for example, is the systematic incorporation into the culture's structures of ideologies that directly and indirectly support the subordination of women (most typically) or men. These subordinating elements are built into the everyday, taken-for-granted way the culture's members live their lives.

- *Ethnocentrism.* Through cross-cultural comparisons, anthropologists have demonstrated that Western culture is not universal. They have exposed our tendency to elevate our own ethnic group and its social and cultural processes over others, a tendency known as **ethnocentrism**. For instance, Western ideals, such as individuality, are built into theories of personality development (Mead, 1935/1950, 1928/1961, 1930/1968; Shweder & LeVine, 1984/1995; Whiting & Whiting, 1975).

Social constructionist perspective, Psychodynamic perspective

- *Cultural symbols.* A **symbol** is something, verbal or nonverbal, that comes to stand for something else. The letters *d-o-g* have come to stand for the animal we call *dog;* the large *M* and a golden arch stand for McDonald's restaurants or hamburgers; water in baptism rites stands for something sacred and holy and moves a person from one state of being to another (D'Andrade, 1984/1995; Kottak, 1994). But as Conrad Kottak (1996, p. 26) points out, "Water is not intrinsically holier than milk, blood or other liquids. . . . A natural thing has been arbitrarily associated with a particular meaning for Catholics" and other religious groups. Race, ethnicity, and gender are symbols that can be thought of in this way as well. For instance, beyond biological differences, what comes to mind when you think of a girl or woman? What about a boy or man? How do the images, thoughts, and feelings you possess about gender influence how you interact with boys and girls, men and women? Gendered thinking undoubtedly influences your assessment of persons, even those you have not actually met. In short, symbols shape perception, or the way a person sees, feels, and thinks about the world, and communicate a host of feelings, thoughts, beliefs, and values that people use to make sense of their daily lives (Ortner, 1973). They are vehicles of culture that facilitate social action. The role of symbols in culture raises questions that social workers face all the time: Do we really know what's going on inside people's heads—what they mean and intend? The idea that symbols express meaning within a culture is part of many recent models of practice in social work and psychology. For example, social constructionists focus on narratives and stories as emotional and behavioral correctives in clinical social work practice.

■ *Worldview and ethos.* A **worldview** is an idea of reality, a "concept of nature, of self, of society" (Geertz, 1973, p. 126). **Ethos** is the "tone, character, and quality of [people's] life, its moral and aesthetic style and mood; it is the underlying attitude toward themselves and their world that life reflects" (Geertz, 1973, p. 126). Worldview is associated with the cognitive domain—how we think about things; ethos is associated more with the emotional or affective and stylistic dimensions of behavior—how we feel about things (Ortner, 1984, p. 129). Both Stan and Tina are adept at using symbols such as clothing, language, and music to convey specific feelings and perceptions that express their worldview and ethos. Exhibit 8.4 compares some additional symbols that convey differences in worldview and ethos.

■ *Cultural innovation.* Culture is not static; it is adapted, modified, and changed through interactions over time. This process is known as cultural innovation. For example, Stan and Tina were described earlier as innovators. Both restyle mainstream clothing to fit with their sense of meaning and with the values of their peers and their community. In addition, in the classroom and with peers, Stan and Tina can switch between Standard English and Black English. The mode of language they use depends on the social and political message or identity they want to convey to listeners.

Conflict perspective ■ *Cultural conflict.* The symbols we use are arbitrary. They can mean one thing to you and something different to others. Therefore, cultural conflict over meanings can easily arise. For example, jeans that are worn low on the hips by many black adolescents and young adults generally signify an ethos of hipness, toughness, and coolness. This is the style, mood, and perspective of their generation. (Some of us who are professionals, or soon will be, have a similar need to fit in with the particular ethos and worldview that is important to us and to the people with whom we interact. We are likely to choose an entirely different style of clothing.) However, the clothing, music, and language of black adolescents convey a different symbolic meaning to law enforcers, school officials,

EXHIBIT 8.4
Sociocultural
Creations

Ask yourself what judgments you make and meanings you attribute in the following areas:

Music:
Classical versus jazz
Rhythm and blues versus bluegrass
Celtic versus rock and roll

Food:
Hamburger versus eel
Ants versus hot dogs
Kangaroo tail versus squid
Pigs' feet versus horse

Household/Domestic Activities:
Parents and children sleeping in separate beds and/or separate rooms versus sleeping in the open

Sexual intercourse in private versus public

Bathing in private versus public

Breast feeding in private versus public

Families living, eating, sleeping in one large room versus separate rooms

Eating with fingers and hands versus forks, spoons, and knives

parents, and even social workers. In today's sociopolitical climate, these authority figures are likely to perceive low-slung jeans as signs of drug and gang culture or as a form of social rebellion, decadence, or incivility.

In sum, culture is both public and private. It has emotional and cognitive components, but these play out in public in our social actions. Symbols are a way of communicating private meaning through public or social action. Furthermore, people's actions express their worldview (how they think about the world) and their ethos (how they feel about the world)—just as Tina and Stan do when they alternate between black and mainstream styles.

These concepts have great relevance to social work. For example, arguments accompanying recent welfare reform legislation reflect shifting meanings regarding

EXHIBIT 8.5

Customary Social Habits Interacting With Social Work Principles, Values, and Ethics, on a Continuum

What are your beliefs about the following interactions with clients and colleagues?

Continuum

Most Professional (Formal) .... *Least Professional (Informal)*

Greetings by handshake .... hugging .... kissing

Use of last name/title .... first name .... nickname
(Mr., Ms., Dr.)

Authority by credentials .... age, experience, ... religion/politics
(BSW, MSW, etc.)   gender, marital status

Sharing no personal .... pertinent information .... open-ended,
information   mutual sharing

Confidentiality .... sharing with professionals/ .... sharing with friends/
                                            family   community members

poverty, single parenting, and work. During the 1960s, it was considered society's moral duty to combat poverty by assisting the poor. Today, *poverty* does not just mean a lack of financial resources for the necessities of life; to many people it symbolizes laziness, the demise of family values, and other characteristics that shade into immorality. Thus, to help people who are poor is now often purported to hurt them by consigning them to immoral behavior.

As social workers, we depend on the NASW Code of Ethics for professional guidance in negotiating these shifts. But what is the source of the values and beliefs that guide our personal lives? And what happens when what we believe and value differs from our clients' beliefs and values? These questions raise the issue of how we form and act on meaning derived from our private cultural leanings into our professional lives. Exhibit 8.5 demonstrates several cultural conflicts that may arise as our personal social habits confront the principles, values, and ethics of professional social workers.

A Contemporary, Holistic Application of Culture

Social workers can better account for the multidimensional nature of human behavior if they understand what culture is and how thinking about culture has evolved. What follows is a discussion of how to apply a multidimensional concept of culture.

To increase our understanding of culture and human behavior, we might ask how it is that Tina's and Stan's ways of living are different from our own. We can apply the same question to immigrants and other groups who differ from the mainstream norm. We need to recognize that their lives may be based on values, beliefs, and rationalizations that we don't fully understand. We could try to understand them, but would we succeed by applying our own cultural frame of reference, our own worldview and ethos? If we limit our quest to our own terms, to our authority and power as social workers to define who they are, what do we achieve? We are likely to learn more about ourselves, our standards, than about people like Stan and Tina. The most we can learn about these students by looking at them from our own frame of reference is how they compare to us. The comparison, however, is in our terms, not theirs. For example, we may well say that Stan is at greater than average risk of failing socially and academically. But he might say that he is more successful than most at negotiating the oppressive structures of school and society.

Ask yourself what would happen if we as social workers combined the views and feelings of clients about their lives and problems with our own views. What would we have to give up and what would we and our clients gain? We need a multidimensional perspective of diversity and human behavior to ground our professional actions in this way. But what should a multidimensional approach to a culture analysis consist of, and what is it trying to explain? These are important questions for social workers.

A Practice Orientation

Thirty-five years ago, the problems of Village Park and Community High School would have been explained largely in terms of a **culture-of-poverty.** Proponents of this theoretical orientation twisted it to suggest that black schools and communities were impoverished because of black people's own beliefs, values, traditions, morals, and frames of reference. Mainstream culture's racism and discrimination were not considered to be factors. That black people faced redlining, a practice that forced them to buy or rent homes only in black communities, was not considered to be a factor. That black people were working in low-income jobs despite qualifications for better ones was not considered to be a factor. That major colleges and universities were denying admission to qualified black applicants was not considered to be a factor either. The list could go on. The culture-of-poverty orientation was used to argue both for and against publicly financed social programs. From time to time, some of my students even today use a culture of poverty line of reasoning to explain people on welfare, poor single parents, and other problems of inner cities.

Contemporary culture scholars (anthropologists, sociologists, psychologists, political scientists, social workers, economists) have also adopted some of the tenets of past theorizing. However, they have taken the better parts of it to develop what has come to be called a **practice orientation** (Berger & Luckmann, 1966; Bourdieu, 1977; Giddens, 1979; Ortner, 1984, 1989, 1996; Sahlins, 1981). *Practice* as used here is different from its use in social work. This theoretical orientation seeks to explain what people do as thinking, intentionally acting persons who face the impact of history and the restraints of structures that are embedded in our society and culture. It asks how social systems shape, guide, and direct people's values, beliefs, and behavior. But it also asks how people, as human actors or agents, perpetuate or shape social systems. The underlying issues, in sum, are about understanding two things:

1. How, through culture, human beings construct meaning, intentionality, and public behavior

2. How human beings produce systemic cultural change or adapt to and maintain the culture

Social
constructionist
perspective,
Conflict perspective

The hope of the practice orientation is—by reflection on history, structure, and agency—to develop a deeper understanding of racism, prejudice associated with ethnicity and social class, and gender relations, among other sociocultural processes.

The issue of poverty offers one example of how the practice orientation can be applied. The practice orientation would not blame poverty's prevalence and influence in Tina's and Stan's community solely on the failings of individuals. Rather, it would seek to identify the structural factors—such as low-income jobs, housing segregation, and racism—that impede upward mobility. It would also seek to determine how poor African Americans perceive their conditions; how nonpoor, nonblack Americans perceive the conditions of poor African Americans; and how all of these perceptions shape the lives and influence the upward mobility of poor African Americans. At the same time, the practice orientation aims to understand how the perceptions and actions of nonpoor, nonblack Americans maintain structures of inequality in the institutions that define and offer educational and economic opportunities. Are poor African Americans as different in values, beliefs, and attitudes as other people think they are? Is there a "culture" of poverty, or do people in dire circumstances adapt their values and beliefs to the demands of survival? These are matters of considerable importance and complexity.

Another example of the types of questions fruitfully addressed through the practice orientation apply to Stan's situation: How have Stan's family and community influenced his behavior in general and his response to racism and classism in school in particular? How have Stan's own responses contributed to his subordination as a black youth, thereby leaving certain oppressive structures in society unchanged? Likewise, how have the values and beliefs encoded through the rules and regulations in public schools like Community High served to perpetuate or reproduce various forms of structural or systemic subjugation? What are the symbolic meanings of school and education, and what role do they play in Stan's behavior? From our position as educated Americans with many mainstream values, we would tend to see schools as intrinsically good because they are largely about academic growth rather than social and cultural relations. But is this the whole, multidimensional picture?

The same questions apply to social work. How have the values, beliefs, and practices of the profession helped to maintain the profession and society as they are? When we label a person or group as having a social problem or dysfunction, are we perpetuating or reproducing subjugation by creating a truth or fact? For better or worse, when social science categorizes human functioning, it does just that. When we label the people we have failed to help as resistant, unmotivated, and pathological, are we carelessly overlooking the ineffectiveness of our modes of understanding and intervention? Are we blaming the victim and reproducing his or her victimization? These and other questions are important for all of us to ponder.

Systems perspective

History, social structure, and human agency are key elements in a practice orientation. I have tried to demonstrate in this chapter how some life events reflect the intertwined influences of history, social structure, and human agency. These kinds of interactions sometimes reflect social strain, and sometimes social solidarity. Sometimes they reflect a conflict between the objective and the subjective nature of what we do and what we believe. In any case, the relationship between human action and social systems is never simple in a political world (Ortner, 1984, 1989).

History. History is made by people, but it is made within the constraints of the social, economic, political, physical, and biological systems in which they are living. History includes, but is not totally defined by, chains of events and experiences to which people simply react. Chains of events like the industrial revolution, World War I, the Great Depression, and World War II are important. So are the specific dates of these important events. Together they link ideas and processes.

However, to understand human diversity and to unearth sociocultural forms of oppression, exploitation, and subjugation, we must take into account the particular form that a society has at a particular moment. We have to consider people's diverse motives and actions as they make and transform the world in which they live (Ortner, 1989, p. 193). We must listen to the memories of official and unofficial observers. We must hear those voices that are represented in the official records and those that are not. We must listen to clients as much as to social workers.

Social Structure. Structure implies the ordered forms and systems of human behavior existing in public life (e.g., capitalism, kinship, public education). It also includes cognitive, emotional, and behavioral frameworks that are mapped onto who we are as people. Structure influences how we construct ourselves—that is, what we make of ourselves based on what things mean to us. We carry forth meanings, values, and beliefs through social, economic, and political practices in our everyday personal lives and the institutions in which we participate. We *reproduce* structures when we assume the rightness of our values, beliefs, and meaning and see no need to change them.

In the end, we must understand the all-encompassing dominance of trends, patterns, and structures in society and the barriers they erect against change. This process is called cultural **hegemony**, or the dominance of a particular way of seeing the world. Most observers of culture in the United States would agree that it is based on the hegemony of Euro American, or Anglo, worldview. People in many other parts of the world have observed a hegemony of the U.S. worldview. As Mike Davis (2000) says at the beginning of his book on Latino influences on U.S. cities, "When you say 'America' you refer to the territory stretching between the icecaps of the two poles. So to hell with your barriers and frontier guards!" As the quote implies, those whose cultures are overtaken by another culture often resent the hegemony.

Humanistic
Perspective

Human Agency. Social, economic, and political structures cannot completely dominate our lives, thanks to the force of human agency. People are not simply puppets, the pawns of history and structure; people are also active participants, capable of exercising their will to shape their lives. Thus, although racism is structured into society, it is not so completely dominant over Tina's and Stan's lives that they have no room for meaningful self-expression in their social and political lives.

Human agency helps to counteract cultural hegemony as well. Consider the influence of African American urban youth culture. Rap music and clothing styles that originated with black teens like Tina and Stan have become popular with white, middle-class young people. In fact, African American music and other social tastes have had considerable influence on the European American mainstream for many years.

Individuals and groups exercise agency in part by constructing culture. They invest the world with their own subjective order, meaning, and value. They rely on their frame of mind or worldview to consciously and unconsciously make choices and take action (Ortner, 1989, p. 18). They construct social and political identities that help them resist and contest cultural hegemony.

However, no individual or group is a fully free agent. We are constrained by external factors such as the climate, disease, natural resources, and population size and growth (Ortner, 1989, p. 14)—although we may be able to modify these constraints through technology. Examples of technologies that modify facts of biology and nature are medicines, agricultural breakthroughs, climate-controlled homes, telecommunications, transportation, and synthetic products that replace the use of wood in furniture and related items.

In sum, human agents are "skilled and intense strategizers" (Ortner, 1996, p. 20). We are constantly stretching the process by which we live and define ourselves. But we do so within the constraints of structures or forces that can never wholly contain us. Human agency is a major source of hope and motivation for social workers who encounter people, organizations, and systems that seem unable to break away from the constraints of daily life.

Cultural Maintenance, Change, and Adaptation

Tina's and Stan's experiences with mainstream schooling provide a good example of how cultural structures are maintained, how they change, and how they adapt. School systems are centered on the norms, values, and beliefs preferred by those who have had the power to decide what is or is not appropriate to learn and use in our lives. Some things we learn in school fit well with the needs of industry. Other things we learn in school fit well with the needs of our social and political institutions. These include the values and workings of family and community life, and of local, state, and national governing bodies. From the outside looking in, schools look like benign or innocent institutions, simply about academics and education. Yet which academic subjects are taught, how they are taught, who teaches them, and how they are to be learned involve an assertion of someone's values and beliefs, whether right or wrong, whether shared by many or few. Exhibit 8.6 lists some of the factors involved in the cultural construction of schooling. As you can see, schooling's influence extends far beyond reading, writing, and arithmetic.

Even in the face of evidence that schools do not work for many of us, they persist. Education is strongly correlated with economic and social success. Therefore, ineffective schools play a role in the persistent poverty we have faced in this country. In

EXHIBIT 8.6
Sociocultural Factors in the Construction of Education and Schooling

---

Politics and Law

Legislation, laws, and regulations regarding attendance and social behavior; educational content; segregation/desegregation; school funding

Family

Socialization regarding gender roles and relations; sex; discipline; health/hygiene/nutrition; recreation; emotional support and development

Religion

Prayer; holidays; family and personal morality and ethics

Social Structure and Economics

Status, opportunities, and rewards associated with knowledge, grades, and credentials; individual versus collective achievement; appropriate versus inappropriate behavior and social skills; media, market, and popular cultural trends and factors

Community

Ethnic representation and attitudes; economic resources and stability; levels of crime addition, if you examine how girls are treated in schools, you will discover correlations with women's subjugation in other domains as well. The experiences of immigrants in schools also raise issues regarding cultural processes in schools and beyond.

Culture provides stability to social life, but it does change over time. It does not change rapidly, however. First we look at some ideas about how culture produces stability, and then we turn to how culture changes over time through immigration and processes of negotiating multicultural community life.

Common Sense, Tradition, and Custom. Over time, the ways in which families, schools, cities, and governments do things have come to seem natural to us. They seem to fit with the common sense, traditions, and customs of most people in the United States.

Keep in mind, however, that **common sense** is a cultural system. It is what people have come to believe everyone in a community or society should know and understand as a matter of ordinary, taken-for-granted social competence. It is based on a set of assumptions that are so unself-conscious that they seem natural, transparent, and an undeniable part of the structure of the world (Geertz, 1983; Swidler, 1986). For example, rain is wet, fire burns, and, as I hear more and more in the general population, as well as from many Community High students, "You can't make it without an education!" "Common sense tells you that you gotta speak English to make it in America," you might overhear a citizen of Charlotte, North Carolina, say about the new Mexicans who have come to the city.

Yet not everyone, especially not members of oppressed, subjugated, or immigrant groups within a society, is likely to share these common schemes of meaning and understanding. Thus, common sense becomes self-serving for those who are in a position of power to determine what it is and who has it. We believe common sense tells us what actions are appropriate in school or in any number of other contexts. But, as a part of culture, common sense is subject to historically defined standards of judgment related to maleness and femaleness, parenting, poverty, work, education, and mental and social (psychosocial) functioning, among other categories of social being. For better or worse, common sense helps to maintain cultures and societies as they are.

We need to approach traditions and customs with the same caution with which we approach common sense. **Traditions** are cultural beliefs and practices so taken for granted that they seem inevitable parts of life (Swidler, 1986). **Customs**, or cultural practices, come into being and persist as solutions to problems of living (Goodenough, 1996, p. 294). Tradition is a process of handing down from one generation to another particular cultural beliefs and practices. In particular, it is a process of ratifying particular beliefs and practices by connecting them to selected social, economic, and political practices. When this is done well, traditions become so taken for granted that they seem "natural" parts of life, as if they have always been here and as if we cannot live without them (Hobsbawm, 1983; Swidler, 1986; Williams, 1977). Some traditions and customs are routine; others, such as special ceremonies, are extraordinary. They are not necessarily followed by everyone in the culture, but they seem necessary and ordained, and they stabilize the culture. They are in a sense collective memories of the group. They reflect meanings at a particular moment in time and serve as guides for the present and future.

Traditions and customs are selective, however. They leave out the experiences, memories, and voices of some group members while highlighting and including others. African American students generally do not experience schooling as reflecting their traditions and customs. In many cases, Latino or Hispanic immigrants in Charlotte will not either. Stan, Tina, and their peers often raised this point in their classes at Community High. And several residents of Village Park have been raising similar issues for many years. In Charlotte I am beginning to see Latino/Hispanic families express similar concerns.

To reflect Village Park's traditions and customs, Community High would have to respect and understand the use of Nonstandard English as students are learning Standard English. Literature and history classes would make salient connections between European traditions and customs and those of West Africans, Afro-Caribbeans, and contemporary African Americans. And processes for including a student's family in schooling processes would include kinship bonds that are not based on legalized blood ties or the rules of state foster care systems. What would a school social worker have to learn to assist schools and immigrant families in having a more successful experience in school?

Traditions and customs, moreover, play a role in the strain that characterizes shifts from old patterns and styles of living to new ones in schools and other institutions in society. To survive, groups of people have to bend their traditions and customs without letting them lose their essence. Nondominant ethnic, gender, religious, and other groups in the United States often have to assimilate or accommodate their host culture if they are to share in economic and political power. In fact, the general survival of the traditions and customs of nondominant groups requires adaptability.

In sum, traditions and customs are parts of a cultural process that are changing ever so subtly and slowly but at times abruptly. Sometimes groups disagree about these changes, and some members deny that they are occurring because they believe they should still do things the old way. Social workers have to understand a group's need to hold on to old ways. Groups hold on to the old ways to protect their worldview about what life means and who they are as a people.

Immigration. It would be foolish to deny that the United States is a nation of immigrants. Immigration to this land began with the gradual migration of prehistoric peoples that anthropologists envision, and picked up speed when Columbus and other Europeans arrived from across the Atlantic Ocean. It continued with the involuntary arrival of Africans and the voluntary and semivoluntary arrivals of various European ethnic groups. Later came Asians and others. Forceful extension of the nation's borders and political influence incorporated Hispanics and Pacific Islanders. There have been many subsequent waves of immigration, with a great influx late in the 20th century and continuing today. Now, more than ever, people are coming to the United States from all over the world. Today we define cultural diversity as a relatively new issue. But the nation's fabric has long included a rich diversity of cultures.

Although diversity has been a feature of life in the United States for centuries, immigration is an especially prominent feature of society today. According to the 2000 U.S. Census, 28.4 million foreign-born residents now reside in the United States (U.S. Census Bureau, 2002). They represent 10.4% of the total U.S. population of 285 million. Fifty-one percent of these immigrants were born in Latin America in general, and 34.5% were born in Central America in particular. They are agents of what the media have called the "browning" of the United States. As for the remaining immigrants, 25.5% of all foreign-born U.S. residents were born in Asia, 15.3% in Europe, and 8.1% in other regions of the world. One of every three foreign-born are naturalized citizens.

These population profiles represent relatively recent immigration trends. For example, 39.5% of immigrants alive today entered the United States in the 1990s, 28.3% entered in the 1980s, 16.2% entered in the 1970s, and the remaining 16.0% arrived before 1970. Each group brings with it its own cultural traditions and languages, which influence its worldview, ethos, and social, economic, and political beliefs and values. Nevertheless, the foreign-born have a few characteristics in common. For example, they are more likely to live in central cities of metropolitan areas, live in larger households than nonimmigrants do, are less likely to have graduated from high school (if 25 or over), and are more likely to be unemployed.

Although many immigrants realize their dream of economic opportunity, many (but not all) encounter resistance from the native-born. Let us consider the case of immigrants from Latin American countries (Central and South America and the Caribbean). This group recently surpassed African Americans as the largest minority in the United States and is therefore the group that social workers are increasingly likely to face. New York City, Los Angeles, Chicago, San Antonio, Houston, and other southwestern cities are traditional sites for the settlement of Hispanic/Latino immigrants. However, they are also settling in increasing numbers in growing metropolitan areas such as Charlotte, where I reside. Charlotte has over 500,000 residents. It has a vibrant economy and is the second largest banking center in the nation (home to Bank of America and First Union Bank). People come to Charlotte because economic opportunities abound.

Like other Americans, Hispanic/Latino immigrants come to Charlotte to get a piece of the economic pie. However, Hispanic/Latino immigrants face a unique set of circumstances. One often hears complaints in Charlotte about "foreigners taking our jobs." African Americans and Latinos/Hispanics face social conflicts over lifestyles in the low-income neighborhoods they share. Social service and law enforcement agencies scramble for Spanish-language workers and interpreters. Banks decry the fact that many new Spanish-language residents don't trust banks and consequently don't open checking and savings accounts.

This situation can be thought of from different perspectives. Is immigration, or are immigrants, inherently a problem? Or are they a problem because of what they mean in the economic, political, and social context of these cities? Who should be more concerned about losing cultural ground: Hispanic/Latino immigrants or long-term U.S. residents? Notions of common sense, tradition, and custom apply in this situation. An understanding of cultural processes also helps social workers interpret the issues they encounter in practice.

Processes of Cultural Change. In multicultural societies, cultural change can be understood in terms of four processes: assimilation, accommodation, acculturation, and bicultural socialization. They describe the individual's or group's response to the dominant culture and have possible implications for clients' well-being.

■   *Assimilation.* **Assimilation** is the process in which the cultural uniqueness of the minority is abandoned and its members try to blend invisibly into the dominant culture (Kottak, 1996). Some culture scholars have noted a prevailing *assimilation ideology* that asserts the ideal of *Anglo conformity* (Gordon, 1964). In keeping with this view, some people have argued that the root of the problems faced by African Americans and by economically marginal immigrants is that they have not assimilated successfully. This argument is greatly oversimplified. First, to the extent that discrimination is based on obvious features such as skin color or lack of facility with Standard English, the ability to assimilate is limited. Second, capitalist economies and societies arbitrarily select different group characteristics as desirable at different times. We have done this, historically, in part, with immigration policies that admit some groups but not others. Many minorities, especially first-generation immigrants, often resist giving up parts of their ethnic identity in order to protect their sense of meaning and purpose in life.

■   *Accommodation.* Accommodation is more common than assimilation is in multicultural, multiethnic society in the United States. **Accommodation** is the process of partial or selective cultural change. Nondominant groups follow the norms, rules, and standards of the dominant culture only in specific circumstances and contexts. When Punjabi Sikh children attend school in Stockton, California, they generally follow the rules of the school (Gibson, 1988). They do not, however, remove their head coverings, socialize with peers of both sexes as is normal in mainstream U.S. society, or live by U.S. cultural standards at home. Some of the Muslim students at Community High could be compared to the Punjabis. Black Muslim girls at Community High, for example, refuse to remove their head coverings or customary long gowns to attend school, even though the school asks them to do so. Increasingly, Latino/Hispanic immigrants and native citizens are refusing to give up Spanish in many settings even though they can and will speak English when necessary.

- *Acculturation.* Acculturation is the other side of accommodation. It too is a more likely outcome when groups with multiple cultural backgrounds interact. *Acculturation* is a mutual sharing of culture (Kottak & Kozaitis, 1999). Although cultural groups remain distinct, certain elements of their culture change and they exchange and blend preferences in foods, music, dances, clothing, and the like. As Charlotte grows in diversity, Mexican, Vietnamese, Asian Indian, and other cuisines are becoming more common. At the same time, these diverse cultural groups are incorporating parts of traditional U.S. southern culture into their lives. Similarly, many U.S. refrigerators now contain salsa and soy sauce, as well as ketchup.

- *Bicultural socialization.* The process of **bicultural socialization** involves a nonmajority group or member mastering both the dominant culture and their own (Robbins, Chatterjee, & Canda, 1998b). Bicultural socialization is necessary in societies that have relatively fixed notions about how a person should live and interact in school, work, court, financial institutions, and the like. A person who has achieved bicultural socialization has, in a sense, a dual identity. Mainstream economic, political, and social success (or crossing over) requires nonmajority musicians, athletes, intellectuals and scholars, news anchors, bankers, and a host of others to master this process of cultural change and adaptation.

Social workers who conduct a multidimensional cultural analysis should seek to uncover the processes by which culture is being maintained, changed, and adapted in the lives of the individuals and groups with whom they work. We must also be alert to the fact that the process of cultural change is not always voluntary, a free and open exchange of culture. We must also pay attention to the political, social, and economic practices that undergird institutional norms and values. If these processes are harmful and oppressive for some people, we have a professional obligation, through our code of ethics, to facilitate change.

Women, people of color, immigrants, and poor people have historically not had a significant say in how cultural change proceeds. But having a limited voice does not eliminate one's voice altogether. Predominantly black schools and institutions have a characteristic flavor that preserves and strengthens elements of African American culture. Organizations dominated by women and feminists, such as NOW (National Organization of Women), give women a voice in a male-dominated culture. Other examples include the aisles of ethnic foods in grocery stores, ethnic and "world" music in music stores, black literature in bookstores, and the influence of Latino/Hispanic/Chicano culture on the social, economic, and political life in cities such as Los Angeles and Houston.

Conflict perspective

As social workers, we must comprehend the process of cultural change affecting our clients and act in accord with such knowledge. We cannot accept only dominant notions about the meaning of the actions of people of color and poor people. We cannot look only to mainstream culture and "traditions of knowledge" to determine the actions we take with nonmajority people. If we do, we are merely reproducing inequality and subjugation and limiting our effectiveness as human service providers.

Diversity

The *practice orientation* is a model for conceptualizing, organizing, and analyzing cultural processes. It helps us to explore different meanings for things we take for granted. It is especially useful for interpreting variation in the social environment. Such variables as race, ethnicity, social class, gender, and family are important symbols in the U.S. psyche and express a host of feelings, beliefs, thoughts, and values about the world around us (Ortner, 1973). They express a legacy that stretches over centuries and across continents.

Race. **Race** is first and foremost a system of social identity. It has been constructed over many years through cultural, social, economic, and political relations. Social and cultural meanings have been mapped onto physical or biological aspects of human variation such as skin color, hair texture, and facial characteristics. Race has become a fundamental principle of social organization, even though it has no validity as a biological category (Omi & Winant, 1993; Shanklin, 1994). The physical or biological characteristics, *phenotypes,* we associate with race are in fact variations resulting from human adaptation to different geographic environments over thousands of years. Some phenotypes have been publicly categorized as European (white), African (black), Asian, Latino/Hispanic, or Native American. However, the physical attributes of each group have no intrinsic or natural relationship to emotional, cognitive, or social capacities. **Racism** is the term for thinking and acting as if phenotype (we like to say "genes") and these other capacities are related and infer inferiority or superiority.

The meanings and uses of race shift, depending on the social, economic, and political context. In one context, for example, being black or African American is an asset, whereas in another it is a deficit. Even among black students and communities, these meanings shift. This variability is a result of the social, political, and economic advantages or disadvantages associated with a black racial identity at a particular moment in time. Race relations and identity issues in the 1960s were somewhat different than they were in the 1990s because the social, economic, and political climates were very different.

Consider the issue of racial identity among Community High students. Today's black students experience less conflict among themselves about "acting white" than did the black students who attended Community High a decade ago (Fordham, 1996; Fordham & Ogbu, 1986; Ogbu, 1991). *Acting white* is the term used to identify behavior that fits with the norms of speech, demeanor, dress, and so on that are preferred and valued by mainstream European American society. "White" norms are perceived to be at play in school activities such as doing homework, carrying books, and speaking in Standard English when answering questions in the classroom. Today, as a decade ago, black students who do "act white" are likely to receive more social, economic, and political acceptance within the larger society. They will also be accorded more privilege and prestige than those who act in accord with what is perceived as distinctly "black" behavior. These judgments are made by both blacks and nonblacks. And the demands of survival require adaptability. Therefore, many families of black students at Community High and many residents in that black community in general are allowing a greater range of flexibility in defining "black" behavior.

Stan and Tina offer examples of the current blurring of distinctions between behaviors that have historically been defined as black or white. Both students borrow from mainstream norms as they shape their ethnic identity. Stan redefines the mainstream meaning of brand-name shirts and biker boots. Tina can speak directly and assertively in class using mainstream Standard English, but her attitude and demeanor are perceived as distinctly black. Both of these students maintain an ethos and world-view seated in the experience of their black community. But at the same time, they are relatively bicultural and accommodating toward mainstream standards. Such changes in meaning and practice are likely to continue in their community in predictable and unpredictable ways.

Ethnicity. Ethnicity is often associated with static traditions, customs, and values that reflect a deep and enduring cultural identity and a desire to keep that identity intact. Ethnic identity has traditionally been asserted through preferences in food, clothing, language, and religion. It is also often tied up with blood relations, geographic location, and nationality. Conflict between Bosnians and Serbs in the 1990s—a matter of nationality and land against a backdrop of religion—is a case in point. Ethnic conflicts in African countries such as Rwanda and Burundi provide further examples. In the United States, ethnic conflict includes more than black-white relations. Now we see conflict between Koreans and blacks, Hispanics/Latinos and blacks, whites and Hispanics/Latinos, Arabs and blacks, Arabs and whites, and so forth.

Ethnic identity is how ethnic groups define themselves and maintain meaning for living individually and as a group. In contemporary industrial societies, ethnic identity is part of a person's social identity (which also includes occupational roles, gender roles, individual and family mobility, and family rituals—regarding meals, for instance).

Ethnic identity also includes methods of solving family problems and social conflicts with schools and other institutions. The meaning of a person's identity shifts, however subtly and slowly, as a result of economic, social, and political processes interacting with individual and collective beliefs and values. Ethnic people, consequently, do not end up practicing the exact particulars of what they espouse about their values, customs, traditions, and other things that make up ethnic identity. You can think back to the process of acculturation discussed earlier.

Such a dilemma might be thought of as the difference between upholding the "spirit" (intentions) versus the "letter" (exact meaning or interpretation) of the law. Ethnic groups in complex societies such as the United States often are better able to uphold the spirit rather than the letter of their values, customs, and beliefs. It is less a matter of truth or fact than one of process, change, and adaptation. When change and adaptation do not occur, ethnic culture may become a "trap" in an inflexible society. A group that is not willing or able to adapt is left economically, socially, and politically disfranchised (Bohannan, 1995). Societies and their institutions could be thought of as trapped as well when they do not support the kind of changes that foster equality among all peoples.

The rejection and disdain that members of some ethnic groups experience in the United States take a toll on identity (Zuniga, 1988). The result is that people of color or members of ethnic groups may need help to sort out their identities. Stan and Tina were able to develop relatively positive identities because they live in communities and families that celebrate and affirm being black or African American. However, those whose ethnicity is not so well supported may need help. Three steps social workers can take are (1) to teach clients about the effects of the political realities of racism, (2) to teach clients how to use the strengths and resources of their own culture in rearing their children, and (3) to organize ethnic communities to seek cultural democracy in dealing with institutions such as schools (Zuniga, 1988).

Conflict Perspective

Social Class. Social class (which includes **socioeconomic status,** or **SES**) is a dirty word among people in the United States, who generally believe that any class differences that may exist are of one's own making. But class differences do exist, and they document another form of cultural inequality, as well as imperfections in our capitalist economic system. Social class is a way of ascribing status, prestige, and power. It is based on education, income, and occupation. Each of these indices—how much education one has, how much money one makes or has, and what one does for a living—carries poignant meanings. These meanings are derived from subjective values and beliefs in interaction with dominant customs, traditions, and notions of common sense. Social scientists do not fully know how or why, but the meanings associated with social class get condensed into our society's fascination with lifestyles.

The terms we commonly use to categorize class status are *upper class, middle class, working class,* and *lower class* or *underclass.* We also talk in terms of jobs that are blue collar (working class), pink collar (supervisory, especially in traditionally female occupations), and white collar (managerial and professional). These categories and their meanings become infused into identities such as race and ethnicity. For instance, Stan's and Tina's identities as African Americans automatically tend to reduce their social class status to the category of lower or underclass. The income, occupation, and education of Stan's and Tina's families, however, would generally place them in the middle class.

To understand the power of class or socioeconomic status, think about the class status of your family of origin when you were living at home. Why was that status assigned? What did it mean in social terms? When did you first recognize that your social class status differed in significant ways from that of some other people? That background colors our values and beliefs throughout life? What do you think of today when a person is referred to as lower class? What are your thoughts about clients who are on welfare?

Gender. Along with race, gender has been and remains a controversial concept. Gender is what our culture symbolizes and means by maleness and femaleness. These terms are further defined through the prescribed roles of men and women, boys and girls, husbands and wives. The physical characteristics of male and female bodies, combined with their sexual and reproductive functions, carry strong symbolic meanings. Physical differences between males and females are perceived by many as an indisputable basis for assigning different gender roles. Some believe "anatomy is destiny."

Conflict perspective

Natural differences translate into inequitable power and opportunity for men and women, as seen in social, economic, and political arenas. In other words, natural differences translate into differences in rank, power, and prestige. This plays out at home, at work, in churches, mosques, or synagogues, and in school and at play.

No doubt, meanings surrounding gender involve historical processes. Gender meanings are also the product of dominant structures reinforced by traditions, customs, and our dominant notions of common sense. A thorough understanding of gender is hindered without consideration of these factors. However, gender meanings are currently in flux in our society.

At Community High, for example, aggressive behavior by boys toward girls has generated a provocative response from girls. Girls have regendered some of their social practices by adopting the aggressive language and posturing of boys as a defense against the boys (Cousins & Mabrey, 1998). Many of Tina's female peers have abandoned ascribed characteristics such as passivity, weakness, and inactivity (lack of agency), which are part of the traditional meanings assigned to female gender roles (Ortner, 1996). One consequence, in school and beyond, is that these girls have been defined as unladylike and "loud" (Fordham, 1993). By contrast, the aggressiveness and loudness of boys have been defined as "toughness" and "boys being boys"—being who they naturally are and doing what they naturally do as males. In the domain of sexual activity, strong traditions and entrenched frames of reference among school staff and some students still define the girls as the polluted or promiscuous participants in sexual liaisons. Sexual activity becomes a social problem for a boy only if the boy gets a venereal disease or the girl gets pregnant. Underlying these gender relations are traditions and customs that have shaped how girls' and boys' bodies and activities are defined. The process of girls redefining themselves in response to social and cultural forces, however, is a good example of human agency, structure, and history in action.

Family. Family and kinship are key symbols in U.S. life (Schneider, 1968; Stacey, 1990). Family may be defined as a set of relationships among two or more people to carry out various social and biological functions, such as support, nurturance, sexual mating, procreation, and child rearing. Family is also an ideological construct on which we impose ideas about intimacy, love, morality, and kinship connections and obligations. Issues of contemporary versus traditional family values, structure, and change can serve as one last example of how culture works as a process, as well as how cultural change and adaptation proceed.

We have been bombarded in recent years by scholarly and public dialogue about the demise of "family values." Many believe this demise leads to the destruction of family life and thereby society (Gallagher, 1996; Popenoe, 1996; Whitehead, 1997). Recent debates about family life and its role in the maintenance of society at large have been fueled by both research and the opinions of influential politicians. On one side is the argument that increases in single parenting, divorce, and out-of-wedlock births are a reflection and a source of moral malaise. They reflect beliefs about misplaced or absent values and the social instability and demise of U.S. society. Families of the past have been presented as the model for families of the present and future. On the other side are arguments attempting to counter the "hysteria" about family values. John Gillis (1996), in particular, notes that neither family change nor anxiety about such change is new. In fact, "diversity, instability, and discontinuity have been part of the European experience of family at least since the late Middle Ages, and continued into the new world" (Skolnick, 1997, p. 87).

At the heart of these debates is a process addressed differently by both sides: if we value family coherence in the form of a stable household consisting of mother, father, and children, why do we have such a high divorce rate, an increase in single parenting, and an increase in nontraditional types of relationships? One side claims that recent trends reflect the absence of morals and virtue in our society; if we punish those who don't have morals and reward those who do, we can fix things. The other side argues that a host of medical and economic changes—including birth control and women working outside the home—have fueled social and cultural changes. At particular issue is the disagreement between the two sides about how women fit into society and family life.

Rational choice perspective

The process of family change and adaptation is complex. Much of it reflects the values we *want* our families to live by versus the values families actually *practice.* Family life is structured by meanings, values, and beliefs that fit our desires and imaginations about what is right and appropriate. But family life is also constructed and lived in a world of competing and interacting meanings and material realities. People do not always do what they intend. They do construct and author their lives, so to speak. But they do so with a host of choices among very real constraints.

Social workers who want to understand and assist families have to understand the processes that create these realities. For instance, Stan and his parents intended for him to be successful in school and avoid criminal behavior. So far, however, Stan's life has not turned out that way. But his experience cannot be reduced solely to psychological, economic, or social factors outside the cultural contexts that shape his life: history, social structure, human agency, common sense, traditions, customs, and the like. All of us, and these processes, are in the embrace of constantly changing social, economic, and political realities of life in society.

The Meaning of Culture

Social workers must not limit themselves to understanding culture only in the terms provided by other academic, scholarly, and professional traditions. We must position ourselves to understand what culture means and how it works in our own terms and in a multidimensional context. Such an understanding of culture challenges simplistic psychological analyses of individual and collective human practices that claim to adequately explain child abuse/neglect, poverty, academic failure, parent/child problems, substance abuse, school dropout, and a host of other psychosocial and social policy issues. We want to know how our world and the worlds of our clients are constructed in all their complexity. Even though this knowledge will inevitably remain incomplete due to the motion of life and the complex world of nature impinging on us and we on it, we must try. Indeed, tools are available for just such an activity: a practice orientation and a multidimensional conceptualization of culture.

Ann Swidler's (1986) definition of culture summarizes what I have tried to express in this chapter. She sees culture as a "tool kit" of symbols, stories, rituals, and worldviews that people may use in varying configurations to solve different kinds of problems. Culture works by suggesting strategies of action or persistent ways of ordering or patterning action through time, rather than only shaping ultimate ends or values toward which action is directed (Swidler, 1986; Rosaldo, 1989/1993).

In the case of Community High students like Stan and Tina, who they have become and how they perform depend on a complex maze of social and psychological processes embedded in European American and African American cultures. The interaction of these processes contributes to Stan's and Tina's ethos and worldview. The extent to which these processes limit and restrain their overall academic and social success is an important question. Neither Stan nor Tina can live outside the meaning of their blackness or their gender in the strained social world they inhabit. Their individual human agency is a factor, however, and it gives them flexibility to interpret or act on such meanings. Tina has managed to transcend culturally insensitive school processes without giving up her ethnic identity. Stan is still finding his way. Still, their interpretations of life events could serve either as motivation or a source of debilitating anxiety and despair. Their interpretations could also generate indignation and ethnic zealotry in the fight for equality in mainstream United States. If they do, will Tina or Stan respond by becoming a race leader? Or will their interpretations result in a loss of self-worth and personal value, leading to a fatalistic dependence on drugs and alcohol to soften the reality of not being powerful and white? Members of immigrant groups face similar questions.

Clearly, U.S. culture and society have a role in this experience. Earlier I talked about cultural hegemony, or how dominant social, economic, and political processes subjugate those who do not comply or fit in. Cultural hegemony skews our search for problems and solutions. If people have a problem, we look to the people for the cause and answer only to culture and society.

What will your interpretations be as a social worker encountering people who differ from the norm? Will you accept the fact that people experience strain and contradictions between the meanings in their heads and the social, economic, and political realities of everyday public life? Will you interpret social and economic problems as largely personal deficits? Will you misinterpret personal functioning due to a one-dimensional understanding of culture? Will your cultural understanding leave out issues of inequality in society and its role in the oppression of people of color; women; people who are poor; immigrants; older adults; those who are physically, mentally and cognitively disabled; or gay and lesbian people?

In summarizing a contemporary paradox of family life, Arlene Skolnick offers us insight into a host of practice and policy issues for social work: "Americans have still not come to terms with the gap between the way we think our families ought to be and the complex, often messy realities of our lives" (Skolnick, 1997, p. 86). Insert *traditions, customs, values,* and so on for the word *families,* and we have a succinct formulation of the simplicity and complexity of culture as a lived process in contemporary industrial societies.

IMPLICATIONS FOR SOCIAL WORK PRACTICE

I learned how the practice orientation works as an ethnographer at Community High, conducting research largely to describe the students' culture from their point of view as well as mine as a researcher. As a social worker, you may be doing ethnographic inquiry without knowing it. Here are a few principles you can follow:

- Recognize the categories of knowledge—social science theories and orientations, folk or common everyday theories and orientations— that you rely on to understand human behavior in the social environment.

- Embrace the traditions, customs, values, and behaviors of disparate groups identified by race, ethnicity, sexual orientation, gender, physical differences, age, nationality, and religion. Avoid approaching these groups in a cookbook, stereotyped, or one-size-fits-all fashion.

- Appreciate the tension between the force of social structure and the resiliency and intentionality of human agency in complex societies such as ours.

- Attempt to understand both personal and social acts of making meaning, and realize how such acts give substance to and obscure our own lives as well as those of our clients.

- Examine culture through the lens of the practice orientation using a "strengths" and person-in-environment perspective that allows you to assess the simultaneous forces of history, social structure, human agency, and the political context in which all of these forces work themselves out in the lives of your clients.

- Use the practice orientation to frame the actions of those who resist being mainstream Americans. This perspective will help you see the creativity and hope, as well as the ugliness and pain, of their resistance.

- Pay attention to processes of cultural change, including assimilation, accommodation, acculturation, and bicultural socialization, in the lives of individuals and groups with whom you work.

- Work to ensure that members of nondominant groups have a significant say in how cultural change proceeds.

accommodation
assimilation
bicultural socialization
biological determinism
common sense
cultural conflict
cultural innovation
cultural relativism
culture
culture of poverty
customs
ethnic identity

ethnocentrism
ethos
hegemony
ideology
practice orientation
race
racism
socioeconomic status (SES)
symbol
traditions
worldview

ACTIVE LEARNING

1. *The Cultural Construction of Schooling.* Compare and contrast Stan's and Tina's experiences at Community High School with your own high school experience, considering the following themes:

- Material and behavioral cultural symbols
- Processes of cultural change (assimilation, accommodation, acculturation, bicultural socialization)
- Ways in which race, ethnicity, social class, and gender play out in the school setting
- Cultural conflict

Next, imagine that you spend a day as a student at Community High and Stan and Tina spend a day at your high school. How do you think you might react to the cultural symbols at Community High? How might Stan and Tina react to the cultural symbols at your high school? How do you account for these reactions?

2. *Cultural Change.* (Adapted from an exercise in Bradshaw, Healey, & Smith, 2001). Either by telephone or face-to-face, interview an adult over the age of 60 for the purpose of learning about cultural change over time.

■ Ask the respondent to reflect on her or his childhood. What favorite activities can the respondent recall from early childhood? What were the favorite toys? What types of clothing were worn? What values were stressed? How was family life structured? What kind of relationship did the respondent have with her or his parents? What type of discipline was used in the family? What was the nature of peer relationships?

■ Ask the respondent to think about the one most important technological change since he or she was a child (e.g., television, Internet, medical technologies). Ask the respondent whether this innovation has been good or bad for children and for family life, and to think about exactly how it has changed the lives of children and families.

■ Ask the respondent to think about the one most important change in customs and traditions of how people go about their everyday lives since he or she was a child (e.g., mothers working outside the home, smaller families). Again, ask the respondent whether this change has been good or bad for children and families, and to think about exactly how it has changed the lives of children and families.

Write a brief paper to summarize the thoughts of your respondent, and your analysis of the responses, based on concepts from this chapter.

WEB RESOURCES

Diversity & Ethnic Studies: Virtual Community

www.public.iastate.edu/~savage/divweb2.htm
Site maintained at Iowa State University contains a collection of links to diversity-related Internet resources on topics such as African Americans, Native Americans, Asian Americans, U.S. Latinos, people with disabilities, lesbians, bisexuals and gays, and general multicultural links.

Multicultural Pavilion

curry.edschool.virginia.edu/go/multicultural
Site maintained at the University of Virginia contains resources, research, awareness activities, and links to multicultural topics.

Diversity Links

www.wesleyan.edu/psych/list/html

Site developed and maintained by the Association of American Colleges and Universities and the University of Maryland contains links to Internet resources on African Americans, Asian Americans, disabilities, European Americans, Latin Americans, Native Americans, lesbians and gays, and women.

CHAPTER 9

Social Institutions and Social Structure

Elizabeth D. Hutchison and Amy Waldbillig

Social Institutions and Social Structure

Elizabeth D. Hutchison
Virginia Commonwealth University

Amy Waldbillig
Virginia Commonwealth University

What are the key social institutions that give pattern to social life in the United States?

What are the major trends in each of these social institutions?

What are the positions in the contemporary debate about social inequality?

Key Ideas

As you read this chapter, take note of these central ideas:

1. Social institutions are patterned ways of solving the problems and meeting the requirements of a particular society.

2. Social structure is a set of interrelated social institutions developed by human beings to impose constraints on human interaction for the purpose of the survival and well-being of the collectivity.

3. Social institutions are relatively stable but also changing. Most of the major U.S. social institutions have undergone extraordinary changes from 1960 to the present.

4. Since 1974, income inequality has grown substantially in the United States.

5. Eight key social institutions in the United States are family and kinship, religion, government and politics, economy, education, social welfare, health care, and mass media. Each of these institutions plays a role in the creation and maintenance of social inequality.

6. Over time, societies have vacillated between a conservative thesis that inequality is the natural order and the radical antithesis that equality is the natural order to answer the question, Is social inequality a good thing or a bad thing?

CASE STUDY

THE MEZA FAMILY'S STRUGGLE TO MAKE IT IN THE UNITED STATES

The Meza family had been getting along well in the United States until the birth of their daughter, Minerva, who was born premature and, now at age 2, experiences some developmental delays. In 1986, Mr. and Mrs. Meza applied to the amnesty program to legalize their immigrant status. They had been in the United States for many years, and their three oldest children, Enrique now age 17, Myra age 15, and Jesus age 11, are all U.S. citizens, having all been born here. During the application process, Mrs. Meza's mother, in the interior of Mexico, became very ill, and Mrs. Meza returned to Mexico to stay with her mother until her death 6 months later. Because of this visit, Mrs. Meza was not able to get her legal documents processed, although her husband was able to develop legal status.

Mr. Meza is grateful for the health insurance coverage he receives from the construction company that employs him; it covered much of the extensive hospitalization expense demanded by Minerva's premature birth. However, Mrs. Meza is not covered because she is not documented. Her lack of legal status often causes stress both for herself and her family, especially when she becomes ill and they have to pay for all her medical expenses. Also, the children are aware of other situations where parents are forced to return to Mexico due to lack of legal immigration status, and in many cases children are left in the United States with relatives. They fear that their mother can be deported if the Immigration and Naturalization Service (INS) finds out. The family also has been afraid to report unethical landlords who failed to return rental deposits as agreed or who had failed to address hazardous plumbing problems that violated housing codes and jeopardized family health. They were afraid that the landlords would report them to the INS.

Mrs. Meza, 42, worked until Minerva's birth at a dry cleaning establishment, where she was exposed to the fumes of toxic cleaning fluids. She feels that she should have obtained a safer job when she discovered she was pregnant. However, her undocumented status prevented her from easily finding other employment. In addition, her employer knew about her lack of documentation, yet paid her as well as others who worked there and were citizens. Moreover, the family had just recently purchased their first home and she was hesitant to seek new employment because she felt that no one would hire a pregnant woman.

Minerva has been hospitalized several times this year, just recently due to pneumonia. The doctor has also recently informed Mrs. Meza that Minerva very likely has cerebral palsy, and Mrs. Meza needs to attend meetings of the multidisciplinary team that oversees Minerva's care. You are the social worker on this team. Mrs. Meza feels that this disability is a way for God to punish her for not placing the health of her unborn over her concern about meeting new house payments. Although she took good care of herself—took vitamins regularly, watched her diet, and tried not to work too hard—she only saw a doctor twice during her pregnancy.

Two months ago, Mrs. Meza returned to work, because the family desperately needed her income. Mr. Meza's mother, age 65, came from Mexico to baby-sit Minerva and help out with housework and meals. Although Grandma has really helped to lift the caregiving burden from Mom, there have been communication issues and conflicts about methods of child care between Mrs. Meza and her mother-in-law. These problems are now causing marital conflict between Mr. and Mrs. Meza because he often sides with his mother. Because his mother raised 10 children, all of whom are healthy, according to her health care beliefs, he argues that she knows what she is doing.

Recently, a real problem arose when Mom picked up Minerva from Grandma, who had been asked to bathe and ready Minerva for a late afternoon appointment Mom had scheduled with the doctor, so she would not lose too much work. When the nurse asked Mom to undress Minerva, Mom discovered Minerva's chest had been wrapped in a poultice that smelled quite strongly. When the doctor asked what the poultice consisted of, Mom was embarrassed that she could not tell him. When the mustard-like substance was wiped away, the physician noted bruising on Minerva's rib cage. Mom was just as surprised as the physician and was not able to explain how the bruising occurred. A referral to child protective services (CPS) resulted in a home call to the Meza household. Both Mr. and Mrs. Meza stayed home from work to try to sort out this embarrassing situation and to explain what had happened.

When Mom returned from the doctor's office, she nervously grilled the grandmother about the poultice. She discovered that the senior Mrs. Meza had taken it upon herself to take Minerva to a *huesero* in a nearby barrio.

CASE STUDY

This man is essentially a masseuse. Grandmother felt that if Minerva's chest was massaged, the phlegm that was causing so much congestion would be loosened and Minerva could breathe more easily. Mr. and Mrs. Meza went to visit the *huesero,* and he explained that he had only rubbed her chest as he normally would any client. He claimed that the child's lack of weight resulted in the bruising.

When all this information was shared with the CPS worker, he informed the family that they could never use this *huesero* again, and if they did, they would be charged with child abuse. Mr. Meza has informed his mother that she cannot undertake any kind of intervention without his knowledge. Mrs. Meza fears that more interactions with CPS might cause her to be identified as undocumented.

Although Mr. Meza is now more supportive of his wife, Mrs. Meza is constantly fearful about the care of Minerva. She calls home several times during the day and has demanded that both Enrique and Myra come home immediately after school each day to attend to Minerva's care. Enrique is a top student and is hoping that his grades and extracurricular activities, like his membership in the Science Club, will result in scholarship opportunities for college. He has a Saturday job tutoring children, which provides a little income. He understands his parents' concerns about Minerva, but feels it should be enough if Myra takes care of Minerva after school. He feels that he has been a good son and has not caused any problems for his parents. He also feels that his parents are not concerned about intruding on his college plans, and he has become irritable and almost disrespectful to his parents and to his grandmother.

Myra, on the other hand, is scared to take care of Minerva by herself, especially when Minerva is ill. She feels that she cannot depend on her grandmother to make correct choices about Minerva's care, particularly if Minerva starts to cough a lot. She also feels that Enrique is trying to dump all responsibility on her and feels that her parents have always let him get away from doing household chores because he is a boy. She has always had to do more around the house, like care for her younger brother, Jesus, because he was very small. She feels it is really unfair that Mexican families do that with their children. The one time she voiced this sentiment her father told her she was acting like she no longer wanted to be Mexican.

Mrs. Meza has lost eight pounds in the 6 weeks since the child abuse report. She has noticed that the night sweats she was already experiencing have increased; she wakes up three to four times a night soaked with perspiration and finds herself exhausted at work the next day. She also feels overwhelmed and has had crying spells both at work and at home. She has tried to hide her feelings from her husband, but he is concerned that something is wrong with her. He wants her to see a doctor, but she feels that she does not want to call any attention to herself after what happened with the child abuse report. Often when she wakes up at night, she thinks about what would happen to her family if she were forced to return to Mexico. She feels that this would destroy her family. Meanwhile, the visitor's permit Grandmother has used to come to the United States will expire soon. Should they try to renew it? Should she stop working? How will they pay their expenses with less income, especially now with the two oldest children costing more money? Maybe buying their home was a bad decision. Maybe the family is becoming too Americanized.

—Maria E. Zuniga

Patterns of Social Life

As you read this story, you are probably aware of both the people and the environments involved. A number of people are involved in the story, and you may be observing how they are interacting with each other and what each contributes to the current situation. Although you do not want to lose sight of the personal dimensions of the Mezas' story, in this chapter we consider the broad patterns of social life that they have encountered and continue to encounter. We want you to see the connections between the personal troubles of the Meza family and social conditions.

A good way to begin to think about broad patterns of social life is to imagine that you and 100 other people have made a space journey to a new planet that has recently, thanks to technological breakthroughs, become inhabitable by humans. You are committed to beginning a new society on this new frontier. How will you work together to be successful in this endeavor? What will you need to do to ensure your survival? Sociologists and anthropologists have given much thought to how people work together to try to ensure the survival of a society. They have identified two concepts—social institution and social structure—as central to understanding those endeavors.

Systems perspective

Social institution and social structure are among the more abstract concepts used by sociologists. Our understanding of these concepts is also complicated by the casual, everyday use of the term *institution* to cover a variety of meanings. In this book, however, we use the definition of **social institutions** as "patterned ways of solving the problems and meeting the requirements of a particular society" (Newman, 1995, p. 30). Another definition is useful as well: social institutions "are solutions that consist of a set of rights and duties, an authority for enforcing them, and some degree of adherence to collective norms of prudent reasonable behavior" (Van de Ven, 1993, p. 142). Rights and duties are organized into statuses and roles and the expected behaviors that accompany them. **Statuses** are specific social positions; roles, as suggested in Chapter 2, are the behaviors of persons occupying particular statuses. Sociologists have identified a set of interrelated social institutions—such as family, religion, government, economy, education—with each institution organizing social relations in a particular sector of social life. We see evidences of each of these institutions in the lives of the Meza family.

Social structure is the concept used to refer to this set of interrelated social institutions. In the broadest sense, social structure is another term for *society,* or simply an acknowledgment that social life is patterned, not random (Babbie, 1994). Although we typically use the term *social structure* to imply a material entity, it is better thought of as a process: "a process of taking away individual freedom and structuring it for corporate action" (Babbie, 1994, p. 13). In other words, **social structure** is a set of interrelated social institutions developed by human beings to impose constraints on human interaction for the purpose of the survival and well-being of the collectivity. Certainly, we can see some of the constraints that various social institutions impose on members of the Meza family.

Sociological treatment of social institutions and social structure emphasizes the ways in which they persist and contribute to social stability. But often they persist despite unintended consequences and evidence that they are ineffective. Thus, social institutions are imperfect solutions to past problems (Van de Ven, 1993). In addition, although social institutions are relatively stable, they also change—whether by accident, by evolution, or by design (Goodin, 1996). Social institutions persist only when they are carried forward by individual actors and only when they are actively monitored (Scott, 1995). This view of social institutions and social structure, as relatively stable but also changing, is consistent with the multidimensional perspective of this book. This view seems justified, given the extraordinary changes in several major social institutions since 1960 in societies around the world (Caplow, 1991; Caplow, Bahr, Modell, & Chadwick, 1991; Farley, 1996; Langlois, 1994; Oberschall, 1996; Zdravomyslova, 1996).

Sociologists commonly identify five interrelated social institutions: family and kinship, religion, government and politics, economy, and education. In addition, they have identified three other key social institutions in modern industrialized societies: social welfare, health care, and mass media (Newman, 1995; Popple & Leighninger, 1993). We can see how important these institutions are in the current lives of the Meza family. The discussion in this chapter includes all eight of these major social institutions. Exhibit 9.1 presents these social institutions and the major functions that they perform for society.

EXHIBIT 9.1
Key Social Institutions
and the Functions
They Perform

Social Institution	Functions Performed
Family and kinship	Regulating procreation
	Conducting initial socialization
	Providing mutual support
Religion	Answering questions about meaning and purpose of life
	Socializing individuals
	Maintaining social control
	Providing mutual support
Government and politics	Making and enforcing societal rules
	Resolving internal and external conflicts
	Mobilizing collective resources to meet societal goals
Economy	Regulating production, distribution, and consumption of goods and services
Education	Passing along formal knowledge from one generation to next
	Socializing individuals
Social welfare	Promoting interdependence
	Dealing with issues of dependence
Health care	Promoting the general health
Mass media	Managing the flow of information, images, and ideas

Contemporary Trends in U.S. Social Institutions

You have plans to become a social worker, so it is probably safe to assume that you have been at least a casual observer of trends in social institutions. As casual observers, we all keep abreast of trends by making personal observations, listening to stories of people in our social network, and consuming the output of the mass media. In our casual observations about trends in social life, we make comparisons between the contemporary social world as we understand it and some past social world as we understand it. This type of comparison provides many opportunities for error. We may view the contemporary world through a lens that is biased by age, gender, social status, religion, or political persuasion, and we may tend to romanticize the past. To avoid these errors, social workers must become professional, not casual, observers of trends in the social world. As planners and administrators, we must design and implement programs that are responsive to trends in social life. Those of us who engage clients directly, to ameliorate problems of living, must understand the changing social situations in which those problems have developed and are being maintained. The purpose of this chapter is to help you observe trends in a more professional way so that you can function more effectively as a social worker.

Because 1960 is often seen as a turning point for contemporary social life (Caplow, 1991; Farley, 1996), we focus for the most part on the trends in social institutions from 1960 to the present. These trends demonstrate the blessings as well as the unresolved problems of industrial capitalism. However, because the profession of social work developed in response to some of the particular problems created by industrial capitalism, we give special attention to social problems related to the current stage of industrialization.

Conflict perspective

Perhaps the most important and troubling trend in contemporary life in the United States is the growing rate of social inequality. In recent years, the United States has enjoyed faster economic growth than any other large industrialized country, but it has also earned the distinction as the most unequal society in the advanced industrial world (Burtless, 2001). We pay particular attention to social inequality because the profession of social work has historically made a commitment to persons and groups who are disadvantaged in the distribution of resources by social institutions. To carry out this commitment, we must have a way of understanding social inequality and its influence on human behavior. Throughout this chapter, we demonstrate how social inequality is created and maintained in eight major interrelated social institutions. But first we take a closer look at inequality in the United States.

In the period 1947 to 1973, income inequality in the United States declined slightly. Since 1974, however, income inequality has grown substantially (Larin & McNichol, 1997; Levy, 1995; Burtless, 2001). Between 1974 and 1995, when adjusted for inflation, the average incomes of families in the lowest income group, the bottom fifth, fell by more than 20%, average incomes for families in the middle fifth fell by about 2%, and incomes for families in the top fifth increased by about 30% (Larin & McNichol, 1997). The growth in income disparities accelerated in the latter half of the 1990s. Exhibit 9.2 shows the rate of income growth between 1993 and 1997 in each income quintile as well as in the top 5% income group and the top 1% income group.

We suggested above that the United States surpasses other advanced industrialized nations in income inequality. Exhibit 9.3 shows the ranking of 19 advanced industrial countries in terms of income inequality, moving from the country with least inequality at the bottom (Austria) to the country with greatest inequality at the top (United States). It was not always easy to make such cross-national comparisons, but in recent years several measures of inequality have been developed and used to make international comparisons. The most commonly used measure, and the one on which Exhibits 9.3

EXHIBIT 9.2

Rate of Income
Growth in U.S.
Income Groups,
1993-1997

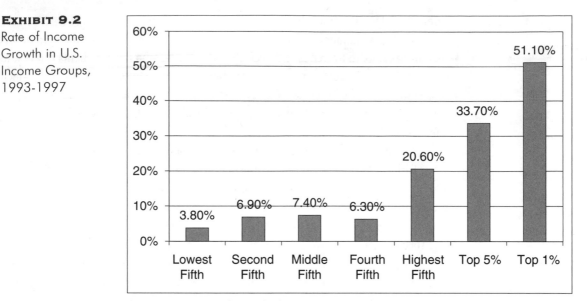

Source: Center on Budget and Policy Priorities, 2001.

and 9.4 are based, is the **Gini index**, which measures the extent to which the distribution of income within a country deviates from a perfectly equal distribution. Gini index scores range from 0 (perfect equality) to 100 (perfect inequality).

Of course, the United States does not have more inequality than all countries in the world. In a general sense, highly industrialized, high-income countries have much lower levels of inequality than nonindustrial or newly industrializing countries (Bradshaw et al., 2001). As demonstrated in Exhibit 9.4, the rate of inequality is much lower in the United States than in many nonindustrialized countries. Overall, the highest rates of inequality can be found in newly industrializing agrarian societies, such as many Latin American countries and some African countries.

The Mezas came to the United States to escape brutal poverty in Mexico. In recent years, Mexico has developed trade agreements with a number of other countries, and has moved from the world's 26th largest economy to the 8th largest. And, yet, real wages in Mexico have declined by about 20% in this period of growth. A large percentage of workers, particularly those in rural areas, are poorly paid with few employment options (Sernau, 2001). You can see from Exhibit 9.4 that Mexico's ratio of inequality is lower than that in Brazil and Nicaragua, but it is still much higher than advanced industrial countries. Although the Mezas are struggling for economic survival in the United States, they do not wish to return to Mexico.

Some social analysts argue that social inequality is the price of economic growth, and suggest that the poorest families in the United States enjoy a much higher standard

EXHIBIT 9.3

Ranking of Social Inequality in 19 Advanced Industrial Countries

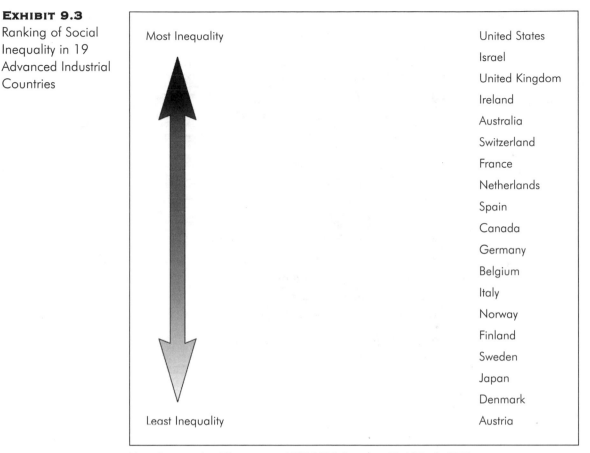

Most Inequality

United States
Israel
United Kingdom
Ireland
Australia
Switzerland
France
Netherlands
Spain
Canada
Germany
Belgium
Italy
Norway
Finland
Sweden
Japan
Denmark

Least Inequality   Austria

Note: Data are for different years, 1987-1998. Based on World Bank, 2002.

of living than poor families in other countries (Rector & Hederman, 1999). In other words, "Rising tides lift all boats." And indeed, the growing number of immigrant families coming from the Latin American countries would seem to support this idea.

But a comparison of the United States with other industrialized countries suggests that societal health is best maintained when economic growth is balanced with attention to social inequality (Burtless, 2001). A growing international research literature suggests that high levels of inequality are bad for the social health of a nation. Let's look at three social indicators for the 19 industrial countries in Exhibit 9.3: childhood mortality (probability of dying before age 5), life expectancy, and secondary school enrollment. In 1960, the United States had a lower childhood mortality rate than 10 of the other countries listed in Exhibit 9.3. By 2000, the United States had the highest childhood mortality rate of the 19 countries. Indeed, the cross-national continuum for childhood mortality looks almost exactly like the continuum of inequality. Thirteen of

EXHIBIT 9.4

Ratings of Income Inequality of Selected Nonindustrial Countries and the United States

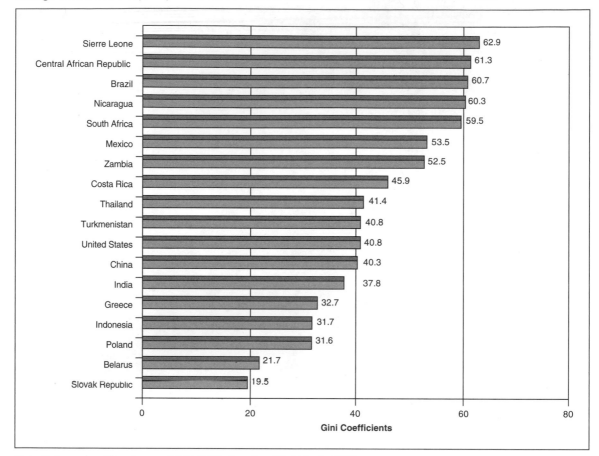

Note: Data are for different years, 1989-1999. Based on World Bank, 2002.

the industrialized countries have longer life expectancy than the United States, and 15 have higher rates of secondary education (UNICEF, 2002). Observers have noted that a "culture of inequality" develops in countries with high rates of inequality. The interests of the rich begin to diverge from the interests of the average family. There is good cross-national evidence that societies with high levels of inequality make smaller investments in public education and other social supports. These societies also have higher levels of violence, less trust and more hostility, and lower levels of involvement in community life (Wilkinson, 2001).

Marc Miringoff and colleagues (1996, 1999) have developed an index that can be used to monitor the social health of the United States. They suggest that we are highly attentive in the United States to economic performance and have access to

Exhibit 9.5

Indicators of Social Health

Children:	Infant mortality
	Child abuse
	Child poverty
Youth:	Youth suicide
	Teenage drug abuse
	High school dropouts
	Teenage births
Adults:	Unemployment
	Wages
	Health care coverage
Older Adults:	Poverty, aged 65+
	Life expectancy, aged 65
All Ages:	Violent crime
	Alcohol-related traffic fatalities
	Affordable housing
	Gap between rich and poor

Source: Based on Miringoff & Miringoff, 1999.

minute-by-minute reports on the economic health of the country through the Dow Jones Industrial Index. It is much harder to get indicators of social health. They recommend the 16 indicators found in Exhibit 9.5 and suggest that these indicators should not be measured against an ideal standard, but rather in comparison to the best year this nation has achieved, a model year. In their research covering the years from 1970 to 1993, they found that the peak years of the Index of Social Health were 1970 to 1973, when the Index averaged 74.6. The worst years were 1982, 1990, and 1991, when it averaged 38.8. It was 40.6 in 1993 and was at about 50 for a few years in the late 1990s (Kawachi & Kennedy, 2001). Between 1970 and 1996, there was improvement in infant mortality, life expectancy, poverty among older adults, and the high school dropout rate. During this same period, however, several social indicators worsened: youth suicide, violent crime, child poverty, inequality, wages, health care coverage, and child abuse. The remaining five indicators have shifted over time with no clear trajectory.

Until the mid-1970s, the Index of Social Health tracked well with the Dow Jones Industrial Average. After the mid-1970s, however, the social health of the United States stagnated while the economic health began a rapid upturn (Miringoff & Miringoff, 1999; Miringoff, Miringoff, & Opdycke, 1996). This decoupling of economic health and social health of the United States coincides with the rise of inequality discussed earlier.

Poverty rates in the United States, one measure of social inequality, demonstrate that social inequality is related to race and ethnicity, age, gender, family structure, and geographic location (U.S. Census Bureau, 2001). Although the majority of people living below the poverty level are white, and people of color can be found in all income groups, blacks, Hispanics, and Native Americans are about three times as likely as whites to be poor. The poverty rate for blacks is 22.1%, for Hispanics 21.2%, for Native Americans 25.9%, for white, non-Hispanics 7.5%, and for Asian and Pacific Islanders 10.8%. The good news is that the differential between whites and groups of color has decreased in recent years. The bad news is that the differential remains quite large. For example, in the 1940s, the median income of black families was about 50% of the median income of white families, and by the end of the 20th century, the median income of black families was only about 60% of white families (Bradshaw et al., 2001). Foreign-born noncitizens (19.4%) have a higher poverty rate than natives (10.7%), but foreign-born citizens (9.7%) have a slightly lower poverty rate than natives. You can see from the Mezas' story how lack of citizenship makes people particularly vulnerable in the labor market.

Over the past 50 years, vulnerability to poverty has shifted from older adults to children. Between 1959 and 2000, the percentage of the population 65 years and older living in poverty decreased from about 35% to about 10% (U.S. Census Bureau, 2001). The proportion of the population under 18 years living in poverty showed a smaller decrease in this same period, from about 27% to about 16%. Since 1974, the poverty rate for persons under 18 has been higher than for the group 65 and over.

Women are more likely than men to be poor. About 22% of unrelated women are poor compared to 16% of unrelated men; many of the unrelated women are in the oldest old category. Single-parent, mother-only families (24.7%) are more likely to live in poverty than two-parent families (4.7%). But in general, families with children (15.7%) are more likely than families without children to live in poverty (9.6%). A cross-national analysis found that more than half of all childless couples, on average, are well-to-do (Smeeding, 1991).

In 1970, poverty was primarily a rural problem. By 1990, poverty was much more of an urban problem. In 2000, 16.1% of people living inside central cities were poor, compared to 14.2% of people in rural areas and 7.8% of people in suburbs (Project Serve, n.d.; U.S. Census Bureau, 2001).

We turn now to analysis of trends in eight major social institutions. We look for the good news in these trends, but we also pay close attention to how social inequality is created and/or maintained in each institution. Unfortunately, by the time you read these words, even the most recent data presented here will already be old. If you have not developed research skills already, this is a good time for you to learn to use your library and the Internet to find social data. Why not make a trip to the library or the information superhighway to see if you can update some of the trends described here? Are trends holding and projections materializing?

Trends in Family and Kinship

You undoubtedly would agree that family and kinship relationships are a very important part of the unfolding story of the Meza family. Family and kinship is perhaps the most basic social institution, and in simple societies it fulfills many of the functions assigned to other social institutions in complex societies. Although the functions of family and kinship have been the subject of some controversy since 1960, modern societies generally agree that the **family and kinship institution** is primarily responsible for the regulation of procreation, for the initial socialization of new members of society, and for mutual support.

The family and kinship institution has experienced some extraordinary changes since 1960, in the United States as well as in other industrial countries. These five changes, taken together, have had a far-reaching impact on human behavior:

1. *Medical advances and court rulings have made childbearing discretionary.* Around 1962, reliable oral contraceptives became generally available, followed shortly by widespread use of surgical sterilization (Caplow, 1991). Then, quite unexpectedly, the U.S. Supreme Court legalized abortion in 1973, in the famous *Roe* v. *Wade* case. These changes, along with changes in other social institutions, have resulted in a sharp decline in fertility; the birthrate dropped from 23.7 births per 1,000 population in 1960 to 14.5 in 1997 (U.S. Department of Health and Human Services, n.d.). People are waiting longer to have children and having fewer children. In addition, people are having children more often outside marriage. In 1996, there were 6 million-plus pregnancies in the United States. Of these pregnancies, 62% resulted in live birth, 22% in abortion, and 16% in miscarriage or stillbirth. Between 1990 and 1996, live births declined 8%, induced abortions declined 16%, and fetal loss by miscarriage or stillbirth was reduced by 4% (National Center for Health Statistics, 2000). The birthrate for married women is almost 10 times their abortion rate. In contrast, for unmarried women, birth and abortion rates are nearly equal. However, in recent years, unmarried women have been increasingly more likely to give birth and less likely to have an induced abortion (National Center for Health Statistics, 2000). Since 1970, the percentage of births to unmarried mothers increased from about 8% to about 33% (U.S. Census Bureau, 2000b). The child-rearing function in the United States has been shifting from the relatively prosperous two-parent family to the lower-income single-parent family.

2. *Unmarried cohabitation is no longer legally prohibited.* Cohabitation may have replaced marriage as the typical way to begin a live-in sexual relationship (Farley, 1996). Prior to the mid-1960s, unmarried cohabitation was discouraged by a combination of local laws and regulations, federal statutes, and unofficial regulations (Caplow, 1991), which made it impossible for unmarried couples to reserve a hotel room, buy a house, or rent an apartment. Between 1965 and 1974, only about 11% of couples

marrying for the first time had lived together prior to marriage (Rodriguez, 1998). Between 1980 and 1984, 44% of marriages included at least one partner who had cohabited prior to marriage. It is estimated that since 1985, about half of all marrying couples have cohabited. In 1990, about one in seven children who were counted in the census as living in single-parent families actually lived in homes with cohabiting parents (Rodriguez, 1998).

3. *The divorce rate increased dramatically.* The divorce rate in the United States has been gradually increasing since 1870, and it is currently much higher than the rates in other advanced industrial societies (Farley, 1996). Until 1966, divorce was granted to couples only when one party was at fault (Caplow, 1991). New York was the first state to develop a no-fault divorce law, and by 1985 all states had some form of no-fault divorce. Between 1965 and 1974, the divorce rate doubled, from 10 to 20 divorces per 1,000 married women per year (Caplow, 1991). Since that time, the divorce rate has leveled off, but there have been fluctuations within each of the recent decades. Divorce rates decline during economic hard times and rise in times of economic prosperity (Ahrons, 1999). About 50% of all first marriages end in divorce, but there are some geographical, racial, ethnic, and religious differences in the divorce rate. States in the western part of the United States have higher divorce rates than states in other regions; the divorce rate of blacks is twice the rate of whites and Hispanics; and divorce is less common among Catholics, Jews, and Muslims than among Protestants (Ahrons, 1999). In the contemporary era, the majority of divorces are initiated by women (Carter & McGoldrick, 1999b). In the United States, some marriages are more prone to divorce than others. The greatest risk factors for divorce are teen marriage, low education, and low income.

4. *Large numbers of women have entered the paid labor force.* Although the increasing employment of women is a long-term trend, the increase during the period 1960-1990 was spectacular, particularly for married women with children under 6. In 1950, women made up 29.6% of the labor force, and by 2001, they made up 46.6% of the labor force. In 1960, 30% of married couples included wives in the paid labor force; by 1997, it was 62% (AFL-CIO, 2001; Farley, 1996). In 1960, 19% of married women with children under 6 were in the labor force; by 2000, the figure had risen to 64.6% (AFL-CIO, 2001; Caplow, 1991). The rates are even higher for divorced and separated mothers. In 1997, 65.3% of separated women and 74.5% of divorced women were in the labor force. This is about the same as the rate of employment for men, which was 74.7% in 2000 (AFL-CIO, 2001; Fullerton & Toossi, 2001).

5. *Average life expectancy has increased.* The average life expectancy in the United States has increased by 60% in the past century. It increased from 68.2 years in 1950 to 76.9 in 2000 (National Center for Health Statistics, 2001, 2002). This increase in longevity, added to the decrease in fertility, is changing the shape of families in late

industrial societies. Families now have more generations but fewer people in each generation. The increase in longevity has also led to an increase in chronic disease and the need for families to provide personal care for members with disabilities.

Two other long-term trends in family relationships are likely to continue: greater valuing of autonomy and self-direction, as opposed to obedience and conformity, in children; and equalization of power between men and women (Caplow, 1991). Not all people agree that these trends are good, and some point to them as causes of the weakening of the family. Other people see these trends as providing possibilities for stabilizing the family in a time of great change in all major social institutions.

Social service programs serving families, children, and older adults need to be responsive to these changing trends. The confluence of declining family size, increasing numbers of single parents, increasing numbers of women in the paid labor force, and an aging population calls for a reexamination, in particular, of our assumptions about family caregiving for dependent persons. Social workers should lead the way in discourse about social policies that can strengthen families and alleviate family stressors. These issues receive greater attention in Chapter 10.

Trends in Religion

Mrs. Meza believes that Minerva's health problems are God's way of punishing her for not placing the health of her unborn over other concerns. This is how she makes meaning of the situation. The **religious institution** is the primary institution for answering these sorts of questions. It also serves important socialization, social control, and mutual support functions.

George Gallup Jr. and Michael Lindsay (1999) suggest that "one cannot understand America if one does not have an awareness and appreciation of the religious underpinnings of our society" (p. 1). International data indicate that Americans have much higher weekly attendance at religious services than Europeans; they spend more time in private devotions and more money on religious activities than residents of other advanced industrial countries (Gallup & Lindsay, 1999; Wald, 1997). For example, 96% of the U.S. population believes in God, compared to 70% of Canadians and 61% of Britons (Gallup & Lindsay, 1999).

In an era of declining confidence in social institutions, opinion polls have indicated that Americans have greater confidence in organized religion than in most other U.S. social institutions. For the past 25 years, organized religion has vied with the military and the Supreme Court for the position of most trusted social institution (Gallup & Lindsay, 1999). (In 2002, however, confidence in the Catholic church was shaken by revelations of sexual abuse by clergy.) It is also important to note that religious organizations receive a large share of philanthropic gifts. Those gifts are a major source of support for social services in the United States. For example, expenditures for welfare activities by Catholic Charities are second only to expenditures by the U.S. government (Wald, 1997). Social workers need to become more aware of the role that religious congregations are playing in social service delivery in the contemporary era (Cnaan, 1997).

On a number of survey measures, the population in the United States has been stable in its attachment to the religious institution over the past half-century. For example, in 1947, 97% of survey respondents believed in God, and 96% reported the same in 1999. The percentage who pray was the same in 1947 and 1999, 47%. Likewise, the percentage with regular church attendance was the same in both years, 40%. Respondents in opinion surveys consistently report that religion is a major source of support in times of trouble (Gallup & Lindsay, 1999). It is important, therefore, that the social work assessment process include assessment of the role of religion in clients' lives.

At the same time, however, opinion poll data indicate a decline, since the 1960s, in confidence that organized religion can make a difference in society. In 1957, 69% of survey respondents thought that religion was increasing its influence on U.S. life. By 1970, only 14% reported a belief that the influence of religion was increasing. Since 1976, approximately 40% of respondents have reported a belief that religion is increasing in influence on U.S. society. Similarly, in 1957, 81% reported that religion is capable of addressing contemporary problems. In contrast, by 1998, only 65% of respondents shared this confidence (Gallup & Lindsay, 1999).

It is unclear whether this trend is cause or effect of another trend noted in opinion poll data, which is that the percentage of persons in the United States with a "deep, lived-out faith" (Gallup & Lindsay, 1999) is much smaller than the general opinion poll data would suggest. Robert Wuthnow (1998) argues that many people in the United States are not willing to embrace a spirituality that is serious, disciplined, and socially responsible. He suggests that many middle-class people use religion as a resource for justifying their privileged position. This is consistent with opinion poll findings that prayer is seen by a large majority (98%) in the United States as a means for acquiring what you want (Gallup & Lindsay, 1999).

Historically, U.S. religious life has been dominated by the Judeo-Christian tradition. That continues to be the case, but since the passage of the Immigration Act of 1965, a growing minority of Buddhists, Muslims, and Hindus inhabit the United States (Wentz, 1998). Exhibit 9.6 shows trends in religious preference between 1947 and 1999, based on surveys conducted by the Gallup Organization (Gallup & Lindsay, 1999; U.S. Census Bureau, 2000b). Religious diversity seems to be increasing, but at present the United States remains a predominantly Christian nation. In contrast, approximately one third of the world's population is estimated to be Christian (U.S. Census Bureau, 1992, p. 60). Muslims and Hindus each make up less than 1% of the population in the

EXHIBIT 9.6
Trends in Religious
Preference,
1947-1999

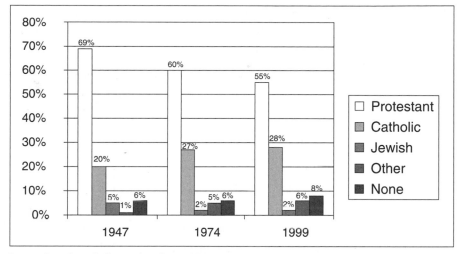

Source: Based on Gallup and Lindsay, 1999; U.S. Census Bureau, 2000, p. 62.

United States, but among nonwhites with postgraduate education, 4% are Muslims and 2% are Hindu (Gallup & Lindsay, 1999).

Christian denominations in the United States exhibit much diversity, and different scholars have classified Christian denominations in different ways. For example, Kenneth Wald (1997) distinguishes between mainline Protestants, evangelical Protestants, black Protestants, and Roman Catholics. Wald suggests that mainline Protestants put top priority on moral teachings about altruism and issues of social justice; evangelical Protestants emphasize personal salvation and put high priority on issues of sexual morality. The evangelical Protestants have been growing while the ranks of mainline Protestants have been declining (Caplow, 1991).

In recent years, a host of controversial issues based in religious beliefs—abortion, homosexuality, pornography, assisted suicide—have stirred passions and dominated political agendas. These issues center on three controversies: the role of women in society, sexual expression, and the meaning of life and death. Wald (1997) found that religious groups are not totally consistent across issues, however:

■ Jews and the nonreligious put the highest value on abortion rights and women's rights; evangelical Protestants and black Protestants are the most opposed to both abortion rights and women's rights; mainline Protestants and Catholics take an intermediate position on these issues.

■ Jews are the most supportive of nondiscrimination against gays and lesbians; evangelical Protestants and mainline Protestants are the least supportive; Catholics and the nonreligious are in an intermediate position. Black Protestants are more favorably disposed to protect gays and lesbians from employment discrimination than to grant them other legal protections.

- Black Protestants are far more favorable toward government programs to assist African Americans than any other religious group. Mainline Protestants and evangelical Protestants are the least supportive of these programs; Jews, the nonreligious, and Catholics are in an intermediate position.

It should be noted that Catholics in the United States are more ethnically diverse than white Protestants. Not surprisingly, different Catholic ethnic groups vary substantially in their religious beliefs. These differences may account for the moderate position of Catholics reported by Wald (Roof & McKinney, 1987). Gallup surveys (Gallup & Lindsay, 1999) suggest that many U.S. Catholics have differences of opinion with Rome. For example,

- 84% believe that Catholics should be allowed to use artificial methods of birth control.

- 78% support allowing divorced Catholics to remarry in the Catholic church.

- 75% believe that priests should be allowed to marry.

- 63% favor the ordination of women as priests.

- 54% would like to see some relaxation of the standards on abortion.

On the other hand, the majority of U.S. Catholics agree with Rome that people who engage in homosexual acts cannot be good Catholics.

Public opinion polls indicate that there are differences in attachment to the religious institution related to gender, race, ethnicity, age, geographic region, and faith tradition. In 1998, 60% of respondents to a public opinion survey rated religion as "very important" in their lives. Two out of three women (67%) and 53% of men reported religion to be very important. There were significant racial and ethnic differences, with 85% of blacks, 75% of Hispanics, and 58% of whites reporting that religion is very important. Religion grew in importance across the phases of adulthood, with 46% of young adults (ages 18 to 29) and 79% of adults ages 65 to 74 reporting that religion is very important. Southerners and people from rural areas were more likely than those in other regions to report that religion is very important in their lives. Protestants (67%) were more likely to report that religion is very important to them than either Catholics (57%) or Jews (22%).

In addition to these group-based differences, several students of religious life in the United States (Gallup & Lindsay, 1999; Roof, 1999; Wald, 1997; Wuthnow, 1998) have noted the intensely personal approaches to religion of the baby boom generation. They suggest that the trend is toward the production of "faith hybrids," noting particularly the rising popularity of Eastern mystical traditions and Native American practices. For example, an increasing minority of the U.S. public believes in reincarnation. There is also a growing trend toward frequent changes in religious allegiance, particularly among Christian Protestant denominations. There is also a growing trend toward religious tolerance. A 1994 survey found that 74% of respondents believed "a person can be a good and ethical person if he or she does not believe in God" (Gallup & Lindsay, 1999, p. 111).

Social workers should not assume that all persons of a religious group hold the same beliefs on social issues. But we must be aware of religious beliefs, both our own and those of clients, when working with controversial social issues.

Trends in Government and Politics

At the current time, Mrs. Meza lives in fear of agents of the government, whether they come from the INS or CPS. She sees the government as a coercive force rather than a supportive force in her life. The **government and political institution** is responsible for how decisions get made and enforced for the society as a whole. It is expected to resolve both internal and external conflicts and mobilize collective resources to meet societal goals.

Systems perspective, Conflict perspective

There is much evidence that the government institution is in a transition period in the United States as well as globally. Changes in the government institution are very intertwined with changes in the economic institution, and these changes taken together are playing a large role in growing inequality globally, but in a more pronounced way in the United States.

In the United States, we take democracy for granted, assuming the permanence of our system of "elected representatives, considerable public debate, electoral account-ability of government leaders to citizens, and extensive personal rights" (Bradshaw et al., 2001). We also have great confidence that democracy is the best form of govern-ment, that it is an idea so good that it will "spread" across the globe. Indeed, we can point to a number of countries that have adopted democratic forms of government since the mid-1970s, including the former Soviet bloc.

Conflict perspective

And yet, beginning in the 1970s, economic globalization began to present serious challenges to nationally based democracies (Bradshaw et al., 2001; Teeple, 2000). For a number of centuries, political and economic life has been organized into national states, which developed strong bureaucracies for maintaining order and mobilizing resources to meet societal needs. One role of strong nation-states has been to tame the excesses of capitalism, to protect workers from exploitation and the insecurities that come from economic cycles of upturn and downturn. Organized labor movements have played a key role in these efforts in most advanced industrial states. Beginning in the 1970s, however, the new information and transportation technologies made possible the development of *transnational corporations,* which carry on production and distribution activities in many nations (Teeple, 2000). These corporations cross national lines to take advantage of cheap labor pools, lax environmental regulations, beneficial tax laws, and new consumer markets. It is hard for any nation-state to monitor or get control over the transnational corporation.

Under these circumstances, governments began to retrench their efforts to monitor and control the economic institution. A **neoliberal philosophy** that governments should keep their hands off the economic institution has taken hold around the world. In this international climate, five major developments can be noted in the government and political institution of societies around the world (Bradshaw et al., 2001; Teeple, 2000):

1. Erosion of the power of nation-states

2. Radical weakening of the bargaining power of workers in national politics

3. Increased attention to immigration issues in the political institution

4. Increased market autonomy and elevated role of economic experts

5. Increased percentage of total tax revenue being paid from individual rather than corporate income

Under these conditions, inequality has grown around the world, but nowhere at the same high rate as in the United States.

Rational choice perspective

As we think about the trials of the Meza family, we are reminded of the increased attention to immigration issues in the political institution. Some observers (Teeple, 2000) have suggested that nation-states compensate for their inability to control the business processes that cross their borders by heightening their attempts to control their physical borders. By controlling borders, a nation-state can get some control of the flow of labor across national boundaries.

It has been noted that countries around the world have been moving federal power downward, upward, and outward (Bradshaw et al., 2001; see Exhibit 9.7):

1. *Upward movement.* The United States played a leadership role in the development of several transnational political and economic organizations and policies at the end of World War II. These organizations and policies have played a significant role in the movement of power upward from nation-states. The United Nations (U.N.) was developed to ensure international "peace and security." The World Bank was developed

EXHIBIT 9.7
Governmental Transfer of Power

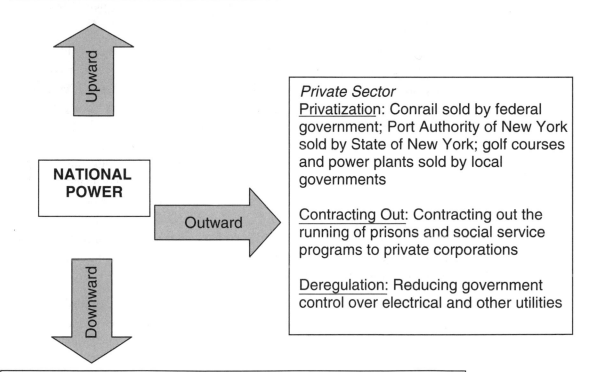

Authorities Above the United States
United Nations (U.N.)
World Bank
International Monetary Fund (IMF)
General Agreement on Tariffs and Trade (GATT)
World Trade Organization (WTO)
North American Free Trade Agreement (NAFTA)

Upward

NATIONAL POWER

Outward

Downward

Private Sector
Privatization: Conrail sold by federal government; Port Authority of New York sold by State of New York; golf courses and power plants sold by local governments

Contracting Out: Contracting out the running of prisons and social service programs to private corporations

Deregulation: Reducing government control over electrical and other utilities

State And Local Governments
Devolution/New Federalism
Block Grants
Flexibility in Federal Mandates
1996 Personal Responsibility and Work Opportunity Reconciliation Act (PRWORA)

Source: Adapted from Bradshaw et al., 2001, p. 367.

to promote reconstruction in war-torn nations but has, in recent years, taken on the concern for poverty. The International Monetary Fund (IMF) was developed to promote international monetary cooperation and a fair balance of trade. The General Agreement on Tariffs and Trade (GATT) was to provide an international forum for developing freer trade across national boundaries; the World Trade Organization (WTO) was developed under GATT in 1995. More recently, the United States, Canada, and Mexico signed the North American Free Trade Agreement (NAFTA) in 1994. European nations joined together as the European Union, adopting a common currency, a set of common legal and economic structures, and other joint endeavors. Similar organizations are in various stages of development in Latin America, Asia, and Africa. These trends are not without controversy. In recent years, there have been conflicts among rich and poor nations at meetings of the WHO and IMF, and activist demonstrations at their meetings.

2. *Downward Movement.* In a period of rising doubt about the ability of nation-states to govern, many of them, including the United States, have been passing policy responsibilities down to regional and local governments. In the United States, **devolution** became the code word for passing responsibilities to state and local governments. This downward movement has also been called **new federalism**. The stated intent of devolution is to improve the responsiveness and efficiency of government. The federal government has used several different mechanisms for devolution, including block grants and increased flexibility for states in complying with federal mandates. As pressures increase on states, some states are beginning to devolve responsibilities to local governments (Watson & Gold, n.d.). Devolution receives more attention when we discuss the welfare institution, because responsibility for public assistance to families with children was devolved to the states with the Personal Responsibility and Work Opportunity Reconciliation Act (PRWORA) in 1996.

3. *Outward Movement.* Growing faith across the world in the wisdom and efficiency of the economic institution has led many nation-states to withdraw from direct control of activities that they have hitherto controlled. They do this in several ways:

■ *Privatization.* Government enterprises that produce goods or deliver services are sold to the private sector. This can be done at any level of government. The U.S. federal government sold Conrail in 1987, and bills have been introduced to sell Amtrak and the U.S. Postal Service. The State of New York sold the Port Authority of New York, and local governments have sold golf courses and power plants (Gibbon, n.d.). President George W. Bush proposed that Social Security be privatized. On the other hand, the U.S. government took over management of airport security from the aviation industry in the months after the September 11, 2001, terrorist attack, a suggestion that the federal government can do some things best.

■ *Contracting out.* The government retains ultimate control over a program but contracts with private organizations for some activities. The most notable example of this type of government retrenchment is state contracts with the private prison industry that has grown up in recent years. Governmental social service agencies also contract out many social service programs to both nonprofit and for-profit organizations. Some school systems have experimented with contracting out public schools to the private sector, in the hopes that the result will be more effective schools.

■ *Deregulation.* Governments give up their claims to the right to regulate particular activities that they have previously regulated but not controlled. The expectation is that deregulation will lead to greater economic growth and lower cost to the consumer. Deregulation of the telephone system is often credited for the proliferation of new services, including wireless telephones. States of the United States began following the global trend to deregulate electricity and other utilities, but the trend may be slowed in the United States by recent revelations that Enron Corporation, an energy trading corporation, may have taken undue advantage of the lack of government oversight. Enron is accused of manipulating California's wholesale energy prices and creating an energy crisis in that state.

Michael Reisch (1997) reminds us that social work has been "at the mercy of political forces throughout its history" (p. 81). Suggesting that this is more the case today than ever before, he argues that social workers cannot afford to ignore processes and trends in the political arena.

Trends in the Economy

As you read the Mezas' story, their economic struggles seem paramount, and yet, both Mr. and Mrs. Meza are employed full time and working hard to provide for their family. The **economic institution** has the primary responsibility for regulating the production, distribution, and consumption of goods and services. In a capitalistic market economy, as in the United States, what one consumes is dependent on how much one is paid for selling goods and services. Most people, if they are not self-employed or independently wealthy, exchange labor for wages, which they then use for consumption. This labor for wages has come to be called *work*. The nature of work has been ever changing since premodern times, but the rate of change has accelerated wildly since the beginning of the industrial revolution.

And indeed, the typical work career at the beginning of the 21st century is very different from the typical work career prior to 1970. For a number of decades prior to 1970, the typical worker began working for a company at relatively low "entry" wages as a young adult, stayed with the company until retirement, and received steady salary increases over the years and a pension upon retirement. That all began to change in the 1970s, when work trajectories became much more disorderly. Now workers must be prepared to change jobs frequently. They must also be prepared to manage their own careers, rather than relying on an employer to do it for them. Workers must therefore have a good social network and good skills in using that network for the purposes of locating work.

Conflict perspective

Seven trends in the economic institution since the 1970s are having a major influence on the work careers and life chances of all of us. These changes, taken together, have created a less stable work life than the one known in the previous era.

1. *The nature of work has undergone a fundamental change.* For several decades, the proportion of workers in the service sector has been increasing and the proportion in manufacturing has been decreasing. This trend is called *economic restructuring.* This shift is important because, overall, wages are lower in the service sector. The loss of manufacturing jobs has led especially to a decline in the average earnings of men, with the effect more severe for men of color.

2. *Many business organizations have been downsized.* When the U.S. economic institution faced difficulties resulting from globalization and the shift to electronic technology, U.S. corporations responded by **downsizing** for greater efficiency. White-collar workers became almost as vulnerable to layoffs as blue-collar workers, as corporations eliminated managerial positions (Bernstein, 1997; Levy, 1995). As demonstrated in Exhibit 9.8, the pace of downsizing seems to have abated, but after several years of deep job cuts, organizations are lean and no longer offer opportunities for employees to build a career ladder of increasing responsibility, status, and reward (Bradshaw et al., 2001).

3. *Employers have been upgrading and deskilling many jobs.* The manufacturing sector of the labor force includes many semiskilled and skilled blue-collar jobs. The service sector, on the other hand, is sharply divided between highly paid technical positions and poorly paid clerical, cleaning, and maintenance jobs. Many of the poorly paid jobs are the result of **deskilling**, or downgrading, as new technologies make the jobs more routine. Some of the well-paid jobs are the result of **skill upgrading**, in which technological and economic change create the need for workers to have more advanced training or to take additional responsibility. Researchers disagree about whether there is more deskilling or skill upgrading in the service sector, but they agree that the net result is sharp increases in socioeconomic inequality (Levy, 1995; Teeple, 2000).

4. *The contingent workforce has been growing.* **Contingent work** is work without a long-term commitment by the employer or work with irregular hours (Reskin & Padavic, 1994, p. 168). Contingent workers include part-time employees, temporary employees, and independent contractors. They lack job security and usually receive no

EXHIBIT 9.8
U.S. Job Cut
Announcements

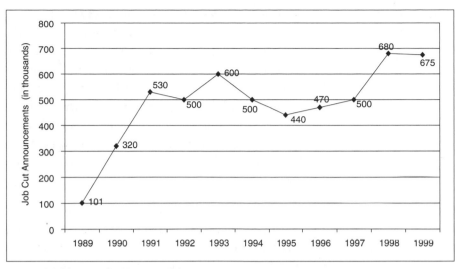

Source: Bradshaw et al., 2001, p. 426.

fringe benefits. In the United States, nearly three workers in ten work in part-time, temporary, on-call, day labor, or short-term jobs, and three quarters of firms report that they make some use of contingent workers (Bradshaw et al., 2001; Fair Jobs, n.d.). There is general agreement that job security will become even more elusive in the future (Teeple, 2000). The job market for semiskilled workers is expected to stay weak, and workers of all educational levels are expected to be highly mobile in the labor market (Levy, 1995).

5. *Labor force diversity is increasing.* Women, minorities, and immigrants make up a growing segment of the labor force. Between 1960 and 2000, the percentage of the labor force that was female increased from 32% to 48%, and experts predict that the participation rates of women and men will continue to converge (Fullerton & Toossi, 2001; Reskin & Padavic, 1994). This trend has enormous implications for social service programs that have been built on the model of a family with a female caregiver at home. As for racial and ethnic diversity, between 1980 and 2000, all minority groups increased their share of the labor force. Hispanics increased their share from 5.7% to 10.9%, Asian and Pacific Islander groups increased their share from 2.3% to 4.7%, and blacks increased their share from 10.2% to 11.8%. During this same period, the percentage of the labor force made up of white non-Hispanic workers decreased from 82% to 73% (Fullerton & Toossi, 2001). These trends do not mean that women and members of racial and ethnic minority groups are doing as well as white men in the labor market. "For every dollar a white man earns, a white woman earns 74 cents, a black man earns 74 cents, a black woman earns 63 cents, a Hispanic male earns 62 cents, and a Hispanic woman earns only 53 cents" (Bradshaw et al., 2001, p. 260).

6. *Organized labor unions have lost power in the political arena.* Since the beginning of industrial capitalism, labor unions have been the force behind governmental protection of workers' rights, working successfully for such protections as workplace safety, a minimum wage, and pensions. Economic globalization has seriously weakened the bargaining power of nationally based labor unions, because companies can always threaten to take their business somewhere else. This diminished power of labor unions has left a vacuum in the struggle for better work conditions and greater job security. Observers have suggested that, to meet the challenges of a global economy, organized labor will need to take a global perspective and address workers' rights in poorer, newly industrializing countries.

7. *Workers in the United States work more hours than workers in other industrialized countries.* Between 1990 and 2000, the average worker in the United States increased the total hours worked per year by almost 1 week, from 1,942 hours in 1990 to 1,978 hours in 2000. Meanwhile, workers in Canada, France, Germany, Japan, and the United Kingdom decreased their total hours worked per year. In 2000, the average worker in Australia, Canada, Japan, and Mexico worked about 100 hours, or 2.5 weeks, less than the average worker in the United States. The average German worker worked almost 500 hours, or 12.5 weeks, less than the average U.S. worker. From 1990 to 2000, labor productivity in the United States also increased, meaning that more work was being done without more compensation to the worker (International Labor Organization, 2001). This extra time spent in the economic institution has a major impact on the family institution as well as community life.

Social workers who participate in policy development must be informed about the serious challenges to job security in the contemporary era. Social workers are also called on to deal with many of the social problems arising out of these changes in the economic institution—problems such as inadequate resources for family caregiving, domestic violence, substance abuse, depression, and anxiety (Rose, 1997). Social workers attached to the workplace need to be skillful in influencing organizational policy and linking the work organization to the wider community, as well as in assessing specific work situations affecting their clients.

Trends in Education

As young as they are, Enrique and Myra Meza understand that educational attainment is becoming increasingly important in the labor market, but Myra complains that their parents take Enrique's education more seriously than hers. Traditionally, the primary purpose of the **educational institution** has been to pass along formal knowledge from one generation to the next—a function that was largely performed by the family, with some help from the church, until the 19th century. In the 20th century, however, the educational institution became increasingly responsible for passing along cultural values and behavioral norms to prepare students for roles as parents, citizens, workers, and consumers. The addition of these socializing functions was not without controversy, however, and many people thought that schools were now performing functions that would more appropriately be performed by family and religion. Perhaps unintentionally, schools also became influential in determining who is economically successful and who is not, and thus in maintaining social inequality.

In the 20th century, average educational attainment increased spectacularly in the United States (Caplow, 1991; Mare, 1995). At the beginning of the century, high school graduation was a privilege experienced only by an elite few, but over the next few decades, high school education was extended to a majority of youth (Caplow et al., 1991). The percentage of adults with high school diplomas increased from 55% in 1970 to 84% in 2000 (U.S. Census Bureau, 2000a). In the same period, the percentage of adults with college degrees more than doubled, from 11% to 26% (Mare, 1995; U.S. Census Bureau, 2000a).

Conflict perspective

Some educational inequalities have been reduced in the contemporary era, but others persist. In the 1980s, as elementary and secondary education became nearly universal, differences in educational attainment based on race and ethnicity almost disappeared at the elementary and secondary school levels (Mare, 1995). Today, however, race and ethnicity interact with income level to produce high dropout rates from secondary school, particularly among low-income students and Hispanic students. In 1998, 7.3% of white youth between the ages of 16 and 24 had dropped out of school, compared to 12.6% of black youth, 28.6% of Hispanic youth, and 4.3% of Asian/Pacific Islander youth (National Center for Education Statistics, 1999). In 1998, youth living in families with incomes in the bottom quintile were four times more likely than youth living in families in the top quintile to drop out of high school. As you can see in Exhibit 9.9, within each racial and ethnic group, low income is associated with higher dropout rates. In addition, being foreign-born increases the likelihood that Hispanic students will drop out of school; 44.2% of these youth dropped out in 1998. Class, race, and ethnic differences in access to and progress through a college education also persist, but gender differences have disappeared. In the 1980s, women pulled ahead of men in the percentages continuing on to college after high school, and in 2000, slightly more women (30%) than men (28%) between the ages of 25 and 29 had completed college.

As this last statistic implies, generational influences also appear in the data on schooling. Robert Mare (1995) has studied the educational attainment of people born between 1940 and 1970, who make up the majority of the current labor force. As shown in Exhibit 9.10, he found racial and ethnic differences in completion of at least some postsecondary education. Mare emphasizes the immigration status of some ethnic groups, because foreign-born individuals may have experienced a very different educational

EXHIBIT 9.9
High School Dropout
Rates by Income
and Race/Ethnicity
(Ages 16-24), 1996

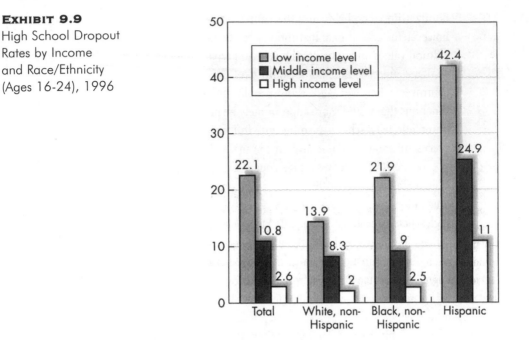

Source: Based on U.S. Department of Education, National Center for Educational Statistics, 1997.

institution than native-born individuals of the same ethnic heritage. He suggests that these racial and ethnic differences in school attainment will perpetuate economic inequalities related to race and ethnicity because the parents' attainment is a big factor in educational opportunities for the next generation. Between 1980 and 1990, educational attainment probabilities grew substantially for Asian Americans and European Americans, but stayed the same for the other groups. Nevertheless, some immigrants, like Mr. and Mrs. Meza, had limited education in their home country but manage to instill in their children the value of a college education.

Racial and ethnic differences in educational attainment have been exacerbated by trends in educational funding. In the 1980s, federal government support for elementary and secondary education was cut by about one third, and state and local governments have needed to increase their support (Reich, 1992). In 2000, only 7% of total spending on education came from federal monies (General Accounting Office, 2001). The result has been growing disparities among states and among local school districts (Kozol, 1991). In the deteriorating central cities, poor and largely minority families, paying the higher tax rates common to urban areas, are sending their children to schools that are seriously substandard. Meanwhile, families in the wealthier suburbs, paying lower tax rates, have access to public schools with highly enriched programs. In 1997 data from Illinois, the average per pupil expenditure was $4,539 in the five most poorly funded

EXHIBIT 9.10
Percentage of
Cohorts Born
1940-1970 with
Postsecondary
Schooling

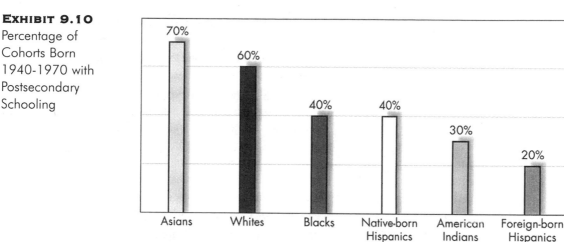

Source: Based on Mare, 1995.

high school districts in the state and $13,753 in the five best funded districts (Illinois Education Association-National Education Association, 1997).

The majority of the children in poorly funded school districts throughout the country are African American and Hispanic American. Even if they graduate from high school and continue into postsecondary education, they will not arrive at college with equal preparation for success. They are further disadvantaged by the dramatic increases in tuition and fees that have been instituted over the past 2 decades, during a period when financial aid was declining (National Center for Education Statistics, n.d.).

In recent years, four issues related to the education institution have received a lot of attention in the government institution:

1. *School vouchers.* With growing concern about the quality of many public schools in the United States, some school systems have experimented with *school vouchers,* a system of providing parents with tax credits or documents to cover tuition at a private school. The value of each voucher has been about $2,500. School vouchers have been very controversial. Proponents of school vouchers argue that parents should be able to send their children to schools of their own choosing, and in general, they tend to favor privatization of many government activities (Heritage Foundation, 2001). Opponents argue that school voucher programs bleed badly needed money away from public schools and will benefit only a small percentage of students in a school district (American Association of University Women, 2002).

2. *Education for limited English proficiency (LEP) students.* With large waves of immigrant groups reaching the United States in recent years, questions have arisen

about the best methods for educating students whose proficiency with the English language is limited. The National Education Association (n.d.) proposes that educational programs for these students should emphasize the development of language proficiency, but the students should receive instruction in other curriculum areas in their native language until English proficiency is achieved. Critics of bilingual and English as a Second Language (ESL) programs, which take this approach, argue for English-only classes. The critics suggest that because English proficiency is necessary for success in the labor market, students who do not learn English as soon as possible are at a disadvantage.

3. *Education for noncollege-bound students.* In 1988, the William T. Grant Foundation issued a report, *The Forgotten Half,* suggesting that reforms are needed in the education institution to provide better job skills for students who do not continue schooling beyond high school. This report was influential in drafting the School-to-Work Opportunities Act of 1994. School systems are experimenting with different types of school-to-work programs (Donahue & Tienda, 2000).

4. *Homeschooling.* In recent years, a small but growing number of parents have chosen to educate their children at home. The U.S. Department of Education surveyed homeschooling parents in 1999 and estimated that 850,000 students, or 1.7% of U.S. students between the ages of 5 and 17, are educated at home. The most common reasons that parents gave for homeschooling were the belief that they could provide a better education at home and religious reasons (U.S. Department of Education, 2001).

Social workers should become active partners in efforts at educational reform, particularly in efforts that equalize educational opportunities. To be effective in these efforts, we need to be informed about trends in the educational institution.

Trends in Social Welfare

The Meza family is facing a number of stressors that are beginning to overwhelm them and tear at their relationships with one another. Although Mrs. Meza is becoming desperate about her situation, because of her undocumented immigrant status she is fearful about trusting anyone outside the family. Her understanding of what social workers do is to "take children away," and you will have a challenge to win her trust. A good understanding of the special stressors of undocumented immigrants will be essential. As social workers, we are well aware of the network of social welfare agencies and programs that could help the Meza family. But others are not so aware, and there is thus some controversy about whether social welfare should be considered a social institution. It is included here because it meets Newman's definition of offering "patterned ways of solving problems and meeting the needs of a particular society."

Systems perspective

Different writers have presented various definitions of the **social welfare institution,** but the definition provided by Philip Popple and Leslie Leighninger (1993, 2001) is particularly compatible with the definition of social institution used in this chapter: the social welfare institution functions to promote interdependence and to deal with issues of dependence. Individuals are interdependent with institutions, as well as with other individuals, for survival and for satisfactory role performance. We depend on our doctors, day care centers, families, friends, neighbors, and so on, and they depend on us. Sometimes, situations occur that increase our need for assistance or decrease the assistance available to us. For example, we may become sick or injured, lose our job, or take on a caregiving role for a newborn infant or a frail parent. In these situations, our ability to successfully fulfill role expectations is jeopardized—a situation that Popple and Leighninger refer to as dependence. In analyzing such problematic situations, social workers must pay attention not only to the behavior of individuals but also to how well social institutions are supporting people in their role performance.

The social work profession and the social welfare institution developed when it became apparent that the existing institutions of family, religion, economy, and government were inadequate for meeting dependency needs in a society that is organized as an industrialized market economy. At first, private service organizations were developed to meet dependency needs, but private organizations were soon followed by social welfare programs run by local governments. The social welfare institution grew dramatically after the federal government assumed social welfare responsibilities during the first administration of Franklin D. Roosevelt (1933-1937). Between 1929 and 1950, the combined state and federal expenditures for social welfare grew from just under $4 billion to nearly $24 billion (Popple & Leighninger, 1993). Since that time, the social welfare institution has grown enormously. A second wave of federal social welfare legislation was enacted from 1964 to 1966 under the administration of Lyndon Johnson, and by 1988, local, state, and federal governments spent more than $885 billion on social welfare programs (Caplow, 1991; Popple & Leighninger, 1993).

The social welfare institution developed in all industrialized countries in the 19th and 20th centuries as these nations tried to cope with the alienation and disruption caused by social inequalities of industrial capitalism (Teeple, 2000). The labor movement played a major role in pushing for an expanded welfare institution (Bradshaw et al., 2001; Teeple, 2000). However, the social welfare institution, like any other social institution, reflects the culture of the society. Many European countries that have come to be known as *welfare states* have been much more trusting than the United States in the notion of a "big state" and high taxes, and they have a more collectivist social philosophy. Consequently, their spending for social welfare has been far more generous, as can be seen in Exhibit 9.11. These countries have higher minimum wages and more generous unemployment compensation than the United States. They also have more generous parental leave, child care, health care, and other supports for children and families. If the

EXHIBIT 9.11

Government
Spending on Social
Welfare in European
"Welfare States"
and the United States

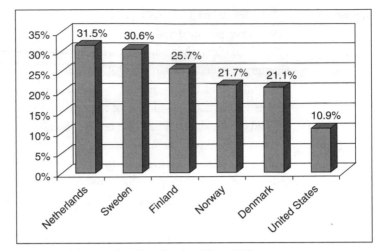

Source: Based on Bradshaw et al., 2001, Graphic 5.9, p. 189.

Mezas lived in Denmark, they might have made use of a family leave policy that allows 18 weeks of maternity leave, including 4 weeks prebirth, at 90% wage replacement. Furthermore, this policy allows up to 52 weeks for either parent until the child's 8th birthday, at 60% wage replacement (Clearinghouse on International Developments in Child, Youth & Family Policies, 2002). Mrs. Meza could use this extra time to work with the multidisciplinary team to stabilize the situation at home.

Beginning in the 1970s, as we noted above, a neoliberal political philosophy took hold in industrialized countries, and nation-states began to take a hands-off approach to the economic institution. Nations began to retrench and even eliminate long-standing social welfare programs and regulatory agencies. Organized labor, situated within national boundaries, was unable to forestall a process that was tied to a global economic institution. In recent years, the social welfare institution in the United States has come under major attack, and concerted efforts have been made to reduce its size, or at least its government support. Although they have not gone as far in retrenching as the United States, the European countries have also begun to examine their welfare policies (Sernau, 2001). Economists at the World Bank and IMF have called for retrenchment of welfare spending in the industrial nations (Tanzi & Schuknecht, 2000).

The social welfare institution in the United States has been influenced by the call to move federal power both downward and outward. PRWORA devolved to the states most of the responsibility for public assistance to needy families and children. The Temporary Assistance to Needy Families (TANF) block grant gives states more flexibility to design their own public assistance programs (Watson & Gold, n.d.). This is a downward movement of power.

Since the 1970s, there has also been a growing trend for government at all levels to develop "purchase of service" contract agreements with private nonprofit organizations to provide social welfare services in "public-private partnerships." This trend has accelerated since the 1980s. Historically, the social welfare institution has had a mix of governmental and nongovernmental monies and activities, but the nature of this mix has changed over time. The government is now playing a smaller role in delivering social service programs, but continues to play a large role in the funding of services through contract agreements.

There is also a long history of faith-based organizations providing social welfare services. Currently, there is much controversy about the "charitable choice provision" of PRWORA, which allows states to contract with religious organizations, as well as other private organizations, for service provision. President George W. Bush has advocated a "faith-based initiative" to expand the role of faith-based organizations in social service delivery. Opinion polls show that 55% of the U.S. public think that government should be more responsible for assisting poor families, 28% think that religious organizations should be more responsible, and 10% think that both should be more responsible (Gallup & Lindsey, 1999).

The most controversial trend in the social welfare institution is the entrance of for-profit organizations into the mix of public-private partnerships, beginning in the 1980s. The for-profit share of social welfare services has continued to grow. By the early 1990s, nearly half of social welfare agencies were for-profit, comprising 22% of social service employment (Lynn, 2002). The for-profit organizations continue to expand their business lines into new service sectors, most recently into welfare-to-work programs. Lockheed Martin Information Management Services, America Works, Maximus, Children's Comprehensive Services, and Youth Services International are just a few of the large, for-profit social welfare organizations on the contemporary scene. Among the serious questions that have been raised by the entrance of for-profit organizations into the social welfare institution is whether these organizations will choose to serve only "easy to serve" client groups, avoiding those with entrenched problems related to poverty (Lynn, 2002; Ryan, 1999).

Conflict perspective

The Meza family is struggling to reorganize itself to cope with Minerva's special needs. They could use help in this effort, but to date, they have experienced the social welfare institution only as a coercive institution, as an institution that tries to control their behavior rather than provide compassionate support. Indeed, the social welfare institution in the United States has always played both a social control function as well as a social reform function (Hutchison, 1987). In recent times, it has moved toward greater attention to social control than to social reform (Hutchison & Charlesworth, 2000; Teeple, 2000). Social workers cannot be active participants in moving that balance back to social reform unless they clearly understand trends in the interrelated social institutions discussed in this chapter.

Trends in Health Care

Health and health care costs are important issues for the Meza family. Mrs. Meza didn't receive much prenatal care, which is relatively inexpensive, when she was pregnant with Minerva because she lacked health insurance. Luckily, Mr. Meza had insurance coverage for Minerva's long postnatal care, which was very expensive. Health is important to this family, but health is also important to a society. Child development, adult well-being, and family stability are all affected by health. The **health care institution** is the primary institution for promoting the general health of a society.

There is much agreement that the health care institution in the United States is in trouble. As demonstrated in Exhibit 9.12, the United States spends a greater percentage of its gross domestic product (GDP) on health care than any other industrial country does. We have the greatest concentration of advanced medical technology. And yet, the World Health Organization ranks the United States 37th among all nations in performance of its health care system (Auerbach & Krimgold, 2001).

Of course, the health care institution is influenced by culture. Health care in the United States reflects the "aggressive 'can do' spirit" (Newman, 1995, p. 83) of the mainstream culture. Compared to European physicians, U.S. physicians recommend more routine examinations and perform many more bypass surgeries and angioplasties than European doctors (Reinhardt et al., 2002). Psychiatrists in the United States often give a diagnosis of clinical depression for situations that British psychiatrists see as normal (Newman, 1995). Although alternative forms of health care have become more respectable in the United States in recent years, they are still considered more suspect in the United States than in European countries (Caplow, 1991). The rapid growth in **therapeutic medicine**—diagnosing and treating disease—has drained resources from the U.S. *public health system,* which focuses on disease prevention and health promotion (Coombs & Capper, 1996). There is also evidence that the United States spends much more on administrative overhead than other countries (Reinhardt et al., 2002).

Even if people in the United States were getting as much for their health care dollars as citizens of other countries do, there is some suggestion that health care spending has been less effective than generally thought. Researchers in the United States and the United Kingdom agree that the impressive decline in mortality in the 20th century was more the result of improvements in the social and physical environments in which people lived than of advances in medical treatment. They note that medical advancements such as therapeutic drugs, immunizations, and surgical procedures were introduced several decades after significant declines in the diseases that they targeted (Auerbach & Krimgold, 2001).

After decades of research showing that health is related to economic status, public health researchers are now taking a serious look at this issue. They are finding that the health of a society is closely linked to the level of inequality in that society

EXHIBIT 9.12

Health Care Spending in Industrialized Countries, 1999

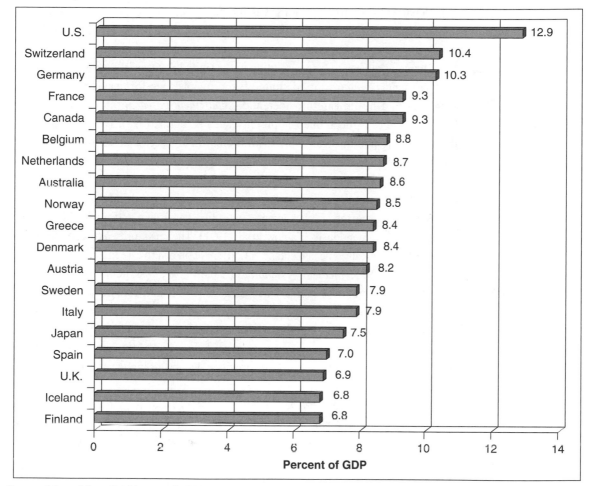

Source: Adapted from Bradshaw et al., 2001, p. 367.

(Kawachi & Kennedy, 2001). Their research is indicating some paths by which societal inequality becomes linked to health:

- Societies with more inequality invest less in public education and other social programs.

- Societies with more inequality have less cohesion and more hostility.

- Societies with more inequality produce more stress for families at the bottom of the social structure.

These researchers are also suggesting that health policy cannot be divorced from economic policy. Creating access to the existing health care institution is only a small part of the solution. They argue that buffering the impact of the market economy on poor and near-poor citizens is necessary to improve the health profile of the United States.

Currently, the health care institution in the United States is in a state of flux. Health care has mainly been organized around two principles: **fee-for-service,** or paying for each visit to a health care provider, and *employment-based insurance,* or obtaining health insurance through one's employer (Gorin & Moniz, 1997). The problem is that this organization of the health care institution prohibits access to health care for some groups. In response to this concern, the U.S. Congress enacted Medicare and Medicaid in 1965 to provide government funding for health care for older adults, people with disabilities, and people living in poverty.

Since that time, the U.S. health care institution has grown and medical technology has advanced tremendously (Caplow et al., 1991). The costs of health care have thus increased dramatically. The percentage of GNP spent on health care increased from 4% in 1950 to 13% in 1993, where it has stabilized (Caplow et al., 1991; Reinhardt et al., 2002).

Efforts to contain the rapidly increasing costs of health care began in the 1970s. During the early 1990s, managed care plans, many of which operate on a for-profit basis, became popular. **Managed care** replaces fee-for-service with a system of *capitation,* in which health care organizations are paid according to the number of people in the system, not the number of services provided. For-profit managed care has become the dominant form of health care delivery in the United States.

Although the fee-for-service principle of health care delivery has been decimated with managed care, the principle of employment-based insurance has not been rejected. But given the trends toward low job security and high workforce mobility, a health care system that relies on people obtaining health insurance through employers has serious shortcomings. U.S. Census data indicate that 13.9% of the U.S. population were without health insurance in 1990; by 1996, this figure had increased to 15.6% (U.S. Census Bureau, 1998). Almost three quarters of the uninsured live in families where at least one person works. Among poor persons, about one third are uninsured and about one fifth of uninsured persons are low-income children (Henry Kaiser Family Foundation, 2000). The evidence suggests that people with chronic illnesses, poor people, and older adults may not fare well in our current for-profit, managed health care system (Gorin & Moniz, 1997).

The near future of health care delivery in the United States is uncertain. Growing public disillusionment with the quality of for-profit, managed health care is reflected in the popular media. Yet Congress failed to pass a plan for universal coverage in 1994. Three years later, in 1997, a Children's Health Insurance Program (CHIP) was enacted to provide government-financed health insurance coverage to children in poor families.

Some states have done better than others in increasing children's health coverage (Children's Defense Fund, 2001).

Social workers must ensure that the voices of poor and other oppressed people are included in the public dialogue about health care reform. In the past, health care social work has been situated in hospitals, but managed care seeks to contain the use of hospitalization. Thus, social workers in the health care institution may increasingly find themselves working as health planners, counselors, educators, advocates, and health promotion experts—in such settings as public health departments, community-based clinics, health centers, and health networks (Gorin & Moniz, 1997).

Trends in Mass Media

In a democratic society with a capitalistic economy, the **mass media institution** is the primary institution for managing the flow of information, images, and ideas among all members of society. Rapid advances in electronic communication technology since the 1950s have resulted in widespread access to multiple forms of mass communication, including newspapers, periodicals, books, radio, television, movies, videocassettes, audiocassettes, compact disks, telephones, fax machines, computer networks, and electronic mail. Electronic media now allow two-way communication, as well as one-way communication, and can store and manipulate vast amounts of information. Like other families in the United States, the Meza family is saturated with images from these media. Some of these images are negative portrayals of Mexican immigrants, which adds to the family's distress.

In totalitarian societies, the flow of information, images, and ideas is controlled by the ruling class. In the United States, we have a long tradition of freedom of the press—a belief that the media must be free to serve as a public watchdog. Traditionally, the emphasis has been on the watchdog role in relation to the government and political institution—in other words, a press that is not controlled by the government. Exposure of the Watergate cover-up during the Nixon presidency is considered a high point in U.S. media history. However, the relationship between government and media is controversial, with some groups calling for more government censorship (e.g., to limit children's access to pornography) and other groups calling for strict adherence to freedom of the press (Croteau & Hoynes, 2000). Increasingly, however, the government and political institution feels pressured to compete with other "would-be opinion makers" (Blumler & Gurevitch, 1996, p. 127)—such as social movements and multinational corporations—for influence with the media. Chapter 14 discusses the important role of the mass media in the mobilization of social movements.

Recently, concern about media censorship has centered on censorship by the economic institution (Bagdikian, 1997; Croteau & Hoynes, 2000; Curran, 1996). A mergers and acquisitions boom in the media institution during the past 3 decades has resulted in powerful media conglomerates, with ownership concentrated in the hands of a few individuals and corporations. For example, Rupert Murdoch's News Corporation— owner of the *Weekly Standard* magazine, Fox News, and HarperCollins Publishers—is a multinational corporation with global power (Croteau & Hoynes, 2000). Some have suggested that Murdoch's strong political views affect which topics are covered and how they are covered in the media outlets over which he has control (Baker, 1998). Media organizations are also increasingly owned by parent companies that do business in areas other than media, and there is evidence that media organizations sometimes refrain from critical investigation of the giant conglomerates that own them (Bagdikian, 1997).

Social psychologists have been interested in the effects of the media on human behavior, focusing particularly on the effects of television, which has become the dominant form of mass media communication. In the United States, 98% of households have at least 1 television set, with an average of 2.3 sets per household. Televisions are turned on in U.S. homes for an average of 7 hours per day. The average child in the United States watches 28 hours of television weekly and, over the course of a year, spends more time in front of the television than in school (Watson, 1996). Busy parents often use television as a surrogate baby-sitter and often fail to monitor what is being viewed.

Fewer families, about one half of all U.S. households, now have computers in the home, and even fewer, about one third of all U.S. households, have access to the Internet (Croteau & Hoynes, 2000). Given the important role of computer technology in the economic institution, this unequal access to computers serves to perpetuate social class standing. Increasing access to the Internet has also raised new questions about the need to prevent minors from gaining access to sexually explicit material and from being exploited by predators on the Internet.

Research on the effects of the media on human behavior is difficult to design, because it is difficult to isolate the effects of specific media forms in changing person/ environment configurations and to capture the cumulative effect of multiple forms. Although the existing research thus contains many contradictions, media scholars agree on a few basic, consistent findings (Croteau & Hoynes, 2000):

- The effect of the media on human behavior is small, when other factors are considered.

- The influence of TV on human behavior increases as time spent watching increases.

- Children and adolescents are more influenced by media presentations than adults.

- Some people are more affected by media presentations than others.

Although it is possible for the media to influence human behavior in both positive and negative ways, the research has focused, for the most part, on negative effects. Social workers and other professionals have been particularly concerned that television provides more models of antisocial than prosocial behavior. Feminists have been concerned about the influence of gender role stereotypes presented in the media (Ang & Hermes, 1996). Members of racial and ethnic minority groups, the disability community, and the gay and lesbian community have also been concerned about stereotypical media presentations of their groups (Croteau & Hoynes, 2000; Newman, 1995).

Mass media critics also suggest that control of the media by political and economic elites results in control of cultural meanings to benefit elites and silence dissident views (Curran, 1996; Livingstone, 1996). The mass media have historically been controlled by white, middle- and upper-class men, who have presented their worldviews. Mass media owners are interested in attracting affluent consumers and choose content with this aim in mind (Croteau & Hoynes, 2000).

Some media scholars, however, emphasize that media consumers are not passive recipients but active interpreters of the messages received, synthesizing messages from a variety of sources and thus keeping media images in perspective (Croteau & Hoynes, 2000; Livingstone, 1996). Social workers can help by working collaboratively with other groups to influence media coverage of vulnerable populations and patterns of social inequality.

Theories of Social Inequality

Throughout this chapter, we have presented information on how social inequality is created and maintained in eight interrelated major social institutions. **Social class** is the term generally used by sociologists to describe "structures of inequality in modern societies" (Crompton, 1993, p. 21). Perhaps no question regarding the human condition has generated more intense and complex controversies and conflicts than the related issues of inequality and distributive justice. Unequal distribution of resources is probably as old as the human species and certainly has existed in all complex societies. Long before the discipline of sociology arose, thoughtful people constructed explanations and justifications for these inequalities (Crompton, 1993; Lenski, 1966; Sernau, 2001). Although social class has been an important topic for sociology, by no means do sociologists agree about the role that social class plays in human behavior.

We have presented inequality as a problem, but as you have probably noted, not everyone agrees with this view. Gerhard Lenski (1966) did a careful study of how societies over time have answered the question, Is inequality a good thing or a bad thing? He divided the way that societies have responded to this question into a conservative thesis and a radical antithesis. In the **conservative thesis**, inequality is the natural, divine order, and no efforts should be made to alter it. In the **radical antithesis**, equality is the natural, divine order; inequality is based on abuse of privilege and should be minimized.

Historical Theories of Social Inequality

Early Hebrew prophets, writing about 800 B.C., denounced the rich and powerful members of society not only for their use of wealth and power but also for the means used in achieving them (see, e.g., the second and third chapters of Micah). A very different view is found in the Laws of Manu, compiled by Hindu priests about 200 B.C., where social inequalities and caste systems are considered to be divinely ordained for the good of the world.

In the classical Greek period, Plato, in his effort to describe the ideal state, noted that people are born with innate differences in capabilities and suggested that a division of labor should be based on what each person is best fitted to do. He saw inequality as inevitable, but proposed ways to alter the distribution of money, status, and power in pursuit of the collective "ideal state" and individual "good life." Plato regarded the family as the key support of institutionalized inequality because individuals are motivated to secure for family members, for whom they feel familial affection, any privileges that they have attained for themselves. He argued that the only way to ensure an egalitarian society was to take children from parents and have the state raise them. He demonstrated his distrust of power and privilege when he suggested that members of the ruling group should be prohibited from holding private property so that they would not be motivated by personal gain in the discharge of their duties (Plato, 1968). Aristotle, Plato's student, reacted against some of the radical positions of his teacher, asserting that "there are by nature free men and slaves, and that servitude is just and agreeable for the latter" (quoted in Dahrendorf, 1969, p. 18).

The Christian religious tradition has vacillated regarding the justice of inequality. Lenski's (1966) historical review suggests that leaders and scholars of the medieval Church saw inequality as a necessary prerequisite for the well-being of society. From the 12th century on, however, a succession of religious movements that criticized wealth flourished. This tradition influenced the development of the social work profession.

According to many scholars, the English revolution of 1648 signaled the demise of a philosophy of inequality as the natural order and the ascent of a philosophy of equality. The philosophy of social equality fostered two major social revolutions, the American and the French, and a massive international political movement, socialism. Equality of political rights, and not of economic status, was the primary objective of the American and French revolutions. But Alexis de Tocqueville (1835/1945) argued that once the idea of equality caught hold, it was irresistible and created greater pressure for economic egalitarianism. Currently, we face the paradox of pressure toward greater equality, as in the feminist and disability movements, along with the breakdown of socialist experiments and a global neoliberal philosophy.

Classical Sociological Theories of Social Inequality

When social inequality was considered to be the natural order and divinely ordained, there was no need to search further for explanations of inequality. But as this traditional assumption gave way to a belief that human beings are born equal, persistent social inequalities required explanation and justification. Explanation of inequality and its relationship to human behavior became central questions for the emerging social and political sciences. Two classical theorists, Karl Marx (1818-1883) and Max Weber (1864-1920), have had lasting impact on the sociological analysis of social inequality.

Marx was both a social theorist and a committed revolutionary. He was interested in explaining the social inequalities of industrial capitalism, but his interests went beyond explanation of inequality to promotion of a more just and equitable society. Marx (1887/1967) emphasized the economic determinants of social class relationships and proposed that class lines are drawn according to roles in the capitalist production system. Although he did not propose a strict two-class system, he suggested a social class division based on a dichotomy of owners and controllers of production (bour-geoisie), on the one hand, and workers who must sell their labor to owners (proletariat), on the other. Marx saw the relationship between the classes to be based on exploitation and domination by the owners and controllers of production and alienation among the workers. He saw social class as a central variable in human behavior and a central force in human history and believed that *class consciousness*—not only the awareness of one's social class but also hostility toward other classes—is what motivates people to transform society.

In contrast to Marx, who was a committed revolutionary, Weber argued for a value-free social science. Weber differed from Marx in other ways as well. Marx saw a class division based on production roles (owners of production and workers); Weber (1947) saw a class division based on "life chances" in the marketplace. *Life chances* reflect the distribution of power within a community. Instead of Marx's dichotomous class system, Weber proposed that life chances fall on a continuum, and that the great variability found along the continuum reflects the multiple sources of power. Weber saw property, skills, and education as primary among these sources. Social class is an important variable in human behavior, but not, as Marx believed, the primary variable.

This difference in perspective on the causal importance of social class reflects the theorists' disagreement about the inevitability of class consciousness or class action. Marx saw class consciousness and communal action related to class as inevitable. Weber saw social class as a possible, but not inevitable, source of identity and communal action.

The Contemporary Debate

Attempts to determine the cause of persistent social inequalities have led to debate among sociologists who embrace functional theories and sociologists who embrace conflict theories. Functional theories of social stratification present structural inequality (social classes) as necessary for society. According to this view, unequal rewards for different types of work guarantee that the most talented persons will work hard and produce technological innovation to benefit the whole society. Conflict theorists, on the other hand, emphasize the role of power, domination, and coercion in the maintenance of inequality. According to this view, persons with superior wealth and income also hold superior social and political power and use that power to protect their privileged positions.

Sociological functionalism was dominant in U.S. sociology during the 1940s and 1950s, but faded in importance after that. However, functionalism was the root for *modernization theory,* which attempted, in the 1960s, to explain why some countries are poor and others are rich (Rostow, 1990). These theorists suggested that poverty is caused by traditional attitudes and technology, by the failure to modernize. The conflict perspective counterargument to modernization theory was *dependency theory,* which argued that poor societies are created by worldwide industrial capitalism, which exploits natural resources and labor (Frank, 1967). These theorists emphasize the tremendous power of foreign multinational corporations to coerce national governments.

The most recent debate has been between neoliberalism and the World Systems perspective. *Neoliberalism* is based in classic economics and argues that free trade and free markets, with limited government interference, will result in a fair distribution of resources. As suggested earlier, this philosophy is dominant across the world today. Economists at the World Bank and IMF have been strong voices in favor of neoliberalism. To counter this view, the *World Systems perspective* suggests that inequality is created and maintained by economic globalization (Wallerstein, 1974/1989). The world is divided into three different sectors: a core sector that dominates the capitalist world-economy and exploits the world's resources, a peripheral sector that provides raw material to the core and is heavily exploited by it, and a semiperipheral sector that is somewhere between the core and periphery and serves to connect them.

Structural Determinism Versus Human Agency

Will knowledge of my social class position help you to predict my attitudes and behaviors? That question, which is highly relevant to social workers, has become a controversial one for contemporary social science. Social scientists who see human behavior as highly determined by one's position in the social class structure *(structural determinism)* are challenged by social scientists who emphasize the capacity of humans

EXHIBIT 9.13
A Model
of Class Structure

Capitalist class: investors, heirs, and executives; typically with a prestigious university education; annual family incomes (1990) over $750,000, mostly from assets

Upper middle class: upper-level managers, professionals, and mid-sized business owners; with a college education, most often with an advanced degree; family incomes of $70,000 or more

Middle class: lower-level managers, semiprofessionals, some sales and skilled craft workers, and foremen and supervisors; with at least a high school education and usually some college, technical training, or apprenticeship; family incomes of about $40,000

Working class: operatives, clerical workers, most retail sales clerks, routinized assembly and factory workers, and related blue-collar employees; high school educated; family incomes of about $25,000

Working poor: poorly paid service workers and laborers, operatives, and clerical workers in low-wage sectors; usually with some high school; family incomes below $20,000

Underclass: persons with erratic job histories and weak attachment to the formal labor force, unemployed, or only able to find seasonal or part-time work; dependent on temporary or informal employment or some form of social assistance

Source: Sernau, 2001, p. 86.

to create their own realities and who give central roles to human actors, not social structures *(human agency)*.

Classical sociology took a very focused approach to the question of structural determinism. Both Marx and Weber asked only whether class consciousness is inevitable. Much of the debate about structural determinism has centered on this question, and not the more general question of how influential social class is on human behavior. Those who suggest that social class is no longer important in social life point out that contemporary social movements are centered around issues other than social class—issues such as the environment, world peace, gender, race, and morality. However, a wealth of contemporary social science research has reported social class as an important, though not singular, predictor of a range of attitudes and behaviors (Crompton, 1993). These findings are reflected throughout this book.

The debate about structural determinism is complicated by the lack of an agreed-on classification system for social class. Although it is not without flaws, we recommend the six-class model found in Exhibit 9.13 (Gilbert & Kahn, 1993; Sernau, 2001). The benefit of this model over other models is that it reflects wealth and education as well as occupation. However, although occupational schemes are not comprehensive measures of social inequality, research indicates that occupation remains the single best measure of material advantage and disadvantage and is significantly associated with a range of attitudes and behavior (Crompton, 1993).

The discussion of the relationship between social structure and human behavior has often turned into a debate between structural determinists and cultural determinists. Cultural determinists, described in Chapter 8, argue that people are poor because they develop a "culture of poverty" that keeps them poor. Attempts have been made in recent years to understand the mutual influences of structure, culture, and behavior. These attempts are consistent with the multidimensional perspective of this book, which suggests that both structure and culture are important and that they influence each other. Unequal material advantage is a social fact, but it is a fact about which people construct meanings—and the meanings that people construct will have some impact on future structures of material advantage. You will recognize this as being very similar to the practice orientation to culture described in Chapter 8.

David Lockwood's (1966) analysis of the inseparable nature of structure and culture helps to explain the persistent findings of an association between social class and a range of attitudes and behaviors. According to Lockwood, individuals "visualise the . . . structure of their society from the vantage points of their own particular *milieu,* and their perceptions of the larger society will vary according to their experiences . . . in the smaller societies in which they live out their daily lives" (Lockwood, 1966, p. 249). Therefore, specific locations in the social structure will have some association with specific societal images or worldviews. This is not to say that social class alone determines worldview; a multidimensional perspective suggests that other factors, such as race, ethnicity, religion, gender, community, and family, mediate the effects of social class. Social workers should recognize that human behavior is forged from complex interactions of multiple dimensions of persons and environments.

IMPLICATIONS FOR SOCIAL WORK PRACTICE

The trends in social institutions and social structure discussed in this chapter suggest several principles for social work practice. These practice principles have greatest relevance for social work planning and administration, but some are relevant for direct social work practice as well.

- Develop adequate information retrieval skills to keep abreast of trends in the interrelated social institutions and the impact of these trends on human interdependence and dependence.

- Review social service programs serving children, older adults, and other dependent persons to ensure that they are responsive to changes in the family and kinship institution, as well as the economic institution.

- Be aware of the role that religious congregations play in social service delivery and the role that religion plays in the lives of clients.

- Monitor the impact of public policies on poverty and inequality.

- Learn to use political processes to promote social services that contribute to the well-being of individuals and communities.

- Be particularly aware of the impact of trends in the economic institution on client resources and functioning.

- Collaborate with other social workers and human service providers to advocate for greater equality of opportunity in the educational institution.

- Consider the extent to which contemporary social welfare programs, especially those with which you are personally involved, are "imperfect solutions to past problems" and how responsive they are to recent changes in the other major social institutions.

- Take the lead in public discourse about the fit between the current social welfare institution and trends in the other major social institutions.

- Work to ensure that the voices of poor and other oppressed people are included in public dialogue about health care reform.

- Collaborate with other social workers and human service providers to influence media coverage of vulnerable populations and patterns of social inequality.

KEY TERMS

conservative thesis
contingent work
deskilling
devolution
downsizing
economic institution
educational institution

family and kinship institution
fee-for-service
Gini index
government and political institution
health care institution
managed care
mass media institution

neoliberal philosophy

new federalism

radical antithesis

religious institution

skill upgrading

social class

social institution

social structure

social welfare institution

status

therapeutic medicine

ACTIVE LEARNING

1. In the case study at the beginning of the chapter, Mr. and Mrs. Meza have been eager to legalize their immigrant status to ensure that they can stay in the United States rather than return to their native Mexico. One way to begin to understand their motivation to stay in the United States is to do a comparative analysis of social indicators in the two countries. To do this, you can make use of some of the many Web resources that contain statistics on global well-being, including the following:

- www.census.gov: Official site of the U.S. Census Bureau. Use search to find the international data base. Click on summary demographic data, which displays data for selected countries. You can select specific countries and get key summary information about the social health of the countries.

- www.unicef.org: Official site of the United Nations Children's Fund. By going to Information Resources and clicking on Statistics, you can access data on the status of children by country.

- www.undp.org: Site of the United Nations Development Program. By clicking on Human Development Reports, then on Statistics, and finally on Human Development Indicators, you can access a wide range of social data by country.

Use these three resources, or other relevant resources, to prepare a statistical overview of the social health of the United States and Mexico. What are the areas of similarity? Main areas of difference? What indicators seem to be the most important in understanding Mr. and Mrs. Meza's motivation to stay in the United States?

2. We have looked at the conservative thesis and the radical antithesis in an ongoing debate about the role of inequality in social life. Talk to at least five people about this issue, including at least one member of your family and at least one friend. Ask each person the following questions:

- Is inequality a good thing for a society?

- If so, in what way, and good for whom?

- If we accept inequality as inevitable, how much inequality is necessary? Should society try to maximize or minimize the amount of inequality?

- On what criteria do we measure inequality?

- If we seek equality, is it equality of opportunity or of outcomes that we seek?

What kinds of positions did people take? How did they support their arguments? Did you find more support for the conservative thesis or the radical antithesis in the responses you heard?

WEB RESOURCES

U.S. Census Bureau

www.census.gov
Official site of the U.S. Census Bureau contains statistics on a wide variety of topics, including race and ethnicity, gender, education, birthrates, disabilities, and many other topics.

United Nations Children's Fund

www.unicef.org
Site maintained by the United Nations Children's Fund contains cross-national information on the well-being of children.

Center for Responsive Politics

www.opensecrets.org
Site maintained by the nonpartisan Center for Responsive Politics contains information on the money collected and spent by major political candidates and links to major interest groups such as the tobacco lobby and the gun lobby.

The National Center for Educational Statistics

govinfo.kerr.orst.edu/sddb-stateis.html
Site presented by the National Center for Educational Statistics contains data on the social, financial, and administrative characteristics of every school district in the United States.

Families

Nancy R. Vosler

Families

Nancy R. Vosler
Washington University, St. Louis

What theoretical perspectives are available to help social workers understand family life and provide avenues for positive change in families?

What competencies do social workers need for working with families from cultures different from their own?

Key Ideas

As you read this chapter, take note of these central ideas:

1. How we define family shapes our view of family membership and our approach to working with different types of families.

2. Recent demographic trends among U.S. families include an increase in single-parent and remarried households; growth of the elderly population; an increase in labor force participation among women, including mothers of very young children; and increases in racial, ethnic, and cultural diversity among the U.S. population as a whole.

3. Theoretical "lenses" for understanding families can be classified into six broad groupings: the psychodynamic perspective, the social behavioral perspective, the family systems and family life cycle perspectives, the ABCX model of family stress and coping, multilevel family practice, and a strengths perspective.

4. Tools for understanding family life and planning interventions include the multi-generational genogram, family time line and chronology, ecomap, monthly household income and expenses table, family access to basic resources (FABR) chart, home visit and neighborhood walk, geographic data map, and agency context diagram.

5. Work with families must take into consideration the diversity of families in today's society. The cultural variant approach values diversity and directs the social worker toward understanding the specific stresses and strengths experienced by families of diverse backgrounds.

6. Further research and knowledge building are necessary to understand how best to work with low-income families stressed by economic and social changes in larger systems.

CASE STUDY

JUNIOR JONES'S COMPLEX FAMILY LIFE

You are a school social worker at Fifth Street Elementary School in a large metropolitan city in the Midwest. Six-year-old Junior has been referred to you for hitting other children in his first grade class, coming to school on several occasions wearing only a light jacket (walking through snow in January), and shouting expletives at his teacher when she reprimands him for his disruptive behavior.

In taking some family background information, you learn that Junior's mother, Angela Jones, age 25, has two younger children, Susan and Ken, who are 3-year-old twins. Angela and her three children currently live in one side of a duplex owned by the mother of the twins' father in an inner-city neighborhood that has experienced increasing drug activity and some drive-by shootings. The twins' father, John, sometimes stays with Angela, but more recently has been staying most of the time with his mother, Ruth, in the housing unit on the other side of the duplex. Junior's father, Roy, lives across town; he occasionally visits Junior and takes him for an "afternoon out"—to an amusement park or a sports event.

Angela is the youngest of four girls in her family of origin. Her father died in jail during a fight when Angela was 5. Her mother died after a long battle with cancer just before Junior's birth. Angela did not do well in school, was sporadically a truant in junior high school, was in juvenile detention for possession of marijuana, and spent nearly 2 years in a residential school when she was 14 and 15. Her mother was very ill during this time and believed that Angela's being in a residential setting was the "best plan" for her. Angela has not completed high school but has worked briefly at several small retail stores. Following Junior's birth when she was 19, Angela began receiving Aid to Families With Dependent Children (AFDC), now Temporary Assistance to Needy Families (TANF), food stamps, and some housing assistance—except for several periods when she was in a training program or was able to get a temporary job.

Angela and Roy, Junior's father, lived together for about 6 months just before and after Junior's birth. They met through a mutual friend and had known each other for nearly a year when Angela became pregnant. Roy dropped out of school in the 11th grade and off and on has done odd jobs such as car washing. He drinks heavily and has done some experimenting with drugs. Not long after Junior was born, when Roy had been drinking most of one Saturday, he hit Angela, blackening her eye and face. She became frightened and moved, with Junior, into her sister Beth's apartment. Roy promised not to hurt her again, so about a week later, she moved back. However, within a few months, he was regularly threatening both her and the baby, and periodically he would become physically violent, throwing an object across the room or hitting Angela. Angela finally went to a shelter to get away, began a program to receive a high school equivalency diploma, and there met John.

Angela notes that she and John "hit it off" immediately and began going out on a regular basis. She had left the shelter after an argument with a staff member and again moved in with her sister Beth. When Beth's landlord threatened to evict Beth for having "too many people" in the apartment, Angela moved into an apartment with John, who at the time was working in construction and making a fairly good wage. She left Junior for several months with Beth and her two children, but after "getting settled" with John, she brought Junior to live with her and John.

John has an older sister in the armed forces. He dropped out of school in the 10th grade, but several years ago, at the urging of his mother, he completed his high school education. John's parents are divorced. His father is on Social Security Disability (SSD) and Supplemental Security Income (SSI) because an accident at work 10 years ago left him in a wheelchair; he periodically drinks heavily and has in the past been violent toward John's mother, Ruth. Ruth inherited from her parents a duplex in an inner-city neighborhood. She works nights for a small company that contracts to clean office buildings. In the past, she has supplemented her low-wage earnings with rent from the second housing unit in the duplex.

Nearly 4 years ago, when Angela found that she was pregnant with twins, John asked Ruth whether they (John, Angela, and Junior) could "rent" the duplex unit. At the time, a tenant had just moved out. Reluctantly, Ruth agreed; however, payment of rent has been sporadic, and conflict and shouting between Ruth and Angela have become much more frequent, especially recently. The birth and care of the twins, Susan and Ken, have been draining for Angela, and she has not wanted to even consider looking for work in the past 3 years. John's work has been sporadic as well, and he has been let go from several jobs for arguing with a boss or coworker. Conflict between John and Angela has also increased, and John is now living most of the time on his mother's side of the duplex, where he still has "his old room."

Angela, Junior, Susan, and Ken currently receive TANF, food stamps, and Medicaid. Occasionally, Roy brings clothes or a toy for his son, Junior, but he is angry with the state for pursuing him for child support, saying that he makes so little already, he cannot afford to "pay the state" anything. John is also being pressured by the state to pay child support; however, both he and Angela clearly believe, like Roy, that any child support money collected (over $50 per month) goes to the state, not to his children.

Because Angela's housing and utilities have essentially been rent-free from Ruth for the past 4 years, Angela has been able to survive with some small assistance from her sister Beth and a food pantry in the neighborhood. However, buying clothes is always a problem, and Angela has been more and more stressed and frustrated. When Junior lost his winter coat recently at school, Angela cried in frustration and then, for several days, let him walk the two blocks to school with only his summer jacket "to teach him a lesson"—until her sister found out and gave Angela a hand-me-down winter coat for Junior from Beth's 8-year-old son.

Angela is angry with John for not supporting her or the children adequately. She is angry with Ruth for "making things worse" with her nagging about the rent. She is angry with Junior for "making trouble" for her at school. She is tired and depressed over feeling alone and overwhelmed with three very active children. She is also aware that TANF regulations require that she find a job within the 2-year time limit, and that the 5-year TANF clock is ticking toward a cut-off of benefits.

The neighborhood in which the Jones family lives has been declining over the past 5 to 10 years. All the factories in the adjacent industrial complex have closed their doors, leaving behind industrial waste and boarded-up buildings. A number of two-story apartment buildings in the area that were two-family dwellings have now been subdivided and converted into four-family apartment buildings. Several apartment fires in the surrounding streets over the past 3 years have resulted in abandoned and boarded-up buildings, which are sometimes broken into and used for drug dealing and other illegal activities. Gang graffiti has appeared on streets, sidewalks, and the sides of buildings. When gunfire is heard in the neighborhood, most residents go inside, close the door, and "hope for the best."

There is a small grocery store on the corner, across from the elementary school. The owner says that he is forced to charge very high prices because of constant thefts. The nearest chain grocery store is 2 miles away, and Angela would have to change buses going and returning if she used public transportation. Usually, at least once a week or so, she can get someone—John or Beth or sometimes even Ruth, depending on whose car is operational at the time—to drive her to the chain store and back. When the twins were babies and Ruth and Angela were on better terms, Angela could do laundry in Ruth's apartment. However, Angela now has to either wash the laundry by hand or walk a block and a half, with three children in tow, to the nearest self-service laundry. The local health center is a 10-minute bus ride away, and Angela notes that each time she has gone there over the past 4 years, she and her children have been seen by a different doctor.

Angela blames John for not being able to "get and keep" a good job. However, she is also aware that "there aren't a lot of good jobs out there anymore." She has no idea what type of work she could do, once she is no longer eligible for "welfare." She is also very concerned about where she could get good-quality child care for the twins and after-school care for Junior—that is, if her employment is a "regular 9-to-5 job." She notes that Beth has been able to get a neighbor to watch out for her two children after school so that Beth could take a 6-month nurse's aide training course. After completion of her training, Beth hopes to get a hospital job "with good wages and benefits" to help her raise her two children. The children's father, from whom Beth is now divorced, lives in a rural area more than 3 hours from the city and has not been paying child support on a regular basis. He lives in the same county as Beth's and Angela's two much older sisters, who, according to Angela, "have a lot of troubles of their own."

You are the only social worker at the elementary school and are new in your job. You want very much to help the 30 children who have been referred to you over the past few months, but with at least one new referral coming across your desk each week, you are unsure how best to proceed toward making a difference in your clients' lives. You do know that to craft a "plan for change" with Junior and his family, you will have to make some assumptions about who his family is and whether or not working with other family members besides Junior is necessary.

U.S. Families Today: Definition of Family

A definition of family may not be the most obvious place to start thinking about an approach to change for Junior. However, if you rely on the traditional definition of family—two biological parents, family ties based on "blood, adoption, or marriage" (Barker, 1987, p. 53)—you may not be able to correctly identify all those who make up Junior's support network. You may make more progress with the following definition of **family** adopted in 1981 by the National Association of Social Workers (NASW): "a grouping that consists of two or more individuals who define themselves as a family and who over time assume those obligations to one another that are generally considered an essential component of family systems" (NASW, 1982, p. 10).

By this definition, certainly the current household consisting of Angela, Junior, Susan, and Ken is a family. In addition, John has perhaps been acting in a kind of step-parent role, and Junior also has contact with his biological father, Roy. Junior has lived with Beth and her family and so may consider them to be family as well. But the extent to which Ruth considers herself family for Junior is not at all clear.

Systems perspective

Understanding both the patterns and the problems in Junior's behavior requires sorting out relationships and boundaries—and consistent rule makers and authority figures—in his family life. Narrow definitions, labeling a family like Junior's as "broken" or "incomplete," constrict our ability to think creatively about families' strengths and potential options for change.

The Family in Historical Perspective

The ways in which we as social workers evaluate Junior, his family, and his current difficulties are embedded in specific cultural and historical contexts (Carter & McGoldrick, 1999a; Milardo, 2001). Until the 1920s in the United States, the extended family tended to be the base for a collective economic enterprise, often requiring family members to defer individual economic and career decisions to the needs of the collective (Hareven, 2000). Some minority and immigrant families continue to operate to some extent out of this extended-family economic understanding (Hines, Preto, McGoldrick, Almeida, & Weltman, 1999). More recently, however, family members are less interdependent than in the past, pursuing individual economic and career interests (Hareven, 2000). Families are now more a base for consumption than for production.

This cultural trend toward "individualization" of family economics is reflected in the ambivalence with which Ruth, Roy, John, and Beth appear to view their relationships with Angela and her children. Previous AFDC entitlements from federal and state governments—though often inadequate—did provide some individual income directly to Angela for her family's consumption needs. With TANF, however, Angela will be expected to be economically "self-sufficient." If her level of personal earnings is not sufficient, additional kinship obligations and support may or may not be adequate to meet her basic needs.

Interestingly, in some respects, Junior's family is quite typical by current U.S. standards. Several important demographic trends in family configurations have emerged over the past decades, as discussed in Chapter 9. One is the increase in the number of single-parent households. There are still many more single-mother than single-father families, but both types have been increasing—in both numbers and percentage of households (see, e.g., Schwartz & Scott, 1994, p. 28; see also Johnson & Wahl, 1995; Benokraitis, 1996). The long-term rise in divorce rates has paralleled the increase in single-parent households (Cherlin, 1992). Only recently have demographers also begun to pay attention to the rise in never-married single-parent households (Moore, 1995). An additional important trend is the high level of remarriage and the resulting increase in stepfamilies, creating potentially very complex family relationships (Vosler & Proctor, 1991). Other trends affecting family relationships include increases in life spans with resulting care needs for elderly family members, increasing labor force participation by mothers with even very young children, and increasing racial, ethnic, and cultural diversity among the U.S. population as a whole (Johnson & Wahl, 1995; see also Vosler, 1996).

Changes in family structure have occurred at the same time as significant shifts in the U.S. economy (also discussed in Chapter 9). These economic changes include more unequal wage distributions, with increasing concentrations at the top and the bottom of the income range and the "hollowing out" of middle levels, especially for men (Ryscavage, 1994). In an increasing number of families, at least one adult is working full time yet not earning enough to bring the household above the U.S. poverty line (Vosler, 1996). As a result, families in the bottom half of the socioeconomic hierarchy must increasingly have at least two wage earners, often both working full time at low-wage jobs (Vosler, 1996). In addition, quality, affordable child care is not available for many families, and many working poor families have no health insurance, as companies have cut costs by shifting to part-time and temporary employees, for whom no benefits or very few benefits are provided.

Recent empirical research has helped us understand some of the effects of these changes on families. Single parenthood is associated with poverty, family instability, and children's risk (McLanahan & Sandefur, 1994; Vosler, 1996). Never-married parenting is also associated with prior economic instability, which affects family stability in turn (Burton, 1995). These are interesting correlations, although causal relationships among poverty, family instability, divorce, never-married parenthood, and risk for negative child outcomes require further study (see Robertson & Vosler, 1997; Vosler & Robertson, 1998).

Theoretical Perspectives
for Understanding Families

With an understanding of societal trends affecting families as background, you can use a number of theoretical "lenses" to understand Junior's problematic behaviors, their connection to family functioning, and avenues for positive change. This section introduces six theoretical perspectives: psychodynamic perspective, social behavioral perspective, family systems and family life cycle perspectives, the ABCX model of family stress and coping, the multilevel family practice model, and a strengths perspective.

Psychodynamic Perspective and Families

Psychodynamic perspective

Psychodynamic approaches to thinking about families are a mix of ideas from psychodynamic and social systems perspectives. Social workers who approach family problems from this perspective assume that current personal and interpersonal problems are the result of unresolved problems in the **family of origin**, the family into which we were born and in which we were raised (Nichols & Schwartz, 2001). They suggest that these unresolved problems continue to be acted out in our current intimate relationships. Patterns of family relationships are passed on from generation to generation, and intergenerational relationship problems must be resolved to improve current problems.

Some social workers who employ the psychodynamic perspective draw heavily on Murray Bowen's (1978) concept of differentiation of self. Bowen suggested that there are two aspects of **differentiation of self** in the family system (see Carter & McGoldrick, 1999b; Lerner, 1986, 2001):

1. *Differentiation between thinking and feeling.* Family members must learn to own and recognize their feelings. But they must also learn to think about and plan their lives rather than reacting emotionally at times that call for clear thinking. It is assumed that many family problems are based on family members' emotional reactivity to each other. This aspect of differentiation is very similar to Daniel Goleman's concept of emotional intelligence, which was discussed in Chapter 4.

2. *Differentiation between the self and other members of the family.* While recognizing their interdependence with other family members, individuals should follow their own beliefs rather than making decisions based on reactivity to the cues of others or the need to win approval. They should do that, however, without attacking others or defending themselves. A clear sense of self allows them to achieve some independence while staying connected to other family members. This aspect of differentiation is

similar to Howard Gardner's concept of interpersonal intelligence, also discussed in Chapter 4.

Another key concept in the psychodynamic perspective on families is triangulation. **Triangulation** occurs when two family members (a family subsystem) inappropriately involve another family member to reduce the anxiety in the dyadic relationship. For example, if a couple is having marital problems, they may focus their energy on a child's school problems to relieve the tension in the marital relationship. The child's school problems then become the stabilizing factor in the marriage, and this problem will not improve until the parents look at their relationship problem (and the origins of it in their own families of origin). In recent years, proponents of this approach have noted that it is not always another family member that gets "triangled in." It may be an addiction, an overinvolvement in work, or an extramarital affair—all used to ease tension in a dyadic relationship.

The psychodynamic perspective has been criticized for its Anglo-American emphasis on individualism versus collectivism. To some, it pathologizes the value of connectedness that prevails in some nondominant cultures. There is some merit to this criticism, but it must be remembered that Bowen's ideal of the differentiated self was perceived to be the best self for maintaining a family relationship. Betty Carter and Monica McGoldrick (1999b) argue, however, that Bowen's approach fails to recognize power relations in families and the broader world. Women and minorities are socialized to "stifle their resentments of slights on an everyday basis" (p. 439) rather than engage in assertive, self-directed behavior that is central to the process of differentiation. Thus, they are often judged as pathological against Bowen's standards for the differentiated self.

If you use a psychodynamic perspective for thinking about the Jones family, you might want to do a multigenerational **genogram,** or graphic picture of the family history (see Exhibit 10.1) to get a picture of the extended family's patterns of relationships. (Females are indicated by circles, males by squares; lines indicate marriages and births.) The genogram could be used to note the intergenerational pattern of gender role performance, with males as "symptom carriers" who play problematic roles in family life. In thinking about the family, you may also note that both Angela and John could benefit from further work on differentiating thinking and feeling, as well as differentiating themselves within their families of origin. Angela faced significant losses in her childhood and adolescence and developed a habit of responding reactively to these emotional wounds. You could explore the possibility that John was triangled in to rescue his mother from his father and may feel torn in his loyalties to his mother and Angela. You may also note the proximity of Junior's birth to Angela's loss of her mother, and wonder about how this accumulation of stressors may still be reverberating in the family's life. These are only a few of the avenues that you could explore from the psychodynamic perspective.

EXHIBIT 10.1

Jones Family Genogram

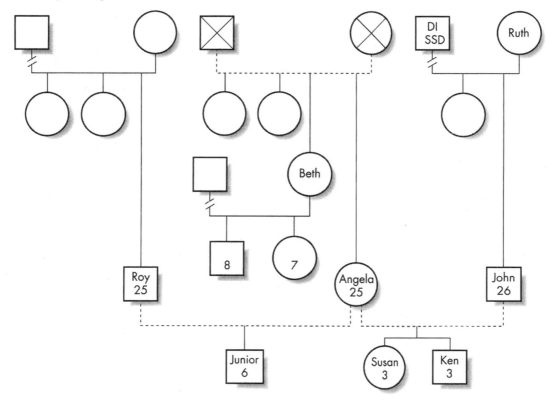

Social Behavioral Perspective and Families

Family therapy often includes behavioral approaches. Social workers who approach family problems from the social behavioral perspective examine communication and family rules, learned patterns of acceptable behaviors, and patterns of rewards for behaviors (who, what, how). Work with the family may involve coaching family members in communication skills, conflict management, and positive reinforcement of desired behaviors.

William Reid's (1985) "task-centered" approach to family problem solving is in this tradition. It involves such in-session activities as "negotiating rules," practicing "positive exchange," and "modifying communication problems" (pp. 202-211), as well as assigning tasks to be carried out at home to reinforce and extend skills learned in the family sessions. Family members are guided toward more effective interaction by defining problematic and desirable behaviors in concrete and observable terms (Walsh, 1993).

Using this approach for understanding Junior's problematic behaviors, the social worker might explore communication and behavioral rules between Junior and Angela, Junior and John, and Junior and Roy—as well as between Angela, Roy, Beth, John, and Ruth. It might also be useful to explore other social contexts from which Junior may be learning what are "acceptable" behavior patterns. For example, Junior spends many afternoons, evenings, and weekends playing in a vacant lot next door to his home, where children of various ages play (and often fight), largely without adult supervision or guidance toward positive activities. In this setting, he may be learning the aggressive behavior and disrespectful language that his teacher has noticed.

Using a behavioral approach, you would want to focus on what Junior has learned in the past—in various contexts—about the behaviors that are considered acceptable and rewarded or are considered unacceptable and punished. Are the behavioral rules in school very different from the explicit and implicit rules in the neighborhood and at home? Does he have to learn different rules for various contexts—for example, with Angela versus with Roy? Also, what roles do his current behaviors play in the rewards and punishments Junior receives both in school and at home? For example, is his "bad" behavior getting him needed attention from an overwhelmed and exhausted Angela? Does he consider negative attention better than no attention at all? Does Junior consider conflict that sometimes escalates into hitting a normal part of living—at home, in the neighborhood, and therefore at school? Do his outbursts at his teacher mirror exchanges he has heard and absorbed from watching conflict between family members (e.g., Roy and Angela, John and Angela, Angela and Ruth)?

In short, analysis of the Jones family from a social behavioral perspective will direct your attention to Junior's learned behavior patterns in family and other contexts. The result, of course, will be that these behavioral patterns and interactions will be the likely focus of your efforts toward positive change.

Family Systems and Family Life Cycle Perspectives

Systems perspective

A behavioral approach tends to focus on the individual, or perhaps on dyadic interchanges. In contrast, a **family systems perspective** adds another lens—that of the family as a social system. As you might imagine, this approach requires a focus on relationships within the family rather than on individual family members (Vosler, 1996). Family members both affect and are affected by other family members; when change occurs for one, all are affected. In this view, families develop boundaries that delineate who is in the family at any given time. Among these members, families develop (sometimes explicitly, sometimes implicitly) organizational structures and roles for accomplishing tasks, commonly shared beliefs and rules, and verbal and nonverbal communication patterns. Necessary structures and roles include family provision ("breadwinners"), leadership and decision making, household maintenance and management, care of dependents, and child rearing (Vosler, 1996).

Developmental perspective

The **family life cycle perspective** expands the concept of "family system" to look at families over time (Carter & McGoldrick, 1999a). It delineates six stages that most U.S. families seem to pass through: single young adults, new couples, families with young children, families with adolescents, families launching children and moving on, and families in later life. Each of these stages involves normative changes and challenging tasks, both for individual family members and for the family system as a whole. In this view, change is inevitable in families, and transitions offer opportunities for positive adaptation and growth. This view may not fit many of the families in today's society, however, including divorced and remarried families.

Ann Hartman and Joan Laird (1983) apply both family systems and family life cycle perspectives in their "family-centered" model for social work practice. In the interdisciplinary field of marriage and family therapy, a number of specialized clinical models have been developed for working with families (see Walsh, 1993, p. 45). In all of these models, the focus for change is the family system itself, with the assumption that changing the patterns of interaction between and among family members will address whatever problem first brought a family member to the attention of a social worker.

The family system and family life cycle perspectives have produced two important tools for assessment:

1. The *multigenerational genogram* (McGoldrick, 1999), which uses visual symbols to represent family members and their relationships across generations (as in Exhibit 10.1)

2. A **family time line** or chronology depicting key dates and events in the family's life (Satir, 1983; Vosler, 1996), which can be used to locate both stressors and strengths (see Exhibit 10.2)

Using this theoretical approach for addressing Junior and his problematic behaviors, you would focus on understanding the family system—the connections and interactional patterns among family members. From the genogram (Exhibit 10.1) and conversation with Angela, you might explore the possibility that this family has unclear boundaries. Is Roy in or out of the family system? Is John in, and if so, for whom? What is the family's understanding of John's relationship to Junior? Is Ruth in or out? What about Beth and her household? If family boundaries are unclear, Junior may be uncertain about who makes which decisions for him. Does Roy have parenting input or authority concerning Junior and his growth and development? Does Angela support—or subvert—Junior's relationship with Roy? Does John attempt to be a father to Junior? How does Junior view such efforts? Is either Ruth or Beth an additional

EXHIBIT 10.2

Jones Family Time Line

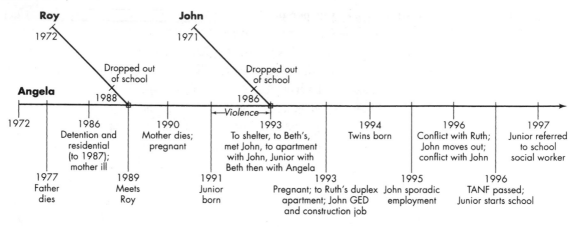

parent for Junior? If so, how does he—and how does Angela—view their parenting efforts?

Organizational structures and roles in this family clearly entail a great deal of anxiety and frustration. Adequate and stable provision for basic family financial needs is an ongoing problem, creating escalating conflict within these multiple family relationships. Unable to manage successfully her multiple tasks and roles, Angela is becoming increasingly angry and frustrated. Attention to her depression is an immediate concern, but antidepressant medication alone is not likely to resolve her difficulties. Family beliefs that John alone should provide for the family financially, with Angela caring for home and children, may not be realistic, given his education and work history to date. Ruth's expectation that she will receive market-rate rent from John and Angela to supplement her low wages is probably unrealistic, at least at present, given their financial situation. Such conflicts over boundaries, roles, beliefs, and rules complicate communication and are likely making problem resolution almost impossible.

From a family life cycle perspective, "family with young children" is the current defining stage of Junior's family. This is normally a period of heavy child-rearing responsibilities, requiring time and energy for both physical and emotional care of quite dependent children. It is not surprising that the care of three active young children is draining for Angela, and letting her know that her experience in this regard is not unusual may provide some perspective on her feelings of being stretched to the limits of her endurance. There are also likely to be unresolved issues around Angela's breakup with Roy, which disrupted the normal development of their family. The "new couple" had moved very quickly into the next stage, being a family with a young child. The addition of a new couple relationship with John—and the addition of two more young children—has complicated relationships for all three of these parents (Angela, John, and Roy). During times of heavy child-rearing responsibilities, supportive relationships with adult friends can be very important for a primary caregiver such as Angela, but there is no indication that Angela has either time or energy for friendships outside the extended family, or for self-care.

Thus, from the family systems and family life cycle perspectives, a primary area for clinical attention might be helping the family to create clear but permeable boundaries, including explicit arenas for family leadership and decision making. For example, discussion with family members could focus on clarifying Angela's role as the primary parent and authority for Junior, with others (John, as well as Beth, Ruth, and Roy) acting to support Angela's decisions and leadership. Additional areas for work might include developing positive communication and problem-solving patterns and delineating clear and age-appropriate rules for Junior's behavior and living situation—including adult time for him and each of his siblings individually and expectations for positive relationships with peers and teachers. This theoretical perspective assumes that work with both primary parenting adults—Angela and John—as well as supportive "kin" (Beth, Ruth, and hopefully Roy) will help the family move toward more consistent and positive interactional patterns, both for family living and for relationships with members of other social systems such as teachers and school personnel.

Often not addressed directly in this perspective, however, is the impact of constraints and changes in larger social systems. Any number of outside forces may subvert the positive new patterns that social workers and family members attempt to develop. For example, welfare-to-work requirements for Angela are likely to leave her with less time and energy available to be a consistent parent for Junior and his siblings.

ABCX Model of Family Stress and Coping

Systems perspective;
Psychodynamic
perspective

You read about theories of individual stress and coping in Chapter 5; the **ABCX model of family stress and coping** addresses family problems. It theorizes that to understand whether an event in the family system (A) becomes a crisis (X), we also need to understand both the family's resources (B) and the family's definitions (C) about the event. This model is based on work by Reuben Hill (1958) and was developed by Hamilton McCubbin and his colleagues (McCubbin et al., 1980; McCubbin & Patterson, 1983).

Systems perspective

The ABCX model describes a "family transition process" following a stressful event. A period of disequilibrium is followed by three possible outcomes: (1) *recovery* to the family's previous level of functioning, (2) *maladaptation,* or permanent deterioration in the family's functioning, or (3) *bonadaptation,* improvement in the family's functioning over and above the previous level. Thus, under certain circumstances, a stressor event can actually be beneficial, if the family's coping process strengthens the family in the long term. They might, for instance, come together to deal with the crisis. One of the key influences on the long-term outcome is the level of resources available to the family both internally and from larger systems in which the family is embedded.

A more complex *double* ABCX model incorporates the concept of **stress pileup** (McCubbin & Patterson, 1983). Over time, a series of crises may deplete the family's resources and expose the family to increasing risk of very negative outcomes (such as divorce, violence, or removal of children from the home). In this view, the balance of stressors and resources is an important consideration. Where there are significant numbers of stressors, positive outcomes depend on a significant level of resources being available to family members and the family as a whole.

Two types of stressors are delineated in the ABCX model (McCubbin & Figley, 1983). **Normative stressors** are the typical family life-cycle transitions, such as the birth of a first child. **Nonnormative stressors** are potentially catastrophic events, such as natural disasters, drug abuse, unemployment, and family violence. These non-normative events can quickly drain the family's resources and may leave family members feeling overwhelmed and exhausted. Lower-level but persistent stress—such as chronic illness or chronic poverty—can also create stress pileup, resulting in instability within the family system and a sense of being out of control on the part of family members.

Two tools are especially useful for discovering patterns of stress, resources, and stress pileup in a family:

1. An *ecomap* uses circles, lines, and arrows to show family relationships and the strength and directional flow of energy and resources to and from the family (Hartman & Laird, 1983; see also Vosler, 1996). Ecomaps help the social worker and the family to identify external sources of stress, conflict, and social support. Exhibit 10.3 is an example of an ecomap.

2. A *family time line* helps to identify times in the family's life when events have "piled up." The social worker and the family can then begin to identify the resources that have been tapped successfully in the past, as well as resource needs in the present. You can refer back to Exhibit 10.2 for an example of a family time line.

As you can see in the Jones family ecomap (Exhibit 10.3), Junior and his family are struggling with multiple stressors and currently have only a few resources to help them cope with the stress. Stress is coming primarily from relationships with Roy, John, Ruth, and Junior's school. The family is also stressed by inadequate income to meet necessary expenses. Not surprisingly, much of the interpersonal conflict revolves around financial needs and expectations, such as inadequate family and child support from Roy and John and failure to pay rent as promised to Ruth.

EXHIBIT 10.3
Jones Family Ecomap

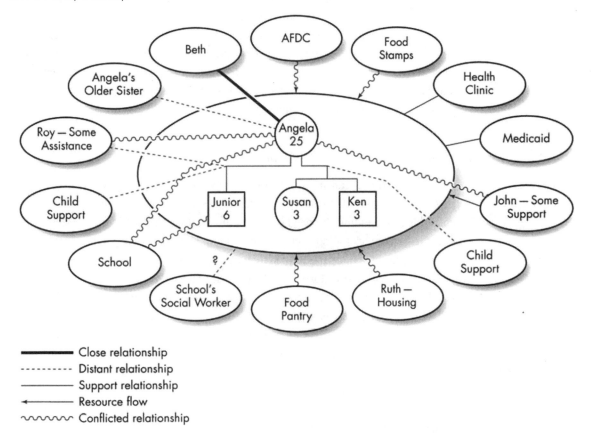

Resources currently available to Angela and her family include Beth's emotional support and limited material support (such as the hand-me-down coat), as well as financial assistance from public sources (TANF, food stamps, Medicaid) and the food pantry. Despite conflict between Angela and Ruth, Ruth has not yet evicted them and thus is providing substantial tangible support in the form of stable housing. Although Angela does not like—or feel good about—receiving public help in the form of TANF, food stamps, Medicaid, and bags of groceries from the food pantry, these resources are providing her with much-needed assistance for the basic necessities of life. It is unclear whether the Jones family will consider you, the school social worker, as another stressor or as a resource for beginning to resolve some of the family's difficulties.

If the ecomap is not enough to convince you, the Jones family time line (Exhibit 10.2) should alert you to the possibility of stress pileup for this family. Previous violence—especially between Roy and Angela—and its consequences may never have been dealt with. Although stable housing has been available to this family for the past 3 years, escalating conflict around John's unemployment, John and Angela's nonpayment of rent, and accumulating effects of chronic poverty (e.g., no budgetary flexibility for a second winter coat for Junior) are likely to be affecting Angela's mental health and therefore her ability to cope with the multitude of household tasks involved in raising three active and needy young children. Simply acknowledging the reality of stress pileup and lack of adequate resources may be a first important step in your establishing a positive relationship with this multiply stressed family.

Multilevel Family Practice Model

Systems perspective   The **multilevel family practice model** (Vosler, 1996) widens the social worker's theoretical framework to include the larger systems in which the family system is embedded—including the neighborhood, the local community, the state, the nation, and the current global socioeconomic system. Thus, the multilevel model is more broadly focused than the family systems perspective, acknowledging the economic, political, and cultural factors that affect which material resources are available to the family and how family members view their current situation and future challenges. This model recognizes, as suggested in Chapter 9, that the family institution is inter-related with other social institutions—religious, political, economic, educational, social welfare, health care, and mass media.

Conflict perspective   This model also incorporates a **developmental social construction view** (Vosler, 1996, p. 30), which alerts the social worker to the fact that current social institutions, along with their policies and programs (or lack of programs), have evolved over time and, therefore, can perhaps be modified. Consider, for example, changes in the past few years in policies and programs designed to support low-income families. "Welfare reform" has assumed that jobs are available at wages that will enable the family provider (breadwinner) to meet basic needs. That view is common among the political and economic elite who benefited from an expanding economy and lower taxes in the 1990s. However, some state and local economies did better than others throughout the 1990s, and this assumption may now be quite untenable for people living in areas of high unemployment or low prevailing wages or for people who lack the skills required in an information economy. Furthermore, basic support structures—such as affordable housing, quality child care, programs for after-school care and youth supervision, and affordable health insurance—may be beyond the means of substantial numbers of working poor families. Even when these supports are supposedly available in a state or even in a specific local community, they may not be truly accessible to a particular family who needs them—because of lack of (or unreliable) transportation or because access requires substantial commitments of time and energy (such as travel outside the neighborhood where the family is currently living).

Social constructionist
perspective

The picture for such families is grim, but it is not totally hopeless. The possibility exists that policy makers and the general public will observe the struggles of the working poor and once again institute policies to help them. However, change can occur only when social workers and other citizens become aware that current societal institutions are socially constructed and therefore, over time, can be modified or changed dramatically—for example, through social and economic development programs and policies. As a nation, the United States has substantially reduced poverty among the elderly population through the Social Security system; however, poverty among children continues to increase.

Several tools are available for assessment of multilevel family stressors and resources:

■ *Monthly household income and expenses* can give the social worker and the family a quick look at current financial stress and resources (see Exhibit 10.4).

■ The *FABR chart* provides a more comprehensive look at potential supports and deficits by examining the family's access to a stable and adequate financial resource base (see Vosler, 1990, 1996).

■ A *home visit and neighborhood walk* provides the social worker with information about resources and stressors within the family's immediate environment.

■ A *geographic data map* examines the neighborhood's or community's patterns of poverty, housing, crime, basic and support services, and public transportation,

EXHIBIT 10.4
Jones Family
Monthly Income
and Expenses

Income		Expenses	
Wages	$0	Rent	$0
Child Support	$0	Utilities	$0
AFDC	$350	Telephone	$25
Food Stamps	$340	Food and Household Supplies (4–5 people)	($28/week) $602
Total	$690	Laundry	$23
		Clothes	$50
		School Supplies	$25
		Transportation (Bus/Car fare)	$25
		Total	$750

Income – Expenses = –$60

providing a more comprehensive understanding of potential resources as well as gaps in services.

■ An *agency context diagram* represents visually a specific agency's links to other agencies and services.

These data sources can also provide information needed for effective program planning and policy changes at state, national, and even global levels.

Let's see how you could use these tools to develop a more accurate picture of the Jones family. Exhibit 10.4, the Jones family's monthly income and expenses, shows that income from TANF and food stamps falls short of the family's basic living expenses by $60 per month—even though they currently have no expenses for rent and utilities. If Ruth forces Angela and her children out of their current housing, they will need at least an additional $400 to $500 monthly plus a deposit to pay for an apartment and utilities. Given TANF requirements (which depend to a large extent on state policies), Angela is likely to be ineligible for this benefit fairly soon (usually within 2 years). She will be expected to find a job that will enable her to be "self-sufficient." However, she will then have additional expenses of child care for the twins, after-school care for Junior, work expenses (including clothing and lunches for herself), transportation, and possibly medical insurance (if her employer does not pay the total premium as a work benefit). Angela's lack of education and work experience make it unlikely that she will be able to find a job at wage and benefit levels that will cover all of the family's basic needs. Thus, she will need to turn to Junior's father, Roy, and the twins' father, John, for child support payments. However, unless the two men have jobs that pay above the minimum wage, they may not be able to provide much in the way of stable financial support. Complicating the current picture is Ruth's limited income, which makes it important for her to receive at least some income from her "renters." On the plus side, once she is employed, Angela will be eligible for the Earned Income Tax Credit (EITC), which will provide very low-level—but needed—support. The **Earned Income Tax Credit (EITC)** is a refundable federal income tax credit for low-income working individuals and families that reduces the amount of federal tax owed. It can result in a tax refund if the EITC exceeds the amount of taxes owed.

Conflict perspective

A home visit and neighborhood walk would reveal additional stressors for Angela and her family, including their weekly walk through a dangerous neighborhood to the crowded and rather run-down laundry; high prices at the local convenience store; and the vacant lot next door—the only neighborhood "park"—where older youth and young adults hang out with unsupervised younger children. The nearest bus stop is two blocks away, and bus connections to other areas of the city involve transfers and long waits for the next bus. The Joneses' neighborhood has no banks, chain grocery stores, or major retail outlets. There is no equipment on the school playground, because school officials assess that "it would just get broken or stolen." Because of their uncertain income and inability to pay rent regularly, many families move into the neighborhood only to move out again 6 to 9 months later. The school reports that at least 50% of the children entering in September will be gone by June, replaced by the same number of new faces—and often by increased numbers of students. Neighborhood residents as well as service providers are frustrated and angry, and at times seem despairing and hopeless.

Theoretically, a number of national, state, and local programs are available to this family. Welfare-to-work programs (for mothers and fathers) and Parents' Fair Share (for fathers) are intended to help parents move from welfare to work through education, job training, and work experience. Some child care is available through the Head Start program; however, there are long waiting lists for a child to be accepted into any of the programs (Early Start, Head Start, Even Start). Counseling, parent education, and support groups funded by the United Way and other nonprofit organizations are not currently available in Angela's immediate neighborhood, and their outreach efforts have not been particularly successful in recruiting low-income clients such as Angela, John, and Roy. The school board has been forced to eliminate funding for after-school activities such as tutoring and sports because of budget deficits and city residents' abhorrence of tax increases. Over the past decade, higher-income families have moved to suburban areas in the surrounding counties, taking with them their tax dollars for schools, parks, playgrounds, and community activities.

The employment that Angela, John, and Roy—and even Ruth—have found over the past several years has for the most part consisted of low-wage jobs without benefits, and the work has often been only temporary or part time. With unstable and inadequate income have come escalating family conflict and family instability. From the perspective of the adult members of this extended family, the future looks neither stable nor hopeful, and talking with the family about planning for positive change is likely to be very difficult.

Strengths Perspective

Humanistic perspective

The final lens for understanding and working with families to be discussed briefly here is the **strengths perspective**. This framework has developed primarily out of work with African American families (Boyd-Franklin, 1989; McAdoo, 1997) and with households headed by women (Miller, 1987). Often in the past, families that did not conform to the "traditional" model—two heterosexual parents with the male as the primary breadwinner and authority figure (Macklin, 1980)—were considered, by definition, to be deficient and potentially pathological. More recently, both researchers and practitioners have begun to document the strengths of nontraditional families and to advocate that social workers identify important stresses and strengths among their clients. Identifying strengths can change the social worker's view of where to begin and create a hopefulness about the future, so that the climate changes from one of despair over an overwhelming multiplicity of problems to an appreciation of how the family meets challenges to the best of its ability. Helping family members identify how they have coped creatively with adversity in the past may help them find hope for making changes in the present.

Although Angela, Junior, Susan, Ken, and John face many difficult stresses and resource deficits, they also—as individuals and as a family—have a number of strengths on which to build. John has completed a GED and has some work experience. Angela has begun work on her GED and has a small amount of work experience as well. In the past, Angela was able to end a violent relationship with Roy, moving herself and Junior to a safe environment. Angela has the support of her sister Beth, both emotionally and at times financially. John's mother Ruth has provided stable housing for this fragile family for nearly 4 years and has continued to support John by allowing him to live at home when conflict escalates between him and Angela.

Despite severe income deficits, Angela has been able to care reasonably well for her three children, combining public supports, help from the children's fathers, and periodic assistance from the neighborhood food pantry. When not overstressed by financial difficulties, John and Angela have a strong positive relationship. John states that he loves both the twins and Junior and is committed to being a good father to all three. Roy also wants to be a good father to his son Junior, and states that he wants to work out a positive coparenting relationship with Angela that will help Junior grow up healthy and strong— "so maybe he won't make some of the mistakes I've made in my life."

The school, as an institution in the neighborhood, may serve as a base for a team of professionals and local residents who work toward identifying neighborhood needs and funding resources for programs and services. You, as a school-based social worker, might spearhead the process of developing local education and training programs, local employment opportunities, counseling and parenting education services, child care, after-school care, youth services, economic development in the neighborhood, health care services, and opportunities for residents to meet around important issues and celebrate renewal of their neighborhood, their families, and their lives.

Diversity in Family Life

As you can see from this review of theoretical perspectives, there is no one way to view a family in order to understand and work effectively with family members toward positive change. The reality today is that a great deal of diversity exists among families, both in the United States and globally. Thus, a final lens that we need to consider as we work to understand families is the lens of diversity and cultural competence in social work practice.

Consider, for example, what assumptions you may have made about the ethnicity, culture, religion, social class, immigrant status, and sexual orientation of (a) Angela and other family members, and (b) the school social worker. How might work with this family be different, given different sets of circumstances with regard to diversity?

For example, if we've assumed that Angela and her other family members are European American, are they connected with any specific culture (e.g., Appalachian), and/or any church or religious group (e.g., Pentecostal)? If the social worker is also European American, is middle-class, female, young, single, lesbian, of English and German ancestry, and grew up Roman Catholic, how might similarities and also differences with regard to Junior and his family affect her ability to establish a working relationship with him, with Angela, and perhaps with other family members? In addition, how might social work with this family be affected if the school and neighborhood are (a) nearly all European American or (b) nearly all European American with a large population of recent immigrants—Bosnian, for example, or (c) mostly African American or (d) nearly half European American and nearly half African American, with a few immigrant families from Bosnia, Vietnam, and Ethiopia scattered through the immediate neighborhood?

Rowena Fong and Sharlene Furuto, in their important work *Culturally Competent Practice* (2001), cite five competencies needed for effective social work across cultures that are important to keep in mind:

1. Be aware of one's own cultural limitations.

2. Be open to cultural differences.

3. Maintain a client-oriented, systematic learning style.

4. Use available cultural resources, such as community members and ethnic festivals.

5. Acknowledge the integrity of all cultures.

The key is to be comfortable with diverse ethnicities (Greene, Jensen, & Jones, 1999). Ideally, social workers would have a good understanding of their clients' cultural backgrounds. However, in light of the great diversity in the United States, that is an impractical goal. A reasonable alternative is to remain curious and open-minded, an attitude that will help social workers to avoid offending clients and to promote their confidence.

Celia Falicov (1998) has developed a guide to multicultural practice that she calls *MECA—multidimensional ecosystemic comparative approach.* Four dimensions are identified for describing and comparing similarities and differences among cultural groups:

1. Migration experience

2. Ecological context of family

3. Family organization

4. Family life cycle

Falicov suggests that consideration of these dimensions will allow social workers and other helping professionals to consider the multiple cultural contexts (race, social class, religion, occupation, language) of the social worker as well as the client group.

The remaining sections focus on families of diverse cultures and social classes, as well as immigrant families and gay and lesbian families. These are the forms of diversity currently receiving the most attention from researchers. However, emerging bodies of empirically based literature are also focusing on families coping with serious illness and disability (Rolland, 1993, 1999), adolescent parents and nonmarital coparenting (Vosler & Robertson, 1998; Seltzer, 2001), families in later life (Walsh, 1999a; Allen, Blieszner, & Roberto, 2001; Brubaker, 1991; Mancini & Blieszner, 1991), and grandparents serving as primary caregivers for grandchildren (Jendrek, 1993, 1994).

As we widen our understanding of "normal" to include these diverse family forms and processes, we must not lose sight of the fact that certain behaviors and arrangements in families are neither normal nor healthy. Behaviors that must always be of grave concern to social workers include abuse and violence, sexual abuse, neglect, and prejudice, discrimination, and systemic oppression—whether based on racism, sexism, sexual orientation, disability, age, class, religion, ethnicity, or other forms of exclusion.

Culture and Family Life

In the past, many of the clinical models for family practice were based on work with primarily middle-class and often two-biological-parent European American families. Family research in the 1960s and 1970s often relied on white middle-class families as subjects and respondents and then generalized findings for this specific population to "all families." A 1980 article reviewing the family scholarship of the previous decade called attention to this "cultural deviant" approach to family research, which relegated culturally different families with a variety of ethnic backgrounds—Asian, African American, Hispanic, and Native American—to the category of deviants. The proposed alternative was a **cultural variant approach**, in which "different" does not necessarily mean "deviant" or "deficient." Since then, others have advocated the cultural variant approach for understanding a wide variety of "different" family forms, including single-parent and remarried households, gay and lesbian families, foster families, families with one or more adopted children, extended family households, and couples without children. As social worker practitioners, we need to examine our understanding of what is "normal" for these various family forms, because our change efforts are inevitably guided by what we consider to be "healthy" or "normal" patterns and behaviors (Walsh, 1993).

There are now a number of helpful guides to cultural diversity among a variety of families. *Ethnicity and Family Therapy* discusses, for example, family differences in beliefs, rules, communication patterns, and organizational norms (McGoldrick, Giordano, & Pearce,1996; see also Mindel, Habenstein, & Wright, 1998; and Hines et al., 1999). Understanding differences as variations on themes rather than "deviations" or "deficiencies" is often a key component in working effectively with a family from an ethnic background different from your own.

A number of important learning resources also focus on a specific population or set of populations. These include Latino families (Falicov, 1998, 1999; Sotomayor, 1991; chapters in Ewalt, Freeman, Fortune, Poole, & Witkin, 1999; and chapters in Fong & Furuto, 2001), African American families (Boyd-Franklin, 1987, 1989; Hines, 1999; chapters in Ewalt et al., 1999; chapters in Fong & Furuto, 2001), First Nations/American Indian/Native American families (chapters in Ewalt et al., 1999; and chapters in Fong & Furuto, 2001), Asian and Pacific Islander families (in both Ewalt et al., 1999, and Fong & Furuto, 2001), and "families of color" (McLoyd, Cauce, Takeuchi, & Wilson, 2001; McAdoo, 1999).

Social Class and Family Life

Up-to-date family research is an important resource to help you understand specific stresses and resource needs among a variety of families. Empirical studies have demonstrated, for example, that children raised in a single-parent or remarried family can grow up physically, mentally, and psychologically healthy (Hetherington, Stanley-Hagan, & Anderson, 1989; Anderson, 1999; McGoldrick & Carter, 1999), but we also know that risks are involved with these family structures. Single-parent families are at risk for poverty and stress pileup (McLanahan & Sandefur, 1994), and remarried families tend to be complex and often must cope with a variety of internal stressors (Hetherington et al., 1989; Vosler & Proctor, 1991).

Interestingly, a review of research on family practice found that traditional family therapy, which focuses on family-level change alone, is not effective with "isolated, impoverished, single-parent families" (Proctor, Davis, & Vosler, 1995), especially in the United States. On the other hand, there is growing evidence that traditional family therapy, especially that based on the social behavioral and family systems perspectives, is effective with nonpoor families for such specific problems as marital discord, substance abuse, schizophrenia, psychosomatic disorders, and juvenile delinquency (Proctor et al., 1995). However, one overview of empirical studies found that only

23% of the 150 possible combinations of therapy method and problem have been evaluated; only 9% have shown a reasonable probability of being effective (Proctor et al., 1995, p. 947). Clearly, much more empirical research remains to be done in this area.

Elsewhere, a small study in Singapore, based on a multilevel family practice approach, found that making resources available in the neighborhood environment of low-income, highly stressed families—connected with a neighborhood-based family service agency, staffed by social work professionals trained in family systems practice—helped to create positive change for some families (Nair, Blake, & Vosler, 1997). Another study describes effective community-based social work practice with a number of overwhelmed individuals and families in the United States today (Hopps, Pinderhughes, & Shankar, 1995). However, further work is clearly needed in evaluating theories and models and in understanding the lives of impoverished families, particularly as poverty increases in the United States and as neighborhoods and local communities struggle with decreasing resources.

Immigrant Families

Interconnected with issues of cultural diversity, immigration is an increasingly important learning area for effective social work practice with families. Consider the sheer size of this population: "Over 7 million people immigrated during the past decade, reflecting consistent increases over previous decades, and these increases are expected to continue. By 2040 one in four Americans will be immigrant (first generation) or the child of immigrants (second generation), and by 2010 children of immigrants will account for 22 percent of the school-aged population" (Padilla, 1999, p. 590; see also Benokraitis, 2001). There are different patterns of immigration in different regions of the United States. California has the highest percentage of foreign-born residents in the United States, 25%, and New York has the second highest percentage, 15% (Hernandez & McGoldrick, 1999). Currently, the United States is averaging 1 million new immigrant arrivals each year; 700,000 of these are legal and the other 300,000 are undocumented (Hernandez & McGoldrick, 1999). You may want to reread the story of the Meza family in Chapter 9 to refresh your memory about some of the special challenges of immigrant families with undocumented members.

To work with immigrant families, social workers need to understand the migration experience and the changes in social networks, socioeconomic status, and culture that result from migration (Hernandez & McGoldrick, 1999). Practitioners also need to know about families' countries of origin, settlement patterns, and immigration policy—including eligibility for mainstream or special education, health and mental health services, and other financial and social services and resources (Padilla, 1999; see also additional chapters in Ewalt et al., 1999). Currently, there is much antiimmigrant sentiment in the United States, as well as in other countries, and this negative sentiment is resulting in declining availability of support programs for immigrant families (Hernandez & McGoldrick, 1999). The most vulnerable immigrant families, the ones with disabled or elderly members or with young children, are left without support in caring for their dependent members.

Gay and Lesbian Families

There is an emerging empirical and practice literature on work with gay and lesbian families (Patterson, 2001; Johnson & Colucci, 1999; Green & Bozett, 1991; Laird, 1993; see also Kanuha, 2001). Overall, these families seem to be adjusting well despite the stressors that affect them (Patterson, 2001).

Thomas Johnson and Patricia Colucci (1999) argue that lesbians and gays are bicultural. They have been reared and socialized in the dominant heterosexual culture and have internalized the norms, values, and beliefs learned in that culture. For the most part, they are members of heterosexually oriented families, and they have hetero-sexual models of family life. At the same time, lesbians and gays participate in a gay culture that copes with homophobia and develops a set of norms and roles for the special circumstances of same-sex partnerships. They must often deal with family of origin reactivity to their sexual orientation and romantic relationships. Johnson and Colucci (1999) suggest that "[f]ollowing this track, we believe that gays and lesbians are part of a complex multigenerational family system consisting of a family of origin, a multi-generational lesbian/gay community, and/or a family of choice that consists of friends, partners, and/or children" (p. 347).

However, these understandings are relatively new in the family studies and practice literatures. Much more work needs to be done to understand gay and lesbian families in the context of current and changing social policies and experiences of oppression, as well as the intersection of sexual orientation with ethnicity and culture (see Kanuha, 2001), religion, and social class. There is much important work to do in all of these areas.

IMPLICATIONS FOR SOCIAL WORK PRACTICE

This discussion of families and family life, in the context of larger social systems, suggests several practice principles:

- Assess families from a variety of theoretical perspectives. Given recent economic shifts, be particularly aware of the impact of changes in larger systems on families' resources and functioning.

- Develop awareness of diversity among families and a commitment to culturally competent practice that involves ongoing learning both about and from families that are different from your own.

- Use appropriate family assessment tools, including the genogram, ecomap, time line, statement of monthly income and expenses, FABR chart, home visit, neighborhood walk, data map, agency context diagram, program evaluation, and policy analysis.

- Understand the neighborhood and local community of each of the families you work with.

- Understand policies and changes at state and national levels and the ways they affect both your own work and the lives of all families—particularly lower-income, stressed families.

- Collaborate with other social workers and human service providers in making needed changes at neighborhood, local, state, and national levels that will support families and enable your work with specific families to be effective.

- Where appropriate, encourage family members to become involved in neighborhood, local, state, and national efforts for positive change.

- As appropriate, work toward your agency's becoming involved in policy and advocacy work on behalf of families, including development of needed programs and services.

- Become involved in continuing efforts to develop up-to-date empirical knowledge about a variety of families and the resources needed by families to grow strong and to raise healthy children.

KEY TERMS

ABCX model of family stress and coping
cultural variant approach
developmental social construction view
differentiation of self
Earned Income Tax Credit (EITC)
family
family life cycle perspective
family of origin
family systems perspective

family time line
genogram
multilevel family practice model
nonnormative stressors
normative stressors
strengths perspective
stress pileup
triangulation

ACTIVE LEARNING

1. *Theory and Your Family.* We have used different theoretical lenses to look at the family of Junior Jones. As the social worker working with the Jones family, you will want to be aware of how your own family experiences influence your practice with families. You can use theory to help you do that as well. To begin this process, reflect on the following questions related to your family of origin when you were a child:

■ What value was placed on connectedness and what value was placed on the differentiated self?

■ What were the important behavioral rules?

■ What were the external boundaries—who was in and who was out of the family? What were the commonly shared beliefs? What roles did family members play? What were the patterns of communication?

■ Can you recall any periods of stress pileup? If so, how did your family cope during those periods?

■ What cultural, economic, and political factors affected stress and coping in your family?

■ What were your family's strengths?

After you have reflected on these questions, write a brief paper addressing the following points:

■ Summarize your reflections on each question.

■ How do you think your experiences in your family of origin might serve as a barrier and/or aid in your work with the Jones family?

2. *Visualizing Your Family.* Sometimes we learn new things about families when we prepare visual representations of them. There are several tools available for doing this. You will use three of them here to visualize your own family.

■ Referring back to Exhibit 2.6, prepare a family ecomap of your *current* family situation.

■ Referring to Exhibit 10.1, prepare a multigenerational genogram of your family, going back to your maternal and paternal grandparents.

■ Referring to Exhibit 10.2, prepare a family time line beginning at the point of your birth, or earlier if you think there were significant earlier events that need to be noted.

After you have prepared these materials, work in small groups in class to discuss how useful each tool was in helping you think about your family of origin. Were any new insights gained from using these visual tools? What is your overall reaction to using tools like these to understand your family?

WEB RESOURCES

The Administration for Children and Families (ACF)

www.acf.dhhs.gov
Site maintained by the Administration for Children and Families, a government agency that is part of the U.S. Department of Health and Human Services, contains fact sheets about children and families and information about ACF programs such as child support enforcement, Head Start, and TANF.

Forum on Child and Family Statistics

childstats.gov
Official Web site of the Federal Interagency Forum on Child and Family Statistics offers easy access to federal and state statistics and reports on children and families, including international comparisons.

Families and Work Institute

www.familiesandwork.org
Site presented by the Families and Work Institute contains information on work-life research, community mobilization forums, information on the Fatherhood Project, and frequently asked questions.

Council on Contemporary Families

www.contemporaryfamilies.org/center.html
Official site of the Council on Contemporary Families, a nonprofit organization that promotes an inclusive view of families, contains information and research on families, along with links to other Internet resources.

Interperson Distance
Density and Crowding
Spatial Arrangements

Implications for Social Work Practice

Key Terms

Active Learning

Web Resources

Small Groups

Elizabeth P. Cramer
Virginia Commonwealth University

Small groups have become a common form of human service delivery. In today's age of managed care and increased human isolation, why would groups be an important form of social work practice?

People find themselves a part of many different formal and informal small groups during their lifetimes. Why might it be helpful for a social worker to know about the groups to which a client belongs?

Key Ideas

As you read this chapter, take note of these central ideas:

1. Small groups are typically defined as collections of individuals who interact with each other, perceive themselves as belonging to a group, are interdependent, join together to accomplish a goal or fulfill a need through joint association, and are influenced by a set of rules and norms.

2. Types of social work groups include therapy, mutual aid, psychoeducational, self-help, and task groups. A group may be a combination of two or more types.

3. Small groups in social work vary in how they develop, how long they last, and how they determine membership.

4. In determining group composition, small groups must resolve issues of inclusion versus exclusion, heterogeneity versus homogeneity, and group cohesiveness.

5. To understand small group processes, social workers may draw on expectation states theory, status characteristics theory, and exchange theory.

6. Both stage theories and process models have been used to understand how small groups develop.

7. Group dynamics are patterns of interactions, including factors such as leadership, roles, and communication networks.

CASE STUDY

TERRY'S SUPPORT GROUP

As she drove to a meeting of her Wednesday night support group, Terry popped a Melissa Etheridge CD into the player. A year ago, she would have barely recognized the singer's name. Now she listens to the tapes incessantly. But much more has changed in Terry's life these past several months. Last year at this time, she was married—to a man. Terry and Brad had an amiable 2-year marriage, but Terry had felt a sense of loneliness and discomfort throughout their marriage. She loved Brad, but could not commit to him deep in her heart. She also felt an unhappiness beyond her marriage to Brad. Terry realized she had to discover what was contributing to her unhappiness. After some serious soul-searching, she joined a support group run for women much like her. The group members have gradually learned much of Terry's history.

In sixth grade, Terry was inseparable from her best friend, Barb. Barb and Terry shared a similar family background—white, middle class, Protestant—and shared many of the preteen developmental stages together: starting menstruation, kissing boys for the first time, being picked on as the youngest children in the middle school, and wearing shirts that show your belly button. Barb loved Terry and Terry loved Barb in that very special way that best friends do.

One night when Terry was sleeping over at Barb's house, Barb suggested that they play the dating game. Terry had played the game before at a boy-girl party. The lights go out, and the boys and the girls pair up to plan a make-believe date. At Barb's house, when Terry protested because there were no boys to play the game with them, Barb suggested that they could switch off playing boys and girls. So Terry and Barb enacted the date themselves, including a long good-night kiss. That was the first and last time Barb and Terry played the dating game. They did not discuss this incident ever again.

Terry went through her preteen and adolescent years dating boys and imagining the kind of guy she might marry. In college, Terry had another sexual experience with a female. She had been at a party with some friends where heavy drinking occurred. The group of friends with whom she went to the party decided to spend the night at the home of the hostess instead of trying to drive home drunk. Bed space was sparse; therefore, beds needed to be shared. Terry and Patricia shared a twin-size bed in a private room. The two women crawled into bed and giggled about the fact that the two of them were sharing this tiny space. The giggling turned into tickling, and the

CASE STUDY

tickling turned into kissing and touching. The next morning, Terry blamed this sexual experience on the alcohol.

After college, Terry worked as a loan officer in a bank. A few years into her job, at age 26, she met Brad. After several relationships with men, she was ready to discontinue the dating scene. Brad and Terry developed a close relationship quickly and were engaged within 9 months of meeting each other. Terry and Brad bought a house, combined their possessions, and began what they both thought would be the rest of their lives together. But that scenario didn't work out.

When Terry came to the women's coming-out support group for the first time, she was petrified. Beverly, a woman on Terry's softball team, promised she would meet Terry in the parking lot and they'd go together. Sure enough, Beverly was in the parking lot with a big smile and hug: "Hey, girl. You'll be all right." They walked to the front of the building, past the sign that read "Gay and Lesbian Community Center" (Terry was sure the sign must have been at least as big as a Ping-Pong table). Beverly rang the doorbell and gave Terry a reassuring look. An African American woman who looked to be in her 50s answered the door: "Hi, Beverly. Hello, Terry . . . I'm Doris. I'm so glad you could make it here tonight. Come on in."

What was so new that evening is now familiar. Terry has told the group that she looks forward to seeing the faces of those faithful members who return each week; she sympathizes with the nervousness and shyness of the new members. Each of the group members' stories is unique. The group includes bisexual women and women questioning their sexual orientation, as Terry did when first attending the group. "Temperature reading"—a review of group members' excitements, concerns, and hopes and wishes—begins each group session. Sometimes, temperature reading is short and superficial; other times, it goes on for nearly the whole meeting, with much disclosure, intensity, and sometimes crying. The facilitators, both lesbians, plan activities for each session but are flexible enough to allow the members to control the flow of the session. They share a good deal about themselves and their own coming-out processes (e.g., how they came to identify themselves as lesbians and to whom they've disclosed their sexual orientation and experiences).

One of the first people in the group to befriend Terry was Kathy, another woman who had been heterosexually married. Kathy approached Terry during social time, an informal gathering after the meeting to schmooze and have refreshments. Kathy shared that she too had questioned her sexual orientation during the time she was married. Kathy and Terry became friends outside the group; in fact, much of Terry's current friendship network has grown out of the group. She often sees group members at gay and lesbian functions that she has begun to attend, such as the gay/lesbian theater company and the monthly women's potlucks. How different her circle of friends has become compared to when she and Brad were together and they socialized primarily with other white, childless, heterosexual couples.

Terry still feels like a "baby dyke" (a woman who has newly emerged in her lesbian identity) around her friends, most of whom have been "out" (open as lesbians/bisexuals) for much longer than she. She still has many questions about lesbian and gay culture, but she feels comfortable to ask them in the group. She has also found that she can help other women who are just beginning to come out by sharing her experiences. Sometimes she is embarrassed by the discussion in the group, however. For example, the facilitators keep an envelope marked "sex questions," where group members can anonymously submit questions about lesbian sex; the facilitators periodically read them to the group to open a discussion. The frankness of such discussions makes Terry's face turn red sometimes, but she's glad she has a place to find answers about these things. Terry also didn't realize some of the differences between the predominantly white lesbian community and the black lesbian community, and has now learned from her friends about some of the issues faced by African American lesbians.

Terry is consistently amazed at the diversity within the group—women of different races, educational backgrounds, socioeconomic classes, disabilities, religions, and ages. Just last week, for example, seven women attended the group: three African Americans, two women who self-identify as bisexual, one who identifies herself as disabled, one woman who is Jewish, and two women younger than 21.

Tonight, Terry tells the group, as she pulled into the parking lot and got out of the car, a woman pulled into the space next to her. Terry hadn't seen her before. The woman stepped out of the car and looked around nervously. Terry walked over to her: "Hi, have you been to the group before?" "No." "C'mon, I'll walk in with you." And now Terry is introducing the new woman to the rest of the group.

Small Groups in Social Work

Small groups play a significant role in our lives. Terry's support group is a type with special relevance to social work practice, but most people also become involved in other

EXHIBIT 11.1
Benefits of
Small Groups

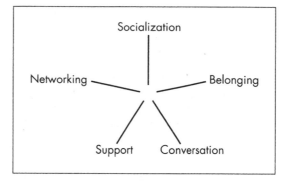

types of small groups: friendship groups, task groups at work, self-help groups, or sports teams, to name but a few.

Humanistic perspective   In a mobile society, where family members may live in different parts of the country and community gathering places (such as a town hall) may be few, groups serve a useful function. They offer individuals an opportunity to meet others and work together to achieve mutual goals. Exhibit 11.1 shows how group members may benefit from belonging to a group. Groups may provide the social support, connection, and healing that various persons (such as clergy) or institutions (such as churches) did in the past (Specht & Courtney, 1994). Identifying with a group is one way that people can "try to find a sense of purpose or meaning" in life (p. 48). In the hustle and bustle of everyday lives, the warmth and sense of "realness" of a productive and healthy group is inviting.

Small groups may be formally defined in a number of ways. A few scholarly definitions of small groups, along with examples from Terry's story, are displayed in Exhibit 11.2. Although these definitions differ, there is general agreement that small groups are more than a collection of individuals who may have similar traits or be in physical proximity. Persons who live on the same block may be in close proximity but have little social interaction and not perceive themselves as a group. Thus, we may define a **small group** as a collection of individuals who interact with each other, perceive themselves as belonging to a group, are interdependent, join together to accomplish a goal or fulfill a need, and are influenced by a set of rules and norms (Johnson & Johnson, 1994).

Social behavioral perspective   A significant element of social work practice today is **group work,** which serves people's needs by bringing them together in small groups. Group work emerged in the United States in the late 1800s and early 1900s. Early group work took place within the settlement houses, YMCA/YWCA, Jewish community centers, and the Boy Scouts and Girl Scouts. These groups focused primarily on recreation, social integration, immigration issues, character building, and social reform. We are now seeing a resurgence in

EXHIBIT 11.2
Definitions of Small Groups

Author(s)	Definition	Example
Shaw (1981)	Two or more individuals who through their interactions influence and are influenced by each other	At the party Terry attended while in college, a group of friends were drinking and chose to stay overnight at the home of the hostess rather than drive after drinking.
Johnson & Johnson (1994)	Two or more individuals who are each aware of membership in the group and of who else belongs to the group, who have a positive interdependence, and who develop and achieve mutual goals	The friends Terry has developed through her association with the coming-out group are aware of themselves as a group of friends, are interdependent, and achieve goals of socialization and companionship through attending gay and lesbian functions together.
Hare, Blumberg, Davies, & Kent (1994)	Two or more individuals who share values that help them maintain an overall pattern of activity, acquire or develop resources and skills to use in that activity, and conform to a set of norms that define roles in the activity, and who have enough cohesiveness and leadership to coordinate their resources and roles in order to accomplish their goals	The coming-out group at the Gay and Lesbian Community Center shares such values as exploration and acknowledgment of sexual orientation, an overall pattern of activity (weekly meetings), resources and skills (Center space, two trained facilitators), norms or roles for the activity (structured group meetings, group guidelines), cohesiveness, and leadership (facilitators).

recreation and social skill-building groups, reminiscent of early group work. Social skills groups with elementary-age children (LeCroy, 1992), hoops groups with adolescent males (Pollio, 1995), and reminiscence and motivation groups for older adults (Link, 1997) are three examples.

By the 1930s and 1940s, formal organizations were promoting group work. In 1935, the Group Work Section of the National Conference on Social Work emerged, and in 1937 the American Association for the Study of Group Work formed. The American Association of Group Workers, formed in 1946, later merged with other organizations to become the National Association of Social Workers (NASW).

During World War II, group work became popular in hospitals and other clinical settings, resulting in some tension between group workers and caseworkers. Following the war, the philosophy of group work shifted from a strengths to a more problem-focused orientation. Nevertheless, group workers continued to attempt to influence the social work profession as a whole. During the 1960s and 1970s, social work education focused on teaching group work, and some students even majored in "group work." But then group work content declined as social work education shifted its focus to individuals and families. Ironically, at the same time, joining groups became more common in the United States. The 1980s and 1990s saw the rise of mutual aid groups (Gitterman & Shulman, 1994), today a popular type of social work group.

Today, in a managed care era, groups are viewed as a financially prudent method of service delivery (Roller, 1997). In addition, empirical studies have shown the effectiveness of groups in addressing a number of social, health, and emotional problems, such as mental illness (Yalom, 1995) and cancer (Spiegel & Classen, 2000). Group work content is coming back into the social work curriculum, and social work students are being exposed to group work through their field placements. Furthermore, graduating students have informed me that potential employers ask if they have had course content on group work.

A number of scholars have established classifications for groups encountered in social work (see, e.g., Corey & Corey, 1992, and Zastrow, 1997). This chapter focuses on five: therapy groups, mutual aid groups, psychoeducational groups, self-help groups, and task groups. Exhibit 11.3 compares these five types of groups on several major features of small groups—purpose, leadership, size of membership, duration—and gives examples of each. As you read about them, remember that groups may not fall exclusively into one category; rather, they may share elements of several group types. For example, a group for parents and friends of seriously mentally ill persons may include psychoeducational material about the nature of mental illness and its impact on family members, provide mutual aid to its members through discussion of taboo areas, and offer a therapeutic component in the examination of family patterns and dynamics.

Therapy Groups

One common type of group is known as the **therapy group,** or psychotherapy group. Group psychotherapy uses the group milieu to enable individuals to work out emotional and behavioral difficulties. The individuals in the group often reproduce their emotional and behavioral problems within the group setting, thus providing the leader and group members an opportunity to provide feedback about those emotional and behavioral problems (Reid, 1997). An example of this type of group is a therapy group for adult incest survivors.

Therapy groups typically have fewer members and meet for a longer duration than self-help, psychoeducational, or mutual aid groups. Such a group may have six or fewer members, may be led by a person who considers herself or himself to be a therapist,

Exhibit 11.3
Types of Groups

Type of Group	Main Purpose	Leadership	Typical Number of Members	Duration	Examples
Therapy	Uses group modality to assist individuals to resolve emotional and behavioral problems.	Typically led by a trained clinician or psychotherapist.	Typically small in size; sometimes six or fewer members.	Brief therapy groups are usually 6 weeks or less. Long-term psychotherapy groups can last years.	Groups for college students run by university counseling centers; groups for adolescent male sexual offenders.
Mutual aid	Uses mutual aid processes to create a helping environment within the group milieu.	Typically led by a facilitator who may be a professional or a layperson trained to lead the group. The leader may or may not have experienced the issue on which the group is focused.	These groups may be small in number (less than 5 persons) or may be large (12 or more), especially if run in a drop-in format.	Drop-in mutual aid groups may be ongoing for a number of years with members coming in and out of the group. Time-limited mutual aid groups typically run for between 4 and 12 weeks.	Groups for cancer survivors; groups in schools for children whose parents are going through a divorce.
Psychoeducational	Focuses on the provision of information about an experience or problem.	Typically led by a trained professional who is knowledgeable about the subject.	Limiting the group size is usually not as critical with these types of groups because of their purpose.	Psychoeducation groups may be offered once on a regular schedule; they might be offered in a series of sessions (e.g., a 4-week educational series); or they be offered on an as-needed basis.	Groups for couples preparing to adopt a child; groups to teach parents how to use adaptive equipment for children with disabilities.

(continued)

EXHIBIT 11.3
Types of Groups (continued)

Type of Group	Main Purpose	Leadership	Typical Number of Members	Duration	Examples
Self-help	Uses the commonality of the problem or issue to build social support among members.	Typically led by a lay person who has experience with the problem (e.g., a person in recovery from alcohol and drug addition).	Typically, since self-help groups operate on a drop-in basis, the group size is not limited.	Most often self-help groups are run on a drop-in basis; however, some self-help groups may be offered in a time-limited format.	Twelve-step groups (e.g., AA, ACOA, NA).
Task	Created to accomplish a specific task.	These groups may be led by professionals or nonprofessionals; leaders may be appointed or elected.	Often limited in size in order to successfully accomplish the task.	Meet until the task has been accomplished.	A committee to examine low-income housing needs that is instructed to submit a report of their findings to the city council.

may meet weekly for a year or more, and may involve intrapsychic exploration of thoughts and emotions. Talk or verbal therapy groups are not the only type of therapy groups. Increasingly popular are art therapy groups, which have demonstrated the standard therapeutic factors of verbal therapy groups as well as some factors unique to art therapy (Shechtman & Perl-Dekel, 2000). In addition, therapy groups do not necessarily meet for long periods. **Brief treatment models**, which usually last 6 weeks or less, are becoming increasingly popular in a managed care environment.

Mutual Aid Groups

In **mutual aid groups,** the members meet to help one another deal with common problems. The members of the group thus become as important to its success as the facilitator is (Gitterman & Shulman, 1994). In Terry's story, we witness many benefits of mutual aid groups:

- *Sharing data*: coming-out stories, events in the lesbian community

- *Engaging in a dialectical process of discovery*: theories about sexual orientation, insight into when one first felt one was not heterosexual

- *Discussing taboo subjects*: the "sex questions" envelope

- *Realizing that one is not alone* (all in the same boat): others who are not heterosexual and have had similar feelings regarding coming-out and disclosure

- *Finding support*: a place to be oneself in a homophobic society

- *Making mutual demands*: gentle challenges to internalized homophobia and unhealthy coping mechanisms, such as alcohol use or thoughts of suicide, that lesbian and bisexual women may use as a way to live in two worlds

- *Problem solving*: disclosure decisions for individuals and the larger issue of self-disclosure of a stigmatized identity

- *Rehearsing new behaviors*: role-playing of disclosure scenarios or confrontations with people who make homophobic jokes

- *Finding strength in numbers*: pride march

In general, mutual aid groups are led by someone, either a professional or a trained individual, who identifies with the population that the group targets. For example, the two facilitators of the women's coming-out group self-identify as lesbians. In fact, some mutual aid groups form as an alternative to professionally led therapy groups. There is no requirement, however, that in order to be an effective leader, one must have "been there."

The groups may be time-limited (for example, a 10-week group for siblings of children with disabilities) or ongoing (such as a weekly support group for incarcerated males).

Mutual aid groups also have the potential for activism. A group of persons may meet initially to gain support and share concerns but may transform some of their healing energy into social change efforts. For instance, mutual aid groups for battered women may attend a Take Back the Night march (to protest violence against women) as a group and then courageously approach the microphone to speak about their own experiences of victimization and empowerment.

Psychoeducational Groups

Psychoeducational groups, in which social workers and other professionals share their expertise with group members, are becoming more common in the United States. The topics include problems such as substance abuse and divorce as well as more general interests, such as child development or the aging process. Those who participate are primarily looking for information rather than treatment of emotional and behavioral problems. Thus, the format of group meetings may be a lecture by the group leader or a guest speaker with minimal group discussion. The group could be a one-time workshop or it could last several sessions.

Although a psychoeducational group is not a therapy group, psychoeducational groups can be therapeutic when members share feelings and concerns. An example would be a one-time group meeting for family and friends of persons in a drug rehabilitation center. The stated purpose may be to provide education about the recovery process to family members and friends, but during the session, group members may share feelings about their loved one's addiction and how it has affected their lives.

Self-Help Groups

In general, **self-help groups** are not professionally led, although a professional may serve in the role of consultant. An informal leader may emerge in a self-help group, or leadership may be rotated among the membership. Self-help groups are often used as a supplement to professional treatment. For example, someone who is receiving outpatient substance abuse treatment may be referred to Alcoholics Anonymous; someone in a family preservation program may be referred to Parents Anonymous. Self-help groups often have no limit on their life span and have rotating membership (people come and go from the group).

Self-help groups have several benefits (Corey & Corey, 1987):

Self-help groups serve a critical need for certain populations that is not met by professional mental-health workers. Such groups, composed of people with a common interest, provide a support system that helps reduce psychological stress and gives the members the incentive to begin changing their life. Self-help groups stress a common identity based on a common life situation to a far greater extent than do most other groups. The members share their experiences, learn from one another, offer suggestions for new members, and provide encouragement for people who sometimes see no hope for their future. (p. 13)

Self-help groups offer their members some of the social functions mentioned in the beginning of this chapter—a chance to meet others and have meaningful interactions, a place to feel as though one belongs and to give support to others. In short, self-help groups offer a social support system. As discussed in Chapter 5, social support has been shown to help people prevent and overcome disease and to maintain good psychological health (Wasserman & Danforth, 1988). In addition, some believe that attending a self-help group is less stigmatizing than a "treatment" or "therapy" group, the latter being more often associated with those who are seriously ill or have major problems in living. Self-help groups also demonstrate helping characteristics (e.g., universality, support, and communication of experiential knowledge) similar to those of mutual aid groups. However, in one study, self-help group members reported more satisfaction with the group and gave higher evaluations for most of the helping characteristics than mutual aid group members did (Schiff & Bargal, 2000).

Another benefit of self-help groups is their potential for activism. In a popular manual used in domestic violence programs (Duluth Domestic Abuse Intervention Project, n.d.), one of the steps in the group process is titled "Options for Actions." These options include personal, institutional, and cultural activities. A vigil in honor of battered women killed by their assailants is an example of such an action. One study found that parents of children with cancer who were members of self-help groups were significantly more involved than other parents of such children in working to improve the medical system in which their children were involved (Chesney & Chesler, 1993).

Task Groups

Most of us have been involved in task groups, such as a committee at school or at work or a task force in the community. In social work practice, task groups are often short term and are formed to accomplish specific goals and objectives. Task groups are used frequently among social workers involved in planning and administration roles but are much less common in other social work roles. An example would be a needs assessment committee formed at an agency to determine the problems and concerns of the population the agency serves. Although members of other types of groups may take on tasks (e.g., researching a subject and presenting it to the group), the **task group** is created with the express purpose of achieving some specific task.

Task groups are often formally led by professionals who are appointed or elected to chair the task group. Leaders may be chosen because of their position in the agency or their expertise in the area.

In task groups as well as other kinds of groups, members fulfill what are commonly referred to as "task and maintenance" roles. The task specialist focuses on the goals set by the group and the tasks needed to accomplish them. These may include providing information to aid group discussion, giving directions for how to proceed with a task, or summarizing members' ideas. Maintenance roles refer to those that enhance the social and emotional bonding within the group. These include inquiring about how close members feel to each other, encouraging open and respectful discussion of conflicts, and inviting reluctant members to participate in group discussion (Zastrow, 1997).

Dimensions of Group Structure

Terry's coming-out group serves a variety of functions. But that one group cannot provide for all of Terry's needs. She also belongs to a group of friends with whom she attends social functions, a group of coworkers, and a softball team. Each group plays a unique part in Terry's life. For example, the softball team provides an outlet for competition and team building, and the work group offers a context for achievement and accomplishment. But all these groups are obviously structured quite differently. They can be categorized along three dimensions:

1. *How they develop.* The types of groups encountered in social work have typically been organized for a purpose. Such **formed groups** have a defined purpose and come about through the efforts of outsiders, such as an agency (Reid, 1997, p. 10). Examples of formed groups include not only therapy groups, mutual aid groups, psychoeducational groups, self-help groups, and task groups but also such groups as college classes, PTAs, and choirs. **Natural groups,** in contrast, "develop in a spontaneous manner on the basis of friendship, location, or some naturally occurring event. Without external initiative, the members simply come together" (Reid, 1997, p. 10). Peer groups, street gangs, and a group of patients who have befriended each other in a psychiatric hospital are examples of natural groups.

2. *How long they last.* A **time-limited group** is one with a set time for termination; an **ongoing group** has no defined endpoint. Both formed and natural groups may be time limited or ongoing, short or long term. A formed group, for example, may last for a 2-hour period (e.g., a focus group) or for months or years (e.g., Terry's coming-out group). A natural group may last a lifetime (a group of close friends from high school) or just through some event (tablemates at a workshop).

3. *How they determine membership.* Finally, both natural and formed groups may be open, closed, or fluctuate between open and closed. **Open groups** permit the addition of new members throughout the group's life. In **closed groups**, the minimum and maximum size of the group is determined in advance, before the group begins or as it is being formed, and others are prohibited from joining once that limit is reached. A group can start off open and then become closed. An example would be a group of persons who have been attending a drop-in support group for women in abusive relationships who decide after a few months that they would like to close the group to do some more intensive work in group sessions. Alternatively, a closed group may open up, as when the number of members has decreased considerably and new members are needed to keep the group going.

These three dimensions of group structure interact in complex ways. The coming-out group that Terry attends, although it is a formed group, is open and ongoing. Attendance has ranged from 3 to 18 persons, and the group may continue indefinitely. An example of a closed natural group is an informal group of middle school girls who call themselves the "lunch bunch." The five girls eat lunch together every day and have let it be known among their peers that no others are welcome. An example of a time-limited closed group is a 12-week group for men and women who are going through a divorce. Interested persons must register prior to the group's beginning, and once the first session begins, no new members are permitted.

An example of an ongoing, open, formed group is a bereavement group that meets every Tuesday evening at the local hospital and allows any person who would like support to join the group on any Tuesday. Another example is a group that spontaneously meets at the basketball courts on Sunday afternoons to play ball. Whoever shows up can get into a game, with no predetermined limit to the number of people allowed to play.

Particular structures and types of groups may lend themselves especially well to group work with certain populations. For example, mutual aid groups of a time-limited or ongoing nature are recommended when working with abused women (Duluth Domestic Abuse Intervention Project, n.d.); groups modeled along the stages of recovery are recommended when doing group work with persons who are addicted to alcohol or other drugs (Rugel, 1991). Funding and space limitations, lack of personnel, and the agency's philosophy of treatment (e.g., brief vs. long term) may also influence the structure and type of group that an agency provides.

Group Composition

Another important element of small groups is their composition—the types of people who are members. Three issues regarding group composition are discussed in this section: inclusiveness/exclusiveness, heterogeneity/homogeneity, and cohesiveness.

Inclusion Versus Exclusion

Terry's coming-out group is relatively inclusive. It is open to any woman who is lesbian, bisexual, or questioning her sexual identity. The members self identify, and the facilitators do not have criteria for determining whether a person is lesbian, bisexual, or questioning. In contrast, the heterosexual couples with whom Terry formerly associated make up a relatively exclusive group. Very few new couples have joined the group over the years, and in fact Terry herself is excluded now that she is no longer part of a heterosexual couple.

Natural groups often have implicit or explicit rules about who gets to belong and who doesn't. Take the previous example of the lunch bunch: the girls determined who would belong. Formed groups have rules of membership too. A sorority or fraternity establishes a process to select who will belong. A group for persons with serious mental illness includes those persons who either define themselves as such or are defined as such by powerful others. Space constraints and personnel issues may determine who gets to belong: the room may only hold eight people, only one social worker may be hired to facilitate the group. Task groups may be composed of those with the most relevant experience to contribute, those who have been appointed by a person in authority, or those who show the greatest interest in the task. Effective task groups often include members with a variety of resources for the task at hand.

Heterogeneity Versus Homogeneity

The degree of heterogeneity/homogeneity of groups may vary along several dimensions, such as age, race, sexual orientation, gender, level of education, coping style, religion, socioeconomic status, disabilities, and problem areas or strengths. Usually groups are homogeneous on one or a few of these dimensions and heterogeneous on the rest. For example, Terry's group is homogeneous regarding gender and sexual orientation but quite heterogeneous on other dimensions, including race, age, socioeconomic status, disabilities, educational status, occupation, age at first awareness of sexual orientation, and amount of disclosure of sexual orientation to others.

Conflict perspective　　　Often heterogeneity/homogeneity is a matter of perception (Chau, 1990; Dufrene & Coleman, 1992). For example, in several studies of racially mixed groups, European American group members had a different perception from African American members regarding the racial balance of the group (Davis, 1984). If the group was in proportion to the population of African Americans in the geographic area, then the European American members perceived the group as balanced. If the group had equal numbers of white and black members, the black members viewed the group as balanced. The white members, however, perceived the group as imbalanced, because the number of African Americans exceeded the psychological threshold of European American members.

Another interesting finding is that proportional representation acts as a significant influence on levels of participation and leadership for those in the numerical minority. In one study, Asian persons showed higher levels of participation and leadership skills in work groups that were racially balanced or all Asian compared to Asians in white-dominated groups (Li, Karakowsky, & Siegel, 1999).

Which is better for group work, heterogeneity or homogeneity? For "long-term intensive interactional group therapy," heterogeneous groups appear to be better (Yalom, 1995, p. 255). Homogeneous groups, on the other hand, are often better for "support or symptomatic relief over a brief period" and "for individuals with monosymptomatic complaints or for the noncompliant patient" (p. 255). Homogeneous groups tend to build commitment more quickly, offer more immediate support to members, and have better attendance and less conflict.

Psychodynamic perspective

Homogeneous groups are generally not beneficial for long-term psychotherapeutic work that involves personality change, because they tend to remain at superficial levels and don't challenge individuals' behavioral patterns and dynamics as much as heterogeneous groups (Yalom, 1995). However, homogeneous groups based on such characteristics as race or sex may be an exception. In group therapy for black women, homogeneous membership allows for more intensive exploration of common problems (Boyd-Franklin, 1987). In a study of 32 group counseling clients at a university counseling center, group members in homogeneous groups (by gender, race, or presenting problem) reported higher levels of commitment to and satisfaction with the group than the heterogeneous group members (Perron & Sedlacek, 2000).

Even heterogeneous groups usually have a homogeneous factor: the purpose or common goal of the group. Differences among people may be overridden by the overall function of groups—a place for people to seek human connection and a sense of belonging (Wasserman & Danforth, 1988). I am reminded of a friend who spoke to me of her experiences attending a support group for family members who had lost their loved ones. As the only African American group member, she said she felt like a "fly in a milk carton," but her fellow group members were the only people she knew who truly understood her grief.

An interesting research finding is that the heterogeneity/homogeneity issue takes on less importance the briefer and more structured the group. Compositional issues are more significant in groups that are less structured and that focus on group interaction (Yalom, 1995). In Terry's group, the homogeneity of sexual orientation provides the safety and support to explore the heterogeneous aspects of the group.

In natural groups, heterogeneity or homogeneity may be affected by such variables as the location (some geographic areas are highly homogeneous), preferences of group members (people tend to form natural groups with those with whom they feel some connection), and social norms and values (acceptance or condemnation of mixed groups).

For task or work groups, heterogeneity has been shown to positively influence group productivity. Among the 42 student project groups examined in one study, racial/ethnic diversity was positively associated with group efficacy (Sargent & Sue-Chan, 2001). The lowest levels of group efficacy occurred in groups with low commitment and less racial/ethnic diversity; conversely, the highest efficacy was in the high-commitment/high-diversity groups.

Another study of work groups assessed diversity by race, age, sex, and functional background in terms of their contribution to quality of innovation (the usefulness of an idea and/or the impact it might have on a business) and quantity of innovation (the number of new ideas that the group produces) (Cady & Valentine, 1999). These four dimensions of diversity had no significant impact on quality of innovation. There were significant differences in quantity of innovation, however. Teams with greater sex diversity had a lower quantity of innovation; teams with greater racial diversity had a higher quantity of ideas. In other words, as the sexual diversity of teams increases, the number of new ideas decreases, whereas when the racial diversity of teams increases, the number of new ideas increases.

Cohesiveness

One important variable related to group composition is **group cohesiveness—**group identity, commitment, and sense of belonging. Groups with a "greater sense of solidarity, or 'we-ness,' value the group more highly, and will defend it against internal and external threats" (Yalom, 1995, p. 48). Groups that are cohesive tend to have higher rates of attendance, participation, and mutual support. But cohesiveness does not mean the absence of conflict or dislike among group members. Even a cohesive group may sometimes experience bickering, frustration, or alienation.

Cohesion is thought to be dynamic: it changes in extent and form throughout the life of a group. Thus, measuring the degree of group cohesiveness across different contexts can be a challenge (see Carron & Brawley, 2000).

Some groups may develop rituals or habits to increase cohesiveness among members. For example, a gang member may receive a tattoo as an initiation rite, the group may name itself (the "lunch bunch"), a member who has been in the group for 6 months may receive a pin, or group members may be expected to call another member when they are having difficulty.

Basic Group Processes

To be effective, group workers need tools for understanding the group processes in which they participate. Group processes are those unique interactions between group members that result from being in a group together. How people behave in groups and why they are of interest to us is because we spend much of our time in groups and groups have a strong influence on our behaviors.

Theories of Group Processes

The fields of social psychology and sociology have been in the forefront of empirical research on group processes. Three of the major theories of group processes are discussed in this section: expectation states theory, status characteristics theory, and exchange theory. Each one helps us understand why and how certain members of a group develop and maintain more power than other members to influence the group's activities.

Rational choice
perspective

Expectation States Theory. Joan and Bob are both members of a task force formed in a housing project community to increase healthy social interactions between the children and beautify the grounds. Joan, a person who is known to be artistic, makes a suggestion that the group involve kids in painting murals on communal buildings and then hold a contest for the best mural. Bob, a person who is not known to be artistic, suggests that the group solicit volunteer contributions from local artists who would donate paintings and other artwork to display on the inside of buildings. **Expectation states theory** suggests that group members will be more willing to go along with Joan's idea than with Bob's because of Joan's greater perceived expertise in artistic matters.

Expectation states theory relies on the concept of **performance expectations**— predictions of how well an act will accomplish a group's task (Meeker, 1994). Group members may have high-performance expectations (the act will help them successfully complete a task) or low-performance expectations (the act will fail to help them complete the task), or mixed expectations.

Group members who have contributed successful suggestions for task accomplishment in the past tend to carry more power and prestige within the group. They are viewed as people "in the know" or people "who have good ideas." Thus, task force members expect Joan, as an artistic individual, to suggest an idea for beautifying the grounds that will be successful. On the other hand, they question the worthiness of Bob's suggestion because of his limited artistic talent. Joan has more power and prestige within the group on this particular subject than Bob.

In Terry's coming-out group, Beverly carries some influence. She has attended for quite a long time and is one of the core members who come to the group consistently.

As an influential member, she is expected to articulate and enforce the group's rules and to assist new members in acclimating to the group. Group members expect Beverly to share her insights about the coming-out process, and perceive her as a knowledgeable person, especially when discussing issues faced by African American lesbians.

In mutual aid groups, certain members may carry more influence than others because of the expectations others have about their contributions. Group members seem to listen to certain members who are expected to offer wise advice or who have the most experience with a certain problem. On the flip side, some group members are consistently ignored or carry little influence with other members. These may be persons who are considered suspect by the rest of the group or who are perceived as having less to offer than others.

Status Characteristics Theory. In the coming-out group, Beverly is perceived as a knowledgeable person regarding coming out and the unique issues faced by African American lesbians. But in another setting, the color of Beverly's skin might negatively influence how she is perceived by other people. Stereotypes about African Americans may cause other people to question Beverly's interests, skills, or values. Such stereotypes are the key to **status characteristics theory,** in which the power and prestige of group members are correlated with their status.

Social constructionist perspective

A central concept in this theory is the **status characteristic**—an attribute considered potentially relevant to the group's task. "Status characteristics reflect cultural beliefs that may or may not be objectively true. . . . [I]t merely is assumed that if people believe something is true, they will act as if it were true, and thus it will tend to be true in its consequences" (Balkwell, 1994, pp. 124-135). For example, if people expect that someone using a wheelchair is incapable of playing basketball for a charity fund-raiser, then they will act as if a person using a wheelchair is unable to play basketball. They may disqualify that person from playing, thereby demoralizing the individual with the disability and preventing the person from contributing to the success of the fund-raiser.

Sometimes, status characteristics are not initially evident. Group members will then search for status differentials as the group interacts. As status characteristics become more obvious, the power and prestige order in the group is formed.

Gender is an influential status characteristic in our society, perhaps because it is so easily discerned. In mixed-gender groups, males have greater participation and influence than females (Balkwell, 1994; Garvin & Reed, 1983), and males or females with traditionally masculine personality traits are likely to exhibit more dominant behavior (Seibert & Gruenfeld, 1992). In same-sex groups, gender is not an initial status differential; instead, members develop expectations of each other based on other status characteristics, such as education, race, or experience. Regardless of gender, a person's perceived ability also affects performance expectations. For example, a female may be perceived as incapable of handling a complex mechanical problem in a work group, but she may be able to develop influence if she shows that she can accomplish the task successfully (Schneider & Cook, 1995).

One assumption of status characteristics theory is that people rely on their stereotypes in the absence of proof that those characteristics are irrelevant (Balkwell, 1994, p. 126). In our example of assumptions people may make about persons using wheelchairs, the burden of proof would be on the persons using wheelchairs to demonstrate that they could indeed play basketball, thus establishing the inapplicability of others' assumptions about the disability.

Rational choice perspective

Exchange Theory. Sometimes in coming-out groups, those who have been out for the longest time have implicit power over those newly out, the baby dykes. A "let me show you the ropes and tell you what this is about" attitude can be used to gain power and influence over another person and to create dependency: "You need me to help you understand what you are getting yourself into." But social power can also be used in a positive way in a coming-out group, as when those who have been in the lesbian community for a long time offer support and information to others with the intention of providing mutual aid. To understand power as a social commodity, we can look to exchange theory (Thibaut & Kelley, 1959), which assumes that human interactions can be understood in terms of rewards and costs.

According to *exchange theory,* social power is what determines who gets valued resources in groups and whether those resources are perceived as being distributed in a just manner. Conflicts within the group often revolve around power issues—those who want the power in the group, those who have power and don't want to give it up, and those who don't want others to have power over them.

Groups are particularly vulnerable to conflicts over power because social power arises within the context of the group itself rather than being an innate quality of an individual. "Sometimes it [power] works within a relationship between two people, but often it works within the complex relationships among a set of three, four, or many more people. Different primary and secondary social networks, where variations occur in who interacts with whom, make up the social situations in which power emerges and produces effects in predictable ways" (Stolte, 1994, p. 173).

Power not only determines the distribution of group resources, but it also influences people's expectations of others' abilities, even when the power results from structural conditions (such as luck) and not from innate personal ability (Lovaglia, 1995). Emotion also influences perceived power and influence, regardless of status. If a person has negative emotions toward a high-status person, the power of the high-status person will lessen (Lovaglia, 1995).

Power differences among group members can create status differences, but not necessarily. Group members may rate more highly the abilities and influences of high-power members, which may in turn influence expectations for high-power members, but negative feelings toward high-power members may mitigate their influence.

Conflict perspective

The exercise of social power often brings with it a concern about justice, fairness, and equality. Most of us would agree that power should not be exercised to the special benefit or detriment of some group members. However, justice is a relative rather than absolute term. Any two persons may have quite different ideas about what constitutes justice. For some, justice would be an equal distribution of resources; for others, justice would be an equitable (but not necessarily equal) distribution.

How persons evaluate the equity of a situation depends on such factors as cultural values, self-interest, the situation, the relationships between those affected, and personal characteristics (Hegtvedt, 1994). People tend to operate more from self-interest in impersonal conditions than when they have personal bonds with others. The status of the person for whom justice claims are being considered also affects the definition of justice, the perception of injustice, and the resolution of injustices. In addition, what may be perceived as fair on an individual level may be perceived as unfair when viewed from a group perspective. For example, suppose a group member is in crisis and asks for extended time in the group. The other five group members agree to give the person an extra 10 minutes because of the crisis. This extension, however, requires each group member to give up 2 minutes of his or her floor time. Giving one individual an extra 10 minutes may not seem like much, but that one action has a cost for five other group members. And what if one group member decides that he or she has a pressing issue to discuss and does not want to give up the 2 minutes? How the group would resolve this dilemma relates to its spoken and unspoken guidelines for handling matters of justice within the group.

Group Development

To understand the unique nature of groups and why they are effective in helping people, we need to examine the ways groups develop. Two common ways of viewing group development are by the stages they pass through and by the processes that facilitate the work of a group. This section provides a brief overview of stage theories and models and then discusses an example of the analysis of processes that facilitate the work of groups.

Developmental perspective

Stage Theories and Models. A variety of scholars have attempted to delineate the life cycle of small groups. But researchers who focus on the stages of group development have reached no consensus as to how many stages there are, the order in which they appear, or the nature of those stages. Exhibit 11.4 displays seven of the models commonly cited in social work literature to describe the development of groups. Note, however, that controlled experiments investigating group stages are rare. Most theories of group

EXHIBIT 11.4

Stage Models of Group Development

Life-Span Metaphor	Bales (1950)	Tuckman (1965)	Sarri & Galinsky (1967)	Hartford (1971)	Garland, Jones, & Kolodny (1973)	Northen (1988)	Levine (1991)
Conception			Origin	Pregroup planning		Planning and intake	
Birth	Orientation	Forming	Formation	Convening	Preaffiliation	Orientation	Parallel relations / Authority crisis
Childhood			Intermediate I	Group formulation			Inclusion
Adolescence	Evaluation	Storming / Norming	Revision / Intermediate II	Integration, disintegration and conflict, reintegration or reorganization, synthesis	Power and control / Intimacy	Exploring and testing	Intimacy crisis
Adulthood (Maturity)	Decision making	Performing	Maturation	Group functioning and group maintenance	Differentiation	Problem solving	Mutuality
Death			Termination	Pretermination / Termination	Separation	Termination	Separation crisis / Termination

Source: Reid, 1997.

stages have been developed by observing patterns and changes in groups, usually after the group has disbanded. Because most of the stage theories have been based on studies of time-limited, closed groups, they may not even be applicable to open-ended or ongoing groups.

Most stage theorists agree, however, on some basic principles: groups don't necessarily move through each stage in order, groups may revert to an earlier stage, stages are not distinct entities but may be a blend or combination, the group's development is influenced by the leader and the members, and groups do not need to reach the most advanced developmental stage in order to be effective (Reid, 1997).

Process Models. If stage theories are inadequate for explaining how groups develop, what are we to use instead? The chief alternative is process models, which identify what goes on in groups and how those processes affect group members and their interactions. The advantage of process analysis is that it focuses on the interactions among group members rather than creating norms for development.

A good example of a process model is the one developed by Irving Yalom, one of the best-known group psychotherapists. Yalom (1995) describes 11 factors that operate in therapeutic groups to shape their functioning. These factors are listed and defined in Exhibit 11.5.

Some of Yalom's therapeutic factors may operate to some extent in groups other than therapy groups. For example, universality and imparting of information are two of the mutual aid processes described earlier in this chapter.

In addition, certain factors may be more significant at particular stages of group development than at others. One study of 12 time-limited outpatient psychotherapy groups found that the development of cohesion varied according to the stage (or phase) of psychotherapy (Budman, Soldz, Demby, Davis, & Merry, 1993). For example, in the earliest stage of the group, members sharing issues about their lives outside the group built cohesion; however, too much focus on the therapist during this stage tended to be counter-cohesive. In Terry's coming-out group, several therapeutic factors are evident at different times. When group members feel they can trust each other, catharsis and interpersonal learning are likely. When new members attend the group, they often desire to experience an instillation of hope, universality, imparting of information, and development of socializing techniques.

Psychodynamic perspective, Social behavioral perspective, Humanistic perspective

Group Dynamics

The overall development of the group is overlaid with patterns of interactions that can be characterized as **group dynamics**—such issues as how leaders are appointed or emerge, which roles members take in groups, and how communication networks affect interactions in groups.

Exhibit 11.5

Therapeutic Factors
Involved in Group
Development

Therapeutic Factor	Definition
Instillation of hope	Confidence and optimism in the ability of the group and individual members to resolve issues and grow
Universality	Sense that others share similar problems and feelings and that one is not alone
Imparting of information	Leader's and group members' sharing of information and guidance around problems and concerns
Altruism	Benefits experienced when one realizes that one has helped another person
Corrective recapitulation of primary family group	(Re)experience of relationship patterns like those in one's family of origin while learning different approaches to relationships
Development of socializing techniques	Examination of patterns of interacting with others and acquisition of new social skills
Imitative behavior	Observation of how other group members handle their problems and feelings and recognition of how those methods apply to one's own situation
Interpersonal learning	Process of learning about oneself through interaction with others
Group cohesiveness	Sense of belonging that group members have and sense of acceptance and support they feel in the group
Catharsis	Sharing of deep and sometimes painful emotions with nonjudgmental acceptance from group members
Existential factors	Search for meaning and purpose in one's life

Source: Yalom, 1995.

Formal and Informal Leadership. Formal leaders are appointed or elected to lead the group by virtue of such characteristics as their position in the organization or community and their interest or expertise in relation to the group's focus. Informal leaders may emerge in groups where no formal leader exists or in ones where formal leaders are established. In the latter case, a group member may feel more comfortable in a helper or leader role than as a client in the group, thereby mimicking the actions of the formal leader.

Both formal and informal group leaders have a binary focus: the individuals in the group and the group as a whole. **Task-oriented leaders** facilitate problem-solving within the context of the group; **process-oriented leaders** identify and manage group relationships (Reid, 1997; Yalom, 1995). Any given leader usually fluctuates from one role to the other, although people tend to be either more task oriented or more process oriented.

In natural groups, leaders may be formal or informal. A friendly softball game at the diamond on a Saturday morning may evolve into a complex hierarchy of leaders and followers as various activities are negotiated—who is on what team, who bats first, how long the game will last, who will decide batting order, and so on—and such process issues as team morale and cohesiveness are promoted.

Systems perspective

Leaders of formed groups also take on various roles, depending on the purpose and structure of the group. A facilitator for a group for children with ADHD is a formal leader who may provide structured activities, support, and guidance for the children. Similarly, the leader of a one-time debriefing group may provide support and information to rescue workers after a fire. Informal leaders of formed groups might include a person who evolves into a leadership role in a work group assigned to some project.

Groups often have coleaders, or one appointed leader and one or more group members who serve as self- or group-appointed coleaders. The coming-out group has two facilitators, both of whom are self-appointed coleaders. Doris is a 52-year-old African American lesbian in a long-term relationship. She tends to be the more nurturing facilitator and has a degree in social work. Marie is a European American, 28, who came out during high school. She considers herself a lesbian/gay activist and works at a clinic for persons with HIV/AIDS. She is more task oriented and does much of the record keeping and information sharing in the group.

Researchers have made a wide range of discoveries about the types of people who tend to become group leaders:

■ They are likely to have personality traits of dominance, friendliness, task orientation, persuasiveness, and intelligence.

■ First-born persons are likely to become task-oriented leaders; later-borns will likely be relationship-oriented leaders (Hare et al., 1994).

Conflict perspective

■ Gender, class, and race influence leadership (both who takes leadership and the perception of leaders by group members). Status differences based on gender influence the behaviors of both male and female group members, including their reactions to male and female group leaders (Garvin & Reed, 1983). Both males and females tend to respect male leadership more quickly and easily. Males in a female-led group tend to challenge the leader(s) and expect female leaders to be more nurturing than male leaders. Persons of color may distrust white leaders "from the system" (Davis, 1995, p. 49), because such leaders may be perceived as not being sensitive or responsive to minorities' needs. In addition, the significant difference in life experiences of persons of color and whites may create a wide gap between white (often middle-class) leaders and group members who are persons of color or poor. White leaders of groups that include minorities may want to prepare themselves for three questions: "1. Are we people of goodwill? 2. Do we have sufficient mastery/skills to help them? 3. Do we understand their social realities?" (Davis, 1995, p. 53). White group leaders should also remember that their behavior should be purposeful and they should demonstrate respect, examine their own attitudes and beliefs regarding clients who are different from them, use culturally and class-appropriate techniques, know the resources that exist in the larger society that may be of help to their group members, make every effort to "get off to a good start" (p. 55), and expect success.

■   Communication content, more than gender, influences leadership emergence in task-oriented groups. One study found task-relevant communication to be the sole significant predictor of emerged leadership, with no significant gender differences in the production of task-relevant communication (Hawkins, 1995).

■   In general, leaders who are elected by members tend to be more favorably perceived than leaders who are self-appointed or appointed by others.

■   Informal leaders may emerge in groups where formal leaders are present. Sometimes an informal leader takes the role of "assistant therapist," the person who "asks leading questions of other members, analyzes behavior, and is always ready with an interpretation" (Reid, 1997, p. 246).

Formal and Informal Roles. In addition to formal and informal leadership roles within the group, group members serve a variety of other roles. Those roles serve a purpose for the group as a whole and simultaneously fulfill group members' personal needs (Reid, 1997, p. 245). Thus, a person's group role often mirrors roles in other arenas. For instance, the group clown is often a clown in other areas of life.

Keep in mind, however, that role is only one element of social interaction: "The other variables include the biological systems of the actors, their personalities, the structure and process of the small groups and organizations that they belong to, and the society, culture, and environment in which these are embedded" (Hare, 1994, pp. 443-444). In other words, role is only one part of the picture.

Systems perspective

Roles of group members may have both positive and negative aspects. The peacemaker, for example, may serve the group function of reducing conflict and anxiety within the group—but perhaps at the cost of suppressing efforts to work through or resolve conflict within the group. The clown or jester reduces anxiety and stress in the group by joking but also enables the group to avoid a painful subject. The scapegoat may remind group members of parts of themselves that they deny or of which they are fearful. The rescuer, who jumps in to defend anyone who appears to be confronted in the group, may be uncomfortable with others' pain or with unfair attacks against the group scapegoat but may also keep the group from sanctioning an unacceptable violation of group norms (Reid, 1997).

From a therapeutic perspective, Yalom (1995) has categorized several types of "problem members," whom he refers to as "problem patients": the monopolist, the silent member, the boring member, the help-rejecting complainer, the psychotic member, the characterologically difficult member, and the borderline member. Yalom observes that he has yet to encounter an unproblematic member; each member has some problems-in-living. Furthermore, the behavior of the problem patient does not exist in a vacuum; "that patient always abides in a dynamic equilibrium with a group that permits or encourages such behavior" (p. 370). The behaviors of the problem members are attempts to cope with underlying feelings. The monopolist, for instance, talks incessantly to handle anxiety and to avoid talking about "real" feelings.

Social constructionist perspective

Roles are not necessarily fixed and rigid. Rather, they develop through give-and-take within the group (Salazar, 1996). Roles are also a social construction. They reflect group members' expectations and both produce and reproduce elements of the social structure.

Communication Networks. Groups function more effectively when the members are able to communicate easily and with competence. Social workers who lead groups can set the tone for the group by being clear, direct, and compassionate in their own communication. The free flow of ideas among members enhances productivity, particularly in task groups.

Communication networks are the links among members—who talks to whom, how information is transmitted, whether communication between members is direct or uses a go-between. Sociograms may be used to depict the physical arrangement of these communication channels. Typically, the formal leader occupies the central position in a communication network, like the hub at the center of spokes on a wheel (Shaw, 1981). However, an informal leader may take the role of information giver and controller.

Group members' satisfaction with a group tends to be higher in "web" networks, where information passes freely among all group members, than in centralized "wheel" networks. (Exhibit 11.6 diagrams these patterns.) Centralized networks are the more efficient configuration for task groups addressing simple problems, however. Decentralized networks are more effective if the group is attempting to solve more complex problems (Shaw, 1981).

The Effects of Physical Environment on Group Processes

The physical environment also influences group interactions. The physical environment includes material aspects, territoriality, interperson distance, density and crowding,

EXHIBIT 11.6

Common
Communication
Patterns in
Groups

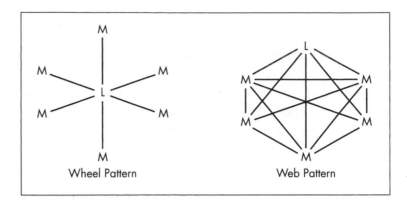

Wheel Pattern   Web Pattern

and spatial arrangements (Shaw, 1981). As you read this section, you might want to refer back to Chapter 7, which discusses the relationship between the physical environment and human behavior.

Material Aspects of the Physical Environment

The coming-out group is held at the Gay and Lesbian Community Center. The group meets in a room large enough for members to sit comfortably. The facilitators are able to control the temperature of the room. Occasionally, a Center volunteer will come into the building, and then the facilitators will shut the door to the group room to ensure privacy. No other group meets at the Center at the same time as the women's coming-out group. These are just a few elements of the material aspects of the physical environment. Material aspects include the structure and contents of the meeting room (size, shape, furniture, arrangement of furniture), lighting, privacy, noise level, colors, and temperature of the space.

Studies of the effects of material aspects on group functioning have revealed the impact of several variables on members' perceptions and interactions. For example, in work groups, walls painted "cool blue" induced more women to complain of being cold with the temperature set at 75 degrees than when the color was changed to "warm yellows and restful greens" at the same temperature. A dimly lit room is perceived as more intimate. Unpredictable noise causes frustration and lowers productivity. Much of this research has been done in the workplace.

Studies have also shown that the attitudes of group members affect their experience of the material aspects of the environment. Persons are more tolerant of an unsatisfactory physical environment when they know that someone is concerned about their welfare and is trying to respond to their concerns about the physical environment—turning up the temperature in a cold room, rearranging furniture to facilitate member interaction, allowing for a food or beverage break to rejuvenate tired group members, closing the door to the group room to reduce outside noise and increase privacy.

Territoriality

Each semester I notice how students "claim" a seat in the class. By the second or third week of the semester, they are referring to a particular chair as "my seat." An unspoken rule is that one does not sit in someone else's seat. Sitting in someone else's seat may be met with a gasp, glare, or a declaration: "Hey, you're in *my* seat!"

People have ways of marking their territory—a jacket thrown over a movie theater seat (this space is reserved) or graffiti on a wall of a subway. Groups also establish territories. For example, gangs who consider a certain part of town under their jurisdiction will defend that territory against rival gangs. Studies of territoriality have found that the permanence of the group's territoriality (how long the group has resided in a place and plans for future residence) influences the degree to which it will be defended (Shaw, 1981). The preferred size of territories may be influenced by such factors as group size, composition, gender (males typically claim more territory than females), and the relationship of members (strangers vs. friends). People generally respect the space boundaries of groups. For example, if a group is talking in a hallway, most people will walk around the group rather than going in between the members, especially when the group members are conversing in an agitated manner (Shaw, 1981).

Interperson Distance

"Get out of my space!" "Get out of my face!" "Move back!" These declarations are verbal attempts to establish a comfortable distance between oneself and others. Persons and groups establish norms about the appropriate distance between themselves and others. **Interperson distance,** to which these norms refer, are influenced by such variables as age, sex, cultural background, relationship between the persons, the interaction situation, and status differences between persons. Interperson distance is the group version of the concept of personal space discussed in Chapter 7.

Studies on interperson distance have found that

- Strangers tend to maintain a greater interperson distance than friends.

- Females prefer closer interperson distances than males.

- Closer interperson distances are more acceptable in such settings as elevators and subways and with service providers like dentists than in situations where close physical proximity is not expected.

- Persons of higher status are more likely to invade the space boundaries of persons of lower status than vice versa (Shaw, 1981).

Norms for interperson distance have considerable influence on our perceptions and behavior. Terry believed that alcohol influenced her to alter her usual norms regarding the proper interperson distance between two females. Terry believed that she would not have shared a bed after a party unless she had been under the influence of alcohol. Considering this incident many years later and in the context of her emerging lesbian identity, Terry realizes that alcohol became the excuse for changing her usual preferences regarding personal space with a person of the same sex.

Researchers observing persons in different size rooms with various furniture arrangements have found that the size of a room and arrangement of chairs may also influence interperson distance. In a small room with tightly packed chairs, persons may experience the sense of not having enough personal space. Even in a large room, a large number of persons may also produce a feeling of discomfort (Shaw, 1981).

Density and Crowding

The coming-out group meets in a small room in the Center. When the attendance at a meeting is high, additional chairs need to be brought into the room, which makes the room seem even smaller. *Population density*—the number of people per unit of space—is correlated with the experience of crowding. The smaller the space and the greater the number of people in it, the more likely it is that one will feel crowded.

The experience of crowding is influenced by other factors, however, such as gender, interperson distance, and the situation. For example, research on the connection between gender and crowding has discovered that women can accept greater stimulation before feeling crowded. All-male groups are more competitive (presumed to be a reaction to crowding) in smaller rooms than in larger rooms; this response may also be related to territoriality (Shaw, 1981).

The comfort that group members feel with one another and each person's need for personal space also affect how crowded the room feels. Rooms can seem especially small when a topic with which one feels uncomfortable is being addressed. In that case, one may feel the need to "get outta here" no matter the size of the room.

Spatial Arrangements

Each semester, it seems, a student asks, "Why do all the black students sit together?" The response usually is, "Why do the white students sit together?" The answer to both questions is that people tend to sit near people with whom they are well acquainted. Seating arrangement has been shown to affect the communication pattern in groups, the quality of interaction, and the reaction to other members (Shaw, 1981).

When chairs are arranged in a circle, communication among group members tends to increase and ratings of self and others tend to be more positive than when chairs are not arranged in a circle. The additional opportunities for eye contact with a circular arrangement increase member-to-member interaction. However, cultural values and norms may influence the level of one's comfort with circle arrangements and direct eye contact (Lum, 1992). For example, Asian Americans generally prefer a greater degree of formality, as indicated by lecture-style rows, because they view the worker/client relationship as formal. Direct eye contact may also be a sign of disrespect for some Asian Americans. Although some Native Americans also may consider direct eye contact a sign of disrespect, those who adhere to native values and customs may still prefer circle seating because of the significance of native healing circle ceremonies (Garrett, Garrett, & Brotherton, 2001).

Persons tend to choose the seats in the room that reflect their perceived status. High-status individuals tend to select chairs at the head of a table or in a central position (Shaw, 1981). This phenomenon could be partially explained by status characteristics theory.

IMPLICATIONS FOR SOCIAL WORK PRACTICE

The overview of formed and natural groups in this chapter suggests a number of principles for social work assessment, intervention, and evaluation.

- In the assessment process with individuals or families, identify any natural or formed groups to which the person or family belongs. Ecomaps or sociograms may be used to identify such groups.

- In the assessment process, determine whether the group modality or another intervention modality would be most appropriate for the client.

- In the assessment process with a potential group member, gather background information such as the motivation for joining the group, the expectations the person has of the leader and other group members, the strengths the person could offer the group, and previous experience with groups.

- Be aware of various groups in your community for referral and networking purposes.

- Develop and implement small groups when it is clear that a group would benefit the population that you serve. Determine what type(s) of groups would be most appropriate for that population. Consider groups for prevention when appropriate.

- Collaborate with colleagues from other disciplines to cofacilitate groups in interdisciplinary settings.

- Seek to build alliances with natural and self-help groups that reinforce or supplement the services that you are providing.

- In the groups that you facilitate, understand the stated and unstated purposes and functions of the group, and pay careful attention to issues of group structure, development, composition, and dynamics.

- Assess the physical environment of groups. Be aware of how material aspects, territoriality, interperson distance, density and crowding, and spatial arrangements may influence the groups you intend to facilitate.

- Determine a method to evaluate the effectiveness of a group prior to its formation. Use the information from this evaluation to make needed changes in the group.

- Be aware of how managed care affects the use of groups as a practice modality.

KEY TERMS

brief treatment model
closed group
communication networks
expectation states theory
formed group
group cohesiveness
group dynamics
group work
interperson distance
mutual aid group
natural group
ongoing group

open group
performance expectations
process-oriented leader
psychoeducational group
self-help group
small group
status characteristic
status characteristics theory
task group
task-oriented leader
therapy group
time-limited group

ACTIVE LEARNING

1. Compare and contrast Terry's support group with a small group of which you are a member in terms of how they developed, how long they are lasting, how membership

was determined, inclusiveness versus exclusiveness, heterogeneity versus homogeneity, cohesiveness, and leadership.

2.   In a small group formed by your instructor, attempt to solve this problem: draw a square. Divide it into four identical squares. Remove the bottom left-hand square. Now divide the resulting shape into four identical shapes.

Work on the problem for 15 minutes. Observe the overall process in the group, the diversity of membership in the group, and the roles of each member while engaged in problem solving. Write up your observations.

WEB RESOURCES

American Self-Help Clearinghouse

www.selfhelpgroups.org
Site that is part of Mental Health Net, edited by Barbara White and Edward Madara, contains links to a wide variety of online self-help groups from adoption to workaholics.

Association for the Advancement of Social Work With Groups (AASWG)

www.aaswg.org
Professional organization advocating in support of group work practice, education, research, and publication; includes links to newsletters, discussion lists, bibliographies, chapter information, syllabi, social work links, and other group work links. To order the association's bibliography on group work (3rd edition), write to AASWG, c/o University of Akron, Akron, OH 44325-8050.

Association for Specialists in Group Work (ASGW)

asgw.educ.kent.edu
Site maintained by a division of the American Counseling Association that promotes quality in group work training, practice, and research.

International Association of Group Psychotherapy

www.iagpweb.org
Includes information about the association, contact information for the board, membership information, and an electronic forum.

Social Work Access Network (SWAN)

www.sc.edu/swan/newsgroups.html

Includes links to various newsgroups on Usenet, including those that are support related.

Support-Group.Com

www.support-group.com

Provides bulletin boards and online chat as well as links to a variety of support groups for persons with health, personal, or relationship issues.

CHAPTER 12

Formal Organizations

Elizabeth D. Hutchison

Formal Organizations

Elizabeth D. Hutchison
Virginia Commonwealth University

How do the major theoretical perspectives on formal organizations help us to understand the functions formal organizations serve in contemporary society and their influence on human behavior?

What are the contemporary trends in the formal organizations in which social workers work?

Key Ideas

As you read this chapter, take note of these central ideas:

1. Formal organizations—collectivities of people, with a high degree of formality of structure, working together to meet a goal or goals—are important influences on human behavior. They help us in many ways and they also cause stress and strain in our lives.

2. Perspectives on formal organizations can be classified into four broad categories: rational perspective, systems perspective, interpretive perspective, and critical perspective.

3. Theories in the rational perspective consider formal organizations to be purposefully designed machines that maximize efficiency and effectiveness.

4. The systems perspective sees the formal organization in constant interaction with multiple environments, and composed of interrelated systems.

5. Both the interpretive and the critical perspectives emphasize human consciousness in creating organizations, but critical theories focus on patterns of domination and oppression in organizations, which interpretive theories ignore or negate.

6. Research in both public sector and business organizations indicates that formal organizations may be hazardous to the health of their members. Burnout—whose symptoms include emotional exhaustion, cynicism, and inefficacy—is the most identified hazard.

7. Social workers work in many diverse types of formal organizations.

CASE STUDY

NEW LEADERSHIP AT BEACON CENTER

Beacon Center (BC) has a short but proud history of providing innovative services to persons who are homeless in River Run, the small midwestern city where it is located. It was established in 1980, thanks to one woman, Martha Green, and her relentless pursuit of a vision.

While serving as executive director of the YWCA, Martha became increasingly concerned about the growing homeless population in River Run. During the 1960s and early 1970s, she had worked in several positions in River Run's antipoverty agency, and she was well known throughout the city for her uncompromising advocacy efforts for families living in poverty. Martha was also a skilled advocate and service planner, and she soon pulled together supporters for a new social service agency to address the special needs of homeless persons. A mix of private and public, federal and local, funds were secured, and BC opened with Martha Green as director, working with the assistance of one staff social worker. The agency grew steadily, and by 1990 it had a staff of 15, as well as several subcontracted programs.

Martha valued client input into program development and made sure that client voices were heard at all levels: at city council meetings, in community discussions of program needs, in Center discussions of program needs and issues, in staff interviews, and at board meetings. She remained uncompromising in advocacy efforts, and she often angered city officials because she was unyielding in her demands for fair treatment of homeless persons. She advocated for their right to receive resources and services from other social service organizations, as well as for their right to congregate in public places.

By the same token, Martha and the staff consistently reminded clients of their obligations as citizens and, gently but firmly, held them to those obligations. Clients were sometimes angered by this call for responsible behavior, but they appreciated the tireless advocacy of Martha and the staff.

They also appreciated that they were kept fully informed about political issues that concerned them, as well as about actions taken by BC in relation to these issues.

Martha also had a vision regarding staff relationships. She was committed to working collaboratively, to trusting front line workers to make their own decisions and to securing the participation of all staff on important policy decisions. This commitment was aided by the fact that Martha and her staff were all of European American heritage and had deep family roots in River Run. Rules were kept to a minimum, and staff relationships were very personal. For example, a staff member needing to keep a medical appointment would make informal arrangements with another staff member to exchange an hour of service, with no need to "go through channels" or invoke formal sick leave. Martha believed in hiring the best-trained and most experienced staff for front line positions and, over the years, hired and retained a highly skilled, committed core staff. She had high expectations of her staff, particularly in terms of their commitment to the rights of homeless persons, but she was also a nurturant administrator who was concerned about the personal well-being and professional development of each staff member. She established a climate of mutual respect where people could risk disagreeing.

Martha spent some time every week working in each program area to ensure that she understood the agency's programs as they were experienced by clients and front line staff. She kept staff fully informed about economic and political pressures faced by BC and about her actions in regard to these issues. She regularly sought their input on these issues, and decisions were usually made by consensus. On occasion, however, around really sensitive issues—such as the choice between forgoing a salary increase or closing a program—she asked staff to vote by secret ballot to neutralize any potential power dynamics.

Martha had a vision, as well, about how a board of directors can facilitate a successful client-centered program. She saw the board as part of the BC system, just as staff and clients are part of the system. She worked hard to ensure that members chosen for the board shared the BC commitment to the rights of homeless persons, and she developed warm, personal relationships with them. She kept the board fully informed about issues facing BC, and she was successful in securing their support and active involvement in advocacy and resource development activities.

Over the years, BC became known as an innovative, client-centered service center, as well as a hardheaded advocacy organization. Staff and board members took pride in being part of what they considered to be a very special endeavor—one that also outstripped other social service organizations in its expertise, commitment, and compassion. Clients were not always satisfied with the services, but generally acknowledged among themselves that they were lucky to have the dedication of BC.

Reactions from the community were more mixed, however. The respect offered up was, in many circles, a grudging respect. Many city officials as well as staff of other social service organizations complained about the self-righteous attitudes and uncompromising posture of Martha and the staff at BC. These detractors acknowledged that the tactics of BC staff were successful in countering discrimination against homeless persons, but suggested that BC succeeded at much cost of goodwill. Although Martha believed in keeping staff, clients, and board members informed about the economic and political pressures faced by BC, she saw it as her job to carry the major responsibility for responding to, and absorbing, those pressures, to protect staff energy for serving clients.

Martha retired in 1995 and relocated with her husband to be closer to their children. An acting director was appointed at BC while a search for a permanent director was under way. The acting director had worked several years at BC and shared much of Martha's administrative and service philosophy. She was not as good, however, at juggling the multiple demands of the position. Staff and clients felt a loss of support; board members lost some of their enthusiasm and confidence; and antagonists in the community saw an opportunity to mute some of BC's advocacy efforts. Staff maintained a strong commitment to the rights of homeless persons, but they lost some of their optimism about making a difference.

After 8 months, Helen Blue, a former community college administrator, was hired as the new executive director. She was also of European American heritage but had only lived in River Run for a few years. She was excited about this new professional challenge, but she had a vision for BC somewhat different from Martha's. She was concerned about the alienation that had resulted, in some circles, from BC's hard-hitting advocacy stance, and she favored a more conciliatory approach. For example, after meeting with city officials, she assigned staff social workers the task of convincing clients to quit congregating in the city park near BC and to stay out of the business district during business hours. After meeting with directors of other social service organizations, she directed staff to be less demanding in their advocacy for clients.

Helen was also concerned about the lack of rules and the looseness of attention to chain of command, and she began to institute new rules and procedures. Staff meetings and open community meetings with clients became presentations by Helen. Staff were no longer allowed to attend board meetings and were not informed about what happened at them. Front line staff often found their decisions overturned by Helen. When the first staff resignation came, Helen hired the replacement with no input from staff, clients, or board members.

Recently, you visited BC to learn more about the services it offers. Overall, you were impressed with the organization. But you overheard a staff member saying, "I don't want to leave this place; I still want to make a difference. But what was once a family to me has become a turbulent place to work. I miss the support, the sense of family, and the pride of being a special kind of place. We spend too much time finding ways to thwart Helen, and that is not why I became a social worker." On the same visit, you overheard a group of clients talking about BC. They agreed that there is no other place to turn, but all nodded agreement when one man suggested, "I knew what I could count on before, but now I can never be sure. It depends on who gets involved."

A Definition of Formal Organizations

You were probably born in a hospital. There is a good chance that you began to attend a house of worship at an early age. You may have enrolled in a child care center by the age of 4. You have, by now, spent close to 2 decades in school. Along the way, you may have joined organizations such as Girl Scouts, Boy Scouts, YMCA, YWCA, or other athletic clubs. You may also have participated in programs offered by civic and social service organizations as a member, recipient of services, or volunteer. You probably manage your finances with the assistance of a bank, and you meet your basic survival needs as well as fulfill your consumer wants through a variety of business organizations. Some of you are, or have been, members of sororities and fraternities, and some may be student members of the National Association of Social Workers (NASW). Most of you have been a paid employee of at least one formal organization, and many of you are currently enrolled in a field practicum in a social service organization like Beacon Center. When you die, a newspaper organization may announce your death, a public organization will issue a death certificate, and your loved ones will probably seek the service of several other organizations to plan your funeral.

Formal organizations are pervasive in our lives. But what, exactly, are they? A **formal organization** is a collectivity of people with a high degree of formality of structure working together to meet a goal or goals (Bozeman, 1987). This definition, like others found in the literature (e.g., Blau & Scott, 1962; Etzioni, 1977; Katz & Kahn, 1978), has three key components: a collectivity of people, a highly formal structure, and the common purpose of working together to meet a goal or goals.

This definition leaves a lot of room for variation. Formal organizations differ in size, structure, culture, and goals. They also perform a variety of functions in contemporary society and influence human behavior in many ways. Exhibit 12.1 is a list of what contemporary organizations do. You can see that formal organizations are intricately woven into the fabric of life in contemporary society, that formal organizations can be both functional and dysfunctional for society or for specific groups, and that some members of organizations benefit more than others from organizational goals and structure. You might want to think about how well the list of functions in Exhibit 12.1 describes Beacon Center, your school of social work, your field agency, and an organization where you have been an employee.

Think too about how much formal organizations influence our behavior. They meet our needs, help us fulfill goals, and nurture our development. They also make stressful demands, thwart our goals, inhibit our holistic development, and constrain our behavior.

The purpose for introducing theory and research about formal organizations in this chapter is twofold: (1) to help you understand the pervasive and multifaceted influence of formal organizations on human behavior, yours as well as your clients', and (2) to assist you in understanding the organizations in which social workers practice.

Perspectives on Formal Organizations

At the current time, ways of thinking about organizations include such a variety of perspectives that the state of organization theory has been described as "more of a weed patch than a well-tended garden" (Pfeffer, 1982, p. 1). Likewise, the research on organizations and the related prescriptions for organizational administration reflect great variety. Nevertheless, three generalizations can be made about the abundant multidisciplinary literature on formal organizations:

Rational choice
perspective

1. Early theories of organizations assumed that a rational organizational structure (bureaucracy) would ensure the effective and efficient accomplishment of organizational goals, which were assumed to be clear and specific. Contemporary theories challenge the rationality of formal organizations, but the image of the modern organization as a rational instrument (machine) of efficiency and predictability has had a

EXHIBIT 12.1

The Functions of Formal Organizations

- *Formal organizations are human facilitators.* Organizations help us get things done and meet our needs. Collective activities are often superior to individual efforts because of speed, accuracy, human connectedness, and other factors.
- *Formal organizations organize society.* Every aspect of contemporary life is systematized and coordinated through formal organizations.
- *Formal organizations are political institutions.* All organizations perform some type of political activity, whether it is personal politics, group politics, interorganizational politics, interest group politics, policy politics, or partisan politics. In addition, all organizations are involved in the promotion of the ideology of the political system in which they operate.
- *Formal organizations are instruments of system maintenance and enhancement.* Organizations engage in activities that maintain or enhance the economic, political, and social systems in which they operate.
- *Formal organizations are change agents.* Although organizations often resist change, they also play a role in societal reform and change.
- *Formal organizations create culture and counterculture.* Organizations produce and promote the general cultural values of the popular culture as well as specific organizational cultural values that run counter to the popular culture. In this way, organizations may play a proactive role in the societies in which they operate.
- *Formal organizations are tools of policy implementation.* Organizations provide some stability and predictability as they implement policy over time.
- *Formal organizations are tools of development.* Organizations produce advancements in science, technology, and other aspects of human functioning. Some of these "advancements" improve the human condition, some aggravate it, and many provide both benefits and costs.
- *Formal organizations are destructive forces.* The processes that organizations use to accomplish organizational goals may create environmental pollution or work conditions that are hazardous to the well-being of organizational members. The goals of the organization may be to develop products for waging war or products detrimental to the health of citizens.
- *Formal organizations are instruments of repression and domination.* Organizations may be, and often are, instruments of control, domination, class rule, and exploitation.
- *Formal organizations are alienators.* In many organizations, hierarchical structures with their arrangements of power generate inequality and alienation.
- *Formal organizations are tension-management systems.* Organizations develop processes for managing the tensions between individual goals and organizational goals, among competing organizational goals, or among competing individual goals. Processes are also developed to manage class tensions related to inequalities in organizational structure.
- *Formal organizations threaten individual rights.* Individual rights are limited, to varying degrees, by organizational roles, rules, and norms.
- *Formal organizations form the administrative state of governance.* Webs of corporate organizations and government organizations create a highly centralized and concentrated social structure.
- *Formal organizations are a forum for discourse.* Their members have multiple perspectives about goals, processes, and structures. Organizations, therefore, become sites for more or less democratic disagreement and negotiation, the active construction of meaning and purpose, and problem resolution.

Source: Based on Farazmand (1994); #15 from Fox and Miller (1995).

lasting influence on theories of organizations (Farazmand, 1994; Morgan, 1997; Pfeffer, 1997).

Systems perspective

2. Early theories focused on what happens inside organizations and ignored all aspects of their environments. In contrast, contemporary theories generally propose some sort of relationship between organization and environment (Hasenfeld, 1992). Attention to the effects of the physical environment, both the external and internal physical environment, on organizational life has especially been lacking (Pfeffer, 1997), suggesting a new direction for organizational theory and research.

Conflict perspective

3. Most organizational theory has been biased toward the interests of owners and managers rather than toward the interests of workers (Carter & Jackson, 1993; Farazmand, 1994; Morgan, 1997). For this reason, you may struggle with the language in this chapter, finding it too mechanistic, aloof, and lacking in intimacy. In recent years, critical theorists have challenged this one-sided view of organizations and raised questions about domination and oppression in organizational life (Farazmand, 1994; Hearn & Parkin, 1993).

Several people have attempted to organize the weed patch of organizational theory into a garden—to bring some order to the diversity of viewpoints without denying the complexity and multifaceted nature of contemporary formal organizations (e.g., Dattalo, 1990; Hasenfeld, 1992; Morgan, 1997; Pfeffer, 1997). Here we use a classification system that includes four perspectives: rational perspective, systems perspective, interpretive perspective, and critical perspective (Farazmand, 1994). None of these perspectives, taken individually, accounts for all 15 functions of organizations listed in Exhibit 12.1, but taken together, they elaborate the multifaceted nature of organizations reflected in the 15 functions. Each perspective encompasses both classical and contemporary theories, and each has relevance for social work practice.

Rational Perspective

Rational choice perspective

When Helen Blue became the executive director at Beacon Center, she was concerned, among other things, about the lack of administrative formality, the lack of rules, and the ambiguous chain of command. She also wanted greater authority over planning and decision making. These concerns reflect the **rational perspective on organizations,** which views the formal organization as a "goal-directed, purposefully designed machine" (Hasenfeld, 1992, p. 25). It assumes that organizations can be designed with structures and processes that maximize efficiency and effectiveness, concepts that are highly valued in this perspective. *Efficiency* is obtaining a high ratio of output to input, achieving the best outcome from the least investment of resources. *Effectiveness* is goal accomplishment. Exhibit 12.2 summarizes the central theories in this perspective.

EXHIBIT 12.2
The Rational
Perspective
on Formal
Organizations

Major theme: The organization is a goal-directed, purposefully designed machine (closed system).

Theory	Central Idea
The ideal-type bureaucracy (Weber).	Formal rationality—rules, regulations, and structures—are essential to goal accomplishment.
Scientific management (Taylor)	The most effective organizations maximize internal efficiency, the "one best way."
Human relations theory	Human relationships are central to organizational efficiency and effectiveness.
Decision theory	Organizational rationality has limits.

The Ideal-Type Bureaucracy. In the modern era, formal organization is often equated with bureaucracy. Indeed, Max Weber, the German sociologist who formulated a theory of bureaucracy at the beginning of the 20th century, saw bureaucracy and capitalism as inseparable (Weber, 1947). Weber proposed a **bureaucracy** as the most efficient form of organization for goal accomplishment. The characteristics of Weber's ideal-type bureaucracy are presented in Exhibit 12.3.

Weber was enthusiastic about the advantages of the ideal-type bureaucracy over other ways of organizing for goal accomplishment, but he did not see bureaucracies as problem free. He was concerned about the dehumanizing potential of bureaucracies—their potential to become an **iron cage of rationality** trapping people and denying many aspects of their humanity. Researchers have noted that the excessive use of rules and procedures often limits the efficiency and effectiveness of bureaucratic organizations.

Despite the potential negative effects of bureaucracies, they are the predominant form of organization in the modern world, and the goal of maximization of efficiency

EXHIBIT 12.3
Weber's Ideal-Type
Bureaucracy

Ideal-Type Bureaucracy

Clear hierarchy and chain of command

Clear division of labor based on specialized skills

Formal rules of operation

Formal and task-oriented communications

Merit-based recruitment and advancement

Keeping of files and records for administrative action

is taken for granted. This is true for human service organizations as well as organizations formed for other purposes (Hasenfeld, 1992). How closely do the social work organizations you have worked in fit the ideal-type bureaucracy? How much emphasis is put on efficiency? Helen Blue wants to move Beacon Center closer to the ideal-type bureaucracy than it was under Martha Green's leadership.

Both Martha Green and Helen Blue might be interested in one researcher's findings that client satisfaction decreased as the level of bureaucracy increased in transitional housing programs for homeless families (Crook, 2001). In addition, conflict among residents increased as the level of organizational bureaucracy increased. The indirect impact of organizational bureaucracy on clients is called trickle-down bureaucracy.

Scientific Management. Another early 20th-century approach to formal organizations has had lasting influence. Fredrick W. Taylor's (1911) **scientific management**, sometimes referred to as Taylorism, was directed toward maximizing internal efficiency. The set of principles that Taylor developed to guide the design of organizations was widely adopted by both industry and government, first in the United States and then worldwide. These principles are listed in Exhibit 12.4.

In his provocative book *The McDonaldization of Society* (1993, 1998), George Ritzer proposes that McDonald's Corporation is a prototype organization, whose organizational style is coming to dominate much of the world (p. 2). This new type of organization, which operates on the combined principles of bureaucratization and scientific management, has four key traits:

1. *Efficiency,* which is valued in a fast-paced society

2. *Quantification,* with an emphasis on saving time and money rather than on quality of product

EXHIBIT 12.4
Taylor's Scientific Management

Scientific Management
Time and motion studies to find the "one best way" to perform each organizational task
Scientific selection and training of workers
Training focused on performing tasks in the standardized one best way
Close managerial monitoring of workers to ensure accurate implementation of task prescriptions and to provide appropriate rewards for compliance
Managerial authority over planning and decision making, with no challenge from workers

3. *Predictability,* with the assurance that a Big Mac will be the same in San Francisco as in Washington, D.C., or Hong Kong

4. *Control,* with workers trained to do a limited number of things exactly as they are told to do them, and with maximum use of nonhuman technology

Ritzer gives many examples of the proliferation of the McDonald's model, including shopping malls; packaged tours; managed medical care; weight loss organizations; the "junk-food journalism" of *USA Today;* the use of machine-graded multiple-choice examinations; reliance on GPAs, PSATs, SATs, and GREs for evaluating educational accomplishment; franchised hotels; planned communities; and franchised child care centers.

Principles of scientific management are frequently followed in social service organizations, and they are becoming more pervasive as managed care arrangements become more prominent in social service delivery. For example, these organizations undertake task and workload analyses to improve effectiveness and efficiency, and managers develop procedures, regulations, and decision trees to be implemented by direct service workers. Have you encountered any of these in your field setting? Although Helen Blue has initiated more procedures and regulations and believes in managerial authority over planning and decision making, she does not share scientific management's enthusiasm for "one best way" of delivering services.

Human Relations Theory. **Human relations theory** introduced a new twist on maximizing organizational efficiency and effectiveness. The theory grew out of a series of studies conducted by Elton Mayo (1933) and associates at the Hawthorne plant of the Western Electric Company in the 1920s and 1930s. Seeking to improve the rationality of the organization, the researchers were studying the effects of working conditions, such as intensity of lighting, on productivity. As expected, the researchers found that productivity increased as the lighting intensity increased. To their surprise, however, productivity continued to increase even when they began to dim the lights in an attempt to confirm their findings. The researchers concluded that *technical rationality*—the development of rational structures, procedures, and processes—is not sufficient to ensure maximum productivity. *Social factors,* they concluded, are as important if not more important than technical factors in accomplishing organizational goals. They based this conclusion, which became the central proposition of a new theory, on their observation that productivity appeared to be related to worker morale and sense of social responsibility to the work group.

This interpretation of the research findings has been criticized on the basis of the **Hawthorne effect**—the tendency of experimental participants to perform in particular ways simply because they know they are being studied. In other words, critics have suggested that the participants in the study may have become more productive simply because they knew that their behavior was being studied.

Regardless of the validity of the initial findings, subsequent research led to the human relations theory of organizational management, which emphasized the heretofore unrecognized importance of human interaction in organizational efficiency and effectiveness. As the theory developed, it also proposed that democratic leadership is more effective than authoritarian management in securing worker cooperation.

The human relations approach is a favorite theory of organizations among social work students, who are after all fundamentally concerned with human interaction (Netting, Kettner, & McMurtry, 1998). The social workers at Beacon Center did indeed respond more cooperatively to Martha Green's democratic leadership than to Helen Blue's more authoritarian leadership. In addition, the organizational philosophy that guides interaction among the employees of a social agency may be directly related to the relationships between staff and clients (Hasenfeld, 1992).

Conflict perspective

It is important to note, however, that human relations theory is still in the rational tradition. Like scientific management, it focuses on maximizing efficiency and effectiveness, and it endorses the interests of owners and managers. Managers must become leaders capable of securing the cooperation of workers, but they are still in control of the organization. Although the consideration of human interaction opens the possibility of nonrational factors in organizational life, human relations theorists still assume that, with "leadership skills," human interactions can be as rationally managed as structures and procedures.

Humanistic Perspective

After losing ground during the 1950s, human relations theory was reinvigorated in the 1960s by **organizational humanism** and a subfield called organizational development. These theories suggest that organizations can maximize efficiency and effectiveness while also promoting individual happiness and well-being. Douglas McGregor (1960), for example, a proponent of organizational humanism, identified two opposing sets of assumptions from which managers view workers (summarized in Exhibit 12.5). McGregor suggested that **Theory X** calls for directive management, but **Theory Y** calls for greater democratization of decision making in organizations. In your work experiences, have you encountered either of these theories about workers? If so, how did you react as a worker?

Some research (e.g., Herzberg, 1966) has supported the overall superiority of Theory Y management over Theory X management, but one much-cited study found that the preferred management approach depends on the nature of the organizational task (Morse & Lorsch, 1970). Tasks that are predictable, repetitive, and technically precise are best accomplished with Theory X management; tasks that are vague and diversified are best accomplished with Theory Y management. This study has been cited as evidence that social service organizations are better suited to Theory

EXHIBIT 12.5

Assumptions
of Theory X and
Theory Y

Assumptions of Theory X	Assumptions of Theory Y
Workers have an inherent dislike of work.	Workers see work as a natural activity.
Workers prefer to be told what to do.	Workers are self-directed when working on projects to which they are committed.
Workers respond to money as the primary motivator.	Workers seek responsibility when organizational goals are congruent with their needs. They have more creative contributions to make than organizations generally allow.

Source: Based on McGregor, 1960.

Y management, because social work tasks are "often loosely defined" (Netting et al., 1998, p. 206).

McGregor's work, like that of other organizational humanists, has a dual focus on individual well-being and organizational efficiency and effectiveness, but it also assumes a fit between individual goals and organizational goals. Critical theorists, as you will see later, criticize the organizational humanists for their failure to recognize conflicting goals and power differentials within organizations. By focusing on individual well-being, however, organizational humanism serves as a bridge to the interpretive and critical perspectives. By focusing on the interdependencies of individuals and organizations, organizational humanism also serves as a bridge to the systems perspective.

Decision-Making Theory. In the 1950s, organizational theorists in the rational tradition began to write about the limits to organizational rationality. Herbert Simon (1957) presented a **decision-making theory** of organizations, focusing on how the decisions of individuals in organizations affect the organization as a whole.

James March and Simon (1958) argued that administrators cannot be perfectly rational in their decision making, because they face many constraints that limit their alternatives: incomplete information about alternatives for action, incomplete understanding of the consequences of those actions, and incapacity to explore more than a limited number of alternatives at a time. March and Simon used the term **bounded rationality** to describe this limited rationality of organizational actors. They also suggested that bounded rationality leads administrators and other organizational actors to **satisfice** rather than maximize when making decisions—to seek satisfactory rather than perfect solutions, and to discontinue the search for alternatives when a satisfactory solution is available.

Systems Perspective

Martha Green and Helen Blue had different styles of managing what happened inside Beacon Center, but they also had different styles of managing external pressures and resources. Martha focused on giving homeless persons a voice in efforts to secure political and economic resources for Beacon Center; Helen focused on conciliation with community and political leaders. In her own way, however, each was attentive to Beacon Center's relationship with its environment. In this respect, they negated the rational perspective's view of the organization as a closed system that can be controlled by careful attention to internal structure and processes. During the 1950s and 1960s, the rationalist view of organizations was challenged by the systems perspective, which seems to inform the efforts of both Martha Green and Helen Blue. All subsequent theorizing about organizations has been influenced by the systems perspective.

The **systems perspective on organizations** builds on the fundamental principle that the organization is in constant interaction with its multiple environments—social, political, economic, cultural, technological—and must be able to adapt to environmental change. Some systems theorists suggest mutual influence between organizations and their environments; other theorists see the influence as unidirectional, with organizational structure and processes being determined by the environment.

A second important principle of the systems perspective is that organizations are composed of interrelated subsystems that must be integrated in order to achieve the organization's goals and meet environmental demands.

Finally, in contrast to the rational approach, the systems perspective holds that there are many different ways, rather than one best way, to reach the same ends. The idea that a system can attain its goals in a variety of ways is known as *equifinality.*

Several systems theories of organizations have been developed over time, but we look at only two here: the political economy model and the learning organization theory. These two theories are summarized in Exhibit 12.6.

Political economy model. The **political economy model** focuses on the dependence of organizations on their environments for necessary resources and on the impact of organization/environment interactions on the internal structure and processes of the organization (Wamsley & Zald, 1973). More specifically, it focuses on two types of resources necessary to organizations: political resources (legitimacy and power) and economic resources. The greater the dependence of the organization on the environment for either of these types of resources, the greater the influence the environment will have on the organization. The political economy model is particularly potent for clarifying how social service organizations resolve such important issues as which clients to serve, which services to provide, how to organize service provision, and how to define staff and client roles (Hasenfeld, 1992). Both Martha Green and Helen Blue are trying to read their political and economic environments as they make these

EXHIBIT 12.6

The Systems
Perspective
on Formal
Organizations

Major theme: The organization is in constant interaction with multiple environments.

Theory	Central Idea
Political economy model	The organization depends on the environment for political and economic resources.
Learning organization theory	The organization must be able to learn and change in a rapidly changing environment.

kinds of decisions, but their different ways of thinking are leading them to attend to different aspects of the environment. The political economy model recognizes clients as resources and as potential players in the political arena. Social workers have an important role to play in facilitating their inclusion in the political process, a role that was part of Martha Green's vision for Beacon Center.

Learning Organization Theory. The **learning organization theory** was developed on the premise that rational planning is not sufficient for an organization to survive in a rapidly changing environment such as the one in which we live. Formal organizations must become complex systems that are capable of constant learning (Argyris & Schon, 1978; Senge, 1990). The learning organization is one that can

■ *Scan the environment, anticipate change, and detect "early warning" signs of trends and patterns.* In a social work context, this facility means understanding services from the points of view of clients as well as from the points of view of a variety of actors in the environment. It seems that Martha Green was more tuned in to the points of view of clients than Helen Blue. On the other hand, Helen Blue seems more sensitive to the points of view of some collaborating agencies.

■ *Question, challenge, and change customary ways of operating.* Certainly, Helen Blue, like many new administrators, is questioning and challenging Martha Green's customary ways of operating. The important issue, however, is whether she is developing ways of operating that allow and encourage ongoing questioning, challenging, and changing. Ongoing growth requires dialogue, expression of conflicting points of view, and some risk taking. Martha Green tried to develop a climate that allowed such dialogue.

■ *Allow the appropriate strategic direction to emerge.* The learning organization needs "a sense of vision, norms, values, limits, or 'reference points'" to guide organizational behavior (Morgan, 1997, p. 95). But these should serve as guideposts, not straitjackets. Even these guideposts must be open for questioning. Ironically, both Martha Green's egalitarian vision and Helen Blue's vision of a more hierarchical organization have the potential to become straitjackets. Organizations need to be willing to look at both the benefits and the downside of their favored ways of operating—and to alter their strategic direction accordingly. Gareth Morgan (1997) emphasizes the importance of organizational limits, the "thou shalt nots" that guide organizational behavior. He suggests that Western organizations have put great emphasis on developing goals and objectives but downplayed the limits that need to guide actions taken to achieve those goals. In light of the news of corporate misbehavior in 2002, this suggestion seems prescient. It now appears that public corporations had too few limits for behavior as they strove to satisfy Wall Street's expectations of their profit margins.

■ *Evolve designs that support continuous learning.* The challenge is to avoid anarchy on one hand and overcentralization on the other hand. The learning organization develops methods for shared decision making and avoids overdefining its members' actions. From this perspective, Beacon Center is more likely to be a learning organization under the leadership of Martha Green than under the leadership of Helen Blue.

As we can see from the experience of Beacon Center, we live in a world that values the kind of order that Helen Blue wants to bring to Beacon Center, and there can be much environmental resistance to the development of learning organizations. But if nothing else, the idea of the learning organization serves as a bridge between the systems perspective and the interpretive perspective.

Interpretive Perspective

Social constructionist perspective

As I have been suggesting, when Helen Blue became executive director at Beacon Center, she wanted to introduce more "rational order" and have fewer internal voices speaking about the kind of place the Center should be. It might be said that she found Martha Green's vision for Beacon Center to be too "interpretive." Theories of organizations within the **interpretive perspective on organizations** are quite diverse, but they all share one basic premise: organizations are creations of human consciousness and reflect the worldviews of the creators; they are social constructions of reality.

The interpretive perspective rejects both the rational and the systems perspectives. Contrary to the rational perspective, the interpretive perspective focuses on processes rather than goals; emphasizes "disorganization, untidiness and flexibility" (Hassard, 1993, p. 3) rather than control and reason; and emphasizes a diversity of approaches rather than one right way. Contrary to the systems perspective, the interpretive perspective emphasizes human agency in creating organizations and challenges the constraining influence of external forces.

In addition to these basic premises, three propositions are common to the interpretive perspective:

1. Organizational survival is based more on "creative confusion" (Gergen, 1992) than on rational order.

2. Organizations are increasingly fragmented into multiple realities and should be studied through multiple voices rather than through the unitary voice of the manager (Linstead, 1993).

3. There is a need for new organizational structures that are more "decentralized, self-regulating, fluid, and flexible" (Thompson, 1993, p. 185). Policy networks, interagency task forces, and "adhocracies" are thought to be the prototype of the organization of the future (Fox & Miller, 1995).

Different interpretive theorists focus on different themes in relation to these basic premises. The four separate approaches summarized in Exhibit 12.7 will give you some sense of these differences.

Social Action Model. One of the most influential contributions to the interpretive study of organizations is that of British sociologist David Silverman, presented in his 1971 book *The Theory of Organizations: A Sociological Framework.* Criticizing both rational and systems perspectives, Silverman proposed an approach to organizations that emphasizes the active role of individual organizational actors in creating the organization—an

EXHIBIT 12.7

The Interpretive Perspective on Formal Organizations

Major theme: The organization is a social construction of reality.

Theory	Central Idea
Social action model (Silverman)	The organization is defined by individual actors.
Organizational culture model	Organizations are cultures with shared experiences and shared meanings.
Managing diversity model	Organizational systems and practices should maximize the potential advantages of diversity in organizational membership.
Discourse theory of public administration	Facilitating discourse about differences among the organization's members is the most effective way to achieve organizational goals.

EXHIBIT 12.8

Silverman's Questions for Studying a Specific Organization (Social Action Model)

Who are the principal actors in the organization?

What goals are the actors trying to achieve?

How are the different actors involved in the organization?

What strategies do they use to achieve their goals?

What are the consequences of their actions for each other and for the development of interactional patterns in the organization?

Source: Silverman, 1971.

approach known as **Silverman's social action model**. He proposed a set of questions, presented in Exhibit 12.8, to ask when studying a specific organization.

In a more recent work, Silverman (1994) criticizes the singular emphasis of his earlier model on organizational actors. He suggests that in reacting against deterministic theories of environmental constraints, he failed to acknowledge the influence of history and social structure. He further suggests that his portrayal of human behavior as free and undetermined failed to acknowledge the influence of cultural scripts and the tendency of humans to see their behavior as freer than it is. This self-critique is consistent with other recent criticisms of the limitations of the interpretive perspective (e.g., Reed, 1993; Thompson, 1993).

Organizational Culture Model. In contrast to Silverman's deemphasis of culture, Edgar Schein (1992) focuses on organizations as cultures whose members have shared experiences that produce shared meanings, or interpretations. Organizations, therefore, exist as much in the heads of their members as in policies, rules, and procedures. The **organizational culture model** views organizations as ongoing, interactive processes of reality construction, involving many organizational actors. Organizational culture is made up of "slogans, evocative language, symbols, stories, myths, ceremonies, rituals, and patterns of tribal behavior" (Morgan, 1986, p. 133) but also of mundane, routine, day-to-day activities. For example, under Martha Green's leadership, the slogan "client input" was an important feature of the Beacon Center culture, buttressed by the day-to-day practice of soliciting client opinions.

When we become new members of an organization, some aspects of its culture are immediately obvious. But other aspects are more difficult to decipher, causing us to feel uncomfortable and confused. For example, after 1 day in a field practicum agency, we may understand the cultural norms about casual versus professional dress and extended versus brief lunch hours, but it may take us several weeks to decipher whether we are in a cooperative or competitive culture. There may be a clear slogan about commitment to clients, but it may take some time to decipher how that commitment is implemented, or whether it is.

Organizational culture is always evolving, and it is not always unitary. In many organizations, like Beacon Center under the administration of Helen Blue, competing beliefs and value systems produce subcultures. Given the evolution of organizational culture and rapid societal changes, it is not unusual to find a split between the old guard and the new guard or to find cultural divisions based on organizational function. For example, members of prevention units in community mental health centers may speak a different language than clinicians in the same agency. The result may be cultural fragmentation or cultural warfare.

According to the organizational culture approach, organizations choose their environments and interact with them based on their interpretive schemes. It could be said that when Martha Green was executive director, Beacon Center saw itself as more humane than, and therefore superior to, other organizations serving homeless persons. Founders, staff, and board members had certain definitions of other agencies and of their client group that they used to influence referring agencies, funding sources, and clientele. They clearly saw themselves as proactive, capable of influencing their environments. This behavior is consistent with the organizational culture premise that organizations, through their interpretive schemes, "often create the constraints, barriers, and situations that cause them problems" (Morgan, 1986, p. 137). Other agencies did feel a certain resentment toward the arrogance and self-righteousness of Beacon Center under Martha Green's leadership. Under Helen Blue, on the other hand, clients and staff resent not being included in decisions.

Criticisms of the organizational culture approach are twofold (Morgan, 1997). One criticism is leveled at theorists who write about managing organizational culture. These theorists are sometimes criticized for being biased in favor of management and potentially exploitative of other employees. They are also criticized for overstating managers' potential to control culture, negating the role of multiple actors in the creation of shared meaning. The second criticism of the organizational culture approach is that it fails to take account of the fact that some members have more power than others to influence the construction of culture.

Managing Diversity Model. In the 1990s, organizational theorists developed an approach to organizational management called the **managing diversity model**. Given the trend toward greater diversity in the labor force, several social scientists (e.g., Cox, 1993; Thomas, 1991) have suggested that contemporary organizations cannot be successful unless they can learn to manage diverse populations.

The purpose in managing diversity is to maximize the advantages of diversity while minimizing its disadvantages. Taylor Cox (1993), a leading proponent of the model, says: "I view the goal of managing diversity as maximizing the ability of all employees to contribute to organizational goals and to achieve their full potential unhindered by group identities such as gender, race, nationality, age, and departmental affiliation" (p. 11). Cox reviews the research relevant to management of diversity and comes to two conclusions: (1) organizations that manage diversity effectively have an advantage in creativity, problem solving, and flexibility, and (2) when diversity in the workforce is not effectively managed, communication problems and decision times increase, and member morale decreases.

In a study of workgroups, one research team found that *informational diversity*, diversity in the knowledge bases of group members, as might happen in multidisciplinary teams, has a positive effect on work group performance (Jehn, Northcraft, & Neale, 1999). On the other hand, *value diversity*, diversity in views about the mission and goal of the work group, is associated with less job satisfaction and commitment to the job.

Gender and age diversity are also associated with improved group member morale. Research findings from the U.S. workforce document higher turnover and absentee rates for women and for men of color than for white men. The cause may be organizational failure to effectively manage diversity (Cox, 1993). Social service organizations are as liable as other types of organizations to fail in this way.

Cox (1993) suggests that effective management of diversity will not happen in many organizations without a more solid commitment to it. Management of diversity is still a young idea and a long distance from the one right way of the rational perspective, which has dominated modern thinking about organizations. Pioneering organizations in the United States have begun to develop specific tools to assist organizations to become more effective at managing diversity. The organizational objectives and the specific tools needed to accomplish those objectives are shown in Exhibit 12.9. How well would Cox say that your field agency is doing in managing diversity? Your school of social work?

Discourse Theory of Public Administration. Charles Fox and Hugh Miller (1995) have proposed what they call a **discourse theory of public administration**. They argue that organizational theory has erred by exaggerating the rationality of human nature, by assuming that organizations are concrete entities, and by assuming consensus about organizational goals. Instead, they say, human behavior is more political than rational, organizations are social constructions created by a struggle over meanings, and differing meanings are reflected in disagreements and tensions about organizational goals. Speaking more specifically, they draw our attention to the widely held myth that in the United States, we operate under a rational model of democracy, in which public policy and administration reflect the wishes of the people. They counter this myth with evidence that the public will is manipulated by the news media, political spin doctors, and special interest groups; that the majority of people do not vote or remain vigilant about public issues; and that the greatest influences on elected officials are lobbyists and special interest groups.

EXHIBIT 12.9

Strategies for Effective Management of Diversity

Model Dimension	Tools
I. Culture *Objective:* Create climate in which members of all identity groups excel	1. Hire or promote people who embrace the new values 2. Reinforce values in rewards and appraisal 3. Educate and communicate
II. Pluralism *Objectives:* Create a two-way socialization process Ensure influence of minority culture perspectives on core organization norms and values	1. Managing/valuing diversity (MVD) training 2. New-member orientation programs 3. Language training 4. Diversity in key committees 5. Explicit treatment of diversity in mission statements 6. Identity-based advisory groups 7. Create flexibility in norm systems
III. Structural integration *Objective:* No correlation between culture group identity and job status	1. Diversity in key committees 2. Education program 3. Affirmative action programs 4. Targeted career development programs
IV. Integration in informal networks *Objective:* Eliminate barriers to entry and participation	1. Mentoring programs 2. Company-sponsored social events 3. Support groups
V. Institutional bias *Objective:* Eliminate bias ingrained in management systems	1. Culture audit 2. Survey feedback 3. Changes in manager performance evaluation and rewards 4. Human Resources policy and benefits changes 5. Task forces
VI. Intergroup conflict *Objectives:* Minimize interpersonal conflict based on group identity Minimize backlash by dominant group members Promote intergroup understanding	1. Survey feedback 2. Conflict management training and conflict resolution techniques 3. MVD training 4. Core groups 5. Equal Employment Opportunity-related training

Source: Cox, 1993, p. 243.

Fox and Miller (1995) suggest that the myth of a rational model of democracy has reinforced an inclination for public agencies to be organized, in large part, according to the principles of Taylor's scientific management and Weber's ideal-type bureaucracy. Fox and Miller argue instead for a new model of public policy and administration that can restore greater democracy to the political process. In their discourse model, public administrators would become midwives, using their skills and commitment to facilitate a more authentic public discourse among disparate groups about public issues. Midwife is a very different metaphor than scientific management. To be eligible to participate in the discourse, persons must be willing to speak sincerely; to take into consideration the "context of the problem, the lives of those affected, and the public interest"(Fox & Miller, 1995, p. 123); to maintain active engagement with the ongoing discourse; and to have a contribution, broadly defined, to make. Fox and Miller (1995) argue that authentic discourse cannot occur among people of unequal status; all participants in the discourse are equal citizens. This last point may have been what Martha Green had in mind when she tried to minimize power differences at Beacon Center.

Critical Perspective

Conflict perspective

Although it may appear that Martha Green administered Beacon Center from an interpretative perspective, it is probably more accurate to describe her worldview as a **critical perspective on organizations**. She tried to minimize the power differences in her organization, and when she asked her staff to vote on sensitive issues, she invoked the secret ballot to neutralize any possible power dynamics. Critical theorists share the interpretive perspective's bias about the role of human consciousness in human behavior, but critical theory undertakes, as its central concern, a critique of the status quo and a vision for change suggested by this critique. More specifically, critical theories of organizations focus on patterns of domination and oppression in organizations. This focus distinguishes the critical perspective from the interpretive perspective, which ignores or negates issues of power and the possibility that persons in power positions can privilege their own versions of reality and marginalize other versions.

Morgan (1997) draws on the work of a diverse group of theorists and researchers to identify several ways in which organizations serve as "instruments of domination":

- Formal organizations create and continually reproduce patterns of social inequality through organizational hierarchies.

- Employees are exposed to work conditions that are hazardous to their health and welfare—such as working with toxic materials or dangerous equipment—and work expectations that interfere with personal health maintenance and family life.

- Employees experience mental health problems caused by job insecurity in a downsizing and globalizing economy.

Exhibit 12.10 summarizes the two critical approaches to formal organizations discussed here: organizations as multiple oppressions and nonhierarchical organizations.

EXHIBIT 12.10
The Critical
Perspective
on Formal
Organizations

Major theme: Organizations are instruments of domination.

Theory	Central Idea
Organizations as multiple oppressions	Organizations exclude and discriminate against multiple groups.
Nonhierarchical organizations	Organizations run by consensus, with few rules and with informality, are least likely to oppress employees.

Organizations as Multiple Oppressions. Have you ever felt oppressed—voiceless, powerless, abused, manipulated, unappreciated—in any of the organizations you have been a member of? Do you think that whole groups of people have felt oppressed in any of those organizations? In the contemporary era, the critical perspective has taken a more focused look at who is oppressed in organizations and the ways in which they are oppressed. This approach was influenced by feminist critiques, during the 1970s and 1980s, of the failure of traditional organizational theories to consider gender issues (Hearn & Parkin, 1993). Feminist critiques led to the recognition that other groups besides women had also been marginalized by formal organizations and by organizational theory.

Jeff Hearn and Wendy Parkin (1993) recommend viewing **organizations as multiple oppressions**—social constructions that exclude and discriminate against some categories of people. Oppression happens through a variety of processes, including "marginalization, domination and subordination, degradation, ignoring, harassment, invisibilizing, silencing, punishment, discipline and violence" (Hearn & Parkin, 1993, p. 153). These processes may also be directed at a variety of organizational actors, including "staff, members, employees, residents, patients and clients" (p. 153). Organizational domination can become compounded by multiple oppressions. Hearn and Parkin cite the example of a children's home where children were being sexually abused and female staff were dissuaded, by intimidation, from reporting the situation.

According to Hearn and Parkin, frequently oppressed groups include women, younger and older people, persons with disabilities, those of lower economic class, persons of color, and sexual minorities. These groups may be excluded from organizations; admitted only in subordinate roles as clients, patients, or students; or admitted but discriminated against within the organization. If groups that are excluded or otherwise oppressed form their own organizations, dominant groups construct a hierarchy of organizations that maintains the oppression, as when a black organization is viewed as inferior to similar white organizations.

Hearn and Parkin suggest that at the current time, the group most marginalized by formal organizations is persons with disabilities. They are often physically excluded from organizations by inaccessible physical environments, and they are further marginalized by a "prevailing ideology . . . of medicine and medication, with people's disabilities being seen as sickness or illness and able-bodied people being seen as able and well, rather [than] the environment being disabling" (Hearn & Parkin, 1993, pp. 157-158).

Critical theory, with its focus on domination and oppression, reminds us that mainstream organizational theory does not provide "organizational theory for the exploited" (Morgan, 1986, p. 316). Therefore, our understanding of organizations is incomplete and biased. If you have felt somewhat alienated in reading about the other theories in this chapter, you may be reacting to this bias. However, critical theory has been criticized for being ideological, giving priority to the voices of oppressed persons, just as Martha Green was criticized for giving too strong a voice to homeless persons. Critical theorists reply that their focus is no more ideological than is recognizing only the voices of the elite.

The critical perspective on organizations has special relevance to social workers. It helps us recognize the ways in which clients' struggles are related to oppressive structures and processes in the formal organizations with which they interact. We must be constantly vigilant about the multiple oppressions within the organizations we provide social services to.

Nonhierarchical Organizations. Helen Blue preferred a more hierarchical organizational structure than the one developed at Beacon Center under Martha Green's leadership. A constant theme in critical theory is that hierarchical organizational structures lead to alienation and internal class conflict. Critical theorists directly challenge the rational perspective argument that hierarchy is needed to maximize efficiency; they point out that in fact hierarchy is often inefficient but that it is maintained because it works well to protect the positions of persons in power. For example, the staff at Beacon Center wastes much time and energy trying to find ways to thwart Helen Blue's decisions.

Humanistic perspective

The idea of the **nonhierarchical organization** is not new. Human relations theorists have recommended "participatory management," which involves lower-level employees in at least some decision making, for several decades. Historical evidence indicates that since the 1840s, experiments with nonhierarchical organizations have accompanied every wave of antimodernist social movements in the United States (Rothschild-Whitt & Whitt, 1986). In recent decades, feminist critiques of organizational theory have helped to stimulate renewed interest in nonhierarchical organizations. Nevertheless, such organizations constitute only a small portion of the population of formal organizations, and research on nonhierarchical organizations constitutes a very small part of the massive body of research on organizations (Iannello, 1992).

EXHIBIT 12.11

Traits of a
Consensual
Model of Formal
Organizations

Authority vested in the membership rather than in an elite at the top of a hierarchy

Decisions made only after issues have been widely discussed by the membership

Rules kept to a minimum

Personal, rather than formal, relationships among members

Leadership based on election, with rotation of leadership positions

No financial reward for leadership roles

No winners and losers in decision making—decisions made based on unchallenged "prevailing sentiment" (consensus)

Source: Iannello, 1992.

Exhibit 12.11 lists the traits of a model of nonhierarchical organization that Kathleen Iannello (1992) calls the consensual model. One study of five nonhierarchical organizations summarized some of the special challenges, both internal and external, faced by consensual organizations (Rothschild-Whitt & Whitt, 1986). Internal challenges include increased time needed for decision making, increased emotional intensity due to the more personal style of relationships, and difficulty incorporating diversity. External challenges are the constraints of social, economic, and political environments that value and reward hierarchy. Almost a decade later, these same challenges were consistent themes in a volume of stories about feminist organizations told by 25 authors (Ferree & Martin, 1995).

On the basis of her study of two successful feminist organizations, Iannello (1992) proposes that the internal challenges of the nonhierarchical organization can be addressed by what she calls a "modified consensual organization" model. Critical decisions continue to be made by the broad membership, but routine decisions are made by smaller groups; members are recognized by ability and expertise, but not by rank and position; there are clear goals, developed through a consensual process.

The two most prominent contemporary examples of organizations based on consensus are feminist organizations and Japanese firms. Both types of organizations typically feature a strong, shared ideology and culture, which should lead to relatively easy consensus. However, the available evidence suggests that feminist organizations in which membership crosses either ideological or cultural lines have not been successful in operating by consensus (Ferree & Martin, 1995; Iannello, 1992). Under Martha Green's administration, most decisions at Beacon Center were made by consensus, but Martha was sometimes criticized for building a staff with little ideological or cultural diversity.

Given the increasing diversity of the workforce in the United States, management of difference and conflict can be expected to become an increasing challenge in organizational life. This is as true for social work organizations as for other organizations. To date, the literature on consensual organizations has failed to address the difficult challenges of diverse ideological and cultural perspectives among organizational members—issues that are the focus of the managing diversity model and the discourse theory. This is an area in which social work should take the lead.

Burnout: A Negative Organizational Outcome

It was suggested at the beginning of this chapter that formal organizations meet our needs, assist us to fulfill goals, and nurture our development—but that they also make stressful demands, thwart our goals, inhibit our holistic development, and constrain our behavior. Robert T. Golembiewski (1994, p. 211) uses more colorful language to talk about the negative effects of organizations, suggesting that "organizational life bends people out of shape, and may even make them crazy." Indeed, some of the staff at Beacon Center have been heard to say, since Helen Blue took over, that they must leave the Center before they go crazy.

In the past 2 decades, researchers have attempted to answer the question, Is organizational membership hazardous to your health? The answer, to date, is that organizational membership is *often* hazardous to health, and burnout is the identified hazard. **Burnout** is a "prolonged response to chronic emotional and interpersonal stressors on the job, and is defined by the three dimensions of exhaustion, cynicism, and inefficacy" (Maslach, Schaufeli, & Leiter, 2001, p. 397). The study of burnout has appeal because it can give voice to individuals who are dominated or exploited in organizations, providing "organizational theory for the exploited" as recommended by Morgan (1986, p. 316).

Burnout is most often studied using the Maslach Burnout Inventory (MBI) (Maslach & Jackson, 1981). The MBI, first developed for use with human service workers and later revised for use with teachers, analyzes three dimensions of burnout: (1) emotional exhaustion, or a feeling of being near the "end of one's rope," (2) depersonalization, or a strong tendency to distance oneself from others, thinking of them as things or objects, and (3) reduced personal accomplishment, which refers to perceptions of doing well on a worthwhile project. In recent years, the MBI has been revised for use in occupations other than human services and education that are not as people oriented. The three dimensions of burnout have been conceptualized in the broader terms found in the previous definition of burnout: exhaustion, cynicism, and inefficacy.

Golembiewski (1994) has built an eight-phase model of burnout based on these three domains, with depersonalization representing the least serious domain of burnout, reduced personal accomplishment a more serious domain, and emotional exhaustion the most serious domain, occurring in late-phase burnout. Golembiewski and colleagues have completed extensive research, with a large number of both public-sector and business organizations, and found several indicators of well-being to be associated with the phases of burnout. With progression through the phases of burnout, research participants report increasingly less work satisfaction, lower self-esteem, greater physical symptoms, lower performance appraisals, and greater hostility, anxiety, and depression.

Golembiewski (1994) found that approximately 45% of 16,476 participants from 55 organizations were in the last three phases of burnout, with high levels of emotional exhaustion, as indicated by their scores on the MBI. Recent international research has noted high levels of burnout among physicians and other health care providers (Bell, Davison, & Sefcik, 2002; Clever, 2002; Jancin, 2002; McManus, Winder, & Gordon, 2002). The high level of hazard in so many settings suggests that social workers need to be attuned to symptoms of job-related burnout, in their clients and in themselves.

Burnout has been found to be associated with absenteeism, turnover, lower productivity and effectiveness at work, decreased job satisfaction, and reduced commitment to the job or the organization. Burnout can be contagious, causing interpersonal conflict and disrupting work.

After 25 years of research on burnout, researchers found six dimensions of work life to be associated with burnout (Maslach et al., 2001):

1. *Workload.* Work overload makes too many demands and exhausts people's capacity to recover. There may also be a workload mismatch in which people are assigned tasks for which they lack skills or interest. The emotional work of people-oriented occupations like social work can be draining if people are required to display emotions that run counter to their feelings. Workload has been found to be directly related to the exhaustion dimension of burnout. Cross-national comparisons have found that workers in North America have higher levels of burnout than workers in Western Europe, particularly higher levels of exhaustion and cynicism (Maslach et al., 2001). As you may recall, we noted in Chapter 9 that workers in the United States work longer hours than workers in Western Europe.

2. *Control.* People may have inadequate control over the resources needed to do their work, or they may be given responsibilities without the authority to do the work. These situations are associated with inefficacy (reduced personal accomplishment). The social workers at Beacon Center miss Martha Green's trust in them to make their own decisions, and they chafe at their diminishing control over their work and the direction of the organization.

3. *Reward.* Organizations may fail to provide appropriate rewards for the work that people do. There may be inadequate financial rewards, but social rewards, such as recognition and appreciation for contributions made, may also be missing. In addition, the work itself may not have intrinsic rewards because it does not feel important and useful. Lack of reward is associated with inefficacy. The social workers at Beacon Center once found that the social rewards more than made up for the poor pay, but they now miss the feeling that they are working in a special place and making a difference.

4. *Community.* In some organizations, people do not have a sense of positive connections to others. People may work in isolation from others, their interactions may be impersonal, or there may be chronic and unresolved conflict with others on the job. Social support from supervisors has been found to be particularly important. It is clear that a sense of community has broken down since Martha Green left Beacon Center.

5. *Fairness.* There may be inequity of workload or pay, or work evaluations and promotions may be handled unfairly. Feelings of being treated unfairly are associated with exhaustion as well as with cynicism about the workplace.

6. *Values.* Sometimes people face situations where the job requires them to compromise their ethical standards. Or they may find that there is a discrepancy between what the organization says it values and the day-to-day activities in the organization. Increasingly, human service organizations face a conflict between the competing values of high-quality service and cost containment. Little research has been done on the role of values in burnout. The social workers at Beacon Center put high value on advocating for their homeless clients, and they are alienated by Helen Blue's request that they become more moderate in those efforts.

The research to date indicates that organizational factors play a bigger role in burnout than individual factors. And yet, greater attention has been given to individual-oriented approaches to preventing burnout than to changing aspects of organizations.

It has been suggested that social work is an occupation with above-average risk of burnout (Hasenfeld, 1983; Jayaratne & Chess, 1984; Pines & Kafry, 1978; Soderfeldt, Soderfeldt, & Warg, 1995). One research team compared the burnout profiles for five occupational groups—teaching, social services, medicine, mental health, and law enforcement—in the United States and Holland (Schaufeli & Enzmann, 1998). They found that the comparisons differed by nation. In the United States, the levels of cynicism were higher for social service workers and mental health workers than for the other occupational groups, but they were about average in Holland. Other than that, the levels of burnout were about average for social service workers in both countries. We know that our work as social workers has many satisfactions as well as many stressors, but further research is needed to discover which way the balance tilts and why.

Social Work and Formal Organizations

You have probably learned already that social work is a diverse profession; we use diverse methods to address a diversity of social problems—and we work in diverse types of organizations. We work in hospitals, outpatient health and mental health clinics, in-home programs, nursing homes and other residential programs, crisis shelters, prisons and jails, government social service agencies, private family and children's agencies, schools, the workplace, community centers, social movement organizations, research centers, planning organizations, and in private practice, among other places.

We can think about the differences among the organizations in which social workers are found in several ways. One is to divide them into host organizations, social work-oriented organizations, and human service organizations (Popple & Leighninger, 1993). In *host organizations*—such as schools, the workplace, correctional facilities, the military, and hospitals—social service is not the primary purpose of the organization. Social workers in these settings work with other disciplines to meet organizational goals, and they often serve as mediators between clients and the organization. In contrast, *social work-oriented organizations* have social service delivery as their purpose and are staffed primarily by social workers. Family and children's agencies and government social service programs are examples of social work-oriented organizations. Social workers also work in *human service organizations,* whose staff come from a variety of disciplines but work in a coordinated fashion to provide an array of services. Community mental health centers and drug treatment programs are examples of human service organizations.

Another way to think about formal organizations in which social workers work has traditionally been to divide them into public and private organizations. *Public social service organizations* are those funded and administered by government; *private social service organizations* are privately funded and administered. This distinction made some sense in earlier eras, but it is not very useful in the contemporary era. Today, many public agencies contract programs out to private organizations, and many private organizations, like Beacon Center, receive public as well as private funding. The Social Security Act of 1935 ushered in an era of government dominance in both the funding and administering of social service programs, but for the past 2 decades, we have seen increasing **privatization** of social services, shifting the administration of programs back to private organizations (Lynn, 2002; Ryan, 1999). This trend is based on a belief that privatization will lead to more efficient and effective service delivery. It has been estimated that more than half of public social service dollars are contracted to private organizations (Ryan, 1999).

Among private service organizations, the distinction between *nonprofit* and *for-profit* organizations is increasingly important. Social workers have a long history with nonprofit organizations, but their involvement in for-profit organizations is more recent and has been increasing steadily since the 1970s (Lynn, 2002; Ryan, 1999). Since the passage of the Personal Responsibility and Work Opportunity Reconciliation Act (PRWORA) of 1996, a number of high-profile for-profit corporations, like Lockheed Martin, have entered the welfare-to-work market (Ryan, 1999). Large for-profit organizations have had the resources to move quickly into new markets and have become serious competitors for nonprofit organizations in vying for government contracts. Some nonprofit organizations are responding by developing partnerships with for-profit organizations; others are changing to for-profit status. There is general agreement that for-profit organizations will continue to have a large presence in the social service landscape in the future.

The entry of for-profit organizations into the social service arena poses questions that have been raised by many observers: Will for-profit organizations, in search of profitable business opportunities, voluntarily serve the common good? Will they engage in advocacy and community building activities that are the hallmark of the social work profession and the history of nonprofit organizations? Historically, social service agencies funded advocacy and community-building activities out of surplus from other programs. Social workers will need to be vigilant to see that these important social work functions do not disappear.

Organizations in which social workers work have not been immune to the economic trends discussed in Chapter 9. Downsizing and the resulting "do more with less" climate have increased work-related stressors, and increasing economic inequality is producing stubborn social problems that must be addressed with shrinking resources. Social workers, like other workers, are increasingly involved in "contingent" labor situations—that is, in part-time, temporary, and contractual arrangements. More and more sectors of the social welfare system are using a managed care model and searching for the one best way. There is increasing evidence that social service organizations are favoring clients who can pay, or who qualify for payment by a third party, and failing to serve people who are poor or have the most challenging problems (Lynn, 2002; Ryan, 1999). The "information revolution" has raised new issues about protection of client confidentiality. Given these challenges, a solid grounding in organizational theory can be an important tool in the social work survival kit.

Culturally Competent Care Systems

Issues of diversity, and managing diversity, are important for all formal organizations, but they take on special urgency in social service organizations. Social workers have a commitment to provide competent service to diverse populations. (We take a broad view of diversity, including, but not limited to, gender, race, ethnicity, social class, religion, disability, age, and sexual orientation.) In recent years, a growing body of literature has recommended ways of providing culturally competent practice (e.g., Devore & Schlesinger, 1999; Green, 1999; Lum, 2003).

Although there is much an individual social worker can do to become more culturally competent, individual efforts will not go far unless the vision of cultural competence is encoded into the fabric of social service organizations. A culturally competent system of care is built by social service organizations with the following traits:

■ The organization is located where it is accessible to the targeted population, and it is decorated in a manner appealing to the population. Particular attention is paid to the accessibility of the physical environment for people with a variety of disabilities.

■ A name is chosen for the organization that is acceptable to the targeted population. For example, for some ethnic groups, mental health services carry a social stigma, and these words should be avoided when naming the organization (Lum, 2003). A name like Beacon Center carries no stigma.

■ Diversity is reflected in the board of directors, administrators, and professional and nonprofessional staff, in accordance with the targeted population. The organization is engaged in an ongoing audit of the diversity represented at all levels from clients to board of directors (Mor Barak, 2000).

■ The organization conducts or supports ongoing training and communication about diversity issues and multicultural communication. Ongoing efforts are made to create a climate where people can recover from multicultural miscommunications (Beckett & Dungee-Anderson, 1998).

■ Ongoing efforts are made to involve minority staff members in information networks and decision-making processes (Mor Barak, 2000).

■ Staff are actively engaged in learning about the community, its norms, values, and formal as well as informal resources. They use what they learn in ongoing program planning. They pay particular attention to the cultural understanding of and preferences for care giving and care receiving (Green, 1999).

■ Staff engage in active outreach, attending local functions, giving talks at community organizations, and so forth, particularly when the targeted population is not inclined to use formal social services. Outreach activities will help build credibility.

■ The staff maintains working relationships with other organizations that serve the same population, such as ethnic agencies, agencies for sexual minority clients, or disability service centers.

IMPLICATIONS FOR SOCIAL WORK PRACTICE

Several principles for social work action are recommended by this discussion of formal organizations:

■ Be alert to the influence of formal organizations on the client's behavior. Be particularly alert to the ways in which the social service organization where you work, as well as other social service organizations to which you frequently refer clients, influences the client's behavior.

- Develop an understanding of the organizational goals of the social service organization where you work and how the tasks that you perform are related to these goals.

- Develop an understanding of the shared meanings in the social service organization where you work and of the processes by which those meanings are developed and maintained.

- Develop an understanding of the forces of inertia and other constraints on rational decision making in the social service organization where you work.

- Develop an understanding of the social, political, economic, cultural, and technological environments of the social service organization where you work.

- Develop an understanding of the sources of legitimacy, power, and economic resources for the social service organization where you work and an understanding of how they influence internal decisions.

- Collaborate with colleagues at the social service organization where you work to understand and enhance the creative use of diversity.

- Collaborate with colleagues at the social service organization where you work to facilitate the inclusion of clients in the political process, internally as well as externally.

- Collaborate with colleagues at the social service organization where you work, and with other relevant parties, to facilitate a more authentic discourse about policy issues among disparate groups.

- Collaborate with colleagues at the social service organization where you work to develop an understanding of multiple oppressions within the organization.

- Be attuned to the symptoms of job-related burnout in yourself, your colleagues, and your clients.

KEY TERMS

bounded rationality
bureaucracy
burnout
critical perspective on organizations

decision-making theory
discourse theory of public
   administration
formal organizations

Hawthorne effect

human relations theory

interpretive perspective on
    organizations

iron cage of rationality

learning organization theory

managing diversity model

nonhierarchical organization

organizational culture model

organizational humanism

organizations as multiple oppressions

political economy model

privatization

rational perspective on organizations

satisfice

scientific management

Silverman's social action model

systems perspective on organizations

Theory X

Theory Y

ACTIVE LEARNING

1. In the case study at the beginning of the chapter, you read about the transition in leadership at Beacon Center. You have also read about four theoretical perspectives on formal organizations. Imagine that you, and not Helen Blue, succeeded Martha Green as executive director at Beacon Center. Write a brief paper covering the following points: What vision would you have for Beacon Center? What would you want to keep the same as it had been and what would you want to change? Use theory to back up your position.

2. Examine aspects of diversity in your workplace, your field practicum agency, or another organization you are familiar with. What can you observe or discover about diversity in the organization on the following variables: gender, age, social class, religion, ethnicity, race, and disability? Compare the diversity found among the management to that among the line workers and clientele. Write a brief paper describing what you found and addressing the following points: How does diversity (or lack of it) appear to affect organizational effectiveness? What changes would you suggest for the organization in terms of diversity? (Based on Strom-Gottfried & Morrissey, 1999).

WEB RESOURCES

ARNOVA

www.arnova.org

Site presented by the Association for Research on Nonprofit Organizations and Voluntary Action (ARNOVA) contains member directory, conference information, publications, partners, and links.

The Alliance

www.allianceonline.org

Site presented by the Alliance for Nonprofit Management contains information on board development, financial management, strategic planning, fund-raising, and risk management as well a newsletter and FAQs.

Center on Nonprofits & Philanthropy

www.urban.org/centers/cnp.html

Site maintained by the Center on Nonprofits & Philanthropy at the Urban Institute contains fact sheets, state profiles, resources, and databases.

CHAPTER 13

Communities

Elizabeth D. Hutchison

Communities

Elizabeth D. Hutchison
Virginia Commonwealth University

Why has there been a revitalization of interest in community social work in the contemporary era?

What are the implications of the different theoretical approaches to community for community social work practice?

Key Ideas

As you read this chapter, take note of these central ideas:

1. After several decades of declining interest, we are currently seeing a resurgence of interest in community.

2. Community consists of people bound either by geography or webs of communication, sharing common ties, and interacting with one another.

3. Sense of community is based on belonging, being important to each other, and having mutual commitment.

4. Both relational communities, based on voluntary association, and territorial communities, based on geography, are relevant to social work.

5. Five approaches to community have relevance for contemporary social work: contrasting types approach, spatial arrangements approach, social systems approach, conflict approach, and social bond approach.

6. Long-standing disagreements about social work's relationships to communities center on four points of tension: community as context for practice versus target of practice, agency orientation versus social action, conflict model versus collaborative model, and expert versus partner in the social change process.

CASE STUDY 13.1

TITO AND THE YMCA GANG
ALTERNATIVES AND INTERVENTION PROGRAM

Seventeen-year-old Tito lives in the Porter Crossing neighborhood of Lakeside, a large midwestern city. Porter Crossing is often called Little Puerto Rico by residents of other city neighborhoods. The main streets of Porter Crossing are crowded with stores whose windows are protected by grillwork and iron bars. Neighborhood walls and fences display spray-painted symbols that mark the territories of over 40 gangs. A few years ago, the gangs of Porter Crossing reigned over a lucrative drug trade, but the drug traffic has now moved elsewhere.

Tito is the leader of the Zs, a Puerto Rican gang. For those in the know, the three spikes in Tito's carefully trimmed goatee readily identify his affiliation with the Zs. Tito says that safety is a major reason that he joined the Zs, because they will "watch my back." On the other hand, his membership in the Zs also can present safety problems. For example, when he had a drug possession charge, the court ordered Tito to attend a special school that had vocational training. Tito was interested in what this school had to offer until he realized that he would have to cross several rival gang territories to attend. He decided that the risk was too great.

The Zs feel very alienated from most social institutions in Porter Crossing; notable exceptions are the YMCA and the church. Schools are places where rival gangs fight over turf, or sometimes places controlled by a rival gang. Tito also thinks that teachers and schools are hostile to gang members, and quickly write them off as people who can't be reached. The police are seen as rival gangs, and gang members view the courts as places that don't understand or care about the safety issues involved in their sentences. The YMCA, on the other hand, operates a program called the Gang Alternatives and Intervention Program (GAIN) that Tito and other Zs see as the only positive opportunity that exists in Porter Crossing.

The Porter Crossing YMCA sits next to Porter Park, which the locals call Death Wish Park, because of the drug trade-related violence that has been so prevalent there in recent years. Still, the Porter Crossing YMCA offers neighborhood residents many of the activities typically offered by YMCAs: swimming lessons, tennis lessons, weight room and aerobics classes, health and child development classes for teen mothers, a Head Start program, and employment training.

GAIN was the idea of YMCA regional director Roberto Colon, who grew up in Porter Crossing. Roberto is committed to providing alternatives and

CASE STUDY 13.1

hope for the youth of the neighborhood, and he does not write off neighborhood members of youth gangs. He had a hard time selling GAIN to many YMCA staff and board members, however, because they saw the gangs as the enemy. He had to promise that gang members would be kept separate from other children and youth at the Porter Crossing YMCA. Roberto also met with leaders and members of the local gangs to get their approval. When it came to hiring staff, Roberto selected former gang members who continue to live in Porter Crossing.

GAIN started with a summer jobs program, funded by the mayor's office, that employed Tito and 16 other gang members to do community cleanup. Among other cleanup duties, the youth painted over gang graffiti on walls and other neighborhood surfaces. Sometimes they simply covered over the graffiti; other times, they created colorful murals to cover the graffiti. As they work in the neighborhood, they wear YMCA staff T-shirts. Roberto explains that these T-shirts serve two functions: they offer an alternative group identity (YMCA staff) to the gang identity and they cover gang-related tattoos.

Besides the summer jobs program, GAIN also provides outreach and case management. One popular outreach program is the gym-and-swim nights for gang members. On these nights, the YMCA closes at the usual time of 9:00 P.M. and reopens a short time later for the members of two or three particular gangs to swim and use the weight room and gym facilities. The schedule for gym-and-swim nights is kept secret, to avoid attacks from rival gangs. Four vans pick up youth in their neighborhoods to avoid the necessity of crossing rival gang territories. Between 50 and 80 gang members attend these nights.

Case managers work one-on-one with gang members, connecting them to jobs or job training. They assist with job applications, provide advice about jobs, and consult about school and other educational opportunities. As needed, they may help with the development of a resume or provide information on how to use the bus system to go downtown. The case managers are tuned in to the special safety needs of gang members and avoid sending them to sites that would endanger them.

Roberto is outraged at the inequities he sees in the distribution of resources for youth across the neighborhoods of Lakeside. He chips away at this inequality where he can, choosing his battles carefully to make good use of his time and energy. He is a member of a number of boards of directors, but one organization that is dear to his heart is Latino Youth Services Network (LYSN), an organization of agency directors from around the state.

CASE STUDY 13.1

With other members of that organization, Roberto has worked hard to address the inequities in the educational system across neighborhoods in Lakeside. One way that he and his colleagues have approached this problem is to discover and publicize accurate figures for school dropout rates for each high school in the city. Roberto and other LYSN members have involved youth in school reform advocacy efforts. One activity organized by the youth was a funeral march of over 1,000 people in front of one high school. Complete with a casket and candles, the funeral march symbolized the death of Lakeside's inner-city youth.

The gang members see Roberto as a local, accessible role model. They know that he is there for them and will fight for them. Roberto is surprised at how readily the youth turned to him as a role model. He is proud of the contributions they have made to improving the physical environment of the neighborhood. He has dreams that activities like gym-and-swim nights can open up dialogue and understanding among rival gangs. In his view, the success of GAIN is based on the knowledge that he and his staff have of the neighborhood and their credibility in it (McLaughlin, Irby, & Langman, 1994).

CASE 13.2

ANN AND EVAN MAXWELL
OF SOUTHERN CALIFORNIA

Ann and Evan Maxwell moved to Laguna Niguel in 1970, to live in the hills above the Pacific Coast. The daunting commute to Evan's journalism job in Los Angeles was offset by the striking natural beauty of Laguna Niguel. The Maxwells became successful coauthors of the Fiddler series of mystery books, and in 1984, Evan decided to leave his journalism job to devote his full energies to writing books. He found that leaving the newspaper was both liberating and unsettling. He cherished the new freedom but was surprised to learn how much he had depended on the support of friends at work and how much his sense of identity was tied up in

CASE STUDY 13.2

the newspaper. Evan talks about leaving the newspaper as a loss of community.

The Maxwells also began to notice that they had lost all sense of community in Laguna Niguel, due to the runaway growth and development that has transformed Southern California. They are planning to leave Laguna Niguel. Although they share a great deal with many of those who live in Laguna Niguel—they're a white, well-educated, upper middle-class couple—they report that they have almost no contact with their neighbors. Laguna Niguel does not seem like their community anymore. Instead, "their community includes writers in Seattle and Indiana, agents and editors in New York, a computer junk man in the Silicon Valley who buys and sells overstock equipment, and a refugee from the Massachusetts Route 128 computer realm who now reconditions covered wagons" (p. 277). Electronic technologies allow them to be in touch with these people on a weekly basis. The Maxwells are delighted that a sense of community can now be easily achieved across great distances.

Ironically, the Maxwells are thinking about moving to the Four Corners region of Colorado, a place of great natural beauty but also a place that operates on old ideas about the connections between people and their geographically based communities (Garreau, 1991).

A Definition of Community

Although the circumstances of their lives are very different, both Tito and the Maxwells appear to see themselves as members of a community. But exactly what is community? Actually, this question has not been an easy one for social scientists. In fact, George Hillery's 1955 review of the sociological literature found 94 distinct definitions of community. Twenty years later, Seymour Sarason (1974) struggled to define the related concept of "sense of community." Sarason concluded that even though "sense of community" is hard to define, "you know when you have it and when you don't" (p. 157).

How should we interpret the fuzziness of the concepts of "community" and "sense of community"? Some suggest that any concept with so many meanings is unscientific and its potential utility is therefore highly suspect. But Larry Lyon (1987) suggests that the multiplicity of definitions of community is evidence that the concept is meaningful to scholars with diverse interests and perspectives. I would certainly agree that a concept such as community should not be discarded simply because it has been hard to define. Over the past 2 decades, sociologists have in fact worked to develop greater agreement about the meaning of *community,* and community psychologists have been equally diligent about developing greater clarity for *sense of community.* Both lines of inquiry are relevant to social work.

Sociological attempts to reach agreement on the definition of community have centered on the report that approximately three fourths of the 94 definitions found in the sociological literature included the same three elements: geographic area, social interaction, and common ties (Hillery, 1955, p. 118). Roberto Colon's understanding of community seems very similar, but Ann and Evan Maxwell would probably question the first of these elements, geographic area.

Historically, community did have a geographic meaning in sociology. More recently, however, two different sociological meanings of community have developed: community as a geographic or territorial concept and community as an interactional or relational concept (Gusfield, 1975). In this chapter, I discuss both meanings of community, because both appear to have relevance for human behavior in the contemporary era. Recently, researchers are finding more similarities than differences in these two types of community (Obst, Zinkiewics, & Smith, 2002a, 2002b). I use the following definition to cover both territorial and relational communities: **community** is people bound either by geography or by webs of communication, sharing common ties, and interacting with one another.

And what do Ann and Evan Maxwell mean when they say that they have lost all sense of community in Laguna Niguel? In 1974, Seymour Sarason proclaimed the enhancement of "psychological sense of community" as the mission of community psychology. He saw the basic characteristics of **sense of community** as "the perception of similarity with others, an acknowledged interdependence with others, a willingness to maintain this interdependence by giving to or doing for others what one expects from them, the feeling that one is part of a larger dependable and stable structure" (p. 157). These characteristics of sense of community are very similar to the "common ties" element of the definition of community. The elements of community and sense of community are presented in Exhibit 13.1. We look more closely at the concept of sense of community in a later section.

Territorial Community and Relational Community

In telling the Maxwells' story, Joel Garreau (1991) argues that community in the contemporary era is based on voluntary interaction (**relational community**), not on geography or territory (**territorial community**). Although the Maxwells no longer feel a sense of connection to their neighbors, they get a personal sense of community from their electronic connections. It appears, however, that Ann and Evan will continue to

EXHIBIT 13.1
Essential Elements
of Community and
Sense of Community

Community *(from community sociology literature)*

- Linked by geography or webs of communication
- Common ties
- Interaction

Sense of Community *(from community psychology literature)*

- Similarity with others
- Interdependence
- Mutual exchanges to fulfill needs
- Sense of belonging

Source: Based on Hillery, 1955, Sarason, 1974, Wellman, 1999.

search for territorial community in Colorado while at the same time staying strongly connected to their electronically based relational community. In contrast, Tito does not have access to ties beyond his neighborhood, and he does have a strong sense of community with the Zs. For Tito, his family, his neighbors, and the members of his gang, the health of the neighborhood is critically intertwined with their own personal well-being. What about for you? Are your strongest supports based on territorial or relational community?

In premodern times, human groups depended, by necessity, on the territorial community to meet their human needs. But each development in communication and transportation technology has loosened that dependency somewhat. Electronic communications now connect people over distant spaces, with a high degree of both immediacy and intimacy. In the past week, I have enjoyed e-mail conversations with several students who live busy lives scattered around the greater Washington, D.C., metropolitan area, friends on the main campus in Richmond, former students who are scattered around the country, a former colleague in Maine, my daughter in Lake Tahoe, my son in Philadelphia, my sister in Atlanta, my publisher in Los Angeles, a best friend from college who just moved from Atlanta to Richmond, a researcher in Australia, and an old friend in Massachusetts.

For a number of years, researchers have been finding that local ties make up a decreasing portion of our social connections, and they have interpreted that finding to mean that territorial community is no longer important in our lives (Hunter & Riger, 1986; Wellman, 1982; Wellman & Wortely, 1990). A more careful look at this research suggests, however, that even highly mobile people like the Maxwells continue to have a lot of contacts in their territorial communities. One study in Toronto (Wellman, 1996) found that if we study *ties,* the number of people with whom we have connections, it is true that the majority of ties for most of us are nonterritorial. However, when we study *contacts,* our actual interactions, two thirds of all contacts are local, in the neighborhood or work setting.

Maybe it is just nostalgic longing, but Garreau's telling of the Maxwells' story suggests that when technology opens the possibilities for relational communities, it does not necessarily spell the death of territorial community. Wendy Griswold (1994, p. 150) proposes that people can have ties to both relational and territorial communities at the same time. Perhaps that is what the Maxwells hope to do once they have relocated to Colorado. Griswold recognizes the possibility that the new technologies will simply allow us to develop and maintain a larger network of increasingly superficial relationships. But she also points out the possibility that the new capacity to be immediately and intimately connected across space could help us to develop more shared meanings and become more tolerant of our differences.

As social workers concerned about social justice, however, we must understand the multiple implications of inequality of access to the new technologies. These technologies open opportunities for relational community and the multitude of resources provided by such communities. Skills in using the new technologies are also increasingly rewarded in the labor market. Unless access to these technologies is equalized, however, territorial community will remain central to the lives of some groups—most notably, young children and their caregivers, older adults, poor families, and many persons with disabilities, who have their own special technological needs. On the other hand, the new technologies may make it easier for some people with disabilities to gain access to relational community, even while inaccessible physical environments continue to block their access to territorial community. One of my African American students has told me that she likes the new technology because it is color blind, and she can have encounters of various kinds without feeling that race got in the way.

Although both territorial and relational communities are relevant to social work, social work's commitment to social justice has recently led to a renewed emphasis on territorial community (Ewalt, Freeman, & Poole, 1998). That same commitment also requires social workers to work toward equalization of access to both territorial and relational community.

Social Workers and Communities: Our History

From the earliest history of social work in the United States, social workers have been interested in the health of communities and in the influence of community on individual behavior (Doherty, 1995; Hardcastle, Wenocur, & Powers, 1997). Social work grew from two different approaches to social problems, one of which—the settlement house movement—was community focused. (The other was the social casework approach, which was focused on individual and family adjustment.) Social workers in the settlement houses provided a wide range of services to help individual poor families cope with the challenges of poverty, including day nurseries, employment bureaus, a place to take a shower, English classes for immigrants, health clinics, pasteurized milk, information on workers' compensation, legal assistance, and emergency financial assistance. Their interests went beyond helping individual families, however; they were also interested in identifying and addressing community conditions that jeopardized the health and well-being of neighborhood families. They campaigned for social reforms such as tenement protection, improved sanitation, and labor reform. In addition, the settlement house social workers were interested in building a sense of mutual support in the poor neighborhoods where they were located. They developed dance, drama, and arts classes, sports and hobby clubs, summer camps, cultural events, and libraries.

Social work's interest in community has ebbed and flowed since then, with more interest shown in some periods than in others. Stanley Wenocur and Steven Soifer (1997) suggest that there have been three peak periods of intense social work interest in community: the Progressive era at the turn of the century, the Depression years of the 1930s, and the Civil Rights era of the 1960s. Contemporary critiques of social work accuse the profession of replacing its original focus on community with a preoccupation with personality problems of individuals (Specht & Courtney, 1994). The social work literature, however, reflects a recent revival of interest in community (e.g., Ewalt, Freeman, & Poole, 1998; Fisher & Karger, 1997; Hardcastle et al., 1997). It is hard to say what mix of societal trends has produced this renewed interest in community social work practice, but some have credited the devolution of policy decisions about social welfare programs to the state and local level, growing social inequality, and social work's renewed commitment to the goal of social justice (see, e.g., Daley & Marsiglia, 2000).

Theoretical Approaches to Community

Social workers traditionally have turned to *community sociology* for theory and research on community. During the 1950s and 1960s, however, community theory and research were scant—almost nonexistent (Lyon, 1987, p. 13). Although this decline in academic interest in community sociology probably had multiple causes, sociologists suggest that it was related in large part to the rising prominence of the concept of mass society (Lyon, 1987; Woolever, 1992). **Mass society** is standardized and homogenized—a society that has no ethnic, class, regional, or local variations in human behavior. Standardized public education, mass media, and residential mobility are cited as the primary mechanisms by which societies become standardized and homogenized. If we assume that mass society has no local or group-based variations in norms, values, and behavior, then community, which is local and group based, loses its relevance to the study of human behavior.

Just as the rising prominence of the concept of mass society contributed to the eclipse of community theory and research, recognition of the limits of mass society as a way of understanding human behavior contributed to the revitalization of community sociology. Beginning in the late 1960s, it became apparent that even though some standardization and homogenization had occurred, mass society had not eradicated ethnic, class, regional, and local variations in human behavior. In the 1980s, a more balanced view of community developed within sociology, a view that recognizes the contributions that both community and mass society make to human behavior (Cuba & Hummon, 1993; Flanagan, 1993; Keane, 1991; Lyon, 1987; Woolever, 1992). In this view, some standardization is present, but local variations still occur. In recent years, scholars from several disciplines have suggested that conflict between communities of competing interests is a more serious problem than the decline of community (Bellah, Madsen, Sullivan, Swidler, & Tipton, 1985; Etzioni, 1993; Hunter, 1994; Newbrough & Chavis, 1986; Rawls, 1993). These scholars identify strong and hotly contested group-based variations in norms, values, and behavior.

At the same time that the concept of community was regaining prominence in sociology, it also emerged as an important concept in psychology. In the midst of concern about the ineffectiveness of existing psychotherapeutic methods, community was discovered—or rediscovered—by the community mental health movement. The field of community psychology developed and became Division 27 of the American Psychological Association (Heller, 1989). Like social workers, community psychologists have turned to the sociological literature for community theory (Heller, 1989; Hunter & Riger, 1986), but they have also developed their own theory of psychological sense of community.

In a 1979 paper presented to the Community Section of the American Sociological Association, Roland Warren (1988) suggested that theorizing about community, like sociological theory in general, includes multiple perspectives. He recommended that multiple theoretical approaches be used to understand communities, because each approach explains particular aspects of community. Two decades later, it still seems wise for social workers to follow Warren's advice and use multiple theoretical approaches for understanding multidimensional community (Flanagan, 1993). That approach is, of course, consistent with the multidimensional approach of this book.

Five perspectives on community seem particularly relevant for social work: contrasting types approach, spatial arrangements approach, social systems approach, conflict approach, and social bond approach. The second of these approaches, the spatial arrangements approach, applies only to territorial communities, but the other four approaches can be applied equally well to both relational and territorial communities. In combination, these five approaches to community should enable you to scan more widely for factors contributing to the problems of living among vulnerable populations, to recognize community resources, and to think more creatively about possible interventions. Using approaches that are not only varied but even discordant should assist you in thinking critically about human behavior and prepare you for the often ambiguous practice situations that you will encounter.

Contrasting Types Approach

Both Roberto Colon and the Maxwells seem concerned about commitment, identification, and relationships within their communities. This concern is at the heart of the oldest theory of community, Ferdinand Tonnies's (1887/1963) concept of gemeinschaft and gesellschaft (translated as community and society). Actually, Tonnies was trying to describe contrasting types of societies, rural preindustrial societies (gemeinschaft) versus urban industrial societies (gesellschaft), but his ideas continue to be used by community sociologists today to understand differences between communities. In **gemeinschaft** communities, relationships are personal and traditional; in **gesellschaft** communities, relationships are impersonal and contractual. The defining characteristics of gemeinschaft and gesellschaft communities are listed in Exhibit 13.2.

Tonnies saw gemeinschaft and gesellschaft as ideal types that will never exist in reality. However, they constitute a hypothetical dichotomy against which the real world can be compared. Although Tonnies's work is more than a century old, the gemeinschaft/gesellschaft dichotomy has proven to be a powerful analytical construct, and it continues to be used and validated in community research. It is also reflected in later typological theories. For example, Charles Cooley (1902/1964) proposed that the social world can be defined in terms of *primary groups* (intimate face-to-face groups to which we form attachments) and *secondary groups* (less intimate, more impersonal groups). Some theorists have envisioned more of a continuum than a dichotomy, such as Robert Redfield's (1947) folk/urban continuum and Howard Becker's sacred/secular (1957) continuum.

Exhibit 13.2
Gemeinschaft and Gesellschaft Communities

Gemeinschaft	Gesellschaft
Strong identification with community	Little identification with community
Authority based on tradition	Authority based on laws and rationality
Relationships based on emotionalism	Relationships based on goal attainment and emotional neutrality
Others seen as whole persons	Others seen as role enactors

Source: Based on Lyon, 1987.

Tonnies shared the view of other early European sociologists, such as Max Weber and Emile Durkheim, that modernization was leading us away from gemeinschaft and toward gesellschaft. We can find evidence of such movement in the stories of Tito and the Maxwells. Capitalism, urbanization, and industrialization have all been proposed as causes of the movement toward gesellschaft. Many typology theorists lament the "loss of community" that occurs in the process. But some theorists suggest that electronic technology is moving us into a third type of community—sometimes referred to as a postgesellschaft, or postmodern, community—characterized by diversity and unpredictability (Lyon, 1987).

Becker sees the evolution of community in a different light. He suggests that modern society does not always move toward the secular but instead moves back and forth a great deal on the sacred/secular continuum. To Becker, the sacred is best characterized by reluctance to change (traditional authority in Tonnies's gemeinschaft) and the secular is best characterized by readiness to change (emotional neutrality in Tonnies's gesellschaft).

Tonnies and other theorists who have studied communities as contrasting types have focused their attention on territorial communities. And indeed, empirical research supports the idea that territorial communities vary along the gemeinschaft/gesellschaft continuum (Cuba & Hummon, 1993; Hunter & Riger, 1986; Keane, 1991; McKinney & Loomis, 1958, cited in Lyon, 1987; Woolever, 1992). More recently, however, Barry Wellman (1999) and research associates have attempted to understand contrasting types of relational communities that are based on networks of interaction rather than territory. In their early work (Wellman, 1979), they identified three contrasting types of communities:

1. *Community lost*: Communities that have lost a sense of connectedness, social support, and traditional customs for behavior

2. *Community saved*: Communities that have retained a strong sense of connectedness, social support, and customs for behavior

3. *Community liberated*: Communities that are loosely knit, with unclear boundaries and a great deal of heterogeneity

They suggested that as societies change, community is not necessarily lost but becomes transformed, and new forms of community develop.

Wellman and associates have continued to study the idea of contrasting types of relational communities for over 20 years, seeking to understand multiple dimensions of communities. Their recent work (e.g., Wellman & Potter, 1999) suggests that it is more important to think in terms of *elements* of communities rather than *types* of communities. Using factor analytic statistical methods, they have identified four important elements of community—contact, range, intimacy, and immediate

EXHIBIT 13.3
Four Elements of
Communities

Contact:	Level of interaction; how accessible community members are for contact and how much contact they actually have
Range:	Size and heterogeneity of community membership
Intimacy:	Sense of relationships being special; desire for companionship among members; interest in being together in multiple social contexts over a long period of time; sense of mutuality in relationships, with needs known and supported
Immediate Kinship/ Friendship:	Proportion of community membership composed of immediate kin (parents, adult children, siblings) versus friends

Source: Based on Wellman & Potter, 1999.

kinship/friendship—which are described in Exhibit 13.3. These elements are config-ured in different ways in different communities, and in the same community at different times.

For example, Ann and Evan Maxwell's electronic community was developed for doing business, but members of this community visit each other whenever they can, inquire about the health of family members, and send gifts and other acknowledg-ments of important family events. Roberto Colon recalls the gemeinschaft roots of his youth in Porter Crossing—the frequent neighborhood contacts and intimate interac-tions—and he thinks that reclaiming some of those roots is essential for the healthy development of the contemporary youth in the neighborhood. He is putting consider-able effort into improving relationships and gang members' sense of identification with Porter Crossing. Social workers might benefit by recognizing both the gemeinschaft and gesellschaft qualities of the communities they serve, as well as the histories of those communities. Approaches like Wellman and Potter's multiple elements of communities could be helpful in this regard.

Spatial Arrangements Approach

If we think about Tito's community in terms of spatial arrangements, we note the bars on the storefront windows, the dilapidated housing, the lack of business and indus-try to provide employment opportunities, and the jeopardized green space of Porter Park. We also note another important spatial dimension, the geographical boundaries of rival gang territories and the visual symbols of those territorial lines found on walls and fences. If we think of the Maxwells' community in terms of spatial arrangements, we note the runaway exurban growth and development and the upper middle-class status of the residents in Laguna Niguel.

Beginning with Robert Park's (1936) human ecology theory, a diverse group of sociological theorists have focused on community as spatial arrangements. Their interests have included city placement, population growth, land use patterns, the process of suburbanization, the development of "edge" cities (newly developed business districts of large scale located on the edge of major cities), and the relationships among central cities, suburbs, and edge cities. They are also interested in variations in human behavior related to the type of spatial community, such as rural area, small town, suburb, or central city.

Social constructionist perspective

Symbolic interactionists have studied how symbolic images of communities—the way people think about their communities—are related to spatial arrangements (Feldman, 1990; Hunter, 1974; Strauss, 1961; Suttles, 1972; Wilson & Baldassare, 1996). A survey of a random sample of Denver employees found that a large majority thought of themselves as either a "city person" or a "suburbanite" (Feldman, 1990). Participants largely agreed about the spatial attributes that distinguish cities from suburbs. In comparison to suburbs, they saw cities as having more heterogeneity of social and physical environment, less nature, poorer maintenance, and "more people, cars, noise, crime, stress, and concerns for safety" (Feldman, 1990, p. 200). On the whole, both city people and suburbanites reported a preference for the type of spatial community in which they resided.

The multidisciplinary theory on human behavior and the physical environment, discussed in Chapter 7, has also been extended to the study of community as spatial arrangements (Cherulnik, 1993; Newman, 1972, 1980; Taylor, 1988). Specifically, social scientists have focused on elements of environmental design that encourage social interaction as well as those that encourage a sense of control and the motivation to "look out" for the neighborhood. They have identified such elements as large spaces broken into smaller spaces, personalized spaces, and spaces for both privacy and congregation. One research team that studied the spatial arrangements in a suburban region found that people who had a sense of adequate privacy from neighbors' houses also reported a greater sense of community (Wilson & Baldassare, 1996).

Early settlement house social workers at Hull House developed community maps for assessing the spatial arrangements of social and economic injustices in Chicago neighborhoods (Wong & Hillier, 2001). Recently, social work planners and administrators have returned to the idea of geographical mapping, making use of advancements in **geographic information system (GIS)** computer technology, which can map the spatial distribution of a variety of social data. Social workers have used GIS to map (a) the distribution of child care facilities in a geographic region (Queralt & Witte, 1998a, 1998b), (b) prior residences of persons admitted to homeless shelters (Culhane, Lee, & Wachter, 1997), and (c) the geographical areas of greatest unmet service needs (Wong & Hillier, 2001). GIS holds much promise for future social work planning, administration, and research. If you have access to GIS technology, you might want to do some mapping of your territorial community: its ethnic makeup, socioeconomic class, crime rate, libraries, parks, hospitals, social services, and so on. If you do not have access to GIS, you can accomplish the same task with a good map blowup and multicolored pushpins.

Thinking about territorial communities as spatial arrangements can help social workers decide which territorial communities to target, for which problems, and with which methods. An interdisciplinary literature has recently focused on the compounding and interrelated nature of problems in deteriorating, impoverished neighborhoods in central cities—neighborhoods like Tito's Porter Crossing. Philanthropic funders have responded with comprehensive community initiatives (CCIs) to fund multifaceted community-building programs that address the economic and physical conditions, as well as social and cultural issues, of these impoverished communities (Ewalt et al., 1998). Typical elements of CCIs are economic and commercial development, education, health care, employment, housing, leadership development, physical revitalization, neighborhood security, recreation, social services, and support networks (Chaskin, Joseph, & Chipenda-Dansokho, 1997; Ewalt, 1997). Many communities are using neighborhood youth for neighborhood cleanup and revitalization, just as Roberto Colon is doing in Porter Crossing (Ross & Coleman, 2000; Twiss & Cooper, 2000).

Social Systems Approach

Systems perspective

A third way to think about communities is as social systems with cultures and patterns of interactions. There are probably many ways in which the cultures and patterns of interaction in Porter Crossing differ from those in Laguna Niguel, and perhaps there are similarities as well. Likewise, there are probably similarities and differences between the Maxwells' territorial and relational communities, and they will also find similarities and differences between Laguna Niguel and their new community in the Four Corners area of Colorado. A closer look at these communities as social systems might help us understand both the differences and similarities. The social systems perspective focuses on social interaction rather than on the physical, spatial aspects of community. Social interaction in a community can be understood in two different ways: as culture and as structure (Griswold, 1994). Exhibit 13.4 shows the differences between these two aspects of community.

Social constructionist perspective

For thinking about community in terms of its culture, symbolic interaction theory is promising (e.g., Snow & Anderson, 1993) because of its emphasis on the development of meaning through interaction. *Ethnography* is also particularly useful for studying community culture. The goal of ethnographic research is to understand the underlying rules and patterns of everyday life, in a particular location or among a particular group, from the "native point of view" (Spradley, 1979) rather than the researcher's point of view. Roberto Colon thinks that it is this local knowledge, the understanding of gang culture from the native point of view, that has led to the success of GAIN.

EXHIBIT 13.4

Aspects of
Community Culture
and Community
Structure

Community Culture

Pattern of meanings
Enduring patterns of communication
Symbols that guide thinking, feelings, and behaviors

Community Structure

Pattern of interactions
Institutions
Economic factors
Political factors

Source: Based on Griswold, 1994.

Community can also be studied in terms of its structure. Roland Warren (1963, 1978, 1987) made significant contributions to the understanding of patterns of interactions in communities. Warren pointed out that members of communities have two distinctive types of interactions. The first of these is interactions that create **horizontal linkage,** or interactions with other members of the community. The second type of interaction is interactions that create **vertical linkage,** or interaction with individuals and systems outside the community. Warren suggested that healthy communities must have both types of interactions. Communities with strong horizontal linkage provide a sense of identity for community members, but without good vertical linkage they cannot provide all the necessary resources for the well-being of community members. Communities with strong vertical linkage but weak horizontal linkage may leave community members searching and yearning for a sense of community.

Researchers have found support for these advantages and disadvantages of horizontal and vertical linkage. But consider also the experiences of the people in the case studies. Tito tells us that many residents of Porter Crossing don't know how to take the bus to leave the neighborhood and get downtown. Roberto Colon knows that. So while he works to create better horizontal linkages in Porter Crossing, he also serves as a bridge to link gang members to the wider world. The Maxwells, on the other hand, derive many personal and professional benefits from their electronic community, which links them vertically across geographies and cultures. But if they were locked out of their house, had car trouble, or developed a medical emergency, horizontal ties to a territorial community would become important.

For the past 2 decades, network theorists and researchers have been using network analysis to study community structure. They suggest that communities, like small groups and organizations, should be thought of as networks of social interaction (Wellman, 1999). They define community as **personal community**, which is composed of ties with friends, relatives, neighbors, workmates, and so on. Community is personal because the makeup of community membership varies from person to person. Another name for personal community is **network**, which has been defined as "the set of social relations or social ties among a set of actors" (Emirbayer & Goodwin, 1994). Network researchers consistently find that the amount of support offered to network members increases as the *range* of the network—size and heterogeneity—increases (Wellman, 1999). This makes sense if we think that increase in size and heterogeneity of network membership brings greater and more varied resources and information into the network. Researchers have also found that densely knit networks, or networks with a great deal of contact among members, are better at providing both emotional and instrumental (material) support to members than networks with sparser contact (Wellman, 1999).

Network analysis has been used to study social ties in both territorial and relational communities. In doing so, researchers have found that for many people, community is based more on relationships than territory. One research team (Lee & Campbell, 1999) did find, however, that barriers of segregation and discrimination make neighborhood relationships more important for blacks than for whites. They found that blacks have more intimate and long-standing ties with neighbors than whites in similar neighborhoods and they engage in more frequent contact with neighbors. Similarly, it would seem that neighborhood is more important to residents of Porter Crossing than to Ann and Evan Maxwell and other residents of Laguna Niguel.

Conflict Approach

Conflict
perspective

Tito and the Zs face daily combat with members of rival gangs. They see the police as a rival gang and the schools as territories for gang warfare. They have little contact with a world beyond Porter Crossing, but they see it as a world that does not welcome them. They feel particularly shut out of the labor market in that world. Roberto Colon is outraged at geographically based inequities of resources for youth in the city. He collaborates with other youth development leaders to chip away at those inequities. Conflict theory's emphasis on dissension, power, and exploitation adds another dimension to our understanding of the Porter Crossing neighborhood.

A conflict approach to community has been problematic for social workers and social scientists, however, because it is hard to integrate with a sense of community. More seriously, conflict theory brings the social work profession face to face with its divergent roles in society. Harry Specht (1994) writes about our historical mission to "help poor people, to improve community life, and to solve difficult social problems" (p. x). The operative CSWE Curriculum Policy Statement and the NASW Code of Ethics emphasize the role of social work in the promotion of social justice. Neo-Marxist theory suggests, however, that social services are increasingly used to smooth over problems and, consequently, allow dominant groups to maintain the status quo (Castells, 1977; Logan & Molotch, 1987). These conflict theories suggest that we cannot make significant improvements in the lives of persons in vulnerable communities without challenging existing patterns of social, economic, and political injustice (Fisher & Shragge, 2000).

Conflict theorists have a point, and indeed the mission of social work is social reform. But social workers do depend for political and financial support on governmental and private philanthropies, which have, for the most part, a heavy investment in the status quo (Wenocur & Soifer, 1997). Emilia Martinez-Brawley (2000) also suggests that social workers working in small communities should keep in mind that memories are usually long in such communities and conflictual relationships established on one issue may have an impact on future issues. She does not argue that social workers should always avoid a conflict approach in small communities, but she does recommend that we should be realistic about the consequences of our confrontational tactics in such communities. The dilemma of social reform versus professionalization is the subject of further discussion in Chapter 14.

Although social workers may envision a world with less conflict and competition, we must recognize that conflict, power, and exploitation are very much a part of contemporary life. In the 21st century, community social workers must be aware of two important ways in which community can be a contest:

1. *Privileged groups seek to protect their privilege, and nonprivileged groups push for change.* This type of contest is consistent with a neo-Marxist approach. Roberto Colon and his colleagues are involved in a contest of this type, as they challenge inequities in education in Lakeside. The struggle over accessible physical environments initiated by the disability community is another example of this type of contest. A final example is the contest between homeless persons and other community groups for valued public space. Robert Fisher and Eric Shragge (2000) argue that the worldwide spread of neoliberal faith in the free market (see discussion in Chapter 9) has "dulled the political edge" (p. 1) of community social workers. They argue for renewed commitment to a form of community social work that is willing to build opposition and use a range of confrontational tactics to challenge privilege and oppression. Given economic globalization, Fisher and Shragge recommend that effective community organizing in the current era will need to be tied to a global social movement. Social movements are the topic of Chapter 14.

2. *Interest groups of relatively equal status compete to control resources or cultural symbols.* Two territorial communities, such as two adjacent suburbs, may compete for funds for housing, or two relational communities may struggle for the hearts and minds of society at large. It is possible that Ann and Evan Maxwell will find themselves embroiled in a conflict between prodevelopment and antidevelopment groups when

they move to Colorado. The sometimes violent struggle between the pro-life and the pro-choice movements is an example of a contest to control cultural symbols about gender roles (Hunter, 1994). As several observers have noted, we need community builders who can help us turn our "culture wars" into culture conversations—respectful conversations based on substance rather than power politics (Etzioni, 1993; Hunter, 1994; Rawls, 1993). Social work is well suited to play a leadership role in developing such respectful conversations. Robert Fisher and Howard Karger (1997) make a similar observation: "Increasingly, social workers are challenged to heal social fractures. Contemporary history suggests that modern societies fracture along various fault lines, including ethnic, religious, racial, tribal, and geographic lines. . . . The effort needed to arrest this phenomenon is herculean, and the more society unravels, the harder it becomes to reweave its diverse social threads" (p. 136). In many areas of life, from race relations to family relations, the mediator role is becoming more prominent for social workers. We will have to become comfortable with conflict if we are to take leadership roles in healing these social fractures.

To work effectively with community conflict, social workers must be able to analyze the structure of community power and influence (Martinez-Brawley, 2000). They must understand who controls which types of resources and how power brokers are related to one another. That means understanding the power held internally in the community as well as the power that resides external to the community. This type of analysis allows social workers to understand both the possibilities and limits of community empowerment. For example, Roberto Colon knows that the youth of Porter Crossing have the power to clean up the neighborhood. On the other hand, power over inequities in school funding lies beyond Porter Crossing, and Roberto Colon wisely finds external partners to help him challenge those entrenched power arrangements while at the same time mobilizing community youth for protest activities.

Social Bond Approach

When the Maxwells talk about sense of community, they are talking about the quality of the connections that community members make with each other and the commitment they feel to one another. They are thinking about community as a social bond that unifies people. Tito has found that social bond with the Zs and is beginning to experience it as well at the YMCA.

It is this idea of community—the tie that binds, the social bond—to which we refer when we lament the loss of community or when we talk longingly about searching for community, strengthening community, or building sense of community. In the early 1990s, Robert Wuthnow (1994) suggested that the small-group movement of the past 2 decades has been a quest for community in the midst of a rapidly changing world.

Participants in his research project reported that they joined small groups because of a "desire for intimacy, support, sharing, and other forms of community involvement" (p. 52), which they were not finding in their neighborhoods and workplaces.

This idea of a social bond among community members is what Seymour Sarason had in mind when he declared the enhancement of *psychological sense of community* (PSOC) as the mission of community psychology. We looked earlier at Sarason's definition of sense of community (see Exhibit 13.1).

Community psychologists David McMillan and David Chavis (1986) turned to the literature on group cohesiveness to understand how to enhance the social bonds of community. They presented a theory of PSOC that identified four essential elements:

1. *Membership* is a sense of belonging, of being part of a collective, something bigger than oneself. It is based on boundaries, emotional safety, personal investment, and a common symbol system. Boundaries clarify who is in and who is out and protect against threat. Personal investment in a community is enhanced when we feel that we have worked for membership. Common symbols facilitate integration of the community, in part by intentionally creating social distance between members and nonmembers. The various tattoos of the different gangs in Porter Crossing serve as such common symbols. However, as we can see with the gang turf wars, communities built on exclusion, rather than inclusion, contribute to the fragmentation of social life (Fisher & Karger, 1997; Hardcastle et al., 1997).

Rational choice perspective

2. *Influence* is bidirectional. On the one hand, members are more attracted to a community where they have some sense of control and influence. On the other hand, to be cohesive, a community has to be able to exert influence over members. In this way, behavioral conformity comes from the need to belong, and conformity promotes cohesiveness. The Porter Crossing YMCA is becoming more attractive to the youth gangs in the neighborhood as they begin to feel that they have some influence there. At the same time, the gang members are willing to abide by the YMCA's requirement that they do not interact with nongang children and youth while at the YMCA. They also willingly wear the YMCA T-shirts, and wearing the T-shirts further enhances their sense of cohesiveness with the YMCA.

Social behavioral perspective

3. *Integration and fulfillment of needs* refers to individual reinforcement or reward for membership. The community must be rewarding to its members, but McMillan and Chavis conclude that "a strong community is able to fit people together so that people meet others' needs while they meet their own" (p. 13). GAIN has created a cleanup project in Porter Crossing that benefits the whole community while also benefiting the youth involved. They are rewarded financially, with a sense of making a contribution, and with the gratitude of neighborhood residents. This sense of being appreciated in

the neighborhood is a new experience for these gang members, who are usually thought of as the enemy.

4. *Shared emotional connection* is based on a shared history and identification with the community. It is enhanced when members are provided with "positive ways to interact, important events to share and ways to resolve them positively, opportunities to honor members, opportunities to invest in the community, and opportunities to experience a spiritual bond among members" (McMillan & Chavis, 1986, p. 14). Clearly, Roberto Colon is trying to encourage positive ways for gang members to interact with each other and with the neighborhood, and the summer jobs program has provided opportunities for the youth to invest in the community.

On the basis of this definition of PSOC, McMillan and Chavis developed a 12-item Sense of Community Index (SCI) that has been used extensively for research on sense of community.

After 10 years of research, David McMillan (1996) made some revisions to the theory of PSOC:

- *Membership* was changed to *spirit*, emphasizing friendship and belonging and downplaying boundaries.

- *Influence* was changed to *trust*, emphasizing the development of community norms that provide order and the importance of equal distribution of power for mutual trust.

- *Fulfillment of needs* was changed to *trade*, emphasizing the rewards of belonging to community as well as the importance of similarity of community members for social bonding.

- *Shared emotional connection* was changed to *art*, emphasizing collective memories and stories of shared moments that represent community values and traditions.

McMillan suggested that art promotes spirit, spirit along with respected authority promotes trust, trust is the basis of social trade, and together these produce a shared history (art).

An Australian research team (Obst et al., 2002a, 2002b) has used McMillan and Chavis's theory of PSOC to compare PSOC in territorial and relational communities. More specifically, the researchers asked 359 science fiction aficionados attending a World Science Fiction Convention to complete questionnaires rating PSOC both for their fandom community and for their territorial community. Research participants reported significantly higher levels of PSOC in their fandom communities than in their territorial communities. They also found that although the ratings on all dimensions of

McMillan and Chavis's four theorized dimensions of PSOC were higher in the fandom communities than in the geographical communities, the dimensions received essentially the same rank ordering in both communities. The researchers also suggest that a fifth dimension, *conscious identification* with the community, should be added to McMillan and Chavis's theory of PSOC. They found this cognitive identification to be an important component of PSOC.

In recent years, the social work literature has paid much attention to the issue of community building (e.g., Ewalt et al., 1998). This literature often focuses broadly on community revitalization, in terms of the economic and physical, as well as the social relationship dimensions of communities (e.g., Beck & Eichler, 2000; Halperin, 2001; Hendricks & Rudich, 2000; Zacharay, 2000). The literature on youth leadership development is particularly noteworthy for its attention to building a sense of community among youth in neighborhoods (Finn & Checkoway, 1998; Twiss & Cooper, 2000). Recent social work literature on community youth development has returned to settlement house roots, recommending the use of arts, humanities, and sports to build a sense of community, as well as to empower youth and help them build skills. Melvin Delgado's (2000) *New Arenas for Community Social Work Practice With Urban Youth: Use of Arts, Humanities, and Sports* is chock full of ideas for enhancing a sense of community among youth.

Before leaving this discussion of community as social bond, I would like to turn to the idea of **unity in diversity,** which has been used by social work scholars in a variety of ways to describe the goal of community social work practice (Fisher & Karger, 1997; Gutierrez, 1997). We live in an increasingly diverse world. And yet, the literature on networks often suggests that birds of a feather flock together; McMillan (1996) suggests that similarity among members is essential for building PSOC. Conformity produces cohesion. Perhaps this is why the study of science fiction fans found that they felt greater sense of community in that community than in their neighborhoods. Science fiction fandom is a community that people join because of a common interest. Neighborhoods—except for ethnic enclaves and the intentional communities that are popping up around the country—are not usually built on common interests.

How then do social workers help communities find unity in diversity? How do we help to ensure that talk of unity is not simply code language for protecting the privileged position of dominant groups? Writing about a social work approach that she calls "multicultural community organizing," Lorraine Gutierrez (1997, p. 250) puts the question this way: "How do we respect diversity and reduce inequality while working toward a common good?" One solution is to promote public activism in the service of inclusiveness and equality (Fisher & Karger, 1997). Although social conflict is an essential component of the process of developing unity in diversity—"of course, it is inappropriate to tell those who do not have power, or whose voices were not heard before, to be less divisive or aggressive in pursuit of their interests and voice" (Fisher & Karger, 1997,

p. 134)—coalition building and healing of social fractures are essential as well. Others also argue that community building and social action are both a part of good community organizing (see Fisher & Shragge, 2000). That seems to be the view of Roberto Colon, who works at building a sense of community among youth in Porter Crossing while also engaging in efforts to reform the educational system across Lakeside.

Social Workers and Communities: Contemporary Issues

As suggested in Chapter 9, modernization, capitalism, industrialization, and urbanization have great costs to society as well as benefits. The profession of social work was developed as one force to minimize the costs—a communal force to correct for extremes of individualism (Falck, 1988). In its efforts to promote the general social welfare, social work has always been involved with communities in some way. But, as suggested earlier, there is renewed interest in community among social workers. This renewed interest has been nurtured by the Association for Community Organization and Social Administration (ACOSA), which was formed in 1987, and by the journal started by ACOSA, *Journal of Community Practice.*

The nature of social work's relationships with communities has changed over time, however, and there are long-standing disagreements about appropriate roles for social workers in communities. These disagreements are evident in recent attempts to reconceptualize community practice for social work (Fisher & Karger, 1997; Hardcastle et al., 1997). Here I summarize the issues involved in four of these points of disagreement.

Community as Context for Practice Versus Target of Practice

Social workers who view community as a context for practice focus on working with individuals and families, although they recognize the ways in which communities provide opportunities and barriers for client behaviors and agency responses. In contrast, social workers who view community as a target of practice focus on enhancing the health of the community.

There seems to be a growing consensus that social work needs to recognize community as both context and target of practice (Fisher & Karger, 1997; Hardcastle et al., 1997; McDonald, Billingham, Conrad, Morgan, & Payton, 1997; Sviridoff & Ryan, 1997). Community agencies are working to help individual families and at the same time to help in building "protective, caring, and connected communities" (McDonald, 1997, p. 115). For example, they are combining family therapy and parent education with community building to help children succeed at school (Feikema, Segalavich, & Jeffries, 1997; McDonald et al., 1997; Webster-Stratton, 1997). Roberto Colon takes this approach. He fears that if community is seen as only the target of practice, and interventions with individual troubled youth are ignored, a whole generation of youth will be written off. Therefore, GAIN provides individual case management as well as neighborhood cleanup.

Even with a combined community practice model, questions still arise about when to intervene with individuals and families and when to focus on larger collectivities and groups. Examples from the social work literature demonstrate this tension. Harry Specht and Mark Courtney (1994) call for putting the social back in social work with a "community-based system of social care" and elimination of the psychotherapeutic role. Carol Swenson (1994) responded thoughtfully, with an appreciation for the communal values articulated by Specht and Courtney. She disagreed, however, with the conclusion that the objectives of community building and psychotherapy are incompatible, recommending instead a continued dual focus on community and individual. She suggests that "it will be difficult to 'help communities create good' if those communities are composed of large numbers of individuals who are alone and purposeless" (p. 198).

In one view, the words "numbers of individuals who are alone and purposeless" suggest the need for strengthening the sense of community, at the collective community level, and would make a poor defense for psychotherapy. In another view, problems of isolation and purposelessness can only be handled one-on-one, with professional helpers. However, although the psychotherapeutic role should not be eliminated from social work's repertoire, social workers may have come to rely too heavily on this role. They may be using it for problems for which it is neither efficient nor effective. An integrated community practice should avoid an overreliance on one-to-one and family sessions, opting, where appropriate, for "collective and group formats" (Fisher & Karger, 1997, p. 50).

Agency Orientation Versus Social Action

Community social work practice has roots in a **social action model** of community organization, which was developed by leaders of the settlement house movement. This model of community practice is political in nature, emphasizing social reform and challenge of structural inequalities. But by the 1930s, this social action model had been replaced by an **agency-based model,** which promoted social agencies and the services they provided (Fisher & Karger, 1997). This model of community practice is nonpolitical and puts little or no emphasis on social change. It is based on the assumption that the best way to strengthen communities is to provide social services. Proponents of the agency-based model of community organizing often focus on coordination of services across agencies (Spergel & Grossman, 1997).

Saul Alinsky, founder of one of the best-known community organizing training centers, was critical of the agency-based model of community social work (Fisher & Karger, 1997). He did not think that social justice is ensured by providing social services. However, agency-based provision of social services, and interagency coordination of services, often does contribute to the well-being of communities. We need social workers who will advocate for the retention of threatened services, as well as the development of new services. Recent initiatives to revitalize impoverished neighborhoods have combined resource development with efforts to strengthen sense of community (Cohen & Phillips, 1997). Bringing community members together for the purposes of building or strengthening the sense of community and identifying community problems and community resources is known as **locality development, or social development**. An integrated approach to community social work practice enhances community-based services, builds a sense of community, and advocates for social reform.

Conflict Model of Practice Versus Collaborative Model

Conflict perspective

Over the years, social work has taken different positions on the question of whether social workers should lean toward conflict or collaboration, ebbing and flowing in its "tradition of nagging the conscience of America" (Fisher & Karger, 1997, p. 188). In liberal times, social work has been more willing to embrace conflict approaches; in conservative times, more collaborative approaches have been preferred. In the early 1900s, social work reformers used social surveys to expose exploitive industries and disseminated the results widely in newspapers and magazines (Fisher & Karger, 1997). Roberto Colon and his colleagues have used a similar tactic to discover accurate school dropout rates and get them published. Today, however, the trend is away from "challenging the establishment" and toward creating partnerships between community groups, government agencies, and corporations (Wenocur & Soifer, 1997).

The contemporary tension between conflict and collaborative models of practice is exemplified by two articles that appeared in the *Journal of Community Practice* during 2000. Robert Fisher, a social work educator from the United States, and Eric Shragge, a social work educator from Canada, contrast social action and community building approaches to practice. *Social action* works for social change by organizing people to put pressure on governments or private organizations. It challenges social inequalities. **Community development** is based on an assumption of shared interests, rather than conflicting interests. It seeks to bring together diverse community interests for the betterment of the community as a whole, with attention to community building and improved sense of community. Fisher and Shragge acknowledge that many community practitioners interweave social action and community development. They suggest, however, that the community development approach to community practice has become dominant. They lament this turn of events, arguing that we are in an era of growing inequality that requires more, not less, social action.

An article by Elizabeth Beck and Michael Eichler (2000) argues the other side of the coin. They propose consensus organizing, based in feminist theory, as a practice model for community building. Consensus organizing has four basic assumptions:

1. Power docs not have to be redistributed; it can be grown.

2. Human behavior is motivated by mutual self-interest, not just individual self-interest.

3. People are basically good, and power holders will make decisions that improve community well-being when given the opportunity.

4. The wealthy and the poor, the powerful and the powerless can be knit together rather than become adversaries.

Like Fisher and Shragge, Beck and Eichler suggest that both social action and community development are needed, but they argue for an emphasis on community work that strengthens relationships. They suggest that social action calls for a redistribution of power, but consensus organizing does not believe that redistribution of power is necessary to end oppression. Indeed, they argue that conflict tactics often don't reach the goal of redistribution of power anyway.

Contemporary social trends call for a contemporary style of community practice that draws on both conflict and collaborative models. Community social workers need skills for exposing and challenging social injustice as well as for resolving conflict and building coalitions. The choice of tactics will depend on the specific person/environment configurations encountered.

Some person/environment configurations call for community social workers to elevate community conflict for the purpose of challenging exploitation and oppression. Throughout this book, we emphasize the need for social workers to take a critical perspective that recognizes power and oppression as important factors in the negotiation of social life. A critical perspective also calls for social workers to challenge existing patterns of domination and oppression. With the trend toward devolution of government responsibilities to the local level, the local territorial community becomes increasingly important to these efforts. Social work research can identify and expose local patterns of exploitation. Community social workers can use consciousness-raising tactics to help oppressed groups understand their situations. They can use a variety of advocacy skills to make appeals for the rights and needs of oppressed groups. Many contemporary social critics "see grassroots community organizations as potentially the most effective progressive balance to the elite domination" (Fisher & Karger, 1997, p. 130).

Other person/environment configurations call for community social workers to resolve community conflicts. Robert Fisher and Howard Karger (1997) remind us that "public life is about difference, and about learning to create a society by interacting with others who have different opinions and experiences" (p. 26). This notion seems to be left out of the community psychology literature on PSOC. Social work's professional organizations have taken a position that values diversity. But they should go beyond that position and value the conflict that accompanies diversity. Communities often need help in negotiating their differences. Social workers can help to develop a civil discourse on controversial issues, a discourse that includes the voices of people who have previously been marginalized and excluded. Community social workers can use a variety of conflict resolution skills to help different community groups understand and respect each other's experiences and to engage in respectful and effective problem-solving activities.

It remains to be seen whether cyber communities, such as the one to which Ann and Evan Maxwell belong, will increase or decrease opportunities for discourse with those who are different from us. Some suggest that we will simply use cyberspace to create communities of like interests to escape our differences in territorial communities (Wellman, 1999).

There is considerable agreement among social work scholars that social workers should focus on helping to develop broad issues that can unite diverse groups in social reform efforts; two examples of such issues are health care and financial security in a global economy (Fisher & Karger, 1997; Gutierrez, 1997; Hardcastle et al., 1997; Wenocur & Soifer, 1997). Recently, demonstrations against the World Trade Organization and International Monetary Fund have suggested that a spark of resistance is alive for the issue of financial security in a global economy. But these efforts are less likely to succeed if they do not build greater solidarity between poor and middle-class people (Fisher & Karger, 1997). Another problem requiring coalition building is the viability of impoverished central-city neighborhoods like Porter Crossing, for which regional solutions will be necessary (Wenocur & Soifer, 1997). Coalitions across cultural groups are also increasingly desirable (Gutierrez, 1997). The social work literature is beginning to grapple with the complexities of coalition building (Dunlop & Angell, 2001; Mizrahi & Rosenthal, 2001).

Expert Versus Partner in the Social Change Process

The **social planning model** of community social work is based on the premise that the complexities of modern social problems require expert planners schooled in a rational planning model. In this model, the community power structure is the author of social change efforts (Fisher & Karger, 1997). This approach is often referred to as a top-down approach to social change.

Locality development and other community building models of community social work take a different view: community practice should support and enhance the ability of community members to identify their own community's needs, assets, and solutions to problems (Daley & Marsiglia, 2000; Lowe, 1997; Naperstek & Dooley, 1997). Social workers work in partnership with community members and groups, and remain open to learning from the community (Gutierrez, 1997). This approach is often known as a bottom-up approach to social change.

Many local community development corporations (CDCs) are experimenting with ways of building partnerships with community members for community revitalization. Laura Ross and Mardia Coleman (2000) provide one model for such partnerships, a model they call Urban Community Action Planning (UCAP). They have adapted this approach from Participatory Rural Appraisal (PRA), a grassroots approach used in rural areas of Africa, Latin America, and Asia. The PRA model is based on three assumptions:

1. *Local knowledge.* Community members have knowledge about local problems, but they need help to organize it.

2. *Local resources.* Community members have resources, but these resources need to be mobilized.

3. *Outside help.* Outside resources are available, but they need to be matched to community-identified priorities.

Roberto Colon talks about the importance of local knowledge for the success of GAIN. He and his staff are mobilizing local resources, and he has been quite successful in attracting outside help.

Efforts at community building often rely heavily on "indigenous leaders" to facilitate meaningful community participation. These efforts do not always run smoothly. Community practitioners have had little guidance on how to choose indigenous leaders and how to prepare them to lead. Recent literature has begun to address this important issue, noting both aids and barriers to effective indigenous leadership (Delgado, 1996a; Zachary, 2000). Seeing that many potential indigenous leaders have limited opportunities to play such roles, some community organizers have suggested a need for preparation or training for the role of indigenous leader.

A social planning model is appropriate for problems requiring specialized technical knowledge. Community members are the experts, however, about community needs and community assets. They also have the capacity to be active partners in identifying solutions to community problems.

IMPLICATIONS FOR SOCIAL WORK PRACTICE

The preceding discussion of community has many implications for social work practice:

■ Be informed about the communities you serve; learn about their readiness to change, their spatial arrangements (for territorial communities), their cultures, their patterns of internal and external relationships, their conflicts, and their sense of community.

■ Avoid overreliance on individual and family sessions; make use of small- and large-group formats where appropriate.

■ When working with individuals and families, assess their opportunities to be supported by and to make contributions to the community, and assess the limits imposed by their territorial and relational communities.

■ Recognize the central role of territorial community in the lives of many young persons and their caregivers, older adults, and poor families.

■ If you are a social work planner or administrator, become familiar with computer-based geographical information systems for mapping social data.

■ Where appropriate, strengthen interaction within the community (horizontal linkages) to build a sense of community and maximize the use of internal resources. Strengthen intercommunity interactions (vertical linkages) to ensure there are adequate resources to meet the community's needs.

■ Where appropriate, advocate for the retention of threatened social services, the coordination of existing services, and the development of new services.

■ Where appropriate, collaborate with others to challenge exploitation and oppression in communities. Use consciousness-raising tactics to help oppressed groups understand their situations.

■ Where appropriate, assist communities to negotiate differences and resolve conflicts.

■ Where appropriate, assist in the development of coalitions to improve the resource base for community problem solving.

- Involve community members in identification of community strengths and community problems, in goal setting, and in intervention activities.

- When working with impoverished communities, work with other individuals and organizations, both inside and outside these communities, to develop comprehensive, multidimensional, integrated strategies.

KEY TERMS

agency-based model

community

community development

gemeinschaft

geographic information systems (GIS)

gesellschaft

horizontal linkage

locality development

mass society

network

personal community

relational community

sense of community

social action model

social development

social planning model

territorial community

unity in diversity

vertical linkage

ACTIVE LEARNING

1. You have read about two geographic communities—the Porter Crossing neighborhood and Laguna Niguel. Now think about your own geographic community. Compare and contrast it with Porter Crossing and Laguna Niguel according to the following characteristics:

- Sense of community

- Physical environment

- Horizontal and vertical linkages

2. One research team has found that the majority of our ties to other people are nonterritorial, but two thirds of our actual interactions are local, in the neighborhood or work setting. To test this idea, for 1 day keep a record of all contacts you have with other

people and the time spent in such contacts—face-to-face contacts as well as telephone and electronic contacts. What percentage of your contacts occur in your neighborhood, at work, or at school?

3.   Visit a neighborhood house or center, a YMCA or YWCA, or another community action organization in your town or city. Interview the director or another staff member about the mission of the organization, asking them to address the following questions:

- Is the focus on working with individuals and families or on enhancing the health of the community?

- Is the focus of the work political in nature, emphasizing social reform and challenge of structure inequalities, or is it on providing and coordinating service?

- Are the methods used confrontational in nature ("challenging the establishment") or collaborative in nature ("creating partnerships")?

- How involved are community members in planning and carrying out the change activities of the organization?

WEB RESOURCES

Association for Community Organization and Social Administration (ACOSA)

www.acosa.org
Site maintained by ACOSA includes recent paper presentations, hot topics, important news about community organizing, and links to other Internet sites.

Association of Community Organizations for Reform Now (ACORN)

www.acorn.org
Site maintained by ACORN includes information about ACORN, ways of getting involved in social reform, and news items.

United Neighborhood Houses of New York Inc.

www.unhny.org
Site maintained by United Neighborhood Houses of New York Inc., a federation of 36 settlement houses in New York City, includes information about the settlement

house movement, current activities of settlement houses in the United States, and job vacancies.

Community Psychology Network

www.communitypsychology.net

An online guide to community psychology maintained by Matthew Cook contains information about the differences between community psychology and sociology, social work, and public health, as well as links to other Internet sites, resources, discussion lists, journals, social policy issues, and professional groups.

The National Community Action Foundation (NCAF)

www.ncaf.org

Site maintained by NCAF, an advocacy group for community action agencies, contains news, events, and current issues.

National People's Action (NPA)

www.npa-us.org

Site maintained by NPA, an advocacy organization that helps neighborhood people take on corporate America and political institutions, contains conference information, issues, and links to other advocacy groups.

The Annie E. Casey Foundation

www.aecf.org

Site maintained by the Annie E. Casey Foundation, a grant-making organization that works to build better futures for disadvantaged children and their families, contains a description of initiatives and projects and publications.

CHAPTER 14

Social Movements

Elizabeth D. Hutchison

Social Movements

Elizabeth D. Hutchison
Virginia Commonwealth University

How might the literature on social movements help social work with its social reform mission?

What are the major theoretical perspectives on social movements?

Key Ideas

As you read this chapter, take note of these central ideas:

1. Social movements are formed when people feel that one or more social institutions are unjust and need to be changed.

2. The profession of social work has its origins in the confluence of two social movements: the charity organization society movement and the settlement house movement.

3. Three theoretical perspectives on social movements have emerged in the past 2 decades: the political opportunities perspective, the mobilizing structures perspective, and the cultural framing perspective. None of these perspectives taken individually is sufficient for understanding social movements, but taken together, they provide a multidimensional understanding of social movements.

4. Social movements are neither completely successful nor completely unsuccessful.

5. Recently, there has been a rise in transnational social movement organizations (TSMOs).

6. Contemporary social work, like historical social work, must manage a tension between professional services and social reform.

CASE STUDY

MARY JO KAHN AND THE
VIRGINIA BREAST CANCER FOUNDATION

Mary Jo Kahn's mother was diagnosed with breast cancer at the age of 39; she died when she was 47—even though she was a member of the privileged white middle class with ample access to health care. Mary Jo was also diagnosed with breast cancer when she was 39, about the same time that her older sister's breast cancer was diagnosed. Mary Jo has two other sisters who have never been diagnosed with breast cancer but who have had prophylactic mastectomies to prevent breast cancer. Mary Jo is the mother of two daughters.

Mary Jo's mother did not have a job outside the home, and she had few opportunities to talk with other women about breast cancer. Breast cancer was a lonely disease for her. When Mary Jo was diagnosed, her situation was very different. She shared the experience of breast cancer with her older sister. She joined a mastectomy support group at the cancer center where she received medical care. She was embedded in a network of women activists who had worked together for several years on a variety of women's issues. Mary Jo had many opportunities to talk with other women about breast cancer, and she was outraged to learn how common the disease was and yet how very little research was being done.

In 1991, Mary Jo began to talk with other women from her mastectomy support group about the need for activist efforts to increase funding for breast cancer research. With the help of friends and family members, they organized a statewide rally for Mother's Day 1991. They were mentored in these efforts by California Breast Cancer Action, which had itself been mentored by an AIDS activist group in the organization of a successful Mother's Day rally in California the previous year. They were also supported by Mary Jo's network of women activists. "We will not die silently anymore" became a theme for their emerging breast cancer movement. For the 1991 Mother's Day rally, Mary Jo's daughters made banners that announced "Hold the line at 1 in 9," referring to the statistic that one in nine women were expected to develop breast cancer at the time.

Soon after the Mother's Day rally, an organizational meeting was held at Mary Jo's house to explore the possibility of formalizing the emerging breast cancer activist movement in Virginia. Twenty people attended the meeting, and for their group they chose the name the Virginia Breast Cancer Foundation. The first public meeting of the Foundation was held in July 1991. Later that year, the National Breast Cancer Coalition was formed, and the Virginia Breast Cancer Foundation became a member of that coalition.

The first national activity of the emerging breast cancer movement was the "Do the Write Thing" letter-writing campaign during the fall of 1991. People were encouraged to write letters to members of Congress and the president calling for more funding for breast cancer research. The campaign organizers set a goal of 180,000 letters, in recognition of the 180,000 women who would be diagnosed with breast cancer in the United States in 1991. To the delight of the organizers, more than 700,000 letters were delivered to the president. In Virginia, the goal was 4,300 letters; Foundation members took buses to Washington to deliver 24,000 letters. The 1992 federal budget, passed in November 1991, contained a $42 million increase for breast cancer research.

In February 1992, breast cancer activists organized a conference and invited breast cancer researchers to present the latest research findings. They asked the researchers how much money would be needed to adequately fund breast cancer research, and the researchers suggested a $300 million increase.

Mary Jo Kahn took on the job of organizing rallies across the country on Mother's Day 1992, and the movement was able to organize 32 rallies—compared with the 2 rallies in 1991. The activists then focused on developing networks of concerned persons. They used these networks to deliver legislative alerts in the summer of 1992 and to publicize their campaign for a $300 million increase in funds for breast cancer research. Once again, the activists were successful.

The original goal of the breast cancer activist movement was to increase funding for breast cancer research. Once the movement began to succeed with this goal, another goal emerged: to ensure that women with breast cancer would have a voice on the committees that made research funding decisions. At first, the federal agencies involved were suspicious, verbalizing their concern that women with cancer would make emotional rather than informed decisions. The activists pressed their goal, however, and the pairing of researchers and women with cancer to make research funding decisions proceeded smoothly. In recent years, the movement has taken on another goal: to gain access for breast cancer treatment for poor women.

There is little doubt that the breast cancer activists benefited from circumstances in the political institution at the time their movement was emerging. A gender gap in political elections had become a serious issue following lawyer Anita Hill's testimony in the hearings to confirm Clarence Thomas as a Supreme Court justice; fervid attacks on Hill's character were considered blatant sexism by many women activists. Issues such as abortion had become highly contentious, and politicians across the political spectrum

CASE STUDY

welcomed a noncontroversial women's issue in 1992. The campaign for a $300 million increase in breast cancer research funds was presented during George H. W. Bush's presidency while he was running for reelection.

At the time of the campaign, congressional mandates prohibited new taxes or the shifting of monies from one federal department to another. The breast cancer activists analyzed the situation this way: to get more money, they had to find a pocket of federal money that politicians would be willing to reappropriate to breast cancer research. The cold war had just ended with the massive changes in Eastern Europe, and there was general agreement that the Department of Defense (DOD) had more money than it needed. So the activists asked for $300 million of the DOD budget. Even the DOD was not opposed to this request, because they were faced with the possibility of laying off a large number of military doctors. So, ironically, the breast cancer activists worked collaboratively with the DOD to develop directions for breast cancer research.

In June 1997, Mary Jo Kahn was recognized by President Bill Clinton for her activism on behalf of women with breast cancer (Mary Jo Kahn, personal communication, August 19, 1997). Today, the National Breast Cancer Coalition (NBCC) continues as a grassroots advocacy organization made up of more than 600 organizations with three main goals: increasing funding for breast cancer research, with an emphasis on prevention and cure; increasing access to treatment and clinical trials for all women, particularly women of limited economic means; increasing the influence of women with breast cancer in decision making about research and treatment. The earlier collaboration with the DOD resulted in the DOD Peer-Reviewed Breast Cancer Research Program, which continues today. By October 1999, this program had received over $1 billion in federal funds (National Breast Cancer Coalition, n.d.). As you become a social worker, you may find the success of this movement an inspiration for your own activism.

A Definition of Social Movements

What happens when a group of people, like these women concerned about breast cancer, think that certain arrangements are unjust and need to be changed? Sometimes they work together to try to bring about the desired changes—not just for themselves but for a large group of people. These joint efforts are **social movements**—ongoing, large-scale, collective efforts to bring about (or resist) social change.

We can think of social movements as either offensive or defensive (Ray, 1993). **Offensive social movements** seek to "try out new ways of cooperating and living together" (Habermas, 1981/1987, p. 394). The breast cancer and Amnesty International movements are examples of offensive social movements. **Defensive social movements**, on the other hand, seek to defend traditional values and social arrangements. Christian and Islamic fundamentalist and property rights movements are examples of defensive social movements. Both types of social movements are common today in the United States and across the world.

The tendency today is to define social movements broadly, to include collective efforts to improve not just society but also individuals' lives. Indeed, self-help groups seem to be much more popular these days than traditional mass movements like the civil rights movement. Some have questioned whether self-help groups—including therapeutic groups, social advocacy/action groups, groups created to support alternative lifestyles, and groups providing havens via a 24-hour live-in situation—can be called social movements, given their emphasis on personal development and revitalization rather than social change. Perhaps the proliferation of self-help groups should be considered a social trend but not a social movement, because the varied self-help groups are not unified into a movement (Katz, 1993). Others have argued, however, that the trend toward self-help groups itself represents a social movement (Wuthnow, 1994). This question of the boundaries of a social movement is one about which social scientists disagree, but certainly, as we saw with the breast cancer advocates, self-help groups can be mobilized to create a social movement.

Social Movements and the History of Social Work

Like many of the world's religions, some nation-states, labor unions, the YMCA/YWCA, and the Boy Scouts and Girl Scouts, the profession of social work is generally considered to have its origin in social movements (Marx & McAdam, 1994). More specifically, the social work profession developed out of the confluence of two social movements: the charity organization society movement and the settlement house movement (Popple & Leighninger, 1993). You have probably studied these social movements in some of your other courses, so they will not be discussed in great detail here. But as social workers, we should recognize how intertwined the history of social work is with social movements.

Both the charity organization society movement and the settlement house movement emerged out of concern during the late 1800s about the ill effects of industrialization, including urban overcrowding and economic instability among low-paid workers. Both social movements developed in England and were transplanted to the United States. But from the beginning, their orientations were very different.

The **charity organization society (COS) movement** developed because private charity organizations became overtaxed by the needs of poor people. Middle- and upper-class people were fearful that a coalition of unemployed people and low-paid workers would revolt and threaten the stability of established political and economic institutions. Leaders of the COS movement saw poverty as based in individual pathology and immorality, and set the goal of coordinating the giving of charity to ensure that no duplication occurred. Volunteer "friendly visitors" were assigned to poor families to help them correct character flaws and develop strong moral fiber. Leaders of the COS movement believed in private, rather than public, charity. Service—the provision of efficient and effective service—was the primary agenda of the COS.

The **settlement house movement** was stimulated by the same social circumstances but was based on very different values and goals. Whereas COS leaders focused on individual pathology, leaders of the settlement house movement focused on environmental hazards. They developed settlement houses in urban neighborhoods where "settlers" lived together as "good neighbors" to poor families and were actively involved in "research, service, and reform" (Popple & Leighninger, 1993, p. 61). The settlers supported labor activities, lobbied for safe and sanitary housing, provided space for local political groups, offered day care, and provided a variety of cultural and educational programs. They published the results of their research widely and used it to push for governmental reform. **Social reform**—the creation of more just social institutions—was the primary agenda of the settlement house movement.

Over time, workers from the two social movements began to interact at annual meetings of the National Conference of Charities and Corrections, and social work as an occupation took shape. With efforts to professionalize the occupation of social work and, later, to win acceptance for the public social welfare institution, the social reform agenda of the settlement house movement lost ground. Direct service became the focus—specifically, individual and family casework in health and welfare agencies, and social work with groups in the settlement houses and YMCA/YWCAs. This transition away from reform toward a service model is not an uncommon trajectory of social movements. However, almost a century later, social work continues to experience a tension between service and social reform.

Although social work emerged from social movements, it is now a profession, not a social movement. Some social workers work for social movement organizations, however, and the social work profession struggles with its relationship to a variety of social movements. For example, Chapter 13 discusses the tensions in community social work around issues of social action. With the profession's emphasis on social justice, we should understand how social movements emerge and become successful. That is why this chapter on social movements is included in this book and why the professional literature is beginning to make use of social movement theory and to call for greater social work involvement with social movements (see, e.g., Fisher & Shragge, 2000; McNair, Fowler, & Harris, 2000).

Perspectives on Social Movements

Conflict perspective

Early social science literature on social movements was based on a relatively unified perspective, commonly called **strain theory**. According to strain theory, social movements develop in response to some form of strain in society, when people's efforts to cope with stress become collective efforts. Different versions of strain theory focus on different types of social strains, such as strain due to rapid social change, strain due to social inequality, strain due to social isolation and lack of community, and strain due to conflicts in cultural beliefs (Hall, 1995; Marx & McAdam, 1994). Discussion in earlier chapters has built a case that each of these types of strain exists in the United States today.

Recent social science theory and research have been critical of social strain theory, however. Critics argue that strain is always present to some degree in all societies, but social movements do not always appear in response, and their intensity does not vary systematically with the level of strain (Hall, 1995; Marx & McAdam, 1994; McAdam, McCarthy, & Zald, 1996). These critics suggest that social strain is a necessary but not sufficient condition to predict the development of a social movement. Any social movement theory must start, they insist, with the condition of social strain, but other theories are needed to understand why a particular social movement develops when it does, what form that movement takes, and how successful the movement is in accomplishing its goals. Without the sense of outrage felt by the breast cancer advocates, the National Breast Cancer Coalition would not have developed, at least not its social reform mission. But the situation of women with breast cancer had not changed suddenly, so why did the social reform movement develop when it did?

Psychodynamic perspective

Instead of focusing on social strains, some social psychologists have looked for psychological factors or attitudes that might explain which individuals are likely to get involved in social movements. A variety of psychological characteristics have been investigated, including authoritarian personality, emotional conflicts with parents, alienation, aggression, and relative deprivation. Empirical investigations have found very little support for a relationship between psychological characteristics and social movement participation, however. Research also indicates that a great many people who never join social movements have similar attitudes about movement goals to those of active movement participants (Marx & McAdam, 1994).

Theory and research about social movements have flourished in the past 3 decades. Throughout the 1970s, social movement scholars in the United States and Europe worked independently of each other and developed different theories and different research emphases (McAdam et al., 1996). In the past 15 years, however, U.S. and European social movement scholars have begun to work together and to engage in comparative analysis of social movements across place and time. Originally, these collaborative efforts focused only on social movements in the United States and Western Europe. Since the momentous political events in Eastern Europe in the late 1980s, however, Eastern European social movements have received extensive and intensive investigation. Social movements scholarship has begun to extend comparative analysis beyond the United States and Europe to nonindustrialized countries as well as to social movements that cross national lines (Smith, Chatfield, & Pagnucco, 1997).

Three perspectives on social movements have emerged out of this lively interest. I will be referring to these perspectives as the political opportunities perspective, the mobilizing structures perspective, and the cultural framing perspective. There is growing agreement among social movement scholars that none of these perspectives taken alone provides adequate tools for understanding social movements (Hall, 1995; McAdam et al., 1996; Marx & McAdam, 1994; Tarrow, 1994, 1998). Each perspective adds important dimensions to our understanding of social movements, however, and taken together they provide a relatively comprehensive theory of social movements. Social movement scholars recommend research that synthesizes concepts across the three perspectives. The recent social movement literature offers one of the best examples of contemporary attempts to integrate and synthesize multiple theoretical perspectives to give a more complete picture of social phenomena.

Political Opportunities Perspective

Mary Jo Kahn and other breast cancer advocates saw political opportunity in the gender gap within the U.S. electorate and in the end of the Cold War. They thought that these circumstances opened the possibility for successful attempts at social reform. These observations are in line with the **political opportunities (PO) perspective**, whose main ideas are summarized in Exhibit 14.1.

Conflict perspective

The PO perspective begins with the assumption that social institutions, particularly political and economic institutions, benefit the more powerful members of society, often called **elites**, and disadvantage many. The elites typically have routine access to institutionalized political channels, whereas disadvantaged groups are denied access. Power disparities make it very difficult for some groups to successfully challenge existing institutions, but the PO perspective suggests that institutions are not consistently invulnerable to challenge by groups with little power. Social movements can at times take advantage of institutional arrangements that are vulnerable to challenge. The breast cancer advocates were convinced that the lack of funding for breast cancer research was related to gender power arrangements, but they astounded even themselves by setting in motion a process that secured Department of Defense funding for

EXHIBIT 14.1
Key Ideas of
the Political
Opportunities
Perspective

Social movements emerge when political opportunities are open.

Political systems differ from each other, and change over time, in their openness to social movements.

A given political system is not equally open or closed to all challengers.

Success of one social movement can open the political system to challenges from other social movements.

A given political system's openness to social movements is influenced by international events.

Opportunities for social movements open at times of instability in political alignments.

Social movements often rely on elite allies.

breast cancer research. Theories of social movements often underestimate the ability of challengers to mount and sustain social movements (Morris, 2000).

The political system itself may influence whether a social movement will emerge at a given time, as well as the form the movement will take. Social movement scholars have identified several influential dimensions of political systems and analyzed the ways in which changes in one or more of these dimensions make the political system either receptive or vulnerable to challenges (Tarrow, 1994, 1998). Here we examine three of those dimensions: openness of the political system, stability of political alignments, and availability of elite allies.

Openness of the Political System. It might seem reasonable to think that activists will undertake collective action when political systems are open and avoid such action when political systems are closed. The relationship of system openness or closure to social movement activity is not that simple, however (Eisinger, 1973). They have instead a curvilinear relationship: neither full access nor its total absence encourages the greatest degree of collective action. Some resistance stimulates movement solidarity, but too much resistance makes collective action too costly for social movement participants (Freeman, 1995; Oberschall, 1992).

More generally, but in a similar vein, democratic states facilitate social movements and authoritarian states repress them (Tarrow, 1994). However, because democratic states invite participation, even criticism, many challenging issues that might spark social movements are "processed" out of existence through electoral processes. It is hard to mount a social movement if it seems that the political system is easily influenced without serious collective action. Democratic states do not treat all challenges in the same manner, however, and are capable of being quite repressive at times. Membership in the Communist party was outlawed in the United States in the 1950s, and black nationalists were ruthlessly suppressed in the 1970s (Tarrow, 1996). On the other hand, the repression found in authoritarian states may serve to radicalize social movement leaders (della Porta, 1996). And as was evident in Eastern Europe in the late 1980s, authoritarian states are not always effective in repressing challenges. The political leadership's efforts to appease the population by offering small liberties had a snowball effect. Relaxation of social control in a previously repressive political system often has the unintended consequence of fueling the fire of long-held grievances (Marx & McAdam, 1994).

Three other propositions associated with the PO perspective about the relationship between social movement activities and the openness of political systems deserve note:

1.   A given political system is not equally open or closed to all challengers at a given time; some social movements are favored over others. Even in a democracy, universal franchise does not mean equal access to the political system; wealth buys access not easily available to poor people's movements (Piven & Cloward, 1977). Indeed, the success of the breast cancer advocates may be, in no small way, related to the middle-class status of the movement's organizers and to their ability to frame breast cancer as an issue that transcends social class.

2.   The success of one social movement can open the political system to the challenge of other social movements. For example, successful legislative action by the black civil rights movement during the 1960s opened the way for other civil rights movements, particularly the women's movement, which benefited from the targeting of women in Title VII of the Civil Rights Act of 1964 (McAdam, 1996a). But the successful movement may also open the way for opponent movements, called **countermovements**, as well as for allied movements. The women's movement has been countered by a variety of antifeminist movements, including the antiabortionist movement and a set of interrelated movements that focus on traditional gender roles for family life.

3.   Since the 18th century, social movements have diffused rapidly across national boundaries, and the fate of national social movements has been influenced by international events. The black civil rights movement in the United States was influenced by international attention to the gap between our national image as champion of human rights and the racial discrimination that permeated our social institutions (McAdam, 1996a). The recent revolution in communication technology, coupled with the globalization of market systems, is expected to quicken the diffusion of collective action, as evidenced by events in Eastern Europe during the late 1980s (Smith et al., 1997; Tarrow, 1998).

Stability of Political Alignments. PO theorists agree that the routine transfer of political power from one group of incumbents to another, as when a different political party takes control of the U.S. presidency or Congress, opens opportunities for the development or reactivation of social movements (McAdam et al., 1996; Marx & McAdam, 1994; Tarrow, 1994, 1996). At such times, some social movements lose favor and others gain opportunity. In both the 1930s and 1960s, changes in political party strength appear to have been related to increased social movement activity among poor people. Some observers note that social movements on the Left mobilized during the Kennedy and Johnson administrations, and social movements on the Right mobilized during the Reagan and Bush administrations and again when the Republicans took over Congress in 1994 (McAdam et al., 1996); social movements on the Right also appear to have gained momentum when George W. Bush became president in 2000.

Disruption of political alliances also occurs at times other than political elections, for both partisan and nonpartisan reasons, and such disruptions produce conflicts and divisions among elites. When elites are divided, social movements can sometimes encourage some factions to take the role of "tribunes of the people" (Tarrow, 1994, p. 88) and support the goals of the movement. The breast cancer advocates were able to capitalize on the desire of politicians across the political spectrum to find a noncontroversial women's issue. Disruptions in political alliances also occur when different branches of the government—such as the executive branch and the legislative branch—are at odds with each other. Such conflict has been the case throughout most of the history of the breast cancer activist movement. New coalitions may be formed, and the uncertainty that ensues may encourage groups to make new or renewed attempts to challenge institutional arrangements, hoping to find new elite allies. The breast cancer advocates found such an opening in their collaborative efforts with the Department of Defense.

The events in Eastern Europe in the late 1980s represent another type of political opportunity—one that has received little attention by social movement scholars—the opportunity that opens when a political regime loses legitimacy with those it governs. A political regime that has lost both legitimacy and effectiveness "is skating on very thin ice" (Oberschall, 1996, p. 98). As reported in Chapter 9, many political analysts suggest that the current era is marked by a reduced capacity of nations to govern and increasing cynicism on the part of citizens about the capacity of governments to govern. Some social movement scholars suggest that this sort of instability is contributing to the global spread of social movement activity (Oberschall, 1996; Smith et al., 1997; Tarrow, 1998).

Availability of Elite Allies. Participants in social movements often lack both power and resources for influencing the political process. But they may be assisted by influential allies who play a variety of supportive roles: "friends in court, guarantors against brutal repression, or acceptable negotiators" (Tarrow, 1996, p. 55). These elite allies may provide financial support, or they may provide name and face recognition that attracts media attention to the goals and activities of the movement. Research indicates a strong correlation between the presence of elite allies and social movement success (Gamson, 1990; Tarrow, 1994). The success of the breast cancer activists was aided by their ability to find allies across the political spectrum.

Social movement participants often have ambivalent relationships with their elite allies, however. On the one hand, powerful allies provide needed resources; on the other hand, they may limit or distort the goals of the movement (Kriesi, 1996). The relationship between participants in the disability movement and actor Christopher Reeve is a good example of the tension that can develop between movement participants and their elite allies. When Christopher Reeve was paralyzed following an equestrian accident, the media quickly assigned him the role of star speaker for the disability community. Many in the disability movement were offended. Reeve's personal agenda is a cure for spinal cord injuries, but the movement's emphasis is on personal assistance for persons with disabilities—on living with disability, not cure (S. Gilson, personal communication, July 25, 1996). People in the disability movement were concerned that the emphasis on cure would undermine their efforts to win public acceptance of their disabilities and to make their environments more accessible.

Mobilizing Structures Perspective

Rational choice perspective

Mary Jo Kahn attributes much of the success of the breast cancer activists to their ability to build a strong movement out of existing networks of mastectomy support groups and women activists. They also benefited from the mentoring provided by AIDS activists. Ms. Kahn suggests, in a more general way, that the involvement of women in paid work, where they come in contact with other women, has facilitated the development of social movements involving women's issues. These views are consistent with the **mobilizing structures (MS) perspective**, which starts from this basic premise: given their disadvantaged position in the political system, social movement leaders must seek out and mobilize the resources they need—people, money, information, ideas, and skills—in order to reduce the costs and increase the benefits of movement activities (Oberschall, 1992; Taylor, 1995). In the MS perspective, social movements have no influence without effective organization of various kinds of **mobilizing structures**—"those collective vehicles, informal as well as formal, through which people mobilize and engage in collective action" (McAdam et al., 1996, p. 3). Mobilizing structures are the collective building blocks of social movements. The main ideas of the MS perspective are summarized in Exhibit 14.2.

Informal and Formal Structures. MS scholars agree that social movements typically do not start from scratch, but build on existing structures. They disagree, however, on the relative importance of informal versus formal structures. The MS perspective has two

EXHIBIT 14.2
Key Ideas of the
Mobilizing Structures
Perspective

Social movements must be able to mobilize various kinds of formal and informal networks.

Resource mobilization theory focuses on the coordination of movement activities through social movement organizations (SMOs).

The political process model focuses on mobilization of the movement through informal networks.

Mobilizing structures have a strong influence on the life course of social movements.

To survive, social movements must be able to attract new members and sustain the involvement of current members.

theoretical building blocks, one that emphasizes formal mobilizing structures and one that emphasizes informal mobilizing structures:

1.   **Resource mobilization theory** focuses on the organization and coordination of movement activities through formal organizations called **social movement organizations (SMOs)** (Zald & McCarthy, 1987). Theorists in this tradition are particularly interested in **professional social movements,** staffed by leaders and activists who make a professional career out of reform causes (Oberschall, 1992, p. 30). The antipoverty movement of the 1960s and various public interest research groups (PIRGs) are examples of professional social movements. Some social movement scholars suggest that professional social movements are more common in the United States than in Europe (Oberschall, 1992; Tarrow, 1998).

2.   The **political process model** focuses on everyday ties between people, in grassroots settings, as the basic structures for the communication and social solidarity necessary for mobilization (McAdam et al., 1996; McCarthy, 1996; Tarrow, 1994). The focus is thus on naturally existing networks based in family, work, and neighborhood relationships. Social networks may "endure longer and are more likely to produce an ongoing social movement when they are rooted in preexisting social ties, habits of collaboration and the zest for planning and carrying out collective action that comes from a common life" (Tarrow, 1994, p. 150). These natural networks are hard to repress and control because, in a democratic society, people have the right to congregate in their private homes and other informal settings (Tarrow, 1994).

Although resource mobilization theory and the political process model disagree about the relative merits of formal and informal structures, they do agree that the costs of mobilizing social movements are minimized by drawing on preexisting structures and networks (McCarthy, 1987; Ray, 1993). The breast cancer activists have now developed formal organizations, but their early efforts depended on their familiar, cohesive informal networks, feminist groups, and mastectomy support groups. This aspect of their experience seems to be quite common. Black churches and black colleges played an important role in the U.S. civil rights movement (McAdam, 1982; Morris, 1981, 1984). The student movements of the 1960s benefited from friendship networks among activists of the civil rights movement (Oberschall, 1992). The radical wing of the women's movement emerged out of informal friendship networks of women who had been active in the civil rights and New Left movements of the 1960s (Evans, 1980). Antiabortion and other New Right movements have benefited from strong ties and commitments found in Catholic and conservative Protestant churches (Oberschall, 1992; Ray, 1993).

In fact, several social movement scholars have noted the particularly "religious roots and character of many American movements" (McAdam et al., 1996, p. 18). They suggest that this link is not surprising, given the higher rates of church affiliation and attendance in the United States than in other comparable Western democracies.

Development perspective

The Life Course of Social Movements. The MS perspective asserts that mobilizing structures have a strong influence on the life course of a social movement, making time an important dimension. Although most social movements fade relatively soon, some last decades (Marx & McAdam, 1994). The typical pattern for the movements that persist is as follows: at the outset, the movement is ill defined, and the various mobilizing structures are weakly organized (Kriesi, 1996; Marx & McAdam, 1994). Once the movement has been in existence for a while, it is likely to become "larger, less spontaneous, better organized" (Marx & McAdam, 1994, p. 95). The mature social movement is typically led by the SMOs that were developed in the course of mobilization. The National Breast Cancer Coalition is currently in this situation, but, as you may recall, it was not always so.

Social movement scholars disagree about whether the increasing role of formal organizations as time passes is a good thing or a bad thing. Many suggest that movements cannot survive without becoming more organized and taking on many of the characteristics of the institutions they challenge (Freeman, 1995; Hall, 1995; Marx & McAdam, 1994; Oberschall, 1992; Tarrow, 1994). On the other hand, this tendency of social movements to become more organized and less spontaneous often dooms them, particularly poor people's movements, to failure (Piven & Cloward, 1977). Organizations that become more formal commonly abandon the oppositional tactics that brought early success and fail to seize the window of opportunity created by the unrest those tactics generated. Thus, one of the most important problems facing social movement organizers is to create mobilizing structures that are sufficiently strong to stand up to opponents but also flexible enough to respond to changing circumstances (Tarrow, 1994).

Jo Freeman (1995, p. 403) asserts that there is "no such thing as a permanent social movement." She suggests that every movement, at some point, changes into something else, often into many other things, through three basic processes:

1. *Institutionalization.* Some movements become part of existing institutions or develop durable SMOs with stable income, staff, and routine operations. The profession of social work is an example of a social movement that became institutionalized.

2. *Encapsulation.* Some social movements, or at least some parts of them, lose their sense of mission and begin to direct their activities inward, to serve members, rather than outward, to promote or resist change. That has been the trajectory of some labor unions (Clemens, 1996). Social work's history also includes periods of encapsulation, when social workers became more concerned about "professional advancement and autonomy, status, and financial security" (Reamer, 1992, p. 12) than about social justice and the public welfare. This appears to be the current state of the social work profession.

3. *Factionalization.* Still other movements fall apart, often disintegrating into contentious, competing factions (Voss, 1996). This was the trajectory of the U.S. student protest movements after the violence at the 1968 Democratic party convention in Chicago (Tarrow, 1994).

It is too early to tell what the long-term trajectory of the breast cancer activist movement will be.

Problems of Movement Membership. To remain vital, social movements must be able to attract new recruits and sustain the morale and commitment of current participants. The successes of the breast cancer activist movement are contributing to a strong membership at the present time, but its continued success will depend on the leaders' ability to continue to attract new recruits and maintain the involvement of current members.

Social movement leaders must manage a variety of membership issues that can threaten or facilitate their success. Three membership issues are particularly important to the success of social movements:

1. **Free riders** are people who stand to benefit from a social movement but make no contributions to its efforts. Social movements must find ways to overcome the free rider tendency and convince people to join and contribute (Oberschall, 1992).

2. **Infiltrators** are people from external groups who make a conscious effort to get inside a social movement and destroy it from within, often by instigating factionalism. Social movement scholars cite evidence of past government infiltration of

a variety of social movements, including the black civil rights movement, the 1960s' student movement, and the Earth First! movement (Balser, 1997; Marx & McAdam, 1994; Oberschall, 1992).

3.   The **radical flank** of a social movement consists of "extremists" within the movement. Research suggests that radical flanks can contribute to the success of a movement, because elites are often more willing to fund, and otherwise support, moderate groups within the movement when confronted by a radical alternative (McAdam et al., 1996). Mary Jo Kahn believes that the early successes of the breast cancer movement were due, in part, to the fact that the cry for breast cancer research looked moderate to political leaders in comparison to the more contentious feminist issues of abortion and sexual harassment. Alternatively, the radical flank may push moderates to become more radical, with the result that outcomes may be more radical than originally expected.

Cultural Framing Perspective

Social constructionist perspective

The **cultural framing (CF) perspective** asserts that a social movement can succeed only when participants develop shared understandings and definitions of the situation. These shared meanings develop through a transactional process of consciousness raising, which social movement scholars call cultural framing. **Cultural framing** involves "conscious strategic efforts by groups of people to fashion shared understandings of the world and of themselves that legitimate and motivate collective action" (McAdam et al., 1996, p. 6). Exhibit 14.3 summarizes the central ideas of the CF perspective.

Social movement leaders and participants engage in a delicate balancing act as they construct cultural frames. To legitimate collective action, cultural frames must impel people to feel aggrieved or outraged about some situation they consider unjust. But to motivate people to engage in collective action, cultural frames must be optimistic about the possibilities for improving the situation. Consider the slogans developed by the breast cancer activists. Some dramatized the severity of their situation and the fairness of their cause: "We will not die silently anymore," "Do the Write Thing." Mary Jo Kahn's daughters also prepared banners that would capture the attention, and inspire the optimism, of their youthful peers: "Hold the line at 1 in 9." Simultaneously, social movements want to draw heavily on existing cultural symbols so that the movement frame will be "culturally resonant to fire people's minds" (Tarrow, 1994, p. 33) while they add new frames to the cultural stock, thus sponsoring new ways of thinking about social conditions. The challenge of this balancing act is "how to put forward a set of unsettling demands for unconventional people in ways that will not make enemies out of potential allies" (Tarrow, 1994, p. 10). Unfortunately, research has provided

EXHIBIT 14.3
Key Ideas of the
Cultural Framing
Perspective

> Social movements must be able to develop shared understandings that legitimate and motivate collective action.
>
> Social movements actively participate in the naming of grievances and injustices.
>
> Social movement leaders must construct a perception that change is possible.
>
> Social movements must articulate goals.
>
> Social movements must identify and create tactical choices for accomplishing goals.
>
> Contests over cultural frames are common in social movements.
>
> Social movements must be able to create cultural frames to appeal to diverse audiences.

movement leaders with little guidance in how to achieve such balance in their slogans and symbols.

Exhibit 14.4 presents some cultural frames provided by social movements in the United States during the past few decades. You may not be familiar with all of these cultural frames, and you might want to check with your classmates to see if, collectively, you can identify the social movement with which each of the frames is associated. How well do you think these cultural frames serve both to legitimate and to motivate collective action? How well do they draw on existing symbols while promoting new ways of thinking?

A further complication in the process of constructing frames is that frames attractive to one audience are likely to be rejected by other audiences. Social movement groups "must master the art of simultaneously playing to a variety of publics, threatening opponents, and pressuring the state, all the while appearing nonthreatening and sympathetic to the media and other publics" (McAdam, 1996b, p. 344). Activists desire media attention because that is the most effective way to reach wide audiences, but they also know that they cannot control the way the movement will be framed by the media. The media are attracted to dramatic, even violent, aspects of a movement, but these aspects are likely to be rejected by other audiences (Tarrow, 1994). Movement activists are particularly concerned about the impact of the media on their **conscience constituency**—people attracted to the movement because it appears just and worthy, not because they will benefit personally.

Social movement framing is never a matter of easy consensus building, and intense **framing contests** may arise among a variety of actors, particularly in the later stages. Representatives of the political system and participants in countermovements

EXHIBIT 14.4
Selected Cultural
Frames Presented
by Social
Movements in the
United States

Pro-life MAKE LOVE, NOT WAR **Deaf Now** CIVIL RIGHTS *12 Steps*

The Color Lavender **I May Be Disabled But I'm Not Dead Yet** Pro Choice

The Peace Sign Stonewall *We Shall Overcome*

A woman's body is her own Family Values *Take Back the Night*

Welfare Rights Unborn Child *Our Homes, Not Nursing Homes* GAY RIGHTS

Every Child a Wanted Child Reverence for Life Piss on Pity

I Have a Dream **Hell No, We Won't Go** *Our Daughters and Our Sons*

black power *Do Not Speak For Me, Listen To Me* **Disability Rights**

influence framing through their own actions and public statements, and internal conflicts become more pronounced. Leaders and followers often have different frames for the movement (Marx & McAdam, 1994), and there are often splits between moderate and radical participants. It is not at all unusual for movements to put forth multiple frames, with different groups sponsoring different frames. For example, in the feminist movement, reformists have focused on employment issues and radicals have sought a fundamental restructuring of gender roles (Carden, 1978). When a movement captures media attention, there is often an intense struggle over who speaks for the movement and which cultural frame is put forward.

Although the CF perspective has generated little empirical research to date, CF theorists have begun to examine the role of cultural framing in social movements. They have found that it provides language, ideology, and symbols for understanding that a problem exists, for recognizing windows of opportunity, for establishing goals, and for identifying pathways for action.

Frames for Understanding That a Problem Exists. Social movements are actively involved in the "naming" of grievances and injustices. They do so in part by drawing on existing cultural symbols, but they also underscore, accentuate, and enlarge current understanding of the seriousness of a situation. In essence, they call attention to contradictions between cultural ideals and cultural realities. For example, the U.S. civil rights movement called attention to the contradiction between democracy and racial discrimination. When the breast cancer activists organized Mother's Day rallies, they called attention to the discrepancy between the high value placed on women's roles as mothers and the failure to protect the health and lives of women.

In the United States, movement frames are often articulated in terms of "rights"— civil rights, disability rights, gay rights, animal rights, children's rights. In Europe, where there is less emphasis on individual liberty, "rights" frames are far less common in social movements (Hastings, 1998; Tarrow, 1994).

In the past decade, fundamentalist religious movements have sprung up in many countries, including the United States. These movements have used "morality" frames, focusing on good and evil rather than justice versus injustice. Compared to Europe, the United States has historically produced a high number of such movements (Marx & McAdam, 1994). Prohibition, abolition, anticommunism, and antiabortionism have all had religious roots. A contemporary religious frame that crosses national boundaries as well as liberal and conservative ideologies is "reverence for life," expressed in such disparate movements as the environmental, health, antiabortion, animal rights, and anticapital punishment movements (Marx & McAdam, 1994).

Frames for Recognizing a Window of Opportunity. The perception of opportunity to change a troublesome situation is also culturally framed to some extent (Gamson & Meyer, 1996). On occasion, it is easy to develop a shared frame that opportunity exists or does not exist, but most situations are more ambiguous. Social movement leaders must successfully construct a perception that change is possible, because an opportunity does not exist unless it is recognized. They typically attempt to overcome concerns about the dangers and futility of activism by focusing on the risks of inaction, communicating a sense of urgency, and emphasizing the openness of the moment. They are intent on "keeping hope alive" (Gamson & Meyer, 1996, p. 286).

Calibrating this type of frame is a difficult task. On the one hand, overstating an opportunity can be hazardous (Piven & Cloward, 1977). Without "fortifying myths," which allow participants to see defeats as mere setbacks, unrealistically high expectations can degenerate into pessimism about possibilities for change (Voss, 1996). On the other hand, "movement activists systematically overestimate the degree of political opportunity, and if they did not, they would not be doing their job wisely" (Gamson & Meyer, 1996, p. 285). Unrealistic perceptions about what is possible can actually make change more possible. A $300 million increase for breast cancer research seemed unrealistic to many women involved in the advocacy movement, but this goal was achieved.

Frames for Establishing Goals. Once it has been established that both problem and opportunity exist, the question of social movement goals arises. Is change to be narrow or sweeping, reformist or revolutionary? Will the emphasis be on providing opportunities for individual self-expression or on changing the social order? U.S. social movements have generally set goals that are more reformist than revolutionary (Marx & McAdam, 1994). Parents, Families and Friends of Lesbians and Gays (PFLAG) is a fairly typical example of a contemporary U.S. social movement that has struck a balance between goals of individual change and changes in the social order. Exhibit 14.5 demonstrates how PFLAG strikes this balance in its statement of goals.

Exhibit 14.5

Goals Statement of
Parents, Families and
Friends of Lesbians
and Gays (PFLAG)

To cope with an adverse society, **PFLAG PROVIDES SUPPORT.** To enlighten a
sometimes frightened and ill-informed public, **PFLAG EDUCATES AND INFORMS.**
To combat discrimination and secure equal rights, **PFLAG ADVOCATES JUSTICE.**

Source: PFLAG, 1995.

Typically, goals are poorly articulated in the early stages of a movement but are clarified through ongoing negotiations about the desired changes. The breast cancer activists began with the goal of increasing funding for research but later added the goal of giving women with breast cancer a voice in research funding decisions. More recently, they have become involved in activism to ensure that genetic testing for breast cancer will not be used to deny health insurance and in advocating for access to treatment by poor women (National Breast Cancer Coalition, n.d.). Manuals for social activism suggest that modest and winnable objectives in the early stages of a movement help to reinforce the possibility of change (Gamson & Meyer, 1996).

Social workers Ray MacNair, Leigh Fowler, and John Harris (2000) suggest that progressive, or offensive, social movements have a three-pronged goal: (1) they must confront oppression, (2) they must attend to the damaged identities of oppressed persons, and (3) they must "renovate" the cultural roles of both oppressor groups and oppressed groups. Three "identity" movements—the black civil rights movement, the women's movement, and the lesbian-gay-bisexual movement—demonstrate the process of goal setting. Each of these movements has a long history of emerging, waning, and reemerging in the United States, changing its framing of the movement's goals along the way. For these three social movements, the framing of goals followed an evolutionary path through six different frames:

1. *Assimilation:* Persuade the mainstream to recognize the capabilities of the oppressed group while also working to "uplift" the oppressed group.

2. *Normative Antidiscrimination:* Place the onus for change completely on oppressor groups and oppressive institutions. Take a confrontational approach of legal challenges and political lobbying. Recognize the positive attributes of the oppressed group.

3. *Militant direct action:* Reject the legitimacy of normal decision-making processes and attempt to disrupt them. Develop a "culture of rebellion" to energize disruptive actions (p. 75).

4. *Separatism:* Avoid oppression by avoiding oppressor groups.

5. *Introspective self-help:* Focus on building a healthy identity.

6. *Pluralistic integration:* Appreciate themselves and promote connections to other cultures.

Frames for Identifying Pathways for Action. Some of the most important framing efforts of a social movement involve tactical choices for accomplishing goals. Social movement scholars generally agree that each society has a supply of forms of collective action that are familiar to social movement participants as well as the elites they challenge (Oberschall, 1992; Tarrow, 1998). New forms are introduced from time to time, and they spread quickly if they are successful. In the United States, for example, marches on Washington have come to be standard fare in collective action, and activist groups exchange information on the logistics of organizing a march on Washington. On the other hand, the sit-down strike is no longer as common as it once was (Zald, 1996). The breast cancer activists have made extensive use of rallies and letter writing campaigns, and also have begun to make use of a relatively new tactic, organized road races. Contemporary social movements draw power from the large selection of forms of collective action currently in the cultural stock, and many movements, notably the women's movement, have wisely used multiple forms of action (Tarrow, 1994).

Just as social movement goals fall on a continuum from reform to revolution, forms of collective action can be arranged along a continuum from conventional to violent, as shown in Exhibit 14.6. Nonviolent forms of collective action are the core of contemporary U.S. movements. Nonviolent disruption of routine activities is today considered the most powerful form of activism in the United States and in other Western democracies with relatively stable governments (McAdam, 1996b; Tarrow, 1994). The power of nonviolent disruption is that it creates uncertainty and some fear of violence, yet provides authorities in democratic societies with no valid argument for repression. Violent collective action, on the other hand, destroys public support for the movement. Martin Luther King was ingenious in recognizing that the best path for the U.S. civil rights movement was "successfully courting violence while restraining violence in his followers" (McAdam, 1996b, p. 349). Consequently, it was the police who lost public favor for their brutality, not the demonstrators.

Social movement scholars agree that for the past 200 years, social movement actions became less violent (Tarrow, 1998). They also suggest, however, that beginning in the 1990s, as the former Soviet empire collapsed, violent social movements began to flourish again around the world. This trend was exemplified by white supremacist armed militias in the United States and militant Islamic fundamentalist movements in the Middle East, Central Asia, and Africa. Out of these two movements have come the bombing of a state building in Oklahoma City and the somber events of September 11, 2001. It is unclear whether the increased violence of social movements will be a

EXHIBIT 14.6
Forms of Collective
Action

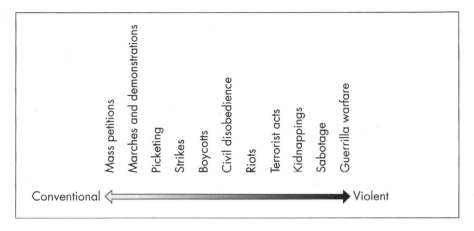

long-term trend, and if so, whether existing theories of social movements will be relevant to the new forms of movement actions.

Social Movement Outcomes

Because social movements are processes, not structures, they are not easy to research. Case study has been the predominant method of study, with recent emphasis on comparative case studies. Unfortunately, one researcher may declare a particular movement a failure while another researcher will see it as having succeeded. Often the impact of a movement cannot be determined until well past its heyday (Tarrow, 1994). Different analyses may be based, in part, on different guidelines for success, but the researchers may also be evaluating the movement from different time perspectives. This is a reminder, again, of the importance of the time dimension in changing person/environment configurations.

Like other human endeavors, social movements are neither completely successful nor completely unsuccessful. In general, however, the most successful social movements have outcomes that are far less radical than their proponents would like and far more radical than their opponents would like. Social movements rarely produce the major redistribution of power that activists desire and movement goals specify. The women's movement has not achieved its goal of equality and nondiscrimination for women. The conservative Christian movement has not reached its goal of restoring traditional family and gender roles. And yet, social movements do have an effect on society (Oberschall, 1992). Thus, their success should perhaps be measured not by their survival but by the institutional changes they influence.

Sidney Tarrow (1998) suggests that the power of social movements is cumulative and can be appreciated only from a long-term historical perspective. Many of the gains of social movements get reversed, but "they often leave behind incremental expansions in participation, changes in popular culture, and residual movement networks" (p. 202). Research on social movements documents a range of direct and indirect effects. Contemporary social movements have accomplished an impressive list of specific federal legislation, including the Civil Rights Act of 1964; Title IX, the federal law that prohibits gender-based discrimination in athletics and educational programs at institutions that receive federal funds; and the Americans With Disabilities Act of 1990. Considered by some scholars to be the most successful social movement in the United States since World War II, the black civil rights movement has served as a model for organizing, opened opportunities, and provided hope for other aggrieved groups. Because of social movements, the political system has become more open and responsive to previously ignored groups, and voicing grievances has become an expected part of life in a democratic country. Many SMOs have become a stable part of the social environment, and activist-oriented networks outlast the movements that spawned them. Research indicates that although individual activists are often temporarily disillusioned at the end of a social movement, in the long term they are empowered and politicized by their participation (Tarrow, 1998).

Although the success of a given social movement depends on its unique configuration of political opportunities, mobilizing efforts, and cultural frames, social movement researchers agree on the factors that influence success or failure. Some of these factors are outside the control of the movement, but some of them can be successfully manipulated by movement leaders. The most obvious factor is the ability to attract a large number of participants. The most successful movements tap into existing networks and associations that have a shared culture, a strong sense of solidarity, and a common identity. These groups are the most likely to be willing to make sacrifices and remain committed over time, and to have the shared symbols to frame the movement (Oberschall, 1992; Tarrow, 1994). Religious movements, for example, benefit from long-lasting and widely cherished religious symbols (Oberschall, 1992). Other forces, however, can serve as serious threats to the success of a social movement. Internal conflicts and factionalism weaken the chances for success, as does a strong opponent. Initial successes may stimulate strong countermovements, or a backlash may develop in reaction to the radical flank of a movement.

The Future of Social Movements

Social movement scholars generally agree that social movements will continue to be a part of the social landscape in the foreseeable future (Oberschall, 1992; Marx & McAdam,

1994; Tarrow, 1998). In fact, some have predicted that we are entering an era of "movement societies," in which challenge and disruption of institutional arrangements will become a routine part of life (Marx & McAdam, 1994; Tarrow, 1994).

Acknowledging that social scientists are, in general, poor prognosticators, Gary Marx and Doug McAdam (1994) nevertheless venture six predictions about the future of social movements:

1. We are entering a period of heightened social movement activity.

2. Ideological conflicts will continue, exacerbated by the growing gap between rich and poor.

3. Social movements will take on an increasingly international character.

4. Race will continue to be a salient issue for protest activity in the United States.

5. In other parts of the world, ethnic nationalist movements will proliferate.

6. Social movements will continue to be based in existing groups or in established communities. (pp. 121-124)

Marx and McAdam project four likely seedbeds for future social movements: churches and other religious institutions, colleges and universities, stable residential neighborhoods, and formal SMOs. They suggest that these are the mobilizing structures most likely to have the necessary resources, preexisting social ties, and shared understandings to mount effective reform movements.

Indeed, in the years since Marx and McAdam made these predictions, there has been a rapid expansion of **transnational social movement organizations (TSMOs)**, or social movement organizations that operate in more than one nation-state. To date, the TSMOs have developed primarily in the areas of human rights, women's rights, environmental protection, and peace (Smith, 1997). Greenpeace, Amnesty International, Service for Peace and Justice (SERPAJ), and Friends of the Earth are examples of TSMOs. One benefit of TSMOs is that they can include people who speak out about an issue in one country while people are silenced in other countries. TSMOs rarely use violent, or even seriously disruptive, methods. Many observers suggest that given the globalization of the economy, any successful labor challenge to growing inequality will have to be international in scope.

Social Movements and Contemporary Social Work

Early in this chapter, I suggested that the professionalization of social work was accomplished by sacrificing the social reform fervor of its settlement house tradition. Social movement scholars have in fact found that it is difficult, if not impossible, to be both a profession and a reform movement (Freeman, 1995). The history of social work is a history of tension between the goal of professional service and the goal of social reform (Popple, 1992). This tension has been quite obvious in recent years. On the one hand, social workers and their professional organizations have devoted a lot of resources to obtaining licensure for clinical social workers and to securing private and public reimbursement for clinical social work services. On the other hand, recent revisions of documents by social work's leading professional organizations, the NASW Code of Ethics and CSWE's Curriculum Policy Statement, have added forceful language about the social justice goals of the profession.

Some social work scholars see a dual focus on professional service and social reform as achievable and even natural (Colcord & Mann, 1930; Lee, 1937; Schwartz, 1963). Others see the two goals as incompatible (Lubove, 1966; Piven & Cloward, 1977). Philip Popple (1992) suggests that each generation of social workers must struggle anew with the tension between a conservative mandate from society for efficient service that manages problems of dependency and a liberal or radical mandate from the profession to promote social justice. He also suggests that social workers experience this tension differently in different political eras. In conservative political times, there is great disparity between the societal mandate for social workers to act as social control agents and the profession's social reform tradition. In such times, the social reform goal is not prominent. In liberal political times, however, there is less tension between the two goals, and social work's social reform goal is more visible. Popple's analysis is consistent with a tenet of the PO perspective on social movements: shifts in political alignments open or close opportunities for social movement activity.

Even though the social work profession's emphasis on social reform at any given time is influenced by political opportunities, the valuing of social justice is a permanent feature of social work in the United States (Popple, 1992). Thus, all social workers should be familiar with developments in social movement theory and research. At least four contemporary trends are increasing the need for social workers to understand how social movements develop and succeed:

1. Rapid changes in social institutions in the current industrial cycle are creating new social problems and patterns of social inequality that call for new solutions to social welfare problems on a global scale.

2. We seem to be entering an era of heightened social movement activity, an era in which groups with long-standing grievances are framing those grievances—such as disabilities rights and gay rights—and organizing to seek reform in social institutions. We should be prepared for the possibility that their grievances will include shortcomings of the social welfare institution and the social work profession. Social workers were

surprised to be considered part of the problem rather than part of the solution in the clients' rights movement of the 1960s, when clients of social service organizations identified ways in which their rights were being violated in the delivery of services (Hutchison, Dattalo, & Rodwell, 1994).

3. Along with economic globalization, there is a trend toward the internationalization of social work, with exchanges between social workers across national boundaries occurring on several levels. To be good partners in this exchange, social workers in the United States will need to know about the political opportunities for social movements in other countries and about the relative emphasis on professional service and social reform in the countries with which they have contact.

4. Social workers are increasingly involved in working with mutual aid groups that have the potential for activism. We need to be aware of these groups as possible networks for social action.

Recent critics of existing social movement theory have suggested that SMOs can be divided into a reform or moderate tradition and a radical tradition (Fitzgerald & Rodgers, 2000). Radical social movement organizations tend to be organized nonhierarchically and operate with little structure. Their goal is usually radical change in social institutions, rather than social reform. Exhibit 14.7 contrasts the characteristics of moderate and radical SMOs. As you can see, existing social movement theories are a better fit with moderate SMOs than with radical SMOs (Fitzgerald & Rodgers, 2000).

This model helps us understand the dimensions of contemporary SMOs but does not capture their changing trajectories over time. After studying six feminist SMOS, Cheryl Hyde (2000) suggests that many social movement agencies fall somewhere between the moderate SMO and radical SMO. The six agencies that she studied had begun as grassroots organizations with traits consistent with the description of radical SMOs. They changed in varying ways over the years, however, falling on a continuum from moderate to radical at the point that she studied them.

Some social workers practice in **social movement agencies,** or *alternative social agencies,* which pursue social change while delivering services (Hyde, 1992). These agencies attempt to change the world by providing revolutionary services that challenge or alter social institutions. Feminist health centers and emergency shelters for battered women are good examples of social movement agencies.

We are living in a time of growing inequality, hot spots of ethnic hatred, and activism based on social identity. It is easy to get overwhelmed and feel powerless about the situations we confront. Social movement theory is an important ingredient in our social work survival kit. It helps us see, as the title of Sidney Tarrow's (1998) book suggests, that there is "power in movement." We may also take inspiration from some contemporary examples of courage and conviction that led to social change (Sernau, 2001):

EXHIBIT 14.7

Characteristics of Moderate and Radical SMOs

	Moderate SMOs	Radical SMOs
Internal structure	Hierarchical leadership; formal bureaucratic organization; development of large membership base for resource generation	Nonhierarchical leadership; participatory democratic organization; egalitarian; "membership" based on involvement; indigenous leadership
Ideology	Reform agenda, emphasis on being a contender in the existing political system; national focus	Radical agenda; emphasis on structural change; flexible ideology; radical networks; global consciousness
Tactics	Nonviolent legal action	Nonviolent direct action; mass actions; innovative tactics
Communication	Mainstream media and communication channels	Either ignored or misrepresented by mainstream media; reliance on alternative forms of communication (music, street theater, pamphlets, newsletters)
Assessment of success	Measured in terms of reform of existing political/economic system; longevity	Measured in terms of contribution to larger radical agenda; subject to intense opposition and government surveillance; may be purposefully short lived

Source: Based on Fitzgerald and Rodgers, 2000, Table 1.

- Rosa Parks, a tired seamstress on a public bus, helped launch the U.S. civil rights movement.

- C. P. Ellis, a former Ku Klux Klan leader, started action that changed the racial climate of an entire community.

- Craig Kielburger, a 12-year-old Canadian boy, began an international movement, Free the Children, to end child labor after reading a story about child workers in Pakistan.

- In 1999, college students around the United States began a boycott of Reebok sports shoes, prompting improved conditions in that company's Indonesian factories.

These are just a few of the empowering stories we can recall in our most discouraged moments.

IMPLICATIONS FOR SOCIAL WORK PRACTICE

This discussion of social movements recommends several principles for social work activism:

■ Become skillful in assessing political opportunities for social reform efforts.

■ Become skillful in recognizing and mobilizing formal and informal networks for social reform activities.

■ In conservative political eras, be vigilant about the temptation to encapsulate and lose sight of social work's social reform mission.

■ Become skillful at attracting new recruits to social reform activities and sustaining the morale and commitment of current participants.

■ Become skillful in managing internal movement conflicts and avoiding factionalism.

■ Become skillful in developing cultural frames that legitimate and motivate collective action.

■ Assist social workers in direct practice to assess the benefits and costs to clients of involvement in social movement activities.

■ Assist social workers in the traditional social welfare institution to recognize the important role that reform social movements play in identifying new or previously unrecognized social injustices and social service needs.

KEY TERMS

charity organization society
   (COS) movement
conscience constituency
countermovement
cultural framing
cultural framing (CF) perspective
defensive social movement
elites
framing contests
free riders

infiltrators
mobilizing structures
mobilizing structures (MS)
   perspective
offensive social movement
political opportunities (PO)
   perspective
political process model
professional social movements
radical flank

resource mobilization theory

settlement house movement

social movement

social movement agencies

social movement organizations (SMOs)

social reform

strain theory

transnational social movement
organization (TSMO)

ACTIVE LEARNING

1. You read about some of the early history of the breast cancer social movement in the case study at the beginning of this chapter. Visit the Web site of the National Breast Cancer Coalition (NBCC) at www.natlbcc.org. What does NBCC present as its public policy activities, grassroots advocacy efforts, programs, positions, and accomplishments? NBCC is just over a decade old. At this point, how do you evaluate its outcomes? How do you explain its successes? What challenges might lie ahead?

2. In this chapter, I suggested that successful social movements often open the way for countermovements. I also suggested that social movements may be either offensive or defensive. In considering these ideas, it is helpful to look at two social movements that hold competing views on issues related to women. Go to the Web sites of the National Organization for Women (NOW) at www.now.org and the National Right to Life Committee (NRLC) at www.nrlc.org. Study carefully the positions that each of these social movement organizations takes on the issue of abortion. What language and symbols does each organization use for framing the issue?

WEB RESOURCES

New Social Movement Network

www.interweb-tech.com/nsmnet

Site maintained by the New Social Movement Network contains links to a number of activist organizations organized topically.

Amnesty International

www.amnesty.org

Site maintained by Amnesty International contains recommendations for protection and promotion of human rights and a time line for accomplishing them, good news, FAQs, and links to other human rights activist groups.

Critical Social Work

www.criticalsocialwork.com

Site is an international, interdisciplinary e-journal whose goal is to promote dialogue about methods for achieving social justice.

Network of Alliances
Bridging Race & Ethnicity (NABRE)

www.jointcenter.org/nabre

Site maintained by NABRE, a project of the Joint Center for Political and Economic Studies (developed to link national community-based organizations working across the country to bridge racial and ethnic differences), contains an executive summary, guiding principles, event calendar, spotlight, and announcements.

Free the Children

www.freethechildren.org

Site maintained by the social movement organization developed by Craig Kielburger when he was 12 years old, contains information about accomplishments, campaigns, planned activities and projects, conferences, and speakers bureau.

National Organizers Alliance (NOA)

www.noacentral.org

Site maintained by NOA, a nonprofit organization with the mission to advance progressive organizing for social, economic, environmental, and racial justice, contains information about national gatherings, job bank, newsletter, calendar of events, and links to other activist organizations.

Greatergood.com

greatergood.com

Site maintained as part of a family of cause-related Web sites operated by Charity USA LLC contains merchandise from over 100 leading online merchants; up to 15% of each purchase goes to a charitable organization of the purchaser's selection.

Margaret Ryan
at Sacred Heart Center

Social Work Practice in a
Multidimensional Environment

Elizabeth D. Hutchison
Virginia Commonwealth University

Margaret Ryan is executive director of Sacred Heart Center (SHC), a nonprofit multiservice community center founded in 1990 to serve an impoverished urban neighborhood. Margaret describes the services provided by SHC as "child centered, family focused, and neighborhood based." They include:

- *Programs for young children.* Licensed day care, Head Start, and early childhood education (K-2)

- *Programs for school-age children.* After-school and summer programs, Boy Scouts and Girl Scouts, recreation programs (soccer, basketball, cheerleading, outdoor adventure, and social and cultural outings)

- *Programs for adolescents.* After-school and summer activities, job skills training, part-time employment placement, and academic support

- *Programs for families*: Family literacy program (with child care provided); parenting skills training; parent support group; job readiness training; baby clothing, food, and equipment; emergency food and fuel assistance

SHC also opens its facilities to community groups.

Margaret clearly sees the environment in which she works as multidimensional. In conversation with her, I heard reference to physical environment, culture, social institutions and social structure, families, small groups, formal organizations, community, and social movements.

A drive around the neighborhood reveals empty lots where housing once stood, dilapidated buildings, five or six storefront churches, several small convenience stores, several Laundromats, and, on the periphery, a grocery store that is a part of a chain developed specifically for central-city residents. There is one elementary school, but children must leave the neighborhood to attend middle and high school.

The city has a redevelopment plan that includes demolishing all public housing units in the neighborhood. The replacement housing will be a mix of low- and middle-income housing, resulting in a diminished stock of low-income housing. Most of the families served by SHC currently live in public housing, and Margaret is concerned about their future.

SHC is affiliated with the Catholic diocese. This affiliation influences Margaret's work. She is sensitive to Catholic theology in her public statements, but she thinks that overall this affiliation is positive. It provides an umbrella that allows her to say and do a lot. She draws heavily on Catholic teaching about social justice and the preferential option for people who are poor. She thinks this makes it possible for her to talk more seriously about social work's social justice mission than she typically hears from other social workers. SHC does not evangelize, but Margaret is proud that the community center is based on the faith perspective of "walking with" people—for the long haul or as long as it takes. Staff acknowledge the spiritual dimension of the people they serve and draw on it as a resource in service provision, when appropriate.

Margaret and the staff at SHC are always looking for new ways to get families involved with SHC's programs for children. Last year, they sponsored a raffle for a car. They celebrated the raffle drawing with a festive party at SHC. Arrangements were made for staff from the Children's Museum to be present with an inviting array of planned activities. Margaret emphasizes that the families who come to SHC really want things to be better for their children. The children represent hope for the future, and the motivation to try.

Every Monday night for the past 3 years, Margaret has led a support group for parents who are trying to improve their parenting. About half of the group's 15 members have been ordered by the courts to attend these meetings because of child abuse or neglect.

SHC works closely with the local Junior League, which has been generous with money and volunteer time to support SHC. Sometimes there is tension about agendas—as there could be about the housing redevelopment plan—but Margaret welcomes that tension. She thinks that social workers should become more comfortable negotiating such tensions—that we too often avoid collaborating with elite sponsors because we are not comfortable with differences in worldviews. In Margaret's view, if we don't actively engage the tensions, we lose opportunities to educate, build bridges, and heal wounds. She comments that she is willing to enter into dialogue with almost anybody—that she starts from the premise that people can agree about the end goal of improving life for families even when they don't agree about means to that end.

Margaret reports that she is constantly aware that her agency and the community it serves exist in an outdoor world that threatens—the mass media present frequent reminders that this neighborhood has the highest crime rate in the city. Margaret regularly makes decisions about how to keep people safe. She and the board of directors of SHC have perpetual discussions about whether to keep SHC's front door locked or unlocked. They continue to leave the door unlocked, because they think that this is an important symbol that signifies that they do not buy into the fear of the environment.

Margaret reports, however, that the violence in the neighborhood has a serious impact on families. Adults who use services at SHC talk about not "messing with people" as the one best way to stay safe. Margaret is concerned that this leads to social isolation. There is little interaction among neighbors, and gathering places are few. Children act the violence out, and SHC must respond with programs that address issues such as anger management and conflict resolution. Neighborhood children get few opportunities to play outside; they are kept inside because the outside is threatening. Recently, student volunteers from a prestigious private high school worked with students at SHC to organize a Children's Walk Against Violence. Participants walked from SHC to city hall, and two participants spoke to the city council about their dream of a safe neighborhood.

Margaret is an active member of an advocacy group that developed in response to "welfare reform" legislation passed over the past few years. Currently, this group is focusing on making sure that clients are fully informed of the appeals process in the social welfare system. They are planning to study child care needs of women leaving welfare and to lobby for policies that put greater focus on training and education.

Margaret was recently appointed chair of the legislative committee of her state chapter of the National Association of Social Workers (NASW). She would like to see this organization put greater emphasis on social conditions and social justice issues—and less emphasis on advocating for the status of the profession.

Something to Think About

Margaret Ryan gives a lot of thought to the multiple dimensions of environment in her work at SHC. The following questions will help you reflect on Margaret's work in this multidimensional environment and consider how you might work in similar situations:

- What evidence do you see that Margaret recognizes the influence of the physical environment on human behavior? What do you learn about the neighborhood culture and the culture of SHC? Which social institutions seem influential in the life of the community served by SHC? How does SHC work with families? What types of small groups are evident? What formal organizations are involved? What communities? Do you see any evidence of or possibilities for social movement activity?

■ Which dimensions of the environment seem most important to Margaret Ryan? If you were the director of SHC, which dimensions of the environment would seem most important to you? Where would you target your interventions? Why?

■ Which perspectives on formal organizations seem to be reflected in Margaret Ryan's work? If you were director of SHC, what theoretical perspectives on formal organizations would seem useful to you? Why?

■ If you were the director of SHC, where would you stand on these issues: community as context of practice versus target of practice, agency orientation versus social action, conflict model of practice versus collaborative model, expert versus partner in the social change process?

WORKS CITED

Abramowitz, L. (1993). Prayer as therapy among the frail Jewish elderly. *Journal of Gerontological Social Work, 19*(3/4), 69-75.

Achterberg, J. (1985). *Imagery in healing: Shamanism and modern medicine.* Boston: Shambhala.

ACOG asseses impact of September 11 on pregnancy. (2002, January 10). *Women's Health Weekly,* p. 18.

Adams, J., & Jacobsen, P. (1964). Effects of wage inequities on work quality. *Journal of Abnormal and Social Psychology, 69,* 19-25.

Ader, R., Felten, D., & Cohen, N. (1990). Interactions between the brain and the immune system. *Annual Review of Pharmacology and Toxicology, 30,* 561-602.

Adler, J. (1995). *Arching backwards: The mystical initiation of contemporary woman.* Rochester, VT: Inner Traditions.

Adler, N. (2001). A consideration of multiple pathways from socioeconomic status to health. In J. Auerbach & B. Krimgold (Eds.), *Income, socioeconomic status, and health: Exploring the relationships* (pp. 56-66). Washington, DC: National Health Policy, Academy for Health Services Research and Health Policy.

Ahrons, C. (1999). Divorce: An unscheduled family transition. In B. Carter & M. McGoldrick (Eds.), *The expanded family life cycle: Individual, family, and social perspectives* (3d ed., pp. 381-398). Boston: Allyn & Bacon.

Aiello, J., Baum, A., & Gormley, F. (1981). Social determinants of residential crowding stress. *Personality and Social Psychology Bulletin, 7,* 643-649.

Ainsman, H., Zaharia, M. D., Meaney, M. J., & Merali, Z. (1998). Do early life events alter behavior and formonal responses to stressors? *International Journal of Developmental Neuroscience, 16*(3/4), 149-164.

Akande, A. (1997). Determinants of personal space among South African students. *Journal of Psychology, 131,* 569-571.

Akbar, N. (1984). Africentric social sciences for human liberation. *Journal of Black Studies, 14,* 395-414.

The Alan Guttmacher Institute. (2001). State-level policies on sexuality, STD education. Retrieved July 7, 2002, from www.agi-usa.org/pubs/ib_5-01.html.

Al-Ansari, E. (2002). Effects of gender and education on the moral reasoning of Kuwait university students. *Social Behavior & Personality, 30*(1), 75-82.

Albrecht, G. L., Seelman, K. D., & Bury, M. (Eds.). (2001). *Handbook of disability studies.* Thousand Oaks, CA: Sage.

Aldwin, C. (1994). *Stress, coping, and development.* New York: Guilford.

Allen, K. R., Blieszner, R., & Roberto, K. A. (2001). Families in the middle and later years: A review and critique of research in the 1990s. In R. M. Milardo (Ed.), *Understanding families into the new millennium* (pp. 130-145). Minneapolis, MN: National Council on Family Relations.

Allen, P. B. (1995). *Art is a way of knowing.* Palo Alto, CA: Shambhala.

Allen-Meares, P., & Lane, B. A. (1987). Grounding social work practice in theory: Ecosystems. *Social Casework, 68,* 517-521.

Altman, I. (1975). *The environment and social behavior: Privacy, personal space, territoriality and crowding.* Monterey, CA: Brooks/Cole.

Altman, I. (1993). Dialectics, physical environments, and personal relationships. *Communication Monographs, 60,* 26-34.

Altman, I., & Rogoff, B. (1987). World views in psychology: Trait, interactional, organismic, and transactional perspectives. In D. Stokols & I. Altman (Eds.), *Handbook of environmental psychology, Vol. 1* (pp. 7-40). New York: Wiley.

Alvarez, L. (2001, January 1). Census director marvels at the new portrait of America. *New York Times,* p. A7.

American Association of University Women. (2002). *School vouchers.* Retrieved October 14, 2002, from www.aauw.org/1000/pospapers/svouchersbd.html.

American Federation of Labor (AFL)-CIO. (2001). *Facts about working women.* Retrieved October 16, 2001, from www.aflcio.org/women/wwfacts.htm.

American Heart Association. (1997a). *High blood pressure statistics.* [Online]. Available from www.americanheart.org/Heart_and_Stroke_A_Z_Guide/hbps.html.

American Heart Association. (1997b). *Statistics.* [Online]. Available from www.americanheart.org/Heart_and_Stroke_ A_Z_Guide/hbps.html.

American Psychiatric Association. (1994). *Diagnostic and statistical manual of mental disorders* (4th ed.). Washington, DC: Author.

American Psychiatric Association. (2000). *Diagnostic and statistical manual of mental disorders* (4th ed.). Washington, DC: Author.

Anderson, C. M. (1999). Single-parent families: Strengths, vulnerabilities, and interventions. In B. Carter & M. McGoldrick (Eds.), *The expanded family life cycle: Individual, family, and social perspectives* (3rd ed., pp. 399-416). Boston: Allyn & Bacon.

Anderson, R., & Carter, I. (1974). *Human behavior in the social environment: A social systems approach.* Chicago: Aldine.

Anderson, T. L. (1994). Drug abuse and identity: Linking micro and macro factors. *Sociological Quarterly, 35,* 159-174.

Ang, I., & Hermes, J. (1996). Gender and/in media consumption. In J. Curran & M. Gurevitch (Eds.), *Mass media and society* (2nd ed., pp. 325-347). New York: Arnold.

Angell, G. B., Dennis, B. G., & Dumain, L. E. (1998). Spirituality, resilience, and narrative: Coping with parental death. *Families in Society, 79*(6), 615-630.

Argyris, C., & Schon, D. (1978). *Organizational learning: A theory of action perspective.* Reading, MA: Addison-Wesley.

Arp, W., & Boeckelman, K. (1997). Religiosity: A source of black environmentalism and empowerment. *Journal of Black Studies, 28*(2), 255-267.

Ashford, J., LeCroy, C., & Lortie, K. (2001). *Human behavior in the social environment* (2nd ed.). Belmont, CA: Wadsworth.

Assagioli, R. (1965). *Psychosynthesis: A manual of principles and techniques.* New York: Viking Penguin.

Assagioli, R. (1973). *The act of will.* New York: Penguin.

Assagioli, R. (1989). Self-realization and psychological disturbances. In S. Grof & C. Grof (Eds.), *Spiritual emergency: When personal transformation becomes a crisis* (pp. 27-48). Los Angeles: Jeremy P. Tarcher.

Association for Community Organization and Social Administration. (n.d.) About ACOSA. Retrieved July 31, 2002, from www. acosa.org.

Auerbach, J., & Krimgold, B. (2001). Improving health: It doesn't take a revolution. In J. Auerbach & B. Krimgold (Eds.), *Income, socioeconomic status, and health: Exploring the relationships* (pp. 1-11). Washington, DC: National Policy Association, Academy for Health Services Research and Health Policy.

Auslander, G., & Litwin, H. (1987). The parameters of network intervention: A social work application. *Social Service Review, 61,* 305-318.

Averill, J. (1980). A constructionist view of emotion. In R. Plutchik & H. Kellerman (Eds.), *Emotion theory, research, and experience: Vol. 1. Theories of emotion.* London: Academic Press.

Babbie, E. (1994). *What is society?* Thousand Oaks, CA: Pine Forge.

Bachelder, J., & Hilton, J. (1994). Implications of the Americans with Disabilities Act of 1990 for elderly persons. *American Journal of Occupational Therapy, 48*(1), 73-81.

Baer, H. A. (1993). The limited empowerment of women in Black spiritual churches: An alternative vehicle to religious leadership. *Sociology of Religion, 54*(1), 65-82.

Bagdikian, B. (1997). *The media monopoly* (5th ed.). Boston: Beacon Press.

Baker, R. (1998, May/June). Murdoch's mean machine. *Columbia Journalism Review.* Retrieved October 14, 2002, from www.cjr.org/year/98/3/murdoch.asp.

Baldwin, J. (1975). Urban criminality and the "problem" estate. *Local Government Studies, 1,* 12-20.

Bales, R. (1950). *Interaction process analysis: A method for the study of small groups.* Cambridge, MA: Addison-Wesley Press.

Balkwell, J. W. (1994). Status. In M. Foshci & E. J. Lawler (Eds.), *Group processes: Sociological analyses* (pp. 119-148). Chicago: Nelson-Hall.

Balser, D. (1997). The impact of environmental factors on factionalism and schism in movement organizations. *Social Forces, 76*(1), 199-228.

Bandura, A. (1977a). Self-efficacy: Toward a unifying theory of behavioral change. *Psychological Review, 84,* 191-215.

Bandura, A. (1977b). *Social learning theory.* Englewood Cliffs, NJ: Prentice-Hall.

Bandura, A. (1986). *Social foundations of thought and action: A social cognitive theory.* Englewood Cliffs, NJ: Prentice-Hall.

Banyard, V. L., & Graham-Bermann, S. A. (1993). Can women cope? A gender analysis of theories of coping with stress. *Psychology of Women Quarterly, 17,* 303-318.

Barker, R. (1968). *Ecological psychology: Concepts and methods for studying the environment of human behavior.* Stanford, CA: Stanford University Press.

Barker, R. L. (1987). *The social work dictionary.* Silver Spring, MD: National Association of Social Workers.

Barker, R., & Gump, P. (1964). *Big school, small school: High school size and student behavior.* Standford, CA: Stanford University Press.

Barma Research Group. (n.d.). *One out of three adults is now unchurched.* Retrieved June 28, 2002, from www. barma.org.

Barnes, C., Mercer, G., & Shakespeare, T. (1999). *Exploring disability: A sociological introduction.* Cambridge, UK: Polity Press.

Barnett, S., & Scotch, R. (2002). *Disability protests.* Washington, DC: Gallaudet.

Barret, R., & Barzan, R. (1996). Spiritual experiences of gay men and lesbians. *Counseling and Values, 41,* 4-15.

Barrett, M. J. (1999). Healing from trauma: The quest for spirituality. In F. Walsh (Ed.), *Spiritual resources in family therapy.* New York: Guilford.

Barusch, A. S. (1999). Religion, adversity, and age: Religious experiences with low-income elderly women. *Journal of Sociology and Social Welfare, 26*(1), 125-142.

Baum, A., & Davis, G. (1980). Reducing the stress of high-density living: An architectural intervention. *Journal of Personality and Social Psychology, 38,* 471-481.

Baum, A., & Valins, S. (1977). *Architecture and social behavior.* Hillsdale, NJ: Erlbaum.

Bechtel, R. (2000). Assumptions, methods, and research problems of ecological psychology. In S. Wapner, J. Demick, T. Yamamoto, & H. Minami (Eds.), *Theoretical perspectives in environment-behavior research: Underlying assumptions, research problems, and methodologies* (pp. 61-66). New York: Kluwer Academic.

Beck, A. T., & Weishaar, M. (1995). Cognitive therapy. In R. J. Corsini & D. Wedding (Eds.), *Current psychotherapies* (5th ed., pp. 229-261). Itasca, IL: Peacock.

Beck, E., & Eichler, M. (2000). Consensus organizing: A practice model for community building. *Journal of Community Practice, 8*(1), 87-102.

Becker, G. (1981). *A treatise on the family.* Cambridge, MA: Harvard University Press.

Becker, G. (2002). Dying away from home: Quandaries of migration for elders in two ethnic groups. *Journals of Gerontology, Series B, 57*(2), S79-95.

Becker, H. (1957). Current sacred-secular theory and its development. In H. Becker & A. Boskoff (Eds.), *Modern sociological theory in continuity and change* (pp. 137-185). New York: Dryden.

Beckett, J., & Dungee-Anderson, D. (1998). Multicultural communication in human services organizations. In A. Daly (Ed.), *Workplace diversity: Issues and perspectives* (pp. 191-214). Washington, DC: NASW Press.

Becvar, D. S. (1997). *Soul healing: A spiritual orientation in counseling and therapy.* New York: Basic Books.

Becvar, D., & Becvar, R. (1996). *Family therapy: A systemic integration* (3rd ed.). Boston: Allyn & Bacon.

Bell, L. (1997). Theoretical foundations for social justice education. In M. Adams, L. Bell, & P. Griffin (Eds.), *Teaching for diversity and social justice* (pp. 1-15). New York: Routledge.

Bell, R., Davison, M., & Sefcik, D. (2002). A first survey: Measuring burnout in emergency medicine physician assistants. *Journal of the American Academy of Physicians Assistants, 15*(3), 40-48.

Bell, T. R., & Bell, J. L. (1999). Help-seeking in the black church: An important connection for social work to make. *Social Work and Christianity, 26*(2), 144-154.

Bell, Y. R., Bouie, C. L., & Baldwin, J. A. (1990). Afrocentric cultural consciousness and African American male-female relationships. *Journal of Black Studies, 21,* 162-189.

Bellah, R., Madsen, R., Sullivan, W., Swidler, A., & Tipton, S. (1985). *Habits of the heart: Individualism and commitment in American life.* Berkeley: University of California Press.

Benedict, J. (1995). Creating sacred space with clients. *Society for Spirituality and Social Work Newsletter,* Spring, 3.

Benedict, R. (1934/1989). *Patterns of culture.* Boston: Houghton Mifflin.

Benedict, R. (1946). *The chrysanthemum and the sword.* Boston: Houghton Mifflin.

Benningfield, M. F. (1997). Addressing spiritual/religious issues in therapy: Potential problems and complications. *Journal of Family Social Work, 2*(4), 25-42.

Benokraitis, N. V. (1996). *Marriages and families: Changes, choices, and constraints* (2nd ed.). Upper Saddle River, NJ: Prentice-Hall.

Benokraitis, N. V. (2001). *Contemporary ethnic families in the United States.* Upper Saddle River, NJ: Prentice-Hall.

Benson, P. L. (1992). Religion and substance abuse. In J. F. Schumaker (Ed.), *Religion and mental health* (pp. 211-221). New York: Oxford University Press.

Benson, P. L., & Donahue, M. J. (1989). Ten-year trends in at-risk behaviors: A national study of black adolescents. *Journal of Adolescent Research, 4*(2), 125-139.

Bentley, K. J., & Walsh, J. (2001). *The social worker & psychotropic medication: Toward effective collaboration with mental health clients, families, and providers* (2nd ed.). Pacific Grove, CA: Brooks/Cole.

Berck, J. (1992). *No place to be: Voices of homeless children.* Boston: Houghton Mifflin.

Berger, P., & Luckmann, T. (1966). *The social construction of reality.* Garden City, NY: Doubleday.

Berlin, S. (1983). Cognitive-behavioral approaches. In A. Rosenblatt & Diana Waldfogel (Eds.), *Handbook of clinical social work* (pp. 1095-1119). San Francisco: Jossey-Bass.

Bernstein, P. (1997). *American work values: Their origin and development.* Albany: State University of New York Press.

Berthold, S. M. (1989). Spiritism as a form of psychotherapy: Implications for social work practice. *Social Casework, 70*(8), 502-509.

Berzoff, J. (1989). From separation to connection: Shifts in understanding women's development. *Affilia, 4,* 45-58.

Besser, G. M., & Thorner, M. O. (1994). *Clinical endocrinology* (2nd ed.). London: Times Mirror International.

Best, J. (1989). Extending the constructionist perspective: A conclusion and introduction. In J. Best (Ed.), *Images of issues: Typifying contemporary social problems* (pp. 243-252). New York: Aldine de Gruyter.

Bilich, M., & Carlson, S. (1994). Therapists and clergy working together: Linking the psychological with the spiritual in the treatment of MPD. *Journal of Christian Healing, 16*(1), 3-11.

Black, H. K. (1999). Life as gift: Spiritual narratives of elderly African American women living in poverty. *Journal of Aging Studies, 13*(4), 441-455.

Blau, P. (1964). *Exchange and power in social life.* New York: Wiley.

Blau, P., & Scott, W. (1962). *Formal organizations.* San Francisco: Chandler.

Bloch, D. P., & Richmond, L. J. (Eds.). (1998). *Finding the work you love, loving the work you have.* Palo Alto, CA: Davies-Black.

Blood, R., & Wolfe, D. (1960). *Husbands and wives: The dynamics of married living.* New York: Free Press.

Bloom, M. (1984). *Configurations of human behavior: Life span development in social environments.* New York: Macmillan.

Blumer, H. (1969). *Symbolic interactionism: Perspective and method.* Englewood Cliffs, NJ: Prentice-Hall.

Blumler, J., & Gurevitch. M. (1996). Media change and social change: Linkages and junctures. In J. Curran & M. Gurevitch (Eds.), *Mass media and society* (2nd ed., pp. 120-137). New York: Arnold.

Boas, F. (1940/1948). *Race, language and culture.* New York: Free Press.

Bohannan, P. (1995). *How culture works.* New York: Free Press.

Bolen, J. S. (1984). *Goddesses in every woman: A new psychology of women.* San Francisco: Harper & Row.

Bolland, K., & Atherton, C. (1999). Chaos theory: An alternative approach to social work practice and research. *Families in Society, 80*(4), 367-373.

Bonaiuto, M., & Bonnes, M. (2000). Social-psychological approaches in environment-behavior studies: Identity theories and discursive approach. In S. Wapner, J. Demick, T. Yamamoto, & H. Minami (Eds.), *Theoretical perspectives in environment-behavior research: Underlying assumptions, research problems, and methodologies* (pp. 67-78). New York: Kluwer Academic.

Borysenko, J. (1996). *A woman's book of life: The biology, psychology, and spirituality of the life cycle.* New York: Riverhead Books.

Boubekri, M., Hull, R., & Boyer, L. (1991). Impact of window size and sunlight penetration on office workers' mood and satisfaction. *Environment and Behavior, 23,* 474-493.

Bourdieu, P. (1977). *Outline of a theory of practice.* New York: Cambridge University Press.

Bowen, M. (1978). *Family therapy in clinical practice.* New York: Aronson.

Boyd-Franklin, N. (1987). Group therapy for black women: A therapeutic support model. *American Journal of Orthopsychiatry, 57,* 394-401.

Boyd-Franklin, N. (1989). *Black families in therapy: A multisystems approach.* New York: Guilford.

Bozeman, B. (1987). *All organizations are public: Bridging public and private organizational theories.* San Francisco: Jossey-Bass.

Bradford, J. (1995). *Caring for the whole child: A holistic approach to spirituality.* London: The Children's Society.

Bradshaw, Y., Healey, J., & Smith, R. (2001). *Sociology for a new century.* Thousand Oaks, CA: Pine Forge.

Brain Injury Association. (2001). *Brain injury awareness month 2001: Awareness kit.* Retrieved January 21, 2002, from www.biausa.org.

Brandon, D. (1976). *Zen in the art of helping.* New York: Delta/Seymour Lawrence.

Braud, A. (1997). Women's history is American religious history. In T. A. Tweed (Ed.), *Retelling U.S. religious history* (pp. 87-107). Berkeley: University of California Press.

Brave Heart, M. Y. H. (2001a). Clinical assessment with American Indians. In R. Fong & S. Furuto (Eds.), *Cultural competent social work practice: Practice skills, interventions, and evaluation* (pp. 63-177). New York: Longman.

Brave Heart, M. Y. H. (2001b). Clinical interventions with American Indians. In R. Fong & S. Furuto (Eds.), *Cultural competent social work practice: Practice skills, interventions, and evaluation* (pp. 285-298). New York: Longman.

Bredy, T., Weaver, I., Champagne, F. C., & Meaney, M. J. (2001). Stress, maternal care, and neural development in the rat. In C. A. Shaw & J. C. McEachern (Eds.), *Toward a theory of neural plasticity* (pp. 288-300). Philadelphia, PA: Psychology Press/Taylor & Francis.

Breitman, B. E. (1995). Social and spiritual reconstruction of self within a feminist Jewish community. *Woman and Therapy: A Feminist Quarterly, 16*(2/3), 73-82.

Breton, M. (1989). Liberation theology, group work, and the right of the poor and oppressed to participate in the life of the community. *Social Work With Groups, 12*(3), 5-18.

Bricker-Jenkins, M., Hooyman, N. R., & Gottlieb, N. (Eds.). (1991). *Feminist social work practice in clinical settings.* Newbury Park, CA: Sage.

Briskin, A. (1996). *The stirrings of soul in the workplace.* San Francisco: Jossey-Bass.

Bronfenbrenner, U. (1989). Ecological systems theory. *Annals of Child Development, 6,* 187-249.

Bronfenbrenner, U. (1999). Environments in developmental perspective: Theoretical and operational models. In S. Friedman, & T. Wachs (Eds.), *Measuring environment across the life span* (pp. 3-28). Washington, DC: American Psychological Association.

Brown, K. A., Jemmott, F. F., Mitchell, H. J., & Walton, M. L. (1998). The Well: A neighborhood-based health promotion model for black women. *Health and Social Work, 23*(2), 146-152.

Brubaker, T. H. (1991). Families in later life: A burgeoning research area. In A. Booth (Ed.), *Contemporary families: Looking forward, looking back* (pp. 226-248). Minneapolis, MN: National Council on Family Relations.

Budman, S. H., Soldz, S., Demby, A., Davis, M., & Merry, J. (1993). What is cohesiveness? An empirical examination. *Small Group Research, 24,* 199-216.

Bullis, R. K. (1996). *Spirituality in social work practice.* Washington, DC: Taylor & Francis.

Burgess, R., & Nielsen, J. (1974). An experimental analysis of some structural determinants of equitable and inequitable exchange relationships. *American Sociological Review, 39,* 427-443.

Burrell, G., & Morgan, G. (1979). *Sociological paradigms and organizational analysis.* London: Heinemann.

Burt, M., & Katz, B. (1987). Dimensions of recovery from rape: Focus on growth outcomes. *Journal of Interpersonal Violence, 2,* 57-82.

Burt, R. (1983). *Corporate profits and cooperation: Networks of market constraints and directorate ties in the American economy.* New York: Academic Press.

Burtless, G. (2001). *Has widening inequality promoted or retarded U.S. growth?* Retrieved July 10, 2002, from www.brook.edu/dybdocroot.

Burton, L. (1981). *A critical analysis and review of the research on Outward Bound and related programs.* Unpublished doctoral dissertation, Rutgers University, New Brunswick, NJ.

Burton, L. M. (1995, September). Family structure and nonmarital fertility: Perspectives from ethnographic research. In U.S. Department of Health and Human Services (Public Health Service, Centers for Disease Control and Prevention, National Center for Health Statistics), *Report to Congress on out-of-wedlock childbearing* (pp. 147-165). (DHHS Pub. No. (PHS) 95-1257). Washington, DC: U.S. Government Printing Office.

Cacioppo, J. T., Bernston, G. G., Sheridan, J. F., & McClintock, M. K. (2000). Multilevel integrative analysis of human behavior: Social neuroscience and the complementary nature of social and biological approaches. *Psychological Bulletin, 126*(6), 829-843.

Cady, S. H., & Valentine, J. (1999). Team innovation and perceptions of consideration: What difference does diversity make? *Small Group Research, 30*(6), 730-750.

Calasanti, T. (1996). Incorporating diversity: Meaning, levels of research, and implications for theory. *The Gerontologist, 36*(2), 147-156.

Cameron, J. (1992). *The artist's way: A spiritual path to higher creativity.* New York: Putnam.

Campbell, D. (1997). *The Mozart effect: Tapping the power of music to heal the body, strengthen the mind, and unlock the creative spirit.* New York: Harper Trade.

Campbell, R. J. (1996). *Psychiatric dictionary* (7th ed.). New York: Oxford University Press.

Canda, E. R. (1983). General implications of shamanism for clinical social work. *International Social Work, 26*(4), 14-22.

Canda, E. R. (1988a). Conceptualizing spirituality for social work: Insights from diverse perspectives. *Social Thought, 14*(1), 30-46.

Canda, E. R. (1988b). Spirituality, religious diversity and social work practice. *Social Casework, 69*(4), 238-247.

Canda, E. R. (1990). A holistic approach to prayer for social work practice. *Social Thought, 16*(3), 3-13.

Canda, E. R. (1997a). Does religion and spirituality have a significant place in the core HBSE curriculum? Yes. In M. Bloom & W. C. Klein (Eds.), *Controversial issues in human behavior in the social environment* (pp. 172-177, 183-184). Boston: Allyn & Bacon.

Canda, E. R. (1997b). Spirituality. *Encyclopedia of social work: 1997 supplement* (19th ed.). Washington, DC: NASW Press.

Canda, E. R. (2001). Buddhism. In M. V. Hook, B. Hugen, & M. Aguilar (Eds.), *Spirituality within religious traditions in social work practice* (pp. 53-72). Pacific Grove, CA: Brooks/Cole.

Canda, E. R., & Furman, L. D. (1999). *Spiritual diversity in social work practice: The heart of helping.* New York: Free Press.

Canda, E. R., & Phaobtong, T. (1992). Buddhism as a support system for Southeast Asian refugees. *Social Work, 37,* 61-67.

Canda, E. R., Shin, S., & Canda, H. (1993). Traditional philosophies of human services in Korea and contemporary social work implications. *Social Development Issues, 15*(3), 84-104.

Canda, E. R., & Yellow Bird, M. J. (1996). Cross-tradition borrowing of spiritual practices in social work settings. *Society for Spirituality and Social Work Newsletter, 3*(1), 1, 7.

Cannon, W. B. (1924). *Bodily changes in pain, hunger, fear, and rage.* New York: Appleton.

Caplan, G. (1990). Loss, stress, and mental health. *Community Mental Health Journal, 26,* 27-48.

Caplow, T. (1991). *American social trends.* Fort Worth, TX: Harcourt Brace Jovanovich.

Caplow, T., Bahr, H., Modell, J., & Chadwick, B. (1991). *Recent social trends in the United States, 1960-1990.* Buffalo, NY: Campus Verlag/McGill-Queen's University Press.

Carden, M. (1978). The proliferation of a social movement: Ideology and individual incentives in the contemporary feminist movement. In L. Kriesberg (Ed.), *Research in social movements, conflicts and change* (Vol. 1). (pp. 179-196). Greenwich, CT: JAI Press.

Carey, J. (Ed.). (1990). *Brain facts: A primer on the brain and nervous system.* Washington, DC: Society for Neuroscience.

Carmody, D. L. (1991). Spirituality as empowerment. *Studies in Formative Spirituality, 12,* 23-33.

Carnes, R., & Craig, S. (1998). *Sacred circles: A guide to creating your own women's spirituality group.* San Francisco: HarperSanFrancisco.

Carolan, M. T., & Allen, K. R. (1999). Commitments and constraints to intimacy for African American couples at midlife. *Journal of Family Issues, 20*(1), 3-24.

Caron, S. L. (1998). *Cross-cultural perspectives on human sexuality.* Boston, MA: Allyn and Bacon.

Carp, F. (1987). Environment and aging. In D. Stokols & I. Altman (Eds.), *Handbook of environmental psychology* (pp. 329-360). New York: Wiley.

Carpenter, M. B. (1991). *Core text of neuroanatomy* (4th ed.). Baltimore: Williams & Wilkins.

Carpman, J., Grant, M., & Simmons, D. (1984). *No more mazes.* Ann Arbor: University of Michigan Hospitals, Office of the Replacement Hospital Program, Patient and Visitor Participation Project.

Carron, A. V., & Brawley, L. R. (2000). Cohesion: Conceptual and measurement issues. *Small Group Research, 31*(1), 89-106.

Carter, B., & McGoldrick, M. (Eds.) (1999a). *The expanded family life cycle: Individual, family, and social perspectives* (3rd ed.). Boston: Allyn & Bacon.

Carter, B., & McGoldrick, M. (1999b). The divorce cycle: A major variation in the American family life cycle. In B. Carter & M. McGoldrick (Eds.), *The expanded family life cycle: Individual, family, and social perspectives* (3rd ed., pp. 373-380). Boston: Allyn & Bacon.

Carter, H., & Glick, P. (1976). *Marriage and divorce: A social and economic study.* Cambridge, MA: Harvard University Press.

Carter, M. V. (1984). Religion in Appalachian cultures: A brief outlook. *Religion: The Cutting Edge, 5*(1), 135-142.

Carter, P., & Jackson, N. (1993). Modernism, postmodernism and motivation, or why expectancy theory failed to come up to expectation. In J. Hassard & M. Parker (Eds.), *Postmodernism and organizations* (pp. 83-100). Newbury Park, CA: Sage.

Castells, M. (1977). *The urban question* (A. Sheridan, Trans.). London: Edward Arnold.

Castex, G. M. (1994). Providing services to Hispanic/Latino populations: Profiles in diversity. *Social Work, 39*(3), 288-296.

Center on Budget and Policy Priorities. (2001). *Recent census data significantly understate the increase in income disparities.* Retrieved July 10, 2002, from www.cbpp.org.

Charon, J. (1998). *Symbolic interactionism: An introduction, an interpretation, and integration* (6th ed.). Englewood Cliffs, NJ: Prentice-Hall.

Chaskin, R., Joseph, M., & Chipenda-Dansokho, S. (1997). Implementing comprehensive community development: Possibilities and limitations. *Social Work, 42*, 435-444.

Chau, K. (1990). Social work with groups in multicultural contexts. *Group Work, 7*(3), 8-21.

Cherlin, A. J. (1992). *Marriage, divorce, remarriage* (rev. ed.). Cambridge, MA: Harvard University Press.

Cherulnik, P. (1993). *Applications of environment-behavior research: Case studies and analysis.* New York: Cambridge University Press.

Chesney, B. K., & Chesler, M. A. (1993). Activism through self-help group membership: Reported life changes of parents of children with cancer. *Small Group Research, 24*, 258-273.

Chestang, L. (1972). *Character development in a hostile environment* (Occasional Paper No. 3). Chicago: University of Chicago, School of Social Service Administration.

Children's Defense Fund. (2001). *The state of America's children: 2001.* Washington, DC: Author.

Chodorow, J. (1991). *Dance therapy and depth psychology: The moving imagination.* London: Routledge.

Choi, G., & Tirrito, T. (1999). The Korean church as a social service provider for older adults. *Arete, 23*(2), 69-83.

Christ, C. P. (1995). *Odyssey with the Goddess: A spiritual quest in Crete.* New York: Continuum Publishing.

Chu, K. F., & Carew, R. (1990). Confucianism: Its relevance to social work with Chinese people. *Australia Social Work, 43*(4), 3-9.

Chung, D. K. (2001). Confucianism. In M. V. Hook, B. Hugen, & M. Aguilar (Eds.), *Spirituality within religious traditions in social work practice* (pp. 73-97). Pacific Grove, CA: Brooks/Cole.

Cingolani, J. (1984). Social conflict perspective on work with involuntary clients. *Social Work, 29*, 442-446.

Clark, C. C. (2002). *Health promotion in communities: Holistic and wellness approaches.* New York: Springer.

Clark, R., Anderson, N., Clark, V., & Williams, D. (1999). Racism as a stressor for African Americans: A biopsychosocial model. *The American Psychologist, 54*(10), 805-816.

Clearinghouse on International Developments in Child, Youth & Family Policies. (2002). *Mother's Day: More than candy and flowers, working parents need paid time-off.* Retrieved October 14, 2002, from www.childpolicyintl.org/issuebrief/issuebrief5.htm.

Clemens, E. (1996). Organizational form as frame: Collective identity and political strategy in the American labor movement, 1880-1920. In D. McAdam, J. McCarthy, & M. Zald (Eds.), *Comparative perspectives on social movements* (pp. 205-226). New York: Cambridge University Press.

Clever, L. (2002). Who is sicker: Patients or residents? *Annals of Internal Medicine, 136*(5), 391-393.

Cnaan, R. (1997). Recognizing the role of religious congregations and denominations in social service provision. In M. Reisch & E. Gambrill (Eds.), *Social work in the 21st century* (pp. 271-284). Thousand Oaks, CA: Pine Forge.

Cohen, C., & Phillips, M. (1997). Building community: Principles for social work practice in housing settings. *Social Work, 42*, 471-481.

Cohen, S., & Wills, T. (1985). Stress, social support, and the buffering hypothesis. *Psychological Bulletin, 98*, 310-357.

Cohn, T. (1997). Art as a healing force: Creativity, healing, and spirituality. *Artweek, 28*, 15-17.

Colcord, J., & Mann, R. (Eds.). (1930). *Mary E. Richmond, the long view: Papers and addresses.* New York: Russell Sage Foundation.

Cole, S. (1992). *Making science: Between nature and society.* Cambridge, MA: Harvard University Press.

Coleman, J. (1990). *Foundations of social theory.* Cambridge, MA: Belknap Press of Harvard University Press.

Coles, R. (1990). *The spiritual life of the child.* Boston: Houghton Mifflin.

Collins, A., & Pancoast, D. (1976). *Natural helping networks.* Washington, DC: National Association of Social Workers.

Collins, R. (1981). On the micro-foundations of macro-sociology. *American Journal of Sociology, 86,* 984-1014.

Collins, R. (1988). *Theoretical sociology.* San Diego, CA: Harcourt Brace Jovanovich.

Collins, R. (1990). Conflict throry and the advance of macro-historical sociology. In G. Ritzer (Ed.), *Frontiers of social theory: The new syntheses* (pp. 68-87). New York: Columbia University Press.

Collins, R. (1994). *Four sociological traditions.* New York: Oxford University Press.

Cook, K. (Ed.). (1987). *Social exchange theory.* Newbury Park, CA: Sage.

Cook, K., O'Brien, J., & Kollock, P. (1990). Exchange theory: A blueprint for structure and process. In G. Ritzer (Ed.), *Frontiers of social theory: The new syntheses* (pp. 158-181). New York: Columbia University Press.

Cooley, C. (1902/1964). *Human nature and the social order.* New York: Scribner's.

Coombs, D., & Capper, S. (1996). *Public health and mortality: Public health in the 1980s.* In D. Peck & J. Hollingsworth (Eds.), *Demographic and structural change: The effects of the 1980s on American society* (pp. 101-126). Westport, CT: Greenwood.

Cooper, B., & Hasselkus, B. (1992). Independent living and the physical environment: Aspects that matter to residents. *Canadian Journal of Occupational Therapy, 59*(1), 6-15.

Corbett, J. M. (1997). *Religion in America* (3rd ed.). Upper Saddle River, NJ: Prentice-Hall.

Corey, M., & Corey, G. (1987). *Groups: Process and practice* (3rd ed.). Pacific Grove, CA: Brooks/Cole.

Corey, M., & Corey, G. (1992). *Groups: Process and practice* (4th ed.). Pacific Grove, CA: Brooks/Cole.

Cornwall, M. (1989). Faith development of men and women over the life span. In S. Bahr and E. Peterson (Eds.), *Aging and the family* (pp. 115-139). Lexington, MA: Lexington Books/DC Heath.

Coser, L. (1956). *The functions of conflict.* New York: Free Press.

Coser, L. (1975). Presidential address: Two methods in search of a substance. *American Sociological Review, 40,* 691-700.

Costas, O. E. (1991). Hispanic theology in North America. In L. M. Getz & R. O. Costa (Eds.), *Strategies for solidarity: Liberation theologies in tension* (pp. 63-74). Minneapolis, MN: Fortress Press.

Cousins, L. (1994). *Community high: The complexity of race and class in a black urban high school* (Doctoral dissertation, University of Michigan, Ann Arbor). Ann Arbor, MI: University Microfilms International.

Cousins, L., & Mabrey, T. (1998). Re-gendering social work practice and education: The case for African American girls. *Journal of Human Behavior in the Social Environment, 1*(2/3), 91-104.

Covington, S. S. (1994). *A woman's way through the twelve steps.* Center City, MN: Hazelden.

Cowley, A. S. (1993). Transpersonal social work: A theory for the 1990s. *Social Work, 38,* 527-534.

Cowley, A. S. (1996). Transpersonal social work. In F. J. Turner (Ed.), *Social work treatment: Interlocking theoretical approaches* (4th ed., pp. 663-698). New York: Free Press.

Cowley, A. S. (1999). Transpersonal theory and social work practice with couples and families. *Journal of Family Social Work, 3*(20), 5-21.

Cowley, A. S., & Derezotes, D. (1994). Transpersonal psychology and social work education. *Journal of Social Work Education, 30,* 32-39.

Cox, G. R. (2000). Children, spirituality, and loss. *Illness, Crisis & Loss, 8*(1), 60-70.

Cox, T., Jr. (1993). *Cultural diversity in organizations: Theory, research, and practice.* San Francisco: Berrett-Koehler.

Crompton, R. (1993). *Class and stratification: An introduction to current debates.* Cambridge, MA: Polity Press.

Crook, W. (2001). Trickle-down bureaucracy: Does the organization affect client responses to programs? *Administration in Social Work, 26*(1), 37-59.

Croteau, D., & Hoynes, W. (2000). *Media society: Industries, images, and audiences* (2nd ed.). Thousand Oaks, CA: Pine Forge Press.

Cuba, L., & Hummon, D. (1993). A place to call home: Identification with dwelling, community, and region. *Sociological Quarterly, 34*(1), 111-131.

Culhane, D., Lee, C., & Wachter, S. (1997). Where the homeless come from: A study of the prior address distribution of families admitted to public shelters in New York City and Philadelphia. In D. Culhane & S. Hornburg (Eds.), *Understanding homelessness: New policy and research perspectives* (pp. 225-263). Washington, DC: Fannie Mae Foundation

Curiel, H. (1995). Hispanics: Mexican Americans. In R. L. Edwards (Ed.), *Encyclopedia of social work* (19th ed., pp. 1233-1244). Washington, DC: NASW Press.

Curran, J. (1996). Mass media and democracy revisited. In J. Curran & M. Gurevitch (Eds.), *Mass media and society* (2nd ed., pp. 81-119). New York: Arnold.

Dahrendorf, R. (1969). On the origin of inequality among men. In A. Beteille (Ed.), *Social inequality* (pp. 16-44). Harmondsworth, Middlesex, UK: Penguin.

Daley, J., & Marsiglia, F. (2000). Community participation: Old wine in new bottles? *Journal of Community Practice, 8*(1), 61-86.

D'Andrade, R. G. (1984/1995). Cultural meaning systems. In R. Shweder & R. LeVine (Eds.), *Culture theory: Essays on mind, self, and emotion* (pp. 88-122). New York: Cambridge University Press.

Das, A. K. (1987). Indigenous models of therapy in traditional Asian societies. *Journal of Multicultural Counseling and Development, 15,* 25-37.

Das, A., & Harries, B. (1996). Validating Fowler's theory of faith development with college students. *Psychological Reports, 78,* 675-679.

Dattalo, P. (1990). Teaching social work students to analyze and apply organizational theory. *Journal of Teaching in Social Work, 4*(2), 127-143.

David, T., & Weinstein, C. (1987). The built environment and children's development. In C. Weinstein & T. David (Eds.), *Spaces for children: The built environment and child development* (pp. 3-18). New York: Plenum.

Davis, D. R., & Jansen, G. G. (1998). Making meaning of Alcoholics Anonymous for social workers: Myths, metaphors, and realities. *Social Work, 43*(2), 169-182.

Davis, L. (1984). Essential components of group work with black Americans. *Social Work With Groups, 7*(3), 97-109.

Davis, L. E. (1995). The crisis of diversity. In M. D. Feit, J. H. Famey, J. S. Wodarski, & A. R. Mann (Eds.), *Capturing the power of diversity* (pp. 47-57). New York: Haworth.

Davis, M. (2000). *Magical urbanism: Latinos reinvent the US city.* New York: Verso.

de Ande, D. (1998). The evaluation of a stress management program for middle school adolescents. *Child and Adolescent Social Work Journal, 15*(1), 73-85.

de la Rosa, M. (1988). Puerto Rican spiritualism: A key dimension for effective social casework practice with Puerto Ricans. *International Social Work, 31*(4), 273-283.

Delgado, M. (1988). Groups in Puerto Rican spiritism: Implications for clinicians. In C. Jacobs & D. D. Bowles (Eds.), *Ethnicity and race: Critical concepts in social work* (pp. 34-37). Silver Spring, MD: NASW Press.

Delgado, M. (1996a). Community asset assessments by Latino youths. *Social Work in Education, 18,* 169-178.

Delgado, M. (1996b). Religion as a caregiving system for Puerto Rican elders with functional disabilities. *Journal of Gerontological Social Work, 26*(3/4), 129-144.

Delgado, M. (2000). *New arenas for community social work practice with urban youth: Use of arts, humanities, and sports.* New York: Columbia University Press.

Delgado, M., & Barton, K. (1998). Murals in Latino communities: Social indicators of community strengths. *Social Work, 43*(4), 346-356.

Delgado, M., & Humm-Delgado, D. (1982). Natural support systems: Sources of strength in Hispanic communities. *Social Work, 27,* 83-89.

della Porta, D. (1996). Social movements and the state: Thoughts on the policing of protest. In D. McAdam, J. McCarthy, & M. Zald (Eds.), *Comparative perspectives on social movements* (pp. 62-92). New York: Cambridge University Press.

Denton, B. (1990). The religiously fundamentalist family: Training for assessment and treatment. *Journal of Social Work Education, 26,* 6-14.

DePree, M. (1997). *Leading without power.* San Francisco: Jossey-Bass.

Derezotes, D. S. (1995). Spirituality and religiosity: Neglected factors in social work practice. *Arete, 20*(1), 1-15.

Derezotes, D. S. (2000). Evaluation of yoga and meditation training with adolescent sex offenders. *Childhood and Adolescent Social Work Journal, 17*(2), 997-1013.

Derezotes, D. S., & Evans, K. E. (1995). Spirituality and religiosity in practice: In-depth interviews of social work practitioners. *Social Thought, 18*(1), 38-56.

Dershimer, R. A. (1990). *Counseling the bereaved.* Elmsford, NY: Pergamon.

de Vaus, D., & McAllister, I. (1987). Gender differences in religion: A test of structural location theory. *American Sociological Review, 52,* 472-481.

Devlin, A. (1992). Psychiatric ward renovation: Staff perception and patient behavior. *Environment and Behavior, 24,* 66-84.

Devore, W., & Schlesinger, E. (1999). *Ethnic-sensitive social work practice* (5th ed.). Boston: Allyn & Bacon.

Dewey, J., & Bentley, A. F. (1949). *Knowing and the known.* Boston: Beacon.

Dionne, E. J. (1996). *They only look dead: Why progressives will dominate the next political era.* New York: Simon & Schuster.

Doherty, W. (1995). Community considerations in psychotherapy. *The Responsive Community, 5*(1), 41-52.

Doka, K., & Morgan, J. (1993). *Death and spirituality.* Amityville, NY: Baywood.

Donahue, D., & Tienda, M. (2000). The transition from school to work: Is there a crisis? What can be done? In S. Danziger & D. Waldfogel (Eds.), *Securing the future: Investing in children from birth to college* (pp. 231-263). New York: Russell Sage Foundation.

DoRosario, L. (1997). Spirituality in the lives of people with disability and chronic illness: A creative paradigm of wholeness and reconstruction. *Disability and Rehabilitation, 19*(10), 427-434.

Dosser, D. A., Smith, A. L., Markowski, E. W., & Cain, H. I. (2001). Including families' spiritual beliefs and their faith communities in systems of care. *Journal of Family Social Work, 5*(3), 63-78.

Dudley, J. R., & Helfgott, C. (1990). Exploring a place for spirituality and religiosity in the social work curriculum. *Journal of Social Work Education, 26,* 287-294.

Dufrene, P. M., & Coleman, V. S. (1992). Counseling Native Americans: Guidelines for group process. *Journal of Specialists in Group Work, 17*(4), 229-234.

Duluth Domestic Abuse Intervention Project. (n.d.). *In our best interest.* Support group manual available from the Duluth Domestic Abuse Intervention Project, 206 W. Fourth Street, Duluth, MN 55806.

Dunlop, J., & Angell, G. B. (2001). Inside-outside: Boundary-spanning challenges in building rural health coalitions. *Professional Development, 4*(1), 40-48.

Duran, E., & Duran, B. (1995). *Native American postcolonial psychology.* Albany: State University of New York Press.

Duvall-Early, K., & Benedict, J. (1992). The relationship between privacy and different components of job satisfaction. *Environment and Behavior, 24,* 670-679.

Earle, A. M. (1987). *An outline of neuroanatomy.* Omaha, NE: University of Nebraska Medical Center.

Eisinger, P. (1973). The conditions of protest behavior in American cities. *American Political Science Review, 67,* 11-28.

Ekeh, P. (1974). *Social exchange theory: The two traditions.* Cambridge, MA: Harvard University Press.

Elder, G. (1998). The life course as developmental theory. *Child Development, 69*(1), 1-12.

Ellis, A. (1989). Is rational emotive therapy (RET) "rationalist or constructivist" In W. Dryden (Ed.), *The essential Albert Ellis* (pp. 199-233). New York: Springer.

Ellison, C. G., & Levin, J. S. (1998). The religion-health connection: Evidence, theory, and future directions. *Health, Education, and Behavior, 25*(6), 700-720.

Ellsworth, P. C. (1991). Some implications of cognitive appraisal theories of emotion. In K. T. Strongman (Ed.), *International review of studies on emotions* (pp. 143-161). New York: Wiley.

Elwan, A. (1999). Poverty and disability: A survey of the literature. Retrieved July 18, 2002, from www.worldbank.org.

Emerson, R. (1972a). Exchange theory: Part I. A psychological basis for social exchange. In J. Berger, M. Zelditch Jr., & B. Anderson (Eds.), *Sociological theories in progress* (Vol. 2, pp. 38-57). Boston: Houghton Mifflin.

Emerson, R. (1972b). Exchange theory: Part II. Exchange relations and networks. In J. Berger, M. Zelditch Jr., & B. Anderson (Eds.), *Sociological theories in progress* (Vol. 2, pp. 58-87). Boston: Houghton Mifflin.

Emirbayer, M., & Goodwin, J. (1994). Network analysis, culture, and the problem of agency. *American Journal of Sociology, 99,* 1411-1454.

Eng, E., & Hatch, J. W. (1992). Networking between agencies and black churches: The lay health advisor model. In K. Pargament, K. Maton, & R. Hess (Eds.), *Religion and prevention in mental health* (pp. 239-252). New York: Haworth Press.

Engel, G. (1977). The need for a new medical model: A challenge for biomedicine. *Science, 196,* 129-136.

Engels, F. (1884/1970). *The origins of the family, private property and the state.* New York: International Publishers.

Erikson, E. (1963). *Childhood and society* (2nd ed.). New York: Norton.

Erikson, E. (1968). *Identity: Youth and crisis.* New York: Norton.

Erikson, K. (1976). *Everything in its path: Destruction of community in the Buffalo Creek flood.* New York: Simon & Schuster.

Etzioni, A. (1977). *Modern organizations.* Englewood Cliffs, NJ: Prentice-Hall.

Etzioni, A. (1993). *The spirit of community.* New York: Crown.

Eugene, T. M. (1995). There is a balm in Gilead: Black women and the black church as agents of a therapeutic community. *Women and Therapy: A Feminist Quarterly, 16*(2/3), 55-71.

Evans, G., & Howard, R. (1973). Personal space. *Psychological Bulletin, 80,* 334-344.

Evans, G., Lepore, S., & Allen, K. (2000). Cross-cultural differences in tolerance for crowding: Fact or fiction? *Journal of Personality and Social Psychology, 79*(2), 204-210.

Evans, G., & Maxwell, L. (1997). Chronic noise exposure and reading deficits: The mediating effects of language acquisition. *Environment and Behavior, 29,* 638-656.

Evans, G., & Saegert, S. (2000). Residential crowding in the context of inner city poverty. In S. Wapner, J. Demick, T. Yamamoto, & H. Minami (Eds.), *Theoretical perspectives in environment-behavior research: Underlying assumptions, research problems, and methodologies* (pp. 247-267). New York: Kluwer Academic.

Evans, S. (1980). *Personal politics.* New York: Vintage.

Ewalt, P. (1997). The revitalization of impoverished communities. *Social Work, 42,* 413-414.

Ewalt, P. L., Freeman, E. M., Fortune, A. E., Poole, D. L., & Witkin, S. L. (Eds.) (1999). *Multicultural issues in social work: Practice and research.* Washington, DC: NASW Press.

Ewalt, P., Freeman, E., & Poole, D. (Eds.). (1998). *Community building: Renewal, well-being, and shared responsibility.* Washington, DC: NASW Press.

Ewert, A., & Heywood, J. (1991). Group development in the natural environment: Expectations, outcomes, and techniques. *Environment and Behavior, 23,* 529-615.

Fair Jobs. (n.d). Contingent work and globalization. Retrieved July 12, 2002, from www.fairjobs.org/resources/points3_global.php.

Falck, H. (1988). *Social work: The membership perspective.* New York: Springer.

Falicov, C. J. (1998). *Latino families in therapy: A guide to multicultural practice.* New York: Guilford.

Falicov, C. J. (1999). The Latino family life cycle. In B. Carter and M. McGoldrick (Eds.), *The expanded family life cycle: Individual, family, and social perspectives* (3rd ed., pp. 141-152). Boston: Allyn & Bacon.

Farazmand, A. (1994). Organization theory: An overview and appraisal. In A. Farazmand (Ed.), *Modern organizations: Administrative theory in contemporary society* (pp. 3-54). Westport, CT: Praeger.

Farley, R. (1996). *The American reality: Who we are, how we got here, where we are going.* New York: Russell Sage Foundation.

Fauri, D. P. (1988). Applying historical themes of the profession in the foundation curriculum. *Journal of Teaching in Social Work, 2,* 17-31.

Federal Emergency Management Agency. (n.d.). Quarterly feature. Retrieved July 17, 2002, from www.fema.gov.

Feikema, R., Segalavich, J., & Jeffries, S. (1997). From child development to community building: One agency's journey. *Families in Society, 78,* 185-195.

Feldman, R. (1990). Settlement-identity: Psychological bonds with home places in a mobile society. *Environment and Behavior, 22*(2), 183-229.

Felty, K., & Poloma, M. (1991). From sex differences to gender role beliefs: Exploring effects on six dimensions of religiosity. *Sex Roles, 23,* 181-193.

Ferree, M. M., & Martin, P. Y. (1995). *Feminist organizations: Harvest of the new women's movement.* Philadelphia, PA: Temple University Press.

Figley, C. (1995). *Compassion: Coping with secondary traumatic stress disorder in those who treat the traumatized.* New York: Brunner/Mazel.

Finn, J., & Checkoway, B. (1998). Young people as competent community builders: A challenge to social work. *Social Work, 43*(4), 335-345.

Fisher, R., & Karger, H. (1997). *Social work and community in a private world.* New York: Longman.

Fisher, R., & Shragge, E. (2000). Challenging community organizing: Facing the 21st century. *Journal of Community Practice, 8*(3), 1-19.

Fitzgerald, J. (1997). Reclaiming the whole: Self, spirit, and society. *Disability and Rehabilitation, 19*(10), 407-413.

Fitzgerald, K., & Rodgers, D. (2000). Radical social movement organizations: A theoretical model. *Sociological Quarterly, 41*(4), 573-592.

Flanagan, L. M. (1996). The theory of self psychology. In J. Berzoff (Ed.), *Inside out and outside in: Psychodynamic clinical theory and practice in contemporary multicultural contexts* (pp. 173-198). Northvale, NJ: Jason Aronson.

Flanagan, W. (1993). *Contemporary urban sociology.* New York: Cambridge University Press.

Fong, R., & Furuto, S. B. C. L. (Eds.) (2001). *Culturally competent practice: Skills, interventions, and evaluations.* Boston: Allyn & Bacon.

Fontana, A. (1984). Introduction: Existential sociology and the self. In J. Kotarba & A. Fontana (Eds.), *The existential self in society* (pp. 3-17). Chicago: University of Chicago Press.

Ford, D., & Lerner, R. (1992). *Developmental systems theory: An integrative approach.* Newbury Park, CA: Sage.

Fordham, S. (1993). Those loud black girls: (Black) women, silence, and gender "passing" in the academy. *Anthropology and Education Quarterly, 2*(1), 3-32.

Fordham, S. (1996). *Blacked out: Dilemmas of race, identity, and success at Capital High.* Chicago: University of Chicago Press.

Fordham, S., & Ogbu, J. (1986). Black students' school success: Coping with the "Burden of 'Acting White.'" *Urban Review, 18*(3), 176-206.

Foucault, M. (1969). *The archaeology of knowledge and the discourse on language.* New York: Harper Colophon.

Fowler, F., Jr. (1981). Evaluating a complex crime control experiment. In L. Bickman (Ed.), *Applied social psychology annual* (Vol. 2, pp. 165-187). Beverly Hills, CA: Sage.

Fowler, J. F. (1981). *Stages of faith: The psychology of human development and the quest for meaning.* San Francisco: Harper.

Fowler, J. F. (1996). *Faithful change: The personal and public challenges of postmodern life.* Nashville: Abindon Press.

Fowler, R., Jr., McCalla, M., & Mangione, T. (1979). *Reducing residential crime and fear: The Hartford neighborhood crime prevention program: Executive summary.* Washington, DC: National Institute of Law Enforcement and Criminal Justice.

Fox, C., & Miller, H. (1995). *Postmodern public administration: Toward discourse.* Thousand Oaks, CA: Sage.

Fox, J. (1997). *Poetic medicine.* Los Angeles: Jeremy P. Tarcher.

Fox, M. (1994). *The reinvention of work: A new vision of livelihood for our time.* San Francisco: HarperSanFrancisco.

Frame, M. W., & Williams, C. B. (1996). Counseling African-Americans: Integrating spirituality into therapy. *Counseling and Values, 41,* 16-28.

Francis, L. J. (1997). The impact of personality and religion on attitudes towards substance use among 13-15 year olds. *Drug and Alcohol Dependence, 44,* 95-104.

Frank, A. (1967). *Capitalism and development in Latin America.* New York: Monthly Review Press.

Frankl, V. E. (1988). *The will to meaning: Foundations and applications of logotherapy.* New York: Meridian.

Franklin, C. (1995). Expanding the vision of the social contructionist debates: Creating relevance for practitioners. *Families in Society, 76,* 395-407.

Franklin, R. M. (1994). The safest place on earth: The culture of black congregations. In J. P. Wind & J. W. Lewis (Eds.), *American congregations* (Vol. 2, pp. 257-260). Chicago: University of Chicago Press.

Franks, D. D. (1991). Mead's and Dewey's theory of emotion and contemporary constructionism. *Journal of Mental Imagery, 15*(1-2), 119-137.

Freeman, J. (1995). From seed to harvest: Transformations of feminist organizations and scholarship. In M. Ferree & P. Martin (Eds.), *Feminist organizations: Harvest of the new women's movement* (pp. 397-408). Philadelphia, PA: Temple University Press.

Freud, S. (1899/1978). *The interpretation of dreams* (A. A. Brill, Trans.). New York: Modern Library.

Freud, S. (1905/1953). Three essays on the theory of sexuality. In J. Strachey (Ed. and Trans.), *The standard edition* (Vol. 7, pp. 135-245). London: Hogarth.

Freud, S. (1928). *The future of an illusion.* London: Horace Liveright.

Fried, M., & Gleicher, P. (1961). Some sources of satisfaction in an urban slum. *Journal of the American Institute of Planners, 27,* 305-315.

Friedman, A. (1976, September). On politics and design. *Contract,* pp. 6, 10, 12.

Fromm, E. (1941). *Escape from freedom.* New York: Avon.

Fromm, E., & Maccoby, M. (1970). *Social character in a Mexican village.* Englewood Cliffs, NJ: Prentice-Hall.

Fukuyama, M. A., & Sevig, T. D. (1999). *Integrating spirituality into multicultural counseling.* Thousand Oaks, CA: Sage.

Fullerton, H., & Toossi, M. (2001). Labor force projections to 2010: Steady growth and changing composition: The labor force will grow steadily as the population and labor force ages; Diversity will continue to increase. *Monthly Labor Review, 124*(11), 21-38.

Furman, L. E., & Chandy, J. M. (1994). Religion and spirituality: A long-neglected cultural component of rural social work practice. *Human Services in the Rural Environment, 17*(3/4), 21-26.

Furushima, R. Y. (1983). Faith development in a cross cultural perspective. *Religious Education, 80,* 414-420.

Furuto, S. M., Biswas, R., Chung, D. K., Murase, K., & Ross-Sherif, F. (Eds.). (1992). *Social work with Asian Americans.* Newbury Park, CA: Sage.

Gallagher, M. (1996). *The abolition of marriage: How we destroy lasting love.* Washington, DC: Regnery.

Gallagher, W. (1993). *The power of place: How our surroundings shape our thoughts, emotions, and actions.* New York: Poseidon.

Gallego, D. T. (1988). Religion as a coping mechanism among Hispanic elderly. In M. Sotomayor & Y. Curiel (Eds.), *Hispanic elderly: A cultural signature* (pp. 117-136). Edinburgh, TX: Pan American University Press.

Gallup, G., & Lindsay, D. M. (1999). *Surveying the religious landscape: Trends in U.S. beliefs.* Harrisburg, PA: Morehouse Publishing.

Galotti, K. M. (1989). Gender differences in self-reported moral reasoning: A review and new evidence. *Journal of Youth and Adolescence, 18,* 475-488.

Gambrill, E. (1987). Behavioral approach. In Anne Minahan (Ed.), *Encyclopedia of social work* (18th ed.) (Vol. 1, pp. 184-194). Silver Spring, MD: NASW Press.

Gambrill, E. (1990). *Critical thinking in clinical practice: Improving the accuracy of judgments and decisions about clients.* San Francisco: Jossey-Bass.

Gambrill, E. D. (1994). Concepts and methods of behavioral treatment. In D. K. Granvold (Ed.), *Cognitive and behavioral treatment: Methods and applications* (pp. 32-62). Pacific Grove, CA: Brooks/Cole.

Gamson, W. (1990). *The strategy of social protest.* Belmont, CA: Wadsworth.

Gamson, W., & Meyer, D. (1996). Framing political opportunity. In D. McAdam, J. McCarthy, & M. Zald (Eds.), *Comparative perspectives on social movements* (pp. 273-290). New York: Cambridge University Press.

Gange-Fling, M. A., & McCarthy, P. (1996). Impact of childhood sexual abuse on client spiritual development: Counseling implications. *Journal of Counseling and Development, 74,* 253-258.

Garbarino, J. (1999). *Lost boys: Why our sons turn violent and how we can save them.* New York: Free Press.

Garbarino, J., & Bedard, C. (1997). Spiritual challenges to children facing violent trauma. *Childhood: A Global Journal of Child Research, 3*(4), 467-478.

Gardner, H. (1983). *Frames of mind: The theory of multiple intelligence.* New York: Basic Books.

Gardner, H. (1999). *Intelligence reframed: Multiple intelligences for the 21st century.* New York: Basic Books.

Gardner, K. (1990). *Sounding the inner landscape.* Rockport, MA: Element Books.

Garland, J., Jones, H., & Kolodny, R. (1973). A model for stages of development in social work groups. In S. Bernstein (Ed.). *Explorations in groupwork* (pp. 17-71). Boston: Milford.

Garreau, J. (1991). *Edge city: Life on the new frontier.* New York: Doubleday.

Garrett, J. T., & Garrett, M. W. (1994). The path of good medicine: Understanding and counseling Native American Indians. *Journal of Multicultural Counseling and Development, 22,* 134-144.

Garrett, M. T., Garrett, J. T., & Brotherton, D. (2001). Inner circle/outer circle: A group technique based on Native American Healing Circles. *Journal for Specialists in Group Work, 26*(1), 17-30.

Garrett, M. T., & Myers, J. E. (1996). The rule of opposites: A paradigm for counseling Native Americans. *Journal of Multicultural Counseling and Development, 24,* 89-104.

Garvin, C. D., & Reed, B. G. (1983). Gender issues in social group work: An overview. *Social Work With Groups, 6*(3/4), 5-18.

Gary, L. E. (1995). African American men's perceptions of racial discrimination: A sociocultural analysis. *Social Work Research, 19,* 207-217.

Geertz, C. (1973). *The interpretation of cultures.* New York: Basic Books.

Geertz, C. (1983). Common sense as a cultural system. In *Local knowledge: Further essays in interpretive anthropology* (pp. 73-93). New York: Basic Books.

Gelberg, L., & Linn, L. S. (1988). Social and physical health of homeless adults previously treated for mental health problems. *Hospital and Community Psychiatry, 39,* 510-516.

General Accounting Office (2001). *The education and protection of the nation's children.* (GAO Strategic Supplement 2002-2007). Washington, DC: Author.

George, L. (1993). Sociological perspectives on life transitions. *Annual Review of Sociology, 19,* 353-373.

Gergen, K. (1985). The social constructionist movement in modern psychology. *American Psychologist, 40,* 266-275.

Gergen, K. (1992). Organization theory in the postmodern era. In M. Reed & M. Hughes (Eds.), *Rethinking organization* (pp. 207-226). Newbury Park, CA: Sage.

Gergen, K. V., & Davis, K. R. (Eds.). (1985). *The social construction of the person.* New York: Springer-Verlag.

Germain, C. (1973). An ecological perspective in casework practice. *Social Casework, 54,* 323-330.

Germain, C. (1978). Space: An ecological variable in social work practice. *Social Casework, 59,* 515-522.

Germain, C. (1981). The physical environment and social work practice. In A. Maluccio (Ed.), *Promoting competence in clients* (pp. 103-124). New York: Free Press.

Germain, C. (1994). Human behavior and the social environment. In R. Reamer (Ed.), *The foundations of social work knowledge* (pp. 88-121). New York: Columbia University Press.

Germain, C., & Gitterman, A. (1980). *The life model of social work practice.* New York: Columbia University Press.

Germain, C., & Gitterman, A. (1996). *The life model of social work practice: Advances in theory and practice* (2nd ed.). New York: Columbia University Press.

Gibbon, H. (n.d.). *Guide for divesting government-owned enterprises.* Retrieved July 12, 2002, from www.privatization.org/Collection/Publications/htg_15-divesting_assets.htm.

Gibbs, L. (1997). Can critical thinking and HBSE course content be taught concurrently? Yes. In M. Bloom & W. Klein (Eds.), *Controversial issues in human behavior in the social environment* (pp. 81-87). Boston: Allyn & Bacon.

Gibson, M. (1988). *Accommodation without assimilation: Sikh immigrants in an American high school.* Ithaca, NY: Cornell University Press.

Giddens, A. (1979). *Central problems in social theory: Action, structure and contradiction in social analysis.* London: MacMillan.

Gifford, R. (1987). *Environmental psychology: Principles and practice.* Boston: Allyn & Bacon.

Gifford, R., & Gallagher, T. (1985). Sociability: Personality, social context, and physical setting. *Journal of Personality and Social Psychology, 48,* 1015-1023.

Gilbert, D., & Kahn, J. (1993). *The American class structure.* Belmont, CA: Wadsworth.

Gilderbloom, J., & Markham, J. (1996). Housing modification needs of the disabled elderly: What really matters? *Environment and Behavior, 28,* 512-535.

Gilligan, C. (1982). *In a different voice.* Cambridge, MA: Harvard University Press.

Gillis, J. (1996). *A world of their own making: Myth, ritual, and the quest for family values.* New York: Basic Books.

Gilson, S. (1996). *The disability movement and federal legislation.* Unpublished manuscript, Richmond, VA.

Gilson, S., & DePoy, E. (2000). Multiculturalism and disability: A critical perspective. *Disability & Society, 15*(2), 207-218.

Gilson, S., & DePoy, E. (2002). Theoretical approaches to disability content in social work education. *Journal of Social Work Education, 37,* 153-165.

Gilson, S. F., Tusler, A., & Gill, C. (1997). Ethnographic research in disability identity: Self-determination and community. *Journal of Vocational Rehabilitation, 9*(1), 7-17.

Gingrich, W., & Eisengart, S. (2000). Solution-focused brief therapy: A review of outcome research. *Family Process, 39*(4), 477-498.

Gitterman, A., & Shulman, L. (1994). *Mutual aid groups, vulnerable populations, and the life cycle* (2nd ed.). New York: Columbia University Press.

Glucksmann, M. (1998). 'What a difference a day makes': A theoretical and historical exploration of temporality and gender. *Sociology, 32*(2), 239-258.

Goffman, E. (1959). *Presentation of self in everyday life.* Garden City, NY: Archer.

Goldberg, N. (1990). *Wild mind: Living the writer's life.* New York: Bantam Books.

Goldman, J. (1996). *Healing sounds: The power of harmonics.* Rockport, MA: Element Books.

Goldstein, D. (1996). Ego psychology theory. In F. Turner (Ed.), *Social work treatment* (4th ed., pp. 191-217). New York: Free Press.

Goldstein, E. (1995). *Ego psychology and social work practice* (2nd ed.). New York: Free Press.

Goleman, D. (1998). *Working with emotional intelligence.* New York: Bantam.

Golembiewski, R. (1994). Is organizational membership bad for your health? Phases of burnout as covariants of mental and physical well-being. In A. Farazmand (Ed.), *Modern organizations: Administrative theory in contemporary society* (pp. 211-227). Westport, CT: Praeger.

Golsworthy, R., & Coyle, A. (1999). Spiritual beliefs and the search for meaning among older adults following partner loss. *Mortality, 4*(1), 21-40.

Goodenough, W. (1996). Culture. In D. Levison & M. Ember (Eds.), *Encyclopedia of cultural anthropology* (Vol. 1, pp. 291-298). New York: Holt.

Goodin, R. (1996). Institutions and their design. In R. Goodin (Ed.), *The theory of institutional design* (pp. 1-53). New York: Cambridge University Press.

Goodson-Lawes, J. (1994). Ethnicity and poverty as research variables: Family studies with Mexican and Vietnamese newcomers. In E. Sherman & W. Reid (Eds.), *Qualitative research in social work* (pp. 22-31). New York: Columbia University Press.

Gordon, M. (1964). *Assimilation in American life: The role of race, religion and national origins.* New York: Oxford University Press.

Gorin, S., & Moniz, C. (1997). Social work and health care in the 21st century. In M. Reisch & E. Gambrill (Eds.), *Social work in the 21st century* (pp. 152-162). Thousand Oaks, CA: Pine Forge.

Gottesman, I. I. (1991). *Schizophrenia genesis.* New York: Freeman.

Gould, S. (1981). *The mismeasure of man.* New York: Norton.

Gourgey, C. (1994). From weakness to strength: A spiritual response to disability. *Journal of Religion in Disability and Rehabilitation, 1*(1), 69-80.

Graham-Poole, J. (1996). Children, death and poetry. *Journal of Poetry Therapy, 9*(3), 129-141.

Granvold, D. K. (1994). Concepts and methods of cognitive treatment. In D. K. Granvold (Ed.), *Cognitive and behavioral treatment: Methods and applications* (pp. 3-31). Pacific Grove, CA: Brooks/Cole.

Gray, E. D. (Ed.). (1988). *Sacred dimensions of women's experience.* Wellesley, MA: Roundtable Press.

Green, G. D., & Bozett, F. W. (1991). Lesbian mothers and gay fathers. In J. C. Gonsiorek & J. D. Weinrich (Eds.), *Homosexuality: Research implications for public policy* (pp. 197-214). Newbury Park, CA: Sage.

Green, J. (1999). *Cultural awareness in the human services: A multi-ethnic approach* (3rd ed.). Boston: Allyn & Bacon.

Greenberg, L. S. (1996). Allowing and accepting of emotional experience. In R. D. Kavanaugh, B. Zimmerberg, & S. Fein (Eds.), *Emotion: Interdisciplinary perspectives* (pp. 315-336). Mahwah, NJ: Lawrence Erlbaum.

Greene, G. J., Jensen, C., & Jones, D. H. (1999). A constructivist perspective on clinical social work practice with ethnically diverse clients. In P. L. Ewalt et al. (Eds.), *Multicultural issues in social work: Practice and research* (pp. 3-16). Washington, DC: NASW Press.

Griswold, W. (1994). *Cultures and societies in a changing world.* Thousand Oaks, CA: Pine Forge.

Grof, S. (1988). *Adventures in self-discovery: Dimensions of consciousness and new perspectives in psychotherapy and inner exploration.* Albany: State University of New York.

Gump, L., Baker, R., & Roll, S. (2000). Cultural and gender differences in moral judgment: A study of Mexican Americans and Anglo-Americans. *Hispanic Journal of Behavioral Sciences, 22*(1), 78-93.

Gump, P. (1987). School and classroom environments. In D. Stokols & I. Altman (Eds.), *Handbook of environmental psychology* (pp. 691-732). New York: Wiley.

Gunnar, M. R., Broderson, L., Nachimas, M., Buss, K., & Rigatuso, J. (1996). Stress reactivity and attachment security. *Developmental Psychobiology, 29*(3), 191-204.

Gusfield, J. R. (1975). *The community: A critical response.* New York: Harper Colophon.

Gutheil, I. (1991). The physical environment and quality of life in residential facilities for frail elders. *Adult Residential Care Journal, 5,* 131-145.

Gutheil, I. (1992). Considering the physical environment: An essential component of good practice. *Social Work, 37,* 391-396.

Gutierrez, L. (1990). Working with women of color: An empowerment perspective. *Social Work, 35*(2), 149-153.

Gutierrez, L. (1994). Beyond coping: An empowerment perspective on stressful life events. *Journal of Sociology and Social Welfare, 21*(3), 201-219.

Gutierrez, L. (1997). Multicultural community organizing. In M. Reisch & E. Gambrill (Eds.), *Social work in the 21st century* (pp. 249-259). Thousand Oaks, CA: Pine Forge.

Habermas, J. (1981/1987). *The theory of communicative action: Vol. 2. Lifeworld and system: A critique of functionalist reason* (T. McCarthy, Trans.). Boston: Beacon Press.

Habermas, J. (1984). *The theory of communicative action: Vol. 1. Reason and the rationalization of society.* Boston: Beacon Press.

Haddad, Y. Y. (1997). Make room for the Muslims? In W. H. Conser Jr. & S. B. Twiss (Eds.), *Religious diversity and American religious history: Studies in traditions and cultures* (pp. 218-261). Athens, GA: University of Georgia Press.

Hagan, J. (1994). *Crime and disrepute.* Thousand Oaks, CA: Pine Forge.

Hag-Brown, C. (1988). *Resistance and renewal: Surviving the Indian residential school.* Vancouver, Canada: Tillacum Library.

Hall, E. (1966). *The hidden dimension.* New York: Doubleday.

Hall, M. (1995). *Poor people's social movement organizations: The goal is to win.* Westport, CT: Praeger.

Halperin, D. (2001). The play's the thing: How social group work and theatre transformed a group into a community. *Social Work With Groups, 24*(2), 27-46.

Hannerz, U. (1992). *Cultural complexity: Studies in the social organization of meaning.* New York: Columbia University Press.

Hansen, L. S. (1997). *Integrative life planning: Critical tasks for career development and changing life patterns.* San Franciso: Jossey-Bass.

Hardcastle, D., Wenocur, S., & Powers, P. (1997). *Community practice: Theories and skills for social workers.* New York: Oxford University Press.

Hardiman, R., & Jackson, B. (1997). Conceptual foundations for social justice courses. In M. Adams, L. Bell, & P. Griffin (Eds.), *Teaching for diversity and social justice* (pp. 16-29). New York: Routledge.

Hare, A. P. (1994). Types of roles in small groups: A bit of history and a current perspective. *Small Group Research, 25,* 433-448.

Hare, A. P., Blumberg, H. H., Davies, M. F., & Kent, M. V. (1994). *Small group research: A handbook.* Norwood, NJ: Ablex.

Hareven, T. K. (2000). *Families, history, and social change: Life-course and cross-cultural perspectives.* Boulder, CO: Westview Press.

Harris, M. (1989). *Dance of the spirit: The seven steps of women's spirituality.* New York: Bantam Books.

Hart, J. (1970). The development of client-centered therapy. In J. T. Hart & T. M. Tomlinson (Eds.), *New directions in client-centered therapy.* Boston: Houghton Mifflin.

Hartford, M. (1971). *Groups in social work.* New York: Columbia University Press.

Hartig, T., Mang, M., & Evans, G. (1991). Restorative effects of natural environment experiences. *Environment and Behavior, 23,* 3-26.

Hartman, A. (1970). To think about the unthinkable. *Social Casework, 51,* 467-474.

Hartman, A. (1995). Diagrammatic assessment of family relationships. *Families in Society, 76,* 111-122.

Hartman, A., & Laird, J. (1983). *Family-centered social work practice.* New York: Free Press.

Hasenfeld, Y. (1983). *Human service organizations.* Englewood Cliffs, NJ: Prentice-Hall.

Hasenfeld, Y. (1992). Theoretical approaches to human service organizations. In Y. Hasenfeld (Ed.), *Human services as complex organizations* (pp. 24-44). Newbury Park, CA: Sage.

Hassard, J. (1993). Postmodernism and organizational analysis: An overview. In J. Hassard & M. Parker (Eds.), *Postmodernism and organizations* (pp. 1-23). Newbury Park, CA: Sage.

Hastings, M. (1998). Theoretical perspectives on social movements. *New Zealand Sociology, 13*(2), 208-238.

Hawkins, K. W. (1995). Effects of gender and communication content on leadership emergence in small task-oriented groups. *Small Group Research, 26,* 234-249.

Hayduk, L. (1983). Personal space: Where we now stand. *Psychological Bulletin, 94,* 293-335.

Healey, J. F. (1995). *Race, ethnicity, gender, and class: The sociology of group conflict and change.* Thousand Oaks, CA: Pine Forge Press.

Hearn, G. (1958). *Theory building in social work.* Toronto: University of Toronto Press.

Hearn, G. (1969). *The general systems approach: Contributions toward an holistic conception of social work.* New York: Council on Social Work Education.

Hearn, J., & Parkin, W. (1993). Organizations, multiple oppressions and postmodernism. In J. Hassard & M. Parker (Eds.), *Postmodernism and organizations* (pp. 148-162). Newbury Park, CA: Sage.

Hegtvedt, K. A. (1994). Justice. In M. Foshci & E. J. Lawler (Eds.), *Group processes: Sociological analyses* (pp. 177-204). Chicago: Nelson-Hall.

Heller, K. (1989). The return to community. *American Journal of Community Psychology, 17*(1), 1-14.

Henderson, L. (2000). The knowledge and use of alternative therapeutic techniques by social work practitioners: A descriptive study. *Social Work in Health Care, 30*(3), 55-71.

Hendricks, C., & Rudich, G. (2000). A community building perspective in social work education. *Journal of Community Practice, 8*(3), 21-36.

Hendricks, G., & Weinhold, B. (1982). *Transpersonal approaches to counseling and psychotherapy.* Denver: Love.

Henry Kaiser Family Foundation (2000). *The uninsured and their access to health care.* Retrieved July 15, 2002, from www.kff.org.

Hepworth, D. H., Rooney, R. H., & Larsen, J. (1997). *Direct social work practice: Theory and skills* (5th ed.). Pacific Grove, CA: Brooks/Cole.

Heritage Foundation. (2001). *The truth about school choice.* Retrieved October 14, 2002, from www.heritage.org/Research/Education/WM9.cfm.

Hernandez, M., & McGoldrick, M. (1999). Migration and the life cycle. In B. Carter & M. McGoldrick, *The expanded family life cycle: Individual, family, and social perspectives* (3rd ed., pp. 169-184). Boston: Allyn & Bacon.

Hertsgaard, L., Gunnar, M. R., Erickson, M. F., & Nachimas, M. (1995). Adrenocortical responses to the strange situation in infants with disorganized/disoriented attachment relationships. *Child Development, 66*(4), 1100-1106.

Herzberg, F. (1966). *Work and the nature of man.* Cleveland, OH: World.

Hetherington, E. M., Stanley-Hagan, M., & Anderson, E. R. (1989). Marital transitions: A child's perspective. *American Psychologist, 44,* 303-312.

Hewitt, J. P. (1994). *Self and society: A symbolic interactionist social psychology* (6th ed.). Boston: Allyn and Bacon.

Hickson, J., & Phelps, A. (1997). Women's spirituality: A proposed practice model. *Journal of Family Social Work, 2*(4), 43-57.

Hill, R. (1958). Generic features of families under stress. *Social Casework, 49,* 139-150.

Hillery, G. (1955). Definitions of community: Areas of agreement. *Rural Sociology, 20,* 111-123.

Hines, P. M. (1999). The family life cycle of African American families living in poverty. In B. Carter and M. McGoldrick (Eds.), *The expanded family life cycle: Individual, family, and social perspectives* (3rd ed., pp. 327-345). Boston: Allyn & Bacon.

Hines, P. M., Preto, N. G., McGoldrick, M., Almeida, R., & Weltman, S. (1999). Culture and the family life cycle. In B. Carter and M. McGoldrick (Eds.), *The expanded family life cycle: Individual, family, and social perspectives* (3rd ed., pp. 69-87). Boston: Allyn & Bacon.

Historical perspective. (2002, January 1). *American Demographics,* p. 11.

Ho, M. K. (1992). *Minority children and adolescents in therapy.* Newbury Park, CA: Sage.

Hobfoll, S., Freedy, R., Lane, C., & Geller, P. (1990). Conservation of social resources: Social support resource theory. *Journal of Social and Personal Relationships, 7,* 465-478.

Hobsbawm, E. (1983). Introduction: Inventing tradition. In E. Hobsbawm & T. Ranger (Eds.), *The invention of tradition* (pp. 1-14). New York: Cambridge University Press.

Hodge, D. R. (2000). Spiritual ecomaps: A new diagrammatic tool for assessing marital and family spirituality. *Journal of Marital and Family Therapy, 26,* 229-240.

Hodge, D. R. (2001). Spiritual genograms: A generational approach to assessing spirituality. *Families in Society, 82,* 35-48.

Hodge, D. R., Cardenas, P., & Montoya, H. (2001). Substance use: Spirituality and religious participation as protective factors among rural youths. *Social Work Research, 25*(3), 153-161.

Hofstede, G. (1998). A case for comparing apples with oranges: International differences in values. *International Journal of Comparative Sociology, 39,* 16-31.

Holahan, C., & Saegert, S. (1973). Behavioral and attitudinal effects of large-scale variation in the physical environment of psychiatric wards. *Journal of Abnormal Psychology, 82,* 454-462.

Holcomb, W. (1987). Promoting collaborative aftercare: Tapping support within the religious community for both mental health clients and agencies. *Psychosocial Rehabilitation Journal, 10*(3), 63-75.

Holder, D. W., Durant, R. H., Harris, T. L., Daniel, J., Obeidallah, D., & Goodman, E. (2000). The association between adolescent spirituality and voluntary sexual activity. *Journal of Adolescent Health, 26*(4), 295-302.

Holm, J., & Bowker, J. (Eds.). (1994). *Women in religion.* New York: Pinter Publishers.

Holman, A., & Silver, R. (1998). Getting "stuck" in the past: Temporal orientation and coping with trauma. *Journal of Personality and Social Psychology, 74*(5), 1146-1163.

Homans, G. (1958). Social behavior as exchange. *American Journal of Sociology, 63,* 597-606.

hooks, b. (1993). *Sisters of the yam: Black women and self-discovery.* Boston: South End Press.

Hopps, J. G., Pinderhughes, E., & Shankar, R. (1995). *The power to care: Clinical practice effectiveness with overwhelmed clients.* New York: Free Press.

Hopson, R. E. (1996). The 12-step program. In E. P. Shafranske (Ed.), *Religion and the clinical practice of psychotherapy* (pp. 533-558). Washington, DC: American Psychological Association.

Horn, L. J. (1991). Rehabilitation in brain disorders: 1. Basic sciences. *Archives of Physical Medicine and Rehabilitation, 72*(4-S), S317-319.

Horney, K. (1939). *New ways in psychoanalysis.* New York: Norton.

Horney, K. (1967). *Feminine psychology.* New York: Norton.

Horsburgh, M. (1997). Towards an inclusive spirituality, wholeness, interdependence and waiting. *Disability and Rehabilitation, 19*(10), 398-406.

House, J. S., Landis, K. R., & Umberson, D. (1988). Social relationships and health. *Science, 241,* 540-545.

Hudson, C. (2000). At the edge of chaos: A new paradigm for social work? *Journal of Social Work Education, 36*(2), 215-230.

Hunter, A. (1974). *Symbolic communities.* Chicago: University of Chicago Press.

Hunter, A., & Riger, S. (1986). The meaning of community in community mental health. *Journal of Community Psychology, 14,* 55-71.

Hunter, J. D. (1994). *Before the shooting begins: Searching for democracy in America's culture wars.* New York: Free Press.

Hurdle, D. E. (1998). The health of Alaska Native women: Significant problems, emerging solutions. *Journal of Poverty, 2*(4), 47-61.

Hurdle, D. E. (2002). Hawaiian traditional healing: Culturally based interventions for social work practice. *Social Work, 47*(2), 183-192.

Hutchison, E. (1987). Use of authority in direct social work practice with mandated clients. *Social Service Review, 61*(4), 581-598.

Hutchison, E., & Charlesworth, L. (2000). Securing the welfare of children: Policies past, present, and future. *Families in Society, 81*(6), 576-586.

Hutchison, E., Dattalo, P., & Rodwell, M. (1994). Reorganizing child protective services: Protecting children and providing family support. *Children and Youth Services Review, 16*(5-6), 319-338.

Hutton, M. S. (1994). How transpersonal psychotherapists differ from other practitioners: An empirical study. *Journal of Transpersonal Psychology, 26*(2), 139-174.

Hyde, C. (1992). The ideational system of social movement agencies: An examination of feminist health centers. In Y. Hasenfeld (Ed.), *Human services as complex organizations* (pp. 121-144). Newbury Park, CA: Sage.

Hyde, C. (2000). The hybrid nonprofit: An examination of feminist social movement organizations. *Journal of Community Practice, 8*(4), 45-67.

Iannello, K. (1992). *Decisions without hierarchy: Feminist interventions in organization theory and practice.* New York: Routledge.

Illinois Education Association-National Education Association. (1997). *IEA-NEA: School funding in Illinois: Supporting documents: Inequities* [Online]. Available from ieanea.org/fundings/sd_inequity.html. Size 2K-4-Mar-97.

Imre, R. (1984). The nature of knowledge in social work. *Social Work, 29,* 41-45.

Ingstad, B., & Whyte, S. (Eds.). (1995). *Disability and culture.* Berkeley: University of California Press.

International Labor Organization (2001). *U.S. leads industrialized world in hours worked, productivity.* Retrieved July 16, 2002, from www.us.ilo.org/news/focus/0110/focus-6.html.

Jackson, M. A. (2002). Christian womanist spirituality: Implications for social work practice. *Social Thought, 21*(1), 63-76.

James, W. (1890). *Principles of psychology.* New York: Holt.

Jancin, B. (2002). Work-family conflict fuels physician burnout. *OB GYN News, 37*(1), 22.

Jayaratne, S., & Chess, W. (1984). Job satisfaction, burnout, and turnover: A national study. *Social Work, 29,* 448-453.

Jehn, K., Northcraft, G., & Neale, M. (1999). Why differences make a difference: A field study of diversity, conflict, and performance in workgroups. *Administrative Science Quarterly, 44*(4), 741-763.

Jendrek, M. P. (1993). Grandparents who parent their grandchildren: Effects on lifestyle. *Journal of Marriage and the Family, 55,* 609-621.

Jendrek, M. P. (1994). Grandparents who parent their grandchildren: Circumstances and decisions. *The Gerontologist, 34*(2), 206-216.

Jenkins, R. (Ed.). (1998). *Questions of competence: Culture, classification and intellectual disability.* New York: Cambridge University Press.

Johnson, D. W., & Johnson, F. P. (1994). *Joining together: Group theory and skills* (5th ed.). Boston: Allyn & Bacon.

Johnson, G. B., & Wahl, M. (1995). Families: Demographic shifts. In R. L. Edwards et al. (Eds.), *Encyclopedia of social work* (19th ed.) (Vol. 2, pp. 936-941). Washington, DC: NASW Press.

Johnson, G. R., Jang, S. J., Larsen, D. B., & De Li, S. (2001). Does adolescent religious commitment matter? A re-examination of the effects of religiosity on delinquency. *Journal on Research in Crime and Delinquency, 38*(1), 22-43.

Johnson, H. C., Atkins, S. P., Battle, S. F., Hernandez-Arata, L., Hesselbrock, M., Libassi, M. F., & Parish, M. S. (1990). Strengthening the "bio" in the biopsychosocial paradigm. *Journal of Social Work Education, 26,* 109-123.

Johnson, M. (Ed.) (1992). *People with disabilities explain it all for you.* Louisville, KY: Advocado Press.

Johnson, S. K. (1997). Does spirituality have a place in rural social work? *Social Work and Christianity, 24*(1), 58-66.

Johnson, T. W., & Colucci, P. (1999). Lesbians, gay men, and the family life cycle. In B. Carter and M. McGoldrick (Eds.), *The expanded family life cycle: Individual, family, and social perspectives* (3rd ed., pp. 346-361). Boston: Allyn & Bacon.

Jones, G. C., & Kilpatrick, A. C. (1996). Wellness theory: A discussion and application to clients with disabilities. *Families in Society, 77*(5), 259-268.

Joseph, M. V. (1987). The religious and spiritual aspects of clinical practice: A neglected dimension of social work. *Social Thought, 13*(1), 12-23.

Joseph, M. V. (1988). Religion and social work practice. *Social Casework, 69,* 443-452.

Jung, C. G. (1933). *Modern man in search of a soul.* New York: Harcourt, Brace & World.

Kahana, B. (1992). Late-life adaptation in the aftermath of extreme stress. In M. Wykel, E. Kahana, & J. Kowal (Eds.), *Stress and health among the elderly* (pp. 5-34). New York: Springer.

Kahn, P. (1999). *The human relationship with nature: Development and culture.* Cambridge, MA: MIT Press.

Kahneman, D., & Tversky, A. (1982). The psychology of preferences. *Scientific American, 246,* 160-173.

Kahneman, D., & Tversky, A. (1984). Choices, values, and frames. *American Psychologist, 39,* 341-350.

Kanuha, V. K. (2001). Individual and family intervention skills with Asian and Pacific Island American lesbians and gay men. In R. Fong & S. B. C. L. Furuto (Eds.), *Culturally competent practice: Skills, interventions, and evaluations* (pp. 313-326). Boston: Allyn & Bacon. .

Kapit, W., Macey, R. I., & Meisami, E. (2000). *The physiology coloring book* (2nd ed.) Cambridge, MA: Harper Collins.

Kaplan, A. J., & Dziegielewski, S. F. (1999). Graduate social work students' attitudes and behaviors toward spirituality and religion: Issues for education and practice. *Social Work & Christianity, 26*(1), 25-39.

Kaplan, H., & Sadock, B. (1998). *Synopsis of psychiatry* (8th ed.). Baltimore: Williams & Wilkins.

Kaplan, R. (1983). The role of nature in the urban context. In I. Altman & J. F. Wohlwill (Eds.), *Behavior and the natural environment* (pp. 127-161). New York: Plenum.

Kaplan, R., & Kaplan, S. (1987). The garden as restorative experience: A research odyssey. In M. Francis & R. T. Hester (Eds.), *The meanings of the garden: Conference proceedings.* Davis: University of California, Center for Design Research.

Kaplan, R., & Kaplan, S. (1989). *The experience of nature: A psychological perspective.* New York: Cambridge University Press.

Karenga, M. (1995). Making the past meaningful: Kwanzaa and the concept of Sankofa. *Reflections: Narratives of Professional Helping, 1*(4), 36-46.

Karls, J. M., & Wandrei, K. E. (Eds.). (1994). *Person-in-environment system: The PIE classification system for social functioning problems.* Washington, DC: National Association of Social Workers.

Kasee, C. R. (1995). Identity, recovery, and religious imperialism: Native American women and the new age. *Women and Therapy: A Feminist Quarterly. 16*(2/3), 83-93.

Katyal, N. (2002). Architecture as crime control. *Yale Law Journal, 111*(5), 1039-1139.

Katz, A. (1993). *Self-help in America: A social movement perspective.* New York: Twayne.

Katz, D., & Kahn, R. (1978). *The social psychology of organizations* (2nd ed.). New York: Wiley.

Kawachi, I., & Kennedy, B. (2001). How income inequality affects health: Evidence from research in the United States. In J. Auerbach & B. Krimgold (Eds.), *Income, socioeconomic status, and health: Exploring the relationships* (pp. 16-28). Washington, DC: National Policy Association. Academy for Health Services Research and Health Policy.

Kaye, V. G. (1985). An innovative treatment modality for elderly residents of a nursing home. *Clinical Gerontologist, 3*(4), 45-51.

Keane, C. (1991). Socioenvironmental determinants of community formation. *Environment and Behavior, 23*(1), 27-46.

Keefe, T. (1996). Meditation and social work treatment. In F. J. Turner (Ed.), *Social work treatment: Interlocking theoretical approaches* (4th ed., pp. 434-460). New York: Free Press.

Kellert, S., & Wilson, E. (Eds.). (1993). *The biophilia hypothesis.* Washington, DC: Island Press.

Kelley, H., & Thibaut, J. (1978). *Interpersonal relations: A theory of interdependence.* New York: Wiley.

Kelly, P. (1996). Narrative theory and social work treatment. In F. Turner (Ed.), *Social work treatment* (4th ed., pp. 461-479). New York: Free Press.

Kennedy, J. E., Davis, R. C., & Taylor, B. G. (1998). Changes and well-being among victims of sexual assault. *Journal for the Scientific Study of Religion, 37,* 322-328.

Kennedy, S., Kiecolt-Glaser, J. K., & Glaser, R. (1988). Immunological consequences of acute and chronic stressors: Mediating role of interpersonal relationships. *British Journal of Medical Psychology, 61,* 77-85.

Kent, S. (1991). Partitioning space: Cross-cultural factors influencing domestic spatial segmentation. *Environment and Behavior, 23,* 438-473.

Kessell, M. J. (1994). Women's adventure group: Experiential therapy in an HMO setting. *Women and Therapy: A Feminist Quarterly, 14*(3/4), 185-203.

Keutzer, C. (1982). Physics and consciousness. *Journal of Humanistic Psychology, 22,* 74-90.

Kilbury, R., Bordieri, J., & Wong, H. (1996). Impact of physical disability and gender on personal space. *Journal of Rehabilitation, 62*(2), 59-61.

Kim, J., Siegel, S., & Patenall, V. (1999). Drug-onset cues as signals: Intraadministration associations and tolerance. *Journal of Experimental Psychology: Animal Behavior Processes, 25*(4), 491-504.

Kimble, M., McFadden, S., Ellor, J., & Seeber, J. (1995). *Aging, spirituality, and religion.* Minneapolis, MN: Fortress Press.

Kinkade, K. (1973). *A Walden Two experiment: The first five years of Twin Oaks Community.* New York: Morrow.

Kirby, D. (1994). *Sexuality and American social policy: Sex education in the schools.* PN: 92-9996-03b. Menlo Park, CA: Henry J. Kaiser Family Foundation.

Kirk, S., & Reid, W. (2002). *Science and social work: A critical appraisal.* New York: Columbia University Press.

Kivel, P. (1991). Men, spirituality, and violence. *Creation Spirituality, 7*(4), 12-14, 50.

Kobayashi, M., & Miura, K. (2000). Natural disaster and restoration housings. In S. Wapner, J. Demick, T. Yamamoto, & H. Minami (Eds.), *Theoretical perspectives in environment-behavior research: Underlying assumptions, research problems, and methodologies* (pp. 39-49). New York: Kluwer Academic.

Koenig, H. G. (1999). *The healing power of faith: Science explores medicine's last great frontier.* New York: Simon and Schuster.

Koenig, H. G. (2001a). Religion and mental health II: Religion, mental health, and related behaviors. *International Journal of Psychiatry in Medicine, 31*(10), 97-109.

Koenig, H. G. (2001b). Religion and medicine IV: Religion, physical health, and clinical implications. *International Journal of Psychiatry in Medicine, 31*(3), 321-336.

Koenig, H. G., Larson, D. B., & Larson, S. S. (2001). Religion and coping with serious medical illness. *Annals of Pharmocotherapy, 35*(3), 352-359.

Koenig, H. G., Larson, D. B., & Weaver, A. J. (1998). Research on religion and serious mental illness. *New Directions for Mental Health Services, 80,* 81-95.

Kohlberg, L. (1969). *Stages in the development of moral thought and action.* New York: Holt, Rinehart, & Winston.

Kosmin, B., & Lachman, S. (1990). *National Survey of Religious Identification, 1990.* Graduate Center of the City of New York. Retrieved June 28, 2002, from www.gc/cuny.edu/studies/aris_index.htm.

Kosmin, B., Mayer, E., & Keysar, A. (2001). *American Religious Identity Survey (2001).* Graduate Center of the City of New York. Retrieved June 28, 2002, from www.gc/cuny/edu/studies/aris_index.htm.

Kottak, C. P. (1994). *Anthropology: The exploration of human diversity.* New York: McGraw-Hill.

Kottak, C. P. (1996). *Mirror for humanity: A concise introduction to cultural anthropology.* New York: McGraw-Hill.

Kottak, C., & Kozaitis, K. (1999). *On being different: Diversity and multiculturalism in the North American mainstream.* Boston: McGraw-Hill.

Kozol, J. (1991). *Savage inequalities: Children in America's schools.* New York: Crown.

Krause, N. (1995). Religiosity and self-esteem among older adults. *Journal of Gerontology, 50,* 236-246.

Kravetz, D. (1982). An overview of content on women for the social work curriculum. *Journal of Education for Social Work, 18*(2), 42-49.

Kriesi, H. (1996). The organizational structure of new social movements in a political context. In D. McAdam, J. McCarthy, & M. Zald (Eds.), *Comparative perspectives on social movements* (pp. 152-184). New York: Cambridge University Press.

Krill, D. (1986). Existential social work. In F. Turner (Ed.), *Social work treatment: Interlocking theoretical approaches* (pp. 181-217). New York: Free Press.

Krill, D. F. (1996). Existential social work. In F. J. Turner (Ed.), *Social work treatment* (4th ed., pp. 250-281). New York: Free Press.

Kroeber, A., & Kluckhohn, C. (1952/1978). *Culture: A critical review of concepts and definitions.* Cambridge, MA: Peabody Museum.

Kroeber, A., & Kluckhohn, C. (1963). *Culture: A critical review of concepts and definitions.* New York: Vintage.

Kropf, N., & Greene, R. (1994). Erikson's eight stages of development: Different lenses. In R. Greene (Ed.), *Human behavior theory: A diversity framework* (pp. 75-114). New York: Aldine de Gruyter.

Kruel, M. (1995). Women's spirituality and healing in Germany. *Women and Therapy: A Feminist Quarterly, 16*(2/3), 135-147.

Kuo, F., Bacaicoa, M., & Sullivan, W. (1998). Transforming inner-city landscapes: Trees, sense of safety, and preference. *Environment and Behavior, 30,* 28-59.

LaDue, R. A. (1994). Coyote returns: Twenty sweats does not an Indian expert make. *Women & Therapy, 15*(1), 93-111.

Laing, R. D. (1967). *The politics of experience.* New York: Ballantine.

Laing, R. D. (1969). *The politics of the family.* New York: Pantheon.

Laird, J. (1984). Sorcerers, shamans, and social workers: The use of ritual in social work practice. *Social Work, 29,* 123-128.

Laird, J. (1993). Lesbian and gay families. In F. Walsh (Ed.), *Normal family processes* (2nd ed., pp. 282-328). New York: Guilford.

Laird, J. (1994). Changing women's narratives: Taking back the discourse. In L. Davis (Ed.), *Building on women's strengths: A social work agenda for the twenty-first century* (pp. 179-210). New York: Haworth.

Lane, H. J. (1984). Self-differentiation in symbolic interactionism and psychoanalysis. *Social Work, 34,* 270-274.

Langer, E., Fiske, S., Taylor, S., & Chanowitz, B. (1976). Stigma, staring, and discomfort: A novel-stimulus hypothesis. *Journal of Experimental Social Psychology, 12,* 451-463.

Langlois, S. (1994). *Convergence or divergence? Comparing recent social trends in industrial societies.* Buffalo, NY: McGill-Queen's University Press.

Lantz, J. E. (1996). Cognitive theory and social work practice. In F. J. Turner (Ed.), *Social work treatment* (4th ed., pp. 94-115). New York: Free Press.

Larin, K., & McNichol, F. (1997). *Pulling apart: A state-by-state analysis of income trends.* Washington, DC: Center on Budget and Policy Priorities.

Larivana, P., Taanila, A., Huttnen, I., Vaesisaenen, E., Moilanen, I., & Kiuttu, J. (2000). From biomedical teaching to biopsychosocial education: A process of change in a Finnish medical school. *Journal of Interprofessional Care, 14*(4), 375-385.

Law, M., & Dunn, W. (1993). Perspectives on understanding and changing the environments of children with disabilities. *Physical and Occupational Therapy in Pediatrics, 13*(3), 1-18.

Lazarus, R. S. (1980). Thoughts on the relations between cognition and emotion. *American Psychologist, 37,* 1019-1024.

Lazarus, R. S. (1993). Coping theory and research: Past, present, and future. *Psychosomatic Medicine, 55,* 234-247.

Lazarus, R. S., & Cohen, J. (1977). Environmental stress. In L. Altman & J. Wohlwill (Eds.), *Human behavior and the environment: Current theory and research.* (Vol. 2, pp. 89-127). New York: Plenum.

Lazarus, R. S., & Lazarus, B. N. (1994). *Passion and reason: Making sense of our emotions.* New York: Oxford University Press.

LeCroy, C. W. (1992). *Case studies in social work practice.* Belmont, CA: Wadsworth.

LeDoux, J. E., & Phelps, E. A. (2000). Emotional networks in the brain. In M. Lewis & J. M. Haviland-Jones (Eds.), *Handbook of emotions* (2nd ed., pp. 157-172). New York: Guilford.

Lee, B., & Campbell, K. (1999). Neighbor networks of black and white Americans. In B. Wellman (Ed.), *Networks in the global village* (pp. 119-146). Boulder, CO: Westview Press.

Lee, J. (2001). *The empowerment approach to social work practice: Building the beloved community.* New York: Columbia University Press.

Lee, P. (1937). *Social work as cause and function, and other papers.* New York: New York School of Social Work.

Leh, D. C., & Corless, I. B. (1988). Spirituality and hospice care. *Death Studies, 12*(2), 101-110.

Leiby, J. (1977). Social welfare: History of basic ideas. In J. B. Turner (Ed.), *Encyclopedia of social work* (17th ed., pp. 1513-1518). Washington, DC: National Association of Social Workers.

Leiby, J. (1985). Moral foundations of social welfare and social work: A historical view. *Social Work, 30,* 323-330.

Lengermann, P. M., & Niebrugge-Brantley, J. (2000). Contemporary feminist theory. In G. Ritzer, *Modern sociological theory* (5th ed., pp. 307-355). Boston: McGraw-Hill.

Lenski, G. (1966). *Power and privilege.* New York: McGraw-Hill.

Lerner, H. (1986). *The dance of anger.* New York: Perennial Library.

Lerner, H. (2001). *The dance of connection.* New York: HarperCollins.

Levi, M., Cook, K., O'Brien, J., & Faye, H. (1990). The limits of rationality. In K. Cook & M. Levi (Eds.), *The limits of rationality* (pp. 1-16). Chicago: University of Chicago Press.

Levin, J. D. (1992). *Theories of the self.* Washington, DC: Hemisphere.

Levine, B. (1991). *Group psychotherapy.* Prospect Heights, IL: Waveland Press.

Levine, S., Coe, C., & Wiener, S. G. (1989). Psychoneuroendocrinology of stress: A psychobiological perspective. In F. R. Brush & S. Levine (Eds.), *Psychoendocrinology* (pp. 341-377). New York: Academic Press.

Levinson, D. (1996). *The seasons of a woman's life.* New York: Knopf.

Levy, F. (1995). Incomes and income inequality. In R. Farley (Ed.), *State of the union: America in the 1990s: Vol. 1. Economic trends* (pp. 1-57). New York: Russell Sage Foundation.

Lewandowski, C. A., & Canda, E. R. (1995). A typological model for the assessment of religious groups. *Social Thought, 18*(1), 17-38.

Lewis, C. (1972). Public housing gardens: Landscapes for the soul. In *Landscape for living* (pp. 277-282). Washington, DC: U.S. Department of Agriculture.

Lewis, C. (1979). Healing in the urban environment: A person/plant viewpoint. *Journal of American Planning Association, 45,* 330-338.

Li, J., Karakowsky, L, & Siegel, J. (1999). The effects of proportional representation on intragroup behavior in mixed-race decision making groups. *Small Group Research, 30*(3), 259-279.

Lifchez, R., & Davis, C. (1987). Living upstairs, leaving home, and at the Moscow Circus. In M. Saxton & F. Howe (Eds.), *With wings: An anthology of literature by and about women with disabilities.* New York: Feminist Press.

Lincoln, Y., & Guba, E. (1985). *Naturalistic inquiry.* Beverly Hills, CA: Sage.

Lindsay, E. W., Kurtz, P. D., Jarvis, S., Williams, N. R., & Nackerud, L. (2000). How runaway and homeless youth navigate troubled waters: Personal strengths and resources. *Clinical and Adolescent Social Work Journal, 17*(2), 115-140.

Link, A. L. (1997). *Group work with elders: 50 therapeutic exercises for reminiscence, validation, and remotivation.* Sarasota, FL: Professional Resource Press.

Linstead, S. (1993). Deconstruction in the study of organizations. In J. Hassard & M. Parker (Eds.), *Postmodernism and organizations* (pp. 49-70). Newbury Park, CA: Sage.

Livingstone, S. (1996). On the continuing problem of media effects. In J. Curran & M. Gurevitch (Eds.), *Mass media and society* (2nd ed., pp. 305-324). New York: Arnold.

Lockwood, D. (1966). Sources of variation in working class images of society. *Sociological Review, 14,* 244-267.

Logan, J., & Molotch, H. (1987). *Urban fortunes: The political economy of place.* Berkeley: University of California Press.

Logan, S. L. (1996). *The black family: Strengths, self-help, and positive change.* Boulder, CO: Westview Press.

Logan, S. L. (1997). Meditation as a tool that links the personal and the professional. *Reflections: Narratives of Professional Helping, 3*(1), 38-44.

Logan, S. L., Freeman, E. M., & McRoy, R. G. (1990*). Social work practice with black families: A culturally specific perspective.* New York: Longman.

Long, P. W. (1996). *Major depressive disorder: Treatment.* [Online]. Available from www.mentalhealth.com.

Longres, J. (2000). *Human behavior in the social environment* (3rd ed.). Itasca, IL.: F. E. Peacock.

Lovaglia, M. J. (1995). Power and status: Exchange, attribution, and expectation states. *Small Group Research, 26,* 400-426.

Low, S., & Altman, I. (1992). Place attachment: A conceptual inquiry. In I. Altman & S. Low (Eds.), *Place attachment* (pp. 1-12). New York: Plenum.

Lowe, J. I. (1997). A social-health model: A paradigm for social work in health care. In M. Reisch & E. Gambrill (Eds.), *Social work in the 21st century* (pp. 209-218). Thousand Oaks, CA: Pine Forge.

Lowenberg, F. M. (1988). *Religion and social work practice in contemporary American society.* New York: Columbia University Press.

Lowery, C. T. (1998). American Indian perspectives on addiction and recovery. *Health & Social Work, 23*(2), 127-135.

Lubin, H., & Johnson, D. R. (1998). Healing ceremonies. *Family Networker, 22*(5), 38-39, 64-67.

Lubove, R. (1966, May 23). Social work and the life of the poor. *Nation,* 609-611.

Luepnitz, D. (1988). *The family interpreted: Feminist theory and clinical practice.* New York: Basic Books.

Luhman, N. (1987). Modern systems theory and the theory of society. In V. Meja, D. Misgeld, & N. Stehr (Eds.), *Modern German sociology* (pp. 173-186). New York: Columbia University Press.

Lum, D. (1992). *Social work practice and people of color: A process-stage approach* (2nd ed.). Pacific Grove, CA: Brooks/Cole.

Lum, D. (2003). *Culturally competent practice: A framework for understanding diverse groups and justice issues* (2nd ed.). Pacific Grove, CA: Brooks/Cole.

Lupien, S. J., King, S., Meaney, M. J., & McEwen, B. S. (2000). Child's stress hormone levels correlate with mother's socioeconomic status and depressive state. *Biological Psychiatry, 48*(10), 976-980.

Lynn, L. (2002). Social services and the state: The public appropriation of private charity. *Social Service Review, 76*(1), 58-83.

Lyon, L. (1987). *The community in urban society.* Philadelphia: Temple University Press.

MacArthur Network on Mind-Body Interactions. (2001). *Vital connections: Science of mind-body interactions: A report on the interdisciplinary conference held at NIH March 26-28, 2001.* Chicago: Author.

Macklin, E. D. (1980). Nontraditional family forms: A decade of research. In F. M. Berardo (Ed.), *Decade review: Family research 1970-1979* (pp. 175-192). Minneapolis, MN: National Council on Family Relations. [Also published as a special issue of *Journal of Marriage and the Family,* 1980, 42(4)]

MacNair, R., Fowler, L., & Harris, J. (2000). The diversity functions of organizations that confront oppression: The evolution of three social movements. *Journal of Community Practice, 7*(2), 71-88.

Mader, S. S. (2001). *Human biology* (7th ed.). Boston: McGraw-Hill.

Magai, C. (1996). Personality theory: Birth, death, and transfiguration. In R. D. Kavanaugh, B. Zimmerberg, & S. Fein (Eds.), *Emotion: Interdisciplinary perspectives* (pp. 171-202). Mahwah, NJ: Lawrence Erlbaum.

Mahoney, M. (1991). *Human change processes: The scientific foundations of psychotherapy.* New York: Basic Books.

Maier, H. W. (1978). *Three theories of child development* (3rd ed.). New York: Harper and Row.

Major branches of religions ranked by number of adherents. (2001). Retrieved June 28, 2002, from www.adherents.com.

Mancini, J. A., & Blieszner, R. (1991). Aging parents and adult children: Research themes in intergenerational relations. In A. Booth (Ed.), *Contemporary families: Looking forward, looking back* (pp. 249-264). Minneapolis, MN: National Council on Family Relations.

Mann, M. (1986). *The sources of social power* (Vol. 1). New York: Cambridge University Press.

March, J., & Simon, H. (1958). *Organizations.* New York: Wiley.

Marcic, D. (1997). *Managing with the wisdom of love: Uncovering virtue in people and organizations.* San Francisco: Jossey-Bass.

Mare, R. (1995). Changes in educational attainment and school enrollment. In R. Farley (Ed.), *State of the union: America in the 1990s* (Vol. 1, pp. 155-243). New York: Russell Sage Foundation.

Markowitz, M. (1997, September). *Protease inhibitors: A new family of drugs for the treatment of HIV infection. What they are, how they work, when to use them* (Rev. ver. 4). [Online]. Available from www.iapac.org/consumer/proinbk.html.

Marlow, C. (2001). *Research methods for generalist social work* (3rd ed.). Belmont, CA: Wadsworth.

Martin, J. G. (1993). Why women need a feminist spirituality. *Women's Studies Quarterly, 1,* 106-120.

Martin, P. Y., & O'Connor, G. G. (1989). *The social environment: Open systems applications.* New York: Longman.

Martinez-Brawley, E. (2000). *Close to home: Human services and the small community.* Washington, DC: NASW Press.

Marty, M. (1980). Social service: Godly and godless. *Social Service Review, 54,* 463-481.

Marx, G., & McAdam, D. (1994). *Collective behavior and social movements: Process and structure.* Englewood Cliffs, NJ: Prentice-Hall.

Marx, K. (1887/1967). *Capital: A critique of political economy* (S. Moore & E. Aveling, Trans.) (Vol. 1). New York: International Publishers.

Maslach, C., & Jackson, S. (1981). *Maslach Burnout Inventory: Research edition.* Palo Alto, CA: Consulting Psychologists Press.

Maslach, C., Schaufeli, W., & Leiter, M. (2001). Job burnout. *Annual Review of Psychology, 52,* 397-422.

Maslow, A. (1962). *Toward a psychology of being.* New York: Van Nostrand.

Maslow, A. (1971). *Farther reaches of human nature.* New York: Viking.

Matheson, L. (1996). Valuing spirituality among Native American populations. *Counseling and Values, 41,* 51-58.

Maton, K. I., & Wells, E. A. (1995). Religion as a community resource for well-being: Prevention, healing, and empowerment pathways. *Journal of Social Issues, 51*(2), 177-193.

Matthews, D. A., McCullough, M. E., Larson, D. B., Koenig, H. G., Swyers, J. P., & Milano, M. G. (1998). Religious commitment and health status: A review of the research and implications for family medicine. *Archives of Family Medicine, 7*(2), 118-124.

Mattison, D., Jayaratne, S., & Croxton, T. (2000). Social workers' religiosity and its impact on religious practice behaviors. *Advances in Social Work, 1*(1), 43-59.

Maturana, H. (1988). Reality: The search for objectivity or the question for a compelling argument. *Irish Journal of Psychology, 9,* 25-82.

Maxwell, L. (1996). Multiple effects of home and day care crowding. *Environment and Behavior, 28,* 494-511.

May, G. G. (1988). *Addiction and grace.* New York: Harper & Row.

Mayhew, P., Clarke, R., Hough, J., & Winchester, S. (1980). Natural surveillance and vandalism to telephone kiosks. In R. Clarke & P. Mayhew (Eds.), *Designing out crime* (pp. 67-74). London: Her Majesty's Stationery Office.

Maynard, F. M. (1998, February 25). *The post-polio syndrome and re-rehabilitation.* [Online]. Available from www.azstarnet.com/~rspear/rehab2.html

Mayo, E. (1933). *The human problems of an industrial civilization.* New York: Macmillan.

McAdam, D. (1982). *Political process and the development of black insurgency, 1930-1970.* Chicago: University of Chicago Press.

McAdam, D. (1996a). Conceptual origins, current problems, future directions. In D. McAdam, J. McCarthy, & M. Zald (Eds.), *Comparative perspectives on social movements* (pp. 23-40). New York: Cambridge University Press.

McAdam, D. (1996b). The framing function of movement tactics: Strategic dramaturgy in the American civil rights movement. In D. McAdam, J. McCarthy, & M. Zald (Eds.), *Comparative perspectives on social movements* (pp. 338-355). New York: Cambridge University Press.

McAdam, D., McCarthy, J., & Zald, M. (1996). Introduction: Opportunities, mobilizing structures, and framing processes: Toward a synthetic, comparative perspective on social movements. In D. McAdam, J. McCarthy, & M. Zald (Eds.), *Comparative perspectives on social movements* (pp. 1-20). New York: Cambridge University Press.

McAdoo, H. P. (Ed.). (1997). *Black families* (3rd ed.). Thousand Oaks, CA: Sage.

McAdoo, H. P. (Ed.). (1999). *Family ethnicity: Strength in diversity* (2nd ed.). Thousand Oaks, CA: Sage.

McCarthy, J. (1987). Pro-life and pro-choice mobilization: Infrastructure deficits and new technologies. In M. Zald & J. McCarthy (Eds.), *Social movements in an organizational society* (pp. 49-66). New Brunswick, NJ: Transaction.

McCarthy, J. (1996). Constraints and opportunities in adopting, adapting, and inventing. In D. McAdam, J. McCarthy, & M. Zald (Eds.), *Comparative perspectives on social movements: Political opportunities, mobilizing structures, and cultural framings* (pp. 141-151). New York: Cambridge University Press.

McCarthy, J., & Zald, M. (1977). Resource mobilization in social movements: A partial theory. *American Journal of Sociology, 82,* 1212-1239.

McCubbin, H. I., & Figley, C. R. (1983). *Stress and the family: Vol. 1: Coping with normative transitions.* New York: Brunner/Mazel.

McCubbin, H. I., Joy, C. B., Cauble, A. E., Comeau, J. K., Patterson, J. M., & Needle, R. H. (1980). Family stress and coping: A decade review. In F. M. Berardo (Ed.), *Decade review: Family research 1970-1979* (pp. 125-141). Minneapolis, MN: National Council on Family Relations. [Also published as a special issue of *Journal of Marriage and the Family,* 1980, 42(4)]

McCubbin, H. I., & Patterson, J. M. (1983). The family stress process: The double ABCX model of adjustment and adaptation. In H. I. McCubbin, M. B. Sussman, & J. M. Patterson (Eds.), *Social stress and the family: Advances and developments in family stress theory and research* (pp. 7-37). New York: Haworth.

McDonald, L. (1997). Building on the strengths and assets of families and communities. *Families in Society, 78,* 115-116.

McDonald, L., Billingham, S., Conrad, T., Morgan, A., Payton, N., & Payton, E. (1997). Families and Schools Together (FAST): Integrating community development with clinical strategies. *Families in Society, 78,* 140-155.

McEwen, B. (1998). Protective and damaging effects of stress mediators. *New England Journal of Medicine, 338,* 614-618.

McGoldrick, M. (1999). History, genograms, and the family life cycle: Freud in context. In B. Carter & M. McGoldrick (Eds.), *The expanded family life cycle: Individual, family, and social perspectives* (3rd ed., pp. 47-68). Boston: Allyn & Bacon.

McGoldrick, M., & Carter, B. (1999). Remarried families. In B. Carter and M. McGoldrick (Eds.), *The expanded family life cycle: Individual, family, and social perspectives* (3rd ed., pp. 417-435). Boston: Allyn & Bacon.

McGoldrick, M., Giordano, J., & Pearce, J. K. (Eds.). (1996). *Ethnicity and family therapy* (2nd ed.). New York: Guilford.

McGregor, D. (1960). *The human side of enterprise.* New York: McGraw-Hill.

McInnis-Dittrick, K. (2002). *Social work with elders: A biopsychosocial appraoch to assessment and intervention.* Boston: Allyn and Bacon.

McIntosh, P. (1988/2001). White privilege: Unpacking the invisible knapsack. In P. Rothenberg (Ed.), *Race, class, and gender in the United States* (5th ed., pp. 163-168). New York: Worth.

McKinney, J., & Loomis, C. (1958). The typological tradition. In J. Roucek (Ed.), *Contemporary sociology.* New York: Philosophical Library.

McLanahan, S., & Sandefur, G. (1994). *Growing up with a single parent: What hurts, what helps.* Cambridge, MA: Harvard University Press.

McLaughlin, M., Irby, M., & Langman, J. (1994). *Urban sanctuaries: Lives and futures of inner-city youth.* San Francisco: Jossey-Bass.

McLoyd, V. C., Cauce, A. M., Takeuchi, D., & Wilson, L. (2001). Marital processes and parental socialization in families of color: A decade review of research. In R. M. Milardo (Ed.), *Understanding families into the new millennium* (pp. 289-312). Minneapolis, MN: National Council on Family Relations.

McManus, I., Winder, B., & Gordon, D. (2002). The causal links between stress and burnout in a longitudinal study of UK doctors. *Lancet, 359*(9323), 2089-2090.

McMillan, D. (1996). Sense of community. *Journal of Community Psychology, 24,* 315-325.

McMillan, D., & Chavis, D. (1986). Sense of community: A definition and theory. *Journal of Community Psychology, 14,* 6-23.

McNeal, K. E. (1999). Affecting experience: Toward a biocultural model of human emotions. In A. L. Hinton (Ed.), *Biocultural approaches to the emotions* (pp. 215-255). Cambridge, UK: Cambridge University Press.

McNeill, J. J. (1995). *Freedom, glorious freedom: The spiritual journey to the fullness of life for gays, lesbians, and everybody else.* Boston: Beacon Press.

McNiff, S. (1992). *Art as medicine: Creating a therapy of the imagination.* Palo Alto, CA: Shambhala.

Mead, G. H. (1934). *Mind, self, and society.* Chicago: University of Chicago Press.

Mead, G. (1959). *The philosophy of the present.* LaSalle, IL: Open Court Publishing.

Mead, M. (1928/1961). *Coming of age in Samoa.* New York: Morrow Quill.

Mead, M. (1930/1968). *Growing up in New Guinea: A comparative study of primitive education.* New York: Dell.

Mead, M. (1935/1950). *Sex and temperament in three primitive societies.* New York: New American Library.

Mechanic, D. (1995). Sociological dimensions of illness behavior. *Social Science and Medicine, 41,* 1207-1216.

Meeker, B. F. (1994). Performance evaluation. In M. Foshci & E. J. Lawler (Eds.), *Group processes: Sociological analyses* (pp. 95-117). Chicago: Nelson-Hall.

Melton, J. G. (1993). *Encyclopedia of American religion.* Detroit, MI: Gale Research.

Mesch, G., & Manor, O. (1998). Social ties, environmental perception, and local attachment. *Environment and Behavior, 30*(4), 504-519.

Meyer, C. (1976). *Social work practice* (2nd ed.). New York: Free Press.

Meyer, C. (Ed.). (1983). *Clinical social work in an eco-systems perspective.* New York: Columbia University Press.

Meyer, C. (1993). *Assessment in social work practice.* New York: Columbia University Press.

Meystedt, D. M. (1984). Religion and the rural populations: Implications for social work. *Social Casework, 65*(4), 219-226.

Middleton, P. (1989). Socialism, feminism and men. *Radical Philosophy, 53,* 8-19.

Mikulincer, M. (1994). *Human learned helplessness: A coping perspective.* New York: Plenum.

Milardo, R. M. (Ed.) (2001). *Understanding families into the new millennium.* Minneapolis, MN: National Council on Family Relations.

Miles, M. (1995). Disability in an Eastern religious context: Historical perspectives. *Disability and Society, 10,* 49-69.

Miller, D. (1987). *Helping the strong: An exploration of the needs of families headed by women.* Silver Spring, MD: NASW Press.

Miller, L., Davies, M., & Greenwald, S. (2000). Religiosity and substance use and abuse among adolescents in the National Comorbidity Survey. *Journal of the American Academy of Child and Adolescent Psychiatry, 19*(9), 1190-1197.

Miller, W. R. (1998). Researching the spiritual dimensions of alcohol and other drug problems. *Addiction, 93*(7), 979-990.

Millison, M. B., & Dudley, J. R. (1990). The importance of spirituality in hospice work: A study of hospice professionals. *Hospice Journal, 6*(3), 63-78.

Minami, H., & Tanaka, K. (1995). Social and environmental psychology: Transaction between physical space and group-dynamic processes. *Environment and Behavior, 27,* 43-55.

Minami, H., & Yamamoto, T. (2000). Cultural assumptions underlying concept-formation and theory building in environment-behavior research. In S. Wapner, J. Demick, T. Yamamoto, & H. Minami (Eds.), *Theoretical perspectives in environment-behavior research: Underlying assumptions, research problems, and methodologies* (pp. 237-246). New York: Kluwer Academic.

Mindel, C. H., Habenstein, R. W., & Wright, R., Jr. (Eds.). (1998). *Ethnic families in America: Patterns and variations* (4th ed.). Upper Saddle River, NJ: Prentice-Hall.

Miringoff, M. L., & Miringoff, M. (1999). *The social health of the nation: How America is really doing.* New York: Oxford University Press.

Miringoff, M. L., Miringoff, M., & Opdycke, S. (1996). The growing gap between standard economic indicators and the nation's social health. *Challenge,* 17-22.

Mischey, E. J. (1981). Faith, identity, and personality in late adolescence. *Character Potential: A Record of Research, 9*(4), 175-185.

Mitka, M. (1998). Getting religion seen as help in being well. *Journal of the American Medical Association, 280*(22), 1896-1897.

Mizrahi, T., & Rosenthal, B. (2001). Complexities of coalition building: Leaders' successes, strategies, struggles, and solutions. *Social Work, 46*(1), 63-78.

Moberg, D. O. (1990). Spiritual maturity and wholeness in the later years. *Journal of Religious Gerontology, 7,* 5-24.

Monette, D., Sullivan, T., & DeJong, C. (1998). *Applied social research: Tool for the human services* (4th ed.). Fort Worth, TX: Harcourt Brace.

Monte, C. (1999). *Beneath the mask: An introduction to theories of personality* (6th ed.). New York: Harcourt Brace.

Montgomery, C. (1994). Swimming upstream: The strengths of women who survive homelessness. *Advances in Nursing Science, 16*(3), 34-45.

Moore, E. (1981). A prison environment's effect on health care service demands. *Journal of Environmental Systems, 11,* 17-34.

Moore, K. A. (1995, September). Executive summary: Nonmarital childbearing in the United States. In U. S. Department of Health and Human Services (Public Health Service, Centers for Disease Control and Prevention, National Center for Health Statistics), *Report to Congress on out-of-wedlock childbearing* (pp. v-xxii). (DHHS Pub. No. (PHS) 95-1257). Washington, DC: U.S. Government Printing Office.

Moore, T. (1992). The African American church: A source of empowerment, mutual help, and social change. In K. Pargament, K. Maton, & R. Hess (Eds.), *Religion and prevention in mental health* (pp. 237-258). New York: Haworth Press.

Mor Barak, M. (2000). The inclusive workplace: An ecosystem approach to diversity management. *Social Work, 45*(4), 339-352.

Morgan, G. (1986). *Images of organization.* Newbury Park, CA: Sage.

Morgan, G. (1997). *Images of organization* (2nd ed.). Thousand Oaks, CA: Sage.

Morgan, J. P. (2002). Dying and grieving are journeys of the spirit. In R. B. Gilbert (Ed.), *Health care and spirituality: Listening, assessing, caring* (pp. 53-64). Amityville, NY: Baywood.

Morreale, D. (Ed.). (1998). *The complete guide to Buddhist America.* Boston: Shambhala.

Morris, A. (1981). The black southern sit-in movement: An analysis of internal organization. *American Sociological Review, 46,* 744-767.

Morris, A. (1984). *The origins of the civil rights movement: Black communities organizing for change.* New York: Free Press.

Morris, A. (2000). Reflections on social movement theory: Criticisms and proposals. *Contemporary Sociology, 29*(3), 445-454.

Morse, J., & Lorsch, J. (1970). Beyond theory Y. *Harvard Business Review, 45,* 61-68.

Mortimer, J. T., & Simmons, R. G. (1978). Adult socialization. *Annual Review of Sociology, 4,* 421-454.

Mueller, P. C., Plevak, D. J., & Rummans, T. A. (2001). Religious involvement, spirituality, and medicine: Implications for clinical practice. *Mayo Clinical Proceedings, 76*(12), 1225-1235.

Muff, J. (1996). Images of life on the verge of death: Dreams and drawings of people with AIDS. *Perspectives in Psychiatric Care, 32*(3), 10-21.

Mulcahy, G. A., & Lunham-Armstrong, Y. (1998). A First Nations approach to healing. In S. N. Madu & P. K. Baguma (Eds.), *In quest of psychotherapy for modern Africa* (pp. 240-256). Sovenga, South Africa: UNIN Press.

Murray, C. (1984). *Losing ground: American social policy, 1950-1980.* New York: Basic Books.

Murray, C., & Herrnstein, R. (1994). *The bell curve: Intelligence and class structure in American life.* New York: Free Press.

Myers, B. K. (1997). *Young children and spirituality.* New York: Routledge.

Nachimas, M., Gunnar, M. R., Mangelsdorf, S., Parritz, R., & Buss, K. (1996). Behavioral inhibition and stress reactivity: Moderating the role of attachment anxiety. *Child Development, 67,* 508-522.

Nagasawa, Y. (2000). The geography of hospitals: A developing approach to the architectural planning of hospitals. In S. Wapner, J. Demick, T. Yamamoto, & H. Minami (Eds.), *Theoretical perspectives in environment-behavior research: Underlying assumptions, research problems, and methodologies* (pp. 217-227). New York: Kluwer Academic.

Nair, S., Blake, M. L., & Vosler, N. R. (1997). Multilevel social systems practice with low-income families in Singapore. *Families in Society, 78*(3), 291-298.

Nakhaima, J. M., & Dicks, B. H. (1995). Social work practice with religious families. *Families in Society, 76,* 360-368.

Naperstek, A., & Dooley, D. (1997). Countering urban disinvestment through community-building initiatives. *Social Work, 42,* 506-514.

Natale, S. M., & Neher, J. C. (1997). Inspiriting the workplace: Developing a values-based management system. In D. P. Bloch & L. J. Richmond (Eds.), *Connections between spirit and work in career development: New approaches and practical perspectives* (pp. 237-255). Palo Alto, CA: Davies-Black.

Nathanson, I. G. (1995). Divorce and women's spirituality. *Journal of Divorce and Remarriage, 22,* 179-188.

National Association of Social Workers. (1982). Changes in NASW family policy. *NASW News, 27*(2), 10.

National Breast Cancer Coalition. (n.d.). *About NBCC.* Retrieved August 11, 2002, from www.natlbcc.org/bin/home.

National Center for Education Statistics. (n.d.). *Societal support for learning.* Retrieved July 13, 2002, from nces.ed.gov/programs/coe/2001/section6/index.html.

National Center for Education Statistics. (1999). *Dropout rates in the United States: 1998.* (NCES 2000-022). Washington, DC: Author.

National Center for Health Statistics. (2000). *NCIIS-2000 fact-sheet.* Retrieved September 20, 2001, from www.cdc.gov/nchs/releases/00facts/trends.htm.

National Center for Health Statistics. (2001). *National vital statistics reports, 49*(12). Hyattsville, MD: Author.

National Center for Health Statistics. (2002). *National vital statistics report, 50*(6). Hyattsville, MD: Author.

National Coalition for the Homeless. (1997a). *NCH fact sheet #2* [Online]. Available from www2.ari.net/home/nch/numbers.html.

National Coalition for the Homeless. (1997b). *NCH fact sheet #3* [Online]. Available from www2.ari.net/home/nch/who.html.

National Education Association. (n.d.). Educational programs for Limited English Proficiency Students. Retrieved July 13, 2002, from www.nea.org.

National Institute of Neurological Disorders and Stroke. (1997). *Post-polio syndrome: Fact sheet.* [Online].

Available from www.ninds.hih.gov/healinfo/disorder/ppolio/ppolio.

Neufeld, P., & Knipemann, K. (2001). Gateway to wellness: An occupational therapy collaboration with the National Multiple Sclerosis Society. *Occupational Therapy in Health Care, 12*(3/4), 67-84.

Nelson, C. A. (1999). How important are the first three years of life? *Applied Developmental Science, 3*(4), 235-238.

Nelson, C. A. (2000). The neurobiological basis of early intervention. In J. P. Shonkoff & S. J. Meisels (Eds.), *Handbook of early childhood intervention* (2nd ed., pp. 204-227). New York: Cambridge University Press.

Nelson, C. A., & Carver, L. J. (1998). The effects of stress and trauma on brain and memory: A view from developmental cognitive neuroscience. *Development & Psychopathology, 10*(4), 793-809.

Netting, F. E., Kettner, P., & McMurtry, S. (1998). *Social work macro practice* (2nd ed.). New York: Longman.

Neufeld, P., & Knipemann, K. (2001). Gateway to wellness: An occupational therapy collaboration with the National Multiple Sclerosis Society. *Occupational Therapy in Health Care, 12*(3/4), 67-84.

Newbrough, J. R., & Chavis, D. M. (1986). Psychological sense of community: I. Foreword. *Journal of Community Psychology, 14,* 3-5.

Newell, P. (1997). A cross-cultural examination of favorite places. *Environment and Behavior, 29,* 495-514.

Newham, P. (1994). *The singing cure: An introduction to voice movement therapy.* Palo Alto, CA: Shambhala.

Newman, D. (1995). *Sociology: Exploring the architecture of everyday life.* Thousand Oaks, CA: Pine Forge.

Newman, O. (1972). *Defensible space.* New York: Macmillan.

Newman, O. (1980). *Community of interest.* Garden City, NY: Anchor/Doubleday.

Nichols, M., & Schwartz, R. (2001). *Family therapy: Concepts and methods* (5th ed.). Boston: Allyn & Bacon.

Nicholson, B. L. (1997). The influence of pre-emigration and postemigration stressors on mental health: A study of Southeast Asian refugees. *Social Work Research, 21,* 19-31.

Niebuhr, R. (1932). *The contribution of religion to social work.* New York: Columbia University Press.

Nobles, W. W. (1980). African philosophy: Foundations for black psychology. In R. L. Jones (Ed.), *Black psychology* (2nd ed., pp. 23-36). New York: Harper & Row.

Noddings, N. (1982). *Caring: A feminine approach to ethics and moral education.* Berkeley: University of California Press.

Noddings, N. (1989). *Women and evil.* Berkeley: University of California Press.

Noll, H., & Langlois, S. (1994). Employment and labour-market change: Toward two models of growth. In S. Langlois (Ed.), *Convergence or divergence? Comparing recent social trends in industrial societies* (pp. 89-113). Buffalo, NY: McGill-Queen's University Press.

Norrell, D., & Walz, T. (1994). Reflections from the field toward a theory and practice of reconciliation in ethnic conflict resolution. *Social Development Issues, 16*(2), 99-111.

Northen, H. (1988). *Social work with groups* (3rd ed.). New York: Columbia University Press.

Novello, A. C. (1993). *Surgeon General's report to the American public on HIV infection and AIDS.* Rockville, MD: CDC National AIDS Clearinghouse.

Nye, I. (Ed.). (1982). *The relationships: Rewards and costs.* Beverly Hills, CA: Sage.

O'Brien, P. J. (1992). Social work and spirituality: Clarifying the concept for practice. *Spirituality and Social Work Journal, 3*(1), 2-5.

O'Brien, P. (2001). Claiming our soul: An empowerment group for African-American women in prison. *Journal of Progressive Human Services, 12*(1), 35-51.

Oberschall, A. (1992). *Social movements: Ideologies, interests, and identities.* New Brunswick, NJ: Transaction.

Oberschall, A. (1996). Opportunities and framing in the Eastern European revolts of 1989. In D. McAdam, J. McCarthy, & M. Zald (Eds.), *Comparative perspectives on social movements: Political opportunities, mobilizing structures, and cultural framings* (pp. 93-121). New York: Cambridge University Press.

Obst, P., Zinkiewics, L., & Smith, S. (2002a). Sense of community in science fiction fandom, Part 1. Understanding sense of community in an international community of interest. *Journal of Community Psychology, 30*(1), 87-103.

Obst, P., Zinkiewicz, L., & Smith, S. (2002b). Sense of community in science fiction fandom, Part 2. Comparing neighborhood and interest group sense of community. *Journal of Community Psychology, 30*(1), 105-117.

Ogbu, J. (1991). Immigrant and involuntary minorities in comparative perspective. In M. Gibson & J. Ogbu (Eds.),

Minority status and schooling: A comparative study of immigrant and involuntary minorities. New York: Garland.

Omi, M., & Winant, H. (1993). On the theoretical status of the concept of race. In C. McCarthy & W. Crichlow (Eds.), *Race, identity, and representation in education.* New York: Routledge.

Ortiz, L. P. A. (1991). Religious issues: The missing link in social work education. *Spirituality and Social Work Journal, 2*(2), 13-18.

Ortner, S. (1973). On key symbols. *American Anthropologist, 75,* 1338-1346.

Ortner, S. (1984). Theory in anthropology since the sixties. *Comparative Studies in History and Society, 26*(1), 126-166.

Ortner, S. (1989). *High religion: A cultural and political history of Sherpa Buddhism.* Princeton, NJ: Princeton University Press.

Ortner, S. (1996). *Making gender: The politics and erotics of culture.* Boston: Beacon Press.

Osmond, H. (1957). Function as the basis of psychiatric ward design. *Mental Hospitals, 8,* 23-29.

Osmond, H. (1959). The relationship between architect and psychiatrist. In C. Goshen (Ed.), *Psychiatric architecture* (pp. 16-20). Washington, DC: American Psychiatric Association.

Osmond, H. (1966). Some psychiatric aspects of design. In L. B. Holland (Ed.), *Who designs America?* Garden City, NY: Anchor.

Ozorak, E. W. (1996). The power, but not the glory: How women empower themselves through religion. *Journal for the Scientific Study of Religion, 35*(1), 17-29.

Padilla, Y. C. (1999). Immigrant policy: Issues for social work practice. In P. L. Ewalt et al. (Eds.), *Multicultural issues in social work: Practice and research* (pp. 589-604). Washington, DC: NASW Press.

Panksepp, J. (1991). Affective neuroscience: A conceptual framework for the neurobiological study of emotions. In K. T. Strongman (Ed.), *International review of studies on emotions* (pp. 59-99). New York: Wiley.

Parappully, J., Rosenbaum, R., van den Daele, L., & Nzewi, E. (2002). Thriving after trauma: The experience of parents of murdered children. *Journal of Humanistic Psychology, 42*(1), 33-70.

Pargament, K. I. (1997). *The psychology of religious coping: Theory, research, practice.* New York: Guilford.

Paris, P. J. (1995). *The spirituality of African peoples: The search for a common moral discourse.* Minneapolis, MN: Fortress Press.

Park, R. (1936). Human ecology. *American Journal of Sociology, 17,* 1-15.

Patterson, C. J. (2001). Family relationships of lesbians and gay men. In R.M. Milardo (Ed.), *Understanding families into the new millennium* (pp. 271-288). Minneapolis, MN: National Council on Family Relations.

Paulino, A. M. (1995a). Death, dying and religion among Dominican immigrants. In J. Parry & A. R. Shen (Eds.), *A cross-cultural look at death, dying, and religion* (pp. 84-101). Chicago: Nelson Hall.

Paulino, A. M. (1995b). Spiritism, santeria, brujeria, and voodooism: A comparative view of indigenous healing systems. *Journal of Teaching in Social Work, 12*(1/2), 105-124.

Payne, B. (1990). Research and theoretical approaches to spirituality and aging. *Generations, 14*(4), 11-14.

Payne, R. (2000). *Relaxation techniques: A practical handbook for the health care professional* (2nd ed.). Edinburgh, NY: Churchill Livingstone.

Pearson, J. (1996) *Discovering the self through drama and movement: The Sesame Approach.* London: Jessica Kingsley Publishers.

Pellebon, D. A., & Anderson, S. C. (1999). Understanding the life issues of spiritual clients. *Families in Society, 80*(3), 229-238.

Perkins, D., Wandersman, A., Rich, R., & Taylor, R. (1993). The physical environment of street crime: Defensible space, territoriality and incivilities. *Journal of Environmental Psychology, 13*(1), 29-49.

Perron, K. M., & Sedlacek, W. E. (2000). A comparison of group cohesiveness and client satisfaction in homogeneous and heterogeneous groups. *Journal for Specialists in Group Work, 25*(3), 243-251.

Perry, B. G. F. (1998). The relationship between faith and well-being. *Journal of Religion and Health, 37*(2), 125-136.

Pert, C. (1997). *Molecules of emotion: Why you feel the way you feel.* New York: Scribner.

Pfeffer, J. (1982). *Organizations and organization theory.* Boston: Pitman.

Pfeffer, J. (1997). *New directions for organizational theory.* New York: Oxford University Press.

Pfeffer, J., & Salancik, G. (1978). *The external control of organizations: A resource dependence perspective.* New York: Harper & Row.

Parents, Families and Friends of Lesbians and Gays (PFLAG). (1995). *Our daughters and sons: Questions and answers for parents of gay, lesbian and bisexual people.* Washington, DC: Author.

Pincus, A., & Minahan, A. (1973). *Social work practice: Model and method.* Itasca, IL: Peacock.

Pines, A., & Kafry, D. (1978). Occupational tedium in the social services. *Social Work, 23,* 499-507.

Piven, F., & Cloward, R. (1977). *Poor people's movements: Why they succeed, how they fail.* New York: Pantheon.

Plato. (1968). *The republic* (A. Bloom, Trans.). New York: Basic Books.

Plutchik, R. (1991). Emotions and evolution. In K. T. Strongman (Ed.), *International review of studies on emotions* (pp. 37-58). New York: Wiley.

Poindexter, C. C., & Linsk, N. L. (1999). "I'm just glad that I'm here": Stories of seven African American HIV-affected grandmothers. *Journal of Gerontological Social Work, 32*(1), 63-81.

Pollio, D. E. (1995). Hoops group: Group work with young "street" men. *Social Work With Groups, 18*(2/3), 107-116.

Popenoe, D. (1996). *Life without father: Compelling new evidence that fatherhood and marriage are indispensable for the good of children and society.* New York: Martin Kessler Books.

Popple, P. (1992). Social work: Social function and moral purpose. In P. Reid & P. Popple (Eds.), *The moral purposes of social work: The character and intentions of a profession* (pp. 141-154). Chicago: Nelson-Hall.

Popple, P., & Leighninger, L. (1990). *Social work, social welfare, and American society.* Boston: Allyn & Bacon.

Popple, P., & Leighninger, L. (1993). *Social work, social welfare, and American society* (2nd ed.). Boston: Allyn & Bacon.

Popple, P., & Leighninger, L. (2001). *The policy-based profession: An introduction to social welfare policy analysis for social workers* (2nd ed.). Boston: Allyn and Bacon.

Potts, R. (1991). Spirits in a bottle: Spirituality and alcoholism treatment in African-American communities. *Journal of Training and Practice in Professional Psychology, 5*(1), 11-14.

Prest, L. A., & Keller, J. F. (1993). Spirituality and family therapy: Spiritual beliefs, myths, and metaphors. *Journal of Marital & Family Therapy, 19*(2), 137-148.

Prewitt, K. (2000, October). Census 2000: *A new picture of America.* Plenary Session at George Warren Brown School of Social Work 75th Anniversary Celebration. St. Louis, MO.

Prichard, D. (1996). *The primary and secondary impact of critical incident stress on police officers and domestic partners.* Unpublished doctoral dissertation, Virginia Commonwealth University, Richmond.

Procidano, M., & Heller, K. (1983). Measures of perceived social support from friends and family: Three validation studies. *American Journal of Community Psychology, 11,* 1-24.

Proctor, E. K., Davis, L. E., & Vosler, N. R. (1995). Families: Direct practice. In R. L. Edwards et al. (Eds.), *Encyclopedia of social work* (19th ed.) (Vol. 2, pp. 941-950). Washington, DC: NASW Press.

Project Serve. (n.d.). *Urban & rural poverty.* University of Michigan Center for Community Service and Learning. Retrieved October 14, 2002, from www.umich.edu/~mserve/ProjectServe/HTML/IEA_poverty.html.

Pulley, M. L. (1997). *Losing your job, reclaiming your soul.* San Francisco: Jossey-Bass.

Queralt, M., & Witte, A. (1998a). Influences on neighborhood supply of child care in Massachusetts. *Social Service Review, 72*(1), 17-46.

Queralt, M., & Witte, A. (1998b). A map for you? Geographic information systems in the social services. *Social Work, 43*(5), 455-469.

Queralt, M., & Witte, A. (1999). Estimating the unmet need for services: A middling approach. *Social Service Review, 73*(4), 524-559.

Ragland, D., Krause, N., Greiner, B., & Fisher, J. (1998). Studies of health outcomes in transit operators: Policy implications of the current scientific database. *Journal of Occupational Health Psychology, 3*(2), 172-187.

Raines, J. (1997). Co-constructing the spiritual tree. *Society for Social Work and Social Work Newsletter, 4*(1), 3, 8.

Ramirez, R. (1985). Hispanic spirituality. *Social Thought, 11*(3), 6-13.

Rapoport, A. (1990). *Meaning of the built environment.* Tucson: University of Arizona Press.

Rappaport, H., Enrich, K., & Wilson, A. (1985). Relation between ego identity and temporal perspective.

Journal of Personality and Social Psychology, 48(6), 1609-1620.

Rathus, S., Nevid, J., & Fichner-Rathus, L. (1998). *Essentials of human sexuality.* Boston, MA: Allyn and Bacon.

Rawls, J. (1993). *Political liberalism.* New York: Columbia University Press.

Ray, L. (1993). *Rethinking critical theory: Emancipation in the age of global social movements.* Newbury Park, CA: Sage.

Reamer, F. (1992). Social work and the public good: Calling or career? In P. Reid & P. Popple (Eds.), *The moral purposes of social work: The character and intentions of a profession* (pp. 11-33). Chicago: Nelson-Hall.

Rector, R., & Hederman, R. (1999). *Income inequality: How census data misrepresent income distribution.* Retrieved July 10, 2002, from www.heritage.org/library/cda/cda99-07.html.

Redfield, R. (1947). The folk society. *American Journal of Sociology, 52,* 293-308.

Reed, M. (1993). Organizations and modernity: Continuity and discontinuity in organization theory. In J. Hassard & M. Parker (Eds.), *Postmodernism and organizations* (pp. 163-182). Newbury Park, CA: Sage.

Reese, D. J., & Kaplan, M. S. (2000). Spirituality, social support, and worry about health: Relationships in a sample of HIV+ women. *Social Thought, 19*(4), 37-52.

Reeves, T. C. (1998). *The empty church: Does organized religion matter anymore?* New York: Simon & Schuster.

Reich, R. (1992). *The work of nations.* New York: Vintage.

Reid, K. E. (1997). *Social work practice with groups: A clinical perspective* (2nd ed.). Pacific Grove, CA: Brooks/Cole.

Reid, W. J. (1985). *Family problem solving.* New York: Columbia University Press.

Reid, W., & Smith, A. (1989). *Research in social work* (2nd ed.). New York: Columbia University Press.

Reilly, P. (1995). The religious wounding of women. *Creation Spirituality, 11*(1), 41-45.

Reinhardt, U., Hussey, P., & Anderson, G. (2002). Cross-national comparisons of health systems using OECD data, 1999. *Health Affairs, 21*(3), 169-181.

Reisch, M. (1997). The political context of social work. In M. Reisch & E. Gambrill (Eds.), *Social work in the 21st century* (pp. 80-92). Thousand Oaks, CA: Pine Forge Press.

Reskin, B., & Padavic, I. (1994). *Women and men at work.* Thousand Oaks, CA: Pine Forge.

Resnick, H., & Jaffee, B. (1982). The physical environment and social welfare. *Social Casework, 63,* 354-362.

Reuther, R. (1983). *Sexism and God-talk: Toward a feminist theology.* Boston, MA: Beacon Press.

Rey, L. D. (1997). Religion as invisible culture: Knowing about and knowing with. *Journal of Family Social Work, 2*(2), 159-177.

Rice, B. (2001). Mind-body interventions. *Diabetes Spectrum, 14*(4), 213-217.

Richards, T. A., & Folkman, S. (1997). Spiritual aspects of loss at the time of a partner's death from AIDS. *Death Studies, 21*(6), 527-552.

Richardson, B. C. (1991). Utilizing the resources of the African-American church: Strategies for counseling professionals. In C. C. Lee & B. L. Richardson (Eds.), *Multicultural issues in counseling: New approaches to diversity* (pp. 65-75). Alexandria, VA: American Association for Counseling and Development.

Richman, J. M., Rosenfeld, L. B., & Hardy, C. J. (1993). The social support survey: A validation study of a clinical measure of the social support process. *Research on Social Work Practice 3,* 288-311.

Richmond, M. (1901). *Charitable cooperation.* In Proceedings of the National Conference of Charities and Corrections. Boston: Elles.

Richmond, M. (1917). *Social diagnosis.* New York: Russell Sage Foundation.

Ringer, B., & Lawless, E. (1989). *Race-ethnicity and society.* New York: Routledge.

Ritter, K. Y., & O'Neill, C. W. (1989). Moving through loss: The spiritual journey of gay men and lesbian women. *Journal of Counseling and Development, 68,* 9-15.

Ritzer, G. (1993). *The McDonaldization of society.* Thousand Oaks, CA: Pine Forge.

Ritzer, G. (1998). *The McDonaldization thesis: Explorations and extensions.* Thousand Oaks, CA: Sage.

Ritzer, G. (2000). *Modern sociological theory* (5th ed.). Boston: McGraw Hill.

Robbins, S., Chatterjee, P., & Canda, E. (1998a). *Contemporary human behavior theory: A critical perspective for social work.* Boston: Allyn & Bacon.

Robbins, S., Chatterjee, P., & Canda, E. (1998b). Theories of assimilation, acculturation, and bicultural socialization. In *Contemporary human behavior theory: A critical perspective for social work* (pp. 118-150). Boston: Allyn & Bacon.

Robertson, J. G., & Vosler, N. R. (1997, July). *Nonmarital parents in St. Louis and Missouri: Report submitted to the Division of Family Services and the Division of Child Support Enforcement of the Missouri Department of Social Services.* St. Louis, MO: Washington University School of Social Work.

Robinson, T. L. (2000). Making the hurt go away: Psychological and spiritual healing for African American women survivors of childhood incest. *Journal of Multi-cultural Counseling and Development, 28*(3), 160-176.

Rodriguez, H. (1998). *Cohabitation: A snapshot.* Retrieved July 11, 2002, from www.clasp.org/pubs/familyformation/cohab.html.

Rogers, C. (1951). *Client-centered therapy.* Boston: Houghton Mifflin.

Rogge, M. (1993). Social work, disenfranchised communities, and the natural environment: Field education opportunities. *Journal of Social Work Education, 29,* 111-120.

Rolland, J. S. (1993). Mastering family challenges in serious illness and disability. In F. Walsh (Ed.), *Normal family processes* (2nd ed., pp. 444-473). New York: Guilford.

Rolland, J. S. (1999). Chronic illness and the family life cycle. In B. Carter and M. McGoldrick (Eds.), *The expanded family life cycle: Individual, family, and social perspectives* (3rd ed., pp. 492-511). Boston: Allyn & Bacon.

Roller, B. (1997). *The promise of group therapy: How to build a vigorous training and organizational base for group therapy in managed behavioral health care.* San Francisco: Jossey-Bass.

Roof, W. (1993). *A generation of seekers: The spiritual journeys of the baby boom generation.* San Francisco: HarperCollins.

Roof, W. (1999). *Spiritual marketplace: Baby boomers and the remaking of American religion.* Princeton, NJ: Princeton University Press.

Roof, W., & McKinney, W. (1987). *American mainline religion: Its changing shape and future.* Rutgers, NJ: State University Press.

Rosaldo, R. (1989/1993). *Culture and truth: The remaking of social analysis.* Boston: Beacon Press.

Rose, N. (1997). The future economic landscape: Implications for social work practice and education. In M. Reisch & E. Gambrill (Eds.), *Social work in the 21st century* (pp. 28-38). Thousand Oaks, CA: Pine Forge.

Rose, S. (1992). *Case management and social work practice.* White Plains, NY: Longman.

Rose, S. (1994). Defining empowerment: A value based approach. In S. P. Robbins (Ed.), *Melding the personal and the political: Advocacy and empowerment in clinical and community practice* (pp. 17-24). Proceedings of the Eighth Annual Social Work Futures Conference, May 13-14, 1993. Houston, TX: University of Houston Graduate School of Social Work.

Roseberry, W. (1989). European history and the construction of anthropological subjects. In *Anthropologies and histories: Essays in culture, history, and political economy.* New Brunswick, NJ: Rutgers University Press.

Rosenzweig, M. R., & Leiman, A. L. (1989). *Physiological psychology* (2nd ed.). Lexington, MA: Heath.

Ross, L., & Coleman, M. (2000). Urban community action planning inspires teenagers to transform their community and their identity. *Journal of Community Practice, 7*(2), 29-45.

Rostow, W. (1990). *The stages of economic growth: A non-communist manifesto.* Cambridge, UK: Cambridge University Press.

Rothberg, D. (1992). Buddhist responses to violence and war: Resources for a socially engaged spirituality. *Journal of Humanistic Psychology, 32*(4), 41-75.

Rothschild-Whitt, J., & Whitt, J. (1986). *The cooperative workplace.* Cambridge, UK: Cambridge University Press.

Rubin, A., & Babbie, E. (1993). *Research methods for social work* (2nd ed.). New York: Columbia University Press.

Rugel, R. P. (1991). Addictions treatment in groups: A review of therapeutic factors. *Small Group Research, 22,* 475-491.

Russel, R. (1998). Spirituality and religion in graduate social work education. *Social Thought: 18*(2), 15-29.

Ryan, W. (1999). The new landscape for nonprofits. *Harvard Business Review, 77*(1), 127-136.

Ryscavage, P. (1994). Gender-related shifts in the distribution of wages. *Monthly Labor Review, 117*(7), 3-15.

Safyer, A. W., & Spies-Karotkin, G. (1988). The biology of AIDS. *Health and Social Work, 13,* 251-258.

Sahlins, M. (1981). *Historical metaphors and mythical realities: Structure in the early history of the Sandwich Islands Kingdom.* Ann Arbor: University of Michigan Press.

Salazar, A. J. (1996). An analysis of the development and evolution of roles in the small group. *Small Group Research, 27,* 475-503.

Saleebey, D. (1985). In clinical social work practice, is the body politic? *Social Service Review, 59,* 578-592.

Saleebey, D. (1992). Biology's challenge to social work: Embodying the person-in-environment perspective. *Social Work, 37*(2), 112-118.

Saleebey, D. (1994). Culture, theory, and narrative: The intersection of meanings in practice. *Social Work, 39,* 351-359.

Saleeby, D. (2001). *Human behavior and social environments. A biopsychosocial approach.* New York: Columbia University Press.

Sampson, R. (1983). Structural density and criminal victimization. *Criminology: An Interdisciplinary Journal, 21,* 276-293.

Saperstein, A. (1996). The prediction of unpredictability: Applications of the new paradigm of chaos in dynamical systems to the old problem of the stability of a system of hostile nations. In L. D. Kiel & E. Elliott (Eds.), *Chaos theory in the social sciences: Foundations and applications* (pp. 139-163). Ann Arbor: University of Michigan Press.

Sarafino, E. P. (2001). *Health psychology: Biopsychosocial interactions* (4th ed.). New York: Wiley.

Sarason, S. (1974). *The psychological sense of community: Prospects for a community psychology.* San Francisco: Jossey-Bass.

Sargent, L. D., & Sue-Chan, C. (2001). Does diversity affect group efficacy? The intervening role of cohesion and task independence. *Small Group Research, 32*(4), 426-450.

Sarri, R., & Galinsky, M. (1967). A conceptual framework for group development. In R. Vinter (Ed.), *Readings in groupwork practice* (pp. 72-94). Ann Arbor, MI: Campus Publisher.

Satir, V. (1983). *Conjoint family therapy* (3rd ed.). Palo Alto, CA: Science and Behavior Books.

Schacter, S., & Singer, J. E. (1962). Cognitive, social, and physiological determinants of emotional states. *Psychological Review, 69,* 379-399.

Schaufeli, W., & Enzmann, D. (1998). *The burnout companion to study and practice: A critical analysis.* London: Taylor and Francis.

Schein, E. (1992). *Organizational culture and leadership* (2nd ed.). San Francisco: Jossey-Bass.

Schiele, J. H. (1996). Afrocentricity: An emerging paradigm in social work practice. *Social Work,* 41(3), 284-294.

Schiff, M., & Bargal, O. (2000). Helping characteristics of self-help and support groups: Their contribution to participants' subjective well-being. *Small Group Research, 31*(3), 275-304.

Schneider, D. (1968). *American kinship: A cultural account.* Englewood Cliffs, NJ: Prentice-Hall.

Schneider, J., & Cook, K. (1995). Status inconsistency and gender: Combining revisited. *Small Group Research, 26,* 372-399.

Schoggen, P. (1989). *Behavior settings.* Stanford, CA: Stanford University Press.

Schriver, J. (2001). *Human behavior and the social environment: Shifting paradigms in essential knowledge for social work practice* (3rd ed.). Boston: Allyn & Bacon.

Schuster, M. A., Stein, B. P., Jaycox, L. H., Collins, R. L., Marshall, G. N., Zhou, A. J., et al. (2001). A national survey of stress reactions after the September 11, 2001, terrorist attacks. *New England Journal of Medicine, 345*(20), 1507-1512.

Schutt, R. (1999). *Investigating the social world* (2nd ed.). Thousand Oaks, CA: Pine Forge Press.

Schutz, A. (1932/1967). *The phenomenology of the social world.* (G. Walsh & F. Lehnert, Trans.) Evanston, IL: Northwestern University Press.

Schwartz, M. (1973). Sexism in the social work curriculum. *Journal of Social Work Education, 9*(3), 65-70.

Schwartz, M. A., & Scott, B. M. (1994). *Marriages and families: Diversity and change.* Englewood Cliffs, NJ: Prentice-Hall.

Schwartz, P. (1999). Quality of life in the coming decades. *Society, 36*(2), 55-59.

Schwartz, W. (1963). Small group science and group work practice. *Social Work, 8,* 40-41.

Scott, A. H., Butin, D. N., Tewfik, D., Burkhardt, A., Mandel, D., & Nelson, L. (2001). Occupational therapy as a means to wellness with the elderly. *Physical and Occupational Therapy in Geriatrics, 18*(4), 3-22.

Scott, R. (1995). *Institutions and organizations.* Thousand Oaks, CA: Sage.

Seabury, B. (1971). Arrangment of physical space in social work settings. *Social Work, 16,* 43-49.

Sebba, R. (1991). The landscapes of childhood: The reflection of childhood's environment in adult memories and in children's attitudes. *Environment and Behavior, 23,* 395-422.

Seibert, S., & Gruenfeld, L. (1992). Masculinity, femininity, and behavior in groups. *Small Group Research, 23,* 95-112.

Seligman, M. (1992). *Helplessness: On depression, development, and death.* New York: Freeman.

Seltzer, J. A. (2001). Families formed outside of marriage. In R. M. Milardo (Ed.), *Understanding families into the new millennium* (pp. 466-487). Minneapolis, MN: National Council on Family Relations.

Senge, P. (1990). *The fifth discipline.* New York: Doubleday.

Sernau, S. (2001). *Worlds apart: Social inequalities in a new century.* Thousand Oaks, CA: Pine Forge Press.

Seyle, H. (1991). History and present status of the stress concept. In A. Monat & R. S. Lazarus (Eds.), *Stress and coping: An anthology* (3rd ed., pp. 21-35). New York: Columbia University Press.

Shanklin, E. (1994). *Anthropology and race.* Belmont, CA: Wadsworth.

Shaw, M. E. (1981). *Group dynamics: The psychology of small group behavior* (3rd ed.). New York: McGraw-Hill.

Shechtman, Z., & Perl-Dekel, O. (2000). A comparison of therapeutic factors in two group treatment modalities: Verbal and art therapy. *Journal for Specialists in Group Work, 24*(3), 288-304.

Sheets, V., & Manzer, C. (1991). Affect, cognition, and urban vegetation: Some effects of adding trees along city streets. *Environment and Behavior, 23,* 285-304.

Sheils, L., & Butler, W. (1992). The development of a stress management and relaxation group in an acute teaching hospital. *Australian Social Work, 45*(4), 27-30.

Sheridan, M. J. (1995). Honoring angels in my path: Spiritually sensitive group work with persons who are incarcerated. *Reflections: Narratives of Professional Helping, 1*(4), 5-16.

Sheridan, M. J. (2000, February). *The use of spiritually-derived interventions in social work practice.* Paper presentation at the 46th annual program meeting of the Council on Social Work Education, New York.

Sheridan, M. J. (2002). Spiritual and religious issues in practice. In A. R. Roberts & G. J. Greene (Eds.), *Social workers' desk reference* (pp. 567-571). New York: Oxford University Press.

Sheridan, M. J., & Amato-von Hemert, K. (1999). The role of religion and spirituality in social work education and practice: A survey of student views and experiences. *Journal of Social Work Education, 35*(1), 125-141.

Sheridan, M. J., & Bullis, R. K. (1991). Practitioners' views on religion and spirituality: A qualitative study. *Spirituality and Social Work Journal, 2*(2), 2-10.

Sheridan, M. J., Bullis, R. K., Adcock, C. R., Berlin, S. D., & Miller, P. (1992). Practitioners' personal and professional attitudes and behavior toward religion and spirituality: Issues for education and practice. *Journal of Social Work Education, 28,* 190-203.

Sheridan, M. J., Wilmer, C., & Atcheson, L. (1994). Inclusion of content on religion and spirituality in the social work curricululm: A study of faculty views. *Journal of Social Work Education, 30,* 363-376.

Sherman, E., & Reid, W. (1994). *Qualitative research in social work.* New York: Columbia University Press.

Shilts, R. (1987). *And the band played on.* New York: St. Martin's Press.

Shmotkin, D. (1991). The role of time orientation in life satisfaction across the life span. *Journal of Gerontology, 46*(5), 243-250.

Shweder, R. (1984/1995). Anthropology's Romantic rebellion against the Enlightenment, or there's more to thinking than reason and evidence. In R. Shweder & R. LeVine (Eds.), *Culture theory: Essays on mind, self, and emotion* (pp. 27-66). New York: Cambridge University Press.

Shweder, R., & LeVine, R. (Eds.). (1984/1995). *Culture theory: Essays on mind, self, and emotion.* New York: Cambridge University Press.

Siegel, A., & Allan, L. (1998). Learning and homeostasis: Drug addiction and the McCollough effect. *Psychological Bulletin, 124*(2), 230-239.

Siegel, S. (1991). Feedforward processes in drug tolerance and dependence. In R. Lister & H. Weingartner (Eds.), *Perspectives on cognitive neuroscience* (pp. 405-416). New York: Oxford University Press.

Siegel, S., Hinson, R., Krank, M., & McCully, J. (1982). Heroin "overdose" death: Contribution of drug-associated environmental cues. *Science, 216,* 436-437.

Silverman, D. (1971). *The theory of organizations: A sociological framework.* New York: Basic Books.

Silverman, D. (1994). On throwing away ladders: Re-writing the theory of organizations. In J. Hassard & M. Parker (Eds.), *Towards a new theory of organizations* (pp. 1-23). New York: Routledge.

Simon, H. (1957). *Administrative behavior* (2nd ed.). New York: Macmillan.

Simpkinson, A. A., & Simpkinson, C. H. (1998). *Soul work: A field guide for spiritual seekers.* New York: Harper Perennial.

Sinetar, M. (1989). *Do what you love, the money will follow: Discovering your right livelihood.* New York: Dell.

Singh, R. (2001). Hinduism. In M. V. Hook, B. Hugen, & M. Aguilar (Eds.), *Spirituality within religious traditions in social work practice* (pp. 34-52). Pacific Grove, CA: Brooks/Cole.

Sinha, S., & Mukherjee, N. (1996). The effect of perceived cooperation on personal space requirements. *Journal of Social Psychology, 136,* 655-657.

Sinha, S., Nayyar, P., & Mukherjee, N. (1995). Perception of crowding among children and adolescents. *Journal of Social Psychology, 135,* 263-268.

Siporin, M. (1975). *Introduction to social work practice.* New York: Macmillan.

Siporin, M. (1985). Current social work perspectives on clinical practice. *Clinical Social Work Journal, 13,* 198-217.

Siporin, M. (1986). Contribution of religious values to social work and the law. *Social Thought, 12*(4), 35-50.

Sistler, A., & Washington, K. S. (1999). Serenity for African-American caregivers. *Social Work With Groups, 22*(1), 49-62.

Skocpol, T. (1979). *States and social revolutions.* New York: Cambridge University Press.

Skolnick, A. (1997). Family values: The sequel. *American Prospect, 32* (May-June), 86-94.

Smeeding, T. (1991). Cross-national comparisons of inequality and poverty. In L. Osberg (Ed.), *Economic inequality and poverty: International perspectives* (pp. 39-59). Armonk, NY: Sharpe.

Smith, D. C. (1993). Exploring the religious-spiritual needs of the dying. *Counseling and Values, 37,* 71-77.

Smith, E. D. (1995). Addressing the psychospiritual distress of death as reality: A transpersonal approach. *Social Work, 40,* 402-413.

Smith, E. D., & Gray, C. (1995). Integrating and transcending divorce: A transpersonal model. *Social Thought, 18*(1), 57-74.

Smith, J. (1997). Characteristics of the modern transnational social movement sector. In J. Smith, C. Chatfield, & R. Pagnucco (Eds.), *Transnational social movements and global politics: Solidarity beyond the state* (pp. 42-58). Syracuse, NY: Syracuse, University Press.

Smith, J., Chatfield, C., & Pagnucco, R. (1997). *Transnational social movements and global politics: Solidarity beyond the state.* Syracuse, NY: Syracuse University Press.

Snipp, C. M. (1998). The first Americans: American Indians. In M. L. Andersen & P. H. Collins (Eds.), *Race, class, and gender: An anthology* (pp. 357-364). Belmont, CA: Wadsworth.

Snow, D., & Anderson, L. (1993). *Down on their luck: A study of homeless street people.* Berkeley: University of California Press.

Soderfeldt, M., Soderfeldt, B., & Warg, L. (1995). Burnout in social work. *Social Work, 40,* 638-646.

Solomon, B. (1976). *Black empowerment: Social work in oppressed communities.* New York: Columbia University Press.

Solomon, B. (1987). Empowerment: Social work in oppressed communities. *Journal of Social Work Practice, 2*(4), 79-91.

Sommer, R. (1969). *Personal space: The behavioral basis of design.* Englewood Cliffs, NJ: Prentice-Hall.

Sommer, R., & Ross, H. (1958). Social interaction on a geriatrics ward. *International Journal of Social Psychiatry, 4,* 128-133.

Sotomayor, M. (Ed.) (1991). *Empowering Hispanic families: A critical issue for the '90s.* Milwaukee, WI: Family Service America.

Specht, H. (1986). Social support, social networks, social exchange, and social work practice. *Social Service Review, 60,* 218-240.

Specht, H. (1994). Preface. In H. Specht & M. Courtney, *How social work has abandoned its mission: Unfaithful angels* (pp. ix-xii). New York: Free Press.

Specht, H., & Courtney, M. E. (1994). *Unfaithful angels: How social work has abandoned its mission.* New York: Free Press.

Spergel, I., & Grossman, S. (1997). The Little Village Project: A community approach to the gang problem. *Social Work, 42,* 456-470.

Spiegel, D., & Classen, C. (2000). *Group therapy for cancer patients: A research-based handbook of psychosocial care.* New York: Basic Books.

Spiritual matters, earthly benefits. (2001, August). *Tufts University Health & Nutrition Letter, 19*(6), 1.

Spradley, J. (1979). *The ethnographic interview.* New York: Holt, Rinehart, & Winston.

St. Clair, M. (1999). Object relations and self psychology: An introduction (3rd ed.). Pacific Grove, CA: Brooks/Cole.

Staral, J. M. (2000). Building on mutual goals: The intersection of community practice and church-based organizing. *Journal of Community, 7*(3), 85-95.

Starhawk. (1979). *The spiral dance: A rebirth of the ancient religion of the great Goddess.* San Francisco: Harper & Row.

Starkey, D., Deleone, H., & Flannery, R. B. (1995). Stress management for psychiatric patients in a state hospital setting. *American Journal of Orthopsychiatry, 65*(3), 446-450.

Stein, H., & Cloward, R. (1958). *Social perspectives on behavior: A reader in social science for social work and related professions.* New York: Free Press.

Stephens, K., & Clark, D. (1987). A pilot study on the effect of visible stigma on personal space. *Journal of Applied Rehabilitation Counseling, 18,* 52-54.

Stocking, G. W., Jr. (1968). *Race, culture, and evolution: Essays on the history of anthropology.* New York: Free Press.

Stoller, E., & Gibson, R. (2000). *Worlds of difference: Inequality in the aging experience* (3rd ed.). Thousand Oaks, CA: Pine Forge.

Stolte, J. F. (1994). Power. In M. Foshci & E. J. Lawler (Eds.), *Group processes: Sociological analyses* (pp. 149-176). Chicago: Nelson-Hall.

Stone, D. (2002). *Policy paradox: The art of political decision making* (rev. ed.). New York: W. W. Norton.

Strand, C. (1997). *Seeds from a birch tree: Writing Haiku and the spiritual journey.* New York: Hyperion.

Strauss, A. (1961). *Images of the American city.* New York: Free Press.

Streeter, C., & Gillespie, D. (1992). Social network analysis. *Journal of Social Service Research, 16,* 201-221.

Strom-Gottfried, K., & Morrissey, M. (1999). The organizational diversity audit. In K. Strom-Gottfried (Ed.), *Social work practice: Cases, activities, and exercises* (pp. 168-172). Thousand Oaks, CA: Pine Forge Press.

Stryker, S. (1980). *Symbolic interactionism: A social structural version.* Menlo Park, CA: Benjamin/Cummings.

Stuart, R. (1989). Social learning theory: A vanishing or expanding presence? *Psychology: A Journal of Human Behavior, 26,* 35-50.

Sturman, A. (1980). Damage on buses: The effects of supervision. In R. Clarke & P. Mayhew (Eds.), *Designing out crime* (pp. 31-38). London: Her Majesty's Stationery Office.

Sue, D. W., & Sue, D. (1990). *Counseling the culturally different: Theory and practice* (2nd ed.). New York: Wiley.

Sundstrom, E., Bell, P., Busby, P., & Asmus, C. (1996). Environmental psychology: 1989-1994. *Annual Review of Psychology, 47,* 485-513.

Suttles, G. D. (1972). *The social construction of communities.* Chicago: University of Chicago Press.

Sviridoff, M., & Ryan, W. (1997). Community-centered family service. *Families in Society, 78,* 128-139.

Swenson, C. (1994). Clinical practice and the decline of community. *Journal of Teaching in Social Work, 10,* 195-212.

Swenson, C. H., Fuller, S., & Clements, R. (1993). Stage of religious faith and reactions to terminal cancer. *Journal of Psychology and Theology, 21,* 238-245.

Swidler, A. (1986). Culture in action: Symbols and strategies. *American Sociological Review, 51,* 273-286.

Swift, D. C. (1998). *Religion and the American experience.* Armonk, NY: Sharpe.

Swinton, J. (1997). Restoring the image: Spirituality, faith, and cognitive disability. *Journal of Religion and Health, 36*(1), 21-27.

Syme, S. L. (2001). Understanding the relationship between socioeconomic status and health: New research initiatives. In J. Auerbach & B. Krimgold (Eds.), *Income, socioeconomic status, and health: Exploring the relationships* (pp. 12-15). Washington, DC: National Policy Association. Academy for Health Services Research and Health Policy.

Tangenberg, K. M. (2001). Surviving two diseases: Addiction, recovery, and spirituality among women living with HIV disease. *Families in Society, 82*(5), 517-524.

Tangenberg, K., & Kemp, S. (2002). Embodied practice: Claiming the body's experience, agency, and knowledge for social work. *Social Work, 47*(1), 9-18.

Tanzi, V., & Schuknecht, L. (2000). *Public spending in the 20th century: A global perspective.* New York: Cambridge University Press.

Tarrow, S. (1994). *Power in movement: Social movements, collective action, and politics.* New York: Cambridge University Press.

Tarrow, S. (1996). States and opportunities: The political structuring of social movements. In D. McAdam, J. McCarthy, & M. Zald (Eds.), *Comparative perspectives on social movements* (pp. 41-61). New York: Cambridge University Press.

Tarrow, S. (1998). *Power in movement: Social movements and contentious politics* (2nd ed.). New York: Cambridge University Press.

Taylor, A., Wiley, A., Kuo, F., & Sullivan, W. (1998). Growing up in the inner city: Green spaces as places to grow. *Environment and Behavior, 30,* 3-27.

Taylor, F. W. (1911). *Principles of scientific management.* New York: Harper & Row.

Taylor, R. (1988). *Human territorial functioning: An empirical, evolutionary perspective on individual and small group territorial cognitions, behaviors, and consequences.* Cambridge, UK: Cambridge University Press.

Taylor, R. J., Ellison, C. G., Chatters, L. M., Levin, J. S., & Lincoln, D. L. (2000). Mental health services in faith communities: The role of clergy in Black churches. *Social Work, 45*(1), 73-87.

Taylor, S., Klein, L, Lewis, B., Gruenewald, T., Gurung, R., & Updegraff, J. (2000). Biobehavioral responses to stress in females: Tend-and-befriend, not fight-or-flight. *Psychological Review, 107*(3), 411-429.

Taylor, S., Lewis, B., Gruenewald, T., Gurung, R., Updegraff, J., & Klein, L. (2002). Sex differences in biobehavioral responses to threat. *Psychological Review, 109*(4), 751-753.

Taylor, V. (1995). Watching for vibes: Bringing emotions into the study of feminist organizations. In M. Ferree & P. Martin (Eds.), *Feminist organizations: Harvest of the new women's movement* (pp. 223-233). Philadelphia, PA: Temple University Press.

Teeple, G. (2000). *Globalization and the decline of social reform: Into the twenty-first century.* Aurora, Ontario, Canada: Garamond Press.

Thibaut, J. W., & Kelley, H. H. (1959). *The social psychology of groups.* New York: Wiley.

Thoits, P. A. (1989). The sociology of emotions. *Annual Review of Sociology, 15,* 317-342.

Thomas, R., Jr. (1991). *Beyond race and gender: Unleashing the power of your total work force by managing diversity.* New York: AMACOM.

Thomas, W., & Thomas, D. (1928). *The child in America: Behavior problems and programs.* New York: Knopf.

Thomason, T. C. (2001). Issues in treatment of Native Americans with alcohol problems. *Journal of Multicultural Counseling and Development, 28*(4), 243-252.

Thomlison, B., & Thomlison, R. (1996). Behavior theory and social work treatment. In F. Turner (Ed.), *Social work treatment* (4th ed., pp. 39-68). New York: Free Press.

Thompson, P. (1993). Postmodernism: Fatal distraction. In J. Hassard & M. Parker (Eds.), *Postmodernism and organizations* (pp. 183-203). Newbury Park, CA: Sage.

Thomson, R. G. (Ed.) (1996). *Freakery: Cultural spectacles of the extraordinary body.* New York: New York University Press.

Thyer, B. (1991). Behavioral social work: It is not what you think. *Arete, 16,* 1-9.

Thyer, B., & Myers, L. (1998). Social learning theory: An empirically-based approach to understanding human behavior in the social environment. *Journal of Human Behavior in the Social Environment, 1*(1), 33-52.

Timberlake, E. M., & Cook, K. O. (1984). Social work and the Vietnamese refugee. *Social Work, 29*(2), 108-114.

Titone, A. M. (1991). Spirituality and psychotherapy in social work practice. *Spirituality and Social Work Communicator, 2*(1), 7-9.

Tocqueville, A. de. (1835/1945). *Democracy in America.* New York: Knopf.

Tolliver, D. E. (2001). African-American female caregivers of family members living with HIV/AIDS. *Families in Society, 82*(2), 145-156.

Tong, R. T. (1998). Feminist thought (2nd ed). Boulder, CO: Westview Press.

Tonnies, F. (1887/1963). *Community and society* (C. P. Loomis, Ed.). New York: Harper & Row.

Torrez, E. (1984). *The folk-healer: The Mexican-American tradition of curanderismo.* Kingsville, TX: Nieves.

Tracy, E., & Whittaker, J. (1990). The social network map: Assessing social support in clinical practice. *Families in Society, 71,* 461-470.

Troiden, R. (1989). The formation of homosexual identities. *Journal of Homosexuality, 17,* 43-73.

Tuckman, B. (1965). Developmental sequence in small groups. *Psychological Bulletin, 63,* 384-399.

Turner, J. H. (1996). The evolution of emotions in humans: A Darwinian-Durkheimian analysis. *Journal for the Theory of Social Behavior, 26*(1), 1-33.

Turner, R. P., Lukoff, D., Barnhouse, R. T., & Lu, F. G. (1995). Religious or spiritual problem: A culturally sensitive diagnostic category in the DSM-IV. *Journal of Nervous and Mental Disease, 183,* 435-444.

Tweed, T. T. (1997). Asian religions in the United States. In W. H. Conser Jr. & S. B. Twiss (Eds.), *Religious diversity and American religious history: Studies in traditions and cultures* (pp. 189-217). Athens, GA: University of Georgia Press.

Twiss, P., & Cooper, P. (2000). Youths revitalizing Main Street: A case study. *Social Work in Education, 22*(3), 162-176.

U.S. Bureau of the Census. (1992). *Statistical abstracts of the United States: 1992* (112th ed.). Washington, DC: Author.

U.S. Bureau of the Census. (1998). *USA Statistics in brief: Health, social welfare, government, employment* [Online]. Available from www.census.gov/statab/www/part3.html.

U.S. Bureau of the Census. (2000a). *Statistical abstract of the United States: 2000. Vital Statistics.* Washington, DC: Author.

U.S. Bureau of the Census. (2000b). *Educational attainment in the United States: Update.* Washington, DC: Author.

U.S. Bureau of the Census. (2001). *Poverty in the United States: 2000.* Washington, DC: Author.

U.S. Bureau of the Census. (2002). *Census brief. Coming to America: A profile of the nation's foreign born (2000 update).* Washington, DC: Author.

U.S. Commission on Human Rights. (1998). Indian tribes: A continuing quest for survival. In P. S. Rothenberg (Ed.), *Race, class and gender in the United States: An integrated study* (4th ed., pp. 378-382). New York: St. Martin's Press.

U.S. Conference of Mayors. (2001). *Status of hunger and homelessness in America's cities.* Retrieved July 18, 2002, from www.nlchp.org/FA_HAPIA.

U.S. Department of Education, National Center for Education Statistics. (1997). *Dropout rates in the United States, 1996* (NCES 98-250). Washington, DC: Author.

U.S. Department of Education. (2001). *Homeschooling in the United States: 1999.* Washington, DC: Author. NCES 2001-033.

U.S. Department of Health and Human Services. (n.d.). *Live births and birth rates, by year.* Retrieved July 11, 2002, from www.dhhs.gov.

U.S. Department of Health and Human Services. (2000, November). *Tracking healthy people 2010.* Washington, DC: U.S. Government Printing Office.

U.S. Department of Housing and Urban Development. (n.d.). *National survey of homeless assistance providers and clients (NSHAPC).* Retrieved July 17, 2002, from www.huduser.org/publications/homeless/homelessness/highlights.html.

Ulrich, R. (1984). View through a window may influence recovery from surgery. *Science, 224,* 420-421.

Ulrich, R. (1993). Biophilia, biophobia, and natural landscapes. In S. Kellert & E. Wilson (Eds.), *The biophilia hypothesis* (pp. 73-137). Washington, DC: Island Press.

UNICEF. (2002). *Official summary: The state of the world's children 2002.* Retrieved July 10, 2002, from www.unicef.org/sowc02summary/table4.html.

The Urban Institute. (2000). *Millions still face homelessness in a booming economy.* Retrieved July 18, 2002, from www.urban.org/news/pressrel/pr000201.html.

Vaillant, G. (2002). *Aging well.* Boston, MA: Little, Brown.

Van de Ven, A. (1993). The institutional theory of John R. Commons: A review and commentary. *Academy of Management Review, 18,* 129-152.

Varela, F. (1989). Reflections on the circulation of concepts between the biology of cognition and systemic family therapy. *Family Process, 28,* 15-24.

Vaux, A. (1988). *Social support: Theory, research, and intervention.* New York: Praeger.

Vaux, A. (1990). An ecological approach to understanding and facilitating social support. *Journal of Social and Personal Relationships, 7,* 507-518.

Vosler, N. R. (1990). Assessing family access to basic resources: An essential component of social work practice. *Social Work, 35,* 434-441.

Vosler, N. R. (1996). *New approaches to family practice: Confronting economic stress.* Thousand Oaks, CA: Sage.

Vosler, N. R., & Proctor, E. K. (1991). Family structure and stressors in a child guidance clinic population. *Families in Society, 72,* 164-173.

Vosler, N. R., & Robertson, J. G. (1998). Nonmarital co-parenting: Knowledge building for practice. *Families in Society, 79*(4), 149-159.

Voss, K. (1996). The collapse of a social movement: The interplay of mobilizing structures, framing, and political opportunities in the Knights of Labor. In D. McAdams, J. McCarthy, & M. Zald (Eds.), *Comparative perspectives on social movements* (pp. 227-258). New York: Cambridge University Press.

Voss, R. W., Douville, V., Little-Soldier, A., & Twiss, G. (1999). Tribal and shamanic-based social work practice: A Lakota perspective. *Social Work, 44*(3), 228-241.

Voss, R. W., Douville, V., Little-Soldier, A., & White Hat, A. (1999). Wo'Lakol kiciyapi: Traditional philosophies of helping and healing among the Lakotas: Toward a Lakota-centric practice of social work. *Journal of Multicultural Social Work, 7*(1/2), 73-93.

Wachs, T. (1992). *The nature of nurture.* Newbury Park, CA: Sage.

Wagner, R. (1981). *The invention of culture.* Chicago: University of Chicago Press.

Wald, K. (1997). *Religion and politics in the United States* (3rd ed.). Washington, DC: Congressional Quarterly.

Walker, B. G. (1990). *Women's rituals: A sourcebook.* San Francisco: Harper.

Wallace, R., & Wolf, A. (1995). *Contemporary sociological theory: Continuing the classical tradition* (4th ed.). Englewood Cliffs, NJ: Prentice-Hall.

Wallerstein, I. (1974-1989). *The modern world system* (Vols. 1-3). New York: Academic Press.

Walsh, F. (1993). Conceptualization of normal family processes. In F. Walsh (Ed.), *Normal family processes* (2nd ed., pp. 3-69). New York: Guilford.

Walsh, F. (1999a). Families in later life: Challenges and opportunities. In B. Carter and M. McGoldrick (Eds.), *The expanded family life cycle: Individual, family, and social perspectives* (3rd ed., pp. 307-326). Boston: Allyn & Bacon.

Walsh, F. (Ed.). (1999b). *Spiritual resources in family therapy.* New York: Guilford.

Walsh, J., & Connelly, P. R. (1996). Supportive behaviors in natural support networks of people with serious mental illness. *Health and Social Work, 21,* 296-303.

Wamsley, G., & Zald, M. (1973). *The political economy of public organizations.* Lexington, MA: Heath.

Wang, C. (1992). Culture, meaning and disability: Injury prevention campaigns and the production of stigma. *Social Science and Medicine, 35,* 1093-1102.

Wapner, S. (1995). Toward integration: Environmental psychology in relation to other subfields of psychology. *Environment and Behavior, 27,* 9-32.

Warren, K., Franklin, C., & Streeter, C. (1998). New directions in systems theory: Chaos and complexity. *Social Work, 43*(4), 357-372.

Warren, R. (1963). *The community in America.* Chicago: Rand McNally.

Warren, R. (1978). *The community in America.* Chicago: Rand McNally.

Warren, R. (1987). *The community in America* (3rd ed.). Chicago: Rand McNally.

Warren, R. (1988). Observations on the state of community theory. In R. Warren & L. Lyon, *New perspectives on the American community* (5th ed., pp. 84-86). Chicago: Dorsey.

Warwick, L. L. (1995). Feminist Wicca: Paths to empowerment. *Women and Therapy: A Feminist Quarterly, 16*(2/3), 121-133.

Wasserman, H., & Danforth, H. E. (1988). *The human bond: Support groups and mutual aid.* New York: Springer.

Watson, G. (1996). *The perils of television.* In Gray Watson's television page [Online]. Available from www.letters. com/~gray/television.html.

Watson, K., & Gold, S. (n.d.). *The other side of devolution: Shifting relationships between state and local governments.* Prepared for Urban Institute, Washington, DC. Retrieved July 12, 2002, from newfederalism.urban. org/html/other.htm.

Weaver, H. N. (1999). Health concerns for Native American youth: A culturally grounded approach to health promotion. *Journal of Human Behavior in the Social Environment, 2*(1/2), 127-143.

Weaver, H. N. (2000). Activism and American Indian issues: Opportunities and roles for social workers. *Journal of Progressive Human Services, 11* (1), 3-22.

Webb, S. J., Monk, C. S., & Nelson, C. A. (2001). Mechanisms of postnatal neurobiological development: Implications for human development. *Developmental Neuropsychology, 19*(2), 147-171.

Weber, M. (1947). *The theory of economic and social organization.* New York: Free Press.

Weber, M. (1904-1905/1958). *The Protestant ethic and the spirit of capitalism* (T. Parsons, Trans.). New York: Scribner's.

Webster-Stratton, C. (1997). From parent training to community building. *Families in Society, 78,* 156-171.

Weick, A. (1986). The philosophical context of a health model of social work. *Social Casework, 67,* 551-559.

Weiner, B. (1985). An attributional theory of achievement motivation and emotion. *Psychological Review, 92,* 548-573.

Weisman, G. (1981). Modeling environment-behavior systems: A brief note. *Journal of Man-Environment Relations, 1*(2), 32-41.

Weitz, R. (2000). *The sociology of health, illness, and health care: A critical approach.* Belmont, CA: Wadsworth.

Wellman, B. (1979). The community question. *American Journal of Sociology, 84,* 1201-1231.

Wellman, B. (1982). Studying personal communities. In P. Marsden & N. Lin (Eds.), *Social structure and network analysis* (pp. 61-80). Beverly Hills, CA: Sage.

Wellman, B. (1996). Are personal communities local? A Dumptarian reconsideration. *Social Networks, 18,* 347-354.

Wellman, B. (1999). The network community: An introduction. In B. Wellman (Ed.), *Networks in the global village* (pp. 1-47). Boulder, CO: Westview Press.

Wellman, B., & Potter, S. (1999). The elements of personal communities. In B. Wellman (Ed.), *Networks in the global village* (pp. 49-81). Boulder, CO: Westview Press.

Wellman, B., & Wortley, S. (1990). Different strokes from different folks: Community ties and social support. *American Journal of Sociology, 96,* 558-588.

Wener, R., Frazier, W., & Farbstein, J. (1985). Three generations of evaluation and design of correctional facilities. *Environment and Behavior, 17,* 71-95.

Wenocur, S., & Soifer, S. (1997). Prospects for community organization. In M. Reisch & E. Gambrill (Eds.), *Social work in the 21st century* (pp. 198-209). Thousand Oaks, CA: Pine Forge.

Wentz, R. (1998). *The culture of religious pluralism.* Boulder, CO: Westview Press.

Werner, C., & Altman, I. (2000). Humans and nature: Insights from a transactional view. In S. Wapner, J. Demick, T. Yamamoto, & H. Minami (Eds.), *Theoretical perspectives in environment-behavior research: Underlying assumptions, research problems, and methodologies* (pp. 21-37). New York: Kluwer Academic.

Werner, C., Altman, I., & Oxley, D. (1985). Temporal aspects of homes: A transactional perspective. In I. Altman & C. Werner (Eds.), *Home environments* (pp. 1-32). New York: Plenum.

Wesley, C. (1975). The women's movement and psychotherapy. *Social Work, 20,* 120-124.

West, M. (1986). *Landscape views and stress responses in the prison environment.* Unpublished master's thesis, University of Washington, Seattle.

Westbrooks, K. L. (1997). Spirituality as a form of functional diversity: Activating unconventional family strengths. *Journal of Family Social Work, 2*(4), 77-87.

Wheeler, H. (Ed.). (1973). *Beyond the punitive society.* San Francisco, CA: Freeman.

Whitehead, B. (1997). *The divorce culture.* New York: Knopf.

Whiting, B., & Whiting, J. (1975). *Children of six cultures: Studies of childrearing.* Cambridge, MA: Harvard University Press.

Wicker, A. (1979). *An introduction to ecological psychology.* Monterey, CA: Brooks/Cole.

Wicker, A. (1987). Behavior settings reconsidered: Temporal stages, resources, internal dynamics, context. In D. Stokols & I. Altman (Eds.), *Handbook of environmental psychology* (Vol. 1, pp. 613-654). New York: Wiley.

Wilber, K. (1977). *The spectrum of consciousness.* Wheaton, IL: Quest.

Wilber, K. (1995). *Sex, ecology, spirituality: The spirit of evolution.* Boston: Shambhala.

Wilber, K. (1996). *A brief history of everything.* Boston: Shambhala.

Wilber, K. (1997). *The eye of spirit: An integral vision for a world gone slightly mad.* Boston: Shambhala.

Wilber, K., Engler, J., & Brown, D. (1986). *Transformations of consciousness: Conventional and contemplative perspectives on development.* Boston: Shambhala.

Wilkinson, R. (2001). Why is inequality bad for health? In J. Auerbach & B. Krimgold (Eds.), *Income, socioeconomic status, and health: Exploring the relationships* (pp. 29-43). Washington, DC: National Policy Association. Academy for Health Services Research and Health Policy.

Willer, D. (1987). *Theory and the experimental investigation of social structures.* New York: Gordon and Breach.

William T. Grant Foundation, Commission on Work, Family, and Citizenship. (1988). *The forgotten half: Pathways to success for America's youth and young families.* New York: Author.

Williams, R. (1977). *Marxism and literature.* Oxford: Oxford University Press.

Williams, R. (1983). *Key words: A vocabulary of culture and society* (rev. ed.). New York: Oxford University Press.

Williamson, J. S., & Wyandt, C. M. (2001). New perspectives on alternative medicines. *Drug Topics, 145*(1), 57-66.

Wilson, E. (1984). *Biophilia.* Cambridge, MA: Harvard University Press.

Wilson, G., & Baldassare, M. (1996). Overall "sense of community" in a suburban region: The effects of localism, privacy, and urbanization. *Environment and Behavior, 28*(1), 27-43.

Wilson, J. Q. (1995). *On character.* Washington, DC: AIE Press.

Wimalasiri, J. (2001). Moral reasoning capacity of management students and practitioners: An empirical study in Australia. *Journal of Managerial Psychology, 16*(8), 614-634.

Witkin, S., & Gottschalk, S. (1988). Alternative criteria for theory evaluation. *Social Service Review, 62,* 211-224.

Wittine, B. (1987, September/October). Beyond ego. *Yoga Journal,* pp. 51-57.

Wolfensberger, W. (1973). *The principle of normalization in human services.* Toronto, Canada: National Institute on Mental Retardation.

Wong, Y., & Hillier, A. (2001). Evaluating a community-based homelessness prevention program: A geographic information system approach. *Administration in Social Work, 25*(4), 21-45.

Wood, M., & Wardell, M. L. (1983). G. H. Mead's social behaviorism vs. the astructural basis of symbolic inter-actionism. *Symbolic Interaction, 6*(1), 85-96.

Woolever, C. (1992). A contextual approach to neighbourhood attachment. *Urban Studies, 29*(1), 99-116.

World Bank. (2002). Distribution of income and consumption. Retrieved July 10, 2002, from worldbank.org.

Wuthnow, R. (1994). *Sharing the journey: Support groups and America's new quest for community.* New York: Free Press.

Wuthnow, R. (1998). *Seeking the spirit: Spirituality in America since the 1950s.* Berkeley: University of California Press.

Yalom, I. D. (1995). *The theory and practice of group psychotherapy* (4th ed.). New York: Basic Books.

Yancey, W. (1971). Architecture, interaction, and social control: The case of a large-scale public housing project. *Environment and Behavior, 2,* 3-21.

Yang, B., & Brown, J. (1992). A cross-cultural comparison of preferences for landscape styles and landscape elements. *Environment and Behavior, 24,* 471-507.

Yattaw, N. (1999). Conceptualizing space and time: A classification of geographic movement. *Cartography and Geographic Information Science, 26*(2), 85-98.

Yellow Bird, M. J. (1995). Spirituality in First Nations story telling: A Sahnish-Hidatsa approach to narrative. *Reflections: Narratives of Professional Helping, 1*(4), 65-72.

Zachary, E. (2000). Grassroots leadership training: A case study of an effort to integrate theory and method. *Journal of Community Practice, 7*(1), 71-93.

Zald, M., & McCarthy, J. (1987). *Social movements in an organizational society.* New Brunswick, NJ: Transaction.

Zastrow, C. (1997). *Social work with groups: Using the class as a group leadership laboratory* (4th ed.). Chicago: Nelson-Hall.

Zdravomyslova, E. (1996). Opportunities and framing in the transition to democracy: The case of Russia. In D. McAdam, J. McCarthy, & M. Zald (Eds.), *Comparative perspectives on social movements* (pp. 122-137). New York: Cambridge University Press.

Zuniga, M. (1988). Chicano self-concept: A proactive stance. In C. Jacobs & D. Bowles (Eds.), *Ethnicity and race: Critical concepts in social work.* Silver Springs, MD: NASW Press.

INDEX/GLOSSARY

that these cross-cutting memberships prevent the development of solidarity among oppressed groups, 56-57

Political economy model   A model of formal organizations that focuses on the organization's dependence on its environments for political and economic resources and, more specifically, on the influence of political and economic factors on the internal workings of the organization, 485-486

Political influences, 16
   case study, 13-15
   See also Government/political institution

Political opportunities (PO) perspective   An approach to social movements that suggests that they develop when windows of political opportunity are open, 549-550, 550 (exhibit)
   alignments, stability of, 551-552
   elite allies and, 552-553
   elites in, 549
   political system openness, 550-551

Political process model   A social movement theory in the mobilizing structures perspective that focuses on the role of grassroots settings in the development and maintenance of social movements

Popple, P., 387, 566

Positivist perspective   The perspective on which modern science is based. Assumes objective reality, that findings of one study should be applicable to other groups, that complex phenomena can be studied by reducing them to some component part, and that scientific methods are value-free, 34

Postconventional morality   In Kohlberg's theory of moral development, a stage in which moral decisions are based on moral principles that transcend those of one's own society, 158

Postpoliomyelitis syndrome (PPS)   Progressive atrophy of muscles in those who once had polio, 134

Post-traumatic stress disorder (PTSD)   A set of symptoms experienced by some trauma survivors that include reliving the traumatic event, avoidance of stimuli related to the event, and hyperarousal, 203, 205

Poverty rates, 368

Power relationships, 56-57, 398, 456-457

Practice orientation   A way of thinking about culture that recognizes the relationships and mutual influences between structures of society and culture, the impact of history, and the nature and impact of human action, 324-325
   applications of, 325-326
   history and, 336

human agency and, 337
   social structure and, 336-337

Preconscious   Mental activity that is out of awareness but can be brought into awareness with prompting, 172-173

Preconventional morality   In Kohlberg's theory of moral development, a stage in which moral decisions are made on the basis of avoiding punishment and receiving rewards, 158

Prewitt, K., 27

Primary emotions   Emotions that developed as specific reactions and signals with survival value for the human species. They serve to mobilize an individual, focus attention, and signal one's state of mind to others. Examples include anger, fear, sadness, joy, and anticipation, 164

Primary territory   A territory that evokes feelings of ownership, that we control on a relatively permanent basis, and that is vital to our daily lives, 293

Privatization   Shifting the administration of programs from government to nongovernment organizations, 378, 389, 500-501

Privilege   Unearned advantage enjoyed by members of some social categories, 28, 398, 525

Problem-focused coping   Coping efforts in which the person attempts to change a stress situation by acting on the environment. Most effective when situations are controllable by action, 201

Process-oriented leader   A leader who identifies and manages group relationships, 460-461

Professional social movements   Social movements that are staffed by leaders and activists who make a professional career out of social reform causes

Program   In behavior settings theories, the consistent, prescribed patterns of behavior that are developed and maintained in a particular behavior settin, 294-295

Proposition   An assertion about a concept or about the relationship between concepts, 33

Psychiatric model, 51, 210, 211 (exhibit)

Psychoanalytic theory   A theory of human behavior and clinical intervention that assumes the primacy of internal drives and unconscious mental activity in determining human behavior, 167-168, 176, 188-189

Psychodynamic perspective   An approach that focuses on how internal processes motivate human behavior, 68-69, 69 (exhibit)
   bias in, 72
   comprehensiveness of, 71
   conflict and, 70-71
   differentiation of self, 413-414
   families and, 413-414, 415 (exhibit)

Socioeconomic status (SES)   Social, economic, and political relations that are developed around educational, economic, and occupational status; social class:

Sociofugal spaces   Physical designs that discourage social interaction, 300-301

Sociopetal spaces   Physical designs that encourage social interaction, 300

Specific immunity   Involves cells (lymphocytes) that not only respond to an infection, but develop a memory of that infection and allow the body to make rapid defense against it in subsequent exposure, 128-129

Spirituality   Search for purpose, meaning, and connection between oneself, other people, the universe, and the ultimate reality, which can be experienced within either a religious or a nonreligious framework, 226, 226 (exhibit)

Staffing   In behavior settings theories, the participants in a particular behavior setting, 295-296

State   A personality characteristic that changes over time depending on the social or stress context, 199

Status   A specific social position, 361

Status characteristic   In status characteristics theory, an attribute considered potentially relevant to a group's task, 455

Status characteristics theory   A theory of basic group process that assumes that status characteristics based on cultural beliefs about certain groups of people will influence the performance expectations group members hold for each other, which in turn influences the amount of power and prestige accorded to group members, 455-456

Stimulation theories   Theories that focus on the physical environment as a source of sensory information that is necessary for human well-being, 291-292

Strain theory   An approach to social movements that sees them as developing in response to some form of societal strain, 195, 548

Strengths perspective   A way of understanding families that focuses on identifying how the family has coped creatively with adversity in the past and on helping family members use these "strengths" to build toward needed change, 425-426

Stress   Any biological, psychological, or social event in which environmental demands or internal demands, or both, tax or exceed the adaptive resources of the individual, 193

Stress/diathesis models   Perspectives on mental and emotional disorders in which a disorder is considered to be the result of interactions of environmental stresses and the person's genetic or biochemical predisposition to the disorde, 196-197

Stress pileup   When a series of crises over time depletes a family's resources and exposes the family to increasing risk of very negative outcomes, 420